Theatre in Theory 1900–2000

Previous Books by David Krasner:

- *American Drama, 1945–2000: An Introduction* (2006)

- *Staging Philosophy: New Approaches to Theater, Performance, and Philosophy* (coeditor with David Saltz, 2006)

- *A Companion to Twentieth-Century American Drama* (editor, 2005)

- *A Beautiful Pageant: African American Theatre, Drama, and Performance, 1910–1927* (2002)
  2002 Finalist for the Theatre Library Association's George Freedley Memorial Award

- *African American Performance and Theater History: A Critical Reader* (coeditor with Harry Elam, 2001)
  Recipient of the 2002 Errol Hill Award from American Society for Theatre Research (ASTR)

- *Method Acting Reconsidered: Theory, Practice, Future* (editor, 2000)

- *Resistance, Parody and Double Consciousness in African American Theatre, 1895–1910* (1997)
  Recipient of the 1998 Errol Hill Award from ASTR

Theatre in Theory 1900–2000

An Anthology

Edited by
David Krasner

Blackwell
Publishing

BLACKWELL PUBLISHING
350 Main Street, Malden, MA 02148-5020, USA
9600 Garsington Road, Oxford OX4 2DQ, UK
550 Swanston Street, Carlton, Victoria 3053, Australia

First published 2008 by Blackwell Publishing Ltd

1   2008

Library of Congress Cataloging-in-Publication Data

Theatre in theory 1900–2000 : an anthology / edited by David Krasner.
    p. cm.
    Includes bibliographical references and index.
    ISBN 978-1-4051-4043-0 (hardcover : alk. paper)—ISBN 978-1-4051-4044-7 (pbk. : alk. paper) 1. Theater—History–20th century. 2. Drama—20th century—History and criticism. I. Krasner, David, 1952–

    PN2189.T494 2008
    792.09′04—dc22

                            2007003785

A catalogue record for this title is available from the British Library.

Set in 10/12.5pt Minion
by SPi Publisher Services, Pondicherry, India.

For further information on
Blackwell Publishing, visit our website at
www.blackwellpublishing.com

Contents

Contents

Acknowledgments

I am grateful to the staff at Blackwell. Emma Bennett has supported this project from its inception. I especially wish to thank and honor the help and dedication of Karen Wilson and the copyeditor, Brigitte Lee. Both have assisted me at every turn of this process. My wife Lynda is, as always, my foundation. Jorge Huerta has been most generous in providing insights into translations. Thelma Carter, Mark Gordon, Marvin Sims, and Doug Moston were four friends, colleagues, students, teachers, and directors who impacted my life and work. They were superb teachers, gifted people of the theatre, and departed much too soon. Their influence can be observed in the excellence of their students. Though I miss their insights and sage advice, their voices resonate. I dedicate this book to them.

The editor and publisher gratefully acknowledge the permission granted to reproduce the copyright material in this book.

Part I   1900–1920

1. August Strindberg, "Preface" (1888) to *Miss Julie*, tr. E. M. Sprinchorn (San Francisco: Chandler Publishing, 1961), xv–xxiv.
2. Excerpts from Oscar Wilde, "The Decay of Lying," first published in *Nineteenth Century* 25 (January 1889), 35–56, reprinted in revised form in Oscar Wilde's *Intentions* (London, 1891), 3–53, and here taken from *Literary Criticism of Oscar Wilde*, ed. S. Weintraub (Lincoln: University of Nebraska Press, 1968), 165–96.
3. Excerpts from Henri Bergson, "Laughter" (*Le Rire*, 1900), in *Comedy*, tr. and ed. Wylie Sypher (Baltimore: Johns Hopkins University Press, 1956, 1980), 63–85.

4. Valery Bryusov, "Against Naturalism in the Theatre" (from "Unnecessary Truth"), originally published in *World of Art* 4 (1902), excerpted from *The Russian Symbolist Theatre: Anthology of Plays and Critical Texts*, tr. and ed. Michael Green (Ann Arbor: Ardis, 1986), 25–30. © 1986 by Ardis Publishers. Reprinted by permission of The Overlook Press.

5. Excerpts from Romain Rolland, *The People's Theatre* [*Le Théâtre du Peuple*] (1903), tr. Barrett H. Clark, in *The Theory of the Modern Stage: An Introduction to Modern Theatre and Drama*, ed. Eric Bentley (New York: Penguin, 1968), 455–70.

6. Maurice Maeterlinck, "The Modern Drama" (1904), from *The Double Garden*, tr. Alfred Sutro (New York: Dodd, Mead, 1911), 115–39.

7. Excerpts from Aida Overton Walker, "Colored Men and Women on the Stage," *Colored American Magazine* 9.4 (October 1905), 571–5.

8. Vsevolod Vaslov Meyerhold, "The Naturalistic Theatre" and "The Theatre of Mood" (1908), first published in *Teatr, Kniga o novom teatre* [*Theatre: A Book about the New Theatre*] (St. Petersburg, 1908), 136–50, reprinted in *O Teatre* (St. Petersburg, 1915), 14–28, 33–47, and excerpted here from *Meyerhold on Theatre*, tr. and ed. Edward Braun (London: Methuen, 1991), 25–34, 49–54. © 1969, 1991 by Edward Braun. Reprinted by permission of Methuen Publishing Ltd.

9. Excerpts from Edward Gordon Craig, "The Actor and the Über-marionette," *The Mask* 1.1 (April 1908), 3–17.

10. W. B. Yeats, "The Tragic Theatre," *The Mask* 3 (October 1910), 77–81.

11. Excerpts from G. B. Shaw, "Preface," in *Three Plays by Brieux* (New York: Brentano's, 1913), vii–liv.

12. F. T. Marinetti, "Futurism and the Theatre: A Futurist Manifesto," tr. D. Nevile Lees, in *Mask* 6.3 (January 1914), 188–93. Originally published in *Lacerba* 1.19 (October 1, 1913).

13. Georg Lukács, "The Sociology of Modern Drama" (1914), tr. Lee Baxandall, copyright Baxandall, 1965; originally appeared in Hungarian in 1909, in German in 1914; reprinted here from *Tulane Drama Review* 9.4 (Summer 1965), 146–70. © 1965 by Lee Baxandall. Reprinted by permission of the author.

14. Emma Goldman, "Foreword," in *The Social Significance of Modern Drama* (1917, reprinted New York: Applause Books, 1987), 1–3.

Part II   1920–1940

15. Luigi Pirandello, "On Comedy" (1920), from a course lecture given by Pirandello in Rome; the first edition appeared in 1908; the second, from which this essay derived, came out in 1920 in Florence. Reprinted here from *Tulane Drama Review* 10.3 (Spring 1966), 46–59, tr. Teresa Novel. © 1966 by Tulane Drama Review. Reprinted by permission of TDR/The Drama Review.

16. Stanislaw Witkiewicz, "On a New Type of Play" (1920), from *The Mother and Other Unsavory Plays*, ed. and tr. Daniel Gerould and C. S. Durer (New York: Applause, 1993), 234–9. © 1966, 1967, 1968, 1993 by Daniel C. Gerould and C. S. Durer.

17. Adolphe Appia, "Organic Unity" (1921), from *The Work of Living Art: A Theory of the Theatre*, tr. H. D. Albright (Coral Gables: University of Miami Press, 1960), 38–58. © 1960 by Walther R. Volbach.

18. Georg Kaiser, "Man in the Tunnel, or: The Poet and the Play" (1923), tr. Joel Agee, reproduced from *Essays on German Theater*, ed. Margaret Herzfeld-Sander (New York: Continuum, 1985), 168–70. Originally from Georg Kaiser, *Werke*, Vol. 4 (Propyläen Verlag, 1971), translated by permission of Verlag Ullstein. © 1985 by the Continuum Publishing Company. Reprinted by permission of The Continuum International Publishing Group.

19. Excerpts from Alain Locke, "The Negro and the American Stage," *Theatre Arts Monthly* 10.2 (February 1926), 112–20, and "The Drama of Negro Life," *Theatre Arts Monthly* 10.10 (October 1926), 701–6.

20. Excerpts from W. E. B. Du Bois, "Krigwa Players Little Negro Theatre," *Crisis* 32.3 (July 1926), 134–6, and "Criteria of Negro Art," *Crisis* 32.6 (October 1926), 290–7. © 1926. Reprinted by permission of Crisis Magazine.

21. Excerpts from Bertolt Brecht, "The Modern Theatre is the Epic Theatre" (1930), "Theatre for Pleasure or Theatre for Instruction" (ca. 1936), and "Alienation Effect in Chinese Acting" (1936), tr. and ed. John Willett, in *Brecht on Theatre: The Development of an Aesthetic* (New York: Hill & Wang, 1957, 2000), 37–9, 69–78, and 91–9. Translation copyright © 1964, renewed 1992 by John Willett. Reprinted by permission of Farrar, Straus, and Giroux, LLC, and Methuen Publishing Ltd.

22. Three essays by Eugene O'Neill from *The American Spectator*: "Memoranda on Masks" (November 1932), 3; "Second Thoughts" (December 1932), 20; and "A Dramatist's Notebook" (January 1933), 2.

23. Excerpts from Gertrude Stein, "Plays" (1934), from Stein, *Last Operas and Plays*, ed. Bonnie Marranca (Baltimore: Johns Hopkins University Press, 1995), xxix–xliv. © 1949 by the Estate of Gertrude Stein. Copyright renewed, 1977. "Plays" taken from *Lectures in America* © 1935 and renewed 1963 by Alice B. Toklas.

24. Zora Neale Hurston, "Characteristics of Negro Expression," in *The Negro*, ed. Nancy Cunard (1934), quoted from a reprint of *The Negro*, ed. and abridged by Hugh Ford (New York: Continuum, 1996), 24–31. © 1970 by Frederick Ungar Publishing Co., Inc. Reprinted by permission of The Continuum International Publishing Group.

25. Federico García Lorca, "The Prophesy of Lorca" (1934), tr. Albert E. Sloman, quoted from *Theatre Arts* 34.10 (October 1950), 38–9. Address delivered after the opening of *Yerma*.

26. Antonin Artaud, "On the Balinese Theatre" and "No More Masterpieces" (1938), from *The Theatre and Its Double*, tr. Mary Caroline Richards (New York: Grove Press, 1958), 53–67, 74–83. © 1958 by Grove Press, Inc. Reprinted by permission of Grove/Atlantic, Inc.

27. Walter Benjamin, "What is Epic Theatre?" (1939), tr. Harry Zohn, from *Illuminations*, ed. Hannah Arendt (New York: Schocken, 1968), 147–54. © 1955 by Suhrkamp Verlag, Frankfurt a. M., English translation by Harry Zohn copyright © 1968 and renewed 1996 by Harcourt, Inc., reprinted by permission of Harcourt, Inc., and The Random House Group Ltd.

28. Maxwell Anderson, "The Essence of Tragedy," in *The Essence of Tragedy and Other Footnotes and Papers* (Washington, DC: Anderson House, 1939), 3–14. Paper read at the Modern Language Association in New York, January 1938.

29. Karel Brušák, "Signs in the Chinese Theatre," originally "Znaky na čínském divadle," *Slovo a slovesnost* (*Word and Poetics*) 5 (1939), tr. Brušák, from *Semiotics of Art*, ed. Ladislav Matejka and Irwin R. Titunik (Cambridge, MA: MIT Press, 1976), 59–73. © 1976 by The Massachusetts Institute of Technology. Reprinted by permission of The MIT Press.

Part III   1940–1960

30. Jindřich Honzl, "Dynamics of the Sign in the Theatre," originally "Pohyb divadelního znaku," *Slovo a slovesnost* (*Word and Poetics*) 6 (1940), tr. I. R. Titunik, from *Semiotics of Art*, ed. Ladislav Matejka and Irwin R. Titunik (Cambridge, MA: MIT Press, 1976), 74–93. © 1976 by The Massachusetts Institute of Technology. Reprinted by permission of The MIT Press.

31. Thornton Wilder, "Some Thoughts on Playwrighting," in *Intent of the Artist*, ed. A. Centeno (Princeton: Princeton University Press, 1941), 83–98. © 1941 by The Wilder Family LLC. All rights reserved. Reprinted by permission of The Barbara Hogenson Agency, Inc.

32. Arthur Miller, "Tragedy and the Common Man," *New York Times* (February 27, 1949), Sec. 2, pp. 1, 3; reprinted in *The Theater Essays of Arthur Miller*, ed. Robert A. Martin (New York: Viking, 1978), 3–7. © 1949, renewed © 1977 by Arthur Miller. Reprinted by permission of Viking Penguin, a division of Penguin Group (USA) Inc.

33. Excerpts from T. S. Eliot, *Poetry and Drama* (Cambridge, MA: Harvard University Press, 1951), 10–17. © 1951 T. S. Eliot. Reprinted by permission of Faber and Faber Ltd and Farrar, Straus, and Giroux, LLC. Originally delivered as Eliot's Theodore Spencer Memorial Lecture, November 21, 1950.

34. Tennessee Williams, "The Timeless World of the Play," in *The Rose Tattoo* (New York: New Directions, 1951), vi–xi. © 1951 by The University of the South. Reprinted by permission of New Directions Publishing Corp. and Methuen Publishing Ltd.

35. Excerpts from John Gassner, "'Enlightenment' and Modern Drama," from *The Theatre in Our Times* (New York: Crown, 1954), 56–66.

36. Excerpts from Friedrich Dürrenmatt, "Problems of the Theatre" (1955), tr. Gerhard Nellhaus, *Tulane Drama Review* 3.1 (October 1958), 3–26. © 1955 by Tulane Drama Review. Reprinted by permission of TDR/The Drama Review. This version was prepared for publication from a lecture delivered by Dürrenmatt in the fall of 1954 and the spring of 1955 in Switzerland and West Germany.

37. Sean O'Casey, "Green Goddess of Realism," in *The Green Crow* (New York: George Braziller, 1956), 73–86. © 1956 by Sean O'Casey. Reprinted by permission of the Estate of Sean O'Casey.

38. Excerpts from Eric Bentley, *What is Theatre? A Point of View* (Boston: Beacon Press, 1956), 264–70. Copyright © 2000 by Eric Bentley. Reprinted by permission of Farrar, Straus, and Giroux, LLC.

39. Northrop Frye, "Specific Forms of Drama," reproduced from the fourth essay, "Rhetorical Criticism: Theory of Genres," in *Anatomy of Criticism: Four Essays* (Princeton: Princeton University Press), 282–93. © 1957 by Princeton University Press, 1985 renewed PUP, 2000 paperback edition. Reprinted by permission of Princeton University Press.

40. Eugène Ionesco, "The Avant-Garde Theatre," *Tulane Drama Review* 5.2 (1960), 44–53. © 1960 by Tulane Drama Review. Reprinted by permission of TDR/The Drama Review.

41. Jean-Paul Sartre, "Beyond Bourgeois Theatre" (1960), tr. R. D. Reck, *Tulane Drama Review* 5.3 (March 1961), 3–11. © 1961 by Tulane Drama Review. Reprinted by permission of TDR/The Drama Review. From a lecture given at the Sorbonne, March 29, 1960. The full version of this lecture, titled "Epic Theater and Dramatic Theater," is contained in *Sartre on Theater*, ed. M. Contat and M. Rybalka (New York: Pantheon, 1976), 77–120.

Part IV 1960–1980

42. Excerpts from Martin Esslin, *Theatre of the Absurd* (New York: Anchor Books, 1961; reprinted New York: Penguin, 1980), 19–26. © 1961 by Martin Esslin. Reprinted by permission of Doubleday, a division of Random House, Inc., and Methuen Publishing Ltd.

43. Excerpts from George Steiner, *The Death of Tragedy* (New York: Oxford University Press, 1961, 1980), 3–10. © 1961, 1980 by George Steiner. Reprinted by permission of Faber and Faber Ltd and Knopf, a division of Random House, Inc.

44. Roland Barthes, "The Task of Brechtian Criticism" (1956) and "Theatre and Signification" (1963), from "Barthes on Theatre," tr. Peter W. Mathers, *Theatre Quarterly* 9.33 (Spring 1979), 25–30.

45. Lionel Abel, "Of Bert Brecht – Not Simple but Simplified," excerpted from Abel, *Metatheatre: A New View of Dramatic Form* (New York: Hill & Wang, 1963), 103–7.

46. Francis Fergusson, "The Notion of 'Action,'" *Tulane Drama Review* 9.1 (Fall 1964), 85–7. © 1964 by Tulane Drama Review. Reprinted by permission of TDR/The Drama Review.

47. Peter Szondi, "The Drama" (1965), from *Theory of the Modern Drama*, tr. and ed. Michael Hays (Minneapolis: University of Minnesota Press, 1987), 7–10. Original work published in German as *Theorie des modernen Dramas*, copyright © 1965 by Suhrkamp Verlag. English translation © 1987 by the University of Minnesota. Reprinted by permission of Polity and Suhrkamp Verlag.

48. Kenneth Burke, "Dramatic Form – And: Tracking Down Implications," *Tulane Drama Review* 10.4 (Summer 1966), 54–63. © 1966 by Tulane Drama Review. Reprinted by permission of TDR/The Drama Review.

49. Jacques Derrida, "Theatre of Cruelty and the Closure of Representation" (1966). Lecture originally delivered as "Le théâtre de la cruauté et la clôture de la représentation" at the Artaud colloquium, International Festival of University Theater, Parma, April 1966, and published in *Critique* 230 (July 1966). Excerpted here from Derrida, *Writing and Difference*, tr. Alan Bass (Chicago: University of Chicago Press, 1978), 232–9. © 1978 by The University of Chicago. Reprinted by permission of The University of Chicago Press and Taylor and Francis Books UK.

50. Jerzy Grotowski, "Towards the Poor Theatre," tr. T. K. Wiewiorowski, *Tulane Drama Review* 11.3 (Spring 1967), 60–5. © 1967 by Tulane Drama Review. Reprinted by permission of TDR/The Drama Review.

51. Raymond Williams, "Drama from Ibsen to Brecht," excerpted from his "Introduction" to *Drama from Ibsen to Brecht* (New York: Penguin, 1968), 1–12. © 1952, 1964, 1968 by Raymond Williams. Reprinted by permission of The Random House Group Ltd.

52. Peter Brook, "The Immediate Theatre," excerpted from *The Empty Space* (New York: Atheneum, 1968), 98–100. Copyright © 1968 by Peter Brook. Copyright renewed 1996 by Peter Brook. All rights reserved. Reprinted with the permission of Scribner, an imprint of Simon & Schuster Adult Publishing Group.

53. Peter Weiss, "Notes on the Contemporary Theatre," tr. Joel Agee, in *Essays on German Theater*, ed. Margaret Herzfeld-Sander (New York: Continuum, 1985), 294–301. © 1985 by the Continuum Publishing Company. Reprinted by permission of The Copyright Clearance Center on behalf of The Continuum Publishing Company. Originally published as "Notizen zum dokumentarischen Theater," *Rapporte* 2 (Frankfurt am Main: Suhrkamp Verlag, 1971).

54. Excerpts from Joyce Carol Oates, *The Edge of Impossibility: Tragic Forms in Literature* (Greenwich, CT: Fawcett Premier Books, 1972), 8–12. © 1972 by Joyce Carol Oates. Reprinted by permission of the author.

55. Luis Valdez, "Notes on Chicano Theater," excerpted from *Guerrilla Theater: Scenarios for a Revolution*, ed. John Weisman (Garden City, NY: Anchor, 1973), 55–8.

56. Augusto Boal, "Empathy or What? Emotion or Reason?" and excerpt from "Experiments with the People's Theatre in Peru," from *Theatre of the Oppressed*, tr. Charles A. and Maria-Odilia Leal McBride (1979; New York: TCG, 1985), 102–4, 122; originally published in Spanish as *Teatro de Oprimido* (1974). Translation © 1979 by Charles A. and Maria-Odilia Leal McBride. Reprinted by permission of Theatre Communications Group.

57. Charles Ludlam, "Ridiculous Theatre, Scourge of Human Folly," *The Drama Review* 19.4 (December 1975), 70. © Charles Ludlam.

58. Michael Kirby, "Manifesto of Structuralism," *The Drama Review* 19.4 (December 1975), 82–3. © 1975 by Tulane Drama Review. Reprinted by permission of TDR/The Drama Review.

59. Wole Soyinka, "Drama and the African World-View," excerpted from *Myth, Literature, and the African World* (Cambridge: Cambridge University Press, 1976), 37–44, 142–7 (appendix). © 1976 by Cambridge University Press. Reprinted by permission of the author and publisher.

60. Robert Wilson, "… I thought I was hallucinating hallucinating," *The Drama Review* 21.4 (December 1977), 76–8. © 1977 by Tulane Drama Review. Reprinted by permission of TDR/The Drama Review.

61. Patrice Pavis, "Languages of the Stage" (1978), in *Languages of the Stage: Essays in the Semiology of Theatre*, tr. Susan Melrose (New York: PAJ, 1982), 39–49. First published in *Silex* 7 (1978). © 1978. Reprinted by permission of Susan Melrose.

62. Heiner Müller, "Reflections on Post-Modernism," tr. Jack Zipes, with B. N. Weber, in *New German Critique* 16 (Winter 1979), reprinted in *Essays on German Theater*, ed.

Margaret Herzfeld-Sander (New York: Continuum, 1985), 345–48. © 1979. Reprinted by permission of Jack Zipes.

63. Ntozake Shange, "Unrecovered losses/black theater traditions," from *Three Pieces* (New York: St. Martin's Press, 1981), ix–xi. © 1981 by Ntozake Shange. Reprinted by permission of St. Martin's Press, LLC.

Part V   1980–2000

64. Tadeusz Kantor, "Theatre Happening 1967" (1982), tr. and ed. Michal Kobialka, first published in 1982 as "Teatr Happening" and reprinted in *TDR* 30.3 (Fall 1986), 135–6. © 1982 by Tadeusz Kantor.

65. Excerpts from Jeffrey E. Huntsman, "Native American Theatre," originally published in *Ethnic Theatre in the United States*, ed. Maxine Schwartz Seller (Westport: Greenwood Press, 1983), reprinted in *American Indian Theater in Performance: A Reader*, ed. Hanay Geiogamah and Jaye T. Darby (Los Angeles: UCLA American Indian Studies Center, 2000), 81–9. © Maxine Schwartz Seller. Reprinted by permission of Greenwood Publishing Group, Inc., Westport, CT.

66. Excerpts from Bert O. States, "The World On Stage," from *Great Reckonings in Little Rooms: On the Phenomenology of Theater* (Berkeley: University of California Press, 1985), 19–47. © 1985 by The Regents of the University of California Press. Reprinted by permission of The Copyright Clearance Center on behalf of University of California Press.

67. Victor Turner, "Images and Reflections: Ritual, Drama, Carnival, Film, and Spectacle in Cultural Performance," in *The Anthropology of Performance* (New York: PAJ Press, 1987), 21–7. © 1987, 1988 PAJ Publications.

68. Eugenio Barba, "Eurasian Theatre," tr. R. Fowler, *TDR* 32.3 (Fall 1988), 126–30. © 1988 by Eugenio Barba. Reprinted by permission of the author.

69. Megumi Sata, "Aristotle's *Poetics* and Zeami's *Teachings on Style and the Flower*," *Asian Theatre Journal* 6.1 (Spring 1989), 47–56, University of Hawai'i Press. © 1989. Reprinted by permission of University of Hawai'i Press.

70. Excerpts from Jill Dolan, "Desire Cloaked in a Trenchcoat," *TDR* 33.1 (Spring 1989), 59–67, reprinted in Dolan, *Presence and Desire: Essays on Gender, Sexuality, Performance* (Ann Arbor: University of Michigan Press, 1993), 121–34. © 1989 by New York University and the Massachusetts Institute of Technology. Reprinted by permission of MIT Press Journals.

71. Judith Butler, "Parody to Politics," in *Gender Trouble: Feminism and the Subversion of Identity* (New York: Routledge, 1990), 142–9. © 1990 by Routledge, Chapman, & Hall, Inc. Reprinted by permission of Taylor and Francis Group LLC.

72. Reza Abdoh, "Los Angeles," *Mime Journal* (1991/1992), annual published by the Pomona College Theatre Department. © 1991 by Mime Journal. Reprinted by permission of Mime, Pomona College Theatre Department.

73. Excerpts from Richard Foreman, "Foundations for a Theater," in *Unbalancing Acts: Foundations for a Theater*, ed. Ken Jordan (New York: TCG, 1992), 3–31. © 1992 by

Richard Foreman. Reprinted by permission of Pantheon Books, a division of Random House, Inc.

74. Suzan-Lori Parks, "Elements of Style" (1994), in Parks, *The American Play and Other Works* (New York: TCG, 1995), 6–18. © 1995 by Suzan-Lori Parks. Reprinted by permission of Theatre Communications Group.

75. Excerpts from Rebecca Schneider, *The Explicit Body in Performance* (London: Routledge, 1997), 1–10 (Introduction). © 1997 by Rebecca Schneider. Reprinted by permission of Taylor and Francis Books UK.

76. Excerpts from Peggy Phelan, *Mourning Sex: Performing Public Memories* (London: Routledge, 1997), 1–5. © 1997 by Peggy Phelan. Reprinted by permission of Taylor and Francis Books UK.

77. Excerpts from Erika Fischer-Lichte, "Written Drama/Oral Performance," in *The Show and the Gaze of Theatre: A European Perspective* (Iowa City: University of Iowa Press, 1997), 319–37. © 1997 by The University of Iowa Press. Reprinted by permission of the publisher.

78. Richard Schechner, "What is Performance Studies Anyway?" in *The Ends of Performance*, ed. Peggy Phelan and Jill Lane (New York: NYU Press, 1998), 357–62. © 1998 by New York University. Reprinted by permission of New York University Press.

79. Alina Troyano, "I, Carmelita Tropicana," excerpted from Alina Troyano, with Ela Troyano and Uzi Parnes, *I, Carmelita Tropicana: PeRforMinG Between CultuRes*, ed. C. A. Norigea (Boston: Beacon Press, 2000), xiii–xxv. © 2000 by Alina Troyano. Reprinted by permission of the author.

80. Excerpts from Herbert Blau, "Limits of Performance: The Insane Root," in *The Dubious Spectacle: Extremities of Theater, 1976–2000* (Minneapolis: University of Minnesota Press, 2002), 307–20. Originally published in *Psychoanalysis and Performance*, ed. Patrick Campbell and Adrian Kear (London: Routledge: 2001), 21–33. © 2001 by Routledge. Reprinted by permission of Taylor and Francis Books UK. The essay is a revised and expanded version of a talk given in May 1999 at the Stanford Presidential Symposium on "Limits of Performance: Sports, Medicine, and the Humanities."

81. Excerpts from Mitsuya Mori, "The Structure of Theater: A Japanese View of Theatricality," in *Substance 98/99: Special Issue, Theatricality* Vol. 31.2 and 3 (2002), 73–93. © 2002. Reprinted by permission of The University of Wisconsin Press.

82. Heisnam Kanhailal, "Ritual Theatre (Theatre of Transition)," in *Theatre India: National School of Drama's Theatre India* 10 (Nov. 2004), 3–16. Reprinted by permission of Heisnam Kanhailal.

Every effort has been made to trace copyright holders and to obtain their permission for the use of copyright material. The publisher apologizes for any errors or omissions in the above list and would be grateful if notified of any corrections that should be incorporated in future reprints or editions of this book.

Introduction

The aim of this anthology is to assist readers in thinking critically about twentieth-century dramatic theory and criticism. The primary sources gathered here are eclectic in content, attesting to the complexity and diversity of theatre and performance theory. The *Oxford English Dictionary* defines "theory" from three Greek sources: θεωρία, which means "a looking at, viewing, contemplation, speculation, sight, and spectacle"; θεωρόα, which means "spectator and looker on"; and θεᾶσθαι, which means "to look on, view, and contemplate." It is noteworthy that the three principal terms used to describe theory – "viewing, looking, contemplating" – also define "theatre." Theatre, derived from the Greek θέᾱτρου, means "a place of viewing."[1] Theory and theatre regarded as "viewing and contemplating" cohere semantically and significantly; both theatre and theory are etymological derivatives of the Greek term *thea* – a place to observe. While theatre has been linked to entertainment, it has traditionally provided a forum of intellectual engagement and philosophical exchange.

The twentieth-century theories set forth in this collection were influenced by developments during the nineteenth century. In theatre there arose the importance of the theatrical director as a source of interpretative intervention and technological advancements in stage lighting, set design, and photography (and later cinema). Europe experienced a shift from rural agrarianism to industrial urbanization, and the aftermath of the Revolution of 1848 ushered in a period of unparalleled technological advances and economic growth, which in turn facilitated bourgeois consumerism, progress, and imperialism. The world shifted, the effects of which ramified across borders and ideas. Amidst the heady times arose the concept of "modernity," eliciting both progressive and chaotic responses and bringing advances in science and medicine, but also causing an increasing awareness of an alienating effect among human relations. In aesthetics, Baudelaire's modernist ambiguity in his art and literary criticism and Zola's naturalism were among several influential theories. Impressionism in art established a then radical style that conveyed not merely a reflection of reality but the observation of reality – the act of perception itself. Light and color coexisted with realistic representation so that the canvas teemed with a palpable determination to examine the tension of portraying reality and the way we see reality. In philosophy there occurred the transition from idealism to modernism, and modernism itself divided along the lines of continental and analytic schools of thought. The former dwelled in speculative metaphysics and phenomenology; the latter dealt with empirical evidence and was directed towards the articulation of meaning. In art, literature, and drama the fin de siècle witnessed the rising avant-garde and the avant-garde's realistic antithesis. A cursory glance at the late nineteenth-century period reveals an elaborate picture of many aims and at times contradictory themes. Theorists had disdain for the ambitions of those preceding them, rejecting eighteenth-century Enlightenment rationalism as well as early nineteenth-century Romantic inwardness. The designation of modernism – a fluid term ranging from one late nineteenth- and early twentieth-century playwright or theatrical event to another – stems from the condition in which tradition was perceived as stifling creativity and the task of making sense of ourselves and the world lacked certainty and authority. Political, social, and economic changes, scientific developments, and artistic inventiveness encouraged the questioning of tradition and validating the "new." For modernists past models had collapsed, convention had inhibited creativity, and formulas were perceived to have thwarted innovation. Modernism broke from seventeenth-century Neoclassicism, which according to modernists had turned Aristotle's *Poetics* into one-size-fits-all dogma, and from Enlightenment's positivist-progressive path to knowledge, which was deemed "totalizing" (relying on a grand theme) and out of step with radical movements inclined towards the marginal and unorthodox. Modernism likewise rebelled against popular melodrama, rejecting its simplistic moralization and avoiding what it saw as its excessive Boulevard razzmatazz and hyped pyrotechnics. Instead intimacy, ambiguity, and fragmentation came into vogue.

At the center of the period's theoretical debate for theatre is mimesis and representation. Theatre historian Patrice Pavis affirms this fact, claiming that the "crisis in mimetism and representation dates back to the end of the nineteenth century, when naturalism and symbolism combined forces under the aegis of the director," resulting in new possibilities of theatre theory apart from the literary. Theatre historian Marvin Carlson adds that "Not until the rise of modern interest in performance was there much thought that a play might be presented in a different contextualization, not as a cousin of such literary forms as the poem or the novel, but of such performance forms as the circus, the sideshow, the parade, or even the wrestling match or the political convention."[2] Indeed, throughout the twentieth century, theatre and performance theory departs from the purely literary and divides along the fault line of theatrical representation. Theatre either levels itself in the dimensions of pure representation liberated from myth, dreams, and metaphysical concerns, or focuses on hidden meanings, spirituality, and the substrata beyond appearances. For theatre theory, the central question is: should theatre remain faithful to real-world representation or challenge the veracity of mimesis by cutting against the grain of realistic presentation? Social reform during the early twentieth century additionally influenced the rise of the Little Theatre Movements across Europe and America, while radical nonconformists influenced Chamber Theatres stressing abstraction, experimentation, formalism, and metatheatrics (theatre calling attention to itself) over psychology and pictorial representations – realistic forms considered shopworn and promoting bourgeois values. Modernists explored narrative techniques, applying avant-garde pressures to the conventions of storytelling in the hopes of creating a new connection between audience and production. The rise of *l'art pour l'art* (art for art's sake) exemplified one of the period's myriad experimentations. Others favoring abstraction but desiring political relevance looked to expressionism and epic theatre as genres inducing social change. The experimental movements by and large rejected fourth-wall convention, the idea that the stage is framed by an imaginary edifice (the proscenium arch) separating audience and actor; content-driven realistic dramas in which the narrative refers to real time and place; and psychological realism, actors embodying characters for the purpose of portraying subconscious motivation. For the avant-garde a critical transcendent form of reality was to be achieved not by replicating the world, but rather by deliberately distorting its representations of people, things, and ideas. Art must not merely mirror reality but make audiences question values as categories of the status quo. Playwrights turned to myth and its archetypes, exploring innovative forms to express interiority. The German director Georg Fuchs (1868–1949) illustrated the challenge to nineteenth-century realism in his *Die Revolution des Theaters* (1909) by positing a desire to "re-theatricalize the theatre." Others, such as playwright and theorist Maurice Maeterlinck (see Chapter 6), sought to convey the tragedy of everyday life (*le tragique quotidien*) by fleshing out not the active but the inactive, inconsequential experiences and processes of daily life that often elude our consciousness. Both realism and experimentalism attempted to expand the theories of theatre, the former through strategically placed symbols and the latter by undermining representation through defamiliarization and the bizarre. The complexity of twentieth-century theatre in theory stems largely from the conflict of (and inability to reconcile) scientific rationalism and artistic autonomy. The former seeks to ground drama in the secular world and the latter stresses theatre's withdrawal into a unique aesthetic realm transcending the everyday.

Still, however much new theories emphasized directorial conceptualization, social conditions, or autonomy from the text, the essays in this anthology frequently revisit antecedent ideas. The meaning of representation (mimesis), for example, was subjected to intense scrutiny by Plato and Aristotle. The European Renaissance and Age of Reason (sixteenth and seventeenth centuries), the Enlightenment (eighteenth century), and the Romantic period (first half of the nineteenth century) yielded influential dramatic theories. Three German philosophers in particular – Kant, Hegel, and Nietzsche – made impressive contributions to aesthetics. While no summary can do justice to the complexity and multiplicity of topics, the following will review mimesis (representation), briefly canvas three key periods (Renaissance, Enlightenment, and Romanticism), especially Kant's influence on aesthetics, and examine Hegel and Nietzsche in setting the stage for twentieth-century theatre in theory. I contend that both the Platonic-Aristotelian divide over theatre and representation and the tripartite influences of Kant, Hegel, and Nietzsche establish the fundamental debates over theatre in theory that extend throughout the twentieth century. Others no doubt inform twentieth-century issues. However, the purpose of this Introduction is to stress the point that the theories of Plato, Aristotle, Kant, Hegel, and Nietzsche provide much of the groundwork for things to come.

Mimesis: Plato and Aristotle

It is often incorrectly asserted that Plato (ca. 427–347 BC) rejected mimesis and representation out of hand. His works indicate various definitions of the term "mimesis," which for
the ancient Greeks meant imitation, representation, emulation, copying, mimicry, art, and
even parody. In *Laws*, for example, Plato considers the "pleasure-giving effect" of music,
noting that the "educative-playful function of the Muses" permits audiences to sit in
judgment. Nevertheless, "A judge who is truly a judge must not learn his verdict from the
audience, letting himself be intimidated into it by the clamor of the multitude and his
own incompetence." The judge, Plato says, "takes his seat not to learn from the audience,
but to teach them, and to set himself against performers who give an audience pleasure in
wrong and improper ways."[3] In *Sophists*, Plato calls art "a man-made dream for waking
eyes" (1014; 266c). He makes a distinction between art that creates "likeness," an example
of which "consists in creating a copy that conforms to the proportions of the original in all
three dimensions and giving moreover proper color to every part," and art that creates
"semblances," which "seems to be a likeness, but is not really so," because it is made like
the original but influenced by the artist (978, 979; 235d, 236b). Both forms of expression,
however, are "deeply involved in perplexity" (979; 236e). Jacques Derrida raises the apt
point that Plato is being evasive here, because "the making of likenesses (the *eikastic*) or
faithful reproduction, and the making of semblances (the *fantastic*) which simulates the
eikastic, pretending to simulate faithfully and deceiving the eye with simulacrum (a
phantasm)" is "an aporia for the philosophical hunter, who comes to a stop before this
bifurcation, incapable of continuing to track down his quarry."[4] Plato, while acknowledging
theatre's mimetic appeal, is skeptical of its value in influencing moral and legal judgments.

In the tenth book of the *Republic* (ca. 373 BC), Plato outright condemns *mímēsis*. The
artist-imitator for Plato is the maker of images as opposed to the maker of reality. Because
the image maker – the imitator-poet – dwells in the realm of illusion, he or she deals in "the
appearance" rather than "the reality and the truth" (821; 596e, 4). The maker of images and
the maker of reality are both removed from the Platonic ideal. However, despite human
error and the ontological inferiority of any imitation, the maker of reality strives (or should
strive) towards the ideal. The maker of images, by contrast, "knows nothing of the reality
but only the appearance" (826; 601c, 1–2), striving neither towards the ideal nor even the
practical. Plato's example, the creation of a bed, illustrates his point that there are three
levels of creators: the ideal, the real, and the illusion maker. The first is nature: the idea
(*eidos*) of a "bed" exists on a lofty plane of nature and represents something which
symbolizes "bed" in its ideal state. The second is utilitarian, the carpenter-bedmaker
(*eikon*) in this case, who strives to make the perfect bed but ultimately falls short by dint
of human imperfection and reliance on facsimile (imitating the ideal). Finally there is the
artist or poet who draws, sculpts, and describes a bed that may not even exist in tangible
form yet whose creation is falsely taken by the public to be real. The artist's mimesis
(*mimos*) is therefore "three removes from reality" (825; 599a, 1), because the artist deals
on a third level: illusion. "Poetry delivers a poor and unreliable knowledge," Arne Melberg
writes, because for Plato "it is a second-hand imitation of an already second-hand imitation."[5] The artist is furthermore driven by inspiration rather than technical ability, deals in
emotions rather than reason, and merely copies what already exists in an imperfect state.

Plato amplifies his criticism by asserting that the artist deceives through phantasm. He sought to preserve the fundamental duality – and capacity to distinguish – between substance, being, and reality on the one hand, and appearance, image, and ephemerality on the other. Duplication, derivation, and representation undermine this duality by creating an illusion of reality through fantasy and brio. Fictional representation is therefore dangerous because it constructs an alternative and seductively appealing narrative to reality (a suspicion of representation that would later be used by the English Puritans and many others in their campaign against theatre). An actor portraying a doctor, for instance, need know nothing of medicine; despite the actor's illusion, the audience is in danger of measuring the quality of doctoring by the behavior of this fictionalized representation. An actor's charming bedside manner will be the yardstick by which real doctors are measured. Plato correctly pinpoints theatre's hoax: the more convincing the actor, the more we are seduced; the allure of the performance – its credibility – is what worries Plato. Performing an imitation overrides substance; its seduction disables our capacity to discern fact from fiction and undermines our judgment of values. Paul Woodruff contends further that in the attractiveness of a performance "we may be beguiled into becoming performers, and therefore into taking deception as *our* aim; and this is morally an unhealthy aim to take."[6] Imitation begets imitation, making cloning the desired aim in lieu of substantive inquiry. It is not that we go to an actor for medical advice, but rather that we might go to a doctor and judge the doctor's diagnosis on the basis of a previously seen actor's performance, or, most egregiously, we might think we know more than the doctor because we copy the actor's ability to dispense facile medical advice. For Plato judgment based on appearance rather than substance derails proper assessment. His reasoning can be summarized as follows: (1) artists sculpt appearances, (2) appearances are deceiving, and (3) deception leads us astray.

Graham Ley observes that for Plato the "painter and imitative poet create works which are poor in relation to the truth, and associate with a part of the soul that is not the best."[7] The artist is a dissembler appealing to the basest part of our being where imagination and playfulness dwell. The imitator, Plato says, "knows nothing worth mentioning of the things he imitates, but that imitation is a form of play (*paidia*), and not anything serious (*spondē*)." Theatre is play and play is puerile. To emphasize his point regarding the performer's optical illusion Plato uses the example of a straight object which appears bent in water. "The same things appear bent and straight to those who view them in water and out, or concave or convex," he notes, "owing to similar errors of vision about colors and there is obviously every confusion of this sort in our souls. And so scene painting in its exploitation of this weakness of our nature falls nothing short of witchcraft, and so do jugglery and so do contrivances" (827; 602c10–11, d1–4). Theatre is legerdemain, untrustworthy and corrupting. Richard McKeon aptly explains that for Plato, dramatic poetry "attains only a small part of the object, and the part it attains is not the object itself but an image capable of deceiving. If the poet were able to produce things he imitates instead of making only images, if he had knowledge of the truth, he would abandon imitation."[8] Mimesis provides no satisfactory substitute for reality; worse, it lacks virtue. In his exemplary study, *Virtues of Authenticity*, Alexander Nehamas writes that for Plato the "inauthentic is the unethical. There is virtue in being authentic, and there is authenticity in all virtue. Nothing fake can be good, and nothing good can be fake."[9] The actor according to Plato takes on the role of authoritarian but lacks sufficient knowledge to assume such responsibility. Even if the imitation is flattering, the imitator-poet for Plato, Nehamas says, "can do no more than imitate the look, not the nature, of things" (260). Plato thus condemns mimetic art on several fronts: because it is a replication masquerading as truth, it is child-like and associated with the basest parts of our soul, and it is potentially deleterious to our well-being.

Plato's criticism of mimesis penetrates twentieth-century theatre theory in two ways. First, his suspicion of mimesis transmogrified into anti-theatrical closet drama (drama read rather than performed). Martin Puchner maintains that "Modern drama and theater is a Platonist theater, by which I mean not a theater of abstract ideas but a theater infused with types of anti-theatricality first developed in Plato's closet dramas."[10] Plato's suspicion of theatricality evolved into playwrights and theorists seeking to limit theatre's illusionary devices and actorial virtuosity. If a play is read and not performed, or performed with minimal intervention by actors, the illusion-making process is contained. As a result the falsehoods Plato decried are kept to a minimum. Second, the ability of language and performance to replicate reality in any accurate way is deemed ludicrous by many twentieth-century theorists: mimesis does not represent the world, but is merely a narrative designed by an author. Realism and mimesis claiming to represent truth labor under the burden of delusion. Like the bourgeois novel of the nineteenth century, the realist theatre has been designated retrograde because its reference to the real world presents reality as fixed, immobile, and determined. One of its most forceful critics, Elin Diamond, writes that theatrical realism, "more than any other form of theater representation, mystifies the process of theatrical signification." Because realism levels the relationship between character and performer, obscuring any break between the setting and the world, realism not only operates in concert with ideology, it "insists on a stability of reference, an objective world that is the source and guarantor of knowledge," and "surreptitiously reinforces (even if it argues with) the arrangements of that world."[11] Diamond's assertion has had an important and powerful influence on late twentieth-century critical thinking, reminding us that Plato's admonitions remain relevant. Despite its claim to project the "mirror up to nature," realism and mimesis are insidious because, as Plato or twentieth-century French poststructural theorists Foucault and Barthes might suggest, their pretense to objectivity obfuscates the backstage strings that manipulate reality. (For the poststructuralists there is no author anyway because writing is basically collaborative, produced by a cultural collective of circulating language.) Realism attempts to mimic what is assumed to be "already there," immutably situated either psychologically or socially in human relations. The debate over the value of mimesis and its detractors begins with Plato and Aristotle, but it does not end with them.

Aristotle (384–322 BC) appears to rebut Plato in his *Poetics* (ca. 335 BC). The *Poetics'* authenticity is difficult to decipher because it comes to us circuitously by way of Arabic and Greek editions.[12] Whether it was actually written by Aristotle or simply notes taken by his students is also uncertain. But the work's enduring significance is undeniable. Mimesis for Aristotle is not so much the conflict between appearance and reality that Plato would have us believe as it is an *imitation of an action*. Aristotle adroitly circumvents Plato's idea that imitation is a crude replica by bypassing the point of mimesis as imitating human beings and situating it squarely on action. Character, in other words, is subsidiary to action: *theatre imitates what people do, not who they are*. The goal of drama is teleological rather than ontological; its characteristics are action and the arrangement of scenes rather than counterfeit entities. In his well-known definition of tragedy he says:

> Tragedy, then, is a representation of an action...in the mode of dramatic enactment, not narrative – and through the arousal of pity and fear effecting the catharsis of such emotions....The most important of these elements [the components of tragedy] is the structure of events, because tragedy is representation not of people as such but of actions and life, and both happiness and unhappiness rest on action. The goal is a certain activity [kind of action], not a qualitative state; and while men do have certain qualities by virtue of their character, it is [through] their actions that they achieve, or fail to achieve, happiness (*eudemonia*). It is not, therefore, the function of the agents' actions to allow the portrayal of their characters; it is, rather, for the sake of their actions that characterization is included. So, the events and the plot-structure are the goal of tragedy, and the goal is what matters most of all.[13]

Aristotle *contra* Plato examines poetry as an applied skill (*téchnē*). He attempts to show how playwrights may achieve excellence at their craft. This craft's aim is to evoke a specific response from audiences, one different from their response to reality. Andrew Ford contends that "What makes Aristotle's theory of *mimēsis* a 'literary' theory is his observation that audiences respond to representation in ways that are different from how they would respond in encountering the originals: in the famous case of tragedy, for example, *imitations* of events that would cause pain to an onlooker in real life can be contemplated (*theorein*) with pleasure."[14] In this way ethical notions may be made explicit in a particularly relevant fashion with a certain critical detachment. In the theatre we are able to observe events that have referentiality to real life, but because they are fictional we enjoy contemplating them without real-life consequences. Furthermore, if life consists of action, then action can serve as a measurement of morality and a form of pedagogy. Theatre provides a way to observe the shape and function of action, which can assist in the betterment of humankind. According to Francis Fergusson, Aristotle divides the concept of *enérgeia* (functioning, activity, and act) into three forms, which Aristotle calls *praxis*, *poiesis*, and *theoria*. Fergusson says that "In *praxis* the motive is 'to do' something." It is the surface action of a play. "In *poiesis* the motive is 'to make' something; it is the action of artists when they are focused upon the play, or the song, or the poem, which they are trying to *make*." In *theoria*, "the motive is 'to grasp and understand' some truth." This final goal, where "the human spirit lives most fully and intensely in the perception of truth," elevates the art of mimesis from mere replica to a desirable and intellectually stimulating objective.[15]

Gerald Else contends that in the *Poetics* the poet is "released from Plato's requirement that he must go to school to philosophy to learn the truth (the Ideas)." Nonetheless, the dramatist "is also condemned to the 'practical' realm and must not claim that he understands the ultimate things. There is in fact not a word in the *Poetics* about the ultimate 'secrets of life,' about why mankind should suffer or be happy, about Fate, or man's relation to God, or any such metaphysical matters. These omissions are not accidental. The proof is that there is nothing about them in Aristotle's discussions of ethics or politics either. He has solved Plato's insistent question about the metaphysical justification of poetry by begging the question: that is, by assuming tacitly that poetry has no metaphysical dimension."[16] Else is correct up to a point. Aristotle does not avoid metaphysics, but rather skillfully shifts the focus from an imitation of a human being to an imitation of an action that a human being makes. This "end-run" around Plato's objection is a subtle but significant difference: through the observation of action we acquire a greater understanding of life.

In his *Poetics* Aristotle describes theatrical theory somewhat like an auto mechanic might describe an automobile. He considers how its parts ought to be made to function, how certain tools and devices make a play run efficiently, and how the unity of the parts can achieve the desired results – catharsis – most effectively. Aristotle brings theatre into the realm of useful art making as opposed to Plato's imagistic and merely inspirational illusion making. Aristotle wants to downplay the mystery of theatre by emphasizing its practical and morally useful side. His notion of mimesis, writes Martha Husain, does not condemn imitation "to third-class ontological status as defective copies of defective copies of perfect transcendent originals. It carries no overtones of deceit, illusion, or counterfeit." Rather, Aristotle is "more respectful of human making, which he considers can produce really new things."[17] Theatre for Aristotle is an active creation; it is not mystical alchemy as Plato might suggest, but rather a skill requiring practice like any other craft that ultimately produces an object. Gunter Gebauer and Christoph Wulf observe that "mimesis produces *fiction*; whatever reference to reality remains is shed entirely of immediacy. The poet creates something that previously did not exist and for which there are no available models. Even in dealing with historical material, the poet must fashion it in accord with his art, raising it to a 'higher' level than is found in reality."[18] Representation does not affirm reality because even if it might parallel portions of reality it deals in origination rather than reflection. As Philip Sidney put it in his *Defense of Poesy* (1583), "for the poet, he nothing affirmeth, and therefore never lieth." For Aristotle the artist represents the shape of human action distilled for the purpose of observing an ethical choice and the consequences derived from that choice. The point of drama and fiction is to reveal the conditions of the world through mimesis: replication is not a replacement for reality but rather sheds a new light on it. Bert O. States affirms the need for representation, noting that "Mental images must be brought outside to this unspecifiable *nonplace* between the self and the empirical world, where they are given duration and audience – where they serve, as it were, as arbitrators of the enigma. For without external representation our subjective understanding of the world remains fleeting and ephemeral, bottled up in the ether of thought, without extension or concrete being – and this is apparently an intolerable loss."[19]

Plato is concerned with the ethical consequences of drama; audiences viewing a convincing portrayal can be diffracted from reality, inspired by the actor's multiple role-playing that diminishes the person imitated and, most importantly for Plato, the person's public stature. The moral order can be further undermined by the imagination. Aristotle is aware of the ethical content underlying drama, saying that tragedy should concern good people, that "poetry is both more philosophical and more serious than history, since poetry speaks more of universals, history of particulars" (41, ch. 9), and that the art of "drama-making" is a skill which, like other skills, requires practice and continual improvement. Rather than mimesis taken to be what Aristotle scholar Stephen Halliwell calls "crudely parasitic on reality," Aristotle "reacts against this view of mimesis…by treating the poet not as an affirmer…but as a skillful maker of dramatic fiction."[20] Aristotle's conception of mimesis interprets reality through action requiring a moral choice. In this way Aristotle stresses the moral dimension, with theatre being a laboratory wherein we witness the unfolding of choices and their consequences. Halliwell remarks that "In the case of tragedy, Aristotle's whole theory suggests that an audience needs to have sufficient experience of life to understand various kinds of action, intention, and character; to be able to distinguish degrees of innocence, responsibility, and guilt; to know, in an effectively mature way, what merits pity and fear; to have a grasp of human successes and failures, of the relationship between status and character, and so forth." Tragedy, he contends, "does not just confirm its audience in preexisting comprehension of the world. It provides them with imaginative opportunities to test, refine, extend, and perhaps even question the ideas and values on which such comprehension rests."[21] Aristotle describes other important features of drama in the *Poetics*, among them the arrangement of plot (*mythos*), the aim of catharsis (purgation), the effects of pity (*eleos*) and fear (*phobos*), peripeteia (a sudden reversal of fortune), anagnorisis (the moment when the protagonist recognizes the crisis), hamartia (missing the mark), the relationship of drama and history, and the roles of happiness (*eudemonia*) and pathos in tragedy. A survey of these conceptions would require a separate book.

Renaissance, Enlightenment, Romanticism

The resurrection of the *Poetics* in the late fifteenth century created a profound shift in European theatre theory. The Roman, medieval, and early Renaissance periods focused on spectacle, the importance of Horace's *Ars Poetica*, which emphasized drama as "utility and pleasure" (*aut prodesse volunt aut delectare poetae*), Plato's stress on forms (primarily among medievalists), and *imitatio* as a rhetorical strategy for moral pedagogy. Throughout the medieval and early Renaissance periods the justification for theatre was its usefulness for moral instruction (*utile dulci*). Matthew Potolsky, commenting on Alexander Pope's "An Essay on Criticism" (1711), says: "Pope's assertion that great art comes from the imitation of role models and not from untutored mirroring of nature is poised at the end of a critical tradition that dominated the literary and intellectual culture of Europe for nearly two thousand years."[22] Religious images were theatrically portrayed as an aid in the remembrance of saints and holy figures, and secular characters exemplified heroes whose deeds inspired virtue. In a largely illiterate European society, dramatized Biblical tales functioned as morality plays for mass edification.

By the sixteenth century, and especially in Italy, an extraordinary examination of the *Poetics* had begun. Coming from at least two sources, Greek and Arabic, the *Poetics* was translated into Latin in 1498 by Giorgio Valla. The widespread interest in it was bolstered further by the commentaries of Julius Caesar Scaliger (1484–1558) and Lodovico Castelvetro (1505–71) in 1561 and 1570, respectively. Despite its fragmentary structure and brevity, the *Poetics* would take center stage in Renaissance dramatic theory. While hardly an unchallenged authority, the *Poetics'* centrality was beyond dispute. The Renaissance simultaneously experienced the rise of *commedia dell' arte* (comedy of the profession), generally consisting of touring companies of street performers committed to improvisation, the carnivalesque, and masked stereotypes. While the former highbrow dramas espoused the spoken text for the social elite, the latter *commedia* troupes facilitated spectacle, archetypes, and the aesthetics of comedy. By the seventeenth century the French scholarly community would follow upon the Italian Neoclassicists Scaliger, Castelvetro, and others in raising the stakes. French playwrights were judged by their fidelity to the *Poetics*, even if some of the ground rules established by the authorities were not always recognizable from Aristotle's text. At the center of the brouhaha were three great French dramatists: Molière, Corneille, and Racine. To varying degrees each was held accountable to the strictures imposed by the *Poetics* or its commentaries. The highly polarized and excessively academic debates concerning, among other things, the significance of a play taking place in one time, at one place, and consisting of one action – referred to as *les trois unités* – had an unintended inhibiting effect. Known as the Cid Controversy (*Querelle du Cid*) because of Corneille's liberality with the Neoclassical rules in his play *Le Cid* (1637), the debate generated a great deal of attention. Ultimately it inspired further debates, known as the *Querelle des Anciens et des Modernes*, which presented the new French Academy its first major test. Although only a handful of critics had maintained the jurisdiction of "rules," the arbiters of the *doctrine classique* of dramatic theory exerted considerable pressure on playwrights to conform to what they believed to be Aristotle's key points: plausibility, verisimilitude, decorum (*bienséance*), propriety, and causality. Mostly the critics latched tenaciously onto the "three unities." Writers and critics took Aristotle's "rules" more literally than Aristotle intended: the fact that Aristotle never mentions one place, and provides merely a passing remark – one revolution of the sun – as stipulation for time, did not deter his epigones. The "rules" were regarded as an aesthetic touchstone of the era, becoming at times restrictive and cumbersome for developing playwrights.

Still, the rules possessed some merit. They applied reason and logic to creative impulses. Defenders of the rules were frequently mathematicians seeking symmetry in dramatic form. They wanted to elevate drama above what they felt to be the common ruck of medieval barbarism represented by sprawling street fairs and unwieldy pageant plays that often endured for several days. Critics of the era condemned Gothic excess; constraints were put in place in order to encourage a rationalized view of dramatic art, induce brevity, and eliminate what they perceived to be the chaotic effect of mixing comedy and tragedy. For the Neo-Aristotelians art can be evaluated by a set of formally applied rules. French society of the seventeenth and pre-Revolutionary eighteenth centuries was an ultra-formal society that imposed elaborate rituals of etiquette, dress codes, and manners. This extended to theatre, creating another set of rules by which to abide. Neoclassicists likewise turned to the *Poetics* as a didactic model: by following strict codes, moral lessons could be implemented. Real-life behaviors were transferred to the stage, creating a theatrical laboratory for epistemological inquiry and social decorum. The traditions originating in the sixteenth century and extending through the seventeenth, writes Donnelee Dox, aimed "at an aesthetic of 'true-to-life' representation and the stimulation of emotions," which "began to define mimesis not in Plato's pejorative terms, with human imitation falling short of ideal forms, but in terms of likeness to what is already known, that which exists in the phenomenonal world."[23] Theorists additionally wanted an elitist drama for a select group opposed to the circus-like theatricality of their Gothic predecessors. Rules were introduced in order to ensure uniformity to rationalism and formal perception. The aesthetics of the time, Ernst Cassirer writes, demanded that art "be measured and tested by the rules of reason, for only such an examination can show whether or not it contains something genuine, lasting, and essential. Such content cannot be attributed to the momentary emotions of pleasure awakened in us by works of art."[24] This thinking would be challenged by the Romantics and Kant, whose ideas we will examine shortly. Debates over rules eventuated in principles of plausibility and causality. Many of the critics included in this collection fall on one side or the other in terms of such conventions.

The mid-seventeenth century experienced a relative decline in respect of rules. Louis Mercier (1740–1814) urged drama towards political activism and personal character studies of the family known as domestic drama. The new emphasis on "subjectivism" required theories of drama capable of gainsaying French Neoclassicism and its stress on high-born tragic heroes. Two significant figures, John Dryden (1631–1700) and later Gottfried Lessing (1729–81), presented a more open-minded investigation of theatre theory. Dryden's *An Essay of Dramatic Poesy* (1668) aims for a certain reasonableness. Dryden creates a dialogue among four characters, taking up the importance of plausibility and causality that had been the raging issues of the day, but modifies them. For Dryden, a play is "a just and lively image of human nature, representing its passions and humours, and the changes of fortune to which it is subject, for the delight and instruction of mankind."[25] He remained under the influence of Horace ("delectation and instruction"), and stressed the importance of mimesis as conceived by the Neoclassicists. Still, he turned to what was to be called "Bardolatry," a term coined by George Bernard Shaw. According to Dryden, Shakespeare ignores rules yet is accorded special status. Shakespeare, he says, "was the man who of all modern, and perhaps ancient poets, had the largest and most comprehensive soul." "When he describes anything," Dryden remarks, "you more than see it, you feel it, too" (48). Shakespeare was held up as the antidote to French unities and classical dramatic traditions. Lessing's *Hamburg Dramaturgy* (1767–9) also raises the specter of Shakespeare as leverage against orthodoxy. For him and a number of other eighteenth-century Enlightenment humanists, the suffering of the tragic hero is less about lofty characters and more about "ordinary" people. The focus shifts from royalty to an emerging middle class. Lessing, likewise Denis Diderot (1713–84), believes in the imitation theory of art, in which dramatic dialogue and characterization coincide with what was deemed "natural." Lessing adds "compassion" (*Mitleid*) to Aristotle's notions of pity and fear. For him, compassion must be a part of tragedy in order for the audience to experience emotional engagement with the play. Compassion, which would later become empathy, is aroused by the sight of undeserved suffering of people "like us." Only if we perceive the protagonist as "like us" can the dramatic experience succeed. Using Aristotle as a point of departure, Lessing says: "It was his [Aristotle's] opinion that the misfortune that becomes the object of our compassion must necessarily be of such a nature that we can fear it might happen as well to us or ours. When this fear is not present compassion does not arise." From this similarity "arises the fear that our destiny might as easily become like his as we feel ourselves to be like him, and this fear it is which would force compassion to full maturity."[26] Despite the implication that the object of our compassion is a prototypical European male, Lessing's important contribution is affirmed. In the twentieth century the idea of compassion is incorporated by many marginalized groups likewise wanting their representation onstage.

One of the most (if not *the* most) important figures in Western aesthetic theory continues to be Immanuel Kant (1724–1804). Because he makes scant reference to theatre and drama (or art in general), and because his aesthetic theory covers considerably contested and difficult terrain, he is largely overlooked in dramatic theory. This is regrettable because his ideas on aesthetics have had widespread influence over all the arts. Alexander Gottlieb Baumgarten (1714–62) coined the term "aesthetic" as an independent intellectual pursuit in his *Philosophical Meditations on Some Conditions of Poetry* (*Meditationes philosophicae de nonnullis ad poema pertinentibus*, 1735) and *Aesthetica* (1750; 1758). Baumgarten distinguished sensual and intellectual cognition as separate sources of knowledge; aesthetic judgment is autonomous (without reference to reason) and falls within the domain of sensuous experience. Following Baumgarten and others (Christian Wolff and Gottfried Leibniz, for instance), Kant takes up aesthetics in his *Critique of Judgment* (1790, second edition 1793). This complex work, referred to as the "third critique," operates on various and sometimes contradictory levels. For Kant, pure reason, the subject of the first critique, and practical reason (freedom, morality, and will), the subject of the second, are inadequate for the treatment of aesthetics, beauty, the sublime, taste, and art. Aesthetics for Kant mediates between reason and morality, and examines freedom and nature (or freedom in nature).

The Critique of Judgment is divided into two sections, "Critique of the Aesthetic Judgment" and "Critique of the Teleological Judgment." The first section is subdivided into the "beautiful" and the "sublime" as they relate to "taste" (*Geschmack*). Kant considers the way in which our autonomous free will can declare something beautiful objectively and universally when our faculties are subjective and inclined to partisanship. He maintains that the "power of judgment in general is the faculty for thinking of the particular (*Besondere*) as contained under the universal (*Allgemeine*). If the universal (the rule, the principle, the law) is given, then the power of judgment, which subsumes the particular under it (even when, as a transcendental power of judgment, it provides the condition *a priori* in accordance with which alone anything can be subsumed under that universal) is determining (*bestimmend*). If, however, only the particular is given, for which the universal is to be found, then the power of judging is merely reflecting (*reflektierend*)."[27] Rules and universal laws are determined. Reflective judgment (i.e., contemplation, not scientific assessment) finds the particular and then constructs a universal. The distinction, Kant says further, "consists in the fact that the idea at issue is not a principle of reason for the understanding, but for the power of judgment, and is thus merely the application of an understanding in general to possible objects of experience, where, indeed, the judgment cannot be determining, but merely reflecting, hence where the object is, to be sure, given in experience, but where it cannot even be determinately (let alone completely appropriately) judged in accordance with the idea, but can only be reflected upon" (275). Kant is attempting to elucidate human understanding "with regard to the power of judgment in its reflection upon things in nature" (275), seeking to define this condition by examining understanding, reason, and judgment. Aesthetic judgment is the power of judgment "to conceive in nature, over and above its mechanical necessity, a purposiveness without the presupposition of which systematic unity in the thoroughgoing classification of particular forms in accordance with empirical laws would not be possible" (21–2). In other words, the systematic unity of nature is a "technique of nature," not "a mechanics of nature." Kant is here describing the difference between machines and art, separating their function, usage, and appreciation as they relate to our apprehension, comprehension, and the manner of presentation of the object. The difference might be described in terms of a cartographical map and a landscape painting: what makes the former "useful" and the latter "aesthetic?" For Kant, nature and art form an organic unity and have a rational plan, although the plan may not be wholly apparent and hardly utilitarian. Aesthetic representations for Kant, Derrida observes, "can certainly give rise to logical judgments when they are related by the judgment to the object, but when the judgment relates to the subject, to the subjective affect – as is the case here – it is and can only be an aesthetic one."[28] Objects themselves or their appearances are not the fount for aesthetic pleasure, but rather it is derived in ourselves. Kant contends that "One only wants to know whether the representation of the object is accompanied with satisfaction in me, however indifferent I might be with regard to the existence of the object of this representation" (90–1). We derive pleasure because the object stimulates our imagination and understanding. Let me briefly try to explain how Kant considers this, and why it is important for theatre (or any art form) in theory.

According to Kant, judgment takes into account particular taste and the role imagination plays in aesthetic judgment, and then judges whether to endow the object as beautiful or not. "In order to decide whether or not something is beautiful," Kant says in separating logic from aesthetics, "we do not relate the representation by means of understanding to the object for cognition, but rather relate it by means of the imagination (perhaps combined with understanding) to the subject and its feeling of pleasure or displeasure. The judgment of taste is therefore not a cognitive judgment, hence not a logical one, but is rather aesthetic, by which is understood one whose determining ground cannot be other than subjective" (89). Aesthetic has its own logic but is not beholden to pure reason. Art and nature induce a particular experience deemed "beautiful." The predicate "the beautiful" occurs when the subject endows an object as "beautiful" along four intersecting lines: subjective pleasure; interest arising from the non-utilitarian nature of the object; attributing purpose to the object (though we may not cognitively know what that purpose is); and the observer assuming that others are in agreement with the aesthetic judgment (thought they, in fact, may be of a different opinion). Kant scholar Paul Guyer asserts that Kant "attempts to show that our aesthetic judgements and practices have a rational foundation even though they cannot be grounded on determinate principles."[29] A work of art, likewise nature, is devised according to some organic plan. In nature and art there is an organic, non-utilitarian unity. Like Aristotle, to some degree, Kant is trying to demystify art and nature, granting art an intellectual foundation albeit dependent upon intuition and imagination invested in the aesthetic experience. Nature's organism for Kant is, according to Frederick C. Beiser, "a necessary idea of reason" though this "reason" comes from outside logic or utility. Since everything in nature "conforms to some intelligent design, or that it has been created according to some rational plan," then the idea of nature (as the Romantics would later stress) "unifies the realms of the noumenal and the phenomenal."[30] Kant's emphasis on aesthetic appraisal is grounded in terms of the beautiful, the agreeable, the good, the sublime, and the worthwhile of the fine arts that are often inscrutable and non-philosophically intelligible by conceptual analysis, yet contain a unique form of rational foundation and organic unity. Subjective judgment combines with an objective assessment based on pleasure, detachment, non-utilitarian purpose, universal agreement, and organic coherence of the object to endow the object with the imprimatur of the "beautiful."

Kant's aesthetic investigation has value for twentieth-century theatre. Subjectivity can be located in numerous essays in this collection; the analysis of interiority is the essential point of expressionism, symbolism, and art for art's sake. Objectivity arises in realistic dramas, and Kant's emphasis on detachment is one of Brecht's key points as well (though Brecht's understanding of detachment is somewhat different). Kant's notion of imaginative "free play" is rooted in eighteenth-century philosophy of mind and stressed what is exquisite and sublime in beauty, but it is also a source of Romanticism's deification of the artist and is influential for dramatic theories of artistic autonomy ("art for art's sake," for example). At the beginning of the twentieth century, Kantian aesthetic judgment was appropriated by the avant-garde, especially in an effort to justify the (at the time) revolutionary style of Cubism. The important art dealer and historian of Cubism, Daniel-Henry Kahnweiler, defended Picasso, Braque, and Gris for creating artworks that no longer required analytic descriptions or mimetic fidelity, but rather advanced a synthesis and conceptualization over verisimilitude. Art historian Mark Cheetham notes that for Kahnweiler, "the analytic/synthetic distinction, the notions of the thing-in-itself and disinterestedness, and the formal autonomy of the work of art provided nothing less than a way of conceptualizing and justifying cubism. Kant's ideas and terminology were also crucial for several of the central French critics who helped to define cubism in its early years."[31] No less so for theatre; practitioners and theorists of the theatre followed art's lead in seeking to detach theatre from descriptive forms, narrative causality, and the well-made-play formula. Theatre, likewise art, used Kantian ideas of artistic autonomy to inspire and motivate radically new theatre forms and theoretical foundations. In addition, the inspirations extracted from Kant were aesthetic as well as morally justifiable. Beauty, Kant says, "is the symbol of the morally good" because it "pleases immediately"in reflection, it pleases "without any interest" (i.e., biases), stimulates the "freedom of imagination," and is "represented as universal" (227–8). For Kant, detaching judgments of taste from the merely idiosyncratic incorporates moral value because, as Mary McCloskey writes, "it is akin to the moral point of view," and this "provides us with a transitional step away from an egocentric outlook towards a fully moral one."[32] The combination of moral and aesthetic judgment further demonstrates Kant's broad influence.

In an oft-quoted passage of the third critique, Kant explicates art's "purpose," saying that in aesthetic judgment "Purposiveness can thus exist without purpose (*Die Zweck-mäßigkeit kann also ohne Zweck sein*), insofar as we do not place the causes of this form in a will, but can still make the explanation of its possibility conceivable to ourselves only by deriving it from a will" (105). We do not perceive art as beautiful because it has practical purpose; this purposiveness creates a harmony in our perception without regard to utilitarian function. An aesthetic judgment tells us nothing about the object's utility; we do not know, or are not interested in, the object's mechanics, nor should we invest personal interest in it. Personal interest, he says, "spoils the judgment of taste and deprives it of its impartiality" (107). An aesthetic judgment tells us about how we, as subjects and observers, are affected by our mental representation of the object – its form – through our pleasurable reaction and through our relationship with the world. Thus, the object that provides aesthetic pleasure is not (or should not be) in a vacuum but ought to be relational. "The judgment of taste," Kant says, "determines its object with regard to satisfaction (as beauty) with a claim to the assent of everyone, as if it were objective" (162).

To understand what Kant means by judgments being relational and objective, we need to consider the way in which he compartmentalizes aesthetic judgment of the sublime. Kant divides an appreciation of the sublime (a popular subject of the eighteenth century) four ways: "universally valid in its quantity, as without interest in its quality, as subjective purposiveness in its relation, and the latter, as far as its modality is concerned, as necessity" (131). These four categories – quantity, quality, subjective purposiveness, and modality – form the nexus of judging the sublime. The first and third of these, an aesthetic judgment "universally valid in its quantity" and "purposiveness in its relation," describes its "interrelatedness." Prior to Kant judgment of the beautiful and the sublime was generally identified as that which realized classical ideals. It was all a matter of following the rules of Neoclassical order and convention. But during the eighteenth century the Anglo-European world moved away from universal judgments proscribed by conventional authority (Church, State, or the French Academy's Neoclassic-dramaturgical "rules" described above) to acceptance of individuality, a surfeit of views, and judgments in the court of public opinion. Judgments of art, too, underwent a concomitant change. By the end of the eighteenth century classical concerns began to break down, transformed by the influence of Rousseau and Romanticism during the early nineteenth century. The result, led by Kant, was a powerful shift in the language of aesthetics that informed the philosophy and theory of the arts.

For Kant art creates objects of pure form, self-contained and complete yet simultaneously intertwined with the public. He examines how art objects relate to other objects, and how their forms can be evaluated in ways that take into account the object's uniqueness as well. The autonomous agent can make judgments independent of others, but for Kant this is unsatisfactory. Only when the individual relinquishes self-interest and considers judgment in light of a universal assessment does the individual acquire "taste." Kant calls this "*sensus communis*," judgment "that in its reflection takes account (*a priori*) of everyone else's way of representing in thought, in order as it were to hold its judgment up to human reason as a whole and thereby avoid the illusion which, from subjective private conditions that could easily be held to be objective, would have a detrimental influence on the judgment" (173–4). Private interest is random, relativistic, and impetuous. Only by submitting oneself to what Terry Eagleton refers to as Kant's "precious form of intersubjectivity, establishing ourselves as a community of feeling subjects linked by a quick sense of our shared capacities," can one acquire taste.[33] Taste therefore assumes four characteristics – objective disinterestedness, subjective pleasure, formal purposiveness without purpose, and an agreed-upon universal liking – in order to remove judgment from either mere "likes" or slavish conformism. Salim Kemal writes that Kant's judgment of taste "must satisfy two criteria – particular judgements must gain confirmation from the community and the confirmed judgement must depend on the subject's autonomous activity in grasping and ordering some material in a pleasurable judgement." This, in effect, "points to a mutual dependence between subject and the community. Neither gains serious employment without the other."[34] Kant's criteria, however, must not be confused with the results of a public opinion poll; he is appealing to an elite judgment and not the lowest common denominator. What might be called Kant's middle ground between subjectivity and objectivity, autonomous pleasure and general consensus, is, according to René Wellek, "subjective, but there is an objectivity in the subjective; in the aesthetic judgment egoism is overcome: we appeal to a general judgment, to a common sense of mankind, but this is achieved by inner experience, not by accepting the opinions of others or consulting them or counting their opinions." It is not an egalitarian agreement but rather "an appeal to humanity, to an ideal totality of judges."[35]

Kant's effort to balance subjectivity and objectivity in imaginative thinking, the "subjective universality" he refers to, establishes the groundwork for modern aesthetic criticism. His "aesthetic universality" is, according to Ernst Cassirer, "the assertion and requirement of a universality of subjectivity itself." The claim to universality does not inhibit the subject's valid claims to subjective judgment of beauty, but does the opposite: "it designates an enlargement of the realm of validity, which is here perfected." We have our subjective tastes, but in the realm of art occurs (or should occur) "a universal feeling of the world and life. The 'self' detaches itself from its individuality when it objectifies itself in a construction of aesthetic fantasy; its individual unique stimulation is nevertheless not destroyed in this construction, but rather dwells powerfully in it and is communicated to all those who are capable of grasping it."[36] Kant therefore distinguishes individual and artistic taste; the former functions in the realm of subjectivity while the latter navigates aesthetic judgment. This relationship, writes Henry Sussman, "is absolutely crucial to Kant's conception of and scenario for art: there are some objective criteria for beauty, but the overall experience of art" must yield "the spontaneity of the experience, its seeming to result from a *free* interplay with the world."[37] Kantian reason and aesthetics ultimately come to grips with the division between the artistic free play of imagination (our autonomy), on the one hand, and the unity of reason that determines a collective consensus (our sociality), on the other.[38]

Kant is seeking to ground an aesthetic theory into a logical system, even if such a system incorporates imagination and transcendental rather than scientific logic. Nature is, for Kant, systematic, even if this system is not wholly dependent on determining principles. "The beautiful," Kant says, "is that which, without concepts, is represented as the object of a *universal* satisfaction" (96). We therefore "speak of the beautiful as if it were a property of the object and the judgment logical," although "it is only aesthetic and contains merely a relation of the representation of the object to the subject, because it still has the similarity with logical judgment that its validity for everyone can be presupposed." As a result, a judgment of taste contains "a claim to validity for everyone without the universality that pertains to objects, i.e., it must be combined with a claim to subjective universality" (97). Kant advances this universality further in what he calls "aesthetic ideas" (*ästhetischer Ideen*), which he describes as "that representation of the imagination that occasions much thinking without it being possible for any determinate thought" (192). An aesthetic idea is not based on determined judgment, but incorporates fresh imagination and "serves that idea of reason instead of logical presentation." The purpose of aesthetic thought is "only to animate the mind by opening up for it the prospect of an immeasurable field of related representations." Art, he says, "gives the imagination the impetus to think more, although in an undeveloped way," i.e., in a non-conceptual, unscientific way (193). Beauty makes us feel as though the natural world conforms to our aims and interests, however much this conceptualization is non-utilitarian. A beautiful sunset, for example, suggests a grand design, though the arrangement of this design is beyond the reach of practical cognition. The sunset is in the "pleasure itself," and that representation stimulates judgment. In representing aesthetic form, he says:

> The consciousness of the merely formal purposiveness in the play of the cognitive powers of the subject in the case of representation through which an object is given is the pleasure itself, because it contains a determining ground of the activity of the subject with regard to the animation of its cognitive powers, thus an internal causality (which is purposive) with regard to cognition in general, but without being restricted to a particular cognition, hence it contains a mere form of subjective purposiveness of a representation in an aesthetic judgment. This pleasure is also in no way practical.... But yet it has a causality in itself, namely that of maintaining the state of the representation of the mind and the occupation of the cognitive powers without a further aim. We linger over the consideration of the beautiful because the consideration strengthens and reproduces itself. (107)

Kant was strongly influenced by Rousseau's notion of neutrality in artistic judgment and unfavorably disposed towards segments of the Romantic Movement. He exhibited his asperity towards the passionate and reckless impetuosity of the rising *Sturm und Drang* and Romantic Movements of his time.[39] (Ironically, despite attempts by Kant to halt the spread of speculative metaphysics and miasmic intuition that were the aesthetic benchmarks of *Sturm und Drang*, Romanticism took root in German idealism during the early nineteenth century and Kant was their theoretical paradigm. Instead of continuing the Enlightenment's preoccupation with science and rationalism, the Romantics, led by Kant's rebellious student Johann Gottfried von Herder [1744–1803], sought a cosmic-religious-spiritualist sense of art and identity, the very thing Kant tried to avoid.) Kant wanted to shift the aesthetic emphasis from the artist as endowed with divination to the audience who, as critical judges, can make determination of art's quality. He did not reject the idea of genius (in fact, he much praised it), but he wanted to lift it from the supercilious. In this way he attempted to combine the artist-genius with audience-judgment. (Coleridge's "willing suspension of disbelief...which constitutes poetic faith" owes much to Kant; the audience is now in control of the will, enabling assessments based on sophisticated faculties of judgment.)[40] As Rodolphe Gasché has observed, for Kant "Pure aesthetic judgments upon the beautiful are possible only in the absence of all determinate concepts, and this condition is met when the concept in man-made art is rendered indeterminate. But whereas an absence of concepts for certain objects of nature is passively experienced by the mind that judges the object beautiful, such an absence for objects of the beautiful arts must be 'actively' engendered in order for them to be judged beautiful, and for the judgments to be aesthetically reflective judgments."[41] Kant's *Critique of Judgment* initiates the path of theoretical criticism of the arts, establishing the idea of the critic as one who judges subjectively and universally.

One of Kant's enduring legacies is his place among formalism and those opposed to it. For the formalists, aesthetic form consists in the harmonious arrangement of parts into the whole. Form is autonomous, its pleasure arising from the play of elements, and its political efficacy derived from its very anti-conventionalism. Kant's judgment of taste, according to one of the twentieth century's leading formalists Theodor Adorno, is informed by a "subjectively directed query" and concerns "the core of objective aesthetics: the question of quality – good and bad, true and false – in the art work." Likewise in his critique of pure reason, Kant, Adorno says, wishes "to ground aesthetic objectivity in the subject rather than displace the former by the latter." Reason gives rise "to one who is capable of discriminating in the object." Taste for Kant, Adorno maintains, "is not defined in Aristotelian fashion by sympathy and fear, the affects provoked in the viewer. The contamination of aesthetic feeling with unmediated psychological emotions by the concept of arousal misinterprets the modification of real experience by artistic experience."[42] For Adorno, form itself is a locale for politics, creating its own political resistance by defying hegemonic convention and calling attention to art qua art, not art qua reality. Adorno's interpretation is controversial, making Kant a formalist of sorts. The transcendental synthesis of Kantian aesthetics also lent weighty authority to apolitical art; art for art's sake provided a fundamental uncertainty to the claim that art creates meaning, leading to an autonomy of art and a retreat from didacticism. At the same time Kant's aesthetic theories have been used to bolster the case for didacticism in art. Beautiful art emerges from the spirit (*Geist*), which, "in an aesthetic significance, means the animating principle in the mind" (192). Mere forms without ideas are sterile exercises in the superficial. Form and content as well as didactic and apolitical art debates have their defenders on both sides and resurface throughout this anthology.

Another of Kant's enduring ideas is the notion of "genius" in art and nature. "Nature was beautiful," he says, "if at the same time it looked like art; and art can only be called beautiful if we are aware that it is art and yet it looks like nature to us" (185). Since nature often produces aesthetic pleasure, and nature has its own rules, then a temporary abeyance of rational rules is necessary for art. Thus, he says, "the purposiveness in the product of beautiful art, although it is certainly intentional, must nevertheless not seem intentional, i.e., beautiful art must be regarded as nature, although of course one is aware of it as art" (185–6). Genius for Kant therefore follows only the rules of nature; genius, he says, "is the talent (natural gift) that gives the rules to art. Since the talent, as an inborn productive faculty of the artists, itself belongs to nature, this could also be expressed thus: Genius is the inborn predisposition of the mind (*ingenium*) through which nature gives the rule to art." Beautiful art, he adds, "does not allow the judgment concerning the beauty of its product to be derived from any sort of rule that has a concept for its determining ground, and thus has as its ground of how it is possible. Thus beautiful art cannot itself think up the rule in accordance with which it is to bring its product into being. Yet since without a proceeding rule a product can never be called art, nature in the subject . . . must give the rule to art, i.e., beautiful art is possible only as a product of genius" (186). Such remarks made it possible for the Romantics to view artists as the heralds of genius – a "natural" endowed with the "gift" – as well as for the "art for art's sake" movement. "The Romantic view of art," Otfried Höffe observes, "picks up on Kant's aesthetic of the genius," and "in the course of the nineteenth century, the notion of the genius is amplified to a universal value and experiences, together with creativity, whose force flows from the unconscious, a veritable deification. The genius becomes the 'hero' of the age."[43] The critic Clement Greenberg, mostly known for his role as the chief advocate of Abstract Expressionist Jackson Pollack, put it best when he said that Kant's "capacity for abstraction enabled him, despite many gaffes, to establish in his *Critique of Aesthetic Judgment* what is the most satisfactory basis for aesthetics we yet have."[44] Although Greenberg's influence waned in the second half of the twentieth century as art criticism departed from Kant's rigid division of the aesthetic and the practical, he shed great light on Kant's significance to aesthetic theory.

Kant, like Plato, considers an aesthetic judgment in relation to the ideal. But Kant, unlike Plato, does not deem imagination the chief dereliction of art. On the contrary, Kant values artistic imagination insofar as it is bound up with judgment. On this basis the Romantics build on Kant's valorization of the imagination in its role of beatification. Kant is not above reproach: his ideas are at times convoluted and fail, in the words of Richard Eldridge, to "point to any neutral, uncontestable procedure for identifying successful work." Kant's focus "on formal elements and the pleasure of apprehending them may underrate the representational and cognitive dimension of some art." Twentieth-century art, Eldridge says, such as "Dada, conceptual art, and performance art," appears "more provocative and 'assertational' than intended to provide pleasure in the apprehension of formal elements."[45] Kant's notion of universality of judgment can additionally lead to authoritarianism. Still, with its emphasis on the uniqueness of art, which promotes the aesthetic free play of the imagination and intuition, Kant's third critique greatly influenced the Romantics and his ideas of autonomous art had a major impact on the twentieth-century avant garde, Abstract Expressionism, ideas of pure form, didacticism, and other modernist theories. His work raises a host of far-reaching implications and questions: when, for example, is theatre aesthetically pleasing? How is it affective (politically or entertainingly)? How do we distinguish its value? By what mechanism of analysis do we penetrate its architectonics, utility or non-utility, and spatial and temporal arrangements? What, to borrow Joseph Roach's prophetic term "surrogation" (see Chapter 78), ascribes the surrogate/embodiment provocation of feelings ("beauty" or otherwise) through the process of judgment? Kant, along with Rousseau, Goethe, Schiller, Diderot, and others, was aware of the great depth and sheer level of changes occurring in society. It was clear to the founders of modernism that if humanity were to be free, humans must be autonomous and informed by a self-imposed and self-regulated condition. The resultant effect of modernism and freedom on theatre theory was an accentuation of the individual either in conflict with society in order to be free (Hegel) or self-delusional in efforts to attain this modernist freedom (Nietzsche).

Realism and Anti-Realism: Hegel and Nietzsche

Georg Wilhelm Friedrich Hegel (1770–1831) and Friedrich Nietzsche (1844–1900) introduced new ideas in dramatic theory from the nineteenth to the twentieth centuries. To a certain degree Hegel shared with the Romantics sympathy for subjectivity. Romanticism was at least in part a rejection of the Enlightenment's self-determining individual exchanging ideas in the public sphere. For the Romantics, self-discovery was not something public but rather something introspective and mystical. Nietzsche, who rejected Romanticism, said: "A romantic is an artist whose great dissatisfaction with himself makes him creative – who looks away, looks back from himself and from his world."[46] If the Enlightenment was social and urbane, Romanticism was inward, folk oriented, idealistic, nationalistic, melancholic, and religious (primarily Christian though with some interest in Buddhism). Enlightenment's salons, journals, and rhetoric considered public discourse, not inwardness and withdrawal, as central. Although Kant is one of the many figures of the Enlightenment, his emphasis on genius (noted above) was appropriated by the Romantics. Romanticism rejected Enlightenment's intellectualism, logic, and science.

What Romanticism did, Isaiah Berlin contends, "was to undermine the notion that in matters of value, politics, morals, aesthetics there are such things as objective criteria which operate between human beings."[47] Instead of objectivity Romanticism sought to defend intuition against reason and place a strong element of mind–body connection at the center of art. Language among Romantics was considered of divine origin and stressed metaphor, image, circumlocution, and inspiration (the "muse") rather than empiricism and fact. Schiller's influential remark in his *Letters on the Aesthetic Education of Man* emphasized the importance of every individual to strive for a "pure idealistic being," creating "the possible realization of the infinite in the finite, and consequently also the possibility of the most sublime humanity." Only beauty for Schiller can combine the sensual and the spiritual, making humans an "entirety," since "the aesthetic communication alone unites society because it applies to what is common to all its members."[48] Schiller led much of the way towards a Romantic notion of harmonious reintegration of a oneness with nature, forging an interpretative link or unity between epistemology and ethics through the aesthetic. This unity would be attained through aesthetic education (*Bildung*), virtue, and human perfection, designed to create a solution to the increasing sense of modernist alienation. Furthermore, the notion of unified inwardness and divination of the aesthetic is, according to Charles Taylor, "as much a part of the modernist sensibility as of the Romantic." For Taylor, the "Romantics made the poet or artist into the paradigm human being. Modernists have only accentuated this."[49] Romanticism's influence on early twentieth-century modernism is evident throughout the following essays.

Hegel agreed with the Romantics that introspection was the state of modern life, but he found pure subjectivity unsatisfactory. Introspection was spiritually incapacitating. The whole apparatus of Enlightenment "feeling" (and the sublime) or Romantic inwardness as the source of aesthetic judgment was for Hegel vapid because feeling is "the indefinite dull region of the mind; what is felt remains wrapped in the form of the most abstract individual subjectivity, and therefore the distinctions of feeling are also quite abstract, and are not distinctions of the actual object-matter itself." Hegel admired Kant for bringing up important observations regarding aesthetics, but was ultimately dissatisfied with what he believed to be Kant's reliance on subjectivity. Kant, he said, "succeeded neither in scientifically unfolding its [aesthetic] genuine essence nor in presenting it as the true and sole reality." Kant recognized "the required unity in what he called the *intuitive understanding*; but here, again, he comes to a standstill in the contradiction of subjectivity and objectivity, so that although he suggests in the abstract a solution of the contradiction of concept and reality, universality and particularity, understanding and sense, and thereby points to the Idea, yet, on the other hand, he makes the solution and reconciliation into a purely subjective one, not one which is true and actual in its nature and on its own merits."[50] For Hegel, art represents an "Idea" or concept that comes to fruition not through subjectivity but through volition and forces opposing the will.

Hegel emphasized the dialectic: the theory of conflicting opposites yielding synthesis. Through conflict ideas can transcend internal inertia and be made visible to a viewing audience. Nietzsche, while sharing an antipathy towards Romanticism, introduced (along with Kierkegaard) existential suffering of the divided modern self. Because modernity has sundered the subject from every organic bond – every social and communicative relationship – art for Hegel must reconcile ethical divides. Nietzsche had little use for Hegelian reconciliation because he had little faith in human agency; volition for Nietzsche was a delusion. Both Hegel and Nietzsche stress Greek tragedy as paradigmatic answers to modernism's malaise; however, as Elliot Jurist observes in his book *Beyond Hegel and Nietzsche*, they diverge on the grounds that tragedy should be "addressed to the spectator qua citizen (Hegel) or qua human being (Nietzsche)." For Nietzsche, Jurist contends, "tragedy forces humans to face the deep, uncomfortable questions about contingency and meaninglessness." Hegel, by contrast, is "uncomfortable with the role that destiny plays in tragedy precisely because it suggests that there are limits to our capacity to understand and control the world."[51] Hegel puts stock in free will, while Nietzsche regards agency as a façade. Hegel and Nietzsche provide the twin pillars of nineteenth-century dramatic theory: the Enlightenment redemptive faith in wholeness and Romanticism's subjectivity give way to Hegelian dialectics of will and the inevitable reconciliation to rationality; and Nietzsche's anguished subject and emphasis on ritual yield a plethora of abstract and surreal theatre theories that incorporate fate and the unknowable.

Hegel systematically explored the self in its manifest relationship to consciousness. For Hegel, the modern self – fragmented and alienated – had replaced that of the Enlightenment's unitary being held together by public discourse. His concept of tragedy evolved in part as a rejection of both Enlightenment optimism and Romantic interiority. Although Hegel's writings on tragedy are scattered, certain themes recur throughout. For Hegel, suffering was a result of a fragmentation produced by modern life. The striving for reconciliation inspired agents to overcome division. He viewed conflict in terms of historical dialectic. He was sympathetic to the Romantic notion that humans do not owe their preconceived values to God or nature, but rather freely create them. But whereas the Romantics considered artists as mystic and clairvoyant arbiters of truth, Hegel expressed an anti-Romantic backlash. For him Romantic inwardness was no cure for modernity's fragmentation but was in fact the disease itself. Rather than Romantic intuition and isolation, Hegel esteemed absolute consciousness (*Geist*) as a way of overcoming modernity's debilitating contradictions.

Greek drama for Hegel, especially Sophocles' *Antigone*, is the paradigmatic drama of modern angst. Dramas of internal division (the root of Romantic drama modeled after *Hamlet*) and dramas of external conflict (the root of Classical drama and *Antigone* as its *ne plus ultra*) represent for him two developments of dialectical conflict. Of the two, Hegel believed the Greeks offered a superior model for tragedy. In favoring external dramatic conflict, he states that dramatic action "is that of individuals in conflict with one another," and the ethical fortitude of each character "supports the course of action."[52] Conflict in drama is conflict among individual wills. Such collision of wills often generates tragedy. According to Hegel, dramatic action "is not confined to the simple, undisturbed implementation of a certain purpose," as the Romantics would have it, "but rather depends throughout on colliding circumstances, passions and characteristics and leads therefore to actions and reactions (*zu Aktionen und Reaktionen*), which in their turn make necessary a further resolution of struggle and conflict (*des Kampfs und Zweispalts*)." The result, he says, are that "what we see before us are the definite ends of individualized purposes in living personalities and conflictual situations" (475–6). "What we see" is a key term; for Hegel ideas must be exposed, not internalized. Internal suffering is not, as Friedrich Schiller contends, tragedy's primary concern which leads to the representation of dignity and moral freedom. "The first law of the tragic art," Schiller says, "was to represent suffering nature. The second law is to represent the resistance of morality opposed to suffering."[53] Tragedy for Hegel is dialectical and external, its themes being moral forces of "ethical substances" colliding. The collision occurs when family and state, parent and child, ruler and ruled clash. *Antigone* embodies this idea insofar as its protagonists represent outward symbols of family and state, ruler and ruled, whose antagonism concludes in mutual destruction. The conflict of wills is held together in thought, i.e., in what Hegel repeatedly calls the absolute consciousness or mind (*Geist*) of the beholder who weighs equally the colliding wills. As I have noted elsewhere, "Within conflicts – that is, within the shifting give and take of dramatic tension based on the relationship between two opposing ethical claims – the Hegelian dialectic introduces the idea that opposites are in fact capable of being held together through the network of thought. Each agent is linked through a struggle to elevate, preserve, and simultaneously negate its opposite. Characters alter their tactics according to the ebb and flow of dramatic action, but they remain steadfast in their ethics and principles. These principles, moreover, must represent the highest ideals."[54]

For Hegel tragedy in its highest attainment is the conflict of two incommensurable claims; the conflict is resolved only by the downfall of both heroes. "Only in the down-fall of both sides alike," Hegel notes, "is absolute right accomplished, and the ethical substance as the negative power which engulfs both sides, that is, omnipotent and righteous Destiny, steps on the scene."[55] The conflict is embedded in the actions between moral values, and what should be the unity of these two ethically right positions is in reality consciousness split in two. Hegel's notion of action is reaffirmed by Amélie Oksenberg Rorty's remarks concerning Aristotle, that "Drama reveals the form and point of the protagonist's action, their sometimes hidden directions and purposes." For Hegel and Aristotle there cannot be action without purpose or pathos, and "we cannot see what an action really is, until we see it contextualized, embedded in the story of which it is an essential part."[56] An action's means and ends are revealed through what the Greeks term *diegesis* (narrative) combined with Hegelian collision, coming to a harmonious resolution only at the play's conclusion. This resolution, Hegel believed, was more than merely an ending of the drama: it should unify the conflicting parties and terminate the stubborn one-sidedness that instigated the conflict.

Johann Wolfgang von Goethe (1749–1832) held views somewhat similar to Hegel in respect of the conflict between moral obligation and individual desire. Goethe remarked that "The Ancient tragedy (*Die alte Tragödie*) is based on an indisputable moral obligation (*Sollen*) which can only intensify and gain momentum if it clashes with an opposing will (*entgegenwirkendes Wollen*)."[57] But Hegel objects to modern drama (Goethe's dramas included) for rendering the conflicts an interior struggle of the protagonist's inner moral conscience and doubt rather than a forceful and external representation of conflicting wills. Hegel, Iván Nyusztay observes, "understandably belittles the tragic phenomenon of vacillation [*Schwank*]. He seems to lay stress on firm and strong-willed characters instead, attributing great initiative to them in under-taking action."[58] It should be noted that Hegel occasionally equivocates, acknowledging the value of internal conflict in characters vacillating over moral dilemmas (Hamlet, for example) through powerful dramas of internal dialectics. Nonetheless, plays of internal struggle evoke sympathy but lack tragic monumentality. In her superb book *Tragedy and Theory*, Michelle Gellrich writes that for Hegel the conflict in Sophocles' *Antigone*, bound up by the different claims between Creon and Antigone, "involves a split between divine law, the unwritten precept existing forever and not made by man, and the human law, the written, civic edicts of a people's communal life. Both of these laws are entitled to expression – their ethical legitimacy is equally balanced – but acting on them gives rise to the crisis in Sophocles' play: by implementing one precept, each character violates the other."[59] This conflict, unlike melodrama's neat division of good and bad, hero and villain, is what A. C. Bradley (brother of British idealist philosopher F. H. Bradley) recognizes as Hegel's central premise of a drama having to do with "good and good." In Hegelian tragedy, Bradley asserts, "there is some sort of collision or conflict – conflict of feelings, modes of thought, desires, wills, purposes; conflict of persons with one another, or with circumstances, or with themselves; one, several, or all of these kinds of conflicts, as the case may be." Tragedy might be the story of suffering, but "Hegel says very little of this [suffering]; partly, perhaps, because it is obvious, but more because the essential point to him is not the suffering but its cause, namely, the action or conflict." Suffering is not tragic itself but is a misfortune: sad but not art. Tragedy appeals to our sense of art because "it is a conflict of the spirit. It is a conflict, that is to say, between powers that rule the world of man's will and action – his 'ethical substance.'" Tragedy is therefore a collision of wills, "not so much the war of good and evil as the war of good with good. Two of these isolated powers face each other, making incompatible demands."[60] What is *tragic* for Hegel is the one-sided and even blind-sided stubbornness of the antagonists. Although each character stands on solid ethical grounds, their uncompromising wills clash tragically. This conflict will lead to the catharsis of modern drama. The collision of inflexible concepts steeped in moral righteousness is the "false one-sidedness" that Hegel sees as the root of modern drama and opens the way to dramatic realism.

Romanticism favored myth, fantasy, and figurative language; by the middle of the nineteenth century, such thinking gave way to realism. Dramatic realism, influenced by the loosely defined political group called the Young Hegelians (Marx among them) and the rise of realistic art and novels, took Hegel's idea of conflict and retooled it from metaphysics to social criticism.[61] European realism opposed Romantic idealism, pastoral adventures, and heroic allegories characteristic of the early nineteenth century. It took literary and dramatic root during the mid-nineteenth century and was founded on detailed observation and the Young Hegelian emphasis on objectivity and detachment. Jürgen Habermas credits the Young Hegelians for bringing about a "situation of consciousness" that remains contemporary. Hegel, Habermas says, "inaugurated the discourse of modernity." When the Young Hegelians of the 1840s "distanced themselves from Hegel and philosophy in general," they "permanently established" modernity's turning point, liberating "the idea of a critique nourished on the spirit of modernity from the burden of the Hegelian concept of reason."[62] Social criticism as advocated by Marxists absorbed Hegel's notions of conflict but rejected his absolute consciousness as mental and purely abstract. The Young Hegelians replaced resolution in the mind with concrete reality; in realism characters were in conflict "on the ground" involving living circumstances. Marx attempts to reverse the order of consciousness, saying that "Life is not determined by consciousness, but consciousness by life." Consciousness is rooted in the concrete: "Its premises are men, not in any fantastic isolation and rigidity, but in their actual, empirically perceptible process of development under definite conditions." In critiquing Hegel's metaphysics, Marx adds, "Where speculation ends – in real life – there real, positive science begins: the representation of the practical activity, of the practical process of development of men."[63]

Marx opposed Hegelian self-consciousness as a fundamental category. For Marx Hegel's emphasis on the speculative over the concrete would lead to an aporia of subjective idealism. Hegel's idea of pure consciousness is "thoroughly subjectivized." The Hegelian clash of family and civil society, Marx says, "is grasped as their *inner imaginary* activity" rather than as social relations in "active forms." When ideas are speculative, civil society and family "become *unactual*."[64] The effort to make dialectical concepts concrete is the basis of dramatic realism. For Marx, Hegel's "conflict" is grounded in reality and manifest in the class struggle. The alienation of the worker "means not only that his labor becomes an object, an *external* existence, but that it exists *outside him*, independently, as something alien to him, and that it becomes a power on its own confronting him."[65] Representing the beleaguered worker and the owner as adversary helped shape the modern conception of realistic conflict in Western drama. From the mid-century onward, realism (later intensified by naturalism) came to the forefront of theatre (Ibsen, early Strindberg, Chekhov, Shaw), literature (Balzac, Tolstoy, Zola, Dickens), and art (Courbet, Manet). It centered on a desire for objective representation of social reality in conflict, unsqueamish in its portrayal of the sordid. René Wellek defines it in comparison to Romanticism, observing that realism "rejects fantasy, the fairy-tale-like, the allegorical and the symbolic, the highly stylized, the purely abstract and decorative," which "implies also a rejection of the improbable, of pure chance, and of extraordinary events, since reality is obviously conceived at that time, in spite of all local and personal differences, as the orderly world of nineteenth-century science, a world of cause and effect, a world without miracle, without transcendence even if the individual may have preserved a personal religious faith. The term 'reality' is also a term of inclusion: the ugly, the revolting, the low are legitimate subjects of art."[66] Realism – the representation of reality through language, description, and image – had existed before the nineteenth century; what made it popular at the time was owing to what Peter Brooks calls "a new valuation of ordinary experience and its ordinary settings and things."[67] The rise of the middle class, photography, and commerce added significantly to the realist vision of novels and plays. Realism, furthermore, emerged in opposition to idealism. The emphasis on the everyday and not the transcendence of ideals as the Romantics might have it became a central subject of art, and theatre proved to be one of the most popular means of conveying the lifelike and everyday.

At the end of the nineteenth century, the differences between realism and idealism that had dominated aesthetic debates throughout most of the nineteenth century transmogrified into an antithesis of realism and modernism (at least the avant-garde version of modernism). However much twentieth-century theatre theory stresses the avant-garde, there is no escaping the fact that the avant-garde's resistance to realism, primarily in theatre theory, was just that – a resistance. Theatre, unlike other arts, relies almost entirely on the human body, the presence of human beings "representing" something. Even if the representation is of oneself (stand-up comedy or soloist storytellers, for instance), a person onstage and an audience situated in a designated place viewing the actor evoke representation. Representation can be downplayed by self-consciously calling attention to itself, negating it (closet readers' theatre), or creating a circus-like atmosphere; but the arrangement of stage, actor, and audience in a specified and material way cannot escape the idea of representing some condition. Referring to art in general, Fredric

Jameson alludes to this conundrum when he remarks that what "precedes modernism," meaning the avant-garde, is "realism, about which it is surely obvious" that it "constitutes the raw material modernism cancels and surcharges." Yet this "cancellation" depends on its antecedent, for if "realism is grasped as the expression of some commonsense experience of a recognizable world, then empirical examination of any work we care to categorize as 'modernist' will reveal a starting point in that conventional real world, a realist core as it were, which the various telltale modernist deformations and 'unrealistic' distortions, sublimations or gross characterizations, take as their pretext and their raw material, and without which their alleged 'obscurity' and 'incomprehensibility' would not be possible."[68]

Nietzsche rebelled against nineteenth-century realism in a way that reverberates to this day. He contested the legitimacy of modernity, especially the Hegelian version that maintains teleological progress through volition and conflict. Such thinking for Nietzsche was mere philistinism. Following Schopenhauer, Nietzsche claimed that human development, rather than being a progressive manifestation of the human spirit, is essentially chaotic, irrational, blind, and ceaselessly craving. Nietzsche's influence on dramatic theory is hard to dispute, but the impact of his *Birth of Tragedy* (1872) has become so absorbed into the fabric of criticism that it is difficult to determine the extent of that influence. Such is the view of Benjamin Bennett, who says that the "dramatic theory of *The Birth of Tragedy* has exercised only a limited direct influence, mainly because it has not been understood; but the idea of the Dionysian, even superficially considered, obviously suggests drama as a form for its expression, for it includes the idea of the communal as opposed to the individual, the idea of art as a revitalized public ritual, the idea of transcending the realistic tendency of nineteenth-century narrative."[69] Indeed, Nietzsche's influence takes root in drama's emphasis on ritual, rejection of mimesis, and laying the groundwork for non-representational theatre. Without Nietzsche, Artaud and others may not have taken the direction they had.

Nietzsche engaged with tragedy in order to come to terms with unredeemable suffering and to oppose the notion, put forth by Hegel and his followers, that all can be made right through reconciliation (*Versöhnung*) and sensible behavior. If Hegel put the concept of ethically conflicting wills and their reconciliation at center stage, Nietzsche challenged the notion that there can be anything resembling moral certitude or objective truth. In a statement that would define his life's work, Nietzsche remarked: "What then is truth? A mobile army of metaphors, metonyms, anthropomorphisms, in short a sum of human relationships, which, poetically and rhetorically are intensified, ornamented, and transferred, and have come to be thought of, after long usage by people, as canonically and bindingly imagined: truths are illusions which one has forgotten that they are illusions, worn-out metaphors now important to stir the senses (*sinnlich kraftlos*), coins which have lost their image (*Bild*) and are considered now only as metal rather than currency."[70] Nietzsche followed Kant's distinction between noumena, being what Kant called "things-in-themselves," and phenomena, the outward appearance manifest in the empirical. The "thing-in-itself" is the interiority that cannot be comprehended, whereas only phenomena can be known. However, for Nietzsche the "thing-in-itself" is no more than rhetoric – "discourse" – based on illusions held together through language. There is for Nietzsche no core reality, only a linguistic parade of recycled ideas and rehashed traditions. History, too, was nothing more than a "monumentalistic conception of the past," creating the illusion that "the greatness that once existed was . . . once *possible* and may thus be possible again."[71] For Hegel, history was a sequence of conflicts and resolution: it progressed through a network of logical arguments, each working out contradictions until a resolution was reached only to confront a new antithesis. The ultimate goal is *Geist* ("spirit"). This was the basis of Hegelian idealism as well as the theories of Marx and others who eschewed the notion of spiritual consciousness but nonetheless retained the core conflict of wills. Hegel and the Romantics (Shelling, Hölderlin, among others) shared the conviction that ideas could change the world, that autonomy envisaged by Kant and Schiller could be put to great use, and that there could emerge a free society based on Athenian ideals. If Goethe and Schiller represented a generation of German Pan-Hellenism, Hegel went further in believing that Germany could surpass the Greek model in art, philosophy, and society. Philosophy and poetry could bridge ideas and reality, healing the fragmentation of the modern self. During the 1840s this optimism climaxed as radical movements that put faith in Hegelian rationality met their demise in the unsuccessful European revolution of 1848. From there the "crisis of reason," to borrow the title of J. W. Barrow's noteworthy book,[72] and the vogue of pessimism, led by Schopenhauer's *World as Will and Representation* (1819), took root. The pessimistic philosophy of renunciation that was exemplified by Baudelaire's notion of the "dandy" – "this solitary mortal endowed with an active imagination … looking for that indefinable something we may be allowed to call 'modernity' "[73] – was carried further by Nietzsche, and his *Birth of Tragedy* became a resource for late nineteenth-century nihilism and early twentieth-century modernism.

For Nietzsche, Greek drama was not, as had been supposed, a theatre of pristine moral debates, stoical rhetoric, and cheerful serenity. The theory of Greek art and drama as rational, contemplative, and psychological was maintained by Johann Joachim Winckelmann (1717–68) and dominated the thinking of classical philologists, philosophers, aestheticists, and critics for two centuries. For Winckelmann, ancient ideas of beauty are characterized by noble simplicity and tranquil grandeur. Nietzsche's theory (and it is pure theory – Nietzsche provides no hard evidence) gainsays such ideas, claiming that Greek tragedy was for the celebration of Dionysiac hedonism. Greek drama for Nietzsche was volatile, chaotic, lustful, intoxicating, orgiastic, and tied to music, the macabre, and the erotic elements within human nature. Music was at the core of drama and was to be given direct access to audiences unmediated by mimetic representation. The Apollonian classicism of refinement and rhetoric had to be balanced with the explosive Dionysian vehicle for the emotions and an emphasis on the body. The Dionysian festivals were collective assemblages – literally the chorus itself – for the renunciation of what Schopenhauer called *principium individuationis*. In place of egoism would come a selfless compliance with the spirit of music. With music as catalyst, the festivals were to merge participants into the oneness of a collective will and jettison at least temporarily the Apollonian view of rationality, orderliness, and dreams. Evoking Eastern philosophy (as consigned by Schopenhauer), Nietzsche writes that in the Dionysiac dithyramb "man is stimulated to the highest intensification of his symbolic powers; something that he has never felt before urgently demands to be expressed: the destruction of the veil of maya, one-ness as the genius of humankind, indeed of nature itself. The essence of nature is bent on expressing itself; a new world of symbols is required, firstly the symbolism of the entire body, not just the mouth, the face, the word, but the full gesture of dance with its rhythmical movement of every limb."[74] From this Nietzsche's influence on modern dance, drama, and the arts in general is easy to ascertain. Tragedy for Nietzsche is self-expression, communal bonding, the disintegration of individualism, a release of passion, and successful reintegration of Dionysian euphoria with Apollonian rationalism. For Nietzsche the Greeks and the moderns had taken rationality and egoism to excess; the Dionysian festivals created tragedy in order to restore the proper balance of rational egoism and the sobering (and for Nietzsche exhilarating) realization of death, chaos, and destruction.

Nietzsche believes tragedy had lost its way owing to Hegelianism. If, as Harold Bloom contends, Shakespeare invented the human,[75] Nietzsche suggests that it is Euripides who first emphasized humanistic autonomy and individuality. This "human invention," however, is nothing to celebrate; it was for Nietzsche mere self-aggrandizement of our rational side. For him, rationality as conveyed by Euripides is the chief culprit; Sophocles began the decline, but it is Euripides who brought the stage down the slippery slope of psychology, egoism, and the false comforts of solipsism. Euripides creates "drama," the Apollonian rationalism that exemplifies dialogue, reason, and argument, which for Nietzsche weakened moral fiber. Nietzsche did not oppose Apollonian rationality per se – true synthesis is a balance of reason and passion, Apollo and Dionysus. However, tragedy had been hijacked by humanists, which for him means Christian moralism, melodramatic ethics (right and wrong), and nineteenth-century realism. Tragedy belongs to the Dionysian realm, to which Dionysus, Gilles Deleuze observes, returns humanity to "primitive unity." Dionysus, the god of wine, fertility, and sex, "shatters the individual, drags him into the great shipwreck and absorbs him into original being."[76]

The rise of individualism taking place in the nineteenth century is characterized by Euripedean-type dramas and is for Nietzsche instrumental in creating obstacles to the expressive joy of tragic suffering. Pain is joyous for Nietzsche: it is life-affirming empowerment. Humanism, with its pretense of individual agency and perfidious healing balm of catharsis, signifies modernism's etiolated malaise. For Nietzsche Hegelian human will in conflict is risible; the individual volition is nothing more than an illusion. Nietzsche's belief in the Buddhist negation of the will – "longing to deny the will as the Buddhist does," and therefore the negation of action – is expressed in the bond forged by Dionysus and Hamlet. For Nietzsche, both Dionysus and Hamlet "have *acquired knowledge* and they find action repulsive, for their actions can do nothing to change the eternal essence of things; they regard it as laughable or shameful that they should be expected to set to rights a world so out of joint." In his key assertion, Nietzsche says: "Knowledge kills action; action requires one to be shrouded in a veil of illusion – this is the lesson of Hamlet." Hamlet for Nietzsche is not some clichéd passive dreamer (a likely countermand to Hegel's nullification of *Hamlet* in favor of *Antigone*), but rather imbued with "true knowledge, insight into the terrible truth, which outweighs every motive for action," existing "both in the case of Hamlet and in that of Dionysiac man." Knowledge will "kill" action because action is fruitless. In a passage anticipating Chekhov's ennui, Artaud's theatre of cruelty, Sartre's nausea, and Beckett's inertia, Nietzsche says: "Once truth has been seen, the consciousness of it prompts man to see only what is terrible or absurd in existence wherever he looks; now he understands the symbolism of Ophelia's fate, now he grasps the wisdom of the wood-god Silenus: he feels revulsion" (*BT* 40). For Nietzsche, representation itself is perceived negatively and dramas of representation – realism – are betrayals of Hellenic tragedy.

If Hegelian-Marxian drama is linear, teleological, historical, progressive, realistic, celebratory of, and dependent on, the individual will, Nietzschean drama is circular, repetitive, ritualistic, and a celebration of the will's demise. Progress in history in the Hegelian sense is for Nietzsche a ruse that ought to be renounced. The world moves by *déjà vu*, and only by accepting arbitrary and repetitive fate can one feel empowered. In a passage titled *Das grösste Schwergewicht* (the "greatest weight" or "greatest stress"), Nietzsche describes his concept of "eternal reoccurrence," the notion of circularity that would come to describe dramas of inaction:

> What if, some day or night a demon were to steal after you into your loneliest loneliness and say to you: "This life as you now live it and have lived it, you will have to live once more and innumerable times more; and there will be nothing new in it, but every pain and every joy and every thought and sigh and everything unutterably small or great in your life will have to return to you, all in the same succession and sequence – even this spider and this moonlight between the trees, and even this moment and I myself. The eternal hourglass of existence is turned upside down again and again, and you with it, speck of dust!"[77]

Nietzsche wants to challenge what he considers the Hegelian myth of progress and agency by revealing the contradictions, absurdities, and radical indeterminacy of the human condition. Life is cyclical and reoccurring; attempts by playwrights to portray sequential arrangements and linear causality are aimless folly. The curse of individuation and history evoke what Julian Young calls Nietzsche's "Schopenhauerian, anti-Hegelian sense that history conceived as a story of evolution or progress is merely 'so-called,' that in a sense history does not exist at all, since all there is is the endless repetition of the same meaningless patterns." For Schopenhauer and Nietzsche, Young notes, "the world lacks teleology: its course resembles that of not an arrow but a circle."[78] For Nietzsche drama does not concern itself as Hegel would have it with a preexisting moral condition which, when it comes in contact with an opposite moral position, results in a dialectically antagonistic stance. Rather, the presence of an audience creates the ritualistic drama merging with the Dionysian spirit. Individualism is the ailment of modern society; Nietzsche nullifies this individuality by suggesting that tragedy merge into the primordial oneness as in a Dionysian ritual. As Nietzsche's biographer put it, "for Nietzsche as well as for Schopenhauer and Nietzsche's Greeks, it is not possible to discern any teleological *justification* of what the individual is thus fated to undergo, either historically or supernaturally. We can look neither to a future utopia nor to a life hereafter that might serve to render endurable and meaningful the terror and horror of existence."[79] Schopenhauer viewed the world as a struggle of uncomprehending forces; human will was amorphous, akin to Rimbaud's drunken boat, careening aimlessly. Nietzsche concurred with this, but his version of the will resists Schopenhauer's retreat from the world. Rather, Nietzsche considers the demise of individuality as a fount of power, a destructive power which is active, not passive, gaining strength in the union of the mythic force that is tragedy.

Nietzsche built his ideas of myth and tragedy from Wagner's efforts to forge an intense bonding of the stage and the audience based on emotionalism and racial unity. Wagner, likewise Nietzsche, favored myth and symbols over rationalism and restraint; struggle and passion facilitate an intensive response on behalf of nationalistic desire. Wagner's *Gesamtkunstwerk* unified staging, acting, music, and set design (especially lighting) under the auspice of one vision and had significant influence not merely on Nietzsche but also on the symbolist and non-rational theories of the early twentieth-century theatrical avant-garde. Whereas Ibsen (and to some extent early Strindberg) exercised an immediate impact on the development of naturalism and realistic social dramas (Shaw, in particular), Wagner sought a stirring folk drama that challenged the limits of rational arguments that were the bailiwick of social problem plays. Ibsen and Wagner can be considered the exemplars of Hegel and Nietzsche in practice, respectively: their works set the tone for things to come.

The Birth of Tragedy might be viewed as a precursor of expressionism, symbolism, and non-representational theatre that seeks to characterize the alienation of society. It argues that alienation is evident in a decadent culture "condemned to exhaust every possibility and to seek meager nourishment from all other cultures." Nietzsche raises the point that the "enormous historical need of dissatisfied modern culture, the accumulation of countless other cultures, the consuming desire for knowledge – what does all this point to, if not to the loss of myth, the loss of a mythical home, a mythical, material womb?" (*BT* 109). It can be said that Nietzsche gainsays Lessing's bourgeois-humanist theatre, nineteenth-century melodrama, and Ibsen's realistic parlor, all of which advance secularist drama and in doing so betray their adherence to the origins of drama's mythic origins. Tragedy – in fact all drama – should emphasize music, myth, and an intoxicating release from the façade of individuality; simply put, drama should strive for something higher than insignificant bickering and anguished nail-biting. Nietzsche's condemnation of modern drama is accomplished through a critique of drama's focus on particularization, mimesis, and realism. Melodramatic suspense common in humanist drama is particularly opprobrious; for Nietzsche the "effect of tragedy never rested on epic suspense, on teasing people and making them uncertain about what will happen now or later, but rather on those great rhetorical and lyrical scenes in which the passion and dialectic of the protagonist swelled into broad and mighty stream. Everything was a preparation for pathos, not for action; and anything that was not a preparation for pathos was held to be objectionable" (*BT* 62). Music, not psychological characterization, is what is tragic, and this "struggle of the spirit of music [is] to be revealed in image and myth" (*BT* 82). In opposition to the spirit of myth, image, and music is character in action, what he calls the "un-Dionysiac," where "the excessive growth in the *presentation of character and of psychological refinement* [is] in tragedy from Sophocles onwards" (*BT* 83–4). Dramas emphasizing character merely dabble in hairsplitting psychology, awash in mundane contretemps and niggling suspense. It is the psychological emphasis that Nietzsche deplores, whereby "Character is not meant to be capable of being expanded into an eternal type; on the contrary, artificial subsidiary features, shading and the fine definition of every line, are all meant to give such an impression of individuality that the spectator no longer senses the myth at all, but only the great fidelity to nature and the imitative skills of the artist" (*BT* 84). Amidst psychological portrayal – the individual's volition and melodramatic intrigue – are lost the quixotic Dionysiac art, "based on play with intoxication, with the state of ecstasy." When the Dionysiac art appears, "the *principium individuationis* is disrupted, subjectivity disappears entirely before the erupting force of the general element in human life, indeed the general element in nature. Not only do the festivals of Dionysos forge a bond between human beings, they also reconcile human beings and nature" (*BT* 120). Only in the spirit of music and the glorious eruption of intoxicating bacchanalia can "man feel himself to be a god." At that point, "What does he now care for images and statues? Man is no longer an artist, he has become a work of art; man himself now moves with the same ecstasy and sublimity with which, in dream, he once saw the gods walk" (*BT* 121). Human life is itself art, occurring in the turbulent atmosphere of its own violable terrain. Performance art and happenings of the late twentieth century are but a few steps away.

Hegel and Nietzsche's opposing theories, among others, took root in the twentieth century, manifesting the debate over representation that Plato and Aristotle had initiated. Stephen Halliwell remarks that it is possible "to draw up an elaborate 'balance-sheet' of twentieth-century thinkers, as well as artistic movements themselves, in terms of their *pro* and *contra* stance toward various (though often reductive) interpretations of artistic mimesis." One of the distinguishing features of the century, Halliwell contends, has been and continues to be "an unresolved, polarized dialectic of values, between whose extremes an entire spectrum of positions, from outright formalism to outright moralism, from pure abstraction to the most engaged styles of *verismo*, has stretched itself out."[80] As the century progressed, wider vistas exploring new directions emerged. The core features of mimesis remained intact, but the debates gained complexity and sophistication. Theatre in theory has, in fact, a more complex progeny than that derived from merely Western ideas. Non-Western theatre has indeed permeated Western philosophy and influenced its aesthetics. Readers will note that as the anthology progresses, chapters increasingly represent thinkers outside the Western canon, conveying new models of form, content, and theories. This suggests that as the twenty-first century comes into view, a global perspective will dominate. Most importantly, what informs this anthology is the belief that there is not a single, universal theory of theatre but many theories, each written from different viewpoints.

About the Anthology

The essays have been chosen because of their intrinsic merit and enduring influence. Some essays are reproduced in their entirety, either because they are succinct or because to abridge them would destroy their meaning. Others have been truncated, either because the specific references they make to people or events have fallen into oblivion or because they have to be edited to keep the anthology from becoming unrealistically long. The goal is to provide as wide a range and as concise an account as possible of twentieth-century theatre in theory. Ellipses in square brackets indicate where I have edited; unbracketed ellipses are either in the original source or the translator's cuts. Wherever possible I aim for consistency (for example, I prefer theatre over theater except in the case of more contemporary authors). However, I honor British spellings when translations occur (neighbour, for example). "Editor's note" or square brackets designate my intervention; all other notes are either the author's (where no additional remarks are made) or the translator's (referred to as "translator's note").

I have distributed the essays across the century as evenly as possible. Each text is accompanied by a brief précis. Although there are occasional footnotes describing references and people, the Internet has made names and events readily accessible. I therefore assert minimal editorial intervention. The essays are arranged chronologically and divided into five sections, each covering two decades. The sections are introduced briefly as a unit in an effort to clarify the prevailing social and historic background. A thematic index appears at the end, offering suggested clusters of readings that might serve as class units; however, each reader is encouraged to cross-reference according to his or her taste. Some of the essays contained in this anthology have rarely, if ever, appeared outside of their original source. Others have appeared in several anthologies. This mix of well-known and underappreciated texts will, it is hoped, embellish the study of theatre in theory.

This collection is indebted to the efforts, translations, and analysis of researchers who greatly aided in disseminating the material. While other anthologies are noted in the bibliography, several individual works deserve special mention. Marvin Carlson's *Theories of the Theatre* (Cornell, 1984, expanded edition, 1993) is an exemplary overview of Western dramatic theory and criticism. It is an essential survey, as is J. L. Styan's three-volume *Modern Drama in Theory and Practice* (Cambridge, 1981). With great detail Shannon Jackson's *Professing Performance: Theatre in the Academy from Philology to Performativity* (Cambridge, 2004) examines the history of performance studies in twentieth-century United States universities. Martin Puchner's highly original *Stage Fright: Modernism, Anti-Theatricality and Drama* (Baltimore, 2002) defines the emergence of modern drama in terms of theatricality's "value." Graham Ley's *From Mimesis to Interculturalism: Readings of Theatrical Theory before and after Modernism* (Exeter, 1999) provides copious references and astute analysis of essential material. Two edited collections, Jenelle Reinelt and Joseph Roach's *Critical Theory and Performance* (Michigan, 1992, expanded edition 2007) and David Krasner and David Z. Saltz's *Staging Philosophy: Intersections of Theater, Performance, and Philosophy* (Michigan, 2006), offer significant and original essays on dramatic theory and performance. Finally, a superb two-volume anthology of primary sources from pre-twentieth-century dramatic criticism is *Sources of Dramatic Theory* edited by Michael J. Sidnell (Cambridge, 1991, 1994). This sourcebook is recommended as complementary to this work, providing texts prior to the twentieth century.

Notes

1 *Oxford English Dictionary* (Oxford, 1989), 2040, 2038.
2 P. Pavis, *Languages of the Stage: Essays in the Semiology of Theatre*, tr. J. Daugherty (New York: PAJ, 1982), 185; M. Carlson, *Performance: A Critical Introduction* (London: Routledge, 1996), 82.
3 Plato, *Laws* II, *The Collected Dialogues*, tr. E. Hamilton and H. Cairns (Princeton: Princeton University Press, 1989), 1252, 1253, 1256 [sections 655, 656, 659].
4 J. Derrida, *Dissemination*, tr. B. Johnson (Chicago: University of Chicago Press, 1981), 186.
5 A. Melberg, *Theories of Mimesis* (Cambridge: Cambridge University Press, 1995), 10.
6 P. Woodruff, "Aristotle on Mimēsis," in *Essays on Aristotle's Poetics*, ed. A. O. Rorty (Princeton: Princeton University Press, 1992), 76.
7 G. Ley, *From Mimesis to Interculturalism: Readings of Theatrical Theory before and after Modernism* (Exeter: University of Exeter Press, 1999), 25.
8 R. McKeon, "The Concept of Imitation in Antiquity," in *Critics and Criticism*, ed. R. S. Crane (Chicago: University of Chicago Press, 1952), 122.
9 A. Nehamas, *Virtues of Authenticity: Essays on Plato and Socrates* (Princeton: Princeton University Press, 1999), xxxiv.

10   M. Puchner, *Stage Fright: Modernism, Anti-Theatricality and Drama* (Baltimore: Johns Hopkins University Press, 2002), 25.

11   E. Diamond, *Unmaking Mimesis: Essays on Feminism and Theater* (London: Routledge, 1977), 4–5.

12   See G. Whalley, "On Translating Aristotle's *Poetics*," in *Aristotle's Poetics* (London: McGill-Queen's University Press, 1997), 3–32.

13   Aristotle, *Poetics*, tr. Stephen Halliwell (Chapel Hill: University of North Carolina Press, 1987), 37 [ch. 6].

14   A. Ford, *The Origins of Criticism: Literary Culture and Poetic Theory in Classical Greece* (Princeton: Princeton University Press, 2002), 95.

15   F. Fergusson, "Introduction," in *Aristotle's Poetics* (New York: Hill & Wang, 1961), 10.

16   G. Else, *Aristotle's Poetics: The Argument* (Cambridge, MA: Harvard University Press, 1957), 306.

17   M. Husain, *Ontology and the Art of Tragedy: An Approach to Aristotle's Poetics* (Albany: State University of New York Press, 2002), 23.

18   G. Gebauer and C. Wulf, *Mimesis: Culture, Art, Society*, tr. D. Reneau (Berkeley: University of California Press, 1992), 55.

19   B. O. States, *The Pleasure of the Play* (Ithaca: Cornell University Press, 1994), 20.

20   S. Halliwell, *Aristotle's Poetics* (Chicago: University of Chicago Press, 1989), 22.

21   S. Halliwell, *The Aesthetics of Mimesis: Ancient Texts and Modern Problems* (Princeton: Princeton University Press, 2002), 168, 201.

22   M. Potolsky, *Mimesis* (New York: Routledge, 2006), 51.

23   D. Dox, *The Idea of the Theater in Latin Christian Thought: Augustine to the Fourteenth Century* (Ann Arbor: University of Michigan Press, 2004), 97.

24   E. Cassirer, *The Philosophy of the Enlightenment* [*Die Philosophie der Aufklärung*, 1932], tr. F. C. A. Koelln and J. P. Pettegrove (Princeton: Princeton University Press, 1951), 279.

25   J. Dryden, *An Essay of Dramatic Poetry*, ed. J. L. Mahoney (New York: Irvington, 1982), 10.

26   G. E. Lessing, *Hamburg Dramaturgy*, tr. V. Lange (New York: Dover, 1962), 180, 181.

27   I. Kant, *Critique of the Power of Judgment*, tr. P. Guyer and E. Matthews (Cambridge: Cambridge University Press, 2000), 66–7. Future references will be cited in the text.

28   J. Derrida, *The Truth in Painting*, tr. G. Bennington and I. McLeod (Chicago: University of Chicago Press, 1987), 44.

29   P. Guyer, "Kant's Ambitions in the Third *Critique*," in *Cambridge Companion to Kant and Modern Philosophy*, ed. Guyer (Cambridge: Cambridge University Press, 2006), 538. For studies in English, see, among others, P. Guyer, *Kant and the Claims of Taste* (Cambridge. MA: Harvard University Press, 1997) and H. E. Allison, *Kant's Theory of Taste* (Cambridge: Cambridge University Press, 2001).

30   F. C. Beiser, *The Romantic Imperative: The Concept of Early German Romanticism* (Cambridge, MA: Harvard University Press, 2003), 81.

31   M. Cheetham, *Kant, Art, and Art History: Moments of Discipline* (Cambridge: Cambridge University Press, 2001), 78.

32   M. McCloskey, *Kant's Aesthetics* (Albany: State University of New York Press, 1987), 156.

33   T. Eagleton, *The Ideology of the Aesthetic* (Oxford: Blackwell, 1990), 75.

34   S. Kemal, *Kant's Aesthetic Theory* (New York: St. Martin's Press, 1997), 122.

35   R. Wellek, *Discriminations: Further Concepts of Criticism* (New Haven: Yale University Press, 1970), 127–8.

36   E. Cassirer, *Kant's Life and Thought*, tr. J. Haden (New Haven: Yale University Press, 1981), 318, 319.

37   H. Sussman, *The Aesthetic Contract: Statutes of Art and Intellectual Work in Modernity* (Stanford: Stanford University Press, 1997), 139.

38   Among exemplary studies of Kant's unity of reason see A. Collins, *Possible Experience: Understanding Kant's Critique of Pure Reason* (Berkeley: University of California Press, 1999);

S. M. Shell, *The Embodiment of Reason: Kant on Spirit, Generation, and Community* (Chicago: University of Chicago Press, 1996); and S. Neiman, *The Unity of Reason: Rereading Kant* (New York: Oxford University Press, 1994).

39 For an examination of Kant's relationship to his student Herder and the *Sturm und Drang* Movement, referred to as the "Pantheism Controversy," see J. H. Zammito, *The Genius of Kant's Critique of Judgment* (Chicago: University of Chicago Press, 1992), 228–47.

40 S. T. Coleridge, *Biographia Literaria* (1812), Vol. II, ed. J. Engell and W. J. Bate (London: Routledge, 1983), 214–15.

41 R. Gasché, *The Idea of Form: Rethinking Kant's Aesthetics* (Stanford University Press, 2003), 185.

42 T. Adorno, *Aesthetic Theory*, tr. R. Hullot-Kentor (Minneapolis: University of Minnesota Press, 1997), 163, 164. For a view of Kant as a pure formalist, see P. de Man, "Kant's Materialism," in *Aesthetic Ideology* (Minneapolis: University of Minnesota Press, 1996), 119–28. For a view opposed see Gasché, *The Idea of Form*.

43 O. Höffe, *Immanuel Kant*, tr. M. Farrier (Albany: State University of New York, 1994), 218.

44 C. Greenberg, *Collected Essays and Criticism*, Vol. 3 (Chicago: University of Chicago Press, 1995), 249. See also T. de Duve, *Kant after Duchamp* (Cambridge, MA: MIT Press, 1996).

45 R. Eldridge, *An Introduction to the Philosophy of Art* (Cambridge, MA: Cambridge University Press, 2003), 55.

46 F. Nietzsche, *The Will to Power*, tr. W. Kaufmann (New York: Vintage, 1968), 445.

47 I. Berlin, *The Roots of Romanticism* (Princeton: Princeton University Press, 1999), 140.

48 F. Schiller, *Aesthetical and Philosophical Essays* (Boston: IndyPublish.com, 2006), 79, 89, no translator noted.

49 C. Taylor, *Sources of the Self: The Making of Modern Identity* (Cambridge, MA: Harvard University Press, 1989), 481.

50 G. W. F. Hegel, *Introductory Lectures on Aesthetics* (1835), tr. B. Bosanquet (New York: Penguin Books, 1993), 37, 63.

51 E. Jurist, *Beyond Hegel and Nietzsche: Philosophy, Culture, and Agency* (Cambridge, MA: MIT Press, 2002), 85.

52 Hegel, *Vorlesungen über die Ästhetik*, III, in *Werke*, Vol. 15 (Frankfurt am Main: Suhrkamp, 1986), 543. Further references will be cited in the text.

53 F. Schiller, *On the Pathetic* (*Über das Pathetische*, 1793), quoted in *Dramatic Theory and Criticism: Greeks to Grotowski*, ed. B. Dukore (New York: Holt, Rinehart, and Winston, 1974), 460.

54 D. Krasner, "Dialogics and Dialectics: Bakhtin, Young Hegelians, and Dramatic Theory," in *Bakhtin: Ethics and Mechanics*, ed. V. Z. Nollan (Evanston: Northwestern University Press, 2004), 9.

55 G. W. F. Hegel, *Phenomenology of Spirit*, tr. A. V. Miller (Oxford: Oxford University Press, 1997), 285.

56 A. O. Rorty, "The Psychology of Aristotelian Tragedy," in *Essays on Aristotle's Poetics*, ed. Rorty, 7.

57 J. W. von Goethe, "Shakespeare und kein Ende" (1815), in *Goethe Frühes Theater*, ed. D. Borchmeyer (Frankfurt am Main: Suhrkamp, 1982), 508.

58 I. Nyusztay, *Myth, Telos, Identity: The Tragic Schema in Greek and Shakespearean Drama* (Amsterdam: Rodopi, 2002), 64.

59 M. Gellrich, *Tragedy and Theory: The Problems of Conflict since Aristotle* (Princeton: Princeton University Press, 1988), 45.

60 A. C. Bradley, "Hegel's Theory of Tragedy," in *Hegel on Tragedy*, ed. A. and H. Paolucci (Garden City, NY: Anchor Books, 1962), 368–9.

61 See W. Breckman, *Marx, the Young Hegelians, and the Origins of Radical Social Theory* (Cambridge: Cambridge University Press, 1999), and W. Essbach, *Die Junghegelianer: Soziologie einer Intellektuellengruppe* (Munich: Wilhelm Fink, 1988).

62   J. Habermas, *The Philosophical Discourse of Modernity*, tr. F. G. Lawrence (Cambridge, MA: MIT Press, 1992), 53.

63   K. Marx, *The German Ideology*, tr. C. J. Arthur (New York: International, 1947), 47, 48.

64   K. Marx, "Feuerbachian Criticism of Hegel," in *Writings of the Young Marx on Philosophy and Society*, tr. L. Easton and K. Guddat (Garden City, NY: Doubleday, 1967), 155.

65   K. Marx, *Economic and Philosophic Manuscripts of 1844*, tr. M. Milligan (New York: International, 1964), 108.

66   R. Wellek, *Concepts of Criticism* (New Haven: Yale University Press, 1963), 241.

67   P. Brooks, *Realist Vision* (New Haven: Yale University Press, 2005), 7.

68   F. Jameson, *A Singular Modernity: Essay on the Ontology of the Present* (London: Verso, 2002), 120.

69   B. Bennett, *Modern Drama and German Classicism: Renaissance from Lessing to Brecht* (Ithaca: Cornell University Press, 1979), 229.

70   F. Nietzsche, *Über Wahrheit und Lüge im Aussermoralischen Sinn* (*On Truth and Falsehood in an Extramoral Sense*), in *Werke*, Vol. 3 (Munich: Carl Hanser, 1973), 314.

71   F. Nietzsche, "On the Uses and Disadvantages of History for Life," in *Untimely Meditations*, tr. R. J. Hollingdale (Cambridge: Cambridge University Press, 1983), 69.

72   J. W. Barrow, *The Crisis of Reason: European Thought, 1848–1914* (New Haven: Yale University Press, 2000).

73   C. Baudelaire, "The Painter of Modern Life," in *Selected Writings on Art and Artists*, tr. P. E. Charvet (New York: Penguin, 1972), 402.

74   F. Nietzsche, *The Birth of Tragedy*, tr. R. Geuss and R. Speirs (Cambridge: Cambridge University Press, 1999), 21. Further references will be cited as *BT* in the text.

75   H. Bloom, *Shakespeare: The Invention of the Human* (New York: Riverhead Books, 1998).

76   G. Deleuze, *Nietzsche and Philosophy*, tr. H. Tomlinson (New York: Columbia University Press, 2006), 11.

77   F. Nietzsche, *The Gay Science*, tr. W. Kaufmann (New York: Vintage, 1974), 273.

78   J. Young, *Nietzsche's Philosophy of Art* (Cambridge: Cambridge University Press, 1992), 39–40.

79   R. Schacht, *Nietzsche* (London: Routledge, 1983), 480.

80   Halliwell, *The Aesthetics of Mimesis*, 370.

Part I

1900–1920

The end of the nineteenth century was a period of artistic experimentation. According to Tom Driver, "To 'experiment' in the theatre has usually meant to break with whatever is the reigning style and method, and in the 1890s breaks were made in many directions. There was a veritable eruption of that modern spirit that insists on rejecting the 'givens.'"[1] As the twentieth century came into view, two directions predominated. Modernism in theatre begins with either the single-minded determination to see the world objectively or the equally concentrated view that the artist's subjectivity must determine theatre's goal. The former avowed no mystery about the world; the stage meant an investigation of society. Theatre was a laboratory to examine social ills without the intervention of fantasy, dreams, illusions, or spirituality. The latter was based on Nietzsche's view of the Dionysian ritual and focused on disrupting logical narrative and challenging the certainty of time and place. For the avant-garde the illusion of stable characters governed by causality and intention was rebuffed, replaced by shifting perspectives, multiple meanings, momentary encounters, and juxtapositions of human and machine.

The divide of mimesis and non-referential theatre is exemplified by two French directors of the period: André Antoine (1858–1943) and Aurélien Lugné-Poe (1869–1940). Although contemporaries (Lugné-Poe briefly worked for Antoine), they sought opposing goals. Antoine was renowned for his realism and utilization of the fourth wall. His productions of Ibsen and early Strindberg paved the way for Stanislavsky's Moscow Art Theatre, which became the symbol if not the nexus of realistic theatre. Lugné-Poe's abstract décor utilized images and evoked symbols. He produced Alfred Jarry's avant-garde play *Ubu Roi* (*King Ubu*) in 1896, as well as Ibsen, Maeterlinck, and Hauptmann during the 1890s, and Claudel's *The Tidings Brought to Mary* in 1912. His works were noted for their intonation, self-conscious performance, and radical departure from realism.

The debates over representation at the end of the nineteenth and into the twentieth centuries influenced Fauvism, Expressionism, Cubism, Futurism, Surrealism, and Dada. These aesthetic debates and theories in turn impacted theatre. But theatre – despite efforts to align with the vogue of modernism – has always had to deal with the actor's body. The actor creates through physical gesture and sound; his material body defies abstraction. How to "abstract" the body was a major concern even for Stanislavsky, who passionately expressed his reservations about the realism he made famous: "'My God!' I cried to myself. Is it possible that we the artists of the stage are fated, due to the materiality of our bodies, to the eternal service and expression of coarse realism and nothing else? Are we not called to go any farther than the realist in painting went in their times? Can it be that we are only forerunners in scenic art?"[2] Christopher Innes remarks along similar lines: "Theatre's intrinsic connection to physical reality and social existence (communicated at a minimum through the bodies of actors and their relationships to each other)," he observes, "makes some of the key modernist principles inapplicable." The modernist aspiration to form and the assertion of the present – the immediate experience of artistic communication undeterred by mimetic representation – was undermined by the actor's "imitation." Abstraction, Innes contends, is possible in theatre "to only a very limited degree."[3] Martin Puchner adds that the "tension between the physical and the metaphysical is always a tension between the theater, dependent as it is on bodies and objects, and that which lies beyond it."[4] This section comprises fourteen essays that, for the most part, follow the trajectory of this tension. On one side are Wilde, Bryusov, Rolland, Meyerhold, Craig, Yeats, and Marinetti, who challenge the prevailing realistic theatre; on the other, Shaw, Lukács, and Goldman defend the left-wing determination to expose injustice. The issues would be revisited throughout the twentieth century.

Notes

1   T. F. Driver, *Romantic Quest and Modern Query: A History of the Modern Theater* (New York: Delecorte, 1970), 73.

2   C. Stanislavsky, *My Life in Art*, tr. J. J. Robins (New York: Theatre Arts Books, 1948), 428.

3   C. Innes, "Modernism in Drama," in *The Cambridge Companion to Modernism*, ed. M. Levinson (Cambridge: Cambridge University Press, 1999), 131, 132.

4   M. Puchner, *Poetry of the Revolution: Marx, Manifestos, and the Avant-Gardes* (Princeton: Princeton University Press, 2006), 202.

Chapter 1

August Strindberg (1849–1912)

August Strindberg was a playwright, director, novelist, painter, photographer, and leading contributor to theatrical modernism. His plays and theories influenced Naturalism, Symbolism, and Expressionism. His naturalistic plays, primarily *Miss Julie* (1888) and *The Father* (1887), were intimate portraits of nuanced psychology and sexual warfare. His experimental plays, especially *Ghost Sonata* (1907, part of his Chamber Plays), *To Damascus* (3 parts, 1900–1), and *A Dream Play* (1900), established a trend in European and American Expressionism. Though his Preface to *Miss Julie* was written in the late nineteenth century, technically setting it outside the boundaries of this collection, its enduring importance renders it worth retaining. Strindberg absorbed considerable criticism for his play *The Father* in 1887. He responded with this Preface as a way of explicating his goals and challenging his critics. Strindberg countered nineteenth-century notions of fixed dramatic characters based on types in favor of more psychologically nuanced characterization. He built his ideas on Nietzsche's notion of multiplicity. For Nietzsche, the idea of a unitary self is a fiction. Strindberg's Preface describes his characters as indeterminate, ambiguous, and vacillating; Julie and Jean experience contradictory feelings of hatred and lust. The characters' conflicting drives are a product of Schopenhauer and Nietzsche's conception of a volatile will, the influence of hypnotic suggestion, and they anticipate Freud's notion of multiple motivations. The fragmentary sense of self also looks forward to late twentieth-century postmodernism's emphasis on an unstable and patchwork sense of self. The modern conception of mind and knowledge developed an abstracted self, severed from the certainty of a stable social world. When in the Preface to *Miss Julie* Strindberg describes his characters as "conglomerations" pasted together from newspaper clippings and books, pieced up from scraps of human lives, and patched

August Strindberg, "Preface" (1888) to *Miss Julie*, tr. E. M. Sprinchorn (San Francisco: Chandler Publishing, 1961), xv–xxiv.

up from the old ball gowns that have become rags like the human soul is, he repeats this notion in his expressionist play, *A Dream Play*, saying that the "characters split, double, multiply, evaporate, condense, disperse, assemble."[1] Within this fragmentation traces of a unified self dissolve. Identity is merely dispersed into diversified and evolving rhetoric, language attempting to hold together a singularity in the face of dissolution.

Strindberg took nothing for granted; no preconceived idea was accepted at face value. His Naturalism was informed by a single-minded determination to see the world objectively. Naturalism (influenced by Zola) advocated objectivity without the interfering sentimentality or moral tidiness that was the bailiwick of melodrama. But Strindberg was also an Impressionist who observed the world subjectively, incorporating light impressions optically. His plays followed the blueprint of naturalism – the descent into sordidness and mental breakdown – but the structural trajectory was hardly linear. Strindberg was too original to follow any form slavishly. He wanted to penetrate beyond surface reality, uncovering the dark contours of sexual combat and moral degeneration. This essay is a groundbreaking outline of theatrical modernism.

Preface to *Miss Julie* (1888)

Like the arts in general, the theatre has for a long time seemed to me a *Biblia Pauperum*, a picture Bible for those who cannot read, and the playwright merely a lay preacher who hawks the latest ideas in popular form, so popular that the middle classes – the bulk of the audiences – can grasp them without racking their brains too much. That explains why the theatre has always been an elementary school for youngsters and the half-educated, and for women, who still retain a primitive capacity for deceiving themselves and for letting themselves be deceived, that is, for succumbing to illusions and responding hypnotically to the suggestions of the author. Consequently, now that the rudimentary and undeveloped mental processes that operate in the realm of fantasy appear to be evolving to the level of reflection, research, and experimentation, I believe that the theatre, like religion, is about to be replaced as a dying institution for whose enjoyment we lack the necessary qualifications. Support for my view is provided by the theatre crisis through which all of Europe is now passing, and still more by the fact that in those highly cultured lands which have produced the finest minds of our time – England and Germany – the drama is dead, as for the most part are the other fine arts.

Other countries, however, have thought to create a new drama by filling the old forms with new contents. But since there has not been enough time to popularize the new ideas the public cannot understand them. And in the second place, controversy has so stirred up the public that they can no longer look on with a pure dispassionate interest, especially when they see their most cherished ideals assailed or hear an applauding or booing majority openly exercise its tyrannical power, as can happen in the theatre. And in the third place, since new forms for the new ideas have not been created, the new wine has burst the old bottles.

In the play that follows [*Miss Julie*] I have not tried to accomplish anything new – that is impossible. I have only tried to modernize the form to satisfy what I believe up-to-date people expect and demand of this art. And with that in mind I have seized upon – or let myself be seized by – a theme which may be said to lie outside current party strife, since the question of being on the way up or the way down the social ladder, of being on the top or on the bottom, superior or inferior, man or woman, is, has been, and will be of perennial interest. When I took this theme from real life – I heard about it a few years ago and it made a deep impression on me – I thought it would be a suitable subject for a tragedy, since it still strikes us as tragic to see a happily favored individual go down in defeat, and even more so to see an entire family line die out. But perhaps a time will come when we shall be so highly developed and so enlightened that we can look with indifference upon the brutal, cynical, and heartless spectacle that life offers us, a time when we shall have laid aside those inferior and unreliable instruments of thought called feelings, which will become superfluous and even harmful as our mental organs develop. The fact that my heroine wins sympathy is due entirely to the fact that we are still too weak to overcome the fear that the same fate might overtake us. The extremely sensitive viewer will of course not be satisfied with expressions of sympathy, and the man who believes in progress will demand that certain positive actions be taken for getting rid of the evil, a kind of program, in other words. But in the first place absolute evil does not exist. The decline of one family is the making of another, which now gets its chance to rise. This alternate rising and falling provides one of life's greatest pleasures, for happiness is, after all, relative. As for the man who has a program for changing the disagreeable circumstance that the eagle eats the dove and that lice eat up the eagle, I should like to ask him why it should be changed? Life is not prearranged with such idiotic mathematical precision that only the larger gets to eat the smaller. Just as frequently the little bee destroys the lion [in Aesop's fable] – or at least drives him wild.

If my tragedy makes most people feel sad, that is their fault. When we get to be as strong as the first French Revolutionists were, we shall be perfectly content and happy to watch the forests being cleared of rotting, superannuated trees that have stood too long in the way of others with just as much right to grow and flourish for a while – as content as we are when we see an incurably ill man finally die.

Recently my tragedy *The Father* was censured for being too unpleasant – as if one wanted amusing tragedies. "The joy of life" is now the slogan of the day. Theatre managers send out orders for nothing but farces, as if the joy of living lay in behaving like a clown and in depicting people as if they were afflicted with St. Vitus's dance or congenital idiocy. I find the joy of living in the fierce and ruthless battles of life, and my pleasure comes from learning something, from being taught something. That is why I have chosen for my play an unusual but instructive case, an exception, in other words – but an important exception of the kind that proves the rule – a choice of subject that I know will offend all lovers of the conventional. The next thing that will bother simple minds is that the motivation for the action is not simple and that the point of view is not single. Usually an event in life – and this is a fairly new discovery – is the result of a whole series of more or less deep-seated causes. The spectator, however, generally chooses the one that puts the least strain on his mind or reflects most credit on his insight. Consider a case of suicide. "Business failure," says the middle-class man. "Unhappy love," say the women. "Physical illness," says the sick man. "Lost hopes," says the down-and-out. But it may be that the reason lay in all of these or in none of them, and that the suicide hid his real reason behind a completely different one that would reflect greater glory on his memory.

I have motivated the tragic fate of Miss Julie with an abundance of circumstances: her mother's basic instincts, her father's improper bringing-up of the girl, her own inborn nature, and her fiancé's sway over her weak and degenerate mind. Further and more immediately: the festive atmosphere of Midsummer Eve, her father's absence, her monthly illness, her preoccupation with animals, the erotic excitement of the dance, the long summer twilight, the highly aphrodisiac influence of flowers, and finally chance itself, which drives two people together in an out-of-the-way room, plus the boldness of the aroused man.

As one can see, I have not concerned myself solely with physiological causes, nor confined myself monomaniacally to psychological causes, nor traced everything to an inheritance from her mother, nor put the blame entirely on her monthly indisposition or exclusively on "immorality." Nor have I simply preached a sermon. For lack of a priest, I have let this function devolve on a cook.

I am proud to say that this complicated way of looking at things is in tune with the times. And if others have anticipated me in this, I am proud that I am not alone in my paradoxes, as all new discoveries are called. And no one can say this time that I am being one-sided.

As far as the drawing of characters is concerned, I have made the people in my play fairly "characterless" for the following reasons. In the course of time the word *character* has acquired many meanings. Originally it probably meant the dominant and fundamental trait in the soul complex and was confused with temperament. Later the middle class used it to mean an automation. An individual who once for all had found his own true nature or adapted himself to a certain role in life, who in fact had ceased to grow, was called a man of character, while the man who was constantly developing, who, like a skillful sailor on the currents of life, did not sail with close tied-sheet sheets but who fell off before the wind in order to luff again, was called a man of no character – derogatorily of course, since he was so difficult to keep track of, to pin down and pigeonhole. This middle-class conception of a fixed character was transferred to the stage, where the middle class has always ruled. A character there came to mean someone who was always one and the same, always drunk, always joking, always moving, and who needed to be characterized only by some physical defect such as a club foot, a wooden leg, or a red nose, or by the repetition of some such phrase as, "That's capital," or "Barkis is willin'." This uncomplicated way of viewing people is still to be found in the great Molière. Harpagon is nothing but a miser, although Harpagon could have been not only a miser but an exceptional financier, a fine father, and a good citizen. Worse still, his "defect" is extremely advantageous to his son-in-law and his daughter who will be his heirs and therefore should not find fault with him, even if they do have to wait a while to jump into bed together. So I do not believe in simple stage characters. And the summary judgments that writers pass on people – he is stupid, this one is brutal, that one is jealous, this one is stingy, and so on – should not pass unchallenged by the naturalists who know how complicated the soul is and who realize that vice has a reverse side very much like virtue.

Since the persons in my play are modern characters, living in a transitional era more hurried and hysterical than the previous one at least, I have depicted them as more unstable, as torn and divided, a mixture of the old and the new. Nor does it seem improbable to me that modern ideas might also have seeped down through newspapers and kitchen talk to the level of the servants. [...]

My souls – or characters – are conglomerations from various stages of culture, past and present, walking scrapbooks, shreds of human lives, tatters torn from former fancy dresses that are now old rags – hodgepodges just like the human soul. I have even supplied a little source history into the bargain by letting the weaker steal and repeat words of the stronger, letting them get ideas (suggestions as they are called) from one another, from the environment (the songbird's blood), and from objects (the razor). [. . .]

I say Miss Julie is a modern character not because the man-hating half-woman has not always existed but because now she has been brought out into the open, has taken the stage, and is making noises. [. . .] The half-woman is a type that forces itself on others, selling itself for power, medals, recognition, diplomas, as formerly it sold itself for money. It represents degeneration. It is not a strong species for it does not maintain itself, but unfortunately it propagates its misery in the following generation. Degenerate men unconsciously select their mates from among these half-women, so that they breed and spread, producing creatures of indeterminate sex to whom life is a torture, but who fortunately are overcome eventually either by hostile reality, or by the uncontrolled breaking loose of their repressed instincts, or else by their frustration in not being able to compete with the male sex. It is a tragic type, offering us the spectacle of a desperate fight against nature; a tragic legacy of romanticism which is now being dissipated by naturalism – a movement which seeks only happiness, and for that strong and healthy species required.

But Miss Julie is also a vestige of the old warrior nobility that is now being superseded by a new nobility of nerve and brain. She is a victim of the disorder produced within a family by a mother's "crime," of the mistakes of a whole generation gone wrong, of circumstances, of her own, defective constitution – all of which put together is equivalent to the fate or universal law of the ancients. The naturalists have banished guilt along with God, but the consequences of the act – punishment, imprisonment, or the fear of it – cannot be banished for the simple reason that they remain whether or not the naturalist dismisses the case from his court. Those sitting on the sidelines can easily afford to be lenient; but what of the injured parties? And even if her father were compelled to forgo taking revenge, Miss Julie would take vengeance on herself, as she does in the play, because of that inherited or acquired sense of honor which has been transmitted to the upper classes from – well, where does it come from? From the age of barbarism, from the first Aryans, from the chivalry of the Middle Ages. And a very fine code it was, but now inimical to the survival of the race. It is the aristocrat's form of hara-kiri, a law of conscience that bids the Japanese to slice his own stomach when someone else dishonors him. The same sort of thing survives, slightly modified, in that exclusive prerogative of the aristocracy, the duel. [. . .] Hence the servant Jean lives on; but not Miss Julie, who cannot live without honor. The advantage that the slave has over his master is that he has not committed himself to this defeatist principle. In all of us Aryans there is enough of the nobleman, or of the Don Quixote, to make us sympathize with the man who takes his own life after having dishonored himself by shameful deeds. And we are all of us aristocrats enough to be distressed at the sight of a great man lying like a dead hulk ready for the scrap pile, even, I suppose, if he were to raise himself up again and redeem himself by honorable deeds.

The servant Jean is the beginning of a new species in which noticeable differentiation has already taken place. He began as the child of a poor worker and is now evolving through self-education into a future gentleman of the upper classes. He is quick to learn, has highly developed senses (smell, taste, sight), and a keen appreciation of beauty. He has already come up in the world, for he is strong enough not to hesitate to make use of other people. He is already a stranger to his old friends, whom he despises as reminders of past stages in his development, and whom he fears and avoids because they know his secrets, guess his intentions, and look with envy on his rise and in joyful expectation toward his fall. Hence his character is unformed and divided. He wavers between an admiration of high positions and a hatred of the men who occupy them. He is an aristocrat – he says so himself – familiar with the ins and outs of good society. He is polished on the outside, but coarse underneath. He wears his frock coat with elegance but gives no assurance that he keeps his body clean.

He respects Miss Julie but he is afraid of Christine, for she knows his innermost secrets. Yet he is sufficiently hard-hearted not to let the events of the night upset his plans for the future. Possessing both the coarseness of the slave and the tough-mindedness of the born ruler, he can look at blood without fainting, shake off bad luck like water, and take calamity by the horns. Consequently he will escape from the battle unwounded, probably ending up as proprietor of a hotel. And if he himself does not get to be a Rumanian count, his son will doubtless go to college and possibly end up as a government official.

Now his observations about life as the lower classes see it, from below, are well worth listening to – that is, they are whenever he is telling the truth, which is not too often, because he is more likely to say what is advantageous to him than what is true. When Miss Julie supposes that everyone in the lower classes must feel greatly oppressed by the weight of the classes above, Jean naturally agrees with her since he wants to win her sympathy. But he promptly takes it all back when he finds it advisable to separate himself from the mob.

Apart from the fact that Jean is coming up in the world, he is also superior to Miss Julie in that he is a man. In the sexual sphere, he is the aristocrat. He has the strength of the male, more highly developed senses, and the ability to take the initiative. His inferiority is merely the result of his social environment, which is only temporary and which he will probably slough off along with his livery.

His slave nature expresses itself in his awe of the Count (the boots) and in his religious superstitions. But he is awed by the Count mainly because the Count occupies the place he wants most in life; and this awe is still there even after he has won the daughter of the house and seen how hollow that beautiful shell was.

I do not believe that any love in the "higher" sense can be born from the union of two such different souls; so I have let Miss Julie's love be refashioned in her imagination as a love that protects and purifies, and I have let Jean imagine that even his love might have a chance to grow under other social circumstances. For I suppose love is very much like the hyacinth that must strike roots deep in the dark earth *before* it can produce a vigorous blossom. Here it shoots up, bursts into bloom, and turns to seed all at once; and that is why it dies so quickly.

Christine – finally to get to her – is a female slave, spineless and phlegmatic after years spent at the kitchen stove, bovinely unconscious of her own hypocrisy, and with a full quota of moral and religious notions that serve as scapegoats and cloaks her sins – which a stronger soul does not require since he is able either to carry the burden of his own sins or to rationalize them out of existence. [...]

Now as far as the dialogue is concerned, I have broken somewhat with tradition in refusing to make my characters into interlocutors who ask stupid questions to elicit witty answers. I have avoided the symmetrical and mathematical design of the artfully constructed French dialogue and have let minds work as irregularly as they do in real life, where no subject is quite exhausted before another mind engages at random some cog in the conversation and governs it for a while. My dialogue wanders here and there, gathers material in the first scenes which is later picked up, repeated, reworked, developed, and expanded like the theme in a piece of music.

The action of the play poses no problems. Since it really involves only two people, I have limited myself to these two, introducing only one minor character, the cook, and keeping the unhappy spirit of the father brooding over the action as a whole. I have chosen this course because I have noticed that what interests people most nowadays is the psychological action. Our inveterately curious souls are no longer content to see a thing happen; we want to see how it happens. We want to see the strings, look at the machinery, examine the double-bottom drawer, put on the magic ring to find the hidden seam, look in the deck for the marked cards. [...]

As far as play construction is concerned, I have made a try at getting rid of act divisions. I was afraid that the spectator's declining susceptibility to illusion might not carry him through the intermission, when he would have time to think about what he has seen and to escape the suggestive influence of the author-hypnotist. I figure my play lasts about ninety minutes. Since one can listen to a lecture, a sermon, or a political debate for that long or even longer, I have convinced myself that a play should not exhaust an audience in that length of time. As early as 1872 in one of my first attempts at the drama, *The Outlaw*, I tried out this concentrated form, although with little success. I had finished the work in five acts when I noticed the disjointed and disturbing effect it produced. I burned it, and from the ashes there arose a single, completely reworked act of fifty pages that would run for less than an hour. This play form is not completely new but seems to be my special property and has a good chance of gaining favor with the public when tastes change. My hope was to get a public so educated that they could sit through a full evening's show in one act. But this whole question must first be probed more deeply. In the meantime, in order to establish resting places for the audience and the actors without destroying the illusion, I have made use of three arts that belong to the drama: the monologue, the pantomime, and the ballet, all of which were part of classic tragedy, the monody having become the monologue and the choral dance, the ballet.

The realists have banished the monologue from the stage as implausible. But if I can motivate it, I make it plausible, and I can then use it to my advantage. Now it is certainly plausible for a speaker to pace the floor and read his speech aloud to himself. It is plausible for an actor to practice his part aloud, for a child to talk to her cat, a mother to babble to her baby, an old lady to chatter to her parrot, and a sleeping man to talk in his sleep. And in order to give the actor a chance to work on his own for once and for a moment not be obliged to follow the author's directions, I have not written out the monologues in detail but simply outlined them. Since it makes very little difference what is said while asleep, or to the parrot or the cat, inasmuch as it does not affect the main action, a gifted player who is in the midst of the situation and mood of the play can probably improvise the monologue better than the author, who cannot estimate ahead of time how much may be said and for how long before the illusion is broken.

Some theatres in Italy have, as we know, returned to the art of improvisation and have thereby trained actors who are truly inventive – without, however, violating the intentions of the author. This seems to be a step in the right direction and possibly the beginning of a new, fertile form of art that will be genuinely productive.

In places where the monologue cannot be properly motivated, I have resorted to pantomime. Here I have given the actor even more freedom to be creative and win honor on his own. Nevertheless, not to try the audience beyond its limits, I have relied on music – well motivated by the Midsummer Eve dance – to exercise its hypnotic powers during the pantomime scene. I beg the music director to select his tunes with great care, so that associations foreign to the mood of the play will not be produced by reminders of popular operettas or current dance numbers or by folk music of interest only to ethnographers.

The ballet that I have introduced cannot be replaced by a so-called crowd scene. Such scenes are always badly acted, with a pack of babbling fools taking advantage of the occasion to "gag it up," thereby destroying the illusion. Inasmuch as country people do not improvise their taunts but make use of material already to hand by giving it a double meaning, I have not composed an original lampoon but have made use of a little known round dance that I noted down in the Stockholm district. The words do not fit the situation exactly, which is what I intended, since the slave in his cunning (that is, weakness) never attacks directly. At any rate, let us have no comedians in this serious story and no obscene smirking over an affair that nails the lid on a family coffin.

As far as the scenery is concerned, I have borrowed from impressionistic painting the idea of asymmetrical and open composition, and I believe that I have thereby gained something in the way of greater illusion. Because the audience cannot see the whole room and all the furniture, they will have to surmise what's missing; that is, their imagination will be stimulated to fill in the rest of the picture. I have gained something else by this: I have avoided those tiresome exits through doors. Stage doors are made of canvas and rock at the slightest touch. They cannot even be used to indicate the wrath of an angry father who storms out of the house after a bad dinner, slamming the door behind him "so that the whole house shakes." (In the theatre it sways and billows.) Furthermore, I have confined the action to one set, both to give the characters a chance to become part and parcel of their environment and to cut down on scenic extravagance. If there is only one set, one has a right to expect it to be as realistic as possible. Yet nothing is more difficult than to make a room look like a room, however easy it may be for the scene painter to create waterfalls and erupting volcanoes. I suppose we shall have to put up with walls made of canvas, but isn't it about time that we stopped painting shelves and pots and pans on the canvas? There are so many other conventions in the theatre which we are told to accept in good faith that we should be spared the strain of believing in painted saucepans.

I have placed the backdrop and the table at an angle to force the actors to play face to face or in half profile when they are seated opposite each other at the table. In a production of *Aida* I saw a flat placed at such an angle, which led the eye out in an unfamiliar perspective. Nor did it look as if it had been set that way simply to be different or to avoid those monotonous right angles.

Another desirable innovation would be the removal of the footlights. I understand that the purpose of lighting from below is to make the actors look more full in the face. But may I ask why all actors should have full faces? Doesn't this kind of lighting wipe out many of the finer features in the lower part of the face, especially around the jaws? Doesn't it distort the shape of nose and throw false shadows above the eyes? If not, it certainly does something else: it hurts the actor's eyes. The footlights hit the retina at an angle from which it is usually shielded (except in sailors who must look at the sunlight reflected in the water), and the result is the loss of any effective play of the eyes. All one ever sees on stage are goggle-eyed glances sideways at the boxes or upward at the balcony, with only the whites of the eyes being visible in the latter case. And this probably also accounts for that tiresome fluttering of the eyelashes that the female performers are particularly guilty of. If an actor nowadays wants to express something with his eyes, he can only do it looking right at the audience, in which case he makes direct contact with someone outside the proscenium arch – a bad habit known justifiably or not as "saying hello to friends."[2]

I should think that the use of sufficiently strong side lights (through the use of reflectors or something like them) would provide the actor with a new asset: an increased range of expression made possible by the play of the eyes, the most expressive part of the face.

I have scarcely any illusions about getting actors to play for the audience and not directly at them, although this should be the goal. Nor do I dream of ever seeing an actor play through all of an important scene with his back to the audience. But is it too much to hope that crucial scenes could be played where the author indicated and not in front of the prompter's box as if they were duets demanding applause? I am not calling for a revolution, only for some small changes. I am well aware that transforming the stage into a real room with the fourth wall missing and with some of the furniture placed with backs to the auditorium would only upset the audience, at least for the present.

If I bring up the subject of make-up, it is not because I dare hope to be heeded by the ladies, who would rather be beautiful than truthful. But the male actor might do well to consider if it is an advantage to paint his face with character lines that remain there like a mask. Let us imagine an actor who pencils in with soot a few lines between his eyes to indicate great anger, and let us suppose that in that permanently enraged state he finds he has to smile on a certain line. Imagine the horrible grimace! And how can the old character actor wrinkle his brows in anger when his false bald pate is as smooth as a billiard ball?

In a modern psychological drama, in which every tremor of the soul should be reflected more by facial expressions than by gestures and grunts, it would probably be most sensible to experiment with strong side lighting on a small stage, using actors without any make-up or a minimum of it.

And then, if we could get rid of the visible orchestra with its disturbing lights and the faces turned toward the public; if the auditorium floor could be raised so that the spectator's eyes are not level with the actor's knees; if we could get rid of the proscenium boxes with their occupants, giggling diners and drinkers; and if we could have it dark in the auditorium during the performance; and if, above everything else, we could have a *small* stage and a *small* auditorium – then possibly a new drama might arise and at least one theatre become a refuge for cultured audiences. While we are waiting for such a theatre, we shall have to write for the dramatic stockpile and prepare the repertory that one day shall come.

Here is my attempt. If I have failed, there is still time to try again!

Notes

1   A. Strindberg, "Preface" to *A Dream Play*, tr. M. Meyer, in *Strindberg: Plays Two* (London: Methuen, 1982), 175.
2   "Counting the house" would be the equivalent in American theatre slang. – Translator's note.

Chapter 2

Oscar Wilde (1854–1900)

Oscar Fingal O'Flahertie Wills Wilde was a dramatist, novelist, poet, critic, and theorist. He was known for promoting aestheticism, anarchistic socialism, art for art's sake, the decadence movement, dandyism, and a radically iconoclastic lifestyle that eventually landed him in jail for what is now famously known as "acts of gross indecency with other male persons." The famous remark in the Oxford University student paper made by Wilde's lover, Lord Alfred Douglas, concerning the "love that dares not speak its name," has had a lasting influence on the twentieth century. Wilde's plays *Lady Windermere's Fan: A Play about a Good Woman* (1892), *An Ideal Husband* (1895), and *The Importance of Being Earnest: A Trivial Comedy for Serious People* (1895) are known for their razor-sharp wit, *bons mots*, double entendres, and palliated innuendoes.

"The Decay of Lying," like Strindberg's Preface to *Miss Julie*, occurs before 1900. But its content places it squarely in the twentieth century. Wilde is drawn to Plato's notion of art as a form of deception; he also borrows Plato's dialogue format. But whereas Plato rejects art because it distorts reality, Wilde celebrates art because it has nothing to do with reality. For Wilde nature is one thing, art quite another. Wilde dismisses realism and nature as irrelevant; art is superior to both. He turns Plato on his head, maintaining that art should not be subservient to nature but the other way around. Imagination creates from originality rather than copying nature's blueprint. In *De Profundis*, a meditative letter to Lord Alfred Douglas concerning his life experiences and art, written while he was incarcerated in Reading Jail in 1897, Wilde remarked that in his work "I treated Art as the supreme reality, and life as a mere mode of fiction; I awoke the imagination of my century so that it created myth and

Excerpts from Oscar Wilde, "The Decay of Lying," first published in *Nineteenth Century* 25 (January 1889), 35–56, reprinted in revised form in Oscar Wilde's *Intentions* (London, 1891), 3–53, and here taken from *Literary Criticism of Oscar Wilde*, ed. S. Weintraub (Lincoln: University of Nebraska Press, 1968), 165–96.

legend around me."[1] For Wilde all instances of beauty need to be displayed; behavior, mannerism, wit, and consciousness illustrate art. Deception is art; life is moribund and quotidian. To conflate life and art is to reduce art to mirroring life, which requires scant creativity and talent. Wilde repudiates realism, with its insistence on interlarding the everyday with art; aesthetics should be as far removed as possible from reality. The everyday pretenses and small hypocrisies required to live were for Wilde philistine concerns when compared to witticism and erudition. Art, in fact, should serve as a model for nature, for art is superior in every way. Wilde made no effort to disguise his elitism: his life was a commitment to aesthetic exceptionalism and he had the talent, education, and savvy to back up his claims. Like Cézanne, Wilde considered art as something more than merely what the eye sees; it is the realization of sensations, forms, and beauty. Wilde's important essay ushers in the pathway to modern dramatic theory's interests in non-referential theatre.

The Decay of Lying: An Observation (1889)

A Dialogue

Persons: Cyril and Vivian[2]
Scene: The Library of a country house in Nottinghamshire.

Cyril: (*coming in through the open window from the terrace*) My dear Vivian, don't coop yourself up all day in the library. It is a perfectly lovely afternoon. The air is exquisite. There is a mist upon the woods like the purple bloom upon a plum. Let us go and lie on the grass, and smoke cigarettes, and enjoy Nature.

Vivian: Enjoy Nature! I am glad to say that I have entirely lost that faculty. People tell me that Art makes us love Nature more than we loved her before; that it reveals her secrets to us; and that after a careful study of Corot and Constable we see things in her that had escaped our observation. My own experience is that the more we study Art, the less we care for Nature. What Art really reveals to us is Nature's lack of design, her curious crudities, her extraordinary monotony, her absolutely unfinished condition. Nature has good intentions, of course, but, as Aristotle once said, she cannot carry them out. When I look at a landscape I cannot help seeing all its defects. It is fortunate for us that Nature is so imperfect, as otherwise we should have had no art at all. Art is our spirited protest, our gallant attempt to teach Nature her proper place. As for the infinite variety of Nature, that is pure myth. It is not to be found in Nature herself. It resides in the imagination, or fancy, or cultivated blindness of the man who looks at her.

Cyril: Well, you need not look at a landscape. You can lie on the grass and smoke and talk.

Vivian: But Nature is so uncomfortable. [...]

Art begins with abstract decoration, with purely imaginative and pleasurable work dealing with what is unreal and nonexistent. This is the first stage. Then Life becomes fascinated with this new wonder, and asks to be admitted into the charmed circle. Art takes life as part of her rough material, recreates it, and refashions it in fresh forms, is absolutely indifferent to fact, invents, imagines, dreams, and keeps between herself and reality the impenetrable barrier of beautiful style, of decorative or ideal treatment. The third stage is when life gets the upper hand, and drives Art out into the wilderness. This is the true decadence, and it is from this that we are now suffering.

Take the case of the English drama. At first in the hands of the monks Dramatic Art was abstract, decorative and mythological. Then she enlists Life in her service, and using some of life's external forms, she created an entirely new race of beings, whose sorrows were more terrible than any sorrow man has ever felt, whose joys were keener than lover's joys, who had the rage of the Titans and the calm of the gods, who had monstrous and marvelous sins, monstrous and marvelous virtues. To them she gave a language different from that of actual use, a language full of resonant music and sweet rhythm, made stately by solemn cadence, or made delicate by fanciful rhyme, jeweled with wonderful words, and enriched with lofty diction. She clothed her children in strange raiment and gave them masks and at her bidding the antique world rose from its marble tomb. A new Caesar stalked through the streets of risen Rome, and with purple sail and flute-led oars another Cleopatra passes up the river to Antioch. Old myth and legend and dream took shape and substance. History was entirely rewritten, and there was hardly one of the dramatists who did not recognize that the object of Art is not simple truth but complex beauty. In this they were perfectly right. Art itself is really a form of exaggeration; and selection, which is the very spirit of art, is nothing more than an intensified mode of overemphasis.

But life soon shattered the perfection of the form. Even in Shakespeare we can see the beginning of the end. It shows itself by the gradual breaking up of the blank verse on later plays, by the predominance given to prose, and by the over-importance assigned to characterization. The passage in Shakespeare – and there are many – where language is uncouth, vulgar, exaggerated, fantastic, obscene even, are entirely due to Life calling for an echo of her own voice, and rejecting the intervention of beautiful style, through which alone should Life be suffered to find expression. Shakespeare is not by any means a flawless artist. He is too fond of going directly to life, and borrowing life's natural utterance. He forgets that when Art surrenders her imaginative medium she surrenders everything. Goethe says somewhere: – ["*In der Beschränkung zeigt sich erst der Meister*"] "It is in the working within limits that the master reveals himself," and the limitation, the very condition of any art, is style. However, we need not linger any longer over Shakespeare's realism. *The Tempest* is the most perfect of palinodes. All that we desire to point out was, that the magnificent work of the Elizabethan and Jacobean artists contained within itself the seeds of its own dissolution, and that, if it drew some of its strength from using life as rough material, it drew all its weakness from using life as an artistic method. As the inevitable result of this substitution of an imitative for a creative medium, this surrender of an im-aginative form, we have the modern English melodrama. The characters in these plays talk on the stage exactly as they would talk off it; they have neither aspirations nor aspirates; they are taken directly from life and reproduce its vulgarity down to the smallest detail; they present the gait, manner, costume, and accent of real people; they would pass unnoticed in a third-class railway carriage. And yet how wearisome the plays are! They do not succeed in producing even the impression of reality at which they aim, and which is their only reason for existing. As a method, realism is a complete failure. [...]

Art finds its own perfection within, and not outside of, herself. She is not to be judged by any external standard of resemblance. She is a veil, rather than a mirror. She has flowers that no forests know of, birds that no woodland possesses. She makes and unmakes many worlds, can draw the moon from heaven with a scarlet thread. Hers are the forms more real than living man, and hers the great archetypes of which things that have existence are but unfinished copies. Nature has, in her eyes, no laws, no uniformity. She can work miracles at her will, and when she calls monsters from the deep they come. [...]

Cyril: [...] I can quite understand your objection to art being treated as a mirror. You think it would reduce genius to the position of a cracked looking-glass. But you don't mean to say that you seriously believe that Life imitates Art, that Life is in fact a mirror, and Art the reality?

Vivian: Certainly I do. Paradox though it may seem – and paradoxes are always dangerous things – it is none the less true that Life imitates Art far more than Art imitates Life. [...]

Cyril: [...] But even admitting this strange imitative instinct on Life and Nature, surely you would acknowledge that Art expresses the temper of its age, the spirit of its time, the moral and social conditions that surround it, and under whose influence it is produced.

Vivian: Certainly not! Art never expresses anything but itself. This is the principle of my new aesthetics. [...]

Cyril: [...] But in order to avoid making any error I want you to tell me briefly the doctrines of the new aesthetics.

Vivian: Briefly, then, they are these. Art never expresses anything but itself. It has an independent life, just as Thought has, and develops purely on its own lines. It is not necessarily realistic in an age of realism, nor spiritual in an age of faith. So far from being the creation of its time, it is usually in direct opposition to it, and the only history that it preserves for us is the history of its own progress. Sometimes it returns upon its footsteps, and revives some antique form, as happened in the archaistic movement of late Greek Art, and in the pre-Raphaelite movement of our own day. At other times it entirely anticipates its age, and produces in one century work that it takes another century to understand, to appreciate, and to enjoy. In no case does it reproduce its age. To pass from the art of a time to the time itself is the great mistake that all historians commit.

The second doctrine is this. All bad art comes from returning to Life and Nature, and elevating them into ideals. Life and Nature may sometimes be used as part of Art's rough material, but before they are of any real service to art they must be translated into artistic conventions. The moment Art surrenders its imaginative medium it surrenders everything. As a method Realism is a complete failure, and the two things that every artist should avoid are modernity of form and modernity of subject-matter. To us, who live in the nineteenth century, any century is a suitable subject for art except our own. The only beautiful things are the things that do not concern us. It is, to have the pleasure of quoting myself, exactly because Hecuba is nothing to us that her sorrows are so suitable a motive for a tragedy. Besides, it is only the modern that ever becomes old-fashioned. M. Zola sits down to give us a picture of the Second Empire.[3] Who cares for the Second Empire now? It is out of date. Life goes faster than Realism, but Romanticism is always in front of Life.

The third doctrine is that Life imitates Art far more than Art imitates Life. This results not merely from Life's imitative instinct, but from the fact that the self-conscious aim of Life is to find expression, and that Art offers it certain beautiful forms through which it may realize that energy. It is a theory that has never been put forward before, but it is extremely fruitful, and throws an entirely new light upon the history of Art.

It follows, as a corollary from this, that external Nature also imitates Art. The only effects that she can show us are effects that we have already seen through poetry, or in paintings. This is the secret of Nature's charm, as well as the explanation of Nature's weakness.

The final revelation is that Lying, the telling of beautiful untrue things, is the proper aim of Art. [...]

Notes

1   O. Wilde, *De Profundis* (New York: Avon, 1962), 118.
2   Cyril and Vivian (also spelled Vyvyan) were Wilde's two sons, born in 1885 and 1886. – Editor's note.
3   Wilde is referring to the Second Empire (1852–1970) and likely Zola's novel, *Nana* (1880). – Editor's note.

Chapter 3

Henri Bergson (1859–1941)

Henri Bergson was a philosopher whose major works included *Time and Free Will* (1889), *Matter and Memory* (1896), *Creative Evolution* (1907), and *The Two Sources of Morality and Religion* (1932). He examined, among other things, the experiential nature of time as an actual duration (*durée réelle*) and the concepts of energy, intuition, and vitalism, which he termed *élan vital*; he also rejected Darwinian biologism in favor of multiple processes of development. For Bergson, *élan vital* reflects the relationship of evolution and creativity, as opposed to Darwin's view of evolution as a biological event. For Bergson spirit and matter collide, and the history of the world "has been the effort of consciousness to raise matter, and of more or less complete overwhelming of consciousness by the matter which has fallen back on it."[1] Creative impulses (not evolution) are the driving force of consciousness which work to resist inert matter and inertia. Bergson's impact on philosophy at the beginning of the century was profound. His status diminished with the appearance of analytic philosophy, which viewed his work as spiritual-irrational mysticism rather than logical empiricism. Nonetheless, Bergson was admired by the American pragmatist William James, among others, for his interest in vital energy and life force.

Bergson considers several important components of laughter. It is a human attribute; it requires detachment; it appeals to our intelligence rather than our emotions; and it is a social event in need of an echo. Laughter is infectious, unfolding in social settings. Most significantly, Bergson posits laughter as a result of physical incongruity. When the body functions as a machine, we are moved to laughter by the incongruity of performer and the machine-like motion. When animals appear human, we likewise laugh at the incongruity. His notion of mechanical movements had a profound impact on early

Excerpts from Henri Bergson, "Laughter" (*Le Rire*, 1900), in *Comedy*, tr. and ed. Wylie Sypher (Baltimore: Johns Hopkins University Press, 1956, 1980), 63–85.

twentieth-century silent movies, primarily those by Buster Keaton and Charlie Chaplin. The actor's mechanical gestures are exemplified in the opening scene of Chaplin's *Modern Times* (1940): the assembly line infects Chaplin's behavior and movement, creating both comic and social commentary.

Laughter (*Le Rire,* 1900)

The first point to which attention should be called is that the comic does not exist outside the pale of what is strictly *human.* A landscape may be beautiful, charming and sublime, or insignificant and ugly; it will never be laughable. You may laugh at an animal, but only because you have detected in it some human attitude or expression. You may laugh at a hat, but what you are making fun of, in this case, is not the piece of felt or straw, but the shape that men have given it, – the human caprice whose mould it has assumed. It is strange that so important a fact, and such a simple one too, has not attracted to a greater degree the attention of philosophers. Several have defined man as "an animal which laughs." They might equally well have defined him as an animal which is laughed at; for if any other animal, or some lifeless object, produces the same effect, it is always because of some resemblance to man, of the stamp he gives it or the use he puts it to.

Here I would point out, as a symptom equally worthy of notice, the *absence of feeling* which usually accompanies laughter. It seems as though the comic could not produce its disturbing effect unless it fell, so to say, on the surface of a soul that is thoroughly calm and unruffled. Indifference is its natural environment, for laughter has no greater foe than emotion. I do not mean that we could not laugh at a person who inspires us with pity, for instance, or even with affection, but in such a case we must, for the moment, put our affection out of court and impose silence upon our pity. In a society composed of pure intelligences there would probably be no more tears, though perhaps there would still be laughter; whereas highly emotional souls, in tune and unison with life, in whom every event would be sentimentally prolonged and re-echoed, would neither know nor understand laughter. Try, for a moment, to become interested in everything that is being said and done; act, in imagination, with those who act, and feel with those who feel; in a word, give your sympathy its widest expansion: as though at the touch of a fairy wand you will see the flimsiest of objects assume importance, and a gloomy hue spread over everything. Now step aside, look upon life as a disinterested spectator: many a drama will turn into a comedy. It is enough for us to stop our ears to the sound of music in a room, where dancing is going on, for the dancers at once to appear ridiculous. How many human actions would stand a similar test? Should we not see many of them suddenly pass from grave to gay, on isolating them from the accompanying music of sentiment? To produce the whole of its effect, then, the comic demands something like a momentary anesthesia of the heart. Its appeal is to intelligence, pure and simple.

This intelligence, however, must always remain in touch with other intelligences. And here is the third fact to which attention should be drawn. You would hardly appreciate the comic if you felt yourself isolated from others. Laughter appears to stand in need of an echo. Listen to it carefully: it is not an articulate, clear, well-defined sound; it is something which would fain be prolonged by reverberating from one to another, something beginning with a crash, to continue in successive rumblings, like thunder in a mountain. Still, this reverberation cannot go on for ever. It can travel within as wide a circle as you please: the circle remains, none the less, a closed one. Our laughter is always the laughter of a group. It may, perchance, have happened to you, when seated in a railway carriage or at *table d'hôte*, to hear travellers relating to one another stories which must have been comic to them, for they laughed heartily. Had you been one of their company, you would have laughed like them, but, as you were not, you had no desire whatever to do so. A man who was once asked why he did not weep at a sermon, when everybody else was shedding tears, replied: "I don't belong to the parish!" What that man thought of tears would be still more true of laughter. However spontaneous it seems, laughter always implies a kind of secret freemasonry, or even complicity, with other laughers, real or imaginary. How often has it been said that the fuller the theatre, the more uncontrolled the laughter of the audience! On the other hand, how often has the remark been made that many comic effects are incapable of translation from one language to another, because they refer to the customs and ideas of a particular social group! It is through not understanding the importance of this double fact that the comic has been looked upon as a mere curiosity in which the mind finds amusement, and laughter itself as a strange, isolated phenomenon, without any bearing on the rest of human activity. Hence those definitions which tend to make the comic into an abstract relation between ideas: "an intellectual contrast," "a palpable absurdity," etc., definitions which, even were they really suitable to every form of the comic, would not in the least explain why the comic makes us laugh. How, indeed, should it come about that this particular logical relation, as soon as it is perceived, contracts, expands and shakes our limbs, whilst all other relations leave the body unaffected? It is not from this point of view that we shall approach the problem. To understand laughter, we must put it back into its natural environment, which is society, and above all must we determine the utility of its function, which is a social one. Such, let us say at once, will be the leading idea of all our investigations. Laughter must answer to certain requirements of life in common. It must have a social signification. [. . .]

A man, running along the street, stumbles and falls; the passers-by burst out laughing. They would not laugh at him, I imagine, could they suppose that the whim had suddenly seized him to sit down on the ground. They laugh because his sitting down is involuntary. Consequently, it is not his sudden change of attitude that raises a laugh, but rather the involuntary element in this change, – his clumsiness, in fact. Perhaps there was a stone on the road. He should have altered his pace or avoided the obstacle. Instead of that, through lack of elasticity, through absentmindedness and a kind of physical obstinacy, *as a result, in fact, of rigidity or of momentum*, the muscles continued to perform the same movement when the circumstances of the case called for something else. That is the reason of the man's fall, and also of the people's laughter.

Now, take the case of a person who attends to the petty occupations of his everyday life with mathematical precision. The objects around him, however, have all been tampered with by a mischievous wag, the result being that when he dips his pen into the inkstand he draws it out all covered with mud, when he fancies he is sitting down on a solid chair he finds himself sprawling on the floor, in a word his actions are all topsy-turvy or mere beating the air, while in every case the effect is invariably one of momentum. Habit has given the impulse: what was wanted was to check the movement or deflect it. He did nothing of the sort, but continued like a machine in the same straight line.

The victim, then, of a practical joke is in a position similar to that of a runner who falls, – he is comic for the same reason. The laughable element in both cases consists of a certain *mechanical inelasticity*, just where one would expect to find the wide-awake adaptability and the living pliableness of a human being. The only difference in the two cases is that the former happened of itself, whilst the latter was obtained artificially. In the first instance, the passer-by does nothing but look on, but in the second the mischievous wag intervenes. [...]

We will now pass from the comic element in *forms* to that in *gestures* and *movements*. Let us at once state the law which seems to govern all the phenomena of this kind. It may indeed be deduced without any difficulty from the considerations stated above.

> *The attitudes, gestures and movements of the human body are laughable in exact proportion as that body reminds us of a mere machine.* [...]

Continuing along this path, we dimly perceive the increasingly important and far-reaching consequences of the law we have just stated. We faintly catch still more fugitive glimpses of mechanical effects, glimpses suggested by man's complex actions, no longer merely by his gestures. We instinctively feel that the usual devices of comedy, the periodical repetition of a word or a scene, the systematic inversion of the parts, the geometrical development of a farcical misunderstanding, and many other stage contrivances, must derive their comic force from the same source, – the art of the playwright probably consisting in setting before us an obvious clockwork arrangement of human events, while carefully preserving an outward aspect of probability and thereby retaining something of the suppleness of life. But we must not forestall results which will be duly disclosed in the course of our analysis. [...]

[...] *Something mechanical encrusted on the living* will represent a cross at which we must halt, a central image from which the imagination branches off in different directions. What are these directions? There appear to be three main ones. We will follow them one after the other, and then continue our onward course.

[...] This view of the mechanical and the living dovetailed into each other makes us incline towards the vaguer image of *some rigidity or other* applied to the mobility of life, in an awkward attempt to follow its lines and counterfeit its suppleness. [...]

Note

1   H. Bergson, *Creative Evolution* [*L' Evolution créatrice*] (1907), tr. A. Mitchell (New York: Holt, 1911), 288.

Chapter 4

Valery Bryusov (1873–1924)

Valery Yakovlevich Bryusov (also Anglicized as Briusov) was a playwright, film writer, poet, editor, spiritualist, and leading symbolist of Russian literature. The first installment of *The Russian Symbolist Anthology* in 1894 marked an important date in Russian literary history, ushering in a new approach to the country's art and culture. Bryusov himself edited several anthologies of symbolist poetry. He was, along with Nikolai Evreinov, Andrei Bley, Leonid Andreyev, Fyodor Sologub, and Alexander Blok (fellow Russian symbolists), part of the "monodrama" movement in Russian theatre, the concept of a single will or monologue holding together the consciousness of the character. Bryusov's symbolism, however, departed somewhat from his contemporaries in that he took his cue from the French and Belgian symbolists, primarily Maeterlinck, Baudelaire, Mallarmé, and Verlaine. The Russian symbolists looked to poetry and art as a means to further philosophical ends; the French hewed closer to art as self-contained. According to Martin Rice, it was "the absence of any mystical philosophy or metaphysics to be served by the new art that distinguished Briusov's brand of Symbolism" from his peers. For Bryusov, art "was not a metaphysic" and "no literary school was an end unto itself, but only a way station along the road of art's eternal evolution."[1]

Bryusov, however, shared with his contemporaries an important departure from the realism of Stanislavsky's Moscow Art Theatre. For Bryusov, the mundane focus on realistic detail denied theatre its artistic possibilities. He criticized the Art Theatre's realistic props, costumes, and acting style, which he believed limited the imagination. Instead of replication, he sought a theatre of mood, image, and the concept of a single

Valery Bryusov, "Against Naturalism in the Theatre" (from "Unnecessary Truth"), originally published in *World of Art* 4 (1902), excerpted from *The Russian Symbolist Theatre: Anthology of Plays and Critical Texts*, tr. and ed. Michael Green (Ann Arbor: Ardis, 1986), 25–30.

consciousness. His play, *The Wayfarer: A Psychodrama in One Act* (1911), is an intense meditation on loneliness and fantasy. Following Nietzsche, the symbolists challenged the realist and naturalist view of a knowable world based on observation, rationalism, and coherence. For the symbolist the surface was mere illusion that disguised deeper truths. Laurence Senelick contends that for Bryusov "the reproduction of externals, as in naturalism, is less important than the communication of the artist's own internal world; the theatre should attempt to present not the phenomenal, but the noumenal." Instead of presenting the pictorial representation of the quotidian, the theatre "should create conventional settings which conduce to and do not distract from the inner meaning of drama."²

Bryusov, however, understood the difficulties in presenting abstractions. In his important work, "Unnecessary Truth," he wrote: "The subject of art lies in the conceptual world, but all the means of art lie in the material world. It is not possible to overcome this fatal contradiction; one can only make it as painless as possible by sharpening, refining, and spiritualizing art."³ His protagonist in *The Wayfarer,* Julia, is an outsider whose existential ennui and isolation (she lives alone in the woods) could easily fold into Chekhov's *Three Sisters.* Yet the character also fantasizes with a stranger who appears to her, both as a wanderer and as in a dream. Bryusov worked closely with Meyerhold, the Russian symbolist director (see Chapter 8), who called Bryusov "the first to stress the futility of the 'truth' which theatres have expended all their efforts in depicting in recent years. Equally, he was the first to indicate the new means of dramatic presentation. He demanded the rejection of the futile 'truth' of the contemporary stage in favour of *conscious stylization*."⁴ Bryusov's notion of conscious stylization or conventionality (*uslovnost*) emphasizes the networking relationship of reality and art.

Against Naturalism in the
Theatre (from "Unnecessary Truth") (1902)

It is three years now that the Art Theatre has been with us in Moscow. Somehow it was an immediate success with everyone – the public, the press, the partisans of the new art and the defenders of the old. Not long ago, it was the custom to cite the Maly Theatre as the model of the Russian stage; these days people only laugh at its routine. And this same Maly Theatre and another Moscow theatre – Korsh's – have begun to adopt the new methods. For Muscovites the Art Theatre has become a kind of idol; they are proud of it, and it is the first thing they hasten to show off to the visitor. When the Art Theatre visited Petersburg, it performed here to packed houses, arousing universal interest. The Art Theatre ventured to stage plays that had failed in other theatres – Chekhov's *Seagull*, for example – and was successful. Most surprising of all, it was the Art Theatre's experimental spirit, its innovations in decor and acting, its daring choice of plays, that won the sympathy of the crowd.

What is the Art Theatre, then? Is it really the theatre of the future, as some have called it? Has it made a step toward the spiritualization of art, toward the overcoming of the fatal contradictions between the essence and the surface of art? Simple probability says no. If the Art Theatre has set itself such tasks, it would hardly have won universal acclaim so quickly. Success attests that what the Art Theatre offers its audience is not the genuinely new, but the old refurbished, that it offers no threat to the deep-rooted habits of the theatregoer. It has only achieved with greater perfection what other theatres, including its rival the Maly, have aimed at. Together with the entire European theatre, with insignificant exceptions, it is on a false path.

Modern theatres aim at the utmost verisimilitude in their depiction of life. They think that if everything on the stage is as it is in reality, then they have worthily fulfilled their function. Actors endeavor to speak as they would in a drawing room, scene painters copy views from nature, costume designers work in accordance with archaeological data. In spite of all this, however, there remains much that the theatre has not succeeded in counterfeiting. The Art Theatre has set itself the aim of reducing this "much." The actors there have begun to sit with their backs to the audience without constraint; they have begun to talk to each other instead of "out" to the audience. In place of the usual box set has appeared the room placed at an oblique angle: other rooms are visible through the open doors, so that an entire apartment is presented to the viewer's gaze. The furniture is arranged as it usually is in people's homes. If a forest or a garden is to be represented, several trees are placed on the forestage. If the play requires rain to fall, the audience is made to listen to the sound of water. If the play is set in winter, snow can be seen falling outside the windows. If it is windy, curtains flutter, and so on.

First of all, one has to say that these innovations are very timid. They are concerned with secondary matters and leave the essential traditions of the theatre undisturbed. And until these traditions, which comprise the essence of any stage production, are changed, no alteration of detail will bring the theatre closer to reality. All theatres, including the Art Theatre, try to make everything on stage visible and audible. Stages are lit by footlights and strip lights, but in real life light either falls from the sky or pours in through windows or is cast by a lamp or a candle. If there is a night scene, the Art Theatre has ventured to leave the stage in greater darkness than is customary, although it has not dared to extinguish all the lights in the theatre; however, if it were really night on stage, the audience would obviously be unable to see anything. Similarly, the Art Theatre is at pains to ensure that all stage conversation is audible to the auditorium. Even if a large gathering is represented, only one actor speaks at a time. When a new group begins to speak, the previous one "moves upstage" and begins gesticulating energetically – and this a quarter of a century after Villiers de l'Isle Adam in his drama *Le nouveau monde* bracketed two pages of dialogue with the direction "Everybody speaks at once!"[5]

But even if the Art Theatre were more daring, it would still fall short of its purpose. To reproduce life faithfully on the stage is impossible. The stage is conventional by its very nature. One set of conventions may be replaced by another, that is all. In Shakespeare's day a board would be set up with the inscription "forest." Not so long ago we used to be content with a backdrop of a forest with side wings depicting trees with branches incomprehensibly intertwined against the sky. In time to come, forests will be constructed from artificial three-dimensional trees with foliage and rounded trunks, or even from living trees with roots hidden in tubs under the stage.... And all this, the last word in stage technique, will, like the Shakespearean inscription, be for the audience no more than a reminder, no more than a symbol of a forest. The modern theatregoer is not in the least taken in by a painted tree – he knows that a particular piece of lathe and canvas is intended to stand for a tree. In much the same way, a signboard meant "forest" to an Elizabethan audience and a stage sapling will mean a tree growing naturally to the audience of the future. The set is no more than a pointer to the imagination. In the Greek theatre, an actor playing someone who had just returned from foreign parts would enter from the left. At the Art Theatre, the actor is admitted to a small vestibule where he divests himself of sheepskin and galoshes as a sign that he has come from afar. But who among the audience is likely to forget that he arrived from the wings? In what way is the convention by which an actor removes his sheepskin more subtle than the one by which it is understood that if he enters from the left he is coming from foreign parts?

Not only the art of the theatre, but art of any kind cannot avoid formal convention, cannot be transformed into a recreation of reality. Never, in looking at a picture by one of the great realist painters, will we be deceived like the birds of Zeuxis into thinking that before us are fruits or an open window through which we may glimpse a distant horizon. By infinitesimal gradations of light and shade, by the most elusive signals, the eye is able to distinguish reality from representation. Never will we bow to the marble bust of an acquaintance. It is unheard of that someone, on reading a story in which the author recounts in the first person how he came to commit suicide, should order a mass to be sung for the repose of his soul. And if there do exist reproductions of people and things that deceive the eye, such, for example, as bridges in a painted panorama or wax figures so convincing that they frighten children, we have difficulty in recognizing these creations as works of art. Not a single one of the spectators sitting in the orchestra and paying three or four rubles for his seat is going to believe that he is really looking at Hamlet, Prince of Denmark, and that in the final scene the prince lies dead.

Each new technical device in art, be it that of the theatre or another, arouses only curiosity and suspicion in the spectator. A certain contemporary artist has, it is said, painted a new series of pictures in which the effect of moonlight is strikingly conveyed. When we see them, our first thought will be: How did he manage to do that? And then we will captiously seek out every discrepancy with reality. Only when we have satisfied our curiosity will we start looking at the picture as a work of art. When an avalanche of wadding descends on the stage, the members of the audience ask each other: How was that done? If Rubek and Irene simply walked off into the wings [in Ibsen's *When We Dead Awaken*], the audience would believe more readily in their destruction than it does now, when before their eyes two straw-stuffed dummies and armfuls of wadding go rolling over the boards. "It faded on the crowing of the cock," someone says of the Ghost in *Hamlet*, and this is enough for the audience to imagine the crowing of the cock. But in *Uncle Vanya* the Art Theatre has a cricket chirping. No one in the audience will imagine that the cricket is real, and the more lifelike the sound, the less convincing the illusion. In time, audiences will become used to the devices they now find so novel and will cease to notice them. But this will not come about because the audience will take wadding for snow in real earnest, or the rope that tugs at the curtains for wind, but because these devices will simply be numbered among the usual theatrical conventions. Would it not then be better to abandon the fruitless battle against the invincible conventions of the theatre, which only spring up with renewed strength, and rather than seeking to eradicate them, attempt to subjugate, to tame, to harness, to saddle them?

There are two kinds of convention. One kind arises from the inability to create successfully. A bad poet says of a beautiful woman: "She is as fresh as a rose." It may be that the poet really understood the vernal freshness of the woman's soul, but he was unable to express his feelings, substituting cliché for genuine expression. In the same way, people want to speak on the stage as they do in life but are unable to, stressing words unnaturally, pronouncing endings too emphatically and so on. But there is another kind of convention – that which is deliberately applied. It is a convention that statues of marble and bronze are left unpainted. They could be painted – at one time they even were – but it is unnecessary, since sculpture is concerned with form, not color. An engraving in which leaves are black and the sky striped observes certain conventions, but it nevertheless affords pure aesthetic enjoyment. Wherever there is art, there is convention. To oppose this is as absurd as to demand that science would dispense with logic and explain phenomena other than by their causal relationship.

It is time that the theatre stopped counterfeiting reality. A cloud depicted in a painting is flat, it does not move or change its form or luminescence – but there is something about it that gives us the same feeling as a real cloud. The stage must provide everything that can most effectively help the spectator to recreate the setting demanded by the play in his imagination. If a battle is to be represented, it is absurd to send on stage a couple of dozen – or even a thousand – extras waving wooden swords: perhaps the audience will be better served by a musical picture from the orchestra. If a wind is called for, there is no need to blow a whistle and tug at the curtain with a rope: the actors themselves must convey the storm by behaving as people do in a strong wind. There is no need to do away with the setting, but it must be deliberately conventionalized. The setting must be, as it were, stylized. Types of setting must be devised that will be comprehensible to everyone, as a received language is comprehensible, as white statues, flat paintings, and black engravings are comprehensible. Simplicity of setting will not be equivalent to banality and monotony. The principle will be changed, and there will be ample scope in particulars for the imagination of Messrs. set designers and technicians.

Dramatists too must in some degree perfect their artistic method. They are sovereign artists only when their work is read; on the stage their plays are only forms into which the actors pour their own content. Dramatists must renounce all superfluous, unnecessary, and ultimately futile copying of life. Everything external in their work must be reduced to a minimum because it has little to do with the conduct of the drama. The drama can convey the external only through an intermediary – through the souls of the *dramatis personae*. The sculptor cannot take soul and emotion in his hands; he has to give the spirit bodily incarnation. The dramatist, on the contrary, should make it possible for the actor to express the physical in the spiritual. Something has already been achieved in the creation of a new drama. The most interesting attempts of this kind are the plays of Maeterlinck and the latest dramas of Ibsen. It is noteworthy that it is in the staging of these plays that the modern theatre has shown itself to be particularly ineffectual.

The ancient theatre had a single permanent set – the palace. With slight alterations it was made to represent the interior of a house, a square, the seashore. Actors wore masks and buskins, which forced them to put aside any thought of imitating everyday life. The chorus sang sacred hymns around the altar and also intervened in the action. Everything was at once thoroughly conventionalized and utterly alive; the audience devoted its attention to the action and not to the setting, "for tragedy," says Aristotle, "is the imitation not of men, but of action." In our day, such simplicity of setting has been preserved in the folk theatre. I chanced to see a performance of [Aleksei Remizov's] *Tsar Maximilian* given by factory workers. The scenery and props consisted of two chairs, the tsar's paper crown and the paper chains of his rebellious son Adolph. Watching this performance, I understood what powerful resources the theatre has at its disposal and how misguided it is in seeking the aid of painters and technicians.

The creative urge is the only reality that exists on earth. Everything external is, in the poet's words, "only a dream, a fleeting dream." Grant that in the theatre we may be partakers of the highest truth, the profoundest reality. Grant the actor his rightful place, set him upon the pedestal of the stage that he may rule it as an artist. By his art he will give content to the dramatic performance. Let your setting aim not at truth, but at the suggestion of truth. I summon you away from the unnecessary truth of the modern stage to the deliberate conventionalization of the ancient theatre.

Notes

1   M. P. Rice, *Valery Briusov and the Rise of Russian Symbolism* (Ann Arbor: Ardis, 1975), 70, 71.
2   L. Senelick, *Russian Dramatic Theory from Pushkin to the Symbolists* (Austin: University of Texas Press, 1981), xlvi.
3   V. Bryusov, "The Unnecessary Truth," in *Meyerhold on Theatre*, tr. and ed. E. Braun (London: Methuen, 1969), 37.
4   V. Meyerhold, "The New Theatre Foreshadowing in Literature," in *Meyerhold on Theatre*, tr. and ed. E. Braun (London: Methuen, 1991), 37.
5   Villiers de l'Isle-Adam (1838–89), French symbolist writer, influenced by Baudelaire and Poe. – Editor's note.

Chapter 5

Romain Rolland (1866–1944)

Romain Rolland was a French novelist who won the Nobel Prize for Literature in 1915. A pacifist after World War I, he was associated with Gandhi and the social movement for world peace. He wrote historical melodramas but is primarily known for this essay, *Le Théâtre du Peuple* (1903). Rolland's melodramas, among them *Danton* (1900) and *Le 14 juillet* (*The July Revolution*, 1902), stressed socialism. For Rolland, theatre must inspire the proletariat to revolution. His was a popular theatre, one that catered to the masses and advocated theatre's political action. He sought a theatre that did not condescend to the people but inspired them through three principles: recreation, energy, and path to intelligence. Like Gandhi, he wanted to reside with the masses while simultaneously elevating them; the theatre for Rolland was a tool for social awareness and entertainment. His ideas would resurface in the work of Luis Valdez's Teatro Campesino (see Chapter 54), the farm workers' theatre troupe that also advocated entertainment and social activism.

The People's Theatre (1903)

Three Requisites

Supposing that the capital is secured and the public ready. What conditions are necessary to a real People's Theatre?

I shall not try to lay down absolute rules of procedure: we must remember that no laws are eternally applicable, the only good laws being made for an epoch that passes and

Excerpts from Romain Rolland, *The People's Theatre* [*Le Théâtre du Peuple*] (1903), tr. Barrett H. Clark, in *The Theory of the Modern Stage: An Introduction to Modern Theatre and Drama*, ed. Eric Bentley (New York: Penguin, 1968), 455–70.

a country that changes. Popular art is essentially changeable. Not only do the people feel in a manner far different from the "cultured" class, there exist different groups among the people themselves: the people of today and the people of tomorrow; those of a certain part of a certain city, and those of a part of another city. We cannot presume to do more than establish an average, more or less applicable to the people of Paris at the present time.

The first requisite of the People's Theatre is that it must be a recreation. It must first of all give pleasure, a sort of physical and moral rest to the working-man weary from his day's work. It will be the task of the architects of the future People's Theatre to see that cheap seats are no instruments of inquisitorial torture. It will be the task of the dramatists to see that their works produce joy, and not sadness and boredom. The greatest vanity or else downright stupidity are the only excuses for offering the people the latest products of a decadent art, which produces evil effects sometimes even on the minds of the torpid. As for the sufferings and doubts of the "cultured," let them keep these to themselves: the people have more than enough already. There is no use adding to their burden. The man of our times who best understood the people – Tolstoy – has not always himself escaped this artistic vice, and he has bravely humbled himself for his pride. His vocation as an apostle, that imperious need of his to impose his faith on others, and the exigencies of his artistic realism, were greater in *The Power of Darkness* than this fundamental goodness. Such plays, it seems to me, discourage rather than help the people. If we offered them no other fare, they would be right in turning their backs on us and seeking to drown their troubles at the cabaret. It would be pitiless of us to try to divert their sad existences with the spectacle of similar existences. If certain of the "cultured few" take pleasure "sucking melancholy as a weasel sucks an egg," we at least cannot demand the same intellectual stoicism from the people. The people are fond of violent acts, provided they do not, as in life, crush the hero. No matter how discouraged or resigned the people are in their lives, they are extravagantly optimistic where their dream-heroes are concerned, and they *suffer* when a play turns out sadly. But does this mean that they want tearful melodramas with uniformly happy endings? Surely not. The crude concoction of lies that forms the basis of most melodrama merely stupefies them, acting as a soporific, and contributes, like alcohol, to general inertia. The factor of amusement which we have desiderated in this art should not be allowed to take the place of moral energy. On the contrary!

The theatre ought to be a source of energy: this is the second requisite. The obligation to avoid what is depressing and discouraging is altogether negative; an antidote is necessary, something to support and exalt the soul. In giving the people recreation, the theatre is obliged to render them better able to set to work on the morrow. The happiness of simple and healthy men is never complete without some sort of action. Let the theatre be an arena of action. Let the people make of their dramatist a congenial traveling-companion, alert, jovial, heroic if need be, on whose arm they may lean, on whose good humor they may count to make them forget the fatigue of the journey. It is the duty of this companion to take the people straight to their destination – without of course neglecting to teach them to observe along the road. This, it seems to me, is the third requisite of our People's Theatre:

The theatre ought to be a guiding light to the intelligence. It should flood with light the terrible brain of man, which is filled with shadows and monsters, and is exceeding narrow and cramped. We have just spoken of the need of guarding against giving every product of the artist to the people; I do not wish, however, to imply that they must be spared all incentive to thought: The working-man does not as a rule think while his body is working. It is good to exercise his brain and, no matter how little he may understand, it will afford him pleasure, just as violent exercise is always gratifying to any normal man after prolonged inaction. He must be taught, then, to see things clearly as well as himself, and to judge.

Joy, energy and intelligence: these are the three fundamental requisites of our People's Theatre. So far as a moral purpose is concerned – lessons, that is, in virtue, social solidarity, and the like – we need not bother much about that. The mere existence of a permanent theatre, where great emotions are shared and shared often, will create at least for the time being a bond of brotherhood. In place of virtue, give them more intelligence, more happiness, and more energy: virtue and moral lessons will take care of themselves. People are not so much downright bad as ignorant: their badness is only the result of ignorance. Our great problem is to bring more light, purer air, and better order into the chaos of the soul. It is enough if we set the people to thinking and doing; let us not think and do for them. Let us above all avoid preaching morality; only too often have the truest friends of the people made art repellent to them by this means. The People's Theatre must avoid these two excesses: moral pedagogy, which seeks to extract lifeless lessons from living works (a stupid thing to do, for the keenly alert will immediately scent the bait and avoid it), and mere impersonal dilettantism, whose only purpose is to amuse the people at any cost – a dishonorable thing, with which the people are not always pleased, for they can judge those who amuse them; and often there is a mixture of disdain in their laughter. No moral purpose, then, and no mere empty amusement, in and for itself. Morality is no more than the hygiene of the heart and the brain.[1] Let us found a theatre full to the brim with health and joy. "*Joy, the abounding strength of nature ... joy, which turns the wheels of the world's clocks; joy, which revolves the spheres in space; joy, which brings forth the flower from the seed, and suns from the firmament!*"...

Note

1   "The ineffable joy we feel when we are perfectly healthy in mind and spirit" (Schiller to Goethe, 7 January 1795).

Chapter 6

Maurice Maeterlinck (1862–1949)

Maurice Polydore Marie Bernard Maeterlinck, the Belgian-born playwright, poet, and essayist, was the leader of the European symbolist movement. He is known for his four plays, *The Intruder* (1890), *The Blind* (1890), *Pelléas and Mélisande* (1892), and *The Blue Bird* (1909). He received the Nobel Prize for Literature in 1911. His essay here first appeared in *Le Figaro* under the title "A propos de Solness le Constructeur" (Solness referring to Ibsen's character in *The Master Builder*). It was revised and expanded, appearing in "Le tragique quotidien," in his collection of essays, *Le Trésor des humbles*, in 1896, and later translated into English.

Maeterlinck advocated a theatre of mood over action. He considered action fruitless; he was concerned with mystical forces that reflected Schopenhauer's notion of an unknowable, elusive, and feckless will. His plays emphasized blindness, shadow, and illusion, and were characterized by a tragic veil masking people's deepest fears and desires. Stéphane Mallarmé (1842–98) notwithstanding, Maeterlinck can be considered symbolism's principal advocate. His brand of symbolism intrigued Chekhov and Ibsen; he anticipated Beckett's theatre of inertia; and his symbolist ideas influenced twentieth-century theories of anti-theatricalism.

Symbolism requires an emphasis on the symbolic object as a gateway to an audience's perception and is intent on opening a parallel and previously unavailable world. The object under investigation exudes metaphor, allegory, and various signs unleashing a path to the subconscious, the mysterious, and the eternal world beyond – the Kantian "thing-in-itself." In symbolist poetry and theatre there exists a ritualistic, incantatory quality stressing rhythm, evocative sounds, scrims, shadows, and penumbra. Symbolists searched for an exquisite, luminous encounter with spirituality. Unlike expressionism,

Maurice Maeterlinck, "The Modern Drama" (1904), from *The Double Garden*, tr. Alfred Sutro (New York: Dodd, Mead, 1911), 115–39.

which tended to be shrill and hyperbolic, symbolist drama was inclined to softer expression. At its core symbolist drama was the concept of language unveiling the hidden consciousness of our existence. It is characterized by the rejection of action in favor of situation, stillness, and reflection. Waiting and inactivity are essential to Maeterlinck's theatre theory.

Maeterlinck and the symbolists considered the actor's body onstage an interference with the dramatist's underlying ideas. For Maeterlinck, writes Patrick McGuinness, the "indirectness, suggestiveness, and purity of Symbolist poetry is destroyed on-stage: the poet's process of abstraction and purification is reversed, so that the indirect, the suggestive, the withheld, become suddenly direct, explicit, and overt."[1] Performance eradicates the symbolic, akin to a living person stepping out of a painting. The mysteriousness and elusiveness of art become flesh and blood, undermining the symbolic in favor of the material. The actor's personality is furthermore forever rising and obscuring the direct link from the artist's creative inception to the audience's reception. Frantisek Deak adds that "To transcend the actor's duplicity, the simultaneous presence of the living body and an emphatic formal body, Maeterlinck suggests that the live actor be replaced by a shadow, a reflection, a sculpture, or a puppet."[2] From here it is only a short step to Edward Gordon Craig's über-marionette, Antonin Artaud's athletic actor, Richard Foreman's stylization, the Wooster Group's use of technology, and Robert Wilson's slow-motion choreography. Reflecting on his early plays, Maeterlinck wrote that the key to his theatre "is dread of the unknown that surrounds us." Echoing Nietzsche, he added, "The problem of existence was answered only by the enigma of annihilation."[3] Maeterlinck laid the foundation for a conceptual theatre that has evolved into various forms but remains indebted to his initial conception.

The Modern Drama (1904)

When I speak of the modern drama, I naturally refer only to those regions of dramatic literature that, sparsely inhabited as they may be, are yet essentially new. Down below, in the ordinary theatre, ordinary and traditional drama is doubtless yielding slowly to the influence of the vanguard; but it were idle to wait for the laggards when we have the pioneers at our call.

The first thing that strikes us in the drama of the day is the decay, one might almost say the creeping paralysis, of external action. Next we note a very pronounced desire to penetrate deeper and deeper into human consciousness, and place moral problems upon a high pedestal; and finally the search, still very timid and halting, for a kind of new beauty that shall be less abstract than was the old.

It is certain that, on the actual stage, we have far fewer extraordinary and violent adventures. Bloodshed has grown less frequent, passions less turbulent; heroism has become less unbending, courage less material and less ferocious. People still die on the stage, it is true, as in reality they still must die, but death has ceased – or will cease, let us hope, very soon – to be regarded as the indispensable setting, the *ultima ratio*, the inevitable end, of every dramatic poem. In the most formidable crises of our life – which, cruel though it may be, is cruel in silent and hidden ways – we rarely look to death for a solution; and for all that the theatre is slower than the other arts to follow the evolution of human consciousness, it will still be at last compelled, in some measure, to take this into account.

When we consider the ancient and tragical anecdotes that constitute the entire basis of the classical drama, the Italian, Scandinavian, Spanish, or mythical stories that provided the plots, not only for all the plays of the Shakespearian period, but also – not altogether to pass over infinitely less spontaneous – for those of French and German Romanticism, we discover at once that these anecdotes are no longer able to offer us the direct interest they presented at a time when they appeared highly natural and possible, at a time when, at any rate, the circumstances, manners, sentiments they recalled were not yet extinct in the minds of those who witnessed their reproduction.

To us, however, these adventures no longer correspond to a living and actual reality. Should a youth of our own time love, and meet obstacles not unlike those which, in another order of ideas and events, beset Romeo's passion, we need no telling that his adventure will be embellished by none of the features that gave poetry and grandeur to the episode of Verona. Gone beyond recall is the entrancing atmosphere of a lordly, passionate life; gone the brawls in picturesque streets, the interludes of bloodshed and splendour, mysterious poisons, the majestic, complaisant tombs! And where shall we look for that exquisite summer's night, which owes its vastness, its savour, the very appeal that it makes to us, to the shadow of an heroic, inevitable death that already lay heavy upon it? Divest the story of Romeo and Juliet of these beautiful trappings, and we have only the very simple and ordinary desire of a noble-hearted, unfortunate youth for a maiden whose obdurate parents deny him her hand. All the poetry, the splendour, the passionate life of this desire, result from the glamour, the nobility, tragedy, that are proper to the environment wherein it has come to flower; nor is there a kiss, a murmur of love, a cry of anger, grief, or despair but borrows its majesty, grace, its heroism, tenderness – in a word, every image that has helped it to visible form – from the beings and objects around it; for it is not in the kiss itself that the sweetness and beauty are found, but in the circumstance, hour, and place wherein it was given. Again, the same objections would hold if we chose to imagine a man of our time who should be jealous as Othello was jealous, possessed of Macbeth's ambition, unhappy as Lear; or, like Hamlet, restless and wavering, bowed down beneath the weight of a frightful and unrealizable duty.

These conditions no longer exist. The adventure of the modern Romeo – to consider only the external events which it might provoke – would provide material for a couple of acts. Against this it may be urged that a modern poet who desires to put on the stage an analogous poem of youthful love is perfectly justified in borrowing from days gone by a more decorative setting, one that shall be more fertile in heroic and tragical incident. Granted; but what can the result be of such an expedient? Would not the feelings and passions that demand for their fullest, most perfect expression and development the atmosphere of today (for the passions and feelings of a modern poet must, in despite of himself, be entirely and exclusively modern), would not these suddenly find them-selves transplanted to a soil where all things prevented their living? They no longer believe, yet are charged with the fear and hope of eternal judgment. In their hours of distress they have discovered new forces to cling to, that seem trustworthy, human and just; and behold them thrust back to a century wherein prayer and the sword decide all! They have profited, unconsciously perhaps, by every moral advance we have made – and they are suddenly flung into abysmal days when the least gesture was governed by prejudices at which they can only shudder or smile. In such an atmosphere, what can they do; how hope that they truly can live there?

But we need dwell no further on the necessarily artificial poems that arise from the impossible marriage of past and present. Let us rather consider the drama that actually stands for the reality of our time, as Greek drama stood for Greek reality, and the drama of the Renaissance for the reality of the Renaissance. Its scene is a modern house, it passes between men and women of today. The names of the invisible protagonists – the passions and ideas – are the same, more or less, as of old. We see love, hatred, ambition, jealousy, envy, greed; the sense of justice and idea of duty; pity, goodness, devotion, piety, selfishness, vanity, pride, etc. But although the names have remained more or less the same, how great is the difference we find in the aspect and quality, the extent and influence, of these ideal actors! Of all their ancient weapons not one is left them, not one of the marvelous moments of olden days. It is seldom that cries are heard now; bloodshed is rare, and tears not often seen. It is in a small room, round a table, close to the fire, that the joys and sorrows of mankind are decided. We suffer, or make others suffer, we love, we die, there in our corner; and it were the strangest chance should a door or a window suddenly, for an instant, fly open, beneath the pressure of extraordinary despair or rejoicing. Accidental, adventitious beauty exists no longer; there remains only an external poetry that has not yet become poetic. And what poetry, if we probe to the root of things – what poetry is there that does not borrow nearly all of its charm, nearly all of its ecstasy, from elements that are wholly external? Last of all, there is no longer a God to widen, or master, the action; nor is there an inexorable fate to form a mysterious, solemn, and tragical background for the slightest gesture of man; nor the sombre and abundant atmosphere that was able to ennoble even his most contemptible weaknesses, his least pardonable crimes.

There still abides with us, it is true, a terrible unknown; but it is so diverse and elusive, it becomes so arbitrary, so vague and contradictory, the moment we try to locate it, that we cannot evoke it without great danger; cannot even, without the mightiest difficulty, avail ourselves of it, though in all loyalty, to raise to the point of mystery the gestures, actions, and words of the men we pass every day. The endeavor has been made; the formidable, problematic enigma of heredity, the grandiose but improbable enigma of inherent justice, and many others beside, have each in their turn been put forward as a substitute for the vast enigma of the Providence or Fatality of old. And it is curious to note how these youthful enigmas, born but of yesterday, already seem older, more arbitrary, more unlikely, than those whose places they took in an access of pride.

Where are we to look, then, for the grandeur and beauty that we find no longer in visible action, or in words, stripped as these are of their attraction and glamour? For words are only a kind of mirror which reflects the beauty of all that surrounds it; and the beauty of the new world wherein we live does not seem as yet able to project its rays on these somewhat reluctant mirrors. Where shall we look for the horizon, the poetry, now that we no longer can seek it in a mystery which, for all that it still exists, does yet fade from us the moment we endeavor to give it a name?

The modern drama would seem to be vaguely conscious of this. Incapable of outside movement, deprived of external ornament, daring no longer to make serious appeal to a determined divinity or fatality, it has fallen back on itself, and seeks to discover, in the regions of psychology and of moral problems, the equivalent of what once was offered by exterior life. It has penetrated deeper into human consciousness but has encountered difficulties there no less strange than unexpected.

To penetrate deeply into human consciousness is the privilege, even the duty, of the thinker, the moralist, the historian, the novelist, and to a degree, of the lyrical poet; but not of the dramatist. Whatever the temptation, he dare not sink into inactivity, become mere philosopher or observer. Do what one will, discover what marvels one may, the sovereign law of the stage, its essential demand, will always be *action*. With the rise of the curtain, the high intellectual desire within us undergoes transformation; and in place of the thinker, psychologist, mystic, or moralist there stands the mere instinctive spectator, the man electrified negatively by the crowd, the man whose one desire it is to see something happen. This transformation or substitution is incontestable, strange as it may seem; and is due, perhaps, to the influence of the *human polypier*,[4] to some undeniable faculty of our soul, which is endowed with a special, primitive, almost unimprovable organ, whereby men can think, and feel, and be moved, *en masse*. And there are no words so profound, so noble and admirable, but they will soon weary us if they leave the solution unchanged, if they lead to no action, bring about no decisive conflict, or hasten no definite solution.

But whence is it that action arises in the consciousness of man? In its first stage it springs from the struggle between diverse conflicting passions. But no sooner has it raised itself somewhat – and this is true, if we examine it closely, of the first stage also – than it would seem to be solely due to the conflict between a passion and a moral law, between a duty and a desire. Hence the eagerness with which modern dramatists have plunged into all the problems of contemporary morality; and it may safely be said that at this moment they confine themselves almost exclusively to the discussion of these different problems.

This movement was initiated by the dramas of Alexandre Dumas *fils*, dramas which brought the most elementary of moral conflicts onto the stage; dramas, indeed, whose entire existence was based on problems such as the spectator, who must always be regarded as the ideal moralist, would never put to himself in the course of his whole spiritual existence, so evident is their solution. Should the faithless husband or wife be forgiven? Is it well to avenge infidelity by infidelity? Has the illegitimate child any rights? Is the marriage of inclination – such is the name it bears in those regions – preferable to the marriage for money? Have parents the right to oppose a marriage for love? Is divorce to be deprecated when a child has been born of the union? Is the sin of the adulterous wife greater than that of the adulterous husband? etc., etc.

Indeed, it may be said here that the entire French theatre of today, and a considerable proportion of the foreign theatre, which is only its echo, exist solely on questions of this kind, and on the entirely superfluous answers to which they give rise.

On the other hand, however, the highest point of human consciousness is attained by the dramas of Björnson, of Hauptmann, and, above all, of Ibsen. Here we touch the limit of the resources of modern dramaturgy. For, in truth, the further we penetrate into the consciousness of man, the less struggle do we discover. It is impossible to penetrate far into any consciousness unless that consciousness be very enlightened; for, whether we advance ten steps, or a thousand, in the depths of a soul that is plunged into darkness, we shall find nothing there that can be unexpected, or new; for darkness everywhere will resemble only itself. But a consciousness that is truly enlightened will possess passions and desires infinitely less exacting, infinitely more peaceful and patient, more salutary, abstract, and general, than are those that reside in the ordinary consciousness. Thence, far less struggle – or at least a struggle of far less violence – between these nobler and wiser passions, and this for the very reason that they have become vaster and loftier; for if there be nothing more restless, destructive, and savage than a dammed-up stream, there is nothing more tranquil, beneficial, and silent than the beautiful river whose banks ever widen.

Again, this enlightened consciousness will yield to infinitely fewer laws, admit infinitely fewer doubtful or harmful duties. There is, one may say, scarcely a falsehood or error, a prejudice, half-truth or convention, that is not capable of assuming, that does not actually assume, when the occasion presents itself, the form of a duty in an uncertain consciousness. It is thus that honour, in the chivalrous, conjugal sense of the word (I refer to the honour of the husband, which is supposed to suffer by the infidelity of the wife), that revenge, a kind of morbid prudishness, pride, vanity, piety to certain gods, and a thousand other illusions have been, and still remain, the unquenchable source of a multitude of duties that are still regarded as absolutely sacred, absolutely incontrovertible, by a vast number of inferior consciousnesses. And these so-called duties are the pivot of almost all the dramas of the Romantic period, as of most of those of today. But not one of these sombre, pitiless duties that so fatally impel mankind to death and disaster can readily take root in the consciousness that a healthy, living light has adequately penetrated; in such there will be no room for honour or vengeance, for conventions that clamor for blood. It will hold no prejudices that exact tears, no injustice eager for sorrow. It will have cast from their throne the gods who insist on sacrifice, and the love that craves for death. For when the sun has entered into the consciousness of him who is wise, as we may hope that it will some day enter into that of all men, it will reveal one duty, and one alone, which is that we should do the least possible harm and love others as we love ourselves; and from this duty no drama can spring.

Let us consider what happens in Ibsen's plays. He often leads us far down into human consciousness, but the drama remains possible only because there goes with us a singular flame, a sort of red light, which, sombre, capricious – unhallowed, one almost might say – falls only on singular phantoms. And indeed nearly all the duties which form the activity principle of Ibsen's tragedies are duties situated no longer within, but without the healthy, illuminated consciousness; and the duties we believe we discover outside this consciousness often come perilously near an unjust pride, or a kind of soured and morbid madness.

Let it not be imagined, however – for indeed this would be wholly to misunderstand me – that these remarks of mine in any way detract from my admiration for the great Scandinavian poet. For, if it be true that Ibsen has contributed few salutary elements to the morality of our time, he is perhaps the only writer for the stage who has caught sight of, and set in motion, a new, though still disagreeable poetry, which he has succeeded in investing with a kind of gloomy beauty, and grandeur (surely too savage and gloomy for it to become general or definitive); as he is the only one who owes nothing to the poetry of the violently illumined drama of antiquity or of the Renaissance.

But, while we wait for the time when human consciousness shall recognize more useful passions and less nefarious duties, for the time when the world's stage shall consequently present more happiness and fewer tragedies, there still remains, in the depths of every heart of loyal intention, a great duty of charity and justice that eclipses all others. And it is perhaps from the struggle of this duty against our egoism and ignorance that the veritable drama of our century shall spring. When this goal has been attained – in real life as on the stage – it will be permissible perhaps to speak of a new theatre, a theatre of peace, and of beauty without tears.

Notes

1 P. McGuinness, *Maurice Maeterlinck and the Making of Modern Theatre* (Oxford: Oxford University Press, 2000), 96.
2 F. Deak, *Symbolist Theater: The Formation of an Avant-Garde* (Baltimore: Johns Hopkins University Press, 1993), 25.
3 Maeterlinck, *The Buried Temple*, tr. K. A. Sutro (London, 1902), n.p.
4 "Polypary," the common stem or supporting structure of a colony of polyps. – Editor's note.

Chapter 7

Aida Overton Walker (1880–1914)

Aida Overton Walker was the leading dancer, actress, singer, and choreographer for the Williams and Walker Theatre Company from 1899 to 1909. She starred in the most successful African American musicals at the beginning of the twentieth century, and also taught the cakewalk dance to whites eager to absorb what they deemed to be the "primitiveness" of black culture. She also dared to perform the Salome Dance in 1908 and 1912 at a time when it was the domain of white performers. As Daphne A. Brooks observes, "Walker entered into this charged cultural context and developed her own version of the dance."[1]

Walker's essay is one of the first theoretical attempts by a black woman to justify a life on the stage. Minstrelsy, which had dominated American entertainment in the nineteenth century, left a residual scar on the representation of African Americans. The notion of performing became something opprobrious for the black middle class, which viewed the theatre as a place where blacks in blackface maintained the derogatory appearance in perpetuity. Walker defended her position against blacks who demurred from the stage, arguing that her work was professional and honorable.

Colored Men and Women on the Stage (1905)

Colored people on the stage have been given very little consideration by our colored writers and critics; perhaps they have considered them unworthy of the attention, or perhaps it has just been a matter of oversight; be that as it may, I beg leave to write briefly on the past, present, and if possible, future of colored men and women on the Stage.

Excerpts from Aida Overton Walker, "Colored Men and Women on the Stage," *Colored American Magazine* 9.4 (October 1905), 571–5.

In the past the profession which I am now following may have merited severe criticism, but like every other calling or profession, the Stage has improved with time, and I am proud to say that there are many clever, honest and well deserving men and women of other races in color in professional life who will compare favorably with men and woman of other races in the profession or other professions. There are good and bad in all vocations, and it does seem rather strange that many outsiders should judge us all alike – bad! When white people refuse to classify, in dealing with us, we get highly indignant and say we should not all be judged alike, and yet we often fail to classify and make distinctions when judging ourselves. Consistency is still a jewel!

Some of our so-called society people regard the Stage as a place to be ashamed of. Whenever it is my good fortune to meet such persons, I sympathize with them for I know they are ignorant as to what is really being done in their own behalf by members of their race on the Stage.

In this age we are all fighting the one problem – that is the color problem! I venture to think and dare to state that our profession does more toward the alleviation of color prejudice than any other profession among colored people. The fact of the matter is this, that we come in contact with more white people in a week than other professional colored people meet in a year and more than some meet in a whole decade.

We entertain thousands of people in the course of a Season. We do a great deal of private entertaining in connection with our public performances and to do it all success-fully requires much hard study. It is quite true that God had blessed us with much ability along musical lines, but even genius requires nursing to be used to good advantage. When a large audience leaves a theatre after a creditable two hour and a half performance by Negroes, I am sure the Negro race is raised in the estimation of the people.

It has been my good fortune to entertain and instruct privately, many members of the most select circles – both in this country and abroad – and I can truthfully state that my profession has given me entree to residences which members of my race in other professions would have a hard task in gaining if they ever did. What I have done, other members of the Williams and Walker Company have also accomplished.

For example: When the Williams and Walker Company played in London, during the Season of 1903–4, Messrs Williams and Walker were invited to the renowned City of Oxford by students of the famous Oxford University, to attend a "stag-party" given in honor of Williams and Walker. Every attention possible was shown to the distinguished colored actors. Students of Oxford entertained the visitors by giving performances from plays written by Oxford men.

I am sure Williams and Walker's visit to Oxford reflected credit on the race and left a lasting impression in the minds of proud and highly cultured Englishmen.

[...] Williams and Walker entertained Sir Thomas and his party at the Hyde Park Hotel in London. Much has been said about the occasion on which the Williams and Walker Company appeared at Buckingham Palace by special comma[n]d from His Most Gracious Majesty King Edward VII., and therefore I need not make further mention of that. I might call attention to many other events in which we have figured, but those mentioned are sufficient to call attention to the work professional colored people have done, and which I am sure has reflected credit on them personally and indirectly on their race.

I do not mention the work of the Williams and Walker Company from an egotistic standpoint, but merely because with them I am better acquainted and know that they have appeared privately as well as publicly before and been appreciated by members of the better class of white people on both sides of the ocean.

As individuals we must strive all we can to show that we are as capable as white people. In all other walks of life when colored people have had fair play, they have proved their ability, those before the lights must do their part for the cause. We must produce good and great actors and actresses to demonstrate that our people move along the progress of the times and improve as they move. Our people are capable and with advantages they will succeed.

As yet our profession is young and as yet we have been permitted to do but little. We are often compelled by sheer force of circumstance to work at a disadvantage, but I think the time is fast approaching when talent will speak for itself and be accepted for its real worth. White people used to allow for us and say "that is good for a colored person," but to-day we are criticized as severely as white actors and actresses, who have every advantage. This is rather a strange fact: the only time white newspaper men speak of us as the equal of white people is when they are severely criticizing us and our ability to act well; when we fall short they cry out and think it strange that our acting is inferior; of course there is a method in all this we know. But at best, when it comes to singing and dancing, our critics find much difficulty in showing us up to disadvantage; they often acknowledge that it is wonderful that we have done so well and accomplished so much in spite of overwhelming difficulties that do not overwhelm.

I have stated that we ought to strive to produce great actors and actresses; in this I do not mean that all our men and women who possess talent for the Stage should commence the study of Shakespeare. Already too many of our people wish to master Shakespeare. This is really a ridiculous notion. There are characteristics and natural tendencies in our people which make just as beautiful studies for the Stage as any to be found in the make up of any other race, and perhaps far better. By carefully studying our own graces we learn to appreciate the noble and the beautiful within us, just as other peoples have discovered the graces and beauty in themselves from studying and by acting that which is noble in them. Unless we learn the lesson of self appreciation and practice it, we shall spend our lives imitating other people and depreciating ourselves. There is nothing so strong as originality, and I think much time is lost in trying to do something that has been done – and "over-done" – much better than you will ever be able to do it.

Morality on the Stage

I do not wish to moralize. I only wish to say a few common sense words in closing this article. I am aware of the fact that many well-meaning people dislike stage life, especially our women. On this point I would say, a woman does not lose her dignity to-day – as used to be the case – when she enters upon Stage life. In claiming Stage life as a profession, the emphasis should not be put upon the avocation, but rather upon the purpose for which you make the choice. If a girl is gay and easily dazzled by the brilliant side of life on the Stage or off, then I should say to that girl: "Choose some other line of work; look to some other profession, for the Stage is certainly no place for you." But if she be a girl of good thoughts and habits, and she chooses the Stage for the love of the profession and professional work, then I should say to her, "Come, for we need so many earnest workers in this field; and by hard work, I am sure the future will repay you and all of us."

One of the greatest needs of the times is a good school in which colored actors and actresses may be properly trained for good acting. With such an institution we could make a great record in the Artistic World. Of course, it takes time to do anything worth while, and especially to carry out great aims and accomplish good work, but when something has been accomplished we consider the time well spent, and so we must go on working in our profession, with the hope that the future will bring us more encouragement and better success and less criticism; not that we cannot stand criticism, for we can; but for the reason that our work is a great work and ought to be encouraged in these days when it needs help and encouragement.

Our Stage work is grand and our lives can be made beautiful. Just think; night after night we entertain people and make them laugh and be happy and forget all the troubles and sorrows with which they are burdened throughout the day. I am sure it is a pleasure to live and work and give pleasure to others as well as to receive pleasure ourselves.

When we look at the Stage from this standpoint, we can appreciate how much it means to ourselves and others. It is rather easy to stand the harsh things some people may say about us when we feel that besides doing good for ourselves and our race, we are using the gifts that God has given us to a good purpose. With this view before us, we are bound to succeed. [...]

Note

1   D. Brooks, *Bodies in Dissent: Spectacular Performances of Race and Freedom, 1850–1910* (Durham, NC: Duke University Press, 2006), 332.

Chapter 8

Vsevolod Vaslov Meyerhold (1874–1940)

Vsevolod Vaslov Meyerhold (born Karl Kazimir Theodor Meyerhold) was Russia's leading stage director and theorist. A student of Stanislavsky at the Moscow Art Theatre (he played Treplev in Chekhov's *The Seagull*, 1898), Meyerhold broke from his teacher during the early twentieth century. His concepts of directing, as exemplified by his early productions of *Hedda Gabler* (1904) and *The Fairground Booth* (1906), were informed by acting, stage design, and the totality of the theatrical experience. He is associated with a number of innovations: scenic constructivism, which utilized Cubism in creating shapes onstage; bio-mechanics, a physical style of acting that incorporates acrobatics and extreme body posture; revising *commedia* and other comedic forms; and stylized directing procedures, known for formalist concepts that revolutionized the theatre. For Meyerhold, stylization is not the pictorial reproduction of a phenomenon but is bound up with convention and symbolism. All means of expression – physical, set pieces, costumes – are to reveal the underlying synthesis of the phenomenon. He defended stylization as the basic principle of theatrical art: the point is not to replicate life, but to improve it. His 1926 production of Gogol's *Revizor* (*Inspector General*) created an elaborately choreographed ending that accentuated the director's expressionist-symbolist vision. This was among many noteworthy productions he directed.

Meyerhold was a dedicated communist, but by the late 1920s and throughout the 1930s his high-profile personality and emphasis on formalism were at odds with Soviet socialist realism. He was unable to conform to the Party's insistence on subdued

Vsevolod Vaslov Meyerhold, "The Naturalistic Theatre" and "The Theatre of Mood" (1908), first published in *Teatr, Kniga o novom teatre* [*Theatre: A Book about the New Theatre*] (St. Petersburg, 1908), 136–50, reprinted in *O Teatre* (St. Petersburg, 1915), 14–28, 33–47, and excerpted here from *Meyerhold on Theatre*, tr. and ed. Edward Braun (London: Methuen, 1991), 25–34, 49–54. © 1969, 1991 by Edward Braun. Reprinted by permission of Methuen Publishing Ltd.

and realistic social content. Meyerhold's theatrical approach eventually led to the banishment of his style and his disappearance (execution) in 1940.

His two essays here are perhaps the clearest articulation of the way a director must tackle the symbolist and constructivist theatre. Meyerhold sought a formalist theatre that reflected the gestures of the machine. If communism was to celebrate the working class, then for Meyerhold the best way to achieve this was not by realism but by representations of another sort. His bio-mechanic acting celebrated the gestures and movements of the assembly line. Meyerhold paid homage to Taylorism – the utilitarian theory of workers' movements that utilized efficiency in the workplace – by reenacting the work's gestures and behavior. In a paper delivered to the American Society of Mechanical Engineers (1895), Frederick W. Taylor (1856–1915) conceptualized the workplace as units of movement and discrete tasks, with each task or action broken down to their individual components. The relationship of these individualized tasks could be logically structured through the formal study of time and motion in the factory. Henry Ford would realize this idea in the creation of the assembly line. At first seen as exploitative, these movements were reconfigured by Meyerhold in a way he thought reverential to the workers in proletarian society. The assembly line gestures accentuated his formal choreography on constructivist sets. Unfortunately, the communist authorities saw things otherwise. Nevertheless, Meyerhold's forty-year career as a director and theorist provided some of the most enduring innovations in twentieth-century theatre.

The Naturalistic Theatre and the Theatre of Mood (1908)

The Moscow Art Theatre has two aspects: the Naturalistic Theatre[1] and the Theatre of Mood.[2] The naturalism of the Art Theatre is the naturalism adopted from the Meiningen Players;[3] its fundamental principle is the *exact representation of life*.

Everything on the stage must be as nearly as possible *real*: ceilings, stucco cornices, fireplaces, wallpaper, stove-doors, air-vents, etc.

A real waterfall flows on the stage and the rain falling is real water. I recall a small chapel built out of real wood, a house faced with thin ply-wood, double windows with cotton-wool padding and panes coated with frost. Every corner of the set is complete in every detail. Fireplaces, tables and dressers are furnished with a mass of oddments visible only through binoculars, and more than the most assiduous and inquisitive spectator could hope to take in during the course of an entire act. The audience is terrified by the din of a round moon being dragged across the sky on wires. Through the window a real ship is seen crossing a fiord. On the stage not only is there a whole set of rooms but it is several storeys high, too, with real staircases and oak doors. Sets are both struck and revolved. The foot-lights glare. There are archways everywhere. The canvas representing the sky is hung in a semicircle. When the play calls for a farmyard the floor is strewn with imitation mud made out of papier mâché. In short, the aim is the same as that of [the Polish genre painter] Jan Styka's panoramas: the merging of the picture and the actual. Like Styka, *the designer of the naturalistic theatre works in close co-operation with the joiner, the carpenter, the property-master and the model-maker*.

In productions of historical plays the naturalistic theatre works on the principle of transforming the stage into a display of authentic museum pieces of the period or, failing that, of copies from contemporary illustrations or museum photographs. The director and the designer attempt to fix as accurately as possible the year, the month and the day of the action. For example, it is not enough for them that the play is set in the "periwig age"; fantastic topiary, fairy-tale fountains, winding, maze-like paths, avenues of roses, clipped chestnuts and myrtle, crinolines and whimsical coiffures – the charm of all this is lost on the naturalistic director. He must establish the exact style of sleeve worn in the time of Louis XV and how the ladies' coiffures during the reign of Louis XVI differed from those of Louis XV's time. Ignoring [Russian symbolist painter Konstantin] Somov's method of stylizing an epoch, he goes in search of fashion magazines of the very year, month and day on which, according to his calculations, the action took place.

That is how *the technique of copying historical styles* was born in the naturalistic theatre. With such a technique it is natural that the rhythmical construction of a play like *Julius Caesar* with its precisely balanced conflict of two opposing forces is completely over-looked and so not even suggested. Not one director realized that a kaleidoscope of "lifelike" scenes and the accurate representation of the plebeian *types* of the period could never convey the synthesis of "Caesarism."

Actors are always made up *true to character* – which means with faces exactly like those we see in real life. Clearly, the naturalistic theatre regards the face as the actor's principal means of conveying his intentions, ignoring completely the other means at his disposal. It fails to realize the fascination of plastic movement, and never insists on the actor training his body; it establishes a theatre school, yet fails to understand that physi-cal culture must be a basic subject if one has any hope of staging plays like [the Moscow Art Theatre's] *Antigone* or *Julius Caesar*, plays which by virtue of their inherent music belong to a different kind of theatre.

One recalls many examples of virtuoso make-up, but not one example of poses or rhythmical movement. In *Antigone*, the director – seemingly unconsciously – felt an urge to group the actors after the style of frescoes and vase drawings, but he was unable to *synthesize, to stylize* the results of his research and succeeded only in representing it photographically. On the stage one saw a series of resurrected tableaux; they resembled a range of hills separated by ravines, for their inner rhythm clashed violently with the "lifelike" gestures and movements of the intervening action.

The naturalistic theatre has created actors most adept in the art of "reincarnation," which requires a knowledge of make-up and the ability to adapt the tongue to various accents and dialects, the voice being employed as a means of sound-reproduction; but in this plasticity plays no part. The actor is expected to lose his self-consciousness rather than develop a sense of aestheticism which might balk at the representation of externally ugly, misshapen phenomena. The actor develops the photographer's ability to *observe the trifles of everyday life.*

In Khlestakov "nothing is sharply indicated," to use Gogol's expression, yet his char-acter is perfectly clear. *There is absolutely no necessity for sharpness of outline in the clear representation of character.*[4]

"The sketches of great masters often produce a stronger impression than their finished paintings...."

"Wax figures have no aesthetic impact even though they represent the closest imitation of nature. It is impossible to regard them as artistic creations, because they leave nothing to the imagination of the spectator." (Schopenhauer.)

The naturalistic theatre teaches the actor to express himself in a finished, clearly defined manner; there is no room for the play of allusion or for conscious understatement. That is why one so often sees overacting in the naturalistic theatre; it knows nothing of the power of suggestion. Yet there were some artists who made use of it, even in the heyday of naturalism: [Meyerhold's leading actress] Vera Komissarzhevskaya's Tarantella in *The Doll's House* [1904; revived in 1906] was no more than a series of expressive poses during which the feet simply tapped out a nervous rhythm. If you watched only the feet, it looked more like running than dancing. What is the effect on the spectator if a naturalistic actress trained by a dancing-master ceases to act and conscientiously dances every step of the Tarantella?

In the theatre the spectator's imagination is able to supply that which is left unsaid. It is this mystery and the desire to solve it which draw so many people to the theatre.

"Works of poetry, sculpture and the other arts contain a rich treasury of the deepest wisdom; through them speaks the very nature of things to which the artist merely gives voice in his own simple and comprehensible language. Of course, everyone who reads or looks at a work of art must further the discovery of this wisdom by his own means. In consequence, each will grasp it according to his latent and actual ability, just as a sailor can plumb his lead only to the depth which his line allows." (Schopenhauer.)

Thus the spectator in the theatre aspires – albeit unconsciously – to that exercise of fantasy which rises sometimes to the level of creativity. Similarly, how can an exhibition of paintings possibly exist except as a spur to the imagination?

It would seem that the naturalistic theatre denies the spectator's capacity to fill in the details with his imagination in the way one does when listening to music. But nevertheless, the capacity is there. In Yartsev's *In the Monastery* [Moscow Art Theatre, 1904], the first act is set inside the inn of a monastery with the sound of the evening chimes outside. There are no windows, but from the chiming of the bells the spectator conjures up a picture of the courtyard with mounds of bluish snow, pines (like a painting by [Mikhail] Nesterov), trampled paths from cell to cell, the golden domes of the church: one spectator sees this picture; another – something different; a third – something different again. The mystery takes hold of the audience and draws it into a world of fantasy. Then, in the second act the director introduces a window and reveals the monastery courtyard to the audience. Where are *their* fir-trees, *their* mounds of snow, *their* gilded domes? The spectator is not only disenchanted but angry, for the mystery has vanished, his dreams are shattered.

This constant insistence on the banishment from the stage of the power of mystery is further demonstrated by *The Seagull*. In the first act of the original production [Moscow Art Theatre, 1898, revived 1905] one couldn't see how the characters left the stage; they crossed the bridge and vanished "somewhere" into the black depths of the wood (at that time the designer was still working without the help of carpenters). But when the play was revived, every corner of the set was laid bare: there was a summer house with a real roof and real columns; there was a real ravine on stage and one could see clearly how the characters made their exits through this ravine. In the original production the window in the third act was placed to one side and the landscape was hidden; when the characters entered the hall in galoshes, shaking out their hats, rugs and scarves, one pictured autumn, a fine drizzle, and puddles in the courtyard covered with squelching boards. In the revival the windows in the improved set faced the spectator so that the landscape was visible. Your imagination was silenced, and whatever the characters said about the landscape, you disbelieved them because it could never be as they described it; it was painted and you could see it. Originally, the departure of the horses with their bells jingling (the finale of the third act) was simply heard offstage and vividly evoked in the spectator's imagination. In the second production, once the spectator saw the veranda from which the people departed, he demanded to see the horses with their bells, too.

"A work of art can influence only through the imagination. Therefore it must constantly stir the imagination." (Schopenhauer.) But it must really stir it, not leave it inactive through trying to show everything. To stir the imagination is "the essential condition of aesthetic activity as well as the basic law of the fine arts. Whence it follows that a work of art must not give *everything to* our senses but only as much as is necessary to direct our imagination on the right track, letting it have the last word." (Schopenhauer.)

"One should reveal little, leaving the spectator to discover the rest for himself, so that sometimes the illusion is strengthened even further; to say too much is to shake the statue and shatter it into fragments, to extinguish the lamp in the magic lantern." (Tolstoy, *On Shakespeare and the Drama.*)

And somewhere in Voltaire: "*Le secret d'être ennuyeux, c'est de tout dire.*" ["The secret of being boring is to tell all."]

If the spectator's imagination is not disillusioned, it becomes even sharper, and art – more refined. How did medieval drama succeed without any stage equipment? Thanks to the lively imagination of the spectator.

The naturalistic theatre denies not only the spectator's ability to imagine for himself, but even his ability to understand clever conversation. Hence, the painstaking *analysis* of Ibsen's dialogue which makes every production of the Norwegian dramatist tedious, drawn-out and doctrinaire.

It is in productions of Ibsen that one sees the *method* of the naturalistic director revealed most clearly. The production is broken up into a series of scenes and each separate part of the action is *analysed* in detail, even the most trifling scenes. Then all the carefully analysed parts are stuck together again.

The assembling of parts to form the whole is an essential aspect of the director's art, but in speaking of this *analysing* by the naturalistic director, I do not mean the combining of the contributions of the poet, the actor, the musician, the designer and the director.

In his didactic poem, *An Essay on Criticism* (1711), the celebrated eighteenth-century critic [Alexander] Pope enumerated the obstacles which prevent the critic from pronouncing true judgment. Amongst them he cited the habit of examining *in detail,* identifying the primary task of the critic as the attempt to place himself in the position of the author, in order that he might view the work *as a whole.* The same might be said of the stage-director.

The naturalistic director subjects all the separate parts of the work to analysis and fails to gain a picture of the *whole.* He is carried away by the filigree work of applying finishing touches to various scenes, the gratifying products of his creative imagination, absolute pearls of verisimilitude; in consequence, he destroys the balance and harmony of the whole.

Time is a very precious element on the stage. If a scene visualized by the author as incidental lasts longer than necessary, it casts a burden on to the next scene which the author may well intend as most significant. Thus the spectator, having spent too long looking at something he should quickly forget, is tired out before the important scene. The director has placed it in a distracting frame. One recalls how the overall harmony was disturbed in the Moscow Art interpretation of Act Three of *The Cherry Orchard*. The author intended the act's leitmotiv to be Ranevskaya's premonition of an approaching storm (the sale of the cherry orchard). Everybody else is behaving as though stupefied: they are dancing happily to the monotonous tinkling of the Jewish band, whirling round as if in the vortex of a nightmare, in a tedious modern dance devoid of enthusiasm, passion, grace, even lasciviousness. They do not realize that the ground on which they are dancing is subsiding under their feet. Ranevskaya alone foresees the disaster; she rushes back and forth, then briefly halts the revolving wheel, the nightmare dance of the puppet show. In her anguish, she urges the people to sin, only not to be "namby-pambies," through sin man can attain grace, but through mediocrity he attains nothing.

The following harmony is established in the act: on the one hand, the lamentations of Ranevskaya with her presentiment of approaching disaster (fate in the new mystical drama of Chekhov); on the other hand, the puppet show (not for nothing does Chekhov make Charlotte dance amongst the "philistines" in a costume familiar in the puppet theatre – a black tail-coat and check trousers). Translated into musical terms, this is one movement of the symphony. It contains the basic elegiac melody with alternating moods in pianissimo, outbursts in forte (the suffering of Ranevskaya), and the dissonant accompaniment of the monotonous cacophony of the distant band and the dance of the living corpses (the philistines). This is the musical harmony of the act, and the conjuring scene is only one of the harsh sounds which together comprise the dissonant tune of the stupid dance. Hence it should blend with the dancing and appear only for a moment before merging with it once more. On the other hand, the dance should be heard constantly as a muffled accompaniment, but only in the background.[5]

The director at the Art Theatre has shown how the harmony of the act can be destroyed. With various bits and pieces of equipment, he makes an entire scene of the conjuring, so that it is long and complicated. The spectator concentrates his attention on it for so long that he loses the act's leitmotiv. When the act ends the memory retains the background melody, but the leitmotiv is lost.

In *The Cherry Orchard*, as in the plays of Maeterlinck, there is a hero, unseen on the stage, but whose presence is felt every time the curtain falls. When the curtain falls at the Moscow Art Theatre one senses no such presence; one retains only an impression of "types." For Chekhov, the characters of *The Cherry Orchard* are the means and not the end. But in the Art Theatre the characters have become the end and the lyrical-mystical aspect of the play remains unrevealed.

Whereas in Chekhov the director loses sight of the whole by concentrating on its parts, because Chekhov's impressionistically treated images happen to lend themselves to portrayal as clearly defined figures (or *types*), Ibsen is considered by the naturalistic director to require *explanation* because he is too obscure for the public.

Firstly, experience has convinced him that the "boring" dialogue must be enlivened by something or other: a meal, tidying the room, putting something away, wrapping up sandwiches, and so on. In *Hedda Gabler*, in the scene between Tesman and Aunt Julie, breakfast was served; I well remember how skillfully the actor playing Tesman ate, but I couldn't help missing the exposition of the plot.

In Ibsen, besides giving a clearly defined sketch of Norwegian *types*, the director excels in emphasizing all sorts of "complicated" (in his opinion) dialogue. One recalls how the essence of *Pillars of the Community* was completely lost in this painstaking analysis of *minor* scenes. Consequently, the spectator who had read the play and knew it well witnessed a completely new play which he didn't understand because he had read something else. The director gave prominence to a number of secondary, parenthetic scenes and brought out their meaning. *But the truth is that the sum of the meaning of all the parenthetic scenes does not add up to the meaning of the whole play.* One decisive moment prominently presented decides the fate of the act in the mind of the audience, even though everything else slips past as though in a fog.

The urge to *show* everything, come what may, the fear of mystery, of leaving anything unsaid, turns the theatre into a mere illustration of the author's words. "There's the dog howling again," says one of the characters, and without fail a dog's howling is reproduced. The spectator concludes the "departure," not only from the retreating sound of the harness bells but from the thundering of hooves on the wooden bridge over the river as well. You hear the rain beating on the iron roof; there are birds, frogs, crickets.

In this connection, let me quote a conversation between Chekhov and some actors (from my diary). On the second occasion (11 September 1898) that Chekhov attended rehearsals of *The Seagull* at the Moscow Art Theatre, one of the actors told him that offstage there would be frogs croaking, dragon-flies humming and dogs barking.

> "Why?" – asked Anton Pavlovich in a dissatisfied tone.
> "Because it's realistic" – replied the actor.
> "Realistic!" – repeated Chekhov with a laugh. Then after a short pause he said: "The stage is art. There's a genre painting by [Ivan] Kramskoy in which the faces are portrayed superbly. What would happen if you cut the nose out of one of the paintings and substituted a real one? The nose would be 'realistic' but the picture would be ruined."

One of the actors proudly told Chekhov that the director intended to bring the entire household, including a woman with a child crying, on to the stage at the close of the third act of *The Seagull*. Chekhov said:

> "He mustn't. It would be like playing pianissimo on the piano and having the lid suddenly crash down."
> "But in life it often happens that the pianissimo is interrupted quite unexpectedly by the forte," retorted one of the actors.
> "Yes, but the stage demands a degree of artifice," said A. P. [Chekhov]. "You have no fourth wall. Besides, the stage is art, the stage reflects the quintessence of life and there is no need to introduce anything superfluous on to it."

One need hardly amplify Chekhov's indictment of the naturalistic theatre implicit in this dialogue. The naturalistic theatre has conducted a never-ending search for the fourth wall which has led it into a whole series of absurdities. The theatre fell into the hands of fabricants who tried to make everything "just like real life" and turned the stage into some sort of antique shop.

Following Stanislavsky's dictum that one day it will be possible to show the audience a real sky in the theatre, every director has racked his brains to raise the roof as high as possible over the stage. Nobody realizes that instead of rebuilding the stage (a most expensive undertaking), it is the fundamental principle of the naturalistic theatre which needs to be broken down. It is this principle alone which has caused the theatre to commit such absurdities.

Nobody believes that it is the wind and not a stage-hand which causes the garland to sway in the first scene of *Julius Caesar*, because the characters' cloaks remain still. The characters in Act Two of *The Cherry Orchard* walk through "real" ravines, across "real" bridges, past a "real" chapel, yet from the sky are suspended two big pieces of blue-painted canvas with tulle frills, which bear no resemblance at all either to sky or clouds. The hills on the battlefield in *Julius Caesar* may be constructed so that they decrease in size towards the horizon, but why don't the characters become smaller, too, as they move away from us towards the hills?

> The usual stage set depicts landscapes of great depth but it is unable to show human figures of corresponding size against these landscapes. Nevertheless, such a set pretends to give a true representation of nature! An actor moves ten or even twenty metres back from the footlights, but he still looks just as tall and is seen in just as much detail as when he was standing close to them. According to the laws of perspective governing decorative art one ought to move the actor as far back as possible and then, in order to relate him correctly to the surrounding trees, houses and mountains, show him considerably reduced in size – sometimes as a silhouette, sometimes as a mere dot. [Meyerhold quotes from Georg Fuchs, *Die Schaubühne der Zukunft*, p. 28.]

A real tree looks crude and unnatural beside a painted one, because its three dimensions strike a discordant note with the two dimensions of art.

One could cite a host of such absurdities, brought about by the naturalistic theatre's policy of the exact representation of nature. The rational definition of a given object, the photographic representation and illustration of the text of a play by means of decorative art, the copying of a historical style: these are the tasks which the naturalistic theatre sets itself.

Whereas naturalism has involved the Russian theatre in complicated stage techniques, the theatre of Chekhov (the other aspect of the Art Theatre), by revealing the power of *atmosphere* on the stage, has introduced that element without which the Meiningen-style theatre would have perished long ago. Yet still the naturalistic theatre has not availed itself of this new element, introduced by Chekhov's "music," to stimulate its further development. Chekhov's art demands a theatre of mood. The Alexandrinsky Theatre's production of *The Seagull* [1896] failed to catch the mood which the author demanded.

The secret lies not in the chirping of crickets, not in dogs barking, not in real doors. When *The Seagull* was performed by the Art Theatre in the Hermitage Theatre [the company performed in this theatre from 1898 to 1920] the stage machinery was not yet perfected and technology had not yet extended its tentacles to all corners of the theatre.

The secret of Chekhov's mood lies in the *rhythm* of his language. It was the rhythm which was captured by the actors of the Art Theatre during the rehearsals of that first production of Chekhov; it was captured because of the actors' love for the author of *The Seagull.*

If the Art Theatre had not captured the rhythm in Chekhov's plays, it would never have succeeded in recreating it on the stage, and would never have acquired that second aspect which secured for it the title of "the theatre of mood." This aspect was the Art Theatre's own, not a mask borrowed from the Meiningen players.

I am firmly convinced that Chekhov himself helped the Art Theatre to succeed in accommodating under one roof both the naturalistic theatre and the theatre of mood; he helped by being present at rehearsals of his plays during which not only frequent discussions with the actors but the sheer fascination of his own personality influenced their taste and their conception of the purpose of art.

The new aspect of the theatre was created by a definite group of actors who became known as "Chekhov's actors." The key to the performance of Chekhov's plays was held by this group which almost invariably acted in them, and which may be regarded as having created Chekhov's rhythm on the stage. Every time I recall the active part which the actors of the Art Theatre played in creating the characters and the mood of *The Seagull* I understand why I believe firmly in the actor as the principal element in the theatre. The atmosphere was created, not by the *mise en scène*, not by the crickets, not by the thunder of horses' hooves on the bridge, but by the sheer musicality of the actors who grasped the rhythm of Chekhov's poetry and succeeded in casting a sheen of moonlight over their creations.

In the first two productions, *The Seagull* and *Uncle Vanya,* when the actors were still free, the harmony remained undisturbed. Subsequently, the naturalistic director first based his productions on "the ensemble" and then lost the secret of performing Chekhov.

Once everything became subordinated to "the ensemble," the creativity of every actor was stilled. The naturalistic director assumed the role of a conductor with full control over the fate of the new tone which the company had discovered; but instead of extending it, instead of penetrating to the heart of the music, he sought to create atmosphere by concentrating on external elements such as darkness, sound effects, properties and characters.

Although he caught the speech rhythms, the director lost the secret of conducting (*The Cherry Orchard,* Act Three), because he failed to see how Chekhov progresses from subtle realism to mystically heightened lyricism.

Having found the key to Chekhov, the theatre sought to impose it like a template on other authors. It began to perform Ibsen and Maeterlinck "à la Chekhov."

We have already discussed Ibsen at the Art Theatre. Maeterlinck was approached, not through the music of Chekhov but through the same process of rationalization. Whilst the people in *The Blind* were broken down into characters, Death in *The Intruder* appeared as a gauze cloud. Everything was most complicated, as is customary in the naturalistic theatre, but not in the least stylized – even though everything in Maeterlinck is stylized.

The Art Theatre had the remedy in its own hands: it could have progressed to the New Theatre through the lyrical power of Chekhov, the musician; but it subordinated his music to the development of all manner of techniques and stage devices; finally it even lost the key to its "own" author – just as the Germans lost the key to Hauptmann once he began to write plays other than domestic dramas, plays which demanded a completely different approach (*Schluck and Jau, And Pippa dances!*).

First Attempts at a Stylized Theatre

The first attempts to realize a Stylized Theatre as conceived by Maeterlinck and Bryusov were made at the Theatre-Studio. In my opinion, this first experimental theatre came very near to achieving ideal stylized drama with its first production, [Maeterlinck's] *The Death of Tintagiles*; so I think it is appropriate to describe the work of the directors, actors and designers on this play, and to consider the lessons learnt during its production.

The theatre is constantly revealing a lack of harmony amongst those engaged in presenting their collective creative work to the public. One never sees an ideal blend of author, director, actor, designer, composer and property-master. For this reason, Wagner's notion of a synthesis of the arts seems to me impossible.[6] Both the artist and the composer should remain in their own fields: the artist in a special *decorative* theatre where he could exhibit canvases which require a stage rather than an art gallery, artificial rather than natural light, several planes instead of just two dimensions, and so on; the composer should concentrate on symphonies like Beethoven's Ninth, for the dramatic theatre, where music has merely an auxiliary role, has nothing to offer him.

These thoughts came to me after our early experiments (*The Death of Tintagiles*) had been superseded by the second phase (*Pelléas and Mélisande*).[7] But even when we started work on *The Death of Tintagiles* I was plagued already by the question of disharmony between the various creative elements; even if it was impossible to reach agreement with the composer and the artist, each of whom was trying instinctively to delineate his own function, at least I hoped to unify the efforts of the author, the director and the actor.

It became clear that these three, the basis of the theatre, could work as one, but only if given the approach which we adopted in the rehearsals of *The Death of Tintagiles* at the Theatre-Studio.

In the course of the usual discussions of the play (before which, of course, the director acquainted himself with it by reading everything written on the subject), the director and actors read through Maeterlinck's verses and extracts from those of his dramas containing scenes corresponding in mood to *The Death of Tintagiles* (the play, itself, was left until we understood how to treat it, lest it became transformed into a mere exercise). The verses and extracts were read by each actor in turn. For them, this work corresponded to the sketches of a painter or the exercises of a musician. The artist must perfect his technique before embarking on a picture. Whilst reading, the actor looked for new means of expression. The audience (everybody, not just the director) made comments and assisted the reader to develop these new means. The entire creative act was directed towards finding those inflections which contained the true ring of the author's own voice. When the author was "revealed" through this collective work, when a single verse or extract "rang true," the audience immediately analysed the means of expression which had conveyed the author's style and tone.

Before enumerating the various new aspects of technique developed through this intuitive method, and while I still retain a clear picture of these combined exercises of director and actors, I should like to mention two distinct methods of establishing contact between the director and his actors: one deprives not only the actor but also the spectator of creative freedom; the other leaves them both free, and forces the spectator to create instead of merely looking on (for a start, by stimulating his imagination).

The two methods may be explained by illustrating the four basic theatrical elements (author, director, actor and spectator) as follows:

1. A triangle, in which the apex is the director and the two remaining corners, the author and the actor. The spectator comprehends the creation of the latter two through the creation of the director. This is method one, which we shall call the "Theatre-Triangle."

2. A straight, horizontal line with the four theatrical elements (author, director, actor, spectator) marked from left to right represents the other method, which we shall call the "Theatre of the Straight Line." The actor reveals his soul freely to the spectator, having assimilated the creation of the director, who, in his turn, has assimilated the creation of the author.

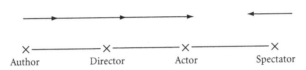

1. In the "Theatre-Triangle" the director explains his *mise en scène* in detail, describes the characters as he sees them, prescribes every pause, and then rehearses the play until his personal conception of it is exactly reproduced in performance. This "Theatre-Triangle" may be likened to a symphony orchestra with the director acting as the conductor.

However, the very architecture of the theatre, lacking any provision for a conductor's rostrum, points to the difference between the two.

People will say that there are occasions when a symphony orchestra plays without a conductor. Let us consider [the celebrated musical conductor of the Leipzig Gewandhaus Orchestra, Arthur] Nikisch and the symphony orchestra which has been playing under him for years with scarcely a change in its personnel; take a composition which it has played several times a year over a period of ten years. If Nikisch were absent from the conductor's rostrum on one occasion, would the orchestra play the composition according to his interpretation? Yes, it is possible that the listener would recognize it as Nikisch's interpretation. But would the performance sound exactly as though Nikisch were conducting? Obviously, it would be worse, although we should still be hearing Nikisch's interpretation.

So I contend this: true, a symphony orchestra without a conductor is possible, but nevertheless it is impossible to draw a parallel between it and the theatre, where the actors invariably perform on the stage without a director. A symphony orchestra without a conductor is possible, but no matter how well rehearsed, it could never stir the public, only acquaint the listener with the interpretation of this or that conductor, and could blend into an ensemble only to the extent that an artist can recreate a conception which is not his own.

The actor's art consists in far more than merely acquainting the spectator with the director's conception. The actor will grip the spectator only if he assimilates both the director and the author and then gives of himself from the stage.

By contrast, an orchestral musician is distinguished by his ability to carry out the conductor's directions precisely, by dint of his virtuoso technique and *by depersonalizing himself.*

In common with the symphony orchestra, the "Theatre-Triangle" must employ actors with virtuoso technique, but at all costs lacking in individuality, so that they are able to convey the director's exact concept.

2. In the "Theatre of the Straight Line," the director, having absorbed the author's conception, conveys his own creation (now a blend of the author and the director) to the actor. The actor, having assimilated the author's conception via the director, stands face to face with the spectator (with director and author behind him), and *freely* reveals his soul to him, thus intensifying the fundamental theatrical relationship of performer and spectator.

In order for the straight line not to bend,[8] the director must remain the sole arbiter of the mood and style of the production, but nevertheless, the actor's art remains free in the "Theatre of the Straight Line."

The director describes his plan during the discussion of the play. The entire production is coloured by his view of it. He inspires the actors with his devotion to the work, and imbues them with the spirit of the author and with his own interpretation. But after the discussion all the performers remain completely independent. Then the director calls a further general meeting to create harmony from all the separate pieces. How does he set about this? Simply by balancing all the parts which have been freely created by the various individuals involved in the collective enterprise. In establishing the harmony vital to the production, he does not insist on the exact representation of his own conception, which was intended only to ensure unanimity and to prevent the work created collectively from disintegrating. Instead he retires behind the scenes at the earliest possible moment and leaves the stage to the actors. Then, either they are out of accord with the director or the author (if, say, they are not of the new school)[9] and "set fire to the ship," or they reveal their souls through almost improvisatory additions, not to the text but to the mere suggestions of the director. In this way the spectator is made to comprehend the author and the director through the prism of the actor's art. *Above all, drama is the art of the actor.* [...]

Notes

1 Repertoire: Pisemsky's *Rule of Will*, Hauptmann's *Henschel*, Naidenov's *Walls*, Gorky's *Children of the Sun*, etc.
2 Repertoire: Chekhov's plays.
3 Georg II, Duke of Saxe-Meiningen (1826–1914), director of the Court Theatre company, noted for his realistic-ensemble detail. – Editor's note.
4 In Gogol's *Inspector General* (1836), Khlestakov is the main character. – Editor's note.

5   Similar instances of dissonant notes emerging fleetingly from the background and encroaching on the act's leitmotiv are: the station-master reading poetry; Yepikhodov breaking his billiard cue; Trofimov falling downstairs. And note how closely and subtly Chekhov interweaves the leitmotiv and the accompaniment:

> Anya (*agitatedly*): And just now someone said that the cherry orchard was sold today.
> Ranevskaya: Sold to whom?
> Anya: He didn't say who; he's gone now. (*Dances* with Trofimov)

6   Wagner's concept of the "total work of art" where all elements are subservient to the director. – Editor's note.

7   First performed on 10 October 1907 at Komissarzhevskaya's Theatre. – Editor's note.

8   Alexander Blok (*Pereval*, Moscow, 1906, no. 2) fears that the actors "might set fire to the ship of the play," but to my mind, discord and disaster could occur only if the straight line were allowed to become crooked. This danger is eliminated if the director accurately interprets the author, accurately transmits him to the actors, and if they accurately understand him.

9   The "Theatre-Triangle" requires non-individualistic actors who none the less are outstanding virtuosi, regardless of their school. In the "Theatre of the Straight Line" individual flair is most important, for without it free creativity is inconceivable. It needs a new school of acting, which must not be a school where new techniques are taught, but rather one which will arise just once to give birth to a free theatre and then die.

"The Theatre of the Straight Line" will grow from a single school as one plant grows from one seed. As each succeeding plant needs a new seed to be sown, so a new theatre must grow every time from a new school.

"The Theatre-Triangle" tolerates schools attached to theatres which provide a regular stream of graduates, who imitate the great actors who founded the theatre, and fill vacancies in the company as they occur. I am convinced that it is these schools which are to blame for the absence of genuine, fresh talent in our theatres.

Chapter 9

Edward Gordon Craig (1872–1966)

Edward Henry Gordon Craig was the son of the famous nineteenth-century actress Ellen Terry. He was a noted actor, designer, director, painter, theorist, draftsman, and a leading advocate of non-representational theatre. His essay *The Art of the Theatre* (1905) became an influential model for non-naturalistic staging. Influenced by the actor Henry Irving, the designer Adolphe Appia, and Richard Wagner's concept of the "total work of art," Craig sought a theatre of light, rhythm, music, and conceptual shapes. His scenic innovations included movable screens and the use of Japanese Nōh theatre techniques. He emphasized mood, shapes, shadows, and visual spectacle in three dimensions. Craig believed that the ideal actor "has so trained his body from head to foot that it would answer the workings of his mind without permitting the emotions even so much to awaken." This, he maintained, was a state of mechanical perfection, making the body "*absolutely* the slave of the mind."[1] The essay here appeared in the first publication of Craig's journal, *The Mask: A Quarterly Journal of the Art of the Theatre*, in 1908. Craig wanted *The Mask* to represent essays of modern theatre as well as articles about art, literature, and society. He illuminates his concepts of acting through his idea of the Über-marionette. For Craig, the actor is not an artist but can achieve a perfect harmony with the scenic representation through gesture, sound, and movement. Rather than psychology, Craig wanted to illuminate form.

The Actor and the Über-marionette (1908)

Inscribed in all affection to my good friends, the actors De Vos and Hevesi.

> To save the Theatre, the Theatre must be destroyed, the actors and actresses must all die of the plague . . . They make art impossible.[2]

Excerpts from Edward Gordon Craig, "The Actor and the Über-marionette," *The Mask* 1.1 (April 1908), 3–17.

It has always been a matter for argument whether or no Acting is an art, and therefore whether the actor is an Artist, or something quite different. There is little to show us that this question disturbed the minds of the leaders of thought at any period, though there is much evidence to prove that had they chosen to approach this subject as one for their serious consideration, they would have applied to it the same method of enquiry as used when considering the arts of Music and Poetry, of Architecture, Sculpture, and Painting.

On the other hand there have been many warm arguments in certain circles on this topic. Those taking part in it have seldom been actors, very rarely men of the theatre at all, and all have displayed any amount of illogical heat, and very little knowledge of the subject. The arguments against acting being an art, and against the actor being an artist, are generally so unreasonable and so personal in their detestation of the actor, that I think it is for this reason the actors have taken no trouble to go into the matter. So now regularly with each season comes the quarterly attack on the actor and on his jolly calling; the attack usually ending in the retirement of the enemy. As a rule it is the literary or private gentlemen who fill the enemy's rank. On the strength of having gone to see plays all their lives, or on the strength of never having gone to see a play in their lives, they attack for some reason best known to themselves. I have followed these regular attacks season by season, and they seem mostly to spring from irritability, personal enmity or conceit.... They are illogical from beginning to end.... There can be no such attack made on the actor or his calling. My intention here is not to join in any such attempt; I would merely place before you what seem to me to be the logical facts of a curious case, and I believe that these admit of no dispute whatever.

Acting is not an art. It is therefore incorrect to speak of the actor as an artist. For accident is an enemy of the artist. Art is the exact antithesis of Pandemonium, and Pandemonium is created by the tumbling together of many accidents; Art arrives only by design. Therefore in order to make any work of art it is clear we may only work in those materials with which we can calculate. Man is not one of those materials.

The whole nature of man tends toward freedom; he therefore carries the proof in his own person, that as *material* for the theatre he is useless. In the modem theatre, owing to the use of the bodies of men and women *as their material*, all which is presented there is of an accidental nature. The actions of the actor's body, the expression of his face, the sounds of his voice, all are at the mercy of the winds of his emotions; these winds which must blow forever round the artist, moving without unbalancing him. But with the actor, emotion *possesses* him; it seizes upon his limbs, moving them whither it will. He is at its beck and call, he moves as one in a frantic dream or as one distraught, swaying here and there; his head, his arms, his feet, if not utterly beyond control, are so weak to stand against the torrent of his passion that they are ready to play him false at any moment. It is useless for him to attempt to reason with himself.... Hamlet's calm directions (the dreamer's not the logician's directions, by the way) are thrown to the winds. His limbs refuse, and refuse again to obey his mind the instant emotion warms, while the mind is all the time creating the heat which shall set these emotions afire. As with his movement, so is it with the expression of his face. The mind struggling and succeeding for a moment, in moving the eyes, or the muscles of the face whither it will;... the mind bringing the face for a few moments into thorough subjection, is suddenly swept aside by the emotion which has grown through the action of the mind.

Instantly, like lightning, and before the mind has time to cry out and protest, the hot passion has mastered the actor's expression. It shifts and changes, sways and turns, it is chased by emotion from the actor's forehead between his eyes and down to his mouth; now he is entirely at the mercy of emotion, and crying out to it: "Do with me what you will!" His expression runs a mad riot hither and thither, and lo! "nothing is coming of nothing." It is the same with his voice as it is with his movements. Emotion cracks the voice of the actor. It sways his voice to join in the conspiracy against his mind. Emotion works upon the voice of the actor, and he produces...the impression of discordant emotion. It is of no avail to say that emotion is the spirit of the gods and is precisely what the artist aims to produce; first of all this is not true, and even if it were quite true, every stray emotion, every casual feeling, cannot be of value. Therefore the mind of the actor, we see, is less powerful than his emotion, for emotion is able to win over the mind to assist in the destruction of that which the mind would produce; and as the mind becomes the slave of the emotion it follows that accident upon accident must be continually occurring. So then, we have arrived at this point;...that emotion is the cause which first of all creates, and secondly destroys. Art as we have said, can admit no accidents. That then which the actor gives us, is not a work of art; it is a series of accidental confessions. In the beginning the human body was not used as material in the art of the theatre. In the beginning the emotions of men and women were not considered as a fit exhibition for the multitude. An elephant and a tiger in an arena suited the taste better, when the desire was to excite. The passionate tussle between the elephant and the tiger gives us all the excitement that we can get from the modern stage, and can give it to us unalloyed. Such an exhibition is not more brutal, it is more delicate; it is more humane; for there is nothing more outrageous than that men and women should be let loose on a platform, so that they may expose that which artists refuse to show except veiled, in the form which their minds create. How it was that man was ever persuaded to take the place which until that time animals had held is not difficult to surmise. [...]

And so the comedy of author and actor commences. The young man appears before the multitude and speaks his lines, and the speaking of them is superb advertisement for the art of literature. After the applause the young man is swiftly forgotten; they even forgive the way he spoke his lines; but as it was an original and new idea at the time, the author found it profitable, and shortly afterwards other authors found it an excellent thing to use the handsome and buoyant men *as instruments*. [...]

The actor looks upon life as a photo-machine looks upon life; and he attempts to make a picture to rival a photograph. He never dreams of his art as being an art such for instance as music. He tries to reproduce nature; he seldom thinks to invent with the aid of nature, and he never dreams of *creating*. As I have said, the best he can do when he wants to catch and convey the poetry of a kiss, the heat of a fight, or the calm of death, is to copy slavishly, photographically...he kisses...he fights...he lies back and mimics death...and when you think of it, is not all this dreadfully stupid? Is it not a poor art and a poor cleverness, which cannot convey the spirit and essence of an idea to an audience, but can only show an artless copy, a facsimile of the thing itself. This is to be an Imitator not an Artist. This is to claim kinship with the Ventriloquist.[3]

There is a stage expression of the actor "getting under the skin of the part." A better one would be getting "*out* of the skin of the part altogether." "What then," cries the red-blooded and flashing actor, "is there to be no flesh and blood in this same art of the theatre of yours? . . . No life?" It depends what you call life, signor, when you use the word in relation with the idea of art. The painter means something rather different to actuality when he speaks of Life in his art, and the other artists generally mean something essentially spiritual; it is only the actor, the ventriloquist or the animal stuffer who, when they speak of putting life into their work, mean some actual and lifelike reproduction, something blatant in its appeal, that it is for this reason I say that it would be better if the actor should get out of the skin of the part altogether. If there is any actor who is reading this, is there not some way by which I can make him realize the preposterous absurdity of this delusion of his, this belief that he should aim to make an actual copy, a reproduction? I am going to suppose that such an actor is here with me as I talk; and I invite a musician and a painter to join us. Let them speak. I have had enough of seeming to decry the work of the actor from trivial motives. I have spoken this way because of my love of the theatre, and because of my hopes and belief that before long an extraordinary development is to raise and revive that which is failing in the theatre, and my hope and belief that the actor will bring the force of his courage to assist in this revival. My attitude toward the whole matter is misunderstood by many in the Theatre. It is considered to be my attitude, mine alone; a stray quarreler I seem to be in their eyes, a pessimist, grumbling; one who is tired of a thing and who attempts to break it. Therefore let the other artists speak with the actor, and let the actor support his own case as best he may, and let him listen to their opinion on matters of art. We sit here conversing, the actor, the musician, the painter, and myself. I who represent an art distinct from all these, shall remain silent.

As we sit here, the talk first turns upon Nature. We are surrounded by beautiful curving hills, trees, vast and towering mountains in the distance covered with snow; around us innumerable delicate sounds of nature stirring . . . Life. "How beautiful," says the painter, "how beautiful the sense of all this!" He is dreaming of the almost impossibility of conveying the full earthly and spiritual value of that which is around him onto his canvas, yet he faces the thing as man generally faces that which is most dangerous.

The musician gazes upon the ground. The actor's is an inward and personal gaze at himself. He is unconsciously enjoying the sense of himself, as representing the main and central figure in a really good scene. He strides across the space between us and the view, sweeping in a half circle, and he regards the superb panorama without seeing it, conscious of one thing only, himself and his attitude. Of course an actress would stand there meek in the presence of nature. She is but a little thing, a little picturesque atom; . . . for picturesque we know she is in every movement, in the sigh which, almost unheard by the rest of us, she conveys to her audience and to herself, that she is there "*little me*," in the presence of the God that made her!! and all the rest of the sentimental nonsense. So we are all collected here, and having taken the attitudes natural to us, we proceed to question each other. And let us imagine that for once we are all really interested in finding out all about the other's interests, and the other's work. (I grant that this is very unusual, and that mind-selfishness, the highest form of stupidity, encloses many a professed artist somewhat tightly in a little square box.) But let us take it for granted that there is a general interest; that the actor and the musician wish to learn something about the art of painting; and that the painter and the musician wish to understand from the actor what his work consists of and whether and why he considers it an art. For here they shall not mince matters, but shall speak that which they believe. As they are looking only for the truth, they have nothing to fear; they are all good fellows, all good friends; not thin-skinned, and can give and take blows. "Tell us," asks the painter, "is it true that before you can act a part properly you must feel the emotions of the character you are representing?" "Oh well, yes and no; it depends what you mean," answers the actor. "We have first to be able to feel and sympathize and also criticize the emotions of a character; we look at it from a distance before we close with it: we gather as much as we can from the text and we call to mind all the emotions suitable for this character to exhibit. After having many times rearranged and selected those emotions which we consider of importance we then practice to reproduce them before the audience; and in order to do so we must feel as little as is necessary; in fact the less we feel, the firmer will our hold be upon our facial and bodily expression." With a gesture of genial impatience, the artist rises to his feet and paces to and fro. He had expected his friend to say that it had nothing whatever to do with emotions, and that he could control his face, features, voice and all, just as if his body were an instrument. The musician sinks down deeper into his chair. "But has there never been an actor," asks the artist, "who has so trained his body from head to foot that it would answer to the workings of his mind without permitting the emotions even so much as to awaken? Surely there must have been one actor, say one out of ten million, who has done this?" "No," says the actor emphatically, "never, never; there never has been an actor who reached such a state of mechanical perfection that his body was *absolutely* the slave of his mind. Edmund Kean of England, Salvini of Italy, Rachel, Eleonora Duse, I call them all to mind and I repeat there never was an actor or actress such as you describe." The artist here asks, "Then you admit that it would be a state of perfection?" "Why of course! But it is impossible; will always be impossible," cries the actor; and he rises…almost with a sense of relief. "That is as much as to say, there never was a perfect actor, there has never been an actor who has not spoiled his performance once, twice, ten times, sometimes a hundred times during the evening? There never has been a piece of acting which could be called even almost perfect and there never will be?" For answer the actor asks quickly, "But has there ever been a painting, or a piece of architecture, or a piece of music which may be called perfect?" "Undoubtedly," they reply, "the laws which control our arts make such a thing possible."

"A picture for instance," continues the artist, "may consist of four lines, or four hundred lines, placed in certain positions; it may be as simple as possible, but it is possible to make it perfect. That is to say, I can first choose that which is to make the lines; I can choose that on which I am to place the lines: I can consider this as long as I like; I can alter it; then in a state which is free from excitement, haste, trouble, nervousness, in fact in any state I choose, (and of course I prepare, wait, and select that also) I can put these lines together…so…now they are in their place. Having my material nothing except my own will can move or alter these; and as I have said my own will is entirely under my control. The line can be straight or it can wave; it can be round if I choose, and there is no fear that when I wish to make a straight line I shall make a curved one, or that when I wish to make a curved one there will be square parts about it. And when it is ready… finished…it undergoes no change but that which time, who finally destroys it, wills." "That is rather an extraordinary thing," replied the actor. "I wish it was possible in my work." "Yes," replies the artist, "*it is a very extraordinary thing, and it is that which I hold* makes the difference between an intelligent statement and a casual or haphazard statement. The most intelligent statement, that is a work of art. The haphazard statement, that is a work of chance. When the intelligent statement reaches its highest possible form it becomes a work of fine art. And therefore I have always held, though I may be mistaken, that your work has not the nature of an art. That is to say (and you have said it yourself) each statement that you make in your work is subject to every conceivable change which emotion chooses to bring about. That which you conceive in your mind, your body is not permitted by nature to complete. In fact, your body, gaining the better of your intelligence, has in many instances on the stage driven out the intelligence altogether. Some actors seem to say, "What value lies in having beautiful ideas. To what end shall my mind conceive a fine idea, a fine thought, for my body which is so entirely beyond my control to spoil? I will throw my mind overboard, let my body pull me and the play through"; and there seems to me to be some wisdom in the standpoint of such an actor. He does not dillydally between the two things which are contending in him, the one against the other. He is not a bit afraid of the result. He goes at it like a man, sometimes a trifle too like a centaur; he flings away all science...all caution...all reason and the result is good spirits in the audience,...and for that they pay willingly. But we are here talking about other things than excellent spirits, and though we applaud the actor who exhibits such a personality as this, I feel that we must not forget that we are applauding his personality... *he* it is we applaud, not what he is doing or how he is doing it; nothing to do with art at all, absolutely nothing to do with art, with calculation, or design.

"You're a nice friendly creature," laughs the actor gaily, "telling me my art's no art! But I believe I see what you mean. You mean to say that before I appear on the stage and before my body commences to come into the question, I am an artist." "Well yes, *you* are, you happen to be, because you are a very bad actor; you're abominable on the stage, but you have ideas, you have imagination; you are rather an exception I should say. I have heard you tell me how you would play Richard III; what you would do; what strange atmosphere you would spread over the whole thing; and that which you have told me you have seen in the play, and that which you have invented and added to it, is so remarkable, so consecutive in its thought, so distinct and clear in form, that *if* you could make your body into a machine, or into a dead piece of material such as clay, and *if* it could obey you in every movement for the entire space of time it was before the audience, and *if* you could put aside Shakespeare's poem, you would be able to make a work of art out of that which is in you. For you would not only have dreamt, you would have executed to perfection; and that which you had executed could be repeated time after time without so much difference as between two farthings." "Ah," sighs the actor, "you place a terrible picture before me. You would prove to me that it is impossible for us ever to think of ourselves as artists. You take away our finest dream and you give us nothing in its place." "No, no, that's not for me to give you. That's for you to find. Surely there must be laws at the roots of the Art of the Theatre, just as there are laws at the roots of all true arts, which if found and mastered, would bring you all you desire?" "Yes, the search would bring the actors to a wall." "Leap it, then!" "Too high!" "Scale it, then!" "How do we know where it would lead?" "Why, up and over." "Yes, but that's talking wildly, talking in the air." "Well, that's the direction you fellows have to go;...fly in the air, live in the air. Something will follow when some of you begin to, I suppose," continued he, "you will get at the root of the matter in time, and then what a splendid future opens before you!

In fact I envy you. I am not sure I do not wish that photography had been discovered before painting, so that we of this generation might have had the intense joy of advancing, showing that photography was pretty good in its way, but there was something better!" "Do you hold that our work is on a level with photography?" "No, indeed, it is not half as exact. It is less of an art even than photography. In fact you and I who have been talking all this time, while the musician has sat silent, sinking deeper and deeper into his chair, our arts by the side of his art, are jokes, games, absurdities." At which the musician must go and spoil the whole thing by getting up and giving vent to some foolish remark. The actor immediately cries out, "But I don't see that that's such a wonderful remark for a representative of the only art in the world to make," at which they all laughed, the musician in a sort of crestfallen, conscious manner. "My dear fellow, that is just because he is a musician. He is nothing except in his music. He is, in fact, somewhat unintelligent, except when he speaks in notes, in tones, and in the rest of it. He hardly knows our language, he hardly knows our world, and the greater the musician, the more is this noticeable; indeed it is rather a bad sign when you meet a composer who is intelligent. And as for the intellectual musician, why that means another...; but we mustn't whisper that name here...he is so popular today. What an actor this man would have been, and what a personality he has. I understand that all his life he had yearnings toward being an actor, and I believe he would have been an excellent comedian, whereas he became a musician...or was it a playwright? Anyhow, it all turned out a great success...a success of personality." "Was it not a success of art?" asks the musician. "Well, which art do you mean?" "Oh, all the arts combined," he replies, blunderingly but placidly. "How can that be? How can all arts combine and make one art? It can only make one joke...one theatre. Things which slowly, by a natural law join together, may have some right in the course of many years or many centuries to ask nature to bestow a new name on their product. Only by this means can a new art be born. I do not believe that the old mother approves of the forcing process; and if she ever winks at it, she soon has her revenge; and so is it with the arts. You cannot co-mingle them and cry out that you have created a new art. *If you can find in nature a new material, one which has never yet been used by man to give form to his thoughts, then you can say that you are on the high road toward creating a new art. For you have found that by which you can create it.* It then only remains for you to begin. The theatre, as I see it, has yet to find that material." And so their conversation ended.

For my part I am with the artist's last statement. My pleasure shall not be to compete with the strenuous photographer and I shall ever aim to get something entirely opposed to life as we see it. This flesh and blood life, lovely as it is to us all, is for me not a thing made to search into, or to give out again to the world, even conventionalized. I think that my aim shall rather be to catch some far off glimpse of that spirit which we call *death*...to recall beautiful things from the imaginary world;...they say they are cold, these dead things,...I do not know...they often seem warmer and more living than that which parades as life. Shades...spirits seem to me to be more beautiful, and filled with more vitality than men and women; cities of men and women packed with pettiness, creatures, inhuman, secret...coldest cold...hardest humanity. For looking too long upon life, may one not find all this to be not the beautiful, nor the mysterious nor the tragic, but the dull, the melodramatic, and the silly: the conspiracy against vitality... against both red heat and white heat; and from such things which lack the sun of life it is not possible to draw inspiration. But from that mysterious, joyous, and superbly complete life which is called Death...that life of shadow and of unknown shapes, where all cannot be blackness and fog as is supposed, but vivid color, vivid light, sharp cut form, and which one finds peopled with strange, fierce, and solemn figures, pretty figures and calm figures, and those figures impelled to some wondrous harmony of movement, all this is something more than a mere matter of fact; from this idea of death which seems a kind of spring, a blossoming – from this land and from this idea can come so vast an inspiration, that with unhesitating exultation I leap forward to it and behold, in an instant, I find my arms full of flowers....I advance but a pace or two and again plenty is around me....I pass at ease on a sea of beauty, I sail whither the winds take me – there, there is no danger. So much for my own personal wish;...but the entire theatre of the world is not represented in me, nor in a hundred artists or actors, but in something far different. Therefore what my personal aim may be is of very little importance. Yet the aim of the theatre as a whole is to restore its art and it should commence by banishing from the theatre this idea of impersonation, this idea of reproducing nature; for while impersonation is in the theatre, the theatre can never become free. The performers should train under the influence of an earlier teaching (if the very earliest and finest principles are too stern to commence with) and they will have to avoid that frantic desire to put "*life*" into their work; for three thousand times against one time, it means the bringing of excessive gesture, swift mimicry, speech which bellows and scene which dazzles, on to the stage, in the wild and vain belief that by such means vitality can be conjured there. And in a few instances, to prove the rule, all this partially succeeds. It succeeds partially with the bubbling personalities of the stage. With them it is a case of sheer triumph *in spite* of the rules, in the very teeth of the rules, and we who look on, throw our hats into the air,...cheer, and cheer again. *We have to*; we don't want to consider or to question; – we go with the tide through admiration and suggestion....That we are hypnotized, our taste cares not a rap....We are delighted to be so moved, and we literally jump for joy. The great personality has triumphed both over us and the art. But personalities such as these are extremely rare, and if we wish to see a personality assert itself in the theatre and entirely triumph as an actor we must at the same time be quite indifferent about the play, the other actors, and Beauty.

Those who do not think with me in this whole matter are the worshipers, or respectful admirers, of the personalities of the stage. It is intolerable to them that I should assert that the stage must be cleared of all its actors and actresses before it will again revive. How could they agree with me? That would include the removal of their favorites...the two or three beings who transform the stage for them from a vulgar joke into an ideal land. But what should they fear? No danger threatens their favorites – for were it possible to put an act into force to prohibit all men and women from appearing before the public upon the stage of a theatre, this would not in the least affect these favorites – these men and women of personality whom the playgoers crown. Consider any one of these personalities born at a period when the stage was unknown; would it in any way have lessened their power...hindered their expression? Not a whit. Personality invents the means and ways by which it shall express itself; and acting is but one (the very least) of the means at the commands of a great personality: and these men and women would have been famous at any time, and in any calling. But if there are many to whom it is intolerable that I should propose to clear the stage of ALL the actors and actresses in order to revive the Art of the Theatre, there are others to whom it seems agreeable.

"The artist," says Flaubert, "should be in his work like God in creation, invisible and all-powerful; he should be felt everywhere and seen nowhere. Art should be raised above personal affection and nervous susceptibility. It is time to give it the perfection of the physical sciences by means of a pitiless method." He is thinking mainly of the Art of Literature; but if he feel this so strongly of the writer, one who is never actually seen, but merely stands half-revealed behind his work, how totally opposed must he have been to the actual appearance of the actor – personality or no personality.

Charles Lamb says; "To see Lear acted ... to see an old man tottering about with a stick, turned out of doors by his daughters on a rainy night, has nothing in it but what is painful and disgusting. We want to take him into shelter, that is all the feeling the acting of Lear ever produced in me. The contemptible machinery by which they mimic the storm which he goes out in, is not more inadequate to represent the horror of the real elements than any actor can be to represent Lear. They might more easily propose to personate the Satan of Milton upon a stage, or one of Michelangelo's terrible figures. ... Lear is essentially impossible to be represented on the stage."

"Hamlet himself seems hardly capable of being acted," says William Hazlitt.

Dante in *La Vita Nuova* tells us that in dream Love in the figure of a youth appeared to him. Discoursing of Beatrice, Dante is told by Love "to compose certain things in rhyme, in the which thou shalt set forth how strong a mastership I have obtained over thee, through her. ... And so write these things that they shall seem rather to be spoken by a third person, and not directly by thee to her, which is scarce fitting." And again "There came upon me a great desire to say somewhat in rhyme; but when I began thinking how I should say it, methought that to speak of her were unseemly, unless I spoke to other ladies 'in the second person.'" We see then that to these men it is wrong that the living person should advance into the frame and display himself upon his own canvas. They hold it as "unseemly" ... "scarce fitting." [...]

The actor must go, and in his place comes the inanimate figure – the über-marionette we may call him, until he has won for himself a better name. Much has been written about the puppet – or marionette. There are some excellent volumes upon him, and he has also inspired several works of art. Today in his least happy period many people have come to regard him as rather a superior doll – and to think he has developed from the doll. This is incorrect. He is a descendant of the stone images or the old Temples – he is today a rather degenerate form of a God. Always the close friend of children he still knows how to select and attract his devotees.

When anyone designs a puppet on paper, he draws a stiff and comic looking thing. Such a one has not even perceived what is contained in the idea which we now call the Marionette. He mistakes gravity of face and calmness of body for blank stupidity and angular deformity. Yet even modern puppets are extraordinary things. The applause may thunder or dribble, their hearts beat no faster, no slower, their signals do not grow hurried or confused; and, though drenched in a torrent of bouquets and love, the face of the leading lady remains as solemn, as beautiful and as remote as ever. There is something more than a flash of genius in the Marionette, and there is something in him more than the flashiness of displayed personality. The Marionette ... appears to me to be the last echo of some noble and beautiful art of a past civilization. But as with all art which has passed into fat or vulgar hands, the puppet has become a reproach. All puppets are now but low comedians. [...]

[...] Then shall we no longer be under the cruel influence of the emotional confessions of weakness which are nightly witnessed by the people and which in their turn create in the beholders the very weaknesses which are exhibited. To that end we must study to remake these images – no longer content with a puppet, we must create an über-marionette. The über-marionette will not compete with life – but will rather go beyond it. Its ideal will not be the flesh and blood but rather the body in Trance – it will aim to clothe itself with a death-like beauty while exhaling a living spirit. Several times in the course of this essay has a word or two about death found its way on to the paper... called there by the incessant clamoring of "Life! Life! Life!" which the Realists keep up. And this might be easily mistaken for an affectation especially by those who have no sympathy or delight in the power and the mysterious joyousness which is in all passionless works of art. If the famous Rubens and the celebrated Raphael made none but passionate and exuberant statements, there were many artists before them and since to whom moderation in their art was the most precious of all their aims, and these more than all others exhibit the true masculine manner. The other flamboyant or drooping artists whose works and names catch the eye of today do not so much speak like men as bawl like animals, or lisp like women. The wise, the moderate masters, strong because of the laws to which they swore to remain ever faithful... their names unknown for the most part... a fine family... the creators of the great and tiny gods of the East and the West, the guardians of those larger times,... these all bent their thoughts forward toward the unknown, searching for sights and sounds in that peaceful and joyous country, that they might raise a figure of stone or sing a verse, investing it with that same peace and joy seen from afar, so as to balance all the grief and turmoil here.

In America we can picture these brothers of that family of masters, living in their superb ancient cities, colossal cities which I ever think of as able to be moved in a single day; cities of spacious tents of silk and canopies of gold under which dwelt their gods; dwellings which contained all the requirements of the most fastidious; those moving cities which, as they traveled from height to plain, over rivers and down valleys, seemed like some vast advancing army of peace. And in each city not one or two men called "artists" whom the rest of the city looked upon as ne'er-do-well idlers, but many men chosen by the community because of their higher powers of perception... artists; for that is what the title of artist means, one who perceives more than his fellows, and who records more than he has seen. And not the least among those artists was the artist of the ceremonies, the creator of the visions, the minister whose duty it was to celebrate their guiding spirit... the spirit of Motion.

In Asia, too, the forgotten masters of the temples and all that those temples contained, have permeated every thought, every mark in their work with this sense of calm motion resembling death... glorifying and greeting it. In Africa (which some of us think we are but now to civilize) this spirit dwelt,... the essence of the perfect civilization. There too dwelt the great masters, not individuals obsessed with the idea of each asserting his personality as if it was a valuable and mighty thing, but content because of a kind of holy patience to move their brains and their fingers only in that direction permitted by the law – in the service of the simple truths. [...]

Notes

1   E. Craig, *On the Art of the Theatre* (London: Heinemann, 1980), 67.

2   Eleonora Dusa, *Studies in Seven Lively Arts*, by Arthur Symons (Constable, 1906).

3   And therefore when any one of these pantomimic gentlemen, who are so clever that they can imitate anything, comes to us, and makes proposal to exhibit himself and his poetry, we will fall down and worship him as a sweet and holy and wonderful being; but we must also inform him that in our State such as he are not permitted to exist; the law will not allow them. And so, when we have anointed him with myrrh, and set a garland of wool upon his head, we shall lead him away to another city. For we mean to employ for our soul's health the rougher and severer poet [...]. (The whole passage being too long to print here, we refer the reader to Plato, *The Republic*, Book III, 395.)

Chapter 10

William Butler Yeats (1865–1939)

William Butler Yeats was Ireland's leading playwright and perhaps the greatest symbolist poet in English. He was also passionately invested in the theatre. Along with John M. Synge and Lady Gregory, he founded Ireland's Abbey Theatre in 1904. The Abbey was a national folk theatre that became a global model for the initiation of the Little Theatre Movement. Among his many important essays are an "Introduction" to the first performance of his *At the Hawk's Well* (1916, reprinted in *Four Plays for Dancer*, 1921), and an "Introduction" to *Certain Noble Plays of Japan* (1916). Yeats was especially inspired by Japanese Nōh theatre, a lyric court drama developed in the fourteenth century. It was marked by simplicity of movement and performed on a specifically designed raised stage, with actors dressed in elaborate costumes, centering on a ritual dance by the masked protagonist, with musicians and a chorus. It was steeped in Buddhist ritual and mythology, evoking the spiritual and material worlds and venerating the noble warrior caste. In his essay "Certain Noble Plays of Japan" (1916), Yeats wrote that "with the help of Japanese plays . . . I have invented a form of drama, distinguished, indirect, and symbolic, and having no need of mob or Press to pay its way – an aristocratic form." For Yeats, Japanese ritual theatre contrasted with realism, which for him was "created for the common people and was always their peculiar delight, and it is the delight today of all those whose minds, educated alone by schoolmasters and newspapers, are without the memory of beauty and emotional subtlety."[1]

This essay appeared in Gordon Craig's *The Mask*. In the first draft Yeats writes the following passage (eventually deleted), which reflects the influence of Wagner's total work of art as well as Craig's artistic synthesis. Dramas, Yeats says, must be subservient to directors; the playwright's task is to "create mechanisms of colour, of sound,

W. B. Yeats, "The Tragic Theatre," *Mask* 3 (October 1910), 77–81.

of shapes of ideas all in elaborate-associative logic, that labyrinth of logic and emotion it brings."[2] The emphasis on image, color, and sound is a guiding motif in his critical essays and dramas. He cultivated a personal style that incorporated Asian theatre techniques, poetry, symbolism, dance, and mask. In this essay, Yeats conveys his theories of pictorial art, examining the manner in which drama may be realized through the use of symbolic scenery, mask, and other non-representational styles.

The Tragic Theatre (1910)

I did not find a word in the printed criticism of Synge's *Deirdre of the Sorrows* about the qualities that made certain moments seem to me the noblest tragedy, and the play was judged by what seemed to me but wheels and pulleys necessary to the effect, but in themselves nothing.

Upon the other hand, those who spoke to me of the play never spoke of these wheels and pulleys, but if they cared at all for the play, cared for the things I cared for. One's own world of painters, of poets, or good talkers, of ladies who delight in Ricard's portraits or Debussy's music, all those whose senses feel instantly every change in our mother the moon, saw the stage in one way; and those others who look at plays every night, who tell the general playgoer whether this play or that play is to his taste, saw it in a way so different that there is certainly some body of dogma – whether in the instincts or in the memory – pushing the ways apart. A printed criticism, for instance, found but one dramatic moment, that when Deirdre in the second act overhears her lover say that he may grow weary of her; and not one – if I remember rightly – chose for praise or explanation the third act which alone had satisfied the author, or contained in any abundance those sentences that were quoted at the fall of the curtain and for days after.

Deirdre and her lover, as Synge tells the tale, returned to Ireland, though it was nearly certain they would die there, because death was better than broken love, and at the side of the open grave that had been dug for one and would serve for both, quarreled, losing all they had given their life to keep. "Is it not a hard thing that we should miss the safety of the grave and we trampling the edge?" That is Deirdre's cry at the outset of a reverie of passion that mounts and mounts till grief itself has carried her beyond grief into pure contemplation. Up to this the play had been a Master's unfinished work, monotonous and melancholy, ill-arranged, little more than a sketch of what it would have grown to, but now I listened breathless to sentences that may never pass away, and as they filled or dwindled in their civility of sorrow, the player, whose art had seemed clumsy and incomplete, like the writing itself, ascended into that tragic ecstasy which is the best that art – perhaps that life – can give. And at last when Deirdre, in the paroxysm before she took her life, touched with compassionate fingers him that had killed her lover, we knew that the player had become, if but for a moment, the creature of that noble mind which had gathered its art in waste islands, and we too were carried beyond time and persons to where passion, living through its thousand purgatorial years, as in the wink of an eye, becomes wisdom; and it was as though we too had touched and felt and seen a disembodied thing.

One dogma of the printed criticism is that if a play does not contain definite character, its constitution is not strong enough for the stage, and that the dramatic moment is always the contest of character with character.

In poetical drama there is, it is held, an antithesis between character and lyric poetry, for lyric poetry – however much it moves you when read out of a book – can, as these critics think, but encumber the action. Yet when we go back a few centuries and enter the great periods of drama, character grows less and sometimes disappears, and there is much lyric feeling, and at times a lyric measure will be wrought into the dialogue, a flowing measure that had well befitted music, or that more lumbering one of the sonnet. Suddenly it strikes us that character is continuously present in comedy alone, and that there is much tragedy, that of Corneille, that of Racine, that of Greece and Rome, where its place is taken by passions and motives, one person being jealous, another full of love or remorse or pride or anger. In writers of tragi-comedy (and Shakespeare is always a writer of tragi-comedy) there is indeed character, but we notice that it is in the moments of comedy that character is defined, in Hamlet's gaiety, let us say; while amid the great moments, when Timon orders his tomb, when Hamlet cries to Horatio "Absent thee from felicity awhile," while Antony names "Of many thousand kisses the poor last," all is lyricism, unmixed passion, "the integrity of fire." Nor does character ever attain to complete definition in these lamps ready for the taper, no matter how circumstantial and gradual the opening of events, as it does in Falstaff, who has no passionate purpose to fulfill, or as it does in Henry V, whose poetry, never touched by lyric heat, is oratorical; nor when the tragic reverie is at its height do we say, "How well that man is realized! I should know him were I to meet him in the street," for it is always ourselves that we see upon the stage, and should it be a tragedy of love, we renew, it may be, some loyalty of our youth, and go from the theatre with our eyes dim for an old love's sake.

I think it was while rehearsing a translation of [Molière's] *Les Fourberies de Scapin* [*The Tricks of Scapin*] in Dublin, and noticing how passionless it all was, that I saw what should have been plain from the first line I had written, that tragedy must always be a drowning and breaking of the dykes that separate man from man, and that it is upon these dykes comedy keeps house. But I was not certain of the site of that house (one always hesitates when there is no testimony but one's own) till somebody told me of a certain letter of [William] Congreve's. He describes the external and superficial expressions of "humor" on which farce is founded and then defines "humor" itself – the foundation of comedy – as a "singular and unavoidable way of doing anything peculiar to one man only by which his speech and actions are distinguished from all other men," and adds to it that "passions are too powerful in the sex to let humor have its course," or, as I would rather put it, that you can find but little of what we call character in unspoiled youth, whatever be the sex, for, as he indeed shows in another sentence, it grows with time like the ash of a burning stick, and strengthens towards middle life till there is little else at seventy years.

Since then I have discovered an antagonism between all the old art and our new art of comedy and understand why I hated at nineteen years Thackeray's novels and the new French painting. A big picture of *cocottes* sitting at little tables outside a café, by some follower of Manet, was exhibited at the Royal Hibernian Academy while I was a student at a life class there, and I was miserable for days. I found no desirable place, no man I could have wished to be, no woman I could have loved, no Golden Age, no lure for secret hope, no adventure with myself for theme out of the endless tale I told myself all day long. Years after, I saw the *Olympia* of Manet at the Luxembourg and watched it without hostility indeed, but as I might some incomparable talker whose precision of gesture gave me pleasure, though I did not understand his language. I returned to it again and again at intervals of years, saying to myself, "Some day I will understand"; and yet it was not until Sir Hugh Lane brought the *Eva Gonzales* to Dublin, and I had said to myself, "How perfectly that woman is realized as distinct from all other women that have lived or shall live," that I understood I was carrying on in my own mind that quarrel between a tragedian and a comedian which the Devil on Two Sticks in Le Sage showed to the young man who had climbed through the window.

There is an art of the flood, the art of Titian when his *Ariosto*, and his *Bacchus and Ariadne*, give new images to the dreams of youth, and of Shakespeare when he shows us Hamlet broken away from life by the passionate hesitations of his reverie. And we call this art poetical, because we must bring more to it than our daily mood if we would take our pleasure; and because it takes delight in the moment of exaltation, of excitement, of dreaming (or in the capacity for it, as in that still face of Ariosto's that is like some vessel soon to be full of wine). And there is an art that we call real, because character can only express itself perfectly in a real world, being that world's creature, and because we understand it best through a delicate discrimination of the senses which is but entire wakefulness, the daily mood grown cold and crystalline.

We may not find either mood in its purity, but in mainly tragic art one distinguishes devices to exclude or lessen character, to diminish the power of that daily mood, to cheat or blind its too clear perception. If the real world is not altogether rejected, it is but touched here and there, and into the places we have left empty we summon rhythm, balance, patter, images that remind us of vast passions, the vagueness of past times, all the chimeras that haunt the edge of trance; and if we are painters, we shall express personal emotion through ideal form, a symbolism handled by the generations, a mask from whose eyes the disembodied looks, a style that remembers many masters that it may escape contemporary suggestion; or we shall leave out some element of reality as in Byzantine painting, where there is no mass, nothing in relief; and so it is that in the supreme moment of tragic art there comes upon one that strange sensation as though the hair of one's head stood up. And when we love, if it be in the excitement of youth, do we not also, that the flood may find no stone to convulse, no wall to narrow it, exclude character or the signs of it by choosing that beauty which seems unearthly because the individual woman is lost amid the labyrinth of its lines as though life were trembling into stillness and silence, or at last folding itself away? Some little irrelevance of line, some promise of character to come, may indeed put us at our ease, "give more interest" as the humor of the old man with the basket does to Cleopatra's dying; but should it come, as we had dreamed in love's frenzy, to our dying for that woman's sake, we would find that the discord had its value from the tune. Nor have we chosen illusion in choosing the outward sign of that moral genius that lives among the subtlety of the passions, and can for her moment make her of the one mind with great artists and poets. In the studio we may indeed say to one another, "Character is the only beauty," but when we choose a wife, as when we go to the gymnasium to be shaped for woman's eyes, we remember academic form, even though we enlarge a little the point of interest and choose "a painter's beauty," finding it the more easy to believe in the fire because it has made ashes.

When we look at the faces of the old tragic paintings, whether it is in Titian or in some painter of mediaeval China, we find there sadness and gravity, a certain emptiness even, as of a mind that waited the supreme crisis (and indeed it seems at times as if the graphic art, unlike poetry which sings the crisis itself, were the celebration of waiting). Whereas in modern art, whether in Japan or Europe, "vitality" (is not that the great word of the studios?), the energy, that is to say, which is under the command of our common moments, sings, laughs, chatters or looks its busy thoughts.

Certainly we have here the Tree of Life and that of the Knowledge of Good and Evil which is rooted in our interests, and if we have forgotten their differing virtues it is surely because we have taken delight in a confusion of crossing branches. Tragic art, passionate art, the drowner of dykes, the confounder of understanding, moves us by setting us to reverie, by alluring us almost to the intensity of trance. The persons upon the stage, let us say, greaten till they are humanity itself. We feel our minds expand convulsively or spread out slowly like some moon-brightened image-crowded sea. That which is before our eyes perpetually vanishes and returns again in the midst of the excitement it creates, and the more enthralling it is, the more do we forget it.

Notes

1   Yeats, "Certain Noble Plays of Japan," in *Essays and Introductions* (New York: Collier, 1961), 221, 227.
2   From Yeats's handwritten notebook, located in the Berg Collection at the New York Public Library (Forty-Second St. and Fifth Ave).

Chapter 11

George Bernard Shaw (1856–1950)

George Bernard Shaw was a prolific author, playwright, and essayist as well as a socialist and vegetarian. At first a novelist, he eventually turned to art and music criticism, and then to theatre. His criticism established ideas of theatre that would soon inform his own plays. Among his critical works were *The Quintessence of Ibsenism* (1891) and *The Perfect Wagnerite* (1898). He was a theatre critic for the *Saturday Review* from 1895 to 1898. Author of over fifty plays, his well-known dramas are *Candida* (1898), *Mrs. Warren's Profession* (1898), *Arms and the Man* (1898), *The Devil's Disciple* (1897), *Caesar and Cleopatra* (1901), *Man and Superman* (1903), with the third act consisting of the "Don Juan" play, *Major Barbara* (1905), *The Doctor's Dilemma* (1906), *Misalliance* (1910), *Androcles and the Lion* (1912), *Pygmalion* (1912), *Heartbreak House* (1919), and *Saint Joan* (1923). He won the Nobel Prize for Literature in 1925.

Shaw was a Fabian socialist, a member of the Fabian Society that sought to bring about socialism in England through peaceful means. In his plays, novels, and essays he examined marital problems, politics, ethics, democracy, music, and evolution. Beginning in 1904 he wrote many of his plays for Harley Granville Barker, who assumed the directorship of the Court Theatre in England. Shaw opposed the longstanding censorship of the Lord Chamberlain and bitterly opposed war after the end of World War I. The following text is from his Preface to three plays by Eugène Brieux (1858–1932), a French author who shared with Shaw a penchant for social dramas. Shaw criticizes the "well-made play," though he regards its essential attributes as crucial for playwriting. For Shaw, drama must engage with the topical issues and social concerns of the times rather than evade them. Social questions, he wrote in his essay "The Problem

Excerpts from G. B. Shaw, "Preface," in *Three Plays by Brieux* (New York: Brentano's, 1913), vii–liv.

Play – A Symposium" (1895), "are produced by the conflict of human institutions with human feelings." Such conflict "affords material for drama" and "drive[s] social questions on to the stage."[1] In the following, Shaw distinguishes between the social problem play and the "well-made-play," the former concerning social matters and the latter a recreation of the trivial. A great admirer of Ibsen, Shaw hoped to influence the theatre as a forum for social debates.

Against the Well-Made Play (1911)

Zolaism as a Superstition

[…] Zola and Ibsen could not, of course, be confined to mere reaction against taboo. Ibsen was to the last fascinating and full of a strange moving beauty; and Zola often broke into sentimental romance. But neither Ibsen nor Zola, after they once took in hand the work of unmasking the idols of the bourgeoisie, ever again wrote a happy or pleasant play or novel. Ibsen's suicides and catastrophes at last produced the cry of "People don't do such things," which he ridiculed through Judge Brack in *Hedda Gabler*.[2] This was easy enough: Brack was so far wrong that people do do such things occasionally. But on the whole Brack was right. The tragedy of Hedda in real life is not that she commits suicide but that she continues to live. If such acts of violent rebellion as those of Hedda and Nora and Rebecca[3] and the rest were the inevitable or even the probable consequences of their unfitness to be wives and mothers, or of their contracting repugnant marriages to avoid being left on the shelf, social reform would be very rapid; and we should hear less nonsense as to women like Nora and Hedda being mere figments of Ibsen's imagination. Our real difficulty is the almost boundless docility and submission to social convention which is characteristic of the human race. What balks the social reformer everywhere is that the victims of social evils do not complain, and even strongly resent being treated as victims. The more a dog suffers from being chained the more dangerous it is to release him: he bites savagely at the hand that dares touch his collar. […] Now the formula of tragedy had come down to the nineteenth century from days in which this was not recognized, and when life was so thoroughly accepted as a divine institution that in order to make it seem tragic, something dreadful had to happen and somebody had to die. But the tragedy of modern life is that nothing happens, and that the resultant dullness does not kill. Maupassant's *Une Vie*[4] is infinitely more tragic than the death of Juliet.

In Ibsen's works we find the old traditions and the new conditions struggling in the same play, like a gudgeon half swallowed by a pike. Almost all the sorrow and the weariness which makes his plays so poignant are the sorrow and the weariness of the mean dull life in which nothing happens; but none the less he provides a final catastrophe of the approved fifth-act-blank-verse type. Hedwig and Hedda shoot themselves; Rosmer and Rebecca throw themselves into the mill-race; Solness and Rubeck are dashed to pieces; Borkman dies of acute stage tragedy without discoverable lesions.[5] I will not say again, as I have said before, that these catastrophes are forced, because a fortunate performance often makes them seem inevitable; but I do submit that the omission of them would leave the play sadder and more convincing.

The Passing of the Tragic Catastrophe and the Happy Ending

Not only is the tradition of the catastrophe unsuitable to modern studies of life; the tradition of an ending, happy or the reverse, is equally unworkable. The moment the dramatist gives up accidents and catastrophes, and takes "slices of life" as his material, he finds himself committed to plays that have no endings. The curtain no longer comes down on a hero slain or married: it comes down when the audience has seen enough of the life presented to it to draw the moral, and must either leave the theatre or miss its last train. [...]

Brieux and the Boulevard

This involves Brieux in furious conflict with the boulevard. Up to quite recent times it was impossible for an Englishman to mention Brieux to a Parisian as the only French playwright who really counted in Europe without being met with astonished assurances that Brieux is not a playwright at all; that his plays are not plays; that he is not (in Sarcey's[6] sense of the phrase) "du théâtre"; that he is a mere pamphleteer without even literary style. And when you expressed your natural gratification at learning that the general body of Parisian dramatists was so highly gifted that Brieux counted for nothing in Paris – when you respectfully asked for the names of a few of the most prominent of the geniuses who had eclipsed him, you were given three or four of which you had never heard, and one or two known to you as those of cynically commercial manipulators of the *ménage à trois*, the innocent wife discovered at the villain's rooms at midnight (to beg him to spare the virtue of a sister, the character of a son, or the life of a father), the compromising letter, the duel, and all the rest of the claptraps out of which dramatic playthings can be manufactured for the amusement of grown-up children. Not until the Académie Française elected Brieux[7] did it occur to the boulevardiers that the enormous difference between him and their pet authors was a difference in which the superiority lay with Brieux.

The Pedantry of Paris

Indeed it is difficult for the Englishman to understand how bigotedly the Parisians cling to the claptrap theatre.

   The English do not care enough about the theatre to cling to its traditions or persecute anyone for their sake; but the French do. [...] Racine and Corneille, who established the alexandrine tradition,[8] deliberately aimed at classicism, taking the Greek drama as their model. Even a foreigner can hear the music of their verse. Corneille wrote alexandrines as Dryden wrote heroic couplets, in a virile, stately, handsome and withal human way; and Racine had tenderness and beauty as well. This drama of Racine and Corneille, with the music of Gluck, gave the French in the seventeenth and eighteenth centuries a body of art which was very beautiful, very refined, very delightful for cultivated people, and very tedious for the ignorant. [...]

   Commercially, the classic play was supplanted by a nuisance which was not a failure: to wit, the "well-made play" of Scribe and his school.[9] The manufacture of well-made plays is not an art: it is an industry. It is not at all hard for a literary mechanic to acquire it: the only difficulty is to find a literary mechanic who is not by nature too much of an artist for the job; for nothing spoils a well-made play more infallibly than the least alloy of high art or the least qualm of conscience on the part of the writer. "Art for art's sake" is the formula of the well-made play, meaning in practice "Success for money's sake." Now great art is never produced for its own sake. It is too difficult to be worth the effort. All the great artists enter into a terrible struggle with the public, often involving bitter poverty and personal humiliation, because they believe they are apostles doing what used to be called the Will of God, and is now called by many prosaic names, of which "public work" is the least controversial. And when these artists have travailed and brought forth, and at last forced the public to associate keen pleasure and deep interest with their methods and morals, a crowd of smaller men – art confectioners, we may call them – hasten to make pretty entertainments out of scraps and crumbs from the masterpieces. Offenbach laid hands on Beethoven's Seventh Symphony and produced *J'aime les militaires*, to the disgust of Schumann, who was nevertheless doing precisely the same thing in a more pretentious way. And these confectioners are by no means mere plagiarists. They bring all sorts of engaging qualities to their work: love of beauty, desire to give pleasure, tenderness, humour, everything except the high republican conscience, the identification of the artist's purpose with the purpose of the universe, which alone makes an artist great.

But the well-made play was not confectionery: it had not even the derived virtue of being borrowed from the great playwrights. Its formula grew up in the days when the spread of elementary schooling produced a huge mass of playgoers sufficiently educated to want plays instead of dog-fights, but not educated enough to enjoy or understand the masterpieces of dramatic art. Besides, education or no education, one cannot live on masterpieces alone, not only because there are not enough of them, but because new plays as well as great plays are needed, and there are not enough Molières and Shakespeares in the world to keep the demand for novelty satisfied. Hence it has always been necessary to have some formula by which men of mediocre talent and no conscience can turn out plays for the theatrical market. [...]

How to Write a Popular Play

The formula for the well-made play is so easy that I give it for the benefit of any reader who feels tempted to try his hand at making the fortune that awaits all successful manufacturers in this line. First, you "have an idea" for a dramatic situation. If it strikes you as a splendidly original idea, whilst it is in fact as old as the hills, so much the better. For instance, the situation of an innocent person convicted by circumstances of a crime may always be depended on. If the person is a woman, she must be convicted of adultery. If a young officer, he must be convicted of selling information to the enemy, though it is really a fascinating female spy who has ensnared him and stolen the incriminating document. If the innocent wife, banished from her home, suffers agonies through her separation from her children, and, when one of them is dying (of any disease the dramatist chooses to inflict), disguises herself as a nurse and attends it through its dying convulsions until the doctor, who should be a serio-comic character, and if possible a faithful old admirer of the lady's, simultaneously announces the recovery of the child and the discovery of the wife's innocence, the success of the play may be regarded as assured if the writer has any sort of knack for his work. Comedy is more difficult, because it requires a sense of humour and a good deal of vivacity; but the process is essentially the same: it is the manufacture of a misunderstanding. Having manufactured it, you place its culmination at the end of the last act but one, which is the point at which the manufacture of the play begins. Then you make your first act out of the necessary introduction of the characters to the audience, after elaborate explanations, mostly conducted by servants, solicitors, and other low life personages (the principals must all be dukes and colonels and millionaires), of how the misunderstanding is going to come about. Your last act consists, of course, of clearing up the misunderstanding, and generally getting the audience out of the theatre as best you can.

Now please do not misunderstand me as pretending that this process is so mechanical that it offers no opportunity for the exercise of talent. On the contrary, it is so mechanical that without very conspicuous talent nobody can make much of a reputation by doing it, though some can and do make a living at it. And this often leads the cultivated classes to suppose that all plays are written by authors of talent. As a matter of fact the majority of those who in France and England make a living by writing plays are unknown and, as to education, all but illiterate. Their names are not worth putting on the playbill, because their audiences neither know nor care who the author is, and often believe that the actors improvise the whole piece, just as they in fact do sometimes improvise the dialogue. To rise out of this obscurity you must be a Scribe or a Sardou,[10] doing essentially the same thing, it is true, but doing it wittily and ingeniously, at moments almost poetically, and giving the persons of the drama some touches of real observed character.

Why the Critics are always Wrong

Now it is these strokes of talent that set the critics wrong. For the talent, being all expended on the formula, at last consecrates the formula in the eyes of the critics. Nay, they become so accustomed to the formula that at last they cannot understand or relish a play that has grown naturally, just as they cannot admire the Venus de Milo because she has neither a corset nor high heeled shoes. [...]

[...] No writer of the first order needs the formula any more than a sound man needs a crutch. In his simplest mood, when he is only seeking to amuse, he does not manu-facture a plot: he tells a story. He finds no difficulty in setting people on the stage to talk and act in an amusing, exciting or touching way. His characters have adventures and ideas which are interesting in themselves, and need not be fitted into the Chinese puzzle of a plot. [...]

How the Great Dramatists torture the Public

Now if the critics are wrong in supposing that the formula of the well-made play is not only an indispensable factor in playwriting, but is actually the essence of the play itself – if their delusion is rebuked and confuted by the practice of every great dramatist even when he is only amusing himself by story-telling, what must happen to their poor formula when it impertinently offers its services to a playwright who has taken on his supreme function as the Interpreter of Life? Not only has he no use for it; but he must attack and destroy it; for one of the very first lessons he has to teach to a play-ridden public is that the romantic conventions on which the formula proceeds are all false, and are doing incalculable harm in these days when everybody reads romances and goes to the theatre. Just as the historian can teach no real history until he has cured his readers of the romantic delusion that the greatness of a queen consists in her being a pretty woman and having her head cut off; so the playwright of the first order can do nothing with his audiences until he has cured them of looking at the stage through the keyhole and sniffing round the theatre as prurient people sniff around the divorce court. The cure is not a popular one. The public suffers from it exactly as a drunkard or a snuff taker suffers from an attempt to conquer the habit. The critics especially, who are forced by their profession to indulge immoderately in plays adulterated with falsehood and vice, suffer so acutely when deprived of them for a whole evening that they hurl disparagements and even abuse and insult at the merciless dramatist who is torturing them. To a bad play of the kind they are accustomed to they can be cruel through superciliousness. [...] But the hatred provoked by deliberately inflicted pain, the frantic denials as of a prisoner at the bar accused of a disgraceful crime, the clamour for vengeance thinly disguised as artistic justice, the suspicion that the dramatist is using private information and making a personal attack: all these are to be found only when the playwright is no mere *marchand de plaisir*, but, like Brieux, a ruthless revealer of hidden truth and a mighty destroyer of idols. [...]

Notes

1   G. B. Shaw, "The Problem Play – A Symposium," in *Shaw on Theatre*, ed. E. J. West (New York: Hill & Wang, 1958), 58, 65.

2   This, the last line in Ibsen's play, is spoken immediately after Hedda's death by Judge Brack, who had hoped to make her his mistress (Act IV). – Editor's note.

3   The heroine of *Hedda Gabler* (1891) shoots herself; Nora Helmer walks out on her marriage in *A Doll's House* (1879); and Rebecca West drowns herself, together with John Rosmer, at the end of *Rosmerholm* (1886). – Editor's note.

4   *Une Vie* (1883), Guy de Maupassant's novel. – Editor's note.

5   Hedwig Ekdal is the 14-year-old girl in *The Wild Duck* (1885) who kills herself after being rejected by her supposed father; Solness, the protagonist of *The Master Builder* (1892), falls to his death from a tower; the sculptor Rubeck perishes in the mountains at the end of *When We Dead Awaken* (1899); the protagonist of *John Gabriel Borkman* (1896) dies of exposure after having been confined to his room for eight years. – Editor's note.

6   Francisque Sarcey (1827–99), French drama critic. – Editor's note.

7   This event took place in 1909. – Editor's note.

8   The 12-syllable alexandrine as the meter for tragedy had been introduced by Etienne Jodelle (1532–73) during the sixteenth century. – Editor's note.

9   Eugène Scribe (1791–1861) was a French playwright who wrote hundreds of plays, vaudeville, operas, and other pieces, alone or in collaboration. He is credited with instituting the well-made play. – Editor's note.

10   Victorien Sardou (1831–1908) was a popular French playwright. Shaw famously attacked Sardou's type of playwriting, calling it "Sardoodledom." – Editor's note.

Chapter 12

F. T. Marinetti (1876–1944)

Filippo Tommaso Emilio (F. T.) Marinetti was a poet and leading advocate of "Futurism." Launched in 1909, Futurism celebrated technology, urban life, and industrialization. Marinetti wrote several documents proclaiming a rejection of the past and exalting militarism and technology – particularly the advent of speed – utilized in art, literature, and painting. Futurism began in Italy and quickly spread across Europe. Art exhibits were organized in Paris, London, and Berlin. Its main premise was that the world moves too quickly to ground truth in static time and place; the artists should strive to represent this rapidity. The arts must make a clean sweep of all stale and useless forms; taste and harmony are fraudulent; and the machine should be celebrated for changing spatial and temporal dynamics. Marinetti first published "The Variety Theatre" in September 1913 as an independent leaflet, and later republished it many times. It was translated into English in the *Daily Mail* in 1913, and was translated by Lees for Craig's *The Mask* also in 1913. Marinetti is attempting to create onstage the sense of traumatic shock that comes with technology. Michael and Victoria Nes Kirby maintain that the key constituents of Marinetti's performance theory "involve an emphasis on concrete or alogical presentation, on the use and combination of physical involvement of the spectators and the destruction of the 'fourth wall' convention." Concrete involves immediate experience rather than representation, and alogical breaks down the concept of a play or opera as a text or narrative. Futurist theatre "tends to *be* rather than to refer," and the actions of the variety performers "are not symbolic but complete and self-sufficient."[1] Marinetti's emphasis on pure presence of the actor, existing not as a symbol or character but rather as he or she exists in the here and now, anticipates many of the theories of Artaud and events such as happenings during

F. T. Marinetti, "Futurism and the Theatre: A Futurist Manifesto," tr. D. Nevile Lees, in *Mask* 6.3 (January 1914), 188–93. Originally published in *Lacerba* 1.19 (October 1, 1913).

the 1960s and performance art during the 1980s. Marinetti advocated "Art as Action," which Günter Berghaus defines as "an artistic-political battle directed *against* an audience he regarded as reactionary, passive, lazy, complacent."[2] Although Futurism's association with fascism has kept it in the shadows of theatre history, illuminating Marinetti's ideas casts considerable light on things to come.

Futurism and the Theatre (1913)

In Praise of the Variety Theatre

We have a profound disgust for the contemporary theatre (verse, prose, and music) because it wavers stupidly between historic reconstruction (a pastiche or a plagiarism) and the photographic reproduction of our daily life.

On the other hand we assiduously frequent the Theatre of Varieties (Music Halls, café-chantants or equestrian circuses), which today offers the only theatrical spectacle worthy of a truly futurist spirit.

Futurism exalts the Variety Theatre because:

1. The Theatre of Variety, born with us, has not, fortunately, any kind of tradition; neither masters nor dogmas, and nourishes itself upon actuality.

2. The Theatre of Variety is absolutely practical because it simply sets out to distract and amuse the public with representations of comicality, of erotic excitation, or of imaginative wonder.

3. The authors, the actors, and the machinists of the Theatre of Variety have one sole motive to exist and to triumph: that of incessantly inventing new elements of wonder. Hence the absolute impossibility of stagnation or repetition; hence a hot rivalry of brains and muscles so as to surpass the various records of agility, velocity, strength, complexity, and grace.

4. The Theatre of Variety, being a lucrative medium for innumerable inventive efforts, naturally generates that which I call Futurist "*marvelousness*" produced by modern mechanism. One finds there at one and the same time: powerful caricatures; depths of absurdity; impalpable and delicious ironies; bewildering and definite symbols; torrents of uncontrollable hilarity; profound analogies between humanity, the animal world, the vegetable world and the mechanical world; conclusions of revealing cynicism, the networks of witty sayings, puns, and riddles which serve agreeably to let in fresh air upon the intelligence, all the gamut of the laugh and smile to stretch the nerves; all the gamut of stupidity, imbecility, blockishness, and absurdity which, insensibly, push to the very border of madness; all the new significations of light, of sound, of noise, and of speech, with their mysterious and inexplicable prolongations in the most unexplored centers of our sensibility.

5. The Theatre of Variety is today the crucible in which are stirring the elements of a new sensibility which is coming into being. Therein is found the ironic decomposition of all the ruined prototypes of the Beautiful, the Great, the Solemn, the Religious, the Ferocious, the Seductive, and the Terrible, and also the abstract elaboration of the new prototypes which shall succeed to these.

The Theatre of Variety is thus the synthesis of all that which humanity has up till now refined in its own nerves so as to divert itself in laughing at material and moral suffering; it is, besides that, the ebullient fusion of all the laughter, of all the smiles, of all the jeers, of all the contortions, of all the raillery of future humanity. Therein may be tasted the gaiety which will move men a hundred years hence, the researches of their painting, of their philosophy, their minds and the upward springing of their architecture.

6. The Theatre of Variety offers the most hygienic of all performances owing to its dynamism of form and color (simultaneous movement of jugglers, dancers, gymnasts, varicolored riding troupers). With its rhythm of swift and languorous dance the Theatre of Variety forcibly draws the slowest souls from their torpor and constrains them to run and leap.

It is, in fact, the only theatre in which the public does not remain inert like a stupid onlooker, but noisily participates in the action, itself singing, accompanying the orchestra, communicating with the actor with unexpected quips and extravagant dialogues.

The action is carried on at the same time on the stage, in the boxes, and in the pit. It then continues at the end of the performance, among the battalions of admirers, sugary youths who crowd at the stage door to dispute the *star*, final double victors; ... a *chic* supper and bed.

7. The Theatre of Variety is an instructive school of sincerity for the male, because it strips from the woman all veils, all the phrases, all the sighs, all the romantic sobs which deform and mask her. It brings into prominence, instead, all the admirable animal qualities of the woman, her powers of capture, of seduction, of perfidy, and of resistance.

8. The Theatre of Variety is a school of heroism by reason of the different records of difficulty to overcome and efforts to be surpassed which create upon the stage the strong and sane atmosphere of danger. (For example: "Looping the loop" on a bicycle, in a motor car, on horseback.)

9. The Theatre of Variety is a school of cerebral subtlety, complication, and synthesis by reason of its clowns, conjurers, thought readers, lightning calculators, mechanicians, imitators and parodists, its musical jugglers and its eccentric Americans, whose fantastic pregnancies bring forth incredible objects and mechanisms.

10. The Variety Theatre is the only school which one can recommend to adolescents and young men of talent, because it explains in an incisive and rapid manner the most mysterious problems and the most complicated political events.

For example: a year ago, at the Folies Bergères, two dancers were representing the wavering discussions of Cambon with Kinderley-Watcher on the question of Morocco and the Congo, by means of a symbolic and significant dance which was worth at least three years of study of foreign politics. The two dancers, turned toward the public, their arms interlaced, the one close beside the other, went on making reciprocal concessions of territory, leaping forward and backward, to right and to left, without ever detaching themselves the one from the other, each keeping his eye fixed upon the object in view, which was, each to entangle the other in turn. They gave an impression of extreme courtesy, of skillful vacillation, of ferocity, of diffidence, of obstinacy, of meticulousness unsurpassably diplomatic.

Besides, the Theatre of Variety explains and luminously illustrates the dominant laws of life:

a) the interweaving of divers rhythms.

b) the fate of lies and contradictions (example: English double-faced dancers; shepherdess and terrible soldier).

c) the synthesis of velocity plus transformations (example: [the Italian quick-change artist and actor soloist Leopoldo] Fregoli).

d) the formation and disintegration of minerals and vegetables; (the blossoming forth and disappearance of luminous advertisements are a most effectual illustration of this).

11. The Theatre of Variety systematically depreciates ideal love and its romantic obsession, repeating to satiety, with the monotony and automaticity of a daily business, the nostalgic languors of passion. It extravagantly mechanicalizes sentiment, depreciates and healthily scorns the obsession of carnal possession, abases voluptuousness to the natural function of coition, deprives it of all mystery, of all anguish, and of all anti-hygienic idealism.

The Theatre of Variety gives instead the sense and the taste of easy light and ironic loves. The spectators of the open-air café-chantants on the terraces of the Casinos afford a most amusing contest between the spasmodic moonlight, tormented by infinite griefs, and the electric light, which strikes violently upon the false jewels, the rouged flesh, the many-colored little skirts, the velvets, the spangles, and the false red of the lips. Naturally the energetic electric light triumphs, and the soft and decadent moonlight is put to rout.

12. The Theatre of Variety is naturally anti-academic, primitive, and ingenuous, hence the more significant owing to the unexpectedness of its researches and the simplicity of its means. (Example: the systematic turn of the stage which the *chanteuses* make, at the end of every couplet, like wild beasts in a cage.)

13. The Theatre of Variety destroys the Solemn, the Sacred, the Serious, the Sublime of Art with a capital *A*. It collaborates in the futurist destruction of the immortal master-pieces, plagiarizing them, parodying them, presenting them just anyhow, without scenery and without compunction just as an ordinary "turn." Thus we approve unconditionally the execution of "Parsifal" in forty minutes which is in preparation for a large London Music Hall.

The Theatre of Variety destroys all our conceptions of time and of space. (Example: a little doorway and gate thirty centimeters high, isolated in the middle of the stage, and through which certain eccentric Americans pass, opening it, and repass, shutting it, in all seriousness, as if they could not do otherwise.)

14. The Theatre of Variety offers us all the "records" attained hitherto: The greatest equilibristic and acrobatic feats of the Japanese, the greatest muscular frenzy of the negroes; the greatest development of the intelligence of animals (trained horses, elephants, seals, dogs, birds); the highest melodic inspiration of the Gulf of Naples and of the Russian steppes, the supreme Parisian spirit, the supreme force, in comparison one with another, of the different races (wrestling and boxing), the greatest anatomical monstrosity, the greatest beauty of women.

15. The Theatre of Variety offers, in short, to all countries which have not one great unique capital (like Italy), a brilliant resume of Paris considered as the sole and obsessing home of ultra refined voluptuousness and pleasure.

Futurism wishes to perfect the Theatre of Variety, by transforming it into,

The Theatre of Wonder and of Record.

1. It is absolutely necessary to destroy all logic in the spectacles in the Theatre of Variety, to exaggerate noticeably its extravagance, to multiply contrasts, and to make the

improbable and the absurd reign as sovereigns on the stage. (Example: oblige the singers to paint their bare necks, their arms, and especially their hair in all the colors hitherto neglected as a means of seduction. Green hair, violet arms, azure breast, orange chignon, etc.; interrupt a singer, making her continue with a revolutionary or anarchistic discourse; sprinkle a romanza with insults and bad words.)

2. To prevent any kind of tradition establishing itself in the Theatre of Variety: For that reason to oppose and abolish the Parisian "Revues" which are as stupid and tedious as the Greek tragedy, their "Compère" and "Commère" which exercise the function of the ancient chorus, and their procession of political personages and events, distinguished with witty sayings, by a most fastidious logic and concatenation. The Theatre of Variety ought not to be, in fact, that which unfortunately it is today, . . . almost always a newspaper, more or less humorous.

3. To make the spectators of the pit, the boxes, and the gallery take part in the action. Here are a few suggestions: put strong glue on some of the stalls, so that the spectator, man or woman, who remains glued down, may arouse general hilarity. (The damaged dress-coat or costume will naturally be paid for on going out.)[3]

Sell the same place to ten different people; hence obstructions, arguments, and altercations.[4]

Offer free seats to ladies and gentlemen notoriously whimsical, irritable, or eccentric, calculated to provoke disturbances by obscene gestures, nudges to the women, and other eccentricities.

Sprinkle the stalls with powders which produce itching, sneezing, etc.

4. Systematically prostitute the whole classic art upon the stage, representing, for example, in a single evening all the Greek, French, and Italian tragedies, condensed and comically mixed up.

Enliven the works of Beethoven, Wagner, Bach, Bellini, Chopin, by introducing into them Neapolitan songs. Put side by side upon the stage Zacconi, Duse and Mayol, Sarah Bernhardt and Fregoli.[5]

Execute a Beethoven symphony backwards, beginning with the last note.[6]

Reduce the whole of Shakespeare to a single act.[7] Do the same with the other most venerated actors. Have *Ernani* performed by actors tied up to the neck in so many sacks. Soap the boards of the stage, to produce amusing tumbles in the most tragic moment.[8]

5. Encourage in every way the *genre* of the American Eccentrics, their effects of exalting grotesque, of terrifying dynamism, their clumsy finds, their enormous brutalities, their waistcoats full of surprises and their pantaloons deep as the holds of ships, from which issue forth, with thousands of other things, the great Futurist hilarity which is to rejuvenate the face of the world.

Because, do not forget, we Futurists are of the "fiery young warriors" as we proclaimed in our manifesto, "let us kill the moonlight."

Notes

1   M. and V. N. Kirby, *Futurist Performance* (New York: PAJ Publications, 1971), 21, 22.
2   G. Berghaus, *Theatre, Performance, and the Historical Avant-Garde* (New York: Palgrave Macmillan, 2005), 103.
3   Yet somehow I hardly see this being done twice to the same public.

4   Haven't we already once too often pulled grandma's chair away from her just as she was sitting down?
5   Who will do the putting?...Don't all speak at once!
6   And then...?
7   And then Marinetti's farces reduced to a single phrase,...what?
8   More than usually considerate!

Chapter 13

Georg Lukács (1885–1971)

Georg (György) Lukács was a Marxist critic and leading advocate of realism in drama and literature. He rejected abstraction and expressionist drama because in his view these movements lacked social commitment. He also rejected naturalism, finding it mere reportage of surface data. Following Marx's concept of exposing reality in all its permutations, Lukács wrote: "If literature is a particular form by means of which objective reality is reflected, then it becomes of crucial importance for it to grasp that reality as it truly is, and not merely to confine itself to reproducing whatever manifests itself immediately on the surface. If a writer strives to represent reality as it truly is, i.e., if he is an authentic realist, then the question of totality plays a decisive role, no matter how the writer actually conceives the problem intellectually."[1] This totality meant incorporating the underlying economic conditions that inform character motivations and social interactions. Lukács believed that Hegelian historical realism embodied in conflicts of proletarian conditions in bourgeois literature (Balzac in particular) offered the correct model for drama. Although the subject matter of bourgeois literature avoids the working class, the conflicts it conveyed could appropriately be transferred to the worker's plight. He was alarmed by expressionism and naturalism, which he felt sensationalized the exotic. These aesthetic movements laid their devices over drama like a patina, creating a gloss which masked a deficiency of the soul. Rather than accentuating form, which modernists sought, the form should reside seamlessly in the background, serving as a function of the conflicts the theme embodies. Although audiences should understand and perhaps even identify with the protagonist, the spectator is to be made aware of the conflicting social issues raised by the play's narrative. For Lukács what

Georg Lukács, "The Sociology of Modern Drama" (1914), tr. Lee Baxandall, copyright Baxandall, 1965; originally appeared in Hungarian in 1909, in German in 1914; reprinted here from *Tulane Drama Review* 9.4 (Summer 1965), 146–70. © 1965 by Lee Baxandall. Reprinted by permission of the author.

mattered in drama is the proper combination of the universal and the particular, the specifics of individuals and their social environment combined with the general creation of "types." This type, he says, is "determined by objective forces at work in society."[2] The author must present a world view (*Weltanschauung*) that takes into account both the individual and surrounding social conditions. Arthur Miller's Willy Loman in *Death of a Salesman* might be said to exemplify the character "type" – the play's protagonist is the prototypical "salesman" concerned with his individual situation, but the play also expresses conflicting social conditions.

The Sociology of Modern Drama (1914)

Modern drama is the drama of the bourgeoisie; modern drama is bourgeois drama. By the end of our discussion, we believe, a real and specific content will have filled out this abstract formulation....

The drama has now taken on new social dimensions.[3] This development became necessary, and necessary at this particular time, because of the specific social situation of the bourgeoisie. For bourgeois drama is the first to grow out of conscious class confrontation; the first with the set intention of expressing the patterns of thought and emotion, as well as the relations with other classes, of a class struggling for power and freedom.... Although in Elizabethan drama the representatives of several classes appear, the true human beings, the dramatic characters, are derived on the whole from a single class. Infrequently, we find a figure that represents the petty nobility, as in *Arden of Feversham*.[4] The lower classes merely take part in comic episodes, or they are on hand simply so their inferiority will highlight the refinements of the heroes. For this reason, class is not decisive in structuring the character and action of these plays....

A new determinant is joined to the new drama: value judgment. In the new drama not merely passions are in conflict, but ideologies, *Weltanschauungen*, as well. Because men collide who come from differing situations, value judgments must necessarily function as importantly, at least, as purely individual characteristics.... The moral outlooks of Hamlet and Claudius, and even of Richard and Richmond, are at bottom identical. Each man is resolute, and feels contemptible if he acts contrary to this moral view. Claudius knows the murder of his brother to be a sin; he is even incapable of seeking motives that might justify his action, and it is inconceivable that he would attempt a relativist justification (as Hebbel's Herod[5] will, following the murder of Aristobolus). Also the "skeptical" and "philosophical" Hamlet never for a moment doubts that he is impelled as though by categorical imperative to seek blood revenge. So long as he remains incapable of acting as he knows he must, he feels sinful and blameworthy. Hegel is therefore correct when he says the deeds of Shakespeare's heroes are not "morally justified." For the ethical value judgment of that epoch rested upon such solid metaphysical foundations, showed such little tolerance for any kind of relativity, and gained universality from such mystic non-analyzable emotions, that no person violating it – for whatever reasons and motive – could justify his act even subjectively. His deed could be explained by his soul's condition, but no amount of reasoning could provide absolution....

The conflict of generations as a theme is but the most striking and extreme instance of a phenomenon new to drama, but born of general emotion. For the stage has turned into the point of intersection for pairs of worlds distinct in time; the realm of drama is one where "past" and "future," "no longer" and "not yet," come together in a single moment. What we usually call "the present" in drama is the occasion of self-appraisal; from the past is born the future, which struggles free of the old and of all that stands in opposition. The end of each tragedy sees the collapse of an entire world. The new drama brings what in fact is new, and what follows the collapse differs qualitatively from the old; whereas in Shakespeare the difference was merely quantitative. Looked at from an ethical perspective, the bad is replaced by the good, or by something better than the old, and at any rate decidedly different in kind. In *Götz von Berlichingen* Goethe depicts the collapse of a world; a tragedy is possible in this case only because Götz was born at that particular time. A century or perhaps even a generation earlier, and he would have become a hero of legend, perhaps rather like a tragi-comic Don Quixote; and a scant generation later as well, this might have been the result....

What we are discussing here is the increased complexity which determines dramatic character. We find it can be viewed from different sides, in numerous perspectives; characters in the new drama are more complicated than in the old, threads that are more intricate run together and knot with one another and with the external world, to express the interrelationship. In turn the concept of the external world grows more relative than ever. We have said of the drama that, in general, destiny is what confronts man from without. In Greek and even in Shakespearean drama we can still easily distinguish between man and his environment, or, speaking from the viewpoint of drama, between the hero and his destiny. But now these lines of division have blurred. So much of the vital centre streams out of the peripheries, and so much streams from there into the vital centre of man, that the concepts which distinguish man from his environment, flesh from spirit, free will from circumstance, hero from destiny, character from situation, are nearly deprived of meaning in the face of the complexity of constant interactions. Destiny is what comes to the hero from without. If we are to continue composing dramas, we must hold to this definition regardless of whether it is true in life; otherwise we would find it impossible to maintain the contending parties in equilibrium (supposing a two-dimension composition), nor would there be foreground or background.... Most simply, what must be located is the equilibrium between man and the external world; the relation of a man to his action is really still his.

The more that circumstances define man, the more difficult this problem seems, and the more the very atmosphere appears to absorb all into itself. Man, distinct contours, no longer exist; only air, only the atmosphere. All that modern life has introduced by way of enriching the perceptions and emotions seems to vanish into the atmosphere, and the composition is what suffers....

To what extent is modern man the enactor of his actions? In his actions man elaborates his entire being, he arrives at himself in them: how much are they really his? How much is the vital centre of man really deep within him? This relation will be the prime determinant of style in every drama. All stylization, all structure bases itself on where the one and the other diverge and coincide, how the one determines the other.... All reflection on the drama comes to this: how does man achieve a tragic action? Is it indeed he who achieves it? By what means? The question truly at the bottom of the theory of tragic guilt is this: did the tragic personage really do his tragic deed, and if he did not, can it be tragic? And the real meaning of "constructing the guilt" exists in building bridges between the deed and the doer, in finding a point from which one will see that all proceeds from within despite every opposition, a perspective which rescues the autonomy of tragic man....

We have to ask whether there can still be a drama. The threat to it is indisputably great, and in naturalism, for instance, we see that it virtually ceases to be dramatic. And yet only the origin of the mutually-opposing forces has been altered; the forces themselves must not be allowed in turn to grow so out of balance that a drama is not possible. In other words, we are faced in the final analysis with a problem of expression, and need not necessarily concern ourselves with the problem of the drama's existence. It matters little whether the will which is set against destiny originates entirely from within; it matters as little whether it is free or constrained, or determined by circumstances of whatever sort. These matters count for little, because a drama remains possible so long as the dynamic force of the will is strong enough to nourish a struggle of life and death dimensions, where the entire being is rendered meaningful.

Hebbel was the first to recognize that the difference between action and suffering is not quite so profound as the words suggest; that every suffering is really an action directed within, and every action which is directed against destiny assumes the form of suffering. Man grows dramatic by virtue of the intensity of his will, by the outpouring of his essence in his deeds, by becoming wholly identical with them. So long as this capacity retains sufficient force to symbolize the entirety of man and his destiny, the displacement earlier noted results merely in a new form of the same relation. The heroes of the new drama – in comparison to the old – are more passive than active; they are acted upon more than they act for themselves; they defend rather than attack; their heroism is mostly a heroism of anguish, of despair, not one of bold aggressiveness. Since so much of the inner man has fallen prey to destiny, the last battle is to be enacted within. We can best summarize by saying that the more the vital motivating centre is displaced outward (i.e., the greater the determining force of external factors), the more the centre of tragic conflict is drawn inward; it becomes internalized, more exclusively a conflict in the spirit. For up to a certain limit, the inner powers of resistance upon which the spirit can depend become greater and more intense in direct proportion to the greatness and intensity of the outwardly opposing forces. And since the hero now is confronted not only with many more external factors than formerly, but also by actions which have become not his own and turn against him, the struggle in which he engages will be heightened into anguish. He must engage in the struggle: something drives him into it which he cannot resist; it is not his to decide whether he even wishes to resist.

This is the dramatic conflict: man as merely the intersection point of great forces, and his deeds not even his own. Instead something independent of him mixes in, a hostile system which he senses as forever indifferent to him, thus shattering his will. And the why of his acts is likewise never wholly his own, and what he senses as his inner motivating energy also partakes of an aspect of the great complex which directs him toward his fall. The dialectical force comes to reside more exclusively in the idea, in the abstract. Men are but pawns, their will is but their possible moves, and it is what remains forever alien to them (the *abstractum*) which moves them. Man's significance consists only of this, that the game cannot be played without him, that men are the only possible hieroglyphs with which the mysterious inscription may be composed....

The new drama is nevertheless the drama of individualism, and that with a force, an intensity and an exclusiveness no other drama ever had. Indeed, one can well conceive an historical perspective on the drama which would see in this the most profound distinction between the old and new drama; such an outlook would place the beginnings of new drama at the point where individualism commences to become dramatic.... We said previously that new drama is bourgeois and historicist; we add now that it is a drama of individualism. And in fact these three formulas express a single point of demarcation; they merely view the parting of ways from distinct vantage-points. The first perspective is the question of sociological basis, the foundation on which the other two are based and from which they grow. It states simply that the social and economic forms which the bourgeoisie opposed to remaining vestiges of the feudal order became, from the eighteenth century onward, the prevailing forms. Also, that life proceeds within this framework, and in the tempo and rhythm it dictates, and thus the problems this fact provokes are precisely the problems of life; in a word, that culture today is bourgeois culture.... Both historicism and individualism have their roots in the soil of this one culture, and though it may seem from several points of view that they would be sharply conflicting, mutually exclusive opposites, we must nevertheless ask how much this opposition really amounts to an antagonism....

In the course of German Romanticism the historicist sense grew to consciousness together with and parallel to Romantic individualism, and the two were never felt to exclude one another. We must regard as no accident the way both of these sensibilities rose to consciousness coincidentally and closely associated with the first great event of bourgeois culture, and perhaps its most decisive, the French Revolution, and all that happened around and because of it....

If we examine even the superficial externals of modern life, we are struck by the degree to which it has grown uniform, though it theoretically has engendered a most extreme individualism. Our clothing has grown uniform, as has the communications system; the various forms of employment, from the employee's viewpoint, have grown ever more similar (bureaucracy, mechanized industrial labour); education and the experiences of childhood are more and more alike (the effect and increasing influence of big-city life); and so on. Parallel to this is the ongoing *rationalizing* of our life. Perhaps the essence of the modern division of labour, as seen by the individual, is that ways are sought to make work independent of the worker's capacities, which, always irrational, are but qualitatively determinable; to this end, work is organized according to production outlooks which are objective, super-personal and independent of the employee's character. This is the characteristic tendency of the economics of capitalism. Production is rendered more objective, and freed from the personality of the productive agent. An objective abstraction, capital, becomes the true productive agent in capitalist economy, and it scarcely has an organic relation with the personality of its accidental owner; indeed, personality may often become superfluous, as in corporations.

Also, scientific methodologies gradually cease to be bound up with personality. In medieval science a single individual personally would command an entire sphere of knowledge (e.g., chemistry, astrology), and masters passed on their knowledge or "secret" to the pupils. The same situation was true in the medieval trades and commerce. But the modern specialized methodologies become continually more objective and impersonal. The relation between work and its performers grows more loose; less and less does the work engage the employee's personality, and conversely, the work is related ever less to the worker's personal qualities. Thus work assumes an oddly objective existence, detached from the particularities of individual men, and they must seek means of self-expression outside their work. The relations between men grow more impersonal as well. Possibly the chief characteristic of the feudal order was the way men's dependencies and relations were brought into unity; by contrast, the bourgeois order rationalizes them. The same tendency to depersonalize, with the substitution of quantitative for qualitative categories, is manifested in the overall state organization (electoral system, bureaucracy, military organization, etc.). Together with all this, man too develops a view of life and the world which is inclined toward wholly objective standards, free of any dependency upon human factors.

The style of the new individualism, especially the aspect of importance to us, is defined by this displacement in the relations of liberty and constraint. The transformation can be briefly formulated: previously, life itself was individualistic; now men, or rather their convictions and their outlooks on life, are. Earlier ideology emphasized constraint, because man felt his place within a binding order to be natural and consistent with the world system; and yet, all occasions of concrete living offered him the opportunity to inject his personality into the order of things by means of his deeds. Hence a spontaneous and continuous individualism of this sort was feasible, whereas today it has grown conscious and problematic as a result of the transformation we have sketched. Previously it was – in Schiller's sense – naïve, and today sentimental. The formulation is this, applied to drama: the old drama, by which we mean here primarily that of the Renaissance, was drama of great individuals, today's is that of individualism. In other words, the realization of personality, its *per se* expression in life, could in no wise become a theme of earlier drama, since personality was not yet problematic. It is, in the drama of today, the chief and most central problem. Though it is true that in most tragedies the action consisted of the clash at some point of someone's maximum attainment with what lay outside him, and the existing order of things refused to let a figure rise to the peak of his possibilities without destroying him, yet this was never associated, consciously at least, with the blunt concept of maximized attainment. The arrangement of the situation was never such that the tragedy had necessarily to result, as it were, from the bare fact of willing, the mere realization of personality. In summary: where the tragedy was previously brought on by the particular *direction* taken by will, the mere *act* of willing suffices to induce it in the new tragedy. Once again Hebbel offers the most precise definition. He stated that it did not matter for the purposes of drama whether the hero's fall was caused by good or bad actions.

The realization and maintenance of personality has become on the one hand a conscious problem of living; the longing to make the personality prevail grows increasingly pressing and urgent. On the other hand, external circumstances, which rule out this possibility from the first, gain ever greater weight. It is in this way that survival as an individual, the integrity of individuality, becomes the vital centre of drama. Indeed the bare fact of being begins to turn tragic. In view of the augmented force of external circumstance, the least disturbance or incapacity to adjust is enough to induce dissonances which cannot be resolved. Just so, the aesthetic of Romanticism regarded tragedy – with a metaphysical rationale and explanation, to be sure – as a consequence of mere being, and the necessary inevitable consequence and natural correlate of individuation. Thus, the contention of these mutually opposed forces is emphasized with increasing sharpness. The sense of being constrained grows, as does its dramatic expression; likewise the longing grows for a man to shatter the bonds which bind men, even though the price he pays is his downfall.

Both these tendencies already had become conscious by the time of *Sturm und Drang* drama, but – in theory at least – they were considered as complementary elements serving to differentiate the genres of art. Lenz saw here the distinction between comedy and tragedy. For him, comedy portrayed society, the men rooted in it, and relationships against which they were incapable of successful struggle; whereas tragedy presented great personalities, who challenged relationships and struggled though it might mean ruin. As early as Goethe's tragedy *Götz* and the first dramas of Schiller, however, relationships are nearly as emphasized as in Lenz's comedies; moreover, what prevents Lenz's comedies from qualifying as real tragedies is not to be found in his idea of what distinguishes the genres (here he was influenced by [Denis] Diderot and [Louis Sébastien] Mercier).

Thus we can say that the drama of individualism (and historicism) is as well the drama of milieu. For only this much-heightened sense of the significance of milieu enables it to function as a dramatic element; only this could render individualism truly problematic, and so engender the drama of individualism. This drama signals the collapse of eighteenth-century doctrinaire individualism. What then was treated as a formal contention between ideologies and life, now becomes a portion of content, an integral part of the historicist drama. Modern life liberates man from many old constraints and it causes him to feel each bond between men (since these are no longer organic) as a bondage. But in turn, man comes to be enclasped by an entire chain of abstract bondages, which are yet more complicated. He feels, whether or not he is conscious of it, that every bond whatsoever is bad and so every bond between men must be resisted as an imposition upon human dignity. In every case, however, the bondage will prove stronger than the resistance. In this perspective Schiller's first play is one typical commencement of the new drama, just as Goethe's play was in another perspective.

Artistically this all implies, in the first place, a paradox in the dramatic representation of character. For in the new drama, compared to the old, character becomes much more important and at the same time much less important. Our perspective alone determines whether we count its formal significance as everything or as nothing. Even as the philosophies of Stirner and Marx are basically drawn from the same source, Fichte, so every modern drama embodies this duality of origin, this dialectic out of the life that gives it birth. (We perhaps see this conflict most clearly in the historical dramas of Grabbe.) Character becomes everything, since the conflict is entirely for the sake of character's vital centre; for it alone and for nothing peripheral, because the force disposed of by this vital centre alone determines the dialectic, that is, the dramatic, quality of drama. Conversely, character becomes nothing, since the conflict is merely *around* and *about* the vital centre, solely for the *principle* of individuality. Since the great question becomes one of to what degree the individual will finds community possible, the direction of the will, its strength, and other specifics which might render it individual in fact, must remain unconsidered. Thus – and the essence of the stylistic problem is here – character is led back to more rational causes than ever before, and becomes at the same time ever more hopelessly irrational. The old drama was founded in a universal sensibility, unifying and meta-rational, which circumscribed as well as permeated its composition and psychology. The old drama's religious origins thus afforded man what was virtually an unconscious and naïve mode of expression. Indeed, to the extent that this drama grew conscious of its tendency, efforts were made to eliminate it. (Euripides is perhaps the best example here.) By contrast, the foundations of the new drama are rational: from its origins it lacks the quality of mystical religious emotion. Only when this emotion once again appears in life does a real drama again appear; to be sure, it reemerges at first as an exclusively artistic demand, but later it seeks to serve as the unifying foundation of life and art. And yet this meta-rational, indissoluble sensibility could never again escape the mark of consciousness, of being *a posteriori*; never could it be once more the unifying, enveloping atmosphere of all things. Both character and destiny had acquired a paradoxical duality, had become at once mystically irrational and geometrically constructed. The expression of the meta-rational becomes in this way more mysterious in psychology than it was earlier, but also, in its technique, more rational and conceptual. The drama comes to be built upon mathematics, a complicated web of abstractions, and in this perspective character achieves significance merely as an intersection; it becomes, as Hofmannsthal once remarked, equivalent to a contrapuntal necessity. And yet, no such systemization can contain the real sum of what humanity makes out of a human being (and drama without human beings is inconceivable). Therefore the dramatic and the characteristic aspects of modern man do not coincide. That which is truly human in the human being must remain to a degree outside the drama. Seen in the perspective of a single life, the personality turns inward, becomes spiritualized, whereas the outward data in turn become abstract and uniform, until a true connection between the two is impossible. The data, actions manifested in the external world, fail to account for the whole man, who in turn is not able to arrive at an action revelatory of his entire self. (Here lies the most profound stylistic contradiction of the intimate drama: as drama increasingly becomes an affair of the spirit, it increasingly misses the vital centre of personality.) This – in context with that indissoluble irrationality whereby man is represented – explains the heavy burden of theory encumbering much of the new drama. Since the vital centre of character and the intersecting point of man and his destiny do not necessarily coincide, supplemental theory is brought in to contrive a dramatic linkage of the two. One could indeed say that the maintenance of personality is threatened by the totality of external data. The data perhaps cannot drain the personality dry – but personality can, by a process of internalization, seek to flee the individual data, avoiding them, keeping out of contact with them.

In sum, life as the subject of poetry has grown more epic, or to be precise, more novelistic than ever (we refer, of course, to the psychological rather than the primitive form of the novel). The transposition of life into the drama is achieved only by the symptomatic rendering of the life data. For the significance of life's external particulars has declined, if we regard them with the task in mind of rendering man dramatic. Thus, the threat to personality becomes almost of necessity the subject of theoretical discussion. Only if the problem is presented abstractly, dialectically, can we succeed in turning the particular event, which is the basic stuff of drama, into an event touching upon, and expressive of, dramatic man's inner essence. The personage must be consciously aware that in the given case directly involving him, the perpetuation of his personality is at stake. The new drama is on this account the drama of individualism: a drama of demands upon personality made conscious. For this reason men's convictions, their ideologies, are of the highest artistic importance, for they alone can lend a symptomatic significance to the naked data. Only they can bring the vital centers of drama and of character into adjustment. However, this adjustment will always remain problematic; it will never be more than a "solution," an almost miraculous coherence of mutually antagonistic forces, for the ideology threatens in turn to reduce character to a "contrapuntal necessity."

Thus heroism in the new drama is quite different from what it was in the old; and the French *tragédie classique* relates most intimately to the old in this regard. Heroism is now more passive, requires less of outward splendour, success, and victory (here again we refer to Hebbel's theory of suffering and action); but on the other hand it is more conscious, judicious and, in expression, more pathetic and rhetorical than was the old. Perhaps we will be somewhat dubious about this last assertion, in view of the sparse simplicity of language in many modern dramas; even so, the essence of the question here concerns not so much rhetoric or its absence in direct expression, but rather the underlying tone in the pathetic scenes, and how much or relatively little this approaches expression. When Hebbel's Clara, Ibsen's Hedda, or even Hauptmann's Henschel dies (to name but the least obtrusively pathetic denouements) the death partakes of the very same tone as did the emotions of heroes in Corneille and Racine. In the face of death, the heroes of Greek and Shakespearean drama were composed; their pathos consists of bravely looking death in the eye, of proudly bearing what is not to be averted. The heroes of the new drama always partake of the ecstatic; they seem to have become conscious of a sense that death can vouchsafe them the transcendence, greatness, and illumination which life withheld (e.g., the *Antigone* of Sophocles compared with that of [Vittorio] Alfieri), and together with this a sense that death will fulfill and perfect their personalities. This sense arose only among the spectators in the old drama. That is why Schopenhauer valued the modern tragedy more highly than the ancient; he called the tone resignation, and regarded it as the essence of tragedy. With this the outer event becomes wholly inward – that is, at the moment when the two vital centres coincide most exactly – and form has in a sense become content. We might well say that the ancients regarded tragedy naïvely. The tragedy is *a posteriori* to the viewpoint of the acting personages and the stylistic means. Thus it is not so important that the problem be thought through to its end. By contrast, in the new tragedies the tragedy is asserted as primary; the various particular phenomena of man, life, and the events of drama are all regarded as tragic; here the tragedy is *a priori* to life.

A dramatic problem exists in this antimony of an individualism which relates to the external world within a reduced scope of expressive significations. It is not the only problem. As we have seen, one of the important new forms of our life results from the slackening and loosening of constraints in the realm of the particular and the immediate, while the abstract constraints correspondingly grow and assume augmented force. The individual's sense of autonomy in his relations with others is ever-increasing, he tolerates less and less any purely personal bond between men, which by its nature will demand more of personality than do those bonds which are purely abstract. Simmel provides an interesting case of this transformation on sensibility. At the beginning of the modern epoch, he states, should an impoverished Spanish nobleman enter the personal service of a rich man (i.e., work as a servant or lackey), he would not lost his title of nobility, whereas he would should he turn to trade. In contrast, a young American woman today is not ashamed to work in a factory, but she does feel shame if she takes up housework in another's employ. Thus relations among men have grown much more complex. For if the realization of personality is not to become a hollow ideology, somebody must achieve it. But since this someone will feel his personal autonomy to be sacred, he will tolerate intrusion upon it no more than will those who aspire to be his master. In this way new conflicts result from the new patterning and sensibility, and this at precisely the juncture where, in the old order of society, the relation of higher to lower rank (master to servant, husband to wife, parents to children, etc.) found stability, the point where a tradition which dated back countless centuries had the energy to confirm and perpetuate tendencies through which the lives of men mingled in the most intimate manner. And so again, and in yet another perspective, the new drama emerges as the drama of individualism. For one of individualism's greatest antimonies becomes its foremost theme: the fact that realization of personality will be achieved only at the price of suppressing the personalities of others (which, in turn, requires for their realization the ruin of the personalities of others).

As a formal relationship, this adds a new development to human relations in drama. Behind a belief that man's full personality is realized in his relationships with others, lies an emotion, a sensibility that suffers all of life. When the emotion vanishes or diminishes, characters whose spirit functions chiefly on the basis of that emotion (the servant, confidante, etc.), will vanish from drama. As the emotion ceases to be universal they become no more than hollow, illusion-disrupting technical properties. This is an evident fact of the French and Spanish drama, and we might better mention that Kent's whole personality is fulfilled in the relationship to Lear, as is Horatio's in his relationship to Hamlet. By contrast, in Goethe's first play, and in Schiller's, we find the theme of a servant at the crucial moment turning against his master (Weislingen – Franz; Franz Moor – Herman), thus ceasing to exist merely in relationship to the master. Here the means elude the one who proposes to use them, they take on new life, become an end. As in many other realms we see here, too, how purely decorative relationships are shattered by the new life; relations become more complex, and where once only gestures made contact, psychological bonds and complex reciprocal effects that are barely expressible are now produced.

The stylistic problem is defined under these conditions, that is, by displacements in the relations among men as caused by the new life (the dramatic material) and by the new ways men have of regarding and evaluating their relationships (the dramatic *principium stilisationis*). Limitations set by these possibilities become the limits of the new drama's expressive potential; and both types of limitation produce the questions which can set the stylistic problem. Perhaps we may briefly formulate these questions: what kind of man does this life produce, and how can he be depicted dramatically? What is his destiny, what typical events will reveal it, how can these events be given adequate dramatic expression?

How does man in the new life relate to the men in the world about him? We must phrase the question thus, if we wish to arrive at a man suitable for drama. Man in isolation is not suited to the drama; no literary art can result from an isolation of human existence which would correspond to the art of portraiture. Literature shows man only in the succession of his feelings and thoughts, which means it cannot entirely exclude the causes of the feelings and thoughts; at most it will somewhat conceal a portion of these causes, that is, the external world, which is their immediate origin. Every other literary form can if it wishes, however, present causes as though sprung straight from the soul of man, as though impressions were drawn but from the soul. They can, in other words, depict arbitrarily the relation of man to his external world, showing it as something other than a web of complex interactions. The dramatic form forbids such an approach, and it moreover focuses relations to the external world in relations to other men. Thus investigation of a man suited for drama coincides with an investigation of the problem of man's relation to other men. (Elsewhere we have discussed, and will discuss again, this relation in its totality, i.e., so-called destiny, the unity that symbolizes this totality.) How do men make contact with one another? Or better, what is their maximum potential for approaching one another, and what is the maximum distance they can place between themselves? Better yet, to what extent is man isolated in modern drama, to what degree is he alone?

Doubtless the old drama offers numerous examples of incomprehension between men. They can be of social origin, resulting because men of low origins and temperament must always see an eternal riddle in all refinement. However, this kind of incomprehension is not an aspect of the problem, for it depends merely upon social distinctions. Other instances are of a moral origin, inasmuch as a refined spirit (Claudius says of Hamlet), "being remiss, most generous, and free from all contriving," just cannot imagine that other men are otherwise. This is the blindness of noble soul, confronted by a calculating evil which sees quite through it. Incomprehension such as this always has a rational basis, either in the qualities of particular men, or in the consequences of certain specific circumstances. It is part of the dramatic groundplan, built in from the first as a "given." As some men will understand one another, others will not, and the one relationship is as absolute and constant as the other. Yet the continued viability of the confidante should be a sign that the potential of absolute understanding among men was never in doubt. Confidantes are almost eliminated in the modern drama, and where they remain, they are felt to function as a disruptive technical device. Now gone out of life is that universal emotion for which alone they could function as symbol, which lifted them above their merely technical function so they might appear as the stylization of a palpable something in reality, rather than a mere convention. The emotion for which they stood could only have been one of the absolute possibility of understanding. If we consider the most complex of these relationships, the one closest to our own emotion, we will see the functioning of Horatio vis-à-vis Hamlet only confirms that no discord of spirits did or could exist between them; all Hamlet's actions and all his motives are rightly regarded and valued by Horatio, in their original sense. [. . .]

A new element is correspondingly introduced into the dialogue – or rather, a new style problem confronts dialogue. . . . What is said becomes ever more peripheral to what is not expressed. The melody in dialogue is ever more submerged in the accompaniment, the openly spoken in the allusion, in silence, in effects achieved by pauses, change in tempo, etc. For the process which proceeds exclusively within, which will not even seek for words, which *can* not, is better expressed by word groupings than by their sense, and better by their associative power rather than compressive energy. The mere lonely men in drama become (and development is ever more in this direction, or at least toward an awareness of it), the more the dialogue will become fragmented, allusive, impressionistic in form rather than specific and forthright. As a form, monologue is not capable of fulfilling this task. . . . A monologue is in fact the compression of a situation, or else a commentary in programmatic form upon what will come later. In a monologue the loneliness of a specific situation is compressed and expressed together with all that must remain unsaid because of the situation; and certain matters at most remain concealed: shame, for instance. But because the monologue always comes either at the start or the end of a dialogue, it cannot express the ever-shifting nuances of understanding and incomprehension which evade formulation and which we speak of here. The new dramatic man is not isolated because he must conceal certain matters for specific reasons, but because he strongly feels he wants, and is aware of wanting, to come together – and knows he is incapable of it. . . .

The only ideology which men will not feel to be an ideology is one which prevails absolutely and tolerates no opposition or doubt; only such a one ceases to be abstract and intellectual and is entirely transformed into feeling, so that it is received emotionally just as though no problem of value-judgment were ever involved (e.g., the medieval ideology of Revenge as still found in Shakespeare, or the dictates of Honour among the Spanish). Until the ideologies motivating men became relativized, a man was right or he was wrong. If right, he recognized no relative justification of his opponents whatsoever; nothing might justify them since they were wrong. Were one to suppose that demonic passions drove them to transgress norms which otherwise were absolutely binding, then the nature of the motivating forces was itself enough to forbid sympathy for the other's state of mind, especially with opponents. The final implication of a struggle between persons was such that one could scarcely see in the opponent anyone less than a mortal enemy, and this is precisely because the struggle was irrational. How different are conflicts where the individual is taken for the mere proxy of something external to him, something objective, conflicts where the pairing of particular opponents is virtually accidental, the result of intersected necessities. This is why the man of Shakespeare's time, ripping and tearing his opponent in the wild grip of unbridled passions, could hardly be thought to conceive a sense of community with those whom he destroyed and who destroyed him. . . .

In the main, this explains why intrigue has become superfluous and even disruptive. When every action can be "understood," man's wickedness (though its forms remain unchanged) can no longer be regarded as the ultimate cause of events (as, e.g., Shakespeare's Iago still was). The Count in Lessing's *Emilia Galotti* represents the first stage of this development; and, after the wild excesses of his initial dramas, Schiller comes to this point almost against his will, in the opinion of Philipp [reference to Schiller's *Don Carlos*]. Again it is Hebbel who grasps the situation in its theoretical purity, when he declares that a dramatist's worth is in inverse ratio to the number of scoundrels he requires. . . . In this way the tragic experience is elevated entirely into the realm of absolute necessity. Everything which is merely personal, merely empirical, disappears from it, even from its form as a phenomenon. Nothing remains but the bare tragic content, a perspective on life in the form of inevitably tragic conflicts. . . . In this way dramatic conflicts grow not merely more profound, but at either side of certain limits they vanish entirely. All becomes a matter of viewpoint. The subjective extreme descends from the acting personages, as it were, and into the very foundations of the play. Whether or not a matter is tragic becomes strictly a matter of viewpoint. The tragi-comedy appears, a genre of art essence is that an event played out before us is, at one and the same time, inseparably comic and tragic. The genre has little positive significance and it is simply impracticable in performance, since the simultaneous duality of vision cannot become spontaneous experience, and the tragic aspect in a comic situation, or the comic in a tragic situation, will only be felt subsequently and then for the most part intellectually. Thus, though this sort of effort may deepen comedy from the perspective of a *Weltanschauung*, it nevertheless disrupts the purity of style and keeps tragedy to the level of the banal and trivial, if indeed it is not distorted into grotesquery. . . .

The conflicts become ever more decisively and exclusively inward, they become so much an affair of man's spirit that they can scarcely by communicated to others; and no data, no actions may be conceived which might express the conflicts, leaving nothing in reserve. Thus does action become not merely superfluous (for the release of tragic emotions does not inherently require it), but it may be felt as positively disruptive.

Often enough action is no more than an accidental instigation of the real event, which occurs somewhere beyond its reach and independent of it. "Our life has become too inward," Hebbel laments, "and, barring a miracle, it will never again become external." Goethe too was aware of the immense advantages which Shakespeare had over him; for in his time the decisive conflicts might still occur in a form which worked strongly upon the senses. . . .

The new life lacks a mythology; what this means is that the thematic material of tragedies must be distanced from life artificially. For the aesthetic significance of mythology is twofold. In the first place it projects, in the concrete symbols of concrete fables, man's vital emotions concerning the most profound problems of his life. These fables are not so rigid that they cannot incorporate displacements of the general sensibility, should these occur. Should it happen, however, the retained elements will always outweigh the added elements; the perceptible event will amount to more than the new way of valuing it. The second aspect, and possibly the more important, is that the tragic situation so expressed is held at a constant natural distance from the public – a constant distance, since the event is projected into vast dark distances of time. A natural distance, since subject and content, and indeed form, have been moulded in the public's midst as something their own life partakes of, something passed along from their ancestors and without which life itself could scarcely be imagined. Whatever can be made into myth is by its nature poetic. This means, in the always paradoxical fashion of every poetic work, that it is both distant and near to life, and bears in itself, without conscious stylization, the real and irreal, the naïve and all-signifying, the spontaneous and symbolic, adornment and simple pathos. At its origins, or in the process of turning the past into myth (as, for instance, Shakespeare with the War of the Roses), everything that is accidental or superfluous or derives from the individual will, or depends for its effect upon the willfulness of individual taste – everything which, despite its "interestingness," renders the profound trivial – is torn from the subjects of poetry. . . .

The bourgeois drama is by nature problematic, as theory and practice both agree, and countless circumstantial and formal signs indicate. Apart from the general stylistic problems of any new drama, drama becomes problematic at its base as soon as its subject is a bourgeois destiny enacted among bourgeois personages. The thematic material of bourgeois drama is trivial, because it is all too near to us; the natural pathos of its living men is non-dramatic and its most subtle values are lost when heightened into drama; the fable is willfully invented and so cannot retain the natural and poetic resonance of an ancient tradition. In consequence, most modern dramas are historical, whether they are set in a definite epoch or the timeless past, and, in view of the foregoing, their historicity gains new meaning. History is meant as a substitute for mythology, creating artificial distances, producing monumentality, clearing away trivia and injecting a new pathos. However, the distance to be gained by projecting back in history is more conscious than formerly, and it is for this reason less spirited and forced to appeal more to the facts, forced, because more timid, to cling more strongly to empirical data. The essence of historical distancing is that it substitutes what happened long ago for what happens today. But always, one event takes the place of another; never does a symbol replace a reality. (Naturally I am not concerned here with trivial "historical truth." A modern fantasy drama is historical; it is less free of the facts than are Shakespeare's historical dramas.) . . .

Tragedy itself has become problematic. There are, that is, no longer any absolute, overriding, external, easily discerned criteria by which one judges whether a given man and a given destiny are tragic. The tragic becomes strictly a matter of viewpoint, and – important as a problem of expression – strictly an inward, spiritual problem. Something becomes tragic only by the suggestive force of expression, and only spiritual intensities can lend the pathos of tragedy to it.... This is why the heroism of the new drama has grown more stylized, more rhetorical, than in the old: the heroism of the hero must be asserted consciously. On the one hand, this serves to hold his tragic experience at the distance of tragedy, as compared to the corresponding events of his life which will refuse to assume a tragic figuration. On the other hand, this affords the possibility of lending a certain force of pathos, of nay-saying significance, to this destiny within the drama, which otherwise lacks the means to render itself objectively conspicuous. What is essential in the hero, what involves him in tragedy, is in this fashion overtly stylized on the plan of a conscious heroism. Dramatic character depiction becomes artificed, hard, places distance between itself and life, whenever it endeavors to rise to tragedy. And the more it aspires to the true tragic peaks of life, or attains them, the more will it be gripped by an obstinate and cold majesty, which will in turn exclude more and more of life's richness and subtleties....

The stylization, however, can no longer be simply the pathos of abstract and conscious heroism. It can be only the stylization of a single quality, exaggerated to a degree beyond any found in life, so that this single quality will be seen to rule the entire man and his destiny as well. To use the language of life, a pathology will be needed. For what does such extremism signify, if not a kind of illness, a pathological overgrowth of a certain specific into the whole life of a man? ...

Pathology is a technical necessity and as such is related to the problems we have sketched – as even Schiller could sense, when he wrote of Goethe's *Iphigenie*: "On the whole, Orestes is the most self-aware among them; without the Furies he would not be Orestes, and yet, since the cause of his condition is not perceptible to the eye, but remains wholly in his spirit, his condition becomes an overly long and unrelieved torment without an object."

When a mythology is absent – which explains why this case is perhaps more striking than others – the basis on which everything must be justified is character. When the motivations are wholly based upon character, however, the wholly inward origin of this destiny will drive the character relentlessly to the limits of pathology. The non-pathological Orestes of Aeschylus was driven from without by what drives Goethe's from within; what once was destiny, becomes character for the modern poets. When we find a pathological trait in one or another personage of the ancient poets (Heracles, Ajax, Lear, Ophelia, etc.), then it is the destiny of that personage to so become and his tragedy is that this is what becomes of him; but his tragedy does not originate in his being so. Even where the tragedy is built upon a pathological situation, as in Phaedra, it is still projected entirely from without: the gods have inflicted it. Perhaps this seems only a technical problem; it may appear to matter little whether Orestes is pursued by the Furies or his own heated imagination, whether it is the witches' enticing words which bring Macbeth's stormy hunger for power to ripeness, or whether Holophernes seeks his own ruin. In practice, however, we will see that what comes from without, what is sent upon man by the gods, is universal; it is destiny. In the same way, to the same degree, it might happen to anyone, and in the final analysis becomes a destiny without reference to the composition of particular character – or at any rate, not solely with reference to it. But when all has become an inner event and can follow only from the character – if, indeed, all is not so infinitely far from the nature of the concerned that they become incapable of dramatic action (as Oswald, Rank) – its intensity must be heightened into an illness if it is to be seen and heard. In pathology and in it alone lies the possibility of rendering undramatic men dramatic. Nothing else is capable of lending them that concentration of action, the intensity of the senses, which will make the act and the situation symbolic and raise the figures above the ordinary, above the everyday. Says [Alfred] Kerr, "in disease we find the permitted poetry of naturalism.... The figure is lent infinitely more dimensions than yet can be justified in reality.".....

We must therefore ask whether today pathology is to be avoided if the content and form of life are to be expressed in dramatic form. It is a tendency destructive of the true dramatic essence, since it relegates causation to the universal and becomes lost in a maze of psychological subtleties and imponderables. But can we see another possibility that remains open to the drama?...

As we see, it is a question transcending the realm of purely artistic or technical problems. To solve this technical task becomes a problem of life itself: it becomes a search for the vital centre of life. For the ancients and their drama, this question offered no problem; the vital centre was their point of departure and everything else grouped itself around it.... Now the vital centre is invented by the poet himself; no longer is it to be discovered, except as an inspiration or vision, as a profound philosophy or the intuition of genius; and even then, on an individual basis, as a particular, thus wholly accidental, insight....

This is the crux of the paradox: the material of drama consists of the interrelatedness of ethical systems, and the dramatic structure which arises from this relationship is aesthetic-formal. From a different viewpoint, what is involved is an equilibrium of forces, of aesthetic interrelations, and this equilibrium can be achieved only in the medium of ethics. More simply, so long as tragedy did not become ethically problematic, either inwardly or outwardly, the pure aesthetics of structure functioned quite naturally: from a given beginning only a single given result can follow, since the ethical structure is a given precondition known to the poet and public alike. But when ethics cease to be a given, the ethical knotting within the drama – thus, its aesthetics – has to be created; whereupon ethics, as the cornerstone of the artistic composition, move necessarily into the vital centre of motivation. In this way the great and spontaneous unity of ethics and aesthetics, within the tragic experience, commences to be the problem.

Notes

1   G. Lukács, "Realism in the Balance," in *Aesthetics and Politics*, tr. R. Livingston (London: Verso, 1977), 33.

2   G. Lukács, *Realism in Our Time*, tr. J. and N. Mander (New York: Harper & Row, 1964), 122.

3   Discussed in detail in a portion of the essay here omitted, which dealt with development of the stage as an institution. Lukács argues that truly bourgeois plays were first written by the Germans Lenz, Grabbe, Goethe, Schiller, and others who were the first dramatists to develop historical ideas. Emphasis upon reasoned argument, together with environmental determinism, is seen to distinguish bourgeois playwrights from their predecessors, who had enjoyed spontaneous communication with their audiences by virtue of shared religious sensibility. [...] – Translator's note.

4   Anonymous Elizabethan tragedy ascribed to Thomas Kyd (1558–94). – Editor's note.

5   *Herod and Marianne* by Friedrich Hebbel (1813–63). – Editor's note.

Chapter 14

Emma Goldman (1869–1940)

Emma Goldman was an anarchist, pacifist, feminist, and socialist. Born in Russia, she emigrated to the United States where she fought for women's emancipation, reproductive rights, and birth control. She returned to Russia after being deported from the United States in the early 1920s, but was soon disillusioned with Soviet communism. Goldman falls in line with other social realists in her effort to defend mimetic representation against the radical avant-garde and conservative critics. Her essay contributes to the ongoing debates of the time, adding a political message to the concerns of drama.

Foreword to *The Social Significance of Modern Drama* (1917)

In order to understand the social and dynamic significance of modern dramatic art it is necessary, I believe, to ascertain the difference between the functions of art for art's sake and art as the mirror of life.

Art for art's sake presupposes an attitude of aloofness on the part of the artist toward the complex struggle of life: he must rise above the ebb and tide of life. He is to be merely an artistic *conjurer* of beautiful forms, a creator of pure fancy.

That is not the attitude of modern art, which is preeminently the reflex, the mirror of life. The artist being a part of life cannot detach himself from the events and occurrences that pass panorama-like before his eyes, impressing themselves upon his emotional and intellectual vision.

The modern artist is, in the words of August Strindberg, "a lay preacher popularizing the pressing questions of his time." Not necessarily because his aim is to proselytize, but because he can best express himself by being true to life.

Emma Goldman, "Foreword," in *The Social Significance of Modern Drama* (1917, reprinted New York: Applause Books, 1987), 1–3.

Millet, Meunier, Turgenev, Dostoyevsky, Emerson, Walt Whitman, Tolstoy, Ibsen, Strindberg, Hauptmann and a host of others mirror in their work as much of the spiritual and social revolt as is expressed by the most fiery speech of the propagandist. And more important still, they compel far greater attention. Their creative genius, imbued with the spirit of sincerity and truth, strikes root where the ordinary word often falls on barren soil.

The reason that many radicals as well as conservatives fail to grasp the powerful message of art is perhaps not far to seek. The average radical is as hidebound by mere terms as the man devoid of all ideas. "Bloated plutocrats," "economic determinism," "class consciousness," and similar expressions sum up for him the symbols of revolt. But since art speaks a language of its own, a language embracing the entire gamut of human emotions, it often sounds meaningless to those whose hearing has been dulled by the din of stereotyped phrases.

On the other hand, the conservative sees danger only in the advocacy of the Red Flag. He has too long been fed on the historic legend that it is only the "rabble" which makes revolutions, and not those who wield the brush or pen. It is therefore legitimate to applaud the artist and hound the rabble. Both radical and conservative have to learn that any mode of creative work, which with true perception portrays social wrongs earnestly and boldly, may be a greater menace to our social fabric and a more powerful inspiration than the wildest harangue of the soapbox orator.

Unfortunately, we in America have so far looked upon the theatre as a place of amusement only, exclusive of ideas and inspiration. Because the modern drama of Europe has till recently been inaccessible in printed form to the average theatregoer in this country, he had to content himself with the interpretation, or rather misinterpretation, of our dramatic critics. As a result the social significance of the Modern Drama has well nigh been lost to the general public.

As to the native drama, America has so far produced very little worthy to be considered in a social light. Lacking the cultural and evolutionary tradition of the Old World, America has necessarily first to prepare the soil out of which sprouts creative genius.

The hundred and one springs of local and sectional life *must* have time to furrow their common channel into the seething sea of life at large, and social questions and problems make themselves felt, if not crystallized, before the throbbing pulse of the big national heart can find its reflex in a great literature – and specifically in the drama – of a social character. This evolution has been going on in this country for a considerable time, shaping the widespread unrest that is now beginning to assume more or less definite social form and expression.

Therefore, America could not so far produce its own social drama. But in proportion as the crystallization progresses, and sectional and national questions become clarified as fundamentally social problems, the drama develops. Indeed, very commendable beginnings in this direction have been made within recent years, among them "The Easiest Way," by Eugene Walter, "Keeping Up Appearances," and other plays by Butler Davenport, "Nowadays" and two other volumes of one-act plays, by George Middleton, – attempts that hold out an encouraging promise for the future.

The Modern Drama, as all modern literature, mirrors the complex struggle of life, – the struggle which, whatever its individual or topical expression, ever has its roots in the depth of human nature and social environment, and hence is, to that extent, universal. Such literature, such drama, is at once the reflex and the inspiration of mankind in its eternal seeking for things higher and better. Perhaps those who learn the great truths of the social travail in the school of life, do not need the message of the drama. But there is another class whose number is legion, for whom that message is indispensable. In countries where political oppression affects all classes, the best intellectual element have made common cause with the people, have become their teachers, comrades, and spokesmen. But in America political pressure has so far affected only the "common" people. It is they who are thrown into prison; they who are persecuted and mobbed, tarred and deported. Therefore another medium is needed to arouse the intellectuals of this country, to make them realize their relation to the people, to the social unrest permeating the atmosphere.

The medium which has the power to do that is the Modern Drama, because it mirrors every phase of life and embraces every strata of society, the Modern Drama, showing each and all caught in the throes of the tremendous changes going on, and forced either to become part of the process or be left behind.

Ibsen, Strindberg, Hauptmann, Tolstoy, Shaw, Galsworthy and the other dramatists contained in this volume represent the social iconoclasts of our time. They know that society has gone beyond the stage of patching up, and that man must throw off the dead weight of the past, with all its ghosts and spooks, if he is to go foot free to meet the future.

This is the social significance which differentiates modern dramatic art from art for art's sake. It is the dynamite which undermines superstition, shakes the social pillars, and prepares men and women for the reconstruction.

Part II

1920–1940

European art and culture experienced new and continuing debates at the close of World War I. The era witnessed such innovations as Bauhaus architecture, *Neue Sachlichkeit* (New Objectivity), Duchamp's ready-mades, and constructivism, the last strongly felt in Russian stage design. There were experiments in newsreel theatre, Négritude, and Joycean stream-of-consciousness. Newsreel theatre coincided with the economic decline of the 1930s. Theatre productions called attention to the worldwide depression. Négritude, which begin in the early 1930s, was initiated by three Francophone poets – Léopold Senghor, Aimé Césaire, and Léon Damas – in their quest to celebrate African cultural identity. Négritude is a humanist-existentialist system of thought created to explain racial differences. It developed descriptives of sensuousness that contrasted with Western-white abstract thought; it valued body over mind and feeling over reason. Négritude posited, in Senghor's words, "the man of nature," signifying "instinctive reason" in contrast to European rationalism.[1] Stream-of-consciousness describes a literary form of subjectivity. The interior monologue has its roots in Dostoyevsky and is associated in English with James Joyce, Virginia Woolf, and William Faulkner.

By the end of the 1920s cinema became talkies and jazz arose, both of these events powerfully influencing the arts. Classical music experimented with modernist atonality and modern dance expressed the abstract. Frank Lloyd Wright transformed architecture, emphasizing the organic relationship of structures and nature, while modern architecture streamlined skyscrapers into geometries of steel, glass, and concrete. Cities teemed with energy and despair; urban dwellers encountered technological advancements but also squalor. Modernism exuded the vectors of depression and utopia, decline and renewal, and ultimately an aesthetic of futility as fascism took hold. The ideas of Freud, Einstein, and Marx instilled theatrical productions with psychology, relativity, and social criticism.

During the period theatre theories expressed human liberation and reform. Marxism, which prevailed in the theatre arts, had numerous adherents and detractors. Especially during the economic hardship of the 1930s, Marxists incorporated agitprop. Others depicted social alienation. Some theorists less revolutionary but equally political turned to folk art, seeing theatre as a way of depicting ordinary experiences. John Dewey's ideas exemplified this turn to the folk. For Dewey, the "task" of art, he said in his important book *Art as Experience* (1934), is to "restore continuity between the refined and intensified forms of experience that are works of art and the everyday events, doings, and sufferings that are universally recognized to constitute experience."[2] The essays by African American theorists Du Bois, Locke, and Hurston represented in this collection reflect Dewey's influence.

Bertolt Brecht is a key constituent of this section. His concepts of theatre aimed at disrupting stage illusion and conventional realism. He encouraged actors to call attention to the fact that they are in the theatre. By using placards, songs, screen projections, addressing the audience, and juxtaposing several images onstage at once, Brecht instituted collage. He advocated a circus or vaudeville-like atmosphere onstage, one in which several different events or episodes might occur either simultaneously or follow each other in rapid succession. He did not abandon narrative realism entirely, but rather shifted its emphasis. Realist drama (especially the melodrama of his time) stressed mood, encouraging the audience to yield to an emotional state. Brecht sought to reverse the pandering to mood by creating a theatrical condition that fostered critical distance from the events onstage. "Gestus" was the term Brecht used as a counterpoint to the prevailing melodramatic ethos. Gestus prevented audiences from following the narrative slavishly and in an unreflecting way. By undermining the stage illusion, Brecht believed he was also unmasking the reality of capitalism. Reminding audiences that they are in the theatre would, he maintained, amplify an awareness of social conditions outside the theatre. He said: "Realism means: discovering the causal complexes of society/unmasking the prevailing view of things as the view of those who are in power/writing from the standpoint of the class which offers the broadest solutions for the pressing difficulties in which human society is caught up/emphasizing the element of development/making possible the concrete, and making possible abstraction from it." Brecht encouraged a new realism, one which allowed the artist "to employ his fantasy, his originality, his humour, his invention." He justifies his call for change with the following: "Methods become exhausted; stimuli no longer work. New problems appear and demand new methods. Reality changes; in order to represent it, modes of representation must also change."[3] The essays in this section (and for the remainder of the century) reflect Brecht's ongoing concern for forms of theatrical representation that might best illuminate social dynamics.

The two-decade period also experienced the beginning of theatre semiotics, a concept that began in the 1930s and would influence theatre theories. Semiotics, Manfred Pfister explains, "interprets the dramatic text as a complex verbal, visual, and acoustic supersign activating various sociocultural codes."[4] It is based on the concept of signifier and referent articulated by Ferdinand de Saussure in his *Course in General Linguistics* (1915) and Charles Sanders Peirce's triad of icon, index, and symbol. According to Peirce the three rubrics (icon, index, and symbol) indicate types of representation (*representamen*), signs that mean something to somebody in their respect or capacity. Signs stand in for an object being represented, marking a reference to an idea or meaning derived from the original object. Icon represents directly; for instance, a box of matches onstage stands for a box of matches. In theatrical terms, the object is represented as an icon by virtue of its similarity to the real thing, both in appearance and in utility. Indices can be either gestural or spatial signs that correspond to feelings, moods, or relationships. Symbolic representations are patterns of convention, fashion, or social context.

Theatre semioticians employed these indicators in decoding performance. In 1931 two important Czechoslovakian studies of theatre semiotics appeared: Otakar Zich's *Aesthetics of the Art of Drama* and Jan Mukařovský's "An Attempted Structural Analysis of the Phenomenon of the Actor." Zich maintained that theatre consists of multiple and interdependent systems, with the written text merely one of many components. The text was one facet of theatre's total dramatic presentation. Mukařovský believed art resides in the public's collective consciousness. Not only the theatre but also the social context of the performance emerge as signs constituting the total effect. Theatre is a structure subordinating all constituents – text, direction, theatre's architecture, sets, etc. – into a unified whole; this includes the importance of the audience as participatory creators of meaning. A production is not just the written text, or the actor's performance, but the totality of text, presentation, representation, and audience. Theatre semiotics will play an important role in the ensuing years of theatre analysis.

Notes

1   Quoted in J. Finn, *Voices of Négritude* (London: Quartet Books, 1988), 58.

2   J. Dewey, *Art as Experience* (New York: Perigee, 1934), 3.

3   B. Brecht, "Popularity and Realism," in *Aesthetics and Politics*, tr. R. Taylor (London: Verso, 1977), 82.

4   M. Pfister, *The Theory and Analysis of Drama*, tr. J. Halliday (Cambridge: Cambridge University Press, 1988), 2.

Chapter 15

Luigi Pirandello (1867–1936)

Luigi Pirandello was a prolific author of plays, novels, and short stories. His well-known dramas – *It Is So If You Think It So* (1917), *Henrico IV* (1922), and his most famous, *Six Characters in Search of an Author* (1921) – examine the elusiveness of identity, the uncertainty of reality, and the modernist challenge to theatrical form. He won the Nobel Prize for Literature in 1934.

Pirandello investigates fantasy, illusions, and the distinction between appearance and identity. He avoided realistic narrative; presenting a story for the sake of story alone, or even symbolism, held little interest for him. He was invested in form, in the way it unfolds, stressing how creativity manifests and operates. In his "Preface" to *Six Characters in Search of an Author,* Pirandello writes: "Creatures of my spirit, these six [characters] were already living a life which was their own and not mine any more, a life which it was not in my power any more to deny them." The emergence of the characters before their *raison d'être* inspired a drama in which the characters arrive in search of the story. "In these six," Pirandello says, "I have accepted the 'being' without the reason for being."[1] Pirandello's *mise en abyme*, the play within a play idea, would become his trademark in dramatic theory. In this essay Pirandello anticipates the theatre of the absurd, examining the discordant tone of comedy.

On Comedy (1920)

Comedy and its opposite lie in the same disposition of feeling, and they are inside the process which results from it. In its abnormality, this disposition is bitterly comical, the condition of a man who is always out of tune; of a man who is at the same time violin and bass; of a man

Luigi Pirandello, "On Comedy" (1920), from a course lecture given by Pirandello in Rome; the first edition appeared in 1908; the second, from which this essay derived, came out in 1920 in Florence. Reprinted here from *Tulane Drama Review* 10.3 (Spring 1966), 46–59, tr. Teresa Novel. © 1966 by Tulane Drama Review. Reprinted by permission of TDR/The Drama Review.

for whom no thought can come to mind unless suddenly another one, its opposite and contrary, intervenes; of a man for whom any one reason for saying yes is at once joined by two or three others compelling him to say no, so that yes and no keep him suspended and perplexed for all his life; of a man who cannot let himself go in a feeling without suddenly realizing something inside which disturbs him, disarranges him, makes him angry....

It is a special psychic phenomenon, and it is absolutely arbitrary to attribute to it any determining cause. It may be the result of a bitter experience with life and man – an experience that doesn't allow one the naïve feeling of putting on wings and flying like a lark chirping in the sunshine: it pulls at the tail when one is ready to fly. On the other hand, it leads to the thought that man's sadness is often caused by life's sadness, by evils so numerous that not everyone knows how to take them. It leads to the reflection that life, though it has not ordained a clear end for human reason, does not require me to wander in the dark, a reflection that is peculiar and illusive for each man, large or small. It is not important, though, since it is not, nor may it be, the real end which all eagerly try to find and which nobody finds – maybe because it does not exist. The important thing is to give importance to something, vain as it might be. It will be valued as much as something serious, and in the end neither will give satisfaction, because it is true, that the ardent thirst for knowledge will always last, the faculty of wishing will never be extinguished – though it cannot be said that man's happiness consists in his progress.

All the soul's fictions and the creations of feeling are subjects for humor; we will see reflection becoming a little devil which disassembles the machine of each image, of each fantasy created by feeling; it will take it apart to see how it is made; it will unwind its spring, and the whole machine will break convulsively. Perhaps humor will do this with the sympathetic indulgence about which those who see only a kind of good humor speak. But it ought not to be trusted....

Every feeling, thought, and idea which arises in the humorist splits itself into contraries. Each yes splits itself into a no, which assumes at the end the same value as the yes. Sometimes the humorist may pretend to take only one side; meanwhile, inside, the other feeling speaks out to him, and appears although he doesn't have the courage to reveal it. It speaks to him and starts by advancing now a faint excuse, an alternative, which cools off the warmth of the first feeling, and then a wise reflection which takes away seriousness and leads to laughter....

Let us start, then, from the construction that illusion offers each of us: the image that everyone has of himself through the work of our illusions. Do we see ourselves in our true reality, as we really are, and not as what we would like to be? Through a spontaneous interior artifice, the result of hidden tendencies or unconscious imitations, don't we believe ourselves to be, in good faith, different from what in substance we are? And we think, work, live according to this factitious but at the same time sincere interpretation of ourselves.

Now, yes, reflection can reveal to the comic and the satirical as well as the humorous writer this concept of illusions. The comic only laughs at it, being pleased to blow away this metaphor of himself created by a spontaneous illusion. The satirical writer will be upset by it. But not the humorist: through the ridiculous side of this perception he will see the serious and grievous side of it. He will analyze the illusion, but not with the intention of laughing at it. Instead of feeling disdain he will, rather, in his laughter, feel commiseration.

The comic and satirical writers know, through reflection, how much nourishment the spider of experience takes from social life to form the web of morality in any person. And they know how often what is called the moral sense remains trapped in this web. In the long run, what *are* arrangements of so-called social convenience? Calculated considerations, in which morality is almost always sacrificed. The humorist goes deeper, and he laughs without disdain on finding out how, with naïveté, with the best good faith, through the spontaneous work of fiction, we are led to interpret as real feeling, as real moral sense in itself, what is nothing but a feeling of *convenience*, that is, of mental calculation. He goes even further, and discovers that even the need to appear worse than what one really is may become conventional, if one is associated with a social group whose characteristic ideas and feelings are inferior to what one might desire for oneself....

Simplicity of soul contradicts the historical concept of the human soul. Its life is a changing equilibrium, a continuous awakening and slumbering of feelings, tendencies, and ideas. It is an incessant fluctuation between contradictory terms, an oscillation between opposite poles: hope and fear, truth and falsehood, beauty and ugliness, right and wrong, and so on. If suddenly in the dark image of the future a brilliant plan of action is drawn, or vaguely a flower of pleasure shines, soon there also appears, as a result of experience, the thought of the past, often dark and sad; or the feeling of the agitated present intervenes to bridle the happy fancy. This conflict of memories, hopes, prophecies, presentiments, perceptions, and ideals can be represented as a conflict of souls among themselves; all are fighting for the definite and full power of personality.

Let's look at an executive, who believes in himself and is a gentleman. The moral is predominant in him. But one day the instinctive soul, which is like a wild beast hidden deep in everybody, gives a kick to his moral soul and the gentleman steals. Now that poor man is the first one who after a while is shocked, cries, and desperately asks himself: "How, how could I have done this?"

But – yes, sir – he has stolen. What about another man? A well-to-do man, indeed a rich man, he has killed. The moral ideal constituted in his personality a soul which was in conflict with his instinctive soul; it constituted an acquired soul which fought with his hereditary soul, which, left free to itself for a while, succeeded in committing crime.

Life is a continuous flow which we continually try to stop, to fix in established and determinate forms outside and inside of ourselves because we are already fixed forms, forms that move among other immovable ones, which follow the flow of life until the point when they become rigid and their movement, slowed, stops. The forms in which we try to stop and fix this continuous flow are the concepts, the ideals, within which we want to keep coherent all the fictions we create, the condition and the status in which we try to establish ourselves. But inside ourselves, in what we call our soul, which is the life in us, the flow continues indistinctly, under the wire, past the limits that we set when we formed consciousness and built a personality. During certain stormy moments, inundated by the flow, all our fictitious forms collapse ignominiously. Even what doesn't flow under the wire and beyond the limits – what is revealed distinctly in us carefully channeled by our feelings, in the duties which we have imposed upon ourselves, in the habits that we have formed – in certain moments of flood overflows and topples everything.

There are some restless spirits, almost in a continuous state of confusion, who do not freeze into this or that personality. But even for the quiet ones, those who find rest in one form or other, fusion is always possible. The flow of life is in everybody.

Therefore, it can be, sometimes, a torture for everyone that, in contrast to the soul that moves and changes, our body should be fixed forever in unchanging features. Why are we made exactly so? We sometimes ask the mirror, "Why this face, this body?" We lift a hand; in the unconscious, the act remains suspended. It seems strange that we have done it. *We see ourselves alive.* In that suspended gesture we look like a statue – like that statue of an ancient orator, for example, whom we see in a niche, climbing the stairs of the Quirinal. He has a scroll in one hand and the other hand lifted in a severe gesture. How sad and surprised that ancient orator seems to be that he has remained there, through so many centuries, suspended in that gesture, while so many persons have climbed, are climbing, and will climb those stairs!

During certain moments of interior silence, during which our soul sheds all habitual functions, and our eyes become sharper and more penetrating, we see ourselves in life and we see life as an arid barrenness. Disconcerted, we feel as if taken by a strange impression, as if, in a flash, a different reality from the one we usually perceive were revealed to us, a living reality beyond human vision, beyond the forms of human vision. Very clearly, then, the facts of daily existence, almost suspended in the vacuum of our interior silence, appear to us meaningless and without scope. That different reality appears horrible to us in its stern and mysterious crudeness because all our fictitious relationships, both of feelings and images, have split and disintegrated in it. The interior vacuum expands, surpasses the limits of our body, becomes a vacuum around ourselves, a strange vacuum like a stop of time and life, as our interior silence plunges itself into the abyss of mystery. With a supreme effort we try, then, to recapture the normal sense of things, to tie ourselves again to the usual relationships, to reassemble ideas, to feel alive in the usual way. But we cannot trust this normal consciousness, these rearranged ideas, any more because we know now that they are deceptions which man needs to save himself from death or insanity. It was an instant, but its impressions will last for a long time, with a dizziness in contrast to the stability, quite specious, of things, ambitions, and miserable appearances. Life, which goes on as usual among these appearances, seems as if it isn't real any more. It seems a mechanical phantasmagoria. How can one give importance to it? How can one respect it?

Today we exist, tomorrow we will not. Which face have they given us to represent part of a living person? An ugly nose? How painful to walk around with an ugly nose for the rest of our life! It is good for us that after a while we don't pay any more attention to it. Then we don't know why other people laugh when they look at us. They are so silly! Let us console ourselves by looking at somebody else's lips, one who doesn't even realize it and doesn't have the courage to laugh at us. Masks, masks. They disappear in a breath, giving way to others. A poor lame man; who is he? Running toward death on crutches. Here life steps on somebody's foot, there it blinds somebody's eye – wooden leg, glass eye, and it goes on. Each one fixes his mask up as he can, the exterior mask.

Because inside there is another one, often contradicting the one outside. Nothing is true! True is: the sea, the mountain, a rock, a blade of grass. But man: always wearing a mask, unwillingly, without knowing it, without wanting it, always masked with that thing which he, in good faith, believes to be handsome, good, gracious, generous, unhappy, and so on.

This is funny, if we stop to think of it. Yes, because a dog, after the first ardor of life is gone, eats and sleeps; he lives as he can, as he ought to. He shuts his eyes, with patience, and lets time go by, cold if it is cold, warm if it is warm. If they kick him he takes it because it means that he deserved it. But what about man? Even when he is old he always has that *fever*; he is delirious and doesn't realize it. He cannot help posing, even in front of himself, in any way, and he imagines so many things which he needs to believe are true, which he needs to take seriously. [...]

From what we have said up to this point about the special activity of reflection in the humorist, the intimate process of humorous art clearly and necessarily develops.

Art, like all ideal or illusory constructions, has the tendency to fix life. It stops it at one moment or in various moments – a statue in a gesture, a landscape in a momentary unchangeable aspect. But what about the perpetual mobility of our successive aspects? What about the continuous fusion in which souls find themselves?

Art in general abstracts and concentrates; that is, it catches and represents only the essential and characteristic ideality of men and things. Now, it appears to the humorist that all this oversimplifies nature; attempting to make life too reasonable, or at least too coherent. It seems to him that art in general does not take into consideration what it ought to, art doesn't consider causes, the real causes which often move this poor human life to strange, absolutely unpredictable actions. For a humorist, causes in real life are never as logical and ordered as in our common works of art, in which all is, in effect, combined and organized to exist within the scope which the writer has in mind. Order? Coherence? What if we have within ourselves four souls fighting among themselves; the instinctive soul, the moral soul, the affective soul, and the social soul? Our consciousness adapts itself according to whichever dominates, and we hold as valid and sincere a false interpretation of our real interior being, which we ignore because it never makes itself manifest as a whole, but now in one way, now in another, according to the circumstances of life.

Yes, an epic or dramatic poet may represent a hero in whom opposite and unacceptable elements are shown fighting; but he will create a character out of these elements and make him coherent in his actions. Well, the humorist will do exactly the reverse: he will take the character apart. While the poet is careful to make him coherent in each action, the humorist is amused by representing him in his incongruities.

A humorist does recognize heroes; even better, he lets others represent them. He, for his own sake, knows what legend is and how it is formed; he knows what history is and how it is formed. They are all compositions more or less ideal; perhaps they are the more ideal if they show a greater pretense of reality. He amuses himself by taking them apart, and one cannot say that this is a pleasant amusement. [...]

And what about the unseen part of life? The abyss which exists in our soul? Don't we often feel a spark inside ourselves, strange thoughts like flashes of folly, illogical thoughts we dare not confide even to ourselves, arising from a soul different from the one we recognize in ourselves? For these, we have in humor research into the most intimate and minute particulars – which might look vulgar or trivial if compared with the ideal syntheses of most art – and work based on contrasts and contradictions in opposition to the coherence sought by the others. We have that disorganized, untied, and capricious element, all the digressions which are seen in a humorous work in opposition to the orderly plan, the *composition*, of most works of art. [...]

Let's conclude: humor is the feeling of polarity aroused by that special activity of reflection which doesn't hide itself, which doesn't become, as ordinarily in art, a form of feeling, but its contrary, following the feelings step by step, however, as the shadow follows the body. A common artist pays attention only to the body. A humorist pays attention to the body and its shadow, sometimes more to the shadow than the body. He sees all the tricks of the shadow; it now assumes length or width, as if to mimic the body, which, meanwhile, doesn't pay any attention to it.

Note

1   L. Pirandello, "Preface to *Six Characters in Search of an Author*," in *Naked Mask: Five Plays by Pirandello*, tr. E. Bentley (1925; New York: E. P. Dutton, 1952), 365–75.

Chapter 16

Stanislaw Witkiewicz (1885–1939)

Polish avant-gardist Stanislaw Ignacy ("Witkacy" – his self-proclaimed nickname) Witkiewicz was a playwright, novelist, painter, photographer, and philosopher. Unheralded in his lifetime, Witkiewicz received acclaim during the 1960s. He wrote over thirty plays. His intellectual colleagues included Jacques Copeau and Benjamin Crémieux, who anticipated the formation of the twentieth century's avant-garde. Witkiewicz's eclectic life militates against any easy classification. He moved from one art form to another, experimented with drugs, and created esoteric dramas that defied comprehension. His plays can be prolix, but his experimentalism is unequivocally important. He was part of a theatrical movement that rejected realism as merely a sidebar of journalism. Like Oscar Wilde, he considered his life a work of art. He walked the streets in harlequin costumes, made lists of friends and enemies, and lived a bohemian life. Witkiewicz, likewise avant-garde author Bruno Schultz, a fellow Pole, was concerned with the idea of form. Daniel Gerould writes that his concept of pure form "is a radical theory of non-realistic drama, according to which the performers and their words, gestures, and actions should serve as sounds, colors, and shapes in a total composition rather than as a depiction of the outside 'real' world. Witkacy wished to free drama from conventional psychology and storytelling and give it the formal possibilities of modern art and music."[1] His life and work laid the foundation for the Theatre of the Absurd and the Theatre of Happenings.

Stanislaw Witkiewicz, "On a New Type of Play" (1920), from *The Mother and Other Unsavory Plays*, ed. and tr. Daniel Gerould and C. S. Durer (New York: Applause, 1993), 234–9. © 1966, 1967, 1968, 1993 by Daniel C. Gerould and C. S. Durer.

On a New Type of Play (1920)

Theatre, like poetry, is a *composite art*, but it is made up of even more elements not intrinsic to it; therefore, it is much more difficult to imagine Pure Form on the stage, essentially independent, in its final result, of the content of human action.

Yet it is not perhaps entirely impossible.

Just as there was an epoch in painting and sculpture when Pure Form was identical with metaphysical content derived from religious concepts, so there was an epoch when performance on stage was identical with myth. Nowadays form alone is the only content of our painting and sculpture, and subject matter, whether concerned with the real world or the fantastic, is only the necessary pretext for the creation of form and has no direct connection with it, except as the "stimulus" for the whole artistic machine, driving it on to creative intensity. Similarly, we maintain that it is possible to write a play in which the performance itself, existing independently in its own right and not as a heightened picture of life, would be able to put the spectator in a position to experience metaphysical feeling, regardless of whether the *fond* of the play is realistic or fantastic, or whether it is a synthesis of both, combining each of their individual parts, provided of course that the play as a *whole* results from a sincere need on the part of the author *to create a theatrical idiom capable of expressing* metaphysical feelings within purely formal dimensions. What is essential is only that the meaning of the play should not necessarily be limited by its realistic or fantastic content, as far as the totality of the work is concerned, but simply that the realistic element should exist for the sake of the purely formal goals – that is, for the sake of the synthesis of all the elements of the theatre: sound, décor, movement on the stage, dialogue, in sum, performance through time, as an uninterrupted whole – so transformed, when viewed realistically, that the performance seems utter nonsense. The idea is to make it possible *to deform either life or the world of fantasy with complete freedom so as to create a whole whose meaning would be defined only by its purely scenic internal construction, and not by the demands of consistent psychology and action according to assumptions from real life. Such assumptions can only be applied as criteria to plays which are heightened reproductions of life.* Our contention is not that a play should necessarily be nonsensical, but only that from now on the drama should no longer be tied down to pre-existing patterns based solely on life's meaning or on fantastic assumptions. The actor, in his own right, should not exist; he should be the same kind of part within a whole as the colour red in a particular painting or the note C-sharp in a particular musical composition. The kind of play under discussion may well be characterized by absolute freedom in the handling of reality, but what is essential is that this freedom, like "nonsensicality" in painting, should be adequately justified and should become valid for the new dimension of thought and feeling into which such a play transports the spectator. At present we are not in a position to give an example of such a play, we are merely pointing out that it is possible if only foolish prejudices can be overcome. But let us assume that someone writes such a play: the public will have to get used to it, as well as to that deformed leg in the painting by Picasso. Although we can imagine a painting composed entirely of abstract forms, which will not evoke any associations with the objects of the external world unless such associations are self-induced, yet it is not even possible for us to imagine such a play, because pure performance in time is possible only in the world of sounds, and a theatre without characters who act, no matter how outrageously and improbably, is inconceivable; simply because theatre is a composite art, and does not have its own intrinsic, *homogeneous* elements, like the part arts: Painting and Music.

The theatre of today impresses us as being something hopelessly bottled up which can only be released by introducing what we have called *fantastic psychology and action*. The psychology of the characters and their actions should only be the pretext for a pure progression of events: therefore, what is essential is that the need for a psychology of the characters and their actions to be consistent and lifelike should not become a bugbear imposing its particular construction on the play. We have had enough wretched logic about characters and enough psychological "truth" – already it seems to be coming out of our ears. Who cares what goes on at 38 Wspólna Street, Apartment 10, or in the castle in the fairy tale, or in past times? In the theatre we want to be in an entirely new world in which the fantastic psychology of characters who are completely implausible in real life, not only in their positive actions but also *in their errors*, and who are perhaps completely unlike people in real life, produces events which by their bizarre interrelationships create a performance in time not limited by any logic except the logic of the form itself of that performance. What is required is that we accept as inevitable a particular movement of a character, a particular phrase having a realistic or only a formal meaning, a particular change of lighting or décor, a particular musical accompaniment, just as we accept as inevitable a particular part of a composition on a canvas or a sequence of chords in a musical work. We must also take into account the fact that such characters' thoughts and feelings are completely unfettered and that they react with complete freedom to any and all events, even though there is no justification for any of this. Still, these elements would have to be suggested on the same level of formal necessity as all the other elements of performance on the stage mentioned above. Of course, the public would have to be won over to this fantastic psychology, as with the square leg in the painting by Picasso. The public has already laughed at the deformed shapes on the canvases of contemporary masters; now they will also have to laugh at the thoughts and actions of characters on the stage, since for the time being these cannot be completely explained. We believe that this problem can be resolved in exactly the same way as it has been in contemporary painting and music: by understanding the essence of art in general and by growing accustomed to it. Just as those who have finally understood Pure Form in painting can no longer even look at other kinds of painting and cannot help understanding correctly paintings which they laughed at before as incomprehensible, so those who become used to the theatre we are proposing will not be able to stand any of the productions of today, whether realistic or heavily symbolic. As far as painting is concerned, we have tested this matter more than once on people who were apparently incapable of understanding Pure Form at the beginning, but who after receiving systematic "injections" over a certain period of time reached a remarkably high level of perfection in making truly expert judgments. There may be a certain amount of perversity in all this, but why should we be afraid of purely artistic perversity? Of course, perverseness in life is often a sad affair, but why should we apply judgments which are reasonable in real life to the realm of art, with which life has essentially so little in common. Artistic perversity (for example, unbalanced masses in pictorial composition, perversely tense movements or clashing colors in a painting) is only a means, and not an end; therefore, it cannot be immoral, because the goal which it enables us to attain – unity within diversity in Pure Form – cannot be subjected to the criteria of good and evil. It is somewhat different with the theatre, because its elements are beings who act; but we believe that in those new dimensions which we are discussing even the most monstrous situations will be no less moral than what is seen in the theatre today.

Of course, even assuming that a certain segment of the public interested in serious artistic experiences will come to demand plays written in the style described above, such plays would still have to result from *a genuine creative necessity* felt by an author writing for the stage. If such a work were only a kind of *schematic nonsense*, devised in cold blood, artificially, without real need, it would probably arouse nothing but laughter, like those paintings with a bizarre form of subject matter which are created by those who do not suffer from a real "insatiable pursuit of new forms," but who manufacture them for commercial reasons or *pour épater les bourgeois*. Just as the birth of a new form, pure and abstract, without a direct religious basis, took place only through deforming our vision of the external world, so the birth of Pure Form in the theatre is also possible only through deforming human psychology and action.

We can imagine such a play as having complete freedom with respect to absolutely everything from the point of view of real life, and yet being extraordinarily closely knit and highly wrought in the way the action is tied together. The task would be to fill several hours on the stage with a performance possessing its own internal, formal logic, independent of anything in "real life": An invented, not *created*, example of such a work can only make our theory appear ridiculous, and from a certain point of view, even absurd (for some, even infuriating or, to put it bluntly, *idiotic*), but let us try.

Three characters dressed in red come on stage and bow to no one in particular. One of them recites a poem (it should create a feeling of urgent necessity at this very moment). A kindly old man enters leading a cat on a string. So far everything has taken place against a background of a black screen. The screen draws apart, and an Italian landscape becomes visible. Organ music is heard. The old man talks with the other characters, and what they say should be in keeping with what has gone before. A glass falls off the table. All of them fall on their knees and weep. The old man changes from a kindly man into a ferocious "butcher" and murders a little girl who has just crawled in from the left. At this very moment a handsome young man runs in and thanks the old man for murdering the girl, at which point the characters in red sing and dance. Then the young man weeps over the body of the little girl and says very amusing things, whereupon the old man becomes once again kindly and good-natured and laughs to himself in a corner, uttering sublime and limpid phrases. The choice of costumes is completely open: period or fantastic – there may be music during some parts of the performance. In other words, an insane asylum? Or rather a madman's brain on the stage? Perhaps so, but we maintain that, *if the play is seriously written and appropriately produced*, this method *can create works of previously unsuspected beauty*; whether it be drama, tragedy, farce, or the grotesque, all in a uniform style and unlike anything which previously existed.

On leaving the theatre, the spectator ought to have the feeling that he has just awakened from some strange dream, in which even the most ordinary things had a strange, unfathomable charm, characteristic of dream reveries, and unlike anything else in the world. Nowadays the spectator leaves the theatre with a bad taste in his mouth, or he is shaken by the purely biological horror and sublimity of life, or he is furious that he has been fooled by a whole series of tricks. For all its variety, the contemporary theatre almost never gives us the other world, other not in the sense of being fantastic, but truly that other world which brings to us an understanding of purely formal beauty. Occasionally something like this happens in the plays of writers of previous ages, plays which after all have their significance and greatness that we certainly do not want to deny them with any fanatical fury. This element which we are discussing can be found in some of the plays of Shakespeare and [the poet Juliusz] Slowacki, for example, but never in its purest form, and therefore, despite their greatness, these plays do not create the desired effect.

The climax and the conclusion of the kind of play which we are proposing may be created in a complete abstraction from what might be called that debasing feeling of pure curiosity about real life, that tension in the pit of the stomach with which we watch a drama of real life, and which constitutes precisely the one and only appeal of plays today. Of course we would have to break this bad habit, so that in a world with which, on the realistic level, we have no contact, we could experience a metaphysical drama similar to the one which takes place among the notes of a symphony or sonata and only among them, so that the dénouement would not be an event of concern to us as part of real life, but only as something comprehensible *as the inevitable conclusion of the purely formal complications of sound patterns, decorative or psychological, free from the causality found in real life.*

The criticism of absolute freedom made against contemporary artists and their works by people who do not understand art can also be applied here. For example, why three characters, not five? Why dressed in red, not green? Of course, we cannot *prove* the necessity for that number and colour, but it should appear inevitable in so far as each element is a necessary part of the work of art once it has been created; while we are watching the play unfold, we ought not to be able to think of any other possible internal interrelationships. And we maintain that, if the work is to be created with complete artistic sincerity, it will have to compel the spectators to accept it as inevitable. It is certainly much more difficult with the theatre than with the other arts, because, as a certain expert on the theatre has asserted, the crowd as it watches and listens is an essential part of the performance itself, and moreover the play has to be a box-office success. But we believe that sooner or later the theatre must embark upon the "insatiable pursuit of new forms," which it has avoided until now, and it is to be hoped that extraordinary works, within the dimensions of Pure Form, still remain to be created, and that there will not simply be more "renaissance" and "purification" or repetition ad nauseam of the old repertoire which really has nothing at all to say to anybody.

We must unleash the slumbering Beast and see what it can do. And if it runs mad, there will always be time enough to shoot it before it is too late.

Note

1   D. Gerould, "Introduction," in *Witkiewicz: Seven Plays* (New York: M. E. Segal Theatre Center, 2004), xix.

Chapter 17

Adolphe Appia (1862–1928)

Adolphe Appia was a theatrical designer whose use of light, shape, and juxtaposition of objects revolutionized the stage. Influenced by Richard Wagner's *Gesamtkunstwerk* (total work of art), he published several books on design. In 1906 he began working with Emile Jaques-Dalcroze (1865–1950), the creator of eurhythmics. He met Edward Gordon Craig in 1914 and Jacques Copeau in 1915, both of whom influenced his work (and vice versa). In his books *La Mise-en-scène du drame Wagnérien* (1895) and *Die Musik und die Inscenierung* (1899), he outlined his design agenda. Although his design output was relatively small, his non-representational style served as a model for the modern theatre.

Appia emphasized the importance of temporal and spatial features in the theatre. The image onstage is made up of units, shapes, and forms in space; a play, however, is not a static entity but rather moves through time. It is a "living art" incorporating the processes of life over the course of time. The design therefore must not merely reflect the organic unity of the play's inner theme, but must also accommodate the movement of the play as its ideas unfold temporarily. According to Richard C. Beacham, Appia used light "to emphasize the living and expressive quality of the human body in rhythmic movement in space," and "to break down the barriers which, traditionally, had governed and restricted the spectators' perception of the work of art in performance."[1] Appia wanted to unify the theatre organically through art, music, dance, acting, design, and the text. His essay calls for this unity, setting the tone for the theory of design through the twentieth century.

Adolphe Appia, "Organic Unity" (1921), from *The Work of Living Art: A Theory of the Theatre*, tr. H. D. Albright (Coral Gables: University of Miami Press, 1960), 38–58. © 1960 by Walther R. Volbach.

Organic Unity (1921)

[...] The dramatic author never considers the stage, as it is offered to him, as definite technical material. He always agrees to accommodate himself to the stage; he even goes so far as to shape his artistic thought according to this sad model, and he does not suffer too much in the process, for this is apparently the only way he can achieve a minimum of harmony. His situation is like that of a painter who is allowed an insufficient number of colors and a canvas of fixed but ridiculous dimensions. It is really worse than that, for a painter of genius will always find the means to express himself, as long as the essential principles of his technique are not perverted; that is to say, as long as he can work with brush, colors, and plane surface. But our modern stage offers the dramatist nonsensical technical material; it is not a medium which can be truly dedicated to dramatic work – only through an inconceivable outrage are we obliged to accept it, or even to consider it, as such a medium. Unfortunately, the habit is formed. It is with this material that we evoke dramatic works and, what is worse, it is with this material that the dramatist conceives these works, fearing lest he be not "theatrical." The term is hallowed: it is never our stage that is accused of not being "theatrical," but always the dramatist himself. That is why he is an artist without a name: he does not dominate a technique; the technique of the stage dominates him. An artist must be free; the dramatist is enslaved. Today he is not – and cannot be – an artist. [...]

Slavery, like all other habits, can become second nature; it has become that for the dramatist and for his public. This is a question of conversion, then, in the truest sense of the word. A function creates its organ. That in psychology and zoology this affirmation is only approximative, matters little here, for it is evident that in art it is profoundly correct. In our day, the function of the dramatist has not created its organ; that is, a work of dramatic art is not presented to our eyes *organically*, but through an artificial, exterior mechanism which does not belong to the dramatic organism. Hence, we must probably seek within the function itself the weak point which has placed the dramatist in dependence and which helps to keep him there.

[...] Should not the dramatist himself have suggested the principles of our stage decoration from the very beginning? And is he not now in danger of further postponing this initiating impulse through sheer inertia and blundering? The indiscriminate use of painting is so characteristic of all our staging that painted canvases and stage decoration are almost synonymous to us. Now, all artists know that the aim of these canvases is not to present an expressive combination of colors and forms, but to "indicate" [...] a group of details and objects. We must suppose that a real need for showing us these objects accounts for the author's seeking help from the painter. The painter, of course, responds eagerly!

If we put ourselves in the place of the author at the moment he chooses his subject, it is evident that this is the precise moment in which his technical liberty or dependence is decided. If the author decides that he can free himself from the means imposed by the stage, he is immediately confronted by the necessity of determining *the essential nature of a subject intended for representation*. From his point of view, a subject is concerned with characters in conflict with one another; from this conflict arise particular circumstances that make the characters react; out of their way of reacting, dramatic interest is born.

To a dramatic author, this is all; dramatic art, consisting entirely of such reactions, is apparently capable of infinite variety. But he soon perceives that such is not the case; that the reactions do not vary infinitely; on the contrary, they are repeated without change; that in this sense human nature is limited; and that each of our passions has a name. As a result, he seeks to vary the interest through diversity in character; and there begin his difficulties – difficulties of dimension. To present a character, one needs time on the stage, space on paper; thus the choice is limited. The novel and the psychological study have an indefinite space – on paper, of course – at their command; a play has but three or four hours.[2]

We must seek elsewhere for variety, then; here the influence of the setting comes into play. The setting is always geographical and historical, dependent on a climate and a culture which are indicated visually by a group of specific objects. Unless the audience can see these objects, the text of the play must convey a quantity of information that will completely paralyze the action. As a result we are forced to represent them in the stage decoration.

There is more to the problem of stage decoration than the mere question of whether or not a setting can be executed. In the theatre we are not at the cinema; the laws that rule the stage are, above all, technical ones. To wish to represent nearly everything on the stage, and to invoke on that account the so-called liberty of the artist, is deliberately to lead dramatic art beyond its own limits and consequently beyond the domain of art. As long as an author remains content to show characters and their reactions, he finds himself relatively independent as far as his work is concerned. But from the moment when he uses the influence of the setting to vary the motifs, he meets with problems of staging and must reckon with them. Under present conditions his only concern is the possibility of representing things on the stage. He will reject all projects that are too difficult to represent; in general, he will confine his choice to places and things that he knows are easy to realize in production and are suitable for maintaining the illusion which is so dear to him. Like the ostrich, he chooses to ignore danger. But how can he help perceiving that decorative technique is regulated by laws other than those of possibility? If he has money to throw out of the window, an author can obtain anything on the stage. The Romans caused a river to pass through the Circus, in the midst of vegetation like that of a virgin forest. The Duke of Meiningen bought museums, apartments, and palaces in order to realize two or three scenes. The results in both cases were artistically regrettable.

No; stage decoration is regulated by the presence of the living body. This body is the final authority concerning the possibility of realization; everything that is incongruous or inconsistent in relation to its presence is "impossible" and suppresses the play.

In the choice of his subject, the author must question, not the director-designer but the actor. Such a generalization, of course, is not meant to suggest that he seek his advice from this actor or that. It is the idea of the living actor – plastic and mobile – that must be his guide. For example, he must ask himself whether a certain setting is in keeping with the presence of the actor, and not merely whether its realization is "possible." From a technical point of view, his choice is concerned with the importance he wishes to – or must – give to the influence of the setting. From both points of view, he must choose with a full knowledge of conditions, and consequently must know perfectly the normal scenic hierarchy and its results.

His technique as an artist determines his choice. The painter is not irked by the fact that plastic relief is denied him; his technique simply does not permit such a possibility.

So must it be for the dramatic author. He need not be distressed by the fact that he cannot place his character in a cathedral, but rather by the fact that he cannot free the character from conditions harmful to its full realization on the stage. The novelist and the epic poet can evoke their heroes by means of description; their work is a story that is told, and the action is placed in the story, since it is not living. But the dramatic author is not merely telling a story; his living action is free, stripped of all drapery. Every indication of specific place tends to bring it nearer to the novel or the epic, and to remove it further from dramatic art. The more "indication" of place is necessary to the action – that is, to make the characters, the events, and the reactions plausible – the more the action will be estranged from *living* art. *The reason is purely and simply a technical one, and no one can change it in any way.*

The more a painter approaches sculpture, the less he will be a painter; the more a sculptor seems for ambience, the less he will be a sculptor. The less the dramatic author makes his characters dependent on the "indications" in the setting, the more he will be a dramatist. For when anyone says "Dramatist," he says "Stage-director" in the same breath; it is a sacrilege to specialize the two activities. We may set up as a rule, then, that if the dramatist does not insist on controlling both, he will be incapable of controlling either – since it is from their mutual correlation that *living art* must be born. Only in very rare exceptions do we yet have this supreme art or its artist. By misplacing the centre of gravity, so to speak, we divide our art; in one respect our dramatic art rests on the author, in another on the director-designer. Sometimes it relies more on the one, sometimes on the other; it should rest simply and clearly on the dramatist himself.

The technical synthesis of the elements of representation finds its source in the initial idea of dramatic art. It depends on the attitude of the author. This attitude frees him; without it, he is not an artist. [...]

The synthesis of the elements of production cannot be determined by and for itself. If we are familiar with these elements, if we know how to measure their power of expression and their respective limits, if we are able to place them in proper relation – then we possess the means to make their use depend exclusively on the author. That is why the idea of a subject now appears of *technical* importance. The unity of the elements will no longer be regulated in advance and imposed upon the dramatist, as it is by the stage of today; the whole responsibility will be his from the beginning. Consequently, he is obliged to be an artist.

However, although the elements he uses are henceforth at his disposal, yet they are not completely in his hands; to realize his artistic dreams, he doubtless needs collaborators. Will this be a new form of slavery? Barely promoted to the rank of an artist – through the complete possession of his own technique – is he going to fall back again into guardianship and lose all the advantages of his many sacrifices? What will be the character of such collaboration? Will this collaboration be merely assistance, or will it penetrate deeper – even to the choice of a subject? Let us put aside for the moment the material services that the electrician, the carpenter and other artisans will be prepared to offer; they go on by themselves, hierarchically concerned with the body of the actor which regulates them. Let us consider for the present only those elements which dictate to the life and the movement of that body. Then, afterwards, we shall turn to the body itself, that marvelous intermediary, dominated by the dramatist, but in its turn dominating space.

Our theatrical habits make it very difficult to imagine what freedom in staging could mean and to visualize a new handling of the elements of production. We cannot conceive of a theatre, it seems, except in terms of the present-day stage – a limited space filled with cut-out paintings, in the midst of which actors pace up and down, separated from us by a clear-cut line of demarcation. Further, the presence of plays and musical scores in our libraries is apparently enough to convince us that a work of dramatic art can exist without actual presentation. Reading the play, or playing over the score on the piano, we are convinced that they are living and that we possess them. Otherwise, how can we account for the renown of a Racine or a Wagner? Is it not evident that their work is on these sheets of paper? What does it matter whether we produce their work or not, since these texts in themselves can remain immortal? There we are! The dramatic author chooses a form of art that is visual, that is meant for our eyes; yet when he writes it down on paper its fame and glory are assured. [...]

The theatre has become intellectualized. Today the body is nothing but the bearer and representative of a literary text; its gestures and movements are not *regulated* by the text but simply *inspired* by it. The actor interprets, according to his own liking, what the author has written; hence his personal importance on the stage is exclusively interpretative rather than technical, with the result that his role is developed according to one conception, while the settings are being painted according to another. Their union is therefore arbitrary and almost accidental. This procedure is repeated for each new play, and the principle remains the same, whatever care we take with the production in other respects.

It is characteristic of theatre reform that all serious effort is instinctively directed toward the *mise en scène*. As for the text of the play, fluctuations of taste result in classicism, romanticism, realism, etc., all of which encroach on each other, combine with each other, approve or disapprove of each other, and make a desperate appeal to the designer-technician without being heard. But in spite of so many varieties of text, we remain in the same place. The detailed scenic indications which the author sometimes adds to the text of his play always have a childish effect, like the little boy who is determined to enter his little countryside of sand and twigs. The presence of the actor overwhelms the artificial construction; the only contact between the two is grotesque since it accentuates the impotence of the author's effort.

But if one courageously directs one's efforts to the *mise en scène* itself, one is surprised to find that one is attacking the *whole dramatic problem*. To be precise: for what existing plays do we wish to reform the stage? What shall be our standard of values? When we consider the stage as something to be stared at, so to speak, as something quite distinct from the audience, it eludes us. What is the stage as a thing apart? Obviously nothing. It is precisely because of this desire to make the stage something in itself that we have strayed so far from Art. At the very start, then, we must clear the table; we must effect in our imagination this apparently difficult conversion, which consists of no longer looking upon our theatres, our stages, our halls, as necessarily existing for spectators. We must completely free the dramatic idea from any such apparently changeless law.

I spoke of halls for spectators. But dramatic art does not exist to present the human being for *others*. The human being is independent of the passive spectator; he is, or ought to be, *living*. And Life is concerned with the *living*. Our first move, then, will be to place ourselves imaginatively in a boundless space, with no witness but ourselves. [...] To set definite proportions in this space, we must walk, then stop, then walk once more, only to stop again. These stopping places will create a sort of rhythm, which will be echoed in us and which will awaken there a need to possess Space. But Space is boundless; the only guide-mark is ourselves. Hence we are – and should be – its centre. Will its measure, then, exist in us? Shall we be the creators of Space? For whom? We are alone. Consequently it will be for ourselves alone that we will create space – that is to say, proportions to be measured by the human body in boundless space.

Soon the hidden rhythm, of which up to now we were unaware, is revealed. From whence does it spring? We know it is there: we even react to it. Under what compulsion? Our inner life grows and develops; it prescribes this gesture rather than another, this deliberate step rather than that uncertain pose. And our eyes are opened at last: they see the step and the gesture that grew out of an inner feeling: they *consider* it. The hand is advanced this far, the foot is placed there: these are the two portions of Space which they have measured. But have they measured these portions consciously and deliberately? No. Then, why just that far and no farther or no nearer? They have been led.

It is not merely mechanically that we possess Space and are its centre: it is because we are living. Space is our life; our life creates Space; our body expresses it. To arrive at that supreme conviction, we have had to walk and to gesticulate, to bend and to straighten up, to lie down and to rise again. In order to move from one point to another, we exerted an effort – however small – corresponding to the beatings of our heart. Those heart beats proportioned our gestures. In Space? No. In Time. In order to proportion Space, our body needs Time! The time duration of our movements, consequently, has determined their extent in space. Our life creates space and time, one through the other. Our living body is the expression of Space during Time, and of Time in Space. Empty and boundless Space – wherein we are placed at the start so that we may effect this essential transformation – no longer exists. We alone exist.

In dramatic art, too, we alone exist. There is no auditorium, no stage, without us and beyond us. There is no spectator, no play, without us, without us alone. We *are* the play and the stage, because it is our living body that creates them. Dramatic art is a spontaneous creation of the body; our body is the dramatic author.

The work of dramatic art is the only one that is truly identified with its author. It is the only art whose existence is certain *without spectators*. Poetry must be read; painting and sculpture, contemplated; architecture, surveyed; music, heard. A work of dramatic art is lived: it is the dramatic author who lives it. A spectator comes to be moved or convinced; therein is the limit of his role.

The work lives for itself – without the spectator. The author expresses it, possesses it, and contemplates it at the same time. A spectator's eyes and ears will never obtain anything but its reflection and echo. The framework of the stage is but a keyhole through which we overhear bits of life never intended for us. [...]

Notes

1 R. C. Beacham, "Appia, Jaques-Dalcroze, and Hellerau, Part Two: 'Poetry in Motion,'" *New Theatre Quarterly* 1.3 (August 1985), 251.

2 To put out on the stage a character whose description and development need a volume of 300 pages is one of the banal monstrosities of our theatre.

Chapter 18

Georg Kaiser (1878–1945)

Georg Kaiser was a playwright best known for his contribution to German Expressionism. Along with Ernst Toller (1893–1939), Kaiser was the most famous Expressionist playwright, though others, including Reinhardt Sorge and Walter Hasenclever, also contributed to the genre. Kaiser wrote over sixty plays, among the most well known being *From Morn till Midnight* (1917), *Gas I* (1918), and *Gas II* (1920).

Expressionism arose globally. However, its firmest roots took hold in Germany. The term was coined by the Czech historian Antonin Matějček, but German Expressionism received its intellectual birth with Wilhelm Worringer's *Abstraktion und Einfühlung* (*Abstraction and Empathy*, 1908) and the artists Kandinsky, Rouault, Beckmann, and Kokoschka. Kandinsky's painting *Der blaue Reiter* (*The Blue Rider*, which also led to a one-issue journal) and Kirchner's *Brücke* (*Bridge*, which inspired the Expressionist movement in Dresden) were precursors. The French version flourished in Paris through "Les fauves" (wild beasts), and in film Expressionism led to *The Cabinet of Dr. Caligari* (1919). By the end of World War I, the artistic movement gave way to Dada.

In theatre, however, Expressionism endured, largely due to the influence of August Strindberg. It spread throughout Europe and America. The defining features of Expressionism were: the stations of the Cross, various places onstage that borrowed from medieval ideas of performing areas (pageant wagons); the actor's *schrei* (cry), an expression of disdain for bourgeois complacency; the emphasis on an anguished soul amidst pretentious piety; and an expression of outrage against the carnage of war. Many of the plays of the Expressionist movement, Richard Murphy observes, responded "to the historical disorder of the times, taking up pronounced melodramatic gestures

Georg Kaiser, "Man in the Tunnel, or: The Poet and the Play" (1923), tr. Joel Agee, reproduced from *Essays on German Theater*, ed. Margaret Herzfeld-Sander (New York: Continuum, 1985), 168–70. Originally from Georg Kaiser, *Werke*, Vol. 4 (Propyläen Verlag, 1971), translated by permission of Verlag Ullstein. © 1985 by the Continuum Publishing Company. Reprinted by permission of The Continuum International Publishing Group.

and attitudes which express analogous longings for a new *revolutionary* order," that nevertheless couched their "idealism in such tentative and 'unrealistic' terms that its full force can only be felt as a general expression of the repressed 'ethical and psychic forces' in society."[1] Expressionist playwrights looked to Strindberg, Frank Wedekind, and Georg Büchner for inspiration. The purpose of Expressionist theatre was to avoid objective reality and depict subjective responses to events. Unlike symbolism, which sought subdued feelings and contemplation, Expressionism's aim was to heighten emotions through the breakdown of language. The fragmented expressions employed a series of exclamations and images that forced audiences to interpret emotionally owing to the lack of logical narrative structure. The subjective world is represented onstage through the vision of one character. This vision is distorted, exaggerated, and jarring; Expressionists used violent applications of theatricality to convey the horrors of the world. Expressionist directors often employed shadows and different applications of light. The director Leopold Jessner (1878–1945), for instance, used extreme levels and steps onstage (what came to be called *Jessnertreppen*) to emphasize physical distortion. He also implemented a rhetorical style of acting that highlighted exaggerated facial expression and gesture in an effort to project the interiority of the character's condition. Although occasionally shrill, the rebelliousness of Expressionism inspired many American dramatists from Arthur Miller to Adrienne Kennedy.

Man in the Tunnel, or: The Poet and the Play (1923)

To write a play is to think a thought through to the end. (One who has exhausted his thinking turns back to his past plays and assists in their theatrical executions: genesis of the exalted master.) An idea without a character remains nonsense: Plato writes the most exciting scenes and in doing so develops his philosophical work. Other philosophical tomes depart further and further from their title with each page (and even the title is nebulous).

One should subject himself – presuming he wants to reflect at all – to the enormous labor of formulating his drama. Whatever can't be presented to my neighbor with a sparse dialogue will float off into stupidity. Man speaks in order to think – thinks in order to speak. Since ancient times the best mouths have preached their way into the *genus humanum* – just listen! You can't keep caning bottoms if what you want is to bring in some light at the top. The human race has undertaken tremendous things in its dramatic thinkers; if they make life hard for you today – the result will triumph in your grandchildren: the individual gives form to his thoughts and takes thought in the making of forms.

Of what value is the play to the poet in the end? He is done with it. The long preoccupation with an idea is already an excessive torment. Ten new ones have shot up since then. But the playwright heroically keeps a grip on the rope until he has groped his way through to the end. That brings his thought to a conclusion. Immediately he sets forth into another area – one must make use of the brief span given hereabouts to brain and blood. (And this gives rise to the image of the dramatist's backside: the playwright who fondly returns to his works, talking about them, pointing at them with lantern-poles, visualizing himself in a highly visible loge before the performance, stuffing his mattress with old laurels that rustle with fame at night under his snoring broadside.)

Once we have seen the multiplicity of unconceived thoughts, there is very little time left for love. (That sounds gloomy – but in a moment I'll pull the loveliest summer sun into my sky.) But no head has an unendurable quantum of thoughtfulness implanted in it. The totality of man is excellently balanced. However, this supreme understanding is required: To stop when you come to the end. Whoever hangs on will lose his life. To live – that's what it's about. That is the meaning of existence. Its exhausting experience. All roads lead there – but all the roads must be trodden. *One* path leads through the head. To travel it, the most severe training is needed: knowing how to think. The shaping of a play is the means – never the goal. (Whoever mistakes the two – see above: exalted master. I am not naming negative examples here; I don't want to fill the following pages with an index of the history of literature – instead, the positive one of Rimbaud, who as a merchant in Egypt laughed at his Parisian poet's fame.) It is villainous to define an excellent human being by *one* of his abilities – and he who accepts this mutilation is ridiculous. It is almost a moral question: remaining a poet.

The goal of existence is: the record. Setting a record in all areas. Man at the peak of his achievements typifies the time that begins tomorrow and never ends. The Hindu model of universal activity through inactivity is being surpassed in our climes: here the universally active man vibrates at a rate that makes his movement visible.

Drama is a passageway – but the springboard directly into completion. After this schooling, a person is excellently equipped to find his place in the world. He hates stupidity – but he no longer exploits it. (Only the idiot wants a bargaining advantage – in commerce and in the life of the mind. He ends up being frequently cheated – viz.: literary history.)

A creator's duty is: to turn away from each of his works and go into the desert; if he reappears, he must bring a great deal with him – but building a villa with garage in the shadow of his sycamores: that won't do. That's pushing shamelessness a bit too far, and entering into infamous competition with the underpaid prostitutes.

Everything is a passageway: but to rest and remain in passageways (tunnels) – good luck to the one who's hardnosed enough to do it and woe to him!

Note

1 R. Murphy, *Theorizing the Avant-Garde: Modernism, Expressionism, and the Problem of Post-modernity* (Cambridge: Cambridge University Press, 1998), 164–5.

Chapter 19

Alain Locke (1886–1954)

Alain Leroy Locke was a philosopher, literary critic, and professor at Howard University in Washington, DC. He was the central figure of the Harlem Renaissance Movement and called attention to its contributions through editing the book *The New Negro*. A Rhodes Scholar and graduate of Harvard (undergraduate and PhD), he sought to elevate African American literary and cultural visibility by sponsoring new ideas in literature, art, and drama. Locke advocated ''folk art'' in drama that had its roots in Romanticism and Johann Gottfried Herder's concept of *Das Volk*. As I have noted elsewhere, folk drama for Locke, ''being the dramatic enactment of text, music, dance, and shared myth, had the character of collective religious performance, binding the community together as participants in a ritual rather than as mere spectators at a theatre.''[1] He looked to the Irish Renaissance, primarily Yeats, Synge, O'Casey, and Ireland's Abbey Theatre, as a paradigm for African American theatre. The American stage had been saturated by minstrelsy, a popular nineteenth-century form that satirized blacks with blackface make-up and exaggerated gestures. Locke, like his contemporaries, set out to overturn minstrelsy's stranglehold on the imagination. He believed that drama can change perceptions, but he rejected the idea of didactic and propagandistic drama. His intellectual rival, W. E. B. Du Bois (see Chapter 20), thought otherwise, maintaining that all art should illustrate politics overtly. Locke took a subtler route; he wanted drama to represent common life. He was invested in realism, mimesis, and language that reflected everyday speech. The two-part essay presented here defines his agenda and sets the tone of African American theatre throughout the century.

Excerpts from Alain Locke, "The Negro and the American Stage," *Theatre Arts Monthly* 10.2 (February 1926), 112–20, and "The Drama of Negro Life," *Theatre Arts Monthly* 10.10 (October 1926), 701–6.

The Negro and the American Stage (1926)

In the appraisal of the possible contribution of the Negro to the American theatre, there are those who find the greatest promise in the rising drama of Negro life. And there are others who see possibilities of a deeper, though subtler influence upon what is after all more vital, the technical aspects of the arts of the theatre. Certainly the Negro influence upon American drama has been negligible. Whereas even under the handicaps of second hand exploitation and restriction to the popular amusement stage, the Negro actor has considerably influenced our stage and its arts. One would do well to imagine what might happen if the art of the Negro actor should really become artistically lifted and liberated. Transpose the possible resources of Negro song and dance and pantomime to the serious stage, envisage an American drama under the galvanizing stimulus of a rich transfusion of essential folk-arts and you may anticipate what I mean. A race of actors can revolutionize the drama quite as definitely and perhaps more vitally than a coterie of dramatists. The roots of drama are after all action and emotion, and our modern drama, for all its frantic experimentation, is an essentially anemic drama, a something of gestures and symbols and ideas and not overflowing with the vital stuff of which drama was originally made and to which it returns for its rejuvenation cycle after cycle.

Primarily the Negro brings to the drama the gift of a temperament, not the gift of a tradition. Time out of mind he has been rated as a "natural born actor" without any appreciation of what that statement, if true, really means. Often it was intended as a disparaging estimate of the Negro's limitations, a recognition of his restriction to the interpretative as distinguished from the creative aspect of drama, a confinement, in terms of a second order of talent, to the status of the mimic and the clown. But a comprehending mind knows that the very life of drama is in dramatic instinct and emotion, that drama begins and ends in mimicry, and that its creative force is in the last analysis the interpretative passion. Welcome then as is the emergence of the Negro playwright and the drama of Negro life, the promise of the most vital contribution of our race to the theatre lies, in my opinion, in the deep and unemancipated resources of the Negro actor, and the folk arts of which he is as yet only a blind and hampered exponent. Dramatic spontaneity, the free use of the body and the voice as direct instruments of feeling, a control of body plastique that opens up the narrow diaphragm of fashionable acting and the conventional mannerisms of the stage – these are indisputably strong points of Negro acting. Many a Negro vaudevillian has greater store of them than finished masters of the polite theatre. And especially in the dawn of the "synthetic theatre" with the singing, dancing actor and the plastic stage, the versatile gifts of the Negro actor seem peculiarly promising and significant.

Unfortunately it is the richest vein of Negro dramatic talent which is under the heaviest artistic impediments and pressure. The art of the Negro actor has had to struggle up out of the shambles of minstrelsy and make slow headway against very fixed limitations of popular taste. Farce, buffoonery and pathos have until recently almost completely overlaid the folk comedy and folk tragedy of a dramatically endowed and circumstanced people. These gifts must be liberated. I do not narrowly think of this development merely as the extension of the freedom of the American stage to the Negro actor, although this must naturally come as a condition of it, but as a contribution to the technical idioms and resources of the entire theatre. [...]

Without invoking analogies, we can see in this technical and emotional endowment great resources for the theatre. In terms of the prevalent trend for the serious development of race drama, we may expect these resources to be concentrated and claimed as the working capital of the Negro Theatre. They are. But just as definitely, too, are they the general property and assets of the American Theatre at large, if once the barriers are broken through. These barriers are slowly breaking down both on the legitimate stage and in the popular drama, but the great handicap, as Carl van Vechten so keenly points out in his *Prescription for the Negro Theatre*, is blind imitation and stagnant conventionalism. Negro dramatic art must not only be liberated from the handicaps of external disparagement, but from its self imposed limitations. It must more and more have the courage to be original, to break with established dramatic convention of all sorts. It must have the courage to develop its own idiom, to pour itself into new moulds; in short, to be experimental. From what quarter this impetus will come we cannot quite predict; it may come from the Negro theatre or from some sudden adoption of the American stage, from the art-theatre or the commercial theatre, from some home source, or first, as so many things seem to have come, from the more liberal patronage and recognition of the European stage. But this much is certain – the material awaits a great exploiting genius.

One can scarcely think of a complete development of Negro dramatic art without some significant artistic re-expression of African life, and the tradition associated with it. It may seem a far cry from the conditions and moods of modern New York and Chicago and the Negro's rapid and feverish assimilation of all things American. But art establishes its contacts in strange ways. The emotional elements of Negro art are choked by the conventions of the contemporary stage; they call for freer, more plastic material. They have no mysterious affinity with African themes or scenes, but they have for any life that is more primitive and poetic in substance. So, if, as seems already apparent, the sophisticated race sense of the Negro should lead back over the trail of the group tradition to an interest in things African, the natural affinities of the material and the art will complete the circuit and they will most electrically combine. Especially with its inherent color and emotionalism, its freedom from body-hampering dress, its odd and tragic and mysterious overtones, African life and themes, apart from any sentimental attachment, offer a wonderfully new field and province for dramatic treatment. Here both the Negro actor and dramatist can move freely in a world of elemental beauty, with all the decorative elements that a poetic emotional temperament could wish. No recent playgoer with the spell of Brutus Jones in the forest underbrush still upon his imagination will need much persuasion about this.[2]

More and more the art of the Negro actor will seek its materials in the rich native soil of Negro life, and not in the threadbare tradition of the Caucasian stage. In the discipline of art playing upon his own material, the Negro has much to gain. Art must serve Negro life as well as Negro talent serve art. And no art is more capable of this service than drama. Indeed the surest sign of a folk renascence seems to be a dramatic flowering. Somehow the release of such self-expression always accompanies or heralds cultural and social maturity. I feel that soon this aspect of the race genius may come to its classic age of expression. Obviously, though, it has not yet come. For our dramatic expression is still too restricted, self-conscious and imitative.

When our serious drama shall become as naïve and spontaneous as our drama of fun and laughter, and that in turn genuinely representative of the folk spirit which it is now forced to travesty, a point of classic development will have been reached. It is fascinating to speculate upon what riotously new and startling may come from this. Dramatic maturings are notably sudden. Usually from the popular sub-soil something shoots up to a rapid artistic flowering. Of course, this does not have to recur with the American Negro. But a peasant folk art pouring out from under a generation-long repression is the likeliest soil known for a dramatic renascence. And the supporters and exponents of Negro drama do not expect their folk temperament to prove the barren exception.

The Drama of Negro Life (1926)

Despite the fact that Negro life is somehow felt to be particularly rich in dramatic values, both as folk experience and as a folk temperament, its actual yield, so far as worth-while drama goes, has been very inconsiderable. There are many reasons behind this paradox; foremost of course the fact that drama is the child of social prosperity and of a degree at least of cultural maturity. Negro life has only recently come to the verge of cultural self-expression, and has scarcely reached such a ripening point. Further than this, the quite melodramatic intensity of the Negro's group experience has defeated its contemporaneous dramatization; when life itself moves dramatically, the vitality of drama is often sapped. But there have been special reasons. Historical controversy and lowering social issues have clouded out the dramatic colors of Negro life into the dull mass contrasts of the Negro problem. Until lately not even good problem drama has been possible, for sentiment has been too partisan for fair dramatic balancing of forces and too serious for either aesthetic interest or artistic detachment. So although intrinsically rich in dramatic episode and substance, Negro life has produced for our stage only a few morally hectic melodramas along with innumerable instances of broad farce and low comedy. Propaganda, pro-Negro as well as anti-Negro, has scotched the dramatic potentialities of the subject. Especially with the few Negro playwrights has the propaganda motive worked havoc. In addition to the handicap of being out of actual touch with the theatre, they have had the dramatic motive deflected at its source. Race drama has appeared to them a matter of race vindication, and pathetically they have pushed forward their moralistic allegories or melodramatic protests as dramatic correctives and antidotes for race prejudice. [...]

The development of Negro drama at present owes more to the lure of the general exotic appeal of its material than to the special program of a racial drama. But the motives of race drama are already matured, and just as inevitably as the Irish, Russian and Yiddish drama evolved from the cultural programs of their respective movements, so must the Negro drama emerge from the racial stir and movement of contemporary Negro life. [...]

But the path of this newly awakened impulse is by no means as clear as its goal. Two quite contrary directions compete for the artist's choice. On the one hand is the more obvious drama of social situation, focusing on the clash of the race life with its opposing background; on the other the apparently less dramatic material of the folk life and behind it the faint panorama of an alluring race history and race tradition. The creative impulse is for the moment caught in this dilemma of choice between the drama of discussion and social analysis and the drama of expression and artistic interpretation. But despite the present lure of the problem play, it ought to be apparent that the real future of Negro drama lies with the development of the folk play. Negro drama must grow in its own soil and cultivate its own intrinsic elements; only in this way can it become truly organic, and cease being a rootless derivative.

Of course the possibilities of Negro problem drama are great and immediately appealing. The scheme of color is undoubtedly one of the dominant patterns of society and the entanglement of its skeins in American life one of its most dramatic features. For a long while strong social conventions prevented frank and penetrating analysis, but now that the genius of O'Neill has broken through what has been aptly called "the last taboo," the field stands open. But for the Negro it is futile to expect fine problem drama as an initial stage before the natural development in due course of the capacity for self-criticism. The Negro dramatist's advantage of psychological intimacy is for the present more than offset by the disadvantage of the temptation to counter partisan and propagandist attitudes. The white dramatist can achieve objectivity with relatively greater ease, though as yet he seldom does, and has temporarily an advantage in the handling of this material as drama of social situation. Proper development of these social problem themes will require the objectivity of great art. Even when the crassest conventions are waived at present, character stereotypes and deceptive formulae still linger; only genius of the first order can hope to penetrate to the materials of high tragedy – and, for that matter, high comedy also – that undoubtedly are there. For with the difference that modern society decrees its own fatalisms, the situations of race hold tragedies and ironies as deep and keen as those of the ancient classics. Eventually the Negro dramatist must achieve a mastery of a detached, artistic point of view, and reveal the inner stresses and dilemmas of these situations as from the psychological point of view he alone can. The race drama of the future will utilize satire for the necessary psychological distance and perspective, and rely upon irony as a natural corrective for the sentimentalisms of propaganda. The objective attack and style of younger contemporary writers like Jean Toomer, who in *Kabnis* has written a cryptic but powerful monologue, promise this not too distantly.

The folk play, on the other hand, whether of the realistic or the imaginative type, has no such conditioned values. It is the drama of free self-expression and imaginative release, and has no objective but to express beautifully and colorfully the folk life of the race. At present, too, influenced perhaps by the social drama, it finds tentative expression in the realistic genre plays of Paul Green, Willis Richardson and others. Later no doubt, after it learns to beautify the native idioms of our folk life and recovers the ancestral folk tradition, it will express itself in a poetic and symbolic style of drama that will remind us of Synge and the Irish Folk Theatre or Ansky and the Yiddish Theatre. [. . .] It seems logical to think that the requisite touch must come in large measure from the Negro dramatists. It is not a question of race, though, but of intimacy of understanding. Paul Green, for example, is a close student of, almost a specialist in, Negro folk life, with unimpeachable artistic motives, and a dozen or more Negro plays to his credit. But the plays of Willis Richardson, the colored playwright, whose *Chip Woman's Fortune* was the first offering of the Chicago Ethiopian Art Theatre under Raymond O'Neill, are very much in the same vein. Though the dialogue is a bit closer to Negro idiom of thought and speech, compensating somewhat for his greater amateurishness of technique and structure, there still comes the impression that the drama of Negro life has not yet become as racy, as gaily unconscious, as saturated with folk ways and the folk spirit as it could be, as it eventually will be. Decidedly it needs more of that poetic strain whose counterpart makes the Irish folk drama so captivating and irresistible, more of the joy of life even when life flows tragically, and even should one phase of it remain realistic peasant drama, more of the emotional depth of pity and terror. This clarification will surely come as the Negro drama shifts more and more to the purely aesthetic attitudes. With life becoming less a problem and more a vital process for the younger Negro, we shall leave more and more to the dramatist not born to it the dramatization of the race problem and concern ourselves more vitally with expression and interpretation. Others may anatomise and dissect; we must paint and create. And while one of the main reactions of Negro drama must and will be the breaking down of those false stereotypes in terms of which the world still sees us, it is more vital that drama should stimulate the group life culturally and give it the spiritual quickening of a native art.

The finest function, then, of race drama would be to supply an imaginative channel of escape and spiritual release, and by some process of emotional reinforcement to cover life with the illusion of happiness and spiritual freedom. Because of the lack of any tradition or art to which to attach itself, this reaction has never functioned in the life of the American Negro except at the level of the explosive and abortive release of buffoonery and low comedy. Held down by social tyranny to the jester's footstool, the dramatic instincts of the race have had to fawn, crouch and be amusingly vulgar. The fine African tradition of primitive ritual broken, with the inhibitions of Puritanism snuffing out even the spirit of a strong dramatic and mimetic heritage, there has been little prospect for the development of strong native dramatic traits. But the traces linger to flare up spectacularly when the touch of a serious dramatic motive once again touches them. No set purpose can create this, only the spontaneous play of the race spirit over its own heritage and traditions. But the deliberate turning back for dramatic material to the ancestral sources of African life and tradition is a very significant symptom. At present just in the experimental stage, with historical curiosity the dominating motive, it heralds very shortly a definite attempt to poetize the race origins and supply a fine imaginative background for a fresh cultural expression. No one with a sense for dramatic values will underestimate the rich resources of African material in these respects. Not through a literal transposing, but in some adaptations of its folk lore, art-idioms and symbols, African material seems as likely to influence the art of drama as much as or more than it has already influenced some of its sister arts. Certainly the logic of the development of a thoroughly racial drama points independently to its use just as soon as the Negro drama rises to the courage of distinctiveness and achieves creative independence.

Notes

1 D. Krasner, *A Beautiful Pageant: African American Theatre, Drama, and Performance in the Harlem Renaissance, 1910–1927* (New York: Palgrave Macmillan, 2002), 130.
2 Locke is referring to the character of Brutus Jones in Eugene O'Neill's *The Emperor Jones* (1920), performed by the great actor Charles Gilpin and later by Paul Robeson. – Editor's note.

Chapter 20

W. E. B. Du Bois (1868–1963)

William Edward Burghardt (W. E. B.) Du Bois was a leading philosopher, sociologist, critic, and activist in the Civil Rights Movement. His advocacy for human rights placed him at the forefront of intellectuals for social change. Du Bois was influenced by Hegel's dialectic (he studied at the University of Berlin in the 1890s) and by William James's pragmatism (James was his teacher at Harvard, where he received his PhD). James's concept of a split consciousness and Hegel's notion of the dialectic led Du Bois to one of his most profound observations: African Americans experience a "double consciousness," he wrote in *The Souls of Black Folk* (1903). This experience was for Du Bois debilitating and rewarding: it created a deep split in the psyche but it also facilitated an expanded vision of the world. In the 1910s Du Bois took an interest in the theatre, producing his pageant, *The Star of Ethiopia* (premiered in 1913 and performed at various times for over a decade). By the 1920s he wrote several essays on theatre and art, two of which are excerpted here. He also produced theatre in Harlem in the 1920s, one of which, the Krigwa Players, became a launching pad for his concept of a propagandistic theatre. His essays reflect his view of didactic art. Propaganda for Du Bois was a way of correcting history's inaccuracies. His essay "Criteria of Negro Art" was first a lecture to historians before it was published in Du Bois's magazine, *Crisis*. This is an important fact, because it emphasizes Du Bois's interest in history. Historical drama, he believed, can portray an alternative reality and set right what had been accepted as common wisdom. August Wilson's dramas owe much to Du Bois's desire to rewrite history from a black perspective. Du Bois's four criteria of "a real Negro theatre" would prove the clarion call of black drama for the twentieth century. His two essays can be interpreted as a rebuttal to Alain Locke's concept of folk theatre (see Chapter 19).

Excerpts from W. E. B. Du Bois, "Krigwa Players Little Negro Theatre," *Crisis* 32.3 (July 1926), 134–6, and "Criteria of Negro Art," *Crisis* 32.6 (October 1926), 290–7. © 1926. Reprinted by permission of Crisis Magazine.

"Krigwa Players Little Negro Theatre": The Story of a Little Theatre Movement (1926)

It is customary to regard Negroes as an essentially dramatic race; and it is probably true that tropical and sub-tropical peoples have more vivid imagination, are accustomed to expressing themselves with greater physical and spiritual abandon than most folk. And certainly, life as black and brown and yellow folk have known it is big with tragedy and comedy. The home life of Africans shows this natural dramatic tendency; the strides of the native African, the ceremony of home and assembly, the intense interest in music and play, all attest this. [...]

Today as the renaissance of art comes among American Negroes, the theatre calls for new birth. But most people do not realize just where the novelty must come in. The Negro is already in the theatre and has been there for a long time; but his presence there is not yet thoroughly normal. His audience is mainly a white audience, and the Negro actor has, for a long time, been asked to entertain this more or less alien group. The demands and ideals of the white group and their conception of Negroes have set the norm for the black actor. He has been a minstrel, comedian, singer and lay figure of all sorts. Only recently has he begun tentatively to emerge as an ordinary human being with everyday reactions. And here he is still handicapped and put forth with much hesitation, as in the case of "The Nigger," "Lulu Belle" and "The Emperor Jones."[1]

In all this development naturally then the best of the Negro actor and the most poignant Negro drama have not been called for. This could be evoked only by a Negro audience desiring to see its own life depicted by its own writers and actors. [...]

The movement which has begun this year in Harlem, New York City, lays down four fundamental principles. The plays of a real Negro theatre must be: 1. *About us.* That is, they must have plots which reveal Negro life as it is. 2. *By us.* That is, they must be written by Negro authors who understand from birth and continual association just what it means to be a Negro today. 3. *For us.* That is, the theatre must cater primarily to Negro audiences and be supported and sustained by their entertainment and approval. 4. *Near us.* The theatre must be in a Negro neighborhood near the mass of ordinary Negro people.

Only in this way can a real folk-play movement of American Negroes be built up.

Criteria of Negro Art (1926)

I do not doubt but there are some in this audience who are a little disturbed at the subject of this meeting, and particularly at the subject I have chosen. Such people are thinking something like this: "How is it that an organization like this, a group of radicals trying to bring new things into the world, a fighting organization which has come up out of the blood and dust of battle, struggling for the right of black men to be ordinary human beings – how is it that an organization of this kind can turn aside to talk about Art? After all, what have we who are slaves and black to do with Art?"

Or perhaps there are others who feel a certain relief and are saying, "After all it is rather satisfactory after all this talk about rights and fighting to sit and dream of something which leaves a nice taste in the mouth."

Let me tell you that neither of these groups is right. The thing we are talking about tonight is part of the great fight we are carrying on and it represents a forward and an upward look – a pushing onward. You and I have been breasting hills; we have been climbing upward; there has been progress and we can see it day by day looking back along blood-filled paths. But as you go through the valleys and over the foothills, so long as you are climbing, the direction, north, south, east or west, is of less importance. But when gradually the vista widens and you begin to see the world at your feet and the far horizon, then it is time to know more precisely whither you are going and what you really want. [. . .]

After all, who shall describe Beauty? What is it? I remember tonight four beautiful things: The Cathedral at Cologne, a forest in stone, set in light and changing shadow, echoing with sunlight and solemn song; a village of the Veys in West Africa, a little thing of mauve and purple, quiet, lying content and shining in the sun; a black and velvet room where on a throne rests, in old and yellowing marble, the broken curves of the Venus of Milo; a single phrase of music in the Southern South – utter melody, haunting and appealing, suddenly arising out of night and eternity, beneath the moon.

Such is Beauty. Its variety is infinite, its possibility is endless. In normal life all may have it and have it yet again. The world is full of it; and yet today the mass of human beings are choked away from it, and their lives distorted and made ugly. This is not only wrong, it is silly. Who shall right this well-nigh universal failing? Who shall let this world be beautiful? Who shall restore to men the glory of sunsets and the peace of quiet sleep?

We black folk may help for we have within us as a race new stirrings; stirrings of the beginning of a new appreciation of joy, of a new desire to create, of a new will to be; as though in this morning of group life we had awakened from some sleep that at once dimly mourns the past and dreams a splendid future; and there has come the conviction that the Youth that is here today, the Negro Youth, is a different kind of Youth, because in some new way it bears this mighty prophecy on its breast, with a new realization of itself, with new determination for all mankind.

What has this Beauty to do with the world? What has Beauty to do with Truth and Goodness – with the facts of the world and the right actions of men? "Nothing," the artists rush to answer. They may be right. I am but a humble disciple of art and cannot presume to say. I am one who tells the truth and exposes evil and seeks with Beauty and for Beauty to set the world right. That somehow, somewhere eternal and perfect Beauty sits above Truth and Right I can conceive, but here and now and in the world in which I work they are for me unseparated and inseparable. [. . .]

I once knew a man and woman. They had two children, a daughter who was white and a daughter who was brown; the daughter who was white married a white man; and when her wedding was preparing the daughter who was brown prepared to go and celebrate. But the mother said, "No!" and the brown daughter went into her room and turned on the gas and died. Do you want Greek tragedy swifter than that?

Or again, here is a little Southern town and you are in the public square. On one side of the square is the office of a colored lawyer and on all the other sides are men who do not like colored lawyers. A white woman goes into the black man's office and points to the white-filled square and says, "I want five hundred dollars now and if I do not get it I am going to scream." [. . .]

With the growing recognition of Negro artists in spite of the severe handicaps, one comforting thing is occurring to both white and black. They are whispering, "Here is a way out. Here is the real solution of the color problem. The recognition accorded Cullen, Hughes, Fauset, White and others shows there is no real color line. Keep quiet! Don't complain! Work! All will be well!"

I will not say that already this chorus amounts to a conspiracy. Perhaps I am naturally too suspicious. But I will say that there are today a surprising number of white people who are getting great satisfaction out of these younger Negro writers because they think it is going to stop agitation of the Negro question. They say, "What is the use of your fighting and complaining; do the great thing and the reward is there." And many colored people are all too eager to follow this advice; especially those who are weary of the eternal struggle along the color line, who are afraid to fight and to whom the money of philanthropists and the alluring publicity are subtle and deadly bribes. They say, "What is the use of fighting? Why not show simply what we deserve and let the reward come to us?" [. . .]

We can go on the stage; we can be just as funny as white Americans wish us to be; we can play all the sordid parts that America likes to assign to Negroes; but for any thing else there is still small place for us.

And so I might go on. But let me sum up with this: Suppose the only Negro who survived some centuries hence was the Negro painted by white Americans in the novels and essays they have written. What would people in a hundred years say of black Americans? Now turn it around. Suppose you were to write a story and put in it the kind of people you know and like and imagine. You might get it published and you might not. And the "might not" is still far bigger than the "might." The white publishers catering to white folk would say, "It is not interesting" to white folk, naturally not. They want Uncle Toms, Topsies, good "darkies" and clowns. I have in my office a story with all the earmarks of truth. A young man says that he started out to write and had his stories accepted. Then he began to write about the things he knew best about, that is, about his own people. He submitted a story to a magazine which said, "We are sorry, but we cannot take it." "Z sat down and revised my story, changing the color of the characters and the locale and sent it under an assumed name with a change of address and it was accepted by the same magazine that had refused it, the editor promising to take anything else I might send in providing it was good enough."

We have, to be sure, a few recognized and successful Negro artists; but they are not all those fit to survive or even a good minority. They are but the remnants of that ability and genius among us whom the accidents of education and opportunity have raised on the tidal waves of chance. We black folk are not altogether peculiar in this. After all, in the world at large, it is only the accident, the remnant, that gets the chance to make the most of itself; but if this is true of the white world it is infinitely more true of the colored world. It is not simply the great clear tenor of Roland Hayes that opened the ears of America. We have had many voices of all kinds as fine as his and America was and is as deaf as she was for years to him. Then a foreign land heard Hayes and put its imprint on him and immediately America with all its imitative snobbery woke up. We approved Hayes because London, Paris and Berlin approved him and not simply because he was a great singer.

Thus it is the bounden duty of black America to begin this great work of the creation of Beauty, of the preservation of Beauty, of the realization of Beauty, and we must use in this work all the methods that men have used before. And what have been the tools of the artist in times gone by? First of all, he has used the Truth not for the sake of truth, not as a scientist seeking truth, but as one upon whom Truth eternally thrusts itself as the highest handmaid of imagination, as the one great vehicle of universal understanding. Again artists have used Goodness – goodness in all its aspects of justice, honor and right – not for sake of an ethical sanction but as the one true method of gaining sympathy and human interest.

The apostle of Beauty thus becomes the apostle of Truth and Right, not by choice but by inner and outer compulsion. Free he is but his freedom is ever bounded by Truth and Justice; and slavery only dogs him when he is denied the right to tell the Truth or recognize an ideal of Justice.

Thus all Art is propaganda and ever must be, despite the wailing of the purists. I stand in utter shamelessness and say that whatever art I have for writing has been used always for propaganda for gaining the right of black folk to love and enjoy. I do not care a damn for any art that is not used for propaganda. But I do care when propaganda is confined to one side while the other is stripped and silent. [...]

Note

1   Popular 1920s plays by white authors. – Editor's note.

Chapter 21

Bertolt Brecht (1898–1956)

One of the most (if not *the* most) important figures of theatrical theory, Bertolt (Eugene Berthold Fredrich) Brecht was a playwright, poet, and stage director. His well-known works, the musical *Threepenny Opera* (1929), *Mother Courage and Her Children* (1939), *The Life of Galileo* (1939, 1947), and *The Caucasian Chalk Circle* (1945), have been reproduced throughout the world. His dramas include didactic-agitprop *Lehrstücke* (learning plays), historical dramas, and dramas of social criticism. His two important works on theory – *Short Organum for the Theatre* (1949) and the unfinished *Messingkauf Dialogues* (1956) – are elaborate expressions of his ideas. He was a vital force internationally during the pre-Nazi period in Weimar, and remained influential during his exile years (ca. 1933–48). During the early 1950s he was a leading figure of East Germany's Berliner Ensemble.

Brecht's theories, from the 1920s to his death in 1956, are an investigation of theatre's apparatus, political efficacy, and theatrical contours. He was a devoted Marxist, but unlike other leftists who turned to social realism (e.g., Lukács), Brecht found the social realistic form outdated. For him nineteenth-century realism inspired inertia rather than action. He believed that a new society needed a new theatre; what was to be gained if socialism perpetuated the status quo, even if it substituted proletarian characters from bourgeois artistic forms? He found the avant-garde equally unsatisfying, dismissing art for art's sake as puerile indulgence. For him expressionism was strident and symbolism apolitical. He wanted to cool down the overheated emotions of expressionism and the histrionics of Stanislavskian melodrama, while simultaneously rejecting the esotericism of the avant-garde. In lieu of a model to build from, Brecht advocated

Excerpts from Bertolt Brecht, "The Modern Theatre is the Epic Theatre" (1930), "Theatre for Pleasure or Theatre for Instruction" (ca. 1936), and "Alienation Effect in Chinese Acting" (1936), tr. and ed. John Willett, in *Brecht on Theatre: The Development of an Aesthetic* (New York: Hill & Wang, 1957, 2000), 37–9, 69–78, and 91–9. Translation copyright © 1964, renewed 1992 by John Willett. Reprinted by permission of Farrar, Straus, and Giroux, LLC, and Methuen Publishing Ltd.

Very academic & thought provoking

"epic" theatre. Epic theatre, a term he borrows from the director Edwin Piscator (1893–1966), is drama containing episodic scenes fashioned after Shakespeare, with each scene a kind of mini-play of its own. Brecht wanted to interrupt the Aristotelian narrative flow because in his view narrative stream-of-consciousness panders to emotions, takes for granted the causal chain of events, and dulls the capacity for audiences to act. He wanted spectators to reflect on the staged event, consider how it took shape in reality, and explore what can be done to change the course of the events. To achieve this end he required theatre artists to isolate or frame specific moments onstage and subject them to analysis.

Brecht was concerned with how a play is transmitted. The prevailing theory was that theatre should elicit empathy, a term first used in the mid-nineteenth century by German aesthetics. It meant "feeling into" (the German term is *Einfühlung*, and sympathy is *Mitfühlung*, feeling with). Empathy first appears in English as a psychological term in 1909. Brecht nullified empathy by estranging the audience, i.e., encouraging them to resist identifying with the protagonist. He wanted instead to stimulate awareness over identification. He called for audience detachment, saying, "If we observe sorrow on the stage and at the same time identify ourselves with it, then this simultaneous observing is a part of our observation. We are sorrowful, but at the same time we are people observing a sorrow – our own – almost as if it were detached from us, in other words like people who aren't sorrowful, because nobody else could observe it so detachedly. In this way we aren't wholly dissolved in sorrow; something solid still remains in us. Sorrow is hostile to thought; it stifles it; and thought is hostile to sorrow."[1]

Brecht borrowed the concept of *Ostranenie* (making strange or defamiliarization) from Russian formalist critic Victor Shklovsky. Shklovsky, Roman Jakobson, and Mikhail Bakhtin were structural literary scholars concerned with art's peculiarity and the way an object is represented. "The technique of art," Shklovsky wrote in 1933, "is to make the object 'unfamiliar,' to make forms difficult, to increase the difficulty and length of perception because the process of perception is an aesthetic end in itself and must be prolonged. *Art is a way of experiencing the artfulness of an object; the object is not important.*"[2] Inserting defamiliar elements into the narrative loosened the certainty of reality and the predictable causality; defamiliarization intends to break the logical coherence and encourage gaps in the audience's perception. Audiences accustomed to seeing things in a routine way are now exposed to the unfamiliar. This artistic device – estrangement – is intended to lead to the audience's questioning of the event and challenging its inevitability.

Brecht created his version of this technique, which he called *Verfremdungseffekt* (translated as alienation effect, or A-effect, although *Verfremdung* actually means estrangement). "If empathy," Brecht says, "makes something ordinary of a special event, alienation [estrangement] makes something special of an ordinary one. The most hackneyed everyday incidents are stripped of their monotony when represented as quite special."[3] The "effect" Brecht sought was meant to stir reflection; he wanted to untangle an incident in order to understand the way the ruling class shrouded and manipulated events for its benefit. Silvija Jestrovic carefully parses the distinction between *Ostranenie* and *Verfremdung*. The former provides a conceptual framework describing the process of making the familiar strange through childlike naïveté, and can apply to absurdism, surrealism, and the grotesque. It is meant to distend and distort the relationship of the signifier and the signified. The latter, for Brecht, "is tied to reality in order to provide historical and ideological grounding for the theatricalized material." Brecht's *Verfremdung*, Jestrovic maintains, "places the material in an artificial framework, and represents it from various angles, but keeps an undistorted, realistic image."[4]

Henri Arvon aptly compares the two Marxist views of theatre, one upheld by Lukács and the other by Brecht. Lukács, Arvon says, "who is seeking to bring about a rapprochement with the liberal bourgeoisie in order to make it an ally of the revolutionary proletariat in the fight against Fascism, describes Socialist Realism as a further development of the critical realism of the bourgeois writers of the nineteenth century." Brecht, by contrast, "is convinced that only a radical break with the decadent bourgeoisie will enable the proletariat to win the battle against Fascism, and therefore flatly condemns the whole of bourgeois literature."[5] Brecht wanted audiences to observe the power dynamics of authority, how it imposed its will through illusion, empathy, and charm.

Brecht's epic theatre is by design disjunctive, deliberately lurching from one scene to another. It is meant to replicate the circus. He advocated a dissonance in music: notes should contrast the mood of a scene (as opposed to Wagner's effort to underscore a scene via leitmotif). He opposed Wagner's *Gesamtkunstwerk* (total work of art), preferring to delineate the separate components of acting, directing, and set design rather than unifying them, and looked to Eastern theatricality for the formalism he desired. Brecht's overarching goal was to cut against the grain by employing what he called "gestus." This describes an actor's gesture that distills the social hierarchy of the haves and the have-nots.

Aristotle became Brecht's dialectical sounding board; he used Aristotelian theory to illuminate his differing ideas. Stanislavsky's effort to connect the feelings of the actor with the role was also used by Brecht to demonstrate differentiation. Asian theatre techniques that distanced the actor from the role were to be encouraged. They enabled the actor to "comment" on the actions of the character rather than accept them at face value. "A definite distance between the actor and the role had to be built into the manner of playing," he said. "The actor had to be able to criticize. In addition to the action of the character, another action had to be there so that selection and criticism were possible."[6] The three essays here illustrate a few of Brecht's many ideas that were to become embedded in the fabric of modern theatre.

The Modern Theatre is the Epic Theatre (1930)

The modern theatre is the epic theatre. The following table shows certain changes of emphasis as between the dramatic and the epic theatre:[7]

DRAMATIC THEATRE	EPIC THEATRE
plot	narrative
implicates the spectator in a stage situation	turns the spectator into an observer, but
wears down his capacity for action	arouses his capacity for action
provides him with sensations	forces him to take decisions

experience	picture of the world
the spectator is involved in something	he is made to face something
suggestion	argument
instinctive feelings are preserved	brought into the point of recognition
the spectator is in the thick of it, shares the experience	
	the spectator stands outside, studies
the human being is taken for granted	the human being is the object of the inquiry
he is unalterable	he is alterable and able to alter
eyes on the finish	eyes on the course
one scene makes another	each scene for itself
growth	montage
linear development	in curves
evolutionary determinism	jumps
man as a fixed point	man as a process
thought determines being	social being determines thought
feeling	reason

When the epic theatre's methods begin to penetrate the opera the first result is a radical *separation of the elements*. The great struggle for supremacy between words, music and production – which always brings up the question "which is the pretext for what?": is the music the pretext for the events on the stage, or are these the pretext for the music? etc. – can simply be bypassed by radically separating the elements. So long as the expression "Gesamtkunstwerk" (or "integrated work of art") means that the integration is a muddle, so long as the arts are supposed to be "fused" together, the various elements will all be equally degraded, and each will act as a mere "feed" to the rest. The process of fusion extends to the spectator, who gets thrown into the melting pot too and becomes a passive (suffering) part of the total work of art. Witchcraft of this sort must of course be fought against. Whatever is intended to produce hypnosis, is likely to induce sordid intoxication, or creates fog, has got to be given up.

Words, music and setting must become more independent of one another.

(a) Music: For the music, the change of emphasis proved to be as follows:

DRAMATIC OPERA	EPIC OPERA
The music dishes up	The music communicates
music which heightens the text	music which sets forth the text
music which proclaims the text	music which takes the text for granted
music which illustrates	which takes up a position
music which paints the psychological situation	
	which gives the attitude

Music plays the chief part in our thesis.

(b) Text

We had to make something straightforward and instructive of our fun, if it was not to be irrational and nothing more. The form employed was that of the moral tableau. The tableau is performed by the characters in the play. The text had to be neither moralizing nor sentimental, but to put morals and sentimentality on view. Equally important was the spoken word and the written word (of the titles). Reading seems to encourage the audience to adopt the most natural attitude towards the work.

(c) Setting

Showing independent works of art as part of a theatrical performance is a new departure. Neher's projections adopt an attitude towards the events on the stage; as when the real glutton sits in front of the glutton whom Neher has drawn. In the same way the stage unreels the events that are fixed on the screen. These projections of Neher's are quite as much an independent component of the opera as are Weill's music and the text. They provide its visual aids.

Of course such innovations also demand a new attitude on the part of the audiences who frequent opera houses.

Theatre for Pleasure or Theatre for Instruction (ca. 1936)

The Epic Theatre

Many people imagine that the term "epic theatre" is self-contradictory, as the epic and dramatic ways of narrating a story are held, following Aristotle, to be basically distinct. The difference between the two forms was never thought simply to lie in the fact that the one is performed by living beings while the other operates via the written word; epic works such as those of Homer and the medieval singers were at the same time theatrical performances, while dramas like Goethe's *Faust* and Byron's *Manfred* are agreed to have been more effective as books. Thus even by Aristotle's definition the difference between the dramatic and epic forms was attributed to their different methods of construction, whose laws were dealt with by two different branches of esthetics. The method of construction depended on the different way of presenting the work to the public, sometimes via the stage, sometimes through a book; and independently of that there was the "dramatic element" in epic works and the "epic element" in dramatic. The bourgeois novel in the last century developed much that was "dramatic," by which was meant the strong centralization of the story, a momentum that drew the separate parts into a common relationship. A particular passion of utterance, a certain emphasis on the clash of forces are hallmarks of the "dramatic." The epic writer Döblin provided an excellent criterion when he said that with an epic work, as opposed to a dramatic, one can as it were take a pair of scissors and cut it into individual pieces, which remain fully capable of life.

This is no place to explain how the opposition of epic and dramatic lost its rigidity after having long been held to be irreconcilable. Let us just point out that the technical advances alone were enough to permit the stage to incorporate an element of narrative in its dramatic productions. The possibility of projections, the greater adaptability of the stage due to mechanization, the film, all completed the theatre's equipment, and did so at a point where the most important transactions between people could no longer be shown simply by personifying the motive forces or subjecting the characters to invisible metaphysical powers.

To make these transactions intelligible the environment in which the people lived had to be brought to bear in a big and "significant" way.

This environment had of course been shown in the existing drama, but only as seen from the central figure's point of view, and not as an independent element. It was defined by the hero's reactions to it. It was seen as a storm can be seen when one sees the ships on a sheet of water unfolding their sails, and the sails filling out. In the epic theatre it was to appear standing on its own.

The stage began to tell a story. The narrator was no longer missing, along with the fourth wall. Not only did the background adopt an attitude to the events on the stage – by big screens recalling other simultaneous events elsewhere, by projecting documents which confirmed or contradicted what the characters said, by concrete and intelligible figures to accompany abstract conversations, by figures and sentences to support mimed transactions whose sense was unclear – but the actors too refrained from going over wholly into their role, remaining detached from the character they were playing and clearly inviting criticism of him.

The spectator was no longer in any way allowed to submit to an experience uncritically (and without practical consequences) by means of simple empathy with the characters in a play. The production took the subject-matter and the incidents shown and put them through a process of alienation: the alienation that is necessary to all understanding. When something seems "the most obvious thing in the world" it means that any attempt to understand the world has been given up.

What is "natural" must have the force of what is startling. This is the only way to expose the laws of cause and effect. People's activity must simultaneously be so and be capable of being different.

It was all a great change.

The dramatic theatre's spectator says: Yes, I have felt like that too – Just like me – It's only natural – It'll never change – The sufferings of this man appall me, because they are inescapable – That's great art; it all seems the most obvious thing in the world – I weep when they weep, I laugh when they laugh.

The epic theatre's spectator says: I'd never have thought it – That's not the way – That's extraordinary, hardly believable – It's got to stop – The sufferings of this man appall me, because they are unnecessary – That's great art: nothing obvious in it – I laugh when they weep, I weep when they laugh.

The Instructive Theatre

The stage began to be instructive.

Oil, inflation, war, social struggles, the family, religion, wheat, the meat market, all became subjects for theatrical representation. Choruses enlightened the spectator about facts unknown to him. Films showed a montage of events from all over the world. Projections added statistical material. And as the "background" came to the front of the stage so people's activity was subjected to criticism. Right and wrong courses of action were shown. People were shown who knew what they were doing, and others who did not. The theatre became an affair for philosophers, but only for such philosophers as wished not just to explain the world but also to change it. So we had philosophy, and we had instruction. And where was the amusement in all that? Were they sending us back to school, teaching us to read and write? Were we supposed to pass exams, work for diplomas?

Generally there is felt to be a very sharp distinction between learning and amusing oneself. The first may be useful, but only the second is pleasant. So we have to defend the epic theatre against the suspicion that it is a highly disagreeable, humorless, indeed strenuous affair.

Well: all that can be said is that the contrast between learning and amusing oneself is not laid down by divine rule; it is not one that has always been and must continue to be.

Undoubtedly there is much that is tedious about the kind of learning familiar to us from school, from our professional training, etc. But it must be remembered under what conditions and to what end that takes place.

It is really a commercial transaction. Knowledge is just a commodity. It is acquired in order to be resold. All those who have grown out of going to school have to do their learning virtually in secret, for anyone who admits that he still has something to learn devalues himself as a man whose knowledge is inadequate. Moreover the usefulness of learning is very much limited by factors outside the learner's control. There is unemployment, for instance, against which no knowledge can protect one. There is the division of labour, which makes generalized knowledge unnecessary and impossible. Learning is often among the concerns of those whom no amount of concern will get any forwarder. There is not much knowledge that leads to power, but plenty of knowledge to which only power can lead.

Learning has a very different function for different social strata. There are strata who cannot imagine any improvement in conditions: they find the conditions good enough for them. Whatever happens to oil they will benefit from it. And: they feel the years beginning to tell. There can't be all that many years more. What is the point of learning a lot now? They have said their final word: a grunt. But there are also strata "waiting their turn" who are discontented with conditions, have a vast interest in the practical side of learning, want at all costs to find out where they stand, and know that they are lost without learning; these are the best and keenest learners. Similar differences apply to countries and peoples. Thus the pleasure of learning depends on all sorts of things; but none the less there is such a thing as pleasurable learning, cheerful and militant learning.

If there were not such amusement to be had from learning the theatre's whole structure would unfit it for teaching.

Theatre remains theatre even when it is instructive theatre, and in so far as it is good theatre it will amuse.

Theatre and Knowledge

But what has knowledge got to do with art? We know that knowledge can be amusing, but not everything that is amusing belongs in the theatre.

I have often been told, when pointing out the invaluable services that modern knowledge and science, if properly applied, can perform for art and specially for the theatre, that art and knowledge are two estimable but wholly distinct fields of human activity. This is a fearful truism, of course, and it is as well to agree quickly that, like most truisms, it is perfectly true. Art and science work in quite different ways: agreed. But, bad as it may sound, I have to admit that I cannot get along as an artist without the use of one or two sciences. This may well arouse serious doubts as to my artistic capacities. People are used to seeing poets as unique and slightly unnatural beings who reveal with a truly godlike assurance things that other people can only recognize after much sweat and toil. It is naturally distasteful to have to admit that one does not belong to this select band. All the same, it must be admitted. It must at the same time be made clear that the scientific occupations just confessed to are not pardonable side interests, pursued on days off after a good week's work. We all know how Goethe was interested in natural history, Schiller in history: as a kind of hobby, it is charitable to assume. I have no wish promptly to accuse these two of having needed these sciences for their poetic activity; I am not trying to shelter behind them; but I must say that I do need the sciences. I have to admit, however, that I look askance at all sorts of people who I know do not operate on the level of scientific understanding: that is to say, who sing as the birds sing, or as people imagine the birds to sing. I don't mean by that I would reject a charming poem about the taste of fried fish or the delights of a boating party just because the writer had not studied gastronomy or navigation. But in my view the great and complicated things that go on in the world cannot be adequately recognized by people who do not use every possible aid to understanding.

Let us suppose that great passions or great events have to be shown which influence the fate of nations. The lust for power is nowadays held to be such a passion. Given that a poet "feels" this lust and wants to have someone strive for power, how is he to show the exceedingly complicated machinery within which the struggle for power nowadays takes place? If his hero is a politician, how do politics work? If he is a business man, how does business work? And yet there are writers who find business and politics nothing like so passionately interesting as the individual's lust for power. How are they to acquire the necessary knowledge? They are scarcely likely to learn enough by going round and keeping their eyes open, though even then it is more than they would get by just rolling their eyes in an exalted frenzy. The foundation of a paper like the *Völkischer Beobachter* or a business like Standard Oil is a pretty complicated affair, and such things cannot be conveyed just like that. One important field for the playwright is psychology. It is taken for granted that a poet, if not an ordinary man, must be able without further instruction to discover the motives that lead a man to commit murder; he must be able to give a picture of a murderer's mental state "from within himself." It is taken for granted that one only has to look inside oneself in such a case; and then there's always one's imagination. . . . There are various reasons why I can no longer surrender to this agreeable hope of getting a result quite so simply. I can no longer find in myself all those motives which the press or scientific reports show to have been observed in people. Like the average judge when pronouncing sentence, I cannot without further ado conjure up an adequate picture of a murderer's mental state. Modern psychology, from psychoanalysis to behaviorism, acquaints me with facts that lead me to judge the case quite differently, especially if I bear in mind the findings of sociology and do not overlook economics and history. You will say: but that's getting complicated. I have to answer that it is complicated. Even if you let yourself be convinced, and agree with me that a large slice of literature is exceedingly primitive, you may still ask with profound concern: won't an evening in such a theatre be a most alarming affair? The answer to that is: no.

Whatever knowledge is embodied in a piece of poetic writing has to be wholly transmuted into poetry. Its utilization fulfills the very pleasure that the poetic element provokes. If it does not at the same time fulfill that which is fulfilled by the scientific element, none the less in an age of great discoveries and inventions one must have a certain inclination to penetrate deeper into things – a desire to make the world controllable – if one is to be sure of enjoying its poetry.

Is the Epic Theatre Some Kind of "Moral Institution?"

According to Friedrich Schiller the theatre is supposed to be a moral institution. In making this demand it hardly occurred to Schiller that by moralizing from the stage he might drive the audience out of the theatre. Audiences had no objection to moralizing in his day. It was only later that Friedrich Nietzsche attacked him by blowing a moral trumpet. To Nietzsche any concern with morality was a depressing affair; to Schiller it seemed thoroughly enjoyable. He knew of nothing that could give greater amusement and satisfaction than the propagation of ideas. The bourgeoisie was setting about forming the ideas of the nation.

Putting one's house in order, patting oneself on the back, submitting one's account, is something highly agreeable. But describing the collapse of one's house, having pains in the back, paying one's account, is indeed a depressing affair, and that was how Friedrich Nietzsche saw things a century later. He was poorly disposed towards morality, and thus towards the previous Friedrich too.

The epic theatre was likewise often objected to as moralizing too much. Yet in the epic theatre moral arguments only took second place. Its aim was less to moralize than to observe. That is to say it observed, and then the thick end of the wedge followed: the story's moral. Of course we cannot pretend that we started our observations out of a pure passion for observing and without any more practical motive, only to be completely staggered by their results. Undoubtedly there were some painful discrepancies in our environment, circumstances that were barely tolerable, and this not merely on account of moral considerations. It is not only moral considerations that make hunger, cold and oppression hard to bear. Similarly the object of our inquiries was not just to arouse moral objections to such circumstances (even though they could easily be felt – though not by all the audience alike; such objections were seldom for instance felt by those who profited by the circumstances in question) but to discover means for their elimination. We were not in fact speaking in the name of morality but in that of the victims. These truly are two distinct matters, for the victims are often told that they ought to be contented with their lot, for moral reasons. Moralists of this sort see man as existing for morality, not morality for man. At least it should be possible to gather from the above to what degree and in what sense the epic theatre is a moral institution.

Can Epic Theatre Be Played Anywhere?

Stylistically speaking, there is nothing all that new about the epic theatre. Its expository character and its emphasis on virtuosity bring it close to the old Asiatic theatre. Didactic tendencies are to be found in the medieval mystery plays and the classical Spanish theatre, and also in the theatre of the Jesuits.

These theatrical forms corresponded to particular trends of their time, and vanished with them. Similarly the modern epic theatre is linked with certain trends. It cannot by any means be practiced universally. Most of the great nations today are not disposed to use the theatre for ventilating their problems. London, Paris, Tokyo, and Rome maintain their theatres for quite different purposes. Up to now favorable circumstances for an epic and didactic theatre have only been found in a few places and for a short period of time. In Berlin Fascism put a very definite stop to the development of such a theatre.

It demands not only a certain technological level but a powerful movement in society which is interested to see vital questions freely aired with a view to their solution, and can defend this interest against every contrary trend.

The epic theatre is the broadest and most far-reaching attempt at large-scale modern theatre, and it has all those immense difficulties to overcome that always confront the vital forces in the sphere of politics, philosophy, science and art.

Alienation Effect in Chinese Acting (1936)

The following is intended to refer briefly to the use of the alienation effect in traditional Chinese acting. This method was most recently used in Germany for plays of a non-Aristotelian (not dependent on empathy) type as part of the attempts [*Versuche*] being made to evolve an epic theatre. The efforts in question were directed to playing in such a way that the audience was hindered from simply identifying itself with the characters in the play. Acceptance or rejection of their actions and utterances was meant to take place on a conscious plane, instead of, as hitherto, in the audience's subconscious.

This effort to make the incidents represented appear strange to the public can be seen in a primitive form in the theatrical and pictorial displays at the old popular fairs. The way the clowns speak and the way the panoramas are painted both embody an act of alienation. The method of painting used to reproduce the picture of "Charles the Bold's flight after the Battle of Murten," as shown at many German fairs, is certainly mediocre; yet the act of alienation which is achieved here (not by the original) is in no wise due to the mediocrity of the copyist. The fleeing commander, his horse, his retinue and the landscape are all quite consciously painted in such a way as to create the impression of an abnormal event, an astonishing disaster. In spite of his inadequacy the painter succeeds brilliantly in bringing out the unexpected. Amazement guides his brush.

Traditional Chinese acting also knows the alienation effect, and applies it most subtly. It is well known that the Chinese theatre uses a lot of symbols. Thus a general will carry little pennants on his shoulder, corresponding to the number of regiments under his command. Poverty is shown by patching the silken costumes with irregular shapes of different colors, likewise silken, to indicate that they have been mended. Characters are distinguished by particular masks, i.e. simply by painting. Certain gestures of the two hands signify the forcible opening of a door, etc. The stage itself remains the same, but articles of furniture are carried in during the action. All this has long been known, and cannot very well be exported.

It is not all that simple to break with the habit of assimilating a work of art as a whole. But this has to be done if just one of a large number of effects is to be singled out and studied. The alienation effect is achieved in the Chinese theatre in the following way.

Above all, the Chinese artist never acts as if there were a fourth wall besides the three surrounding him. He expresses his awareness of being watched. This immediately removes one of the European stage's characteristic illusions. The audience can no longer have the illusion of being the unseen spectator at an event which is really taking place.

A whole elaborate European stage technique, which helps to conceal the fact that the scenes are so arranged that the audience can view them in the easiest way, is thereby made unnecessary. The actors openly choose those positions which will best show them off to the audience, just as if they were acrobats. A further means is that the artist observes himself. Thus if he is representing a cloud, perhaps, showing its unexpected appearance, its soft and strong growth, its rapid yet gradual transformation, he will occasionally look at the audience as if to say: isn't it just like that? At the same time he also observes his own arms and legs, adducing them, testing them and perhaps finally approving them. An obvious glance at the floor, so as to judge the space available to him for his act, does not strike him as liable to break the illusion. In this way the artist separates mime (showing observation) from gesture (showing a cloud), but without detracting from the latter, since the body's attitude is reflected in the face and is wholly responsible for its expression. At one moment the expression is of well-managed restraint; at another, of utter triumph. The artist has been using his countenance as a blank sheet, to be inscribed by the gest of the body.

The artist's object is to appear strange and even surprising to the audience. He achieves this by looking strangely at himself and his work. As a result everything put forward by him has a touch of the amazing. Everyday things are thereby raised above the level of the obvious and automatic. A young woman, a fisherman's wife, is shown paddling a boat. She stands steering a non-existent boat with a paddle that barely reaches to her knees. Now the current is swifter, and she is finding it harder to keep her balance; now she is in a pool and paddling more easily. Right: that is how one manages a boat. But this journey in the boat is apparently historic, celebrated in many songs, an exceptional journey about which everybody knows. Each of this famous girl's movements has probably been recorded in pictures; each bend in the river was a well-known adventure story, it is even known which particular bend it was. This feeling on the audience's part is induced by the artist's attitude; it is this that makes the journey famous. The scene reminded us of the march to Budejovice in Piscator's production of *The Good Soldier Schweik*. Schweik's three-day-and-night march to a front which he oddly enough never gets to was seen from a completely historic point of view, as no less noteworthy a phenomenon than, for instance, Napoleon's Russian expedition of 1812. The performer's self-observation, an artful and artistic act of self-alienation, stopped the spectator from losing himself in the character completely, i.e. to the point of giving up his own identity, and lent a splendid remoteness to the events. Yet the spectator's empathy was not entirely rejected. The audience identifies itself with the actor as being an observer, and accordingly develops his attitude of observing or looking on.

The Chinese artist's performance often strikes the Western actor as cold. That does not mean that the Chinese theatre rejects all representation of feelings. The performer portrays incidents of utmost passion, but without his delivery becoming heated. At those points where the character portrayed is deeply excited the performer takes a lock of hair between his lips and chews it. But this is like a ritual, there is nothing eruptive about it. It is quite clearly somebody else's repetition of the incident: a representation, even though an artistic one. The performer shows that this man is not in control of himself, and he points to the outward signs. And so lack of control is decorously expressed, or if not decorously, at any rate decorously for the stage. Among all the possible signs certain particular ones are picked out, with careful and visible consideration. Anger is naturally different from sulkiness, hatred from distaste, love from liking; but the corresponding fluctuations of feeling are portrayed economically. The coldness comes from the actor's holding himself remote from the character portrayed, along the lines described. He is careful not to make its sensations into those of the spectator. Nobody gets raped by the individual he portrays; this individual is not the spectator himself but his neighbour.

The Western actor does all he can to bring his spectator into the closest proximity to the events and the character he has to portray. To this end he persuades him to identify himself with him (the actor) and uses every energy to convert himself as completely as possible into a different type, that of the character in question. If this complete conversion succeeds, then his art has been more or less expended. Once he has become the bank-clerk, doctor or general concerned, he will need no more art than any of these people need "in real life."

This complete conversion operation is extremely exhausting. Stanislavsky puts forward a series of means – a complete system – by which what he calls "creative mood" can repeatedly be manufactured afresh at every performance. For the actor cannot usually manage to feel for very long on end that he really is the other person; he soon gets exhausted and begins just to copy various superficialities of the other person's speech and hearing, whereupon the effect on the public drops off alarmingly. This is certainly due to the fact that the other person has been created by an "intuitive" and accordingly murky process which takes place in the subconscious. The subconscious is not at all responsive to guidance; it has as it were a bad memory.

These problems are unknown to the Chinese performer, for he rejects complete conversion. He limits himself from the start to simply quoting the character played. But with what art he does this! He only needs a minimum of illusion. What he has to show is worth seeing even for a man in his right mind. What Western actor of the old sort (apart from one or two comedians) could demonstrate the elements of his art like the Chinese actor Mei Lan-fang,[8] without special lighting and wearing a dinner jacket in an ordinary room full of specialists? It would be like the magician at a fair giving away his tricks, so that nobody ever wanted to see the act again. He would just be showing how to disguise oneself; the hypnotism would vanish and all that would be left would be a few pounds of ill-blended imitation, a quickly-mixed product for selling in the dark to hurried customers. Of course no Western actor would stage such a demonstration. What about the sanctity of Art? The mysteries of metamorphosis? To the Westerner what matters is that his actions should be unconscious; otherwise they would be degraded. By comparison with Asiatic acting our own art still seems hopelessly parsonical. None the less it is becoming increasingly difficult for our actors to bring off the mystery of complete conversion; their subconscious's memory is getting weaker and weaker, and it is almost impossible to extract the truth from the uncensored intuitions of any member of our class society even when the man is a genius.

For the actor it is difficult and taxing to conjure up particular inner moods or emotions night after night; it is simpler to exhibit the outer signs which accompany these emotions and identify them. In this case, however, there is not the same automatic transfer of emotions to the spectator, the same emotional infection. The alienation effect intervenes, not in the form of absence of emotion, but in the form of emotions which need not correspond to those of the character portrayed. On seeing worry the spectator may feel a sensation of joy; on seeing anger, one of disgust. When we speak of exhibiting the outer signs of emotion we do not mean such an exhibition and such a choice of signs that the emotional transference does in fact take place because the actor has managed to infect himself with the emotions portrayed, by exhibiting the outer signs; thus, by letting his voice rise, holding his breath and tightening his neck muscles so that the blood shoots to his head, the actor can easily conjure up a rage. In such a case of course the effect does not occur. But it does occur if the actor at a particular point unexpectedly shows a completely white face, which he has produced mechanically by holding his face in his hands with some white make-up on them. If the actor at the same time displays an apparently composed character, then his terror at this point (as a result of this message, or that discovery) will give rise to an alienation effect. Acting like this is healthier and in our view less unworthy of a thinking being; it demands a considerable knowledge of humanity and worldly wisdom, and a keen eye for what is socially important. In this case too there is of course a creative process at work; but it is a higher one, because it is raised to the conscious level.

The alienation effect does not in any way demand an unnatural way of acting. It has nothing whatever to do with ordinary stylization. On the contrary, the achievement of an A-effect absolutely depends on lightness and naturalness of performance. But when the actor checks the truth of his performance (a necessary operation, which Stanislavsky is much concerned with in his system) he is not just thrown back on his "natural sensibilities," but can always be corrected by a comparison with reality (is that how an angry man really speaks? is that how an offended man sits down?) and so from outside, by other people. He acts in such a way that nearly every sentence could be followed by a verdict of the audience and practically every gesture is submitted for the public's approval.

The Chinese performer is in no trance. He can be interrupted at any moment. He won't have to "come round." After an interruption he will go on with his exposition from that point. We are not disturbing him at the "mystic moment of creation," when he steps on to the stage before us the process of creation is already over. He does not mind if the setting is changed around him as he plays. Busy hands quite openly pass him what he needs for his performance. When Mei Lang-fang was playing a death scene a spectator sitting next to me exclaimed with astonishment at one of his gestures. One or two people sitting in front of us turned round indignantly and sshhh'd. They behaved as if they were present at the real death of a real girl. Possibly their attitude would have been all right for a European production, but for a Chinese it was unspeakably ridiculous. In their case the A-effect had misfired.

It is not entirely easy to realize that the Chinese actor's A-effect is a transportable piece of technique: a conception that can be pried loose from the Chinese theatre. We see this theatre as uncommonly precious, its portrayal of human passions as schematized, its idea of society as rigid and wrong-headed; at first sight this superb art seems to offer nothing applicable to a realistic and revolutionary theatre. Against that, the motives and objects of the A-effect strike us as odd and suspicious.

When one sees the Chinese acting it is at first very hard to discount the feeling of estrangement which they produce in us as Europeans. One has to be able to imagine them achieving an A-effect among their Chinese spectators too. What is still harder is that one must accept the fact that when the Chinese performer conjures up an impression of mystery he seems uninterested in disclosing a mystery to us. He makes his own mystery from the mysteries of nature (especially human nature): he allows nobody to examine how he produces the natural phenomenon, nor does nature allow him to understand as he produces it. We have here the artistic counterpart of a primitive technology, a rudimentary science. The Chinese performer gets his A-effect by association with magic. "How it's done" remains hidden; knowledge is a matter of knowing the tricks and is in the hands of a few men who guard it jealously and profit from their secrets. And yet there is already an attempt here to interfere with the course of nature; the capacity to do so leads to questioning; and the future explorer, with his anxiety to make nature's course intelligible, controllable and down-to-earth, will always start by adopting a standpoint from which it seems mysterious, incomprehensible and beyond control. He will take up the attitude of somebody wondering, will apply the A-effect. Nobody can be a mathematician who takes it for granted that "two and two makes four"; nor is anybody one who fails to understand it. The man who first looked with astonishment at a swinging lantern and instead of taking it for granted found it highly remarkable that it should swing, and swing in that particular way rather than any other, was brought close to understanding the phenomenon by this observation, and so to mastering it. Nor must it simply be exclaimed that the attitude here proposed is all right for science but not for art. Why shouldn't art try, by its *own* means of course, to further the great social task of mastering life?

In point of fact the only people who can profitably study a piece of technique like Chinese acting's A-effect are those who need such a technique for quite definite social purposes.

The experiments conducted by the modern German theatre led to a wholly independent development of the A-effect. So far Asiatic acting has exerted no influence.

The A-effect was achieved in the German epic theatre not only by the actor, but also by the music (choruses, songs) and the setting (placards, film etc.). It was principally designed to historicize the incidents portrayed. By this is meant the following:

The bourgeois theatre emphasized the timelessness of its objects. Its representation of people is bound by the alleged "eternally human." Its story is arranged in such a way as to create "universal" situations that allow Man with a capital M to express himself: man of every period and every color. All its incidents are just one enormous cue, and this cue is followed by the "eternal" response: the inevitable, usual, natural, purely human response. An example: a black man falls in love in the same way as a white man: the story forces him to react with the same expression as the white man (in theory this formula works as well the other way round); and with that the sphere of art is attained. The cue can take account of what is special, different; the response is shared, there is no element of difference in it. This notion may allow that such a thing as history exists, but is none the less unhistorical. A few circumstances vary, the environments are altered, but Man remains unchanged. History applies to the environment, not to Man. The environment is remarkably unimportant, is treated simply as a pretext; it is a variable quantity and something remarkably inhuman; it exists in fact apart from Man, confronting him as a coherent whole, whereas he is a fixed quantity, eternally unchanged. The idea of man as a function of the environment and the environment as a function of man, i.e. the breaking up of environment into relationships between men, corresponds to a new way of thinking, the historical way. Rather than be sidetracked into the philosophy of history, let us give an example. Suppose the following is to be shown on the stage: a girl leaves home in order to take a job in a fair-sized city (Piscator's *American Tragedy*). For the bourgeois theatre this is an insignificant affair, clearly the beginning of a story; it is what one has to have been told in order to understand what comes after, or to be keyed up for. The actor's imagination will hardly be greatly fired by it. In a sense the incident is universal: girls take jobs (in the case in question one can be keyed up to see what in particular is going to happen to her). Only in one way is it particular: this girl goes away (if she had remained what comes after would not have happened). The fact that her family lets her go is not the object of the inquiry; it is understandable (the motives are understandable). But for the historicizing theatre everything is different. The theatre concentrates entirely on whatever in this perfectly everyday event is remarkable, particular and demanding inquiry. What! A family letting one of its members leave the nest to earn her future living independently and without help? Is she up to it? Will what she has learnt here as a member of the family help her to earn her living? Can't families keep a grip on their children any longer? Have they become (or remained) a burden? Is it like that with every family? Was it always like that? Is this the way of the world, something that can't be affected? The fruit falls off the tree when ripe: does this sentence apply here? Do children always make themselves independent? Did they do so in every age? If so, and if it's something biological, does it always happen in the same way, for the same reasons and with the same results? These are the questions (or a few of them) that the actors must answer if they want to show the incident as a unique, historical one: if they want to demonstrate a custom which leads to conclusions about the entire structure of a society at a particular (transient) time. But how is such an incident to be represented if its historic character is to be brought out? How can the confusion of our unfortunate epoch be striking? When the mother, in between warnings and moral injunctions, packs her daughter's case – a very small one – how is the following to be shown: So many injunctions and so few clothes? Moral injunctions for a lifetime and bread for five hours? How is the actress to speak the mother's sentence as she hands over such a very small case – "There, I guess that ought to do you" – in such a way that it is understood as a historic dictum? This can only be achieved if the A-effect is brought out. The actress must not make the sentence her own affair, she must hand it over to criticism, she must help us to understand its causes and protest. The effect can only be got by long training. In the New York Yiddish Theatre, a highly progressive theatre, I saw a play by S. Ornitz showing the rise of an East Side boy to be a big crooked attorney. The theatre could not perform the play. And yet there were scenes like this in it: the young attorney sits in the street outside his house giving cheap legal advice. A young woman arrives and complains that her leg has been hurt in a traffic accident. But the case has been bungled and her compensation has not yet been paid. In desperation she points to her leg and says: "It's started to heal up." Working without the A-effect, the theatre was unable to make use of this exceptional scene to show the horror of a bloody epoch. Few people in the audience noticed it; hardly anyone who reads it will remember that cry. The actress spoke the cry as if it were something perfectly natural. But is it exactly this – the fact that this poor creature finds such a complaint natural – that she should have reported to the public like a horrified messenger returning from the lowest of all hells. To that end she would of course have needed a special technique which would have allowed her to underline the historical aspect of a specific social condition. Only the A-effect makes this possible. Without it all she can do is to observe how she is not forced to go over entirely into the character on the stage.

In setting up new artistic principles and working out new methods of representation we must start with the compelling demands of a changing epoch; the necessity and the possibility of remodeling society loom ahead. All incidents between men must be noted, and everything must be seen from a social point of view. Among other effects that a new theatre will need for its social criticism and its historical reporting of completed transformations is the A-effect.

Notes

1 B. Brecht, *The Messingkauf Dialogue*, tr. J. Willett (London: Methuen, 1965), 47.
2 V. Shklovsky, "Art as Technique," tr. L. T. Lemon and M. J. Teis, in *Literary Aesthetics: A Reader*, ed. A. Singer and A. Dunn (Oxford: Blackwell, 2000), 225–6.
3 Brecht, *Messingkauf Dialogue*, 76.
4 S. Jestrovic, *Theatre of Estrangement: Theatre, Practice, Ideology* (Toronto: University of Toronto Press, 2006), 26, 40.
5 H. Arvon, *Marxist Aesthetics*, tr. H. Lane (Ithaca: Cornell University Press, 1973), 105.
6 B. Brecht, "Notes on Stanislavsky," *Tulane Drama Review* 9.2 (1964), 156.
7 This table does not show absolute antitheses but mere shifts of accent. In a communication of fact, for instance, we may choose whether to stress the element of emotional suggestion or that of plain rational argument.
8 Mei Lan-fang (1894–1961), Chinese actor, one of the first actors to introduce Eastern style to the West. Brecht observed his work in 1935. – Editor's note.

Chapter 22

Eugene O'Neill (1888–1953)

Eugene Gladstone O'Neill was a dramatist who experimented in various styles. His early realistic plays helped form the Little Theatre Movement in America, and he was one of the first American dramatists to experiment with expressionism in his *Emperor Jones* (1920) and *Hairy Ape* (1921). He used masks in *The Great God Brown* (1925), recreated Greek tragedy in a modern milieu in *Mourning Becomes Electra* (1929–31), examined the conflicts of race relations in *All God's Chillun Got Wings* (1924), and developed interior monologues spoken aloud in *Strange Interlude* (1926–7). His two greatest plays, *Long Day's Journey into Night* and *The Iceman Cometh* (published posthumously), are poignant dramas examining family, illusion, and the tenuous bonds of human relationships. He won the Nobel Prize for Literature in 1936.

O'Neill had a lifelong interest in masks. The series of essays reproduced here explicate his attempt to define masks in a modern idiom. O'Neill was concerned with self-deception, how we don masks in our everyday lives in order to disguise our feelings not only from others, but also from ourselves. The theatre was for O'Neill a laboratory exploring the use of illusion and whether or not illusion comforts people from harsh reality. Influenced by Ibsen, Strindberg, and Nietzsche, O'Neill expressed the conflict between reality and illusion, thematically returning to the arguments begun by Plato.

Memoranda on Masks (1932)

Not masks for all plays, naturally. Obviously not for plays conceived in purely realistic terms. But masks for certain types of plays, especially for the new modern play, as yet only dimly foreshadowed in a few groping specimens, but which must inevitably be written in

Three essays by Eugene O'Neill from *The American Spectator*: "Memoranda on Masks" (November 1932), 3; "Second Thoughts" (December 1932), 20; and "A Dramatist's Notebook" (January 1933), 2.

the future. For I hold more and more surely to the conviction that the use of masks will be discovered eventually to be the freest solution of the modem dramatist's problem as to how – with the greatest possible dramatic clarity and economy of means – he can express those profound hidden conflicts of the mind which the probings of psychology continue to disclose to us. He must find some method to present this inner drama in his work, or confess himself incapable of portraying one of the most characteristic preoccupations and uniquely significant, spiritual impulses of his time. With his old – and more than a bit senile! – standby of realistic technique, he can do no more than, at best, obscurely hint at it through a realistically disguised surface symbolism, superficial and misleading. But that, while sufficiently beguiling to the sentimentally mystical, is hardly enough. A comprehensive expression is demanded here, a chance for eloquent presentation, a new form of drama projected from a fresh insight into the inner forces motivating the actions and reactions, of men and women (a new and truer characterization, in other words) – a drama of souls, and the adventures of "free wills," with the masks that govern them and constitute their fates.

For what, at bottom, is the new psychological insight into human cause and effect but a study in masks, an exercise in unmasking? Whether we think the attempted unmasking has been successful, or has only created for itself new masks, is of no importance here. What is valid, what is unquestionable, is that this insight has uncovered the mask, has impressed the idea of mask as a symbol of inner reality upon all intelligent people of today; and I know they would welcome the use of masks in the theatre as a necessary, dramatically revealing new convention, and not regard them as any "stunt," resurrection of archaic props.

This was strikingly demonstrated for me in practical experience by *The Great God Brown*, which ran in New York for eight months, nearly all of that time in Broadway theatres – a play in which the use of masks was an integral part of the theme. There was some misunderstanding, of course. But so is there always misunderstanding in the case of every realistic play that attempts to express anything beyond what is contained in a human-interest newspaper story. In the main, however, *The Great God Brown* was accepted and appreciated by both critics and public – a fairly extensive public, as its run gives evidence.

I emphasize this play's success because the fact that a mask drama, the main values of which are psychological, mystical, and abstract, could be played in New York for eight months, has always seemed to me a more significant proof of the deeply responsive possibilities in our public than anything that has happened in our modern theatre before or since.

[2]

Looked at from even the most practical standpoint of the practicing playwright, the mask *is* dramatic in itself, *has always* been dramatic in itself, *is* a proven weapon of attack. At its best, it is more subtly, imaginatively, suggestively dramatic than any actor's face can ever be. Let anyone who doubts this study the Japanese Noh masks, or Chinese theatre masks, or African primitive masks – or right here in America the faces of the big marionettes Robert Edmond Jones made for the production of Stravinsky's *Oedipus*, or [Polish painter Waldystaw Teodor] Benda's famous masks, or even photographs of them.

[3]

Dogma for the new masked drama. One's outer life passes in a solitude haunted by the masks of others; one's inner life passes in a solitude hounded by the masks of oneself.

[4]

With masked mob a new type of play may be written in which the Mob as King, Hero, Villain, or Fool will be the main character – The Great Democratic Play!

[5]

Why not give all future Classical revivals entirely in masks? *Hamlet*, for example. Masks would liberate this play from its present confining status as exclusively a "star vehicle." We would be able to see the great drama we are not only privileged to read, to identify ourselves with the figure of Hamlet as a symbolic projection of a fate that is in each of us, instead of merely watching a star giving us his version of a great acting role. We would even be able to hear the sublime poetry as the innate expression of the spirit of the drama itself, instead of listening to it as realistic recitation – or ranting by familiar actors.

[6]

Consider Goethe's *Faust*, which, psychologically speaking, should be the closest to us of all the Classics. In producing this play, I would have Mephistopheles wearing the Mephisto-phelean mask of the face of Faust. For is not the whole of Goethe's truth for our time just that Mephistopheles and Faust are one and the same – are Faust?

Second Thoughts (1932)

What would I change in past productions of my plays if I could live through them again?

Many things. In some plays, considerable revision of the writing of some of the scenes would strike me as imperative. Other plays – *The First Man, Gold, Welded, The Fountain* – I would dismiss as being too painfully bungled in their present form to be worth producing at all.

But one thing I most certainly would not change: the use of masks in *The Hairy Ape*, in my arrangement of Coleridge's "Ancient Mariner," in *All God's Chillun Got Wings* (the symbol of the African primitive mask in the last part of the play, which, in the production in Russian by the Moscow Kamerny Theatre I saw in Paris, is dramatically intensified and emphasized), in *The Great God Brown* and, finally, in *Lazarus Laughed*, in which all the characters except Lazarus remain masked throughout the play. I regard this use of masks as having been uniformly successful.

The change I would make would be to call for more masks in some of these productions and to use them in other productions where they were not used before. In *The Emperor Jones*, for example. All the figures in Jones's flight through the forest should be masked. Masks would dramatically stress their phantasmal quality, as contrasted with the unmasked

Jones, intensify the supernatural menace of the tomtom, give the play a more complete and vivid expression. In *The Hairy Ape*, a much more extensive use of masks would be of the greatest value in emphasizing the theme of the play. From the opening of the fourth scene, where Yank begins to think, he enters into a masked world; even the familiar faces of his mates in the forecastle have become strange and alien. They should be masked, and the faces of everyone he encounters thereafter, including the symbolic gorilla's.

In *All God's Chillun Got Wings*, all save the seven leading characters should be masked; for all the secondary figures are part and parcel of the Expressionistic background of the play, a world at first indifferent, then cruelly hostile, against which the tragedy of Jim Harris is outlined. In *The Great God Brown* I would now make the masks symbolize more definitely the abstract theme of the play instead of, as in the old production, stressing the more superficial meaning that people wear masks before other people and are mistaken by them for their masks.

In *Marco Millions* all the people of the East should be masked – Kublai, the Princess Kokachin, all of them! For anyone who has been in the East, or who has read Eastern philosophy, the reason for this is obvious. It is an exact dramatic expression of West confronted by East. Moreover, it is the only possible way to project this contrast truthfully in the theatre, for Western actors cannot convey Eastern character realistically, and their only chance to suggest it convincingly is with the help of masks.

As for *Strange Interlude*, that is an attempt at the new masked psychological drama which I have discussed before, without masks – a successful attempt, perhaps, in so far as it concerns only surfaces and their immediate sub-surfaces, but not where, occasionally, it tries to probe deeper.

With *Mourning Becomes Electra*, masks were called for in one draft of the three plays. But the Classical connotation was too insistent. Masks in that connection demand great language to speak – which let me out of it with a sickening bump! So I had to discard them. There was a realistic New England insistence in my mind, too, which would have barred great language even in a dramatist capable of writing it, an insistence on the clotted and clogged and inarticulate. So it evolved ultimately into the "masklike faces," which expressed my intention tempered by the circumstances. However, I should like to see *Mourning Becomes Electra* done entirely with masks, now that I can view it solely as a psychological play, quite removed from the confusing preoccupations the Classical derivation of its plot once caused me. Masks would emphasize the drama of the life and death impulses that drive the characters on to their fates and put more in its proper secondary place, as a frame, the story of the New England family.

A Dramatist's Notebook (1933)

I advocate masks for stage crowds, mobs – wherever a sense of impersonal, collective mob psychology is wanted. This was one reason for such an extensive use of them in *Lazarus Laughed*. In masking the crowds in that play, I was visualizing an effect that, intensified by dramatic lighting, would give an audience visually the sense of the Crowd, not as a random collection of individuals, but as a collective whole, an entity. When the Crowd speaks, I wanted an audience to hear the voice of Crowd mind, Crowd emotion, as one voice of a body composed of, but quite distinct from, its parts.

And, for more practical reasons, I wanted to preserve the different crowds of another time and country from the blighting illusion-shattering recognitions by an audience of the supers on the stage. Have you ever seen a production of *Julius Caesar*? Did the Roman mob ever suggest to you anything more Roman than a gum-chewing Coney Island Mardi Gras or, in the case of a special all-star revival, a gathering of familiar-faced modern actors masquerading uncomfortably in togas? But with masks – and the proper intensive lighting – you would have been freed from these recognitions; you would have been able to imagine a Roman mob; you would not even have recognized the Third Avenue and Brooklyn accents among the supers, so effectively does a mask change the quality of a voice.

It was interesting to watch, in the final rehearsals of *The Great God Brown*, how after using their masks for a time the actors and actresses reacted to the demand made by the masks that their bodies become alive and expressive and participate in the drama. Usually it is only the actors' faces that participate. Their bodies remain bored spectators that have been dragged off to the theatre when they would have much preferred a quiet evening in the upholstered chair at home.

Meaning no carping disrespect to our actors. I have been exceedingly lucky in having had some exceptionally fine acting in the principal roles in my plays, for which I am exceedingly grateful. Also some damned poor acting. But let that pass. Most of the poor acting occurred in the poor plays, and there I hold only myself responsible. In the main, wherever a part challenged the actors' or actresses' greatest possibilities, they have reacted to the challenge with a splendid creative energy and skill. Especially, and this is the point I want to make now, where the play took them away from the strictly realistic parts they were accustomed to playing. They always welcomed any opportunity that gave them new scope for their talents. So when I argue here for a non-realistic imaginative theatre I am hoping, not only for added scope for playwright and director and scenic designer, but also for a chance for the actor to develop his art beyond the narrow range to which our present theatre condemns it. Most important of all, from the standpoint of future American culture, I am hoping for added imaginative scope for the audience, a chance for a public I know is growing yearly more numerous and more hungry in its spiritual need to participate in imaginative interpretations of life rather than merely identify itself with faithful surface resemblances of living.

I harp on the word "imaginative" – and with intention! But what do I mean by an "imaginative" theatre – (where I hope for it, for example, in the subtitle of *Lazarus Laughed*: A Play for an Imaginative Theatre)? I mean the one true theatre, the age-old theatre, the theatre of the Greeks and Elizabethans, a theatre that could dare to boast – without committing a farcical sacrilege – that it is a legitimate descendant of the first theatre that sprang, by virtue of man's imaginative interpretation of life, out of his worship of Dionysus. I mean a theatre returned to its highest and sole significant function as a Temple where the religion of a poetical interpretation and symbolical celebration of life is communicated to human beings, starved in spirit by their soul-stifling daily struggle to exist as masks among the masks of living!

But I anticipate the actors' objection to masks: that they would extinguish their personalities and deprive them of their greatest asset in conveying emotion by facial expression. I claim, however, that masks would give them the opportunity for a totally new kind of acting, that they would learn many undeveloped possibilities of their art if they appeared, even if only for a season or two, in masked roles. After all, masks did not extinguish the Greek actor, nor have they kept the acting of the East from being an art.

Chapter 23

Gertrude Stein (1874–1946)

Gertrude Stein was a poet, playwright, feminist, and author. American born, she spent most of her life in France. The sister of art critic Leo Stein, she lived in the hub of Parisian modernism. In 1907 she met her lifelong partner, Alice B. Toklas, and also befriended Picasso. In the 1920s her Paris salon was the center of modern art and literature, attracting authors, painters, and philosophers. She coined the term "lost generation" in describing the American ex-patriots who came to Paris. Her most reproduced play is *Four Saints in Three Acts* (1934). Stein's literary work explored several themes, but her main concern was language, its meaning and form. She focused on what Sarah Bay-Cheng calls "her use of non-linear plot, repetition, the fragmentation or complete elimination of character, simultaneity, and her own unique, 'continuous present.' " Stein was influenced by the avant-garde cinema, attempting to turn the theatre into a metaphor for "ambiguous images, fractured and multiplicative characters, and words collaged or edited in nonlinear progression or, more often, stagnation."[1] Stein was also concerned with the geography of theatre, how the stage space informed images and projections. Like the Cubist painters with whom she was closely associated, Stein used the theatre of shapes to create a panorama of ideas. She influenced important twentieth-century directors such as Frank Galati, Al Carmines, Robert Wilson, Elizabeth LeCompte, and Anne Bogart, and theatres such as the Living Theatre, Judson Poets Theatre, and the Wooster Group.

Excerpts from Gertrude Stein, "Plays" (1934), from Stein, *Last Operas and Plays*, ed. Bonnie Marranca (Baltimore: Johns Hopkins University Press, 1995), xxix–xliv. © 1949 by the Estate of Gertrude Stein. Copyright renewed, 1977. "Plays" taken from *Lectures in America* © 1935 and renewed 1963 by Alice B. Toklas.

Plays (1934)

In a book I wrote called *How To Write* I made a discovery which I considered fundamental, that sentences are not emotional and that paragraphs are. I found out about language that paragraphs are emotional and sentences are not and I found out something else about it. I found out that this difference was not a contradiction but a combination and that this combination causes one to think endlessly about sentences and paragraphs because the emotional paragraphs are made up of unemotional sentences.

I found out a fundamental thing about plays. The thing I found out about plays was too a combination and not a contradiction and it was something that makes one think endlessly about plays.

That something is this.

The thing that is fundamental about plays is that the scene as depicted on the stage is more often than not one might say it is almost always in syncopated time in relation to the emotion of anybody in the audience.

What this says is this.

Your sensation as one in the audience in relation to the play played before you your sensation I say your emotion concerning that play is always either behind or ahead of the play at which you are looking and to which you are listening. So your emotion as a member of the audience is never going on at the same time as the action of the play.

This thing the fact that your emotional time as an audience is not the same as the emotional time of the play is what makes one endlessly troubled about a play, because not only is there a thing to know as to why this is so but also there is a thing to know why perhaps it does not need to be so.

This is a thing to know and knowledge as anybody can know is a thing to get by getting.

And so I will try to tell you what I had to get and what perhaps I have gotten in plays and to do so I will tell you all that I have ever felt about plays or about any play.

Plays are either read or heard or seen.

And there then comes the question which comes first and which is first, reading or hearing or seeing a play.

I ask you.

What is knowledge. Of course knowledge is what you know and what you know is what you do know.

What do I know about plays.

In order to know one must always go back.

What was the first play I saw and was I then already bothered bothered about the different tempo there is in the play and in yourself and your emotion in having the play go on in front of you. I think I may say I may say I know that I was already troubled by this in that my first experience at a play. The thing seen and the emotion did not go on together.

This that the thing seen and the thing felt about the thing seen not going on at the same tempo is what makes the being at the theatre something that makes anybody nervous.

The jazz bands made of this thing, the thing that makes you nervous at the theatre, they made of this thing an end in itself. They made of this different tempo a something that was nothing but a difference in tempo between anybody and everybody including all those doing it and all those hearing and seeing it. In the theatre of course this difference in tempo is less violent but still it is there and it does make anybody nervous.

In the first place at the theatre there is the curtain and the curtain already makes one feel that one is not going to have the same tempo as the thing that is there behind the curtain. The emotion of you on one side of the curtain and what is on the other side of the curtain are not going to be going on together. One will always be behind or in front of the other.

Then also beside the curtain there is the audience and the fact that they are or will be or will not be in the way when the curtain goes up that too makes for nervousness and nervousness is the certain proof that the emotion of the one seeing and the emotion of the thing seen do not progress together.

Nervousness consists in needing to go faster or to go slower so as to get together. It is that that makes anybody feel nervous.

And is it a mistake that that is what the theatre is or is it not.

There are things that are exciting as the theatre is exciting but do they make you nervous or do they not, and if they do and if they do not why do they and why do they not.

Let us think of three different kinds of things that are exciting and that make or do not make one nervous. First any scene which is a real scene something real that is happening in which one takes part as an actor in that scene. Second any book that is exciting, third the theatre at which one sees an exciting action in which one does not take part.

Now in a real scene in which one takes part at which one is an actor what does one feel as to time and what is it that does or does not make one nervous.

And is your feeling at such a time ahead and behind the action the way it is when you are at the theatre. It is the same and it is not. But more not.

If you are taking part in an actual violent scene, and you talk and they or he or she talk and it goes on and it gets more exciting and finally then it happens, whatever it is that does happen then when it happens then at the moment of happening is it a relief from the excitement or is it a completion of the excitement. In the real thing it is a completion of the excitement, in the theatre it is a relief from the excitement, and in that difference the difference between completion and relief is the difference between emotion concerning a thing seen on the stage and the emotion concerning a real presentation that is really something happening. [...]

This [...] is the fundamental difference between excitement in real life and on the stage, in real life it culminates in a sense of completion whether an exciting act or an exciting emotion has been done or not, and on the stage the exciting climax is a relief. And the memory of the two things is different. As you go over the detail that leads to culmination of any scene in real life, you find that each time you cannot get completion, but you can get relief and so already your memory of any exciting scene in which you have taken part burst it into the thing seen or heard not the thing felt. You have as I say as the result relief rather than culmination. Relief from excitement, rather than the climax of excitement. In this respect an exciting story does the same only in the exciting story, you so to speak have control of it as you have in your memory of a really exciting scene, it is not as it is on the stage a thing over which you have no real control. You can with an exciting story find out the end and so begin over again just as you can in remembering an exciting scene, but the stage is different, it is not real and yet it is not within your control as the memory of an exciting thing is or the reading of an exciting book. No matter how well you know the end of the stage story it is nevertheless not within your control as the memory of an exciting thing is or as the written story of an exciting thing is or even in a curious way the heard story of an exciting thing is. And what is the reason for this difference and what does it do to the stage. It makes for nervousness that of course, and the cause of nervousness is the fact that the emotion of the one seeing the play is always ahead or behind the play.

Beside all this there is a thing to be realized and that is how you are being introduced to the characters who take part in an exciting action even when you yourself are one of the actors. And this too has to be very much thought about. And thought about in relation to an exciting real thing to an exciting book, to an exciting theatre. How are you introduced to the characters.

There are then the three ways of having something be exciting, and the excitement may or may not make one nervous, a book being read that is exciting, a scene in which one takes part or an action in which one takes part and the theatre at which one looks on.

In each case the excitement and the nervousness and me being behind or ahead in one's feeling is different.

First anything exciting in which one takes part. There one progresses forward and back emotionally and at the supreme crisis of the scene the scene in which one takes part, in which one's hopes and loves and fears take part at the extreme crisis of this thing one is almost one with one's emotions, the action and the emotion go together, there is but just a moment of this coordination but it does exist otherwise there is no completion as one has no result, no result of a scene in which one has taken part, and so instinctively when any people are living an exciting moment one with another they go on and on and on until the thing has come together the emotion the action the excitement and that is the way it is when there is any violence either of loving or hating or quarreling or losing or succeeding. But there is, there has to be the moment of it all being abreast the emotion, the excitement and the action otherwise there would be no succeeding and no failing and so no one would go on living, why yes of course not.

That is life the way it is lived.

Why yes of course and there is a reasonable and sometimes an unreasonable and very often not a reasonable amount of excitement in everybody's life and when it happens it happens in that way.

Now when you read a book how is it. Well it is not exactly like that no not even when a book is even more exciting than any excitement one has ever had. In the first place one can always look at the end of the book and so quiet down one's excitement. The excitement having been quieted down one can enjoy the excitement just as any one can enjoy the excitement of anything having happened to them by remembering and so tasting it over and over again but each time less intensely and each time until it is all over. Those who like to read books over and over get continuously this sensation of the excitement as if it were a pleasant distant thunder that rolls and rolls and the more it rolls well the further it rolls the pleasanter until it does not roll any more. That is until at last you have read the book so often that it no longer holds any excitement not even ever so faintly and then you have to wait until you have forgotten it and you can begin it again.

Now the theatre has still another way of being all this to you, the thing causing your emotion and the excitement in connection with it.

Of course lots of other things can do these things to lots of other people that is to say excite lots of people but as I have said knowledge is what you know and I naturally tell you what I know, as I do so very essentially believe in knowledge.

So then once again what does the theatre do and how does it do it.

What happens on the stage and how and how does one feel about it. That is the thing to know, to know and to tell it as so.

Is the thing seen or the thing heard the thing that makes most of its impression upon you at the theatre. How much has the hearing to do with it and how little. Does the thing heard replace the thing seen. Does it help or does it interfere with it.

And when you are taking part in something really happening that is exciting, how is it. Does the thing seen or does the thing heard effect you and effect you at the same time or in the same degree or does it not. Can you wait to hear or can you wait to see and which excites you the most. And what has either one to do with the completion of the excitement when the excitement is a real excitement that is excited by something really happening. And then little by little does the hearing replace the seeing or does the seeing replace the hearing. Do they go together or do they not. And when the exciting something in which you have taken part arrives at its completion does the hearing replace the seeing or does it not. Does the seeing replace the hearing or does it not. Or do they both go on together.

All this is very important, and important for me and important, just important. It has of course a great deal to do with the theatre a great great deal. [...]

Note

1   S. Bay-Cheng, *Mama Dada: Gertrude Stein's Avant-Garde Theater* (New York: Routledge, 2005), 18.

Chapter 24

Zora Neale Hurston (1891–1960)

Zora Neale Hurston was a novelist, dramatist, critic, anthropologist, and essayist who rose to prominence during the 1930s and 1940s, only to fall into obscurity by the 1950s. By the 1970s, interest in Hurston was revived, and she once again received the attention she deserved. During her lifetime she managed to alienate many, reveling in her iconoclasm in both the black and white community. Hurston firmly believed in the values of the rural, southern, African American life – its art and culture – and feared that urban modernism was overtaking their artistic contributions. Although primarily known as a novelist, she was a playwright, director, choreographer, designer, and drama teacher at several colleges and universities. Throughout her work she emphasized "the real Negro theatre," which she believed existed in jook joints (roadside shacks converted into bars and music clubs), the turpentine camps of black workers, and the daily existence of blacks whose creativity often occurred on the front porches of rural southern homes. She took umbrage at urban modernism, considering its art and theatre as watered-down images of African American life. Her form of realism was regional, particular, and endemic to the working class. Although her politics were sometimes conservative – she opposed integration and rejected socialism – her identification with the working class derived from her life in Eatonville, Florida, the first all-black town to be incorporated and chartered in the United States.

Her essay, "Characteristics of Negro Expression," was an outgrowth of her Columbia University PhD dissertation in anthropology under the tutelage of Franz Boas. Boas encouraged Hurston to do field work by traveling back to her roots in the rural South. This she did with alacrity, returning with data, interviews, and observations. Hurston placed a great premium on getting theatre aligned with reality. Although she argues that black southern culture is always changing, she nevertheless challenged her colleagues to represent the essence of this culture. This essay, published in Nancy Cunard's *Negro* in 1934, pronounces the dramatic traits of the people she examined. Her concept of "drama," Hurston scholar Lynda Marion Hill notes, is meant to be "a model – a world-as-stage metaphor – to explain patterns of expressive behavior."[1] Hurston's ideas of "Negro identity" are a mixture derived from her research and epitomize the irony and tongue-in-cheek language of everyday life. The text is characteristic of Hurston's literary output: rich in double entendre, innuendo, humor, and vitality. Hurston is criticizing the pretensions of the elite, whom she believed claimed to know African Americans but were in fact ignorant of working-class life (what she termed the "lowest down"). She calls attention to the collective rituals of African Americans, contending that "Negro expression" is a communal art. It combines the everyday as "experience" and a detachment that produces a conscious self-creation. At the same time, Barbara Johnson writes, Hurston "deplored the appropriation, dilution, and commodification of black culture (through spirituals, jazz, etc.) by the pre-Depression white world, and she constantly tried to explain the difference between a reified 'art' and a living culture in which the distinctions between the spectator and spectacle, rehearsal and performance, experience and representation, are not fixed."[2] Performance for Hurston requires an audience to complete its meaning. Hurston, like Gertrude Stein (see Chapter 23), enjoyed her nonconformity. Fiercely independent, Stein and Hurston made their ways in an intellectual world not always receptive to their ideas.

Characteristics of Negro Expression (1934)

Drama

The Negro's universal mimicry is not so much a thing in itself as evidence of something that permeates his entire self. And that thing is drama.

His very words are action words. His interpretation of the English language is in terms of pictures. One act described in terms of another. Hence the rich metaphor and simile.

The metaphor is of course very primitive. It is easier to illustrate than it is to explain because action came before speech. Let us make a parallel. Language is like money. In primitive communities actual goods, however bulky, are bartered for what one wants. This finally evolves into coin, the coin being not real wealth but a symbol of wealth. Still later, even coin is abandoned for legal tender, and still later cheques for certain usages.

Every phase of Negro life is highly dramatized. No matter how joyful or how sad the case there is sufficient poise for drama. Everything is acted out. Unconsciously for the most part of course. There is an impromptu ceremony always ready for every hour of life. No little moment passes unadorned.

Now the people with highly developed languages have words for detached ideas. That is legal tender. "That-which-we-squat-on" has become "chair." "Groan-causer" has evolved into "spear" and so on. Some individuals even conceive of the equivalent of cheque words, like "ideation" and "pleonastic." Perhaps we might say that *Paradise Lost* and *Sartor Resartus* are written in cheque words.

The primitive man exchanges descriptive words. His terms are all close fitting. Frequently the Negro, even with detached words in his vocabulary – not evolved in him but transplanted on his tongue by contact – must add action to it to make it do. So we have "chop-axe," "sitting-chair," and "cook-pot" and the like because the speaker has in his mind the picture of the object in use. Action. Everything illustrated. So we can say the white man thinks in a written language and the Negro thinks in hieroglyphics.

A bit of Negro drama familiar to all is the frequent meeting of two opponents who threaten to do atrocious murder one upon the other.

Who has not observed a robust young Negro chap posing upon a street corner, possessed of nothing but his clothing, his strength, and his youth? Does he bear himself like a pauper? No, Louis XIV could be no more insolent in his assurance. His eyes say plainly "Female, halt!" His posture exults "Ah, female, I am the eternal male, the giver of life. Behold in my hot flesh all the delights of this world. Salute me, I am strength." All this with a languid posture, there is no mistaking his meaning.

A Negro girl strolls past the corner lounger. Her whole body panging [pangs of hunger] and posing. A slight shoulder movement that calls attention to her bust, that is all of a dare. A hippy undulation below the waist that is a sheaf of promises tied with conscious power. She is acting out "I'm a darned sweet woman and you know it."

These little plays by strolling players are acted out daily in a dozen streets in a thousand cities, and no one ever mistakes the meaning.

Will To Adorn

The will to adorn is the second most notable characteristic in Negro expression. Perhaps his idea of ornament does not attempt to meet conventional standards, but it satisfies the soul of its creator.

In this respect the American Negro has done wonders to the English language. This is true, but it is equally true that he has made over a great part of the tongue to his liking and has his revision accepted by the ruling class. No one listening to a Southern white man talk could deny this. Not only has he softened and toned down strongly consonanted words like "aren't" to "ain't" and the like, he has made new force words out of old feeble elements. Examples of this are "ham-shanked," "battle-hammed," "double-teen," "bodaciously," "muffle-jawed."

But the Negro's greatest contribution to the language is: (1) the use of metaphor and simile, (2) the use of the double descriptive, (3) the use of verbal nouns. [. . .]

The stark, trimmed phrases of the Occident seem too bare for the voluptuous child of the sun, hence the adornment. It arises out of the same impulse as the wearing of jewelry and the making of sculpture – the urge to adorn.

On the walls of the home of the average Negro one always finds a glut of gaudy calendars, wall pockets and advertising lithographs. The sophisticated white man or Negro would tolerate none of these, even if they bore a likeness to the Mona Lisa. No commercial art for decoration. Neither the calendar nor the advertisement spoils the picture for this lowly man. He sees the beauty in spite of the declaration of the Portland Cement Works or the butcher's announcement. I saw in Mobile a room in which there was an over-stuffed mohair living-room suite, an imitation mahogany bed and chifferobe, a console victrola. The walls were gaily papered with Sunday supplements of the *Mobile*

Register. There were seven calendars and three wall pockets. One of them was decorated with a lace doily. The mantel-shelf was covered with a scarf of deep home-made lace, looped up with a huge bow of pink crepe paper. Over the door was a huge lithograph showing the Treaty of Versailles being signed with a Waterman fountain pen.

It was grotesque, yes. But it indicated a desire for beauty. And decorating a decoration, as in the case of the doily on the gaudy wall pocket, did not seem out of place to the hostess. The feeling back of such an act is that there can never be enough of beauty, let alone too much. Perhaps she is right. We each have our standards of art, and thus we are all interested parties and so unfit to pass judgment upon the art concepts of others.

Whatever the Negro does of his own volition he embellishes. His religious service is for the greater part excellent prose poetry. Both prayers and sermons are tooled and polished until they are true works of art. The supplication is forgotten in the frenzy of creation. The prayer of the white man is considered humorous in its bleakness. The beauty of the Old Testament does not exceed that of a Negro prayer.

Angularity

After adornment the next most striking manifestation of the Negro is Angularity. Everything that he touches becomes angular. In all African sculpture and doctrine of any sort we find the same thing.

Anyone watching Negro dancers will be struck by the same phenomenon. Every posture is another angle. Pleasing, yes. But an effect achieved by the very means which a European strives to avoid.

The pictures on the walls are hung at deep angles. Furniture is always set at an angle. I have instances of a piece of furniture in the *middle* of a wall being set with one end nearer the wall than the other to avoid the simple straight line.

Asymmetry

Asymmetry is a definite feature of Negro art. I have no samples of true Negro painting unless we count the African shields, but the sculpture and carvings are full of this beauty and lack of symmetry. It is present in the literature, both prose and verse. [...]

It is the lack of symmetry which makes Negro dancing so difficult for white dancers to learn. The abrupt and unexpected changes. The frequent changes of key and time are evidences of this quality in music (Note the St. Louis Blues).

The dancing of the justly famous Bo-Jangles and Snake Hips are excellent examples.

The presence of rhythm and lack of symmetry are paradoxical, but there they are. Both are present to a marked degree. There is always rhythm, but it is the rhythm of segments. Each unit has a rhythm of its own, but when the whole is assembled it is lacking in symmetry. But easily workable to a Negro who is accustomed to the break in going from one part to another, so that he adjusts himself to the new tempo.

Dancing

Negro dancing is dynamic suggestion. No matter how violent it may appear to the beholder, every posture gives the impression that the dancer will do much more. For example, the performer flexes one knee sharply, assumes a ferocious face mask, thrusts the upper part of the body forward with clenched fists, elbows taut as in hard running or grasping a thrusting blade. That is all. But the spectator himself adds the picture of ferocious assault, hears the drums and finds himself keeping time with the music and tensing himself for the struggle. It is compelling insinuation. That is the very reason the spectator is held so rapt. He is participating in the performance himself – carrying out the suggestions of the performer.

The difference in the two arts is: the white dancer attempts to express fully; the Negro is restrained, but succeeds in gripping the beholder by forcing him to finish the action the performer suggests. Since no art can ever express all the variations conceivable, the Negro must be considered the greater artist, his dancing is realistic suggestion, and that is about all a great artist can do.

Negro Folklore

Negro folklore is not a thing of the past. It is still in the making. Its great variety shows the adaptability of the black man: nothing is too old or too new, domestic or foreign, high or low, for his use. God and the Devil are paired, and are treated no more reverently than Rockefeller and Ford. Both of these men are prominent in folklore. Ford being particularly strong, and they talk and act like good-natured stevedores or mill-hands. Ole Massa is sometimes a smart man and often a fool. The automobile is ranged alongside of the oxcart. The angels and the apostles walk and talk like section hands. And through it all walks Jack, the greatest culture hero of the South; Jack beats them all – even the Devil, who is often smarter than God. [...]

Originality

It has been said so often that the Negro is lacking in originality that it has almost become a gospel. Outward signs seem to bear this out. But if one looks closely its falsity is immediately evident.

It is obvious that to get back to original sources is much too difficult for any group to claim very much as a certainty. What we really mean by originality is the modification of ideas. The most ardent admirer of the great Shakespeare cannot claim first source even for him. It is his treatment of the borrowed material.

So if we look at it squarely, the Negro is a very original being. While he lives and moves in the midst of a white civilization, everything that he touches is reinterpreted for his own use. He has modified the language, mode of food preparation, practice of medicine, and most certainly the religion of his new country, just as he adapted to suit himself the Sheik haircut made famous by Rudolph Valentino.

Everyone is familiar with the Negro's modification of the whites' musical instruments, so that his interpretation has been adopted by the white man himself and then re-interpreted. In so many words, Paul Whiteman is giving an imitation of a Negro orchestra making use of white-invented instruments in a Negro way. Thus has arisen a new art in the civilized world, and thus has our so called civilization come. The exchange and re-exchange of ideas between groups.

Imitation

The Negro, the world over, is famous as a mimic. But this in no way damages his standing as an original. Mimicry is an art in itself. If it is not, then all art must fall by the same blow that strikes it down. When sculpture, painting, dancing, literature neither reflect nor suggest anything in nature or human experience we turn away with a dull wonder in our hearts at why the thing was done. Moreover, the contention that the Negro imitates from a feeling of inferiority is incorrect. He mimics for the love of it. The group of Negroes who slavishly imitate is small. The average Negro glories in his ways. The highly educated Negro the same. The self-despisement lies in a middle class who scorns to do or be anything Negro. "That's just like a Nigger" is the most terrible rebuke one can lay upon this kind. He wears drab clothing, sits through a boresome church service, pretends to have no interest in the community, holds beauty contests, and otherwise apes all the mediocrities of the white brother. The truly cultured Negro scorns him, and the Negro "farthest down" is too busy "spreading his junk" in his own way to see or care. He likes his own things best. Even the group who are not Negroes but belong to the "sixth race," buy such records as "Shake dat thing" and "Tight lak dat." They really enjoy hearing a good bible-beater preacher, but wild horses could drag no such admission from them. Their readymade expression is: "We done got away from all that now." Some refuse to coun- tenance Negro music on the grounds that it is niggerism, and for that reason should be done away with. Roland Hayes was thoroughly denounced for singing spirituals until he was accepted by white audiences. Langston Hughes is not considered a poet by this group because he writes of the man in the ditch, who is more numerous and real among us than any other.

But, this group aside, let us say that the art of mimicry is better developed in the Negro than in other racial groups. He does it as the mocking-bird does it, for the love of it, and not because he wishes to be like the one imitated. I saw a group of small Negro boys imitating a cat defecating and the subsequent toilet of the cat. It was very realistic, and they enjoyed it as much as if they had been imitating a coronation ceremony. The dances are full of imitations of various animals. The buzzard lope, walking the dog, the pig's hind legs, holding the mule, elephant squat, pigeon's wing, falling off the log, seabord (imitation of an engine starting), and the like.

Absence of the Concept of Privacy

It is said that Negroes keep nothing secret, that they have no reserve. This ought not to seem strange when one considers that we are an outdoor people accustomed to commu- nal life. Add this to all-permeating drama and you have the explanation.

There is no privacy in an African village. Love, fights, possessions are, to misquote Woodrow Wilson, "Open disagreements openly arrived at." The community is given the benefit of a good fight as well as a good wedding. An audience is a necessary part of any drama. We merely go with nature rather than against it.

Discord is more natural than accord. If we accept the doctrine of the survival of the fittest, there are more fighting honors than there are honors for other achievements. Humanity places premiums on all things necessary to its well-being, and a valiant and good fighter is valuable in any community. So why hide the light under a bushel? Moreover, intimidation is a recognized part of warfare the world over, and threats certainly must be listed under that head. So that a great threatener must certainly be considered an aid to the fighting machine. So then if a man or woman is a facile hurler of threats, why should he or she not show their wares to the community? Hence, the holding of all quarrels and fights in the open. One relieves one's pent-up anger and at the same time earns laurels in intimidation. Besides, one does the community a service. There is nothing so exhilarating as watching well-matched opponents go into action. The entire world likes action, for that matter. Hence prize-fighters become millionaires.

Likewise love-making is a biological necessity the world over and an art among Negroes. So that a man or woman who is proficient sees no reason why the fact should not be moot. He swaggers. She struts hippily about. Songs are built on the power to charm beneath the bed-clothes. Here again we have individuals striving to excel in what the community considers an art. Then if all of his world is seeking a great lover, why should he not speak right out loud?

It is all in a view-point. Love-making and fighting in all their branches are high arts, other things are arts among groups where they brag about their proficiency just as brazenly as we do about these things that others consider matters for conversation behind closed doors. At any rate, the white man is despised by Negroes as a very poor fighter individually, and a very poor lover. One Negro, speaking of white men, said, "White folks is alright when dey gits in de bank and on de law bench, but dey sho' kin lie about wimmen folks." [...]

The Jook

Jook is the word for a Negro pleasure house. It may mean a bawdy house. It may mean a house set apart on public works where the men and women dance, drink, and gamble. Often it is a combination of all these. [...]

The Negro dances circulated over the world were also conceived inside the Jooks. They too make the round of Jooks and public works before going into the outside world.

In this respect it is interesting to mention the Black Bottom. I have read several false accounts of its origin and name. One writer claimed that it got its name from the black sticky mud on the bottom of the Mississippi River. Other equally absurd statements gummed the press. Now the dance really originated in the Jook section of Nashville, Tennessee, around Fourth Avenue. This is a tough neighborhood known as Black Bottom – hence the name.

The Charleston is perhaps forty years old and was danced up and down the Atlantic seaboard from North Carolina to Key West, Florida. The Negro social dance is slow and sensuous. The idea in the Jook is to gain sensation, and not so much exercise. So that just enough foot movement is added to keep the dancers on the floor. A tremendous sex stimulation is gained from this. But who is trying to avoid it? The man, the woman, the time and place have met. Rather, little intimate names are indulged in to heap fire on fire.

These too have spread to all the world.

The Negro theatre, as built up by the Negro, is based on Jook situations, with women, gambling, fighting and drinking. Shows like "Dixie to Broadway" are only Negro in cast, and could just as well have come from pre-Soviet Russia.

Another interesting thing – Negro shows before being tampered with did not specialize in octoroon chorus girls. The girl who could hoist a Jook song from her belly and lam it against the front door of the theatre was the lead, even if she were as black as the hinges of hell. The question was "Can she jook?" She must also have a good belly wobble, and her hips must, to quote a popular work song, "Shake like jelly all over and be so broad, Lawd, Lawd, and be so broad." So that the bleached chorus is the result of a white demand and not the Negro's. [...]

Speaking of the use of Negro material by white performers, it is astonishing that so many are trying it, and I have never seen one yet entirely realistic. They often have all the elements of the song, dance, or expression, but they are misplaced or distorted by the accent falling on the wrong element. Everyone seems to think that the Negro is easily imitated when nothing is further from the truth. Without exception I wonder why the black-face comedians are black-face; it is a puzzle, good comedians, but darn poor niggers. Gershwin and the other "Negro" rhapsodists come under this same axe. Just about as Negro as caviar or Ann Pennington's athletic Black Bottom. When the Negroes who knew the Black Bottom in its cradle saw the Broadway version they asked each other, "Is you learnt dat new Black Bottom yet?" Proof that it was not *their* dance.

And God only knows what the world has suffered from the white damsels who try to sing Blues.

The Negroes themselves have sinned also in this respect. In spite of the goings up and down on the earth, from the original Fisk Jubilee Singers down to the present, there has been no genuine presentation of Negro songs to white audiences. The spirituals that have been sung around the world are Negroid to be sure, but so full of musicians' tricks that Negro congregations are highly entertained when they hear their old songs so changed. They never use the new style songs, and these are never heard unless perchance some daughter or son has been off to college and returns with one of the old songs with its face lifted, so to speak. [...]

To those who want to institute the Negro theatre, let me say it is already established. It is lacking in wealth, so it is not seen in the high places. A creature with a white head and Negro feet struts the Metropolitan boards. The real Negro theatre is in the jooks and the cabarets. Self-conscious individuals may turn away the eye and say, "Let us search elsewhere for our dramatic art." Let 'em search. They certainly won't find it. Butter Beans and Susie, Bo-Jangles and Snake Hips are the only performers of the real Negro school it has ever been my pleasure to behold in New York. [...]

Notes

1   L. M. Hill, *Social Rituals and the Verbal Art of Zora Neale Hurston* (Washington, DC: Howard University Press, 1996), 9.
2   B. Johnson, *A World of Difference* (Baltimore: Johns Hopkins University Press, 1987), 159.

Chapter 25

Federico García Lorca (1899–1936)

During the 1930s Federico García Lorca was Spain's leading poet and dramatist. He enjoyed a productive relationship with the avant-garde and at the height of his creative powers wrote his most enduring plays. *Blood Wedding* (1933), *Yerma* (1934), and *The House of Bernarda Alba* (1936) mixed poetic language with the conflict between passion and duty. Lorca's homosexuality and his wish to remain closeted influenced the emotional intensity and anguish of his works. At the outbreak of the Spanish Civil War he was executed by the Fascist Falangist militia in 1936. Much of his work was banned, and his most popular play, *The House of Bernarda Alba*, received its first production in 1945.

Lorca's passion for political reform and liberation of the soul informs his art and stagecraft. He used theatre to advance his belief in socialism and human rights. He stressed the realism of ''folk language'' in his dramas but also mixed into his work were the influences of Salvador Dali and Louis Buñuel. His brief but productive life gave birth to notable dramas, and his theories of a politically motivated theatre broke ground for dramas of social action.

The Prophecy of Lorca (1934)

My Dear Friends: Some time ago I made a solemn promise to refuse every kind of tribute, banquet, or celebration which might be made in my honor, first, because I know that each of them drives another nail into our literary coffin, and second, because I have found that

Federico García Lorca, "The Prophesy of Lorca" (1934), tr. Albert E. Sloman, quoted from *Theatre Arts* 34.10 (October 1950), 38–9. Address delivered after the opening of *Yerma*.

there is nothing more depressing than a formal speech made in our honor, and nothing sadder than organized applause, however sincere.

Besides, between ourselves, I hold that banquets and scrolls bring bad luck upon the one who receives them, bad luck springing from the relief of his friends who think: "Now we have done our duty by him."

A banquet is a gathering of professional people who eat with us and where we find thrown together every kind of person who likes us least.

Rather than do honor to poets and dramatists, I should prepare challenges and attacks, in which we should be told roundly and passionately: "Are you afraid of doing this?" "Are you incapable of expressing a person's anguish at the sea?" "Daren't you show the despair of soldiers who hate war?"

Necessity and struggle, grounded on a critical love, temper the artist's soul, which easy flattery makes effeminate and destroys. The theatres are full of deceiving sirens, garlanded with hothouse roses, and the public is content, and applauds dummy hearts and super-ficial dialogue; but the dramatic poet who wishes to save himself from oblivion must not forget the open fields with their wild roses, fields moistened by the dawn where peasants toil, and the pigeon, wounded by a mysterious hunter, which is dying amongst the rushes with no one to hear its grief.

Shunning sirens, flattery, and congratulations, I have accepted nothing in my honor, on the occasion of the first night of *Yerma*; but it has been the greatest pleasure of my short life as a writer to learn that the theatre world of Madrid was asking the great Margarita Xirgu, an actress with an impeccable artistic career, luminary of the Spanish theatre, and admirable interpreter of the part of Yerma, together with the company which so brilliantly supports her, for a special production.

For the interest and attention in a notable theatrical endeavor which this implies, I wish, now that we are all together, to give to you my deepest and sincerest thanks. I am not speaking tonight as an author, nor as a poet, nor as a simple student of the rich panorama of man's life, but as an ardent lover of the theatre of social action. The theatre is one of the most useful and expressive instruments for a country's edifica-tion, the barometer which registers its greatness or its decline. A theatre which in every branch, from tragedy to vaudeville, is sensitive and well oriented, can in a few years change the sensibility of a people, and a broken-down theatre, where wings have given way to cloven hoofs, can coarsen and benumb a whole nation.

The theatre is a school of weeping and of laughter, a rostrum where men are free to expose old and equivocal standards of conduct, and explain with living examples the eternal norms of the heart and feelings of man.

A nation which does not help and does not encourage its theatre is, if not dead, dying; just as the theatre which does not feel the social pulse, the historical pulse, the drama of its people, and catch the genuine color of its landscape and of its spirit, with laughter or with tears, has no right to call itself a theatre, but an amusement hall, or a place for doing that dreadful thing known as "killing time." I am referring to no one, and I want to offend no one; I am not speaking of actual fact, but of a problem that has yet to be solved.

Every day, my friends, I hear about the crisis in the theatre, and I feel always that the defect is not one before our eyes, but deep down in its very nature; it is not a defect of the flower we have before us, of a play, that is, but deeply rooted; in short, a defect of organization. Whilst actors and authors are in the hands of managements that are completely commercial, free, without either literary or state control of any kind, managements devoid of all judgment and offering no kind of safeguard, actors, authors, and the whole theatre will sink lower every day, beyond all hope of salvation.

The delightful light theatre of revue, vaudeville, and farce, forms of which I am a keen spectator, could maintain and even save itself; but plays in verse, the historical play, and the so-called Spanish *zarzuela*, will suffer more and more setbacks, because they are forms which make great demands and which admit of real innovations, and there is neither the authority nor the spirit of sacrifice to impose them on a public which has to be overruled from above, and often contradicted and attacked. The theatre must impose itself on the public, not the public on the theatre. To do this, authors and actors must, whatever the cost, again assume great authority, because the theatre-going public is like a school child; it reveres the stern, severe teacher who demands justice and sees justice done; and puts pins on the chairs of the timid and flattering ones who neither teach themselves nor allow anyone else to teach.

The public can be taught – I say public, of course, not people – it can be taught; for, some years ago, I saw Debussy and Ravel howled down, and I have been present since at loud ovations given by a public of ordinary people to the very works which were earlier rejected. These authors were imposed by the high judgment of authority, superior to that of the ordinary public, just as were Wedekind in Germany and Pirandello in Italy, and so many others.

This has to be done for the good of the theatre and for the glory and status of its interpreters. Dignity must be maintained, in the conviction that such dignity will be amply repaid. To do otherwise is to tremble behind the flies, and kill the fantasies, imagination, and charm of the theatre, which is always, always an art, and will always be a lofty art, even though there may have been a time when everything which pleased was labeled art, so that the tone was lowered, poetry destroyed, and the stage itself a refuge for thieves.

Art above all else. A most noble art, and you, my actor friends, artists above all else. Artists from head to foot, since through love and vocation, you have risen to the make-believe and pitiful world of the boards. Artists by occupation and by preoccupation. From the smallest theatre to the most eminent, the word "Art" should be written in auditoriums and dressing rooms, for if not we shall have to write the word "Commerce" or some other that I dare not say. And distinction, discipline, and sacrifice and love.

I don't want to lecture you, because I should be the one receiving a lecture. My words are dictated by enthusiasm and conviction. I labor under no delusion. As a good Andalusian I can think coolly, because I come of an ancient stock. I know that truth does not lie with him who says, "Today, today, today," eating his bread close to the hearth, but with him who watches calmly at a distance the first light of dawn in the country.

I know that those people who say, "Now, now, now," with their eyes fixed on the small jaws of the box office are not right, but those who say, "Tomorrow, tomorrow, tomorrow," and feel the approach of the new life which is hovering over the world.

Chapter 26

Antonin Artaud (1896–1949)

Antonin Artaud was a poet, actor, director, and theorist. He belonged to several avant-garde groups in the 1920s, from surrealists to experimental theatre companies. He acted in films and drifted among theatre groups in France and Mexico. With directors Roger Vitrac and Robert Aron, he founded the Theatre of Alfred Jarry. In the 1930s Artaud commenced a period of creative activity, as well as lecturing and writing manifestos. He wrote *Le Jet de sang* (*Spurt of Blood*) in 1925 and produced *Les Cenci* in 1935. Artaud's *Les Cenci* was modeled after Shelley's five-act tragedy (1819) and Stendhal's translation in 1837. The collection of his papers would collocate into his extraordinary contribution, *Le Théâtre et son double* (*The Theatre and Its Double*, 1938), which contains a preface and thirteen essays. Two are reproduced here.

Artaud attacks theatre's dependence on the "text." Recreating the words of fossilized scripts made theatre little more than fusty museum experiences. Rather than reproducing "masterpieces," he focuses instead on the danger of the stage; by deconstructing formulas that lead to a reassuring theatre, Artaud condemned the bourgeoisie. He wanted to create a new language for the stage, "the almost mystical sense of which the metteur en scène ought to possess."[1] For Artaud, according to Eric Sellin, this "completely new language belonged to the theatre itself, not merely the illusionistic representations of novels or staged dialogues" (82). He primarily wanted to impose creative gestures that reject predictable mannerisms, calling for a theatre that resembles the plague – his "theatre of cruelty." The plague was a delirium, a combination of cruelty and ecstasy, and informed by Artaud's own physical disabilities. Martin Esslin notes that Artaud's theatre of cruelty was meant "to swoop down upon a crowd of

Antonin Artaud, "On the Balinese Theatre" and "No More Masterpieces" (1938), from *The Theatre and Its Double*, tr. Mary Caroline Richards (New York: Grove Press, 1958), 53–67, 74–83. © 1958 by Grove Press, Inc. Reprinted by permission of Grove/Atlantic, Inc.

spectators with all the awesome horror of the plague, the Black Death of the Middle Ages, with all its shattering impact, creating a complete upheaval, physical, mental, and moral, among the population it struck." This ambitious project displayed "the fanatical fury with which Artaud pursued his objective, a commitment of truly mad heroism."[2] In his production of *The Conquest of Mexico*, for example, the "wall of the stage is crammed unevenly with heads, with throats. . . . Flying vessels cross a Pacific of purplish indigo. . . . The space is stacked high with swirling gestures, horrible faces, glaring eyes, closed fists, plumes, armour, heads, bellies falling like hailstones pelting the earth with supernatural explosions."[3]

To create his theatre Artaud believed that the stage must first be emancipated from petty psychology and melodramatic conundrums. He called for physical gestures intended to create a kind of hieroglyphics of body language. Gesture must represent ideas rather than dead thoughts from the past. It is a theatre that would evolve into the "happenings" of the 1960s. His "theatre of cruelty" destroys the habitual body and remakes theatre into pain, illumination, and incantatory rants. Artaud was impressed by the Balinese theatre, which for him used physicality, signs, and elaborate costumes. Artaud was also exhilarated by Balinese dancers' extraordinary versatility and suppleness. Like Witkiewicz, he inspired the counterculture's effort to merge theatre and life.

On the Balinese Theatre (1938)

The spectacle of the Balinese theatre, which draws upon dance, song, pantomime – and a little of the theatre as we understand it in the Occident – restores the theatre, by means of ceremonies of indubitable age and well-tried efficacity, to its original destiny which it presents as a combination of all these elements fused together in a perspective of hallucination and fear.

It is very remarkable that the first of the little plays which compose this spectacle, in which we are shown a father's remonstrances to his tradition-flouting daughter, begins with an entrance of phantoms; the male and female characters who will develop a dramatic but familiar subject appear to us first in their spectral aspect and are seen in that hallucinatory perspective appropriate to every theatrical character, before the situations in this kind of symbolic sketch are allowed to develop. Here indeed situations are only a pretext. The drama does not develop as a conflict of feelings but as a conflict of spiritual states, themselves ossified and transformed into gestures – diagrams. In a word, the Balinese have realized, with the utmost rigor, the idea of pure theatre, where everything, conception and realization alike, has value, has existence only in proportion to its degree of objectification *on the stage*. They victoriously demonstrate the absolute preponderance of the director (*metteur en scène*) whose creative power *eliminates words*. The themes are vague, abstract, extremely general. They are given life only by the fertility and intricacy of all the artifices of the stage which impose upon our minds like the conception of a metaphysics derived from a new use of gesture and voice.

What is in fact curious about all these gestures, these angular and abruptly abandoned attitudes, these syncopated modulations formed at the back of the throat, these musical phrases that break off short, these flights of elytra, these rustlings of branches, these sounds of hollow drums, these robot squeakings, these dances of animated manikins, is this: that through the labyrinth of their gestures, attitudes, and sudden cries, through the gyrations and turns which leave no portion of the stage space un-utilized, the sense of a new physical language, based upon signs and no longer upon words, is liberated. These actors with their geometric robes seem to be animated hieroglyphs. It is not just the shape of their robes which, displacing the axis of the human figure, create beside the dress of these warriors in a state of trance and perpetual war a kind of second, symbolic dress and thus inspire an intellectual idea, or which merely connect, by all the intersections of their lines, with all the intersections of perspective in space. No, these spiritual signs have a precise meaning which strikes us only intuitively but with enough violence to make useless any translation into logical discursive language. And for the lovers of realism at all costs, who might find exhausting these perpetual allusions to secret attitudes inaccessible to thought, there remains the eminently realistic play of the double who is terrified by the apparitions from beyond. In this double – trembling, yelping childishly, these heels striking the ground in cadences that follow the very automatism of the liberated unconscious, this momentary concealment behind his own reality – *there* is a description of fear valid in every latitude, an indication that in the human as well as the superhuman the Orientals are more than a match for us in matters of reality.

The Balinese, who have a vocabulary of gesture and mime for every circumstance of life, reinstate the superior worth of theatrical conventions, demonstrate the forcefulness and greater emotional value of a certain number of perfectly learned and above all masterfully applied conventions. One of the reasons for our delight in this faultless performance lies precisely in the use these actors make of an exact quantity of specific gestures, of well-tried mime at a given point, and above all in the prevailing spiritual tone, the deep and subtle study that has presided at the elaboration of these plays of expression, these powerful signs which give us the impression that their power has not weakened during thousands of years. These mechanically rolling eyes, pouting lips, and muscular spasms, all producing methodically calculated effects which forbid any recourse to spontaneous improvisation, these horizontally moving heads that seem to glide from one shoulder to the other as if on rollers, everything that might correspond to immediate psychological necessities, corresponds as well to a sort of spiritual architecture, created out of gesture and mime but also out of the evocative power of a system, the musical quality of a physical movement, the parallel and admirably fused harmony of a tone. This may perhaps shock our European sense of stage freedom and spontaneous inspiration, but let no one say that this mathematics creates sterility or uniformity. The marvel is that a sensation of richness, of fantasy and prodigality emanates from this spectacle ruled with a maddening scrupulosity and consciousness. And the most commanding interpenetrations join sight to sound, intellect to sensibility, the gesture of a character to the evocation of a plant's movement across the scream of an instrument. The sighs of wind instruments prolong the vibrations of vocal cords with a sense of such oneness that you do not know whether it is the voice itself that is continuing or the identity which has absorbed the voice from the beginning. A rippling of joints, the musical angle made by the arm with the forearm, a foot falling, a knee bending, fingers that seem to be coming loose from the hand, it is all like a perpetual play of mirrors in which human limbs seem resonant with echoes, harmonies in which the notes of the orchestra, the whispers of wind instruments evoke the idea of a monstrous aviary in which the actors themselves would be the fluttering wings. Our theatre which has never had the idea of this metaphysics of gesture nor known how to make music serve such immediate, such concrete dramatic ends, our purely verbal theatre, unaware of everything that makes theatre, of everything that exists in the air of the stage, which is measured and circumscribed by that air and has a density in space – movements, shapes, colors, vibrations, attitudes, screams – our theatre might, with respect to the unmeasurable, which derives from the mind's capacity for receiving suggestion, be given lessons in spirituality from the Balinese theatre. This purely popular and not sacred theatre gives us an extraordinary idea of the intellectual level of a people who take the struggles of a soul preyed upon by ghosts and phantoms from the beyond as the basis for their civic festivals. For it is indeed a purely interior struggle that is staged in the last part of the spectacle. And we can remark in passing on the degree of theatrical sumptuousness which the Balinese have been able to give this struggle: their sense of the plastic requirements of the stage is equaled only by their knowledge of physical fear and the means of unleashing it. And there is in the truly terrifying look of their devil (probably Tibetan) a striking similarity to the look of a certain puppet in our own remembrance, a puppet with swollen hands of white gelatine and nails of green foliage, which was the most beautiful ornament of one of the first plays performed by Alfred Jarry's theatre.

This spectacle is more than we can assimilate, assailing us with a superabundance of impressions, each richer than the next, but in a language to which it seems we no longer have the key; and this kind of irritation created by the impossibility of finding the thread and tracking the beast down – the impossibility of putting one's ear closer to the instrument in order to hear better – is one charm the more to the credit of this spectacle. And by language I do not mean an idiom indecipherable at first hearing, but precisely that sort of theatrical language foreign to every *spoken tongue*, a language in which an overwhelming stage experience seems to be communicated, in comparison with which our productions depending exclusively upon dialogue seem like so much stuttering.

What is in fact most striking in this spectacle – so well contrived to disconcert our Occidental conceptions of theatre that many will deny it has any theatrical quality, whereas it is the most beautiful manifestation of pure theatre it has been our privilege to see – what is striking and disconcerting for Europeans like ourselves is the admirable intellectuality that one senses crackling everywhere in the close and subtle web of gestures, in the infinitely varied modulations of voice, in this sonorous rain resounding as if from an immense dripping forest, and in the equally sonorous interlacing of movements. There is no transition from a gesture to a cry or a sound: all the senses interpenetrate, as if through strange channels hollowed out in the mind itself!

Here is a whole collection of ritual gestures to which we do not have the key and which seem to obey extremely precise musical indications, with something more that does not generally belong to music and seems intended to encircle thought, to hound it down and lead it into an inextricable and certain system. In fact everything in this theatre is calculated with an enchanting mathematical meticulousness. Nothing is left to chance or to personal initiative. It is a kind of superior dance, in which the dancers were actors first of all.

Repeatedly they seem to accomplish a kind of recovery with measured steps. Just when they appear to be lost in the middle of an inextricable labyrinth of measures or about to overturn in the confusion, they have their own way of recovering equilibrium, a particular buttressing of the body, of the twisted legs, which gives the impression of a sopping rag being wrung out in tempo; – and on three final steps, which lead them ineluctably to the middle of the stage, the suspended rhythm is completed, the measure made clear.

Everything is thus regulated and impersonal; not a movement of the muscles, not the rolling of an eye but seem to belong to a kind of reflective mathematics which controls everything and by means of which everything happens. And the strange thing is that in this systematic depersonalization, in these purely muscular facial expressions, applied to the features like masks, everything produces a significance, everything affords the maximum effect.

A kind of terror seizes us at the thought of these mechanized beings, whose joys and griefs seem not their own but at the service of age-old rites, as if they were dictated by superior intelligences. In the last analysis it is this impression of a superior and prescribed Life which strikes us most in this spectacle that so much resembles a rite one might profane. It has the solemnity of a sacred rite – the hieratic quality of the costumes gives each actor a double body and a double set of limbs – and the dancer bundled into his costume seems to be nothing more than his own effigy. Over and beyond the music's broad, overpowering rhythm there is another extremely fragile, hesitant, and sustained music in which, it seems, the most precious metals are being pulverized, where springs of water are bubbling up as in the state of nature, and long processions of insects file through the plants, with a sound like that of light itself, in which the noises of deep solitudes seem to be distilled into showers of crystals, etc. . . .

Furthermore all these sounds are linked to movements, as if they were the natural consummation of gestures which have the same musical quality, and this with such a sense of musical analogy that the mind finally finds itself doomed to confusion, attributing to the separate gesticulations of the dancers the sonorous properties of the orchestra – and vice versa.

An impression of inhumanity, of the divine, of miraculous revelation is further provided by the exquisite beauty of the women's headdresses: this series of banked luminous circles, made from combinations of multicolored feathers or from pearls of so beautiful a coloration that their combination has a quality of *revelation*, and the crests of which tremble rhythmically, responding *consciously*, or so it seems, to the tremblings of the body. – There are also the other headdresses of sacerdotal character, in the shape of tiaras and topped with egret crests and stiff flowers in pairs of contrasting, strangely harmonizing colors.

This dazzling ensemble full of explosions, flights, secret streams, detours in every direction of both external and internal perception, composes a sovereign idea of the theatre, as it has been preserved for us down through the centuries in order to teach us what the theatre never should have ceased to be. And this impression is doubled by the fact that this spectacle – popular, it seems, and secular – is like the common bread of artistic sensations among those people.

Setting aside the prodigious mathematics of this spectacle, what seems most surprising and astonishing to us is this aspect of *matter as revelation*, suddenly dispersed in signs to teach us the metaphysical identity of concrete and abstract and to teach us this *in gestures made to last*. For though we are familiar with the realistic aspect of matter, it is here developed to the nth power and definitively stylized.

*

In this theatre all creation comes from the stage, finds its expression and its origins alike in a secret psychic impulse which is Speech before words.

*

It is a theatre which eliminates the author in favor of what we would call, in our Occidental theatrical jargon, the director; but a director who has become a kind of manager of magic, a master of sacred ceremonies. And the material on which he works, the themes he brings to throbbing life are derived not from him but from the gods. They come, it seems, from elemental interconnections of Nature which a double Spirit has fostered.

What he sets in motion is the *manifested*.

This is a sort of primary Physics, from which Spirit has never disengaged itself.

*

In a spectacle like that of Balinese theatre there is something that has nothing to do with entertainment, the notion of useless, artificial amusement, of an evening's pastime which is the characteristic of our theatre. The Balinese productions take shape at the very heart of matter, life, reality. There is in them something of the ceremonial quality of a religious rite, in the sense that they extirpate from the mind of the onlooker all idea of pretense, of cheap imitations of reality. This intricately detailed gesticulation has one goal, an immediate goal which it approaches by efficacious means, whose efficacity we are even meant to experience immediately. The thoughts it aims at, the spiritual states it seeks to create, the mystic solutions it proposes are aroused and attained without delay or circumlocution. All of which seems to be an exorcism to make our demons flow.

*

There is a low hum of instinctual matters in this theatre, but they are wrought to that point of transparency, intelligence, and ductility at which they seem to furnish us in physical terms some of the spirit's most secret insights.

The themes selected derive, one might say, from the stage itself. They have reached such a point of objective materialization that one cannot imagine them outside this close perspective, this confined and limited globe of performing space.

This spectacle offers us a marvelous complex of pure stage images, for the comprehension of which a whole new language seems to have been invented: the actors with their costumes constitute veritable living, moving hieroglyphs. And these three-dimensional hieroglyphs are in turn brocaded with a certain number of gestures – mysterious signs which correspond to some unknown, fabulous, and obscure reality which we here in the Occident have completely repressed.

There is something that has this character of a magic operation in this intense liberation of signs, restrained at first and then suddenly thrown into the air.

A chaotic boiling, full of recognizable particles and at moments strangely orderly, crackles in this effervescence of painted rhythms in which the many fermatas unceasingly make their entrance like a well-calculated silence.

Of this idea of pure theatre, which is merely theoretical in the Occident and to which no one has ever attempted to give the least reality, the Balinese offer us a stupefying realization, suppressing all possibility of recourse to words for the elucidation of the most abstract themes – inventing a language of gesture to be developed in space, a language without meaning except in the circumstances of the stage.

The stage space is utilized in all its dimensions and, one might say, on all possible planes. For in addition to an acute sense of plastic beauty, these gestures always have as their final goal the elucidation of a spiritual state or problem.

At least that is the way they appear to us.

No point of space and at the same time no possible suggestion has been lost. And there is a philosophical sense, so to speak, of the power which nature has of suddenly hurling everything into chaos.

*

One senses in the Balinese theatre a state prior to language and which can choose its own: music, gestures, movements, words.

*

It is certain that this aspect of pure theatre, this physics of absolute gesture which is the idea itself and which transforms the mind's conceptions into events perceptible through the labyrinths and fibrous interlacings of matter, gives us a new idea of what belongs by nature to the domain of forms and manifested matter. Those who succeed in giving a mystic sense to the simple form of a robe and who, not content with placing a man's double next to him, confer upon each man in his robes a double made of clothes – those who pierce these illusory or secondary clothes with a saber, giving them the look of huge butterflies pinned in the air, such men have an innate sense of the absolute and magical symbolism of nature much superior to ours, and set us an example which it is only too certain our own theatre technicians will be powerless to profit from. [. . .]

*

In the performances of the Balinese theatre the mind has the feeling that conception at first stumbled against gesture, gain its footing in the midst of a whole ferment of visual or sonorous images, thoughts as it were in a pure state. To put it briefly and more clearly, something akin to the musical state must have existed for this *mise en scène* where everything that is a conception of the mind is only a pretext, a virtuality whose double has produced this intense stage poetry, this many-hued spatial language.

*

This perpetual play of mirrors passing from color to gesture and from cry to movement leads us unceasingly along roads rough and difficult for the mind, plunges us into that state of uncertainty and ineffable anguish which is the characteristic of poetry.

These strange games of flying hands, like insects in the green air of evening, communicate a sort of horrible obsession, an inexhaustible mental ratiocination, like a mind ceaselessly taking its bearings in the maze of its unconscious.

And what this theatre makes palpable for us and captures in concrete signs are much less matters of feeling than of intelligence.

And it is by intellectual paths that it introduces us into the re-conquest of the signs of what exists.

From this point of view the gesture of the central dancer who always touches his head at the same place, as if wishing to indicate the position and existence of some unimaginable central eye, some intellectual egg, is highly significant.

*

What occurs as a highly colored reference to physical impressions of nature is taken up again on the level of sounds, and the sound itself is only the nostalgic representation of something else, a sort of magic state where sensations have become so subtle that they are a pleasure for the spirit to frequent. And even the imitative harmonies, the sound of the rattlesnake and rustlings of dried insects against each other, suggest the glade of a swarming landscape ready to hurl itself into chaos. – And these dancers dressed in dazzling clothes, whose bodies beneath seem wrapped in swaddling-bands! There is something umbilical, larval in their movement. And at the same time we must remark on the hieroglyphic aspect of their costumes, the horizontal lines of which project beyond the body in every direction. They are like huge insects full of lines and segments drawn to connect them with an unknown natural perspective of which they seem nothing more than a kind of detached geometry.

These costumes which encircle their abstract rotations when they walk, and the strange crisscrossings of their feet!

Each of their movements traces a line in space, completes some unknown rigorous figure in the ritual of a hermetic formula which an unforeseen gesture of the hand completes.

And the folds of these robes, curving above the buttocks, hold them as if suspended in air, as if pinned to the depths of the theatre, and prolong each of their leaps into a flight.

These howls, these rolling eyes, this continuous abstraction, these noises of branches, noises of the cutting and rolling of wood, all within the immense area of widely diffused sounds disgorged from many sources, combine to overwhelm the mind, to crystallize as a new and, I dare say, concrete conception of the abstract.

And it must be noted that when this abstraction, which springs from a marvelous scenic edifice to return into thought, encounters in its flight certain impressions from the world of nature, it always seizes them at the point at which their molecular combinations are beginning to break up: a gesture narrowly divides us from chaos.

*

The last part of the spectacle is – in contrast to all the dirt, brutality, and infamy chewed up by our European stages – a delightful anachronism. And I do not know what other theatre would dare to pin down in this way as *if true to nature* the throes of a soul at the mercy of phantasms from the Beyond.

*

These metaphysicians of natural disorder who in dancing restore to us every atom of sound and every fragmentary perception as if these were now about to rejoin their own generating principles, are able to wed movement and sound so perfectly that it seems the dancers have hollow bones to make these noises of resonant drums and woodblocks with their hollow wooden limbs.

Here we are suddenly in deep metaphysical anguish, and the rigid aspect of the body in trance, stiffened by the tide of cosmic forces which besiege it, is admirably expressed by that frenetic dance of rigidities and angles, in which one suddenly feels the mind begin to plummet downwards.

As if waves of matter were tumbling over each other, dashing their crests into the deep and flying from all sides of the horizon to be enclosed in one minute portion of tremor and trance – to cover over the void of fear.

*

There is an absolute in these constructed perspectives, a real physical absolute which only Orientals are capable of envisioning – it is in the loftiness and thoughtful boldness of their goals that these conceptions differ from our European conceptions of theatre, even more than in the strange perfection of their performances.

Advocates of the division and partitioning of genres can pretend to see mere dancers in the magnificent artists of the Balinese theatre, dancers entrusted with the representation of unexplained, lofty Myths whose very elevation renders the level of our modern Occidental theatre unspeakably gross and childish. The truth is that the Balinese theatre suggests, and in its productions *enacts*, themes of pure theatre upon which the stage performance confers an intense equilibrium, a wholly materialized gravity.

*

Everything in this theatre is immersed in a profound intoxication which restores to us the very elements of ecstasy, and in ecstasy we discover the dry seething, the mineral friction of plants, vestiges and ruins of trees illuminated on their faces.

Bestiality and every trace of animality are reduced to their spare gesture: mutinous noises of the splitting earth, the sap of trees, animal yawns.

The dancers' feet, in kicking aside their robes, dissolve thoughts and sensations, permitting them to recover their pure state.

And always this confrontation of the head, this Cyclops' eye, the inner eye of the mind which the right hand gropes for.

The sign language of spiritual gestures which measure, prune, fix, separate, and subdivide feelings, states of the soul, metaphysical ideas.

This theatre of quintessences in which things perform a strange about-face before becoming abstractions again.

＊

Their gestures fall so accurately upon this rhythm of the hollow drums, accent it, and seize it in flight with such sureness and at such climactic moments that it seems the very abyss of their hollow limbs which the music is going to scan.

＊

And the women's stratified, lunar eyes:

Eyes of dreams which seem to absorb our own, eyes before which we ourselves appear to be *fantôme.*

＊

Utter satisfaction from these dance gestures, from these turning feet mingling with states of the soul, from these little flying hands, these dry and precise tappings.

＊

We are watching a mental alchemy which makes a gesture of a state of mind – the dry, naked, linear gesture all our acts could have if they sought the absolute.

＊

It happens that this mannerism, this excessively hieratic style, with its rolling alphabet, its shrieks of splitting stones, noises of branches, noises of the cutting and rolling of wood, compose a sort of animated material murmur in the air, in space, a visual as well as audible whispering. And after an instant the magic identification is made: *We know it is we who were speaking.*

Who, after the formidable battle between Arjuna and the Dragon, will dare to say that the whole of theatre is not on the stage, i.e., beyond situations and words?

The dramatic and psychological situations have passed here into the very sign language of the combat, which is a function of the mystic athletic play of bodies and the so to speak undulatory use of the stage, whose enormous spiral reveals itself in one perspective after another.

The warriors enter the mental forest rocking with fear, overwhelmed by a great shudder, a voluminous magnetic whirling in which we can sense the rush of animal or mineral meteors.

It is more than a physical tempest, it is a spiritual concussion that is signified in the general trembling of their limbs and their rolling eyes. The sonorous pulsation of their bristling heads is at times excruciating – and the music sways behind them and at the same time sustains an unimaginable space into which real pebbles finally roll.

And behind the Warrior, bristling from the formidable cosmic tempest, is the Double who struts about, given up to the childishness of his schoolboy gibes, and who, roused by the repercussion of the turmoil, moves unaware in the midst of spells of which he has understood nothing.

No More Masterpieces (1938)

One of the reasons for the asphyxiating atmosphere in which we live without possible escape or remedy – and in which we all share, even the most revolutionary among us – is our respect for what has been written, formulated, or painted, what has been given form, as if all expression were not at last exhausted, were not at a point where things must break apart if they are to start anew and begin fresh.

We must have done with this idea of masterpieces reserved for a self-styled elite and not understood by the general public; the mind has no such restricted districts as those so often used for clandestine sexual encounters.

Masterpieces of the past are good for the past: they are not good for us. We have the right to say what has been said and even what has not been said in a way that belongs to us, a way that is immediate and direct, corresponding to present modes of feeling, and understandable to everyone.

It is idiotic to reproach the masses for having no sense of the sublime, when the sublime is confused with one or another of its formal manifestations, which are moreover always defunct manifestations. And if, for example, a contemporary public does not understand *Oedipus Rex*, I shall make bold to say that it is the fault of *Oedipus Rex* and not of the public.

In *Oedipus Rex* there is the theme of incest and the idea that nature mocks at morality and that there are certain unspecified powers at large which we would do well to beware of, call them destiny or anything you choose.

There is in addition the presence of a plague epidemic which is a physical incarnation of these powers. But the whole in a manner and language that have lost all touch with the rude and epileptic rhythm of our time. Sophocles speaks grandly perhaps, but in a style that is no longer timely. His language is too refined for this age; it is as if he were speaking beside the point.

However, a public that shudders at train wrecks, that is familiar with earthquakes, plagues, revolutions, wars, that is sensitive to the disordered anguish of love, can be affected by all these grand notions and asks only to become aware of them, but on condition that it is addressed in its own language, and that its knowledge of these things does not come to it through adulterated trappings and speech that belong to extinct eras which will never live again.

Today as yesterday, the public is greedy for mystery: it asks only to become aware of the laws according to which destiny manifests itself, and to divine perhaps the secret of its apparitions.

Let us leave textual criticism to graduate students, formal criticism to aesthetes, and recognize that what has been said is not still to be said; that an expression does not have the same value twice, does not live two lives; that all words, once spoken, are dead and function only at the moment when they are uttered; that a form, once it has served, cannot be used again and asks only to be replaced by another; and that the theatre is the only place in the world where a gesture, once made, can never be made the same way twice.

If the public does not frequent our literary masterpieces, it is because those masterpieces are literary, that is to say, fixed; and fixed in forms that no longer respond to the needs of the time.

Far from blaming the public, we ought to blame the formal screen we interpose between ourselves and the public, and this new form of idolatry, the idolatry of fixed masterpieces which is one of the aspects of bourgeois conformism.

This conformism makes us confuse sublimity, ideas, and things with the forms they have taken in time and in our minds – in our snobbish, precious, aesthetic mentalities which the public does not understand.

How pointless in such matters to accuse the public of bad taste because it relishes insanities, so long as the public is not shown a valid spectacle; and I defy anyone to show me *here* a spectacle valid – valid in the supreme sense of the theatre – since the last great romantic melodramas, i.e., since a hundred years ago.

The public, which takes the false for the true, has the sense of the true and always responds to it when it is manifested. However, it is not upon the stage that the true is to be sought nowadays, but in the street; and if the crowd in the street is offered an occasion to show its human dignity, it will always do so.

If people are out of the habit of going to the theatre, if we have all finally come to think of theatre as an inferior art, a means of popular distraction, and to use it as an outlet for our worst instincts, it is because we have learned too well what the theatre has been, namely, falsehood and illusion. It is because we have been accustomed for four hundred years, that is since the Renaissance, to a purely descriptive and narrative theatre – storytelling psychology; it is because every possible ingenuity has been exerted in bringing to life on the stage plausible but detached beings, with the spectacle on one side, the public on the other – and because the public is no longer shown anything but the mirror of itself.

Shakespeare himself is responsible for this aberration and decline, this disinterested idea of the theatre which wishes a theatrical performance to leave the public intact, without setting off one image that will shake the organism to its foundations and leave an ineffaceable scar.

If, in Shakespeare, a man is sometimes preoccupied with what transcends him, it is always in order to determine the ultimate consequences of this preoccupation within him, i.e., psychology.

Psychology, which works relentlessly to reduce the unknown to the known, to the quotidian and the ordinary, is the cause of the theatre's abasement and its fearful loss of energy, which seems to me to have reached its lowest point. And I think both the theatre and we ourselves have had enough of psychology.

I believe furthermore that we can all agree on this matter sufficiently so that there is no need to descend to the repugnant level of the modern and French theatre to condemn the theatre of psychology.

Stories about money, worry over money, social careerism, the pangs of love unspoiled by altruism, sexuality sugar-coated with an eroticism that has lost its mystery have nothing to do with the theatre, even if they do belong to psychology. These torments, seductions, and lusts before which we are nothing but Peeping Toms gratifying our cravings, tend to go bad, and their rot turns to revolution: we must take this into account.

But this is not our most serious concern.

If Shakespeare and his imitators have gradually insinuated the idea of art for art's sake, with art on one side and life on the other, we can [stick to] this feeble and lazy idea only as long as the life outside endures. But there are too many signs that everything that used to sustain our lives no longer does so, that we are all mad, desperate, and sick. And I call for us to react.

This idea of a detached art, of poetry as a charm which exists only to distract our leisure, is a decadent idea and an unmistakable symptom of our power to castrate.

Our literary admiration for Rimbaud, Jarry, Lautréamont, and a few others, which has driven two men to suicide, but turned into café gossip for the rest, belongs to this idea of literary poetry, of detached art, of neutral spiritual activity which creates nothing and produces nothing; and I can bear witness that at the very moment when that kind of personal poetry which involves only the man who creates it and only at the moment he creates it broke out in its most abusive fashion, the theatre was scorned more than ever before by poets who have never had the sense of direct and concerted action, nor of efficacity, nor of danger.

We must get rid of our superstitious valuation of texts and *written* poetry. Written poetry is worth reading once, and then should be destroyed. Let the dead poets make way for others. Then we might even come to see that it is our veneration for what has already been created, however beautiful and valid it may be, that petrifies us, deadens our responses, and prevents us from making contact with that underlying power, call it thought-energy, the life force, the determinism of change, lunar menses, or anything you like. Beneath the poetry of the texts, there is the actual poetry, without form and without text. And just as the efficacity of masks in the magic practices of certain tribes is exhausted – and these masks are no longer good for anything except museums – so the poetic efficacity of a text is exhausted; yet the poetry and the efficacity of the theatre are exhausted least quickly of all, since they permit the *action* of what is gesticulated and pronounced, and which is never made the same way twice.

It is a question of knowing what we want. If we are prepared for war, plague, famine, and slaughter we do not even need to say so, we have only to continue as we are; continue behaving like snobs, rushing en masse to hear such and such a singer, to see such and such an admirable performance which never transcends the realm of art (and even the Russian ballet at the height of its splendor never transcended the realm of art), to marvel at such and such an exhibition of painting in which exciting shapes explode here and there but at random and without any genuine consciousness of the forces they could rouse.

This empiricism, randomness, individualism, and anarchy must cease. Enough of personal poems, benefiting those who create them much more than those who read them.

Once and for all, enough of this closed, egoistic, and personal art.

Our spiritual anarchy and intellectual disorder are a function of the anarchy of everything else – or rather, everything else is a function of this anarchy.

I am not one of those who believe that civilization has to change in order for the theatre to change; but I do believe that the theatre, utilized in the highest and most difficult sense possible, has the power to influence the aspect and formation of things: and the encounter upon the stage of two passionate manifestations, two living centers, two nervous magnetisms is something as entire, true, even decisive, as, in life, the encounter of one epidermis with another in a timeless debauchery.

That is why I propose a theatre of cruelty. – With this mania we all have for depreciating everything, as soon as I have said "cruelty," everybody will at once take it to mean "blood." But "theatre of cruelty" means a theatre difficult and cruel for myself first of all. And, on the level of performance, it is not the cruelty we can exercise upon each other by hacking at each other's bodies, carving up our personal anatomies, or, like Assyrian emperors, sending parcels of human ears, noses, or neatly detached nostrils through the mail, but the much more terrible and necessary cruelty which things can exercise against us. We are not free. And the sky can still fall on our heads. And the theatre has been created to teach us that first of all.

Either we will be capable of returning by present-day means to this superior idea of poetry and poetry-through-theatre which underlies the Myths told by the great ancient tragedians, capable once more of entertaining a religious idea of the theatre (without meditation, useless contemplation, and vague dreams), capable of attaining awareness and a possession of certain dominant forces, of certain notions that control all others, and (since ideas, when they are effective, carry their energy with them) capable of recovering within ourselves those energies which ultimately create order and increase the value of life, or else we might as well abandon ourselves now, without protest, and recognize that we are no longer good for anything but disorder, famine, blood, war, and epidemics.

Either we restore all the arts to a central attitude and necessity, finding an analogy between a gesture made in painting or the theatre, and a gesture made by lava in a volcanic explosion, or we must stop painting, babbling, writing, or doing whatever it is we do.

I propose to bring back into the theatre this elementary magical idea, taken up by modern psychoanalysis, which consists in effecting a patient's cure by making him assume the apparent and exterior attitudes of the desired condition.

I propose to renounce our empiricism of imagery, in which the unconscious furnishes images at random, and which the poet arranges at random too, calling them poetic and hence hermetic images, as if the kind of trance that poetry provides did not have its reverberations throughout the whole sensibility, in every nerve, and as if poetry were some vague force whose movements were invariable.

I propose to return through the theatre to an idea of the physical knowledge of images and the means of inducing trances, as in Chinese medicine, which knows, over the entire extent of the human anatomy, at what points to puncture in order to regulate the subtlest functions.

Those who have forgotten the communicative power and magical mimesis of a gesture, the theatre can reinstruct, because a gesture carries its energy with it, and there are still human beings in the theatre to manifest the force of the gesture made.

To create art is to deprive a gesture of its reverberation in the organism, whereas this reverberation, if the gesture is made in the conditions and with the force required, incites the organism and, through it, the entire individuality, to take attitudes in harmony with the gesture.

The theatre is the only place in the world, the last general means we still possess of directly affecting the organism and, in periods of neurosis and petty sensuality like the one in which we are immersed, of attacking this sensuality by physical means it cannot withstand.

If music affects snakes, it is not on account of the spiritual notions it offers them, but because snakes are long and coil their length upon the earth, because their bodies touch the earth at almost every point; and because the musical vibrations which are communicated to the earth affect them like a very subtle, very long massage; and I propose to treat the spectators like the snake charmer's subjects and conduct them *by means of their organisms* to an apprehension of the subtlest notions.

At first by crude means, which will gradually be refined. These immediate crude means will hold their attention at the start.

That is why in the "theatre of cruelty" the spectator is in the center and the spectacle surrounds him.

In this spectacle the sonorization is constant: sounds, noises, cries are chosen first for their vibratory quality, then for what they represent.

Among these gradually refined means, light is interposed in its turn. Light which is not created merely to add color or to brighten, and which brings its power, influence, suggestions with it. And the light of a green cavern does not sensually dispose the organism like the light of a windy day.

After sound and light there is action, and the dynamism of action: here the theatre, far from copying life, puts itself whenever possible in communication with pure forces. And whether you accept or deny them, there is nevertheless a way of speaking which gives the name of "forces" to whatever brings to birth images of energy in the unconscious, and gratuitous crime on the surface.

A violent and concentrated action is a kind of lyricism: it summons up supernatural images, a bloodstream of images, a bleeding spurt of images in the poet's head and in the spectator's as well.

Whatever the conflicts that haunt the mind of a given period, I defy any spectator to whom such violent scenes will have transferred their blood, who will have felt in himself the transit of a superior action, who will have seen the extraordinary and essential movements of his thought illuminated in extraordinary deeds – the violence and blood having been placed at the service of the violence of the thought – I defy that spectator to give himself up, once outside the theatre, to ideas of war, riot, and blatant murder.

So expressed, this idea seems dangerous and sophomoric. It will be claimed that example breeds example, that if the attitude of cure induces cure, the attitude of murder will induce murder. Everything depends upon the manner and the purity with which the thing is done. There is a risk. But let it not be forgotten that though a theatrical gesture is violent, it is disinterested; and that the theatre teaches precisely the uselessness of the action which, once done, is not to be done, and the superior use of the state unused by the action and which, *restored*, produces a purification.

I propose, then, a theatre in which violent physical images crush and hypnotize the sensibility of the spectator seized by the theatre as by a whirlwind of higher forces.

A theatre which, abandoning psychology, recounts the extraordinary, stages natural conflicts, natural and subtle forces, and presents itself first of all as an exceptional power of redirection. A theatre that induces trance, as the dances of Dervishes induce trance, and that addresses itself to the organism by precise instruments, by the same means as those of certain tribal music cures which we admire on records but are incapable of originating among ourselves.

There is a risk involved, but in the present circumstances I believe it is a risk worth running. I do not believe we have managed to revitalize the world we live in, and I do not believe it is worth the trouble of clinging to; but I do propose something to get us out of our [malaise] instead of continuing to complain about it, and about the boredom, inertia, and stupidity of everything.

Notes

1   E. Sellin, *The Dramatic Concepts of Antonin Artaud* (Chicago: University of Chicago Press, 1968), 82.
2   M. Esslin, *Antonin Artaud* (New York: Penguin, 1976), 76.
3   In C. Schumacher, *Artaud on Theatre* (London: Methuen, 1989), 82.

Chapter 27

Walter Benjamin (1892–1940)

Walter Benjamin was a Marxist literary and pioneering cultural critic. His major work, *The Origin of German Tragic Drama* (1925), a densely written study of allegory, language, and Judaic mysticism, was to serve as his entry into German university professorship. The book, however, was roundly rejected. Free to pursue the life of a freelance critic, Benjamin wrote on numerous and original themes, among them observations on the *flâneur* (''stroller'') in modern life, *passages* (urban byways appealing to Benjamin's sense of cultural detritus where nostalgic charm imprints its deepest secrets), language that transcends meaning, and his important essay, ''The Work of Art in the Age of Mechanical Reproduction'' (1936), in which he argues that the key turn from the premodern to the modern age was the demise of artistic ''aura.'' Works of art had enjoyed a uniqueness observed only by attending to the object itself. With mechanical reproduction, primarily photography and film, the notion of an ''original'' artwork's importance diminishes, diluted by the availability of reproduction. Rather than protest modernism's technological encroachment, Benjamin celebrates technology's capacity to expand art's reach and deemphasize the idea of an ''original.'' Benjamin, a friend to Brecht, found Brecht's notion of didacticism and epic theatre superior for the implementation of revolutionary socialism. Much of Benjamin's work consists of unfinished projects, but his impact on academic scholarship in the last quarter of the twentieth century is unequivocal. Benjamin sought to combine Marxist materialism with spirituality, and to consider history ''from the bottom up.''

Walter Benjamin, "What is Epic Theatre?" (1939), tr. Harry Zohn, from *Illuminations*, ed. Hannah Arendt (New York: Schocken, 1968), 147–54. © 1955 by Suhrkamp Verlag, Frankfurt a. M., English translation by Harry Zohn copyright © 1968 and renewed 1996 by Harcourt, Inc., reprinted by permission of Harcourt, Inc., and The Random House Group Ltd.

What is Epic Theatre? (1939)

The Relaxed Audience

"There is nothing more pleasant than to lie on a sofa and read a novel," wrote a nineteenth-century narrator, indicating the great extent to which a work of fiction can relax the reader who is enjoying it. The common image of a man attending a theatrical performance is the opposite: one pictures a man who follows the action with every fiber of his being at rapt attention. The concept of the epic theatre, originated by Brecht as the theoretician of his poetic practice, indicates above all that this theatre desires an audience that is relaxed and follows the action without strain. This audience, to be sure, always appears, as a collective, and this differentiates it from the reader, who is alone with his text. Also, this audience, being a collective, will usually feel impelled to react promptly. This reaction, according to Brecht, ought to be a well-considered and therefore a relaxed one – in short, the reaction of people who have an interest in the matter. Two objects are provided for this interest. The first is the action; it has to be such that the audience can keep a check on it at crucial places on the basis of its own experience. The second is the performance; it should be mounted artistically in a pellucid manner. (This manner of presentation is anything but artless; actually, it presupposes artistic sophistication and acumen on the part of the director.) Epic theatre appeals to an interest group who "do not think without reason." Brecht does not lose sight of the masses, whose limited practice of thinking is probably described by this phrase. In the endeavor to interest the audience in the theatre expertly, but definitely not by way of mere cultural involvement, a political will has prevailed.

The Plot

The epic theatre purposes to "deprive the stage of its sensation derived from subject matter." Thus an old story will often do more for it than a new one. Brecht has considered the question of whether the incidents that are presented by the epic theatre should not already be familiar. The theatre would have the same relationship to the plot as a ballet teacher has to his pupil: his first task would be to loosen her joints to the greatest possible extent. This is how the Chinese theatre actually proceeds. In his essay "The Fourth Wall of China" (*Life and Letters Today*, Vol. XV, No. 6, 1936), Brecht states what he owes to this theatre. If the theatre is to cast about for familiar events, "historical incidents would be the most suitable." Their epic extension through the style of acting, the placards and captions, is intended to purge them of the sensational.

In this vein Brecht takes the life of Galileo as the subject of his latest play. Brecht presents Galileo primarily as a great teacher who not only teaches a new physics, but does so in a new way. In his hands, experiments are not only an achievement of science, but a tool of pedagogy as well. The main emphasis of this play is not on Galileo's recantation; rather, the truly epic process must be sought in what is evident from the labeling of the penultimate scene: "1633 to 1642. As a prisoner of the Inquisition, Galileo continues his scientific work until his death. He succeeds in smuggling his main works out of Italy."

Epic theatre is in league with the course of time in an entirely different way from that of the tragic theatre. Because suspense belongs less to the outcome than to the individual events, this theatre can cover the greatest spans of time. (The same is true of the earlier mystery plays. The dramaturgy of *Oedipus* or *The Wild Duck* constitutes the counterpole of epic dramaturgy.)

The Untragic Hero

The French classical theatre made room in the midst of the players for persons of rank, who had their armchairs on the open stage. To us this seems inappropriate. According to the concept of the "dramatic element" with which we are familiar, it seemed inappropriate to attach to the action on the stage a nonparticipating third party as a dispassionate observer or "thinker." Yet Brecht often had something like that in mind. One can go even further and say that Brecht made an attempt to make the thinker, or even the wise man, the hero of the drama. From this very point of view one can define his theatre as epic theatre. This attempt is taken furthest in the character of Galy Gay, the packer. Galy Gay, the protagonist of the play *A Man's a Man*, is nothing but an exhibit of the contradictions which make up our society. It may not be too bold to regard the wise man in the Brechtian sense as the perfect showcase of its dialectics. In any case, Galy Gay is a wise man. Plato already recognized the undramatic quality of that most excellent man, the sage. In his Dialogues he took him to the threshold of the drama; in his *Phaidon*, to the threshold of the passion play. The medieval Christ, who also represented the wise man (we find this in the Early Fathers), is the untragic hero *par excellence*. But in the secular drama of the West, too, the search for the untragic hero has never ceased. In always new ways, and frequently in conflict with its theoreticians, this drama has differed from the authentic – that is, the Greek – form of tragedy. This important but poorly marked road, which may here serve as the image of a tradition, went via Roswitha and the mystery plays in the Middle Ages, via Gryphius and Calderón in the Baroque age; later we may trace it in Lenz and Grabbe, and finally in Strindberg. Scenes in Shakespeare are its roadside monuments, and Goethe crosses it in the second part of *Faust*. It is a European road, but a German one as well – provided that we may speak of a road and not of a secret smugglers' path by which the legacy of the medieval and the Baroque drama has reached us. It is this mule track, neglected and overgrown, which comes to light today in the dramas of Brecht.

The Interruption

Brecht differentiates his epic theatre from the dramatic theatre in the narrower sense, whose theory was formulated by Aristotle. Appropriately, Brecht introduces his art of the drama as non-Aristotelian, just as Riemann introduced a non-Euclidian geometry. This analogy may bring out the fact that it is not a matter of competition between the theatrical forms in question. Riemann eliminated the parallel postulate; Brecht's drama eliminated the Aristotelian catharsis, the purging of the emotions through empathy with the stirring fate of the hero.

The special character of the relaxed interest of the audience for which the performances of the epic theatre are intended is the fact that hardly any appeal is made to the empathy of the spectators. Instead, the art of the epic theatre consists in producing astonishment rather than empathy. To put it succinctly: instead of identifying with the characters, the audience should be educated to be astonished at the circumstances under which they function.

The task of the epic theatre, according to Brecht, is not so much the development of actions as the representation of conditions. This presentation does not mean reproduction as the theoreticians of Naturalism understood it. Rather, the truly important thing is to discover the conditions of life. (One might say just as well: to alienate [*verfremden*] them.) This discovery (alienation) of conditions takes place through the interruption of happenings. The most primitive example would be a family scene. Suddenly a stranger enters. The mother was just about to seize a bronze bust and hurl it at her daughter; the father was in the act of opening the window in order to call a policeman. At that moment the stranger appears in the doorway. This means that the stranger is confronted with the situation as with a startling picture: troubled faces, an open window, the furniture in disarray. But there are eyes to which even more ordinary scenes of middle-class life look almost equally startling.

The Quotable Gesture

In one of his didactic poems on dramatic art Brecht says: "The effect of every sentence was waited for and laid bare. And the waiting lasted until the crowd had carefully weighed our sentence." In short, the play was interrupted. One can go even further and remember that interruption is one of the fundamental devices of all structuring. It goes far beyond the sphere of art. To give only one example, it is the basis of quotation. To quote a text involves the interruption of its context. It is therefore understandable that the epic theatre, being based on interruption, is, in a specific sense, a quotable one. There is nothing special about the quotability of its texts. It is different with the gestures which fit into the course of the play.

"Making gestures quotable" is one of the substantial achievements of the epic theatre. An actor must be able to space his gestures the way a typesetter produces spaced type. This effect may be achieved, for instance, by an actor's quoting his own gesture on the stage. Thus we saw in *Happy End* how Carola Neher, acting a sergeant in the Salvation Army, sang, by way of proselytizing, a song in a sailors' tavern that was more appropriate there than it would have been in a church, and then had to quote this song and act out the gestures before a council of the Salvation Army. Similarly, in *The Measures Taken* the party tribunal is given not only the report of the comrades, but also the acting out of some of the gestures of the comrade they are accusing. What is a device of the subtlest kind in the epic theatre generally becomes an immediate purpose in the specific case of the didactic play. Epic theatre is by definition a gestic theatre. For the more frequently we interrupt someone in the act of acting, the more gestures result.

The Didactic Play

In every instance, the epic theatre is meant for the actors as much as for the spectators. The didactic play is a special case largely because it facilitates and suggests the interchange between audience and actors and vice versa through the extreme paucity of the mechanical equipment. Every spectator is enabled to become a participant. And it is indeed easier to play the "teacher" than the "hero."

In the first version of *Lindberghflug* (Lindbergh's Flight), which appeared in a periodical, the flier was still presented as a hero. That version was intended as his glorification. The second version – and this is revealing – owes its origin to the fact that Brecht revised himself. What enthusiasm there was on both continents on the days following this flight! But this enthusiasm petered out as a mere sensation. In *The Flight of the Lindberghs* Brecht endeavors to refract the spectrum of the "thrill" (*Erlebnis*) in order to derive from it the hues of "experience" (*Erfahrung*) – the experience that could be obtained only from Lindbergh's effort, not from the excitement of the public, and which was to be conveyed to "the Lindberghs."

T. E. Lawrence, the author of *The Seven Pillars of Wisdom*, wrote to Robert Graves when he joined the air force that such a step was for modern man what entering a monastery was for medieval man. In this remark we perceive the same tension that we find in *The Flight of the Lindberghs* and the later didactic plays. A clerical sternness is applied to instruction in a modern technique – here, that of aviation; later, that of the class struggle. This second application may be seen most fully in *Mother*. It was a particularly daring undertaking to keep a social drama free of the effects which empathy produces and which the audience was accustomed to. Brecht knew this and expressed it in an epistolary poem that he sent to a New York workingmen's theatre when *Mother* was produced there. "We have been asked: Will a worker understand this? Will he be able to do without his accustomed opiate, his mental participation in someone else's uprising, the rise of others; the illusion which whips him up for a few hours and leaves him all the more exhausted, filled with vague memories and even vaguer hopes?"

The Actor

Like the pictures in a film, epic theatre moves in spurts. Its basic form is that of the shock with which the single, well-defined situations of the play collide. The songs, the captions, the lifeless conventions set off one situation from another. This brings about intervals which, if anything, impair the illusion of the audience and paralyze its readiness for empathy. These intervals are reserved for the spectators' critical reaction – to the actions of the players and to the way in which they are presented. As to the manner of presentation, the actor's task in the epic theatre is to demonstrate through his acting that he is cool and relaxed. He too has hardly any use for empathy. For this kind of acting the "player" of the dramatic theatre is not always fully prepared. Perhaps the most open-minded approach to epic theatre is to think of it in terms of "putting on a show."

Brecht wrote: "The actor must show his subject, and he must show himself. Of course, he shows his subject by showing himself, and he shows himself by showing his subject. Although the two coincide, they must not coincide in such a way that the difference between the two tasks disappears." In other words: an actor should reserve for himself the possibility of stepping out of character artistically. At the proper moment he should insist on portraying a man who reflects about his part. It would be erroneous to think at such a moment of Romantic Irony, as employed by Tieck in his *Puss in Boots*. This irony has no didactic aim. Basically, it demonstrates only the philosophic sophistication of the author who, in writing his plays, always remembers that in the end the world may turn out to be a theatre.

To what extent artistic and political interests coincide on the scene of epic theatre will become manifest in the style of acting appropriate to this genre. A case in point is Brecht's cycle *The Private Life of the Master Race*. It is easy to see that if a German actor in exile were assigned the part of an SS man or a member of the People's Court, his feelings about it would be quite different from those of a devoted father and husband asked to portray Molière's Don Juan. For the former, empathy can hardly be regarded as an appropriate method, since he presumably cannot identify with the murderers of his fellow fighters. Another mode of performance, which calls for detachment, would in such cases be right and fitting and particularly successful. This is the epic stagecraft.

Theatre on a Dais

The aims of the epic theatre can be defined more easily in terms of the stage than of a new drama. Epic theatre allows for a circumstance which has been too little noticed. It may be called the filling in of the orchestra pit. The abyss which separates the players from the audience as it does the dead from the living; the abyss whose silence in a play heightens the sublimity, whose resonance in an opera heightens the intoxication – this abyss, of all elements of the theatre the one that bears the most indelible traces of its ritual origin, has steadily decreased in significance. The stage is still raised, but it no longer rises from an unfathomable depth; it has become a dais. The didactic play and the epic theatre are attempts to sit down on a dais.

Chapter 28

Maxwell Anderson (1888–1959)

Maxwell Anderson was a playwright and theorist. Among his successful plays were *What Price Glory?* (1924, co-written with Lawrence Stallings), the Pulitzer Prize-winning *Both Your Houses* (1933), *Winterset* (1935), *High Tor* (1937), and *Key Largo* (1939), as well as historical dramas such as *Elizabeth the Queen* (1930) and *Mary of Scotland* (1933). In his essay "The Essence of Tragedy," Anderson weighs in on Aristotle's *Poetics* and the possibility of tragedy in the modern age. It is one of the first attempts by an American author to grapple with the meaning of tragedy, an idea that will resurface considerably in Part III.

The Essence of Tragedy (1939)

Anybody who dares to discuss the making of tragedy lays himself open to critical assault and general barrage, for the theorists have been hunting for the essence of tragedy since Aristotle without entire success. There is no doubt that playwrights have occasionally written tragedy successfully, from Aeschylus on, and there is no doubt that Aristotle came very close to a definition of what tragedy is in his famous passage on catharsis. But why the performance of a tragedy should have a cleansing effect on the audience, why an audience is willing to listen to tragedy, why tragedy has a place in the education of men, has never, to my knowledge, been convincingly stated. I must begin by saying that I have not solved the Sphinx's riddle which fifty generations of skillful brains have left in shadow. But I have one suggestion which I think might lead to a solution if it were put to laboratory tests by those who know something about philosophical analysis and dialectic.

Maxwell Anderson, "The Essence of Tragedy," in *The Essence of Tragedy and Other Footnotes and Papers* (Washington, DC: Anderson House, 1939), 3–14. Paper read at the Modern Language Association in New York, January 1938.

There seems no way to get at this suggestion except through a reference to my own adventures in playwriting, so I ask your tolerance while I use myself as an instance. A man who has written successful plays is usually supposed to know something about the theory of playwriting, and perhaps he usually does. In my own case, however, I must confess that I came into the theatre unexpectedly, without preparation, and stayed in it because I had a certain amount of rather accidental success. It was not until after I had fumbled my way through a good many successes and an appalling number of failures that I began to doubt the sufficiency of dramatic instinct and to wonder whether or not there were general laws governing dramatic structure which so poor a head for theory as my own might grasp and use. I had read the *Poetics* long before I tried playwriting, and I had looked doubtfully into a few well-known handbooks on dramatic structure, but the maxims and theories propounded always drifted by me in a luminous haze – brilliant, true, profound in context, yet quite without meaning for me when I considered the plan for a play or tried to clarify an emotion in dialogue. So far as I could make out every play was a new problem, and the old rules were inapplicable. There were so many rules, so many landmarks, so many pitfalls, so many essential reckonings, that it seemed impossible to find your way through the jungle except by plunging ahead, trusting to your sense of direction and keeping your wits about you as you went.

But as the seasons went by and my failures fell as regularly as the leaves in autumn I began to search again among the theorists of the past for a word of wisdom that might take some of the gamble out of playwriting. What I needed most of all, I felt, was a working definition of what a play is, or perhaps a formula which would include all the elements necessary to a play structure. A play is almost always, probably, an attempt to recapture a vision for the stage. But when you are working in the theatre it's most unsatisfactory to follow the gleam without a compass, quite risky to trust "the light that never was on sea or land" without making sure beforehand that you are not being led straight into a slough of despond. In other words you must make a choice among visions, and you must check your chosen vision carefully before assuming that it will make a play. But by what rules, what maps, what fields of reference can you check so intangible a substance as a revelation, a dream, an inspiration, or any similar nudge from the subconscious mind?

I shan't trouble you with the details of my search for a criterion, partly because I can't remember it in detail. But I reread Aristotle's *Poetics* in the light of some bitter experience, and one of his observations led me to a comparison of ancient and modern playwriting methods. In discussing construction he made a point of the recognition scene as essential to tragedy. The recognition scene, as Aristotle isolated it in the tragedies of the Greeks, was generally an artificial device, a central scene in which the leading character saw through a disguise, recognized as a friend or as an enemy, perhaps as a lover or a member of his own family, some person whose identity had been hidden. Iphigenia, for example, acting as priestess in an alien country, receives a victim for sacrifice and then recognizes her own brother in this victim. There is an instant and profound emotional reaction, instantly her direction in the play is altered. But occasionally, in the greatest of the plays, the recognition turned on a situation far more convincing, though no less contrived. Oedipus, hunting savagely for the criminal who has brought the plague upon Thebes, discovers that he is himself that criminal – and since this is a discovery that affects not only the physical well-being and happiness of the hero, but the whole structure of his life, the effect on him and on the direction of the story is incalculably greater than could result from the more superficial revelation made to Iphigenia.

Now scenes of exactly this sort are rare in the modern drama except in detective stories adapted for the stage. But when I probed a little more deeply into the memorable pieces of Shakespeare's theatre and our own I began to see that though modern recognition scenes are subtler and harder to find, they are none the less present in the plays we choose to remember. They seldom have to do with anything so naïve as disguise or the unveiling of a personal identity. But the element of discovery is just as important as ever. For the mainspring in the mechanism of a modern play is almost invariably a discovery by the hero of some element in his environment or in his own soul of which he has not been aware – or which he has not taken sufficiently into account. Moreover, nearly every teacher of playwriting has had some inkling of this, though it was not until after I had worked out my own theory that what they said on this point took on accurate meaning for me. I still think that the rule which I formulated for my own guidance is more concise than any other, and so I give it here: A play should lead up to and away from a central crisis, and this crisis should consist in a discovery by the leading character which has an indelible effect on his thought and emotion and completely alters his course of action. The leading character, let me say again, must make the discovery; it must affect him emotionally; and it must alter his direction in the play.

Try that formula on any play you think worthy of study, and you will find that, with few exceptions, it follows this pattern or some variation of this pattern. The turning point of *The Green Pastures*, for example, is the discovery of God, who is the leading character, that even he must learn and grow, that a God who is to endure must conform to the laws of change. The turning point of *Hamlet* is Hamlet's discovery, in the play-scene, that his uncle was unquestionably the murderer of his father. In *Abe Lincoln in Illinois* Lincoln's discovery is that he has been a coward that he has stayed out of the fight for the Union because he was afraid. In each case, you will note, the discovery has a profound emotional effect on the hero, and gives an entirely new direction to his action in the play.

I'm not writing a disquisition on playwriting and wouldn't be competent to write one, but I do want to make a point of the superlative usefulness of this one touchstone for play-structure. When a man sets out to write a play his first problem is his subject and the possibilities of that subject as a story to be projected from the stage. His choice of subject matter is his personal problem, and one that takes its answer from his personal relation to his times. But if he wants to know a possible play subject when he finds it, if he wants to know how to mould the subject into play form after he has found it, I doubt that he'll ever discover another standard as satisfactory as the modern version of Aristotle which I have suggested. If the plot he has in mind does not contain a playable episode in which the hero or heroine makes an emotional discovery, a discovery that practically dictates the end of the story, then such an episode must be inserted – and if no place can be found for it the subject is almost certainly a poor one for the theatre. If this emotional discovery is contained in the story, but is not central, then it must be made central, and the whole action must revolve around it. In a three-act play it should fall near the end of the second act, though it may be delayed till the last; in a five-act play it will usually be found near the end of the third, though here also it can be delayed. Everything else in the play should be subordinated to this one episode – should lead up to or away from it.

Now this prime rule has a corollary which is just as important as the rule itself. The hero who is to make the central discovery in a play must not be a perfect man. He must have some variation of what Aristotle calls a tragic fault – and the reason he must have it is that when he makes his discovery he must change both in himself and in his action – and he must change for the better. The fault can be a very simple one – a mere unawareness, for example – but if he has no fault he cannot change for the better, but only for the worse, and for a reason which I shall discuss later, it is necessary that he must become more admirable, and not less so, at the end of the play. In other words, a hero must pass through an experience which opens his eyes to an error of his own. He must learn through suffering. In a tragedy he suffers death itself as a consequence of his fault or his attempt to correct it, but before he dies he has become a nobler person because of his recognition of his fault and the consequent alteration of his course of action. In a serious play which does not end in death he suffers a lesser punishment, but the pattern remains the same. In both forms he has a fault to begin with, he discovers that fault during the course of the action, and he does what he can to rectify it at the end. In *The Green Pastures* God's fault was that he believed himself perfect. He discovered that he was not perfect, and he resolved to change and grow. Hamlet's fault was that he could not make up his mind to act. He offers many excuses for his indecision until he discovers that there is no real reason for hesitation and that he has delayed out of cowardice. Lincoln, in *Abe Lincoln in Illinois*, has exactly the same difficulty. In the climactic scene it is revealed to him that he had hesitated to take sides through fear of the consequences to himself, and he then chooses to go ahead without regard for what may be in store for him. From the point of view of the playwright, then, the essence of a tragedy, or even of a serious play, is the spiritual awakening, or regeneration, of his hero.

When a playwright attempts to reverse the formula, when his hero makes a discovery which has an evil effect, or one which the audience interprets as evil, on his character, the play is inevitably a failure on the stage. In *Troilus and Cressida* Troilus discovers that Cressida is a light woman. He draws from her defection the inference that all women are faithless – that faith in woman is the possession of fools. As a consequence he turns away from life and seeks death in a cause as empty as the love he has given up, the cause of the strumpet Helen. All the glory of Shakespeare's verse cannot rescue the play for an audience, and save in *Macbeth* Shakespeare nowhere wrote so richly, so wisely, or with such a flow of brilliant metaphor.

For the audience will always insist that the alteration in the hero be for the better – or for what it believes to be the better. As audiences change the standards of good and evil change, though slowly and unpredictably, and the meanings of plays change with the centuries. One thing only is certain: that an audience watching a play will go along with it only when the leading character responds in the end to what it considers a higher moral impulse than moved him at the beginning of the story, though the audience will of course define morality as it pleases and in the terms of its own day. It may be that there is no absolute up or down in this world, but the race believes that there is, and will not hear of any denial.

And now at last I come to the point toward which I've been struggling so laboriously. Why does the audience come to the theatre to look on while an imaginary hero is put to an imaginary trial and comes out of it with credit to the race and to himself? It was this question that prompted my essay, and unless I've been led astray by my own predilections there is a very possible answer in the rules for playwriting which I have just cited. The theatre originated in two complementary religious ceremonies, one celebrating the animal in man and one celebrating the god. Old Greek Comedy was dedicated to the spirits of lust and riot and earth, spirits which are certainly necessary to the health and continuance of the race. Greek tragedy was dedicated to man's aspiration, to his kinship with the gods, to his unending, blind attempt to lift himself above his lusts and his pure animalism into a world where there are other values than pleasure and survival. However unaware of it we may be, our theatre has followed the Greek patterns with no change in essence, from Aristophanes and Euripides to our own day. Our more ribald musical comedies are simply our approximation of the Bacchic rites of Old Comedy. In the rest of our theatre we sometimes follow Sophocles, whose tragedy is always an exaltation of the human spirit, sometimes Euripides, whose tragicomedy follows the same pattern of an excellence achieved through suffering. The forms of both tragedy and comedy have changed a good deal in non-essentials, but in essentials – and especially in the core of meaning which they must have for audiences – they are in the main the same religious rites which grew up around the altars of Attica long ago.

It is for this reason that when you write for the theatre you must choose between your version of a phallic revel and your vision of what mankind may or should become. Your vision may be faulty, or shallow, or sentimental, but it must conform to some aspiration in the audience, or the audience will reject it. Old Comedy, the celebration of the animal in us, still has a place in our theatre, as it had in Athens, but here, as there, that part of the theatre which celebrated man's virtue and his regeneration in hours of crisis is accepted as having the more important function. Our comedy is largely the Greek New Comedy, which grew out of Euripides' tragicomedy, and is separated from tragedy only in that it presents a happier scene and puts its protagonist through an ordeal which is less than lethal.

And since our plays, aside from those which are basically Old Comedy, are exaltations of the human spirit, since that is what an audience expects when it comes to the theatre, the playwright gradually discovers, as he puts plays before audiences, that he must follow the ancient Aristotelian rule: he must build his plot around a scene wherein his hero discovers some mortal frailty or stupidity in himself and faces life armed with a new wisdom. He must so arrange his story that it will prove to the audience that men pass through suffering purified, that, animal though we are, despicable though we are in many ways, there is in us all some divine, incalculable fire that urges us to be better than we are.

It could be argued that what the audience demands of a hero [is] only conformity to race morality, to the code which seems to the spectators most likely to make for race survival. In many cases, especially in comedy, and obviously in the comedy of Molière, this is true. But in the majority of ancient and modern plays it seems to me that what the audience wants to believe is that men have a desire to break the moulds of earth which encase them and claim a kinship with a higher morality than that which hems them in. The rebellion of Antigone, who breaks the laws of men through adherence to a higher law of affection, the rebellion of Prometheus, who breaks the law of the gods to bring fire to men, the rebellion of God in *The Green Pastures* against the rigid doctrine of the Old Testament, the rebellion of Tony in *They Knew What They Wanted* against the convention that called on him to repudiate his cuckold child, the rebellion of Liliom against the heavenly law which asked him to betray his own integrity and make a hypocrisy of his affection, even the repudiation of the old forms and the affirmation of new by the heroes of Ibsen and Shaw, these are all instances to me of the groping of men toward an excellence dimly apprehended, seldom possible of definition. They are evidence to me that the theatre at its best is a religious affirmation, an age-old rite restating and reassuring man's belief in his own destiny and his ultimate hope. The theatre is much older than the doctrine of evolution, but its one faith, asseverated again and again for every age and every year, is a faith in evolution, in the reaching and the climb of men toward distant goals, glimpsed but never seen, perhaps never achieved, or achieved only to be passed impatiently on the way to a more distant horizon.

Chapter 29

Karel Brušák (1913–2004)

Karel Antonin Brušák taught Czech language and literature at Cambridge University. His essay, "Signs in the Chinese Theatre," was one of the first works to emerge from the 1930s Prague Linguistic Circle (sometimes referred to as the Prague structuralism) concerning theatre. The theories arising from this group (which began in 1926) can partly be considered as a continuation of the Russian formalisms of the 1920s. The major figures of the Prague School were Jan Mukařovský, Otakar Zich, and Roman Jakobson, the last arriving in Prague from Russia and bringing with him the ideas of Russian formalism. The structuralists were concerned with the inner unification of the literary and dramatic work by examining the mutual relation of its parts. Prague structuralists rejected the union of interrelated signs and themes as holistic; for them such aggregation was an outdated residue of Hegelian positivism and Wagner's total work of art. Instead, the concept of structure for the Prague School, Michael Quinn informs us, "always implies the idea of a system – a group of interdependent relations."[1] The relationship could be symmetrical or asymmetric, in agreement or contradictory, but the concept of structure implies the idea of a system of interdependent relations.

The importance of Brušák's essay is twofold: it opened the way to a general study of semiotics during the twentieth century, and it stressed the importance of performance over text. In the theatre, according to semioticians, every costume, gesture, sound, or formation of the stage has specific properties of its own. It is both an independent coded sign and sign interconnecting with other signs. A few strategically placed trees, for instance, can imply a forest. The spatial and temporal setting of the theatre creates a unique series of rules governing the stage. The stage, in short, has

Karel Brušák, "Signs in the Chinese Theatre," originally "Znaky na čínském divadle," *Slovo a slovesnost* (*Word and Poetics*) 5 (1939), tr. Brušák, from *Semiotics of Art*, ed. Ladislav Matejka and Irwin R. Titunik (Cambridge, MA: MIT Press, 1976), 59–73. © 1976 by The Massachusetts Institute of Technology. Reprinted by permission of The MIT Press.

its own language equal in importance to the written text. For Brušák, the enduring system of Chinese theatre created a paradigm of what Kier Elam calls "the actor's strictly codified gesture."[2] The signs of Chinese theatre are not meant to represent reality, but rather function to solidify the conventional actions in the acoustical and gestural world of the theatre. A few of the many significant works emanating from the study of semiotics onstage are Marvin Carson, *Theatre Semiotics: Signs of Life* (1990), Elam, *The Semiotics of Theatre and Drama* (1980), Marco De Marinis, *The Semiotics of Performance* (1993), Quinn, *The Semiotic Stage: Prague School Theater Theory* (1995), Fernando de Toro, *Theatre Semiotics: Text and Staging in Modern Theatre* (1995), and H. Schmid and A. van Kesteren (eds.), *Semiotics of Drama and Theatre: New Perspectives in the Theory of Drama and the Theatre* (Amsterdam, 1984). The last book contains a dated but highly useful bibliography by van Kesteren.

Signs in the Chinese Theatre (1939)

Chinese theatre has devised a complicated and precise system of signs carrying a large and categorically diverse range of meaning. The emergence of the system was made possible by the nature of the repertoire; the number of plays is relatively small and they are familiar to most of the audience. The Chinese play is of little significance from the literary point of view; performance is paramount. The components of the structure appear simple enough, but individual elements within the structure carry numerous obligatory signs standing for referents that are often very complex.

The stage is a rectangular raised platform flanked on three sides by the audience. The rear is formed by a backcloth with two apertures. These provide the only access to the stage; the opening on the spectators' left is the entrance, that on the right, the exit. Where an actor is coming from or going to is shown by his choice of aperture. If he both enters and leaves by "the entrance," the audience knows he is going back to the same place; if two actors enter and depart by different apertures, this shows they have come from different places and are returning thence, and so forth. Court theatres, which presented numerous plays involving the appearance of supernatural beings, had their stages built on two levels, mortals figuring on the lower level and spirits on the upper. Chinese stage sets are not made up of painted scenery or architectural structures as in the West but employ only a small number of separate articles, in particular a table and chairs, which then function as specific signs according to their position on the stage. The set is further elaborated by specific elements in the player's performance. Thus equipped the Chinese stage has survived for centuries and still operates unchanged in the classical Chinese theatre of today.

Until recently the development of the theatre has been examined almost exclusively from the angle of literature; the significance of the text has been overestimated. Nowadays it is generally accepted that the words form only the basis of a complicated structure made up of two interrelated series, one acoustic and one visual. The visual side of any dramatic performance apprehended by the spectator can be termed dramatic space. We can distinguish two qualities in it. The first is furnished by the mere existence of its members and is therefore static; the second is created and characterized only by their change and movement and is therefore kinetic. Of the static aspects of dramatic space the most permanent is the architectural element – the stage. Upon this is erected from performance to performance a variable space in the narrow sense of the word, formed by the scenery, scenic contrivances, and so on – the scene. Within this space of arbitrary duration there is formed a nonmaterial and transitory fictitious space, conjured up by the movement of actors, by the movements and color changes of light, by the moving images of a film, and so forth – the action space. In highly developed theatrical systems the stage used to have a conventional form. The Greek theatre had its orchestra and proscenium; the humanist, Elizabethan and Chinese theatres had their platform; the nineteenth-century theatre had a hollow cube minus the front wall, in the folklore theatre the stage is formed anew for each performance. The scene may be identical with the stage if the acting is without scenery, but usually it is an independent structure built upon it. The stage, in its ideally perfect form, is an inner space, limited by the structure of the theatre, and the scene is a fictitious space depicting or suggesting a real space. In the conception of the scene we must include not only the scenery and scenic contrivances but also the actors' costumes and masks. The lighting belongs to the scene only in so far as it renders it visible, contributes to the definition of place or time, or creates an impression. If it belongs dramatically in the performance, emphasizing the movements of the actors or forming an independent action, we may include it in the action space. In the same way a film, if shown as part of the scenery, belongs to the scene. But it may be shown to supplement the actions of the actors, as Piscator used to do in his crowd scenes or as an equal partner to their actions, a method invented by the Czech producer E. F. Burian and called by him "theatre-graph."

Consequently, the signs of Chinese theatre may be roughly divided into two groups: visual, that is, those associated with the dramatic space, and acoustic, that is, those associated with the dialogue, music, and sound effects.

The Visual Signs

This group comprises on the one hand signs related to the scene, on the other hand signs belonging to the concept of action space. Let us deal first with the signality of those elements forming the scene, namely (a) scenic articles, (b) costumes, and (c) makeup.

I   The Scene

(a) Scenic Articles: Articles on set are normally summarized under the general heading of stage properties. This term is, however, too imprecise in the context of Chinese theatre. In addition to the usual characterizing and functional types of stage properties, we have to deal here with articles that, while resembling these, are nevertheless quite distinct in their own right; they function as elementary signs, symbols standing for referents composing the scene.

The hierarchy of articles on set can be determined if they are considered in terms of their various functions. The most significant, dramatically active, are those that partici-pate in the player's performance, for example, swords, goblets, and so forth; they represent a point of transition from scene to action space and can be termed *scenic articles* in the proper sense of the word. After these come articles not brought into active use; their function is passively to complement the character of the scene or dramatis personae (for example, boulders, trees, armor, accoutrement, rings, and so on); they particularize the place of action (in time, history, society, and so forth) and are closely allied to scenery – these are *complementary articles*. As two distinct functions are involved, the borderline between the two types of article is clear enough. Nevertheless, an article on set may combine both functions; scenic articles may be and usually are also complementary articles (chairs, and so on) or, alternatively, articles previously considered as merely complementary may enter the play at some point as scenic articles. The latter is a less common occurrence and therefore dramatically extremely effective. The signification of these two types of articles on set is self-evident. An object may appear on set either in reality or in representation. If the object itself is displayed, it presents, both as a whole and in its individual qualities, the same series of signs as in real life (for example, a specific piece of furniture may be, in relation to its owner, a sign of his social standing, taste, upbringing, state of health, habits, and so forth). While in real life the utilitarian function of an object is usually more important than its signification, on a theatrical set the signification is all important. A real object may be substituted on the set by a symbol if this symbol is able to transfer the object's own signs to itself. To satisfy this condition, it is sufficient for the symbol to possess only a few of the basic characteristics of the represented object. The article on set as a theatrical sign of the object itself takes on the sign duties of the object represented; thus articles on set are theatrical signs of signs and frequently very complex.

Chinese theatre however possesses articles of a special kind, exceptional in their relationship to actors and set. These are *object signs*, able to represent all aspects of the scene alone and unaided. On a stage without scenery or lighting effects these serve to denote the locale of the play. They are elementary theatrical signs and, as such, distinct from scenic articles and complementary articles, that is to say, they are neither signs of signs nor a structure of signs; they are signs not of particular objects but of objects in general.

The most important of these are a table and chair that are almost never absent from the Chinese stage. If the table and chair are standing in the usual manner, then the set is an interior. On the other hand, a chair placed side on the ground or on its back signifies an embankment or earthwork; overturned it signifies a hill or mountain; standing on the table, it signifies a city tower. Apart from the table and chair the Chinese theatre uses articles that, while resembling the scenery of Western theatre, differ in that they remain the same for each play they are required for and are consciously interpreted as theatrical signs. A mountainous or desolate area is sometimes represented by a board with a stylized drawing of a mountain; city battlements are represented by a length of blue material held by theatre assistants; sometimes a gate and wall masonry are depicted on it, and sometimes it is simply a plain rectangular piece of cloth, unadorned by drawing.

These object signs are also used in the Chinese theatre to portray natural phenomena. Black pennants waved by theatre assistants are a sign for wind; a hammer and mirror signify a thunderstorm; a sign for blizzard is confetti falling from black pennants that unfurl as the assistants wave them. Chinese theatre does not alter the brightness or color of the lighting; the onset of dusk and night is marked by a theatre assistant carrying on a lit lamp or lantern. An object, pennant, or piece of material showing the stylized drawing of a wave and fish is a sign for water; the actor playing a drowning person leaps between the assistants bearing these signs, and all go off together.

The Chinese theatre does, however, also have objects on set which we have termed scenic articles; for our purposes we shall distinguish articles that are adjuncts to the actor's performance and articles that are signs characterizing his dramatic personality.

The elaborate system of signs evolved has enabled the Chinese actor to give a comprehensible portrayal of the most varied actions without having to recreate reality on the stage. He is able to manage with a few props, chiefly relying on his own performance. For example, to act riding on horseback he uses a whip that represents the horse. The color of the whip denotes the color of the horse. Thrown at random on stage, the whip represents a horse grazing. Riding by carriage is indicated by an assistant carrying a banner on both sides of the actor, usually a yellow banner marked with a circle, the sign of a wheel; to indicate alighting, the assistant raises the banner. To indicate a trip in a boat, it is enough for the actor to carry an oar with which he performs a great variety of exactly defined motions while walking about the stage. If an execution is to be enacted, a packet encased in red silk signifies the severed head; the man executed runs off the stage, and an assistant displays the packet to the audience.

Characterizing signs are those articles worn visibly and continuously by the player; they form a point of transition to costume and generally comprise banners, coils of silk, pieces of material. The use of scenic articles linked to costume comprehensibly delineates the character of the personage while obviating the necessity for explanatory passages in the dialogue. Spirits are revealed by black or red veils or paper tassels, a sick person is marked by a stripe of yellow material tied round the head and running down onto the back, a captive wears a long silk cord round his neck. The sign for the rank of general is a collection of triangular shaped bannerets, usually four, embroidered with dragons, flowers, and phoenixes, fastened on the actor's back; a special banner is reserved for a general in command, another for a general on concluding peace. Special coils of yellow silk denote an imperial order or imperial safe-conduct, and its bearer may enter places forbidden to others; a board cased in yellow silk denotes an official seal, and so forth.

(b) Costumes: Four types of character are most frequent on the Chinese stage: i. heroes of shining character, loyal and honorable men (shēng), ii. villains, cruel and faithless men, coarse soldiers, servants (jìng), iii. clowns; dancers, and acrobats (chǒu), iv. female characters (dàn). All these roles admit of many nuances according to age, situation, and so on; the second group (jìng) is distinguished from the first (shēng) by its actors wearing makeup on their faces. Religious reasons prevented women playing in the Chinese theatre; female parts were formerly distinguished only by the actor playing a woman wearing a blue tulle band around his head, but later this simple sign was replaced by a more elaborate form of dress, makeup, and hairstyle.

Each of these types wears a costume appropriate in material, color, cut, and design to the character's meaning. Chinese theatrical costume observes strict conventions, but in contrast to Chinese object signs, which are elementary signs, it is a complicated structure of signs. It differs from Western theatrical costume not only by its plurisignification but also by the nature of the referents. It reveals not merely the wearer's social status, age, and so forth, but his worth, character, and so on. This purely theoretical aspect has its practical consequences. It reveals an interesting interdependence between aesthetic outlook and questions of technique. For the costumes used are always made from high quality, expensive materials painstakingly put together to fulfill to perfection the demands of stern convention, while at the same time upholding the immutability of that same convention by their own durability. Chinese theatrical costume, however, has another important task to fulfill – that of forming the scene. The object signs are very restrained; besides, the Chinese classical theatre is without lighting effects. This gives rise to the magnificence of Chinese theatrical costume, whose variegated colors, sophisticated cut, and intricate embroidery are the most splendid in the world.

We may distinguish three types of costume according to cut and design: ceremonial garb (mǎng), everyday wear (diéz), and military uniform (kǎikào). Any of these may be worn by either male or female characters, situation being the only determining factor. Alongside these, however, there exists a large series of separate items of dress which function as distinct autonomous signs. Chinese costume in its function as sign adopts those elements of ordinary dress which are signs standing for specific referents but simplifies or adapts them. Thus, for instance, the beggar's costume stems from its counterpart in everyday reality but is converted into an autonomous theatrical sign; the beggar in the Chinese theatre wears an everyday silk dress (diéz) spangled with multi-colored silk patches. A mandarin is distinguished by his long coat and thick-soled shoes, and so on. Occasionally the meaning of the sign varies according to situation; a cape worn early in the morning betrays the fact that the character returned home late at night; worn later in the day, however, it indicates the wearer's laziness and slovenliness. A woman's skirt signifies dress that is not too clean and as such is common with women of the lower class; if worn by a wealthy woman, it shows either that the person in question is on a journey and unable therefore to care for her appearance or that we are dealing with a disguise.

(c) Makeup: An actor is still more closely identified with the character represented by his makeup. Makeup in Chinese theatre is used as a sign that sets apart complex and exceptional characters. Not all players are given makeup, only those acting second or third group parts (jìng and chǒu); honorable men (shēng) and women (dàn) are never made up. The makeup used is unimitative and independent entirely of matters of physiognomy; it forms a self-contained, artificial sign system. It is strikingly similar to the ancient war mask of the Chinese; theatrical makeup was evidently derived from it when evil and cruel personages were being represented and the need arose to find some way of clearly marking them apart from other characters. These masks, portraying spirits and demons intended to overawe the enemy in battle, had a long tradition behind them and boasted a suitably strict symbolism, but they were too stiff and rigid to be suitable in themselves for the flexible and constantly changing dramatic space of the Chinese theatre. This most probably gave rise to the idea of painting them directly on the skin of the face, which was then still able to use its expressive resources beneath the colorful abstract patterns of the makeup. Pattern and color of makeup are signs of the character of the personage represented by the actor. In the course of time, though, signs, which in the original system had universal validity and permitted of random combination, grouped themselves into schematic units, ideographs, connected with specific heroes of individual plays; within these schemes, however, the signs retained their original values. The scheme painted on the actor's face is, in fact, a chart of the moral qualities of the dramatic persona.

The patterns employed are several and diverse in meaning. Most widespread is a form of makeup dividing the actor's face into three sections, roughly in the shape of a Y, consisting of the forehead and both cheeks; the chin is generally covered with a beard and has no special function in this regard. Old men are characterized by evenly painted eyebrows extended to the ears. The wounded have their face covered with irregular drawing and multifarious colors. The parts of clowns are marked by makeup distorting the features, with irregular placing of nose and eyes, or alternatively the forehead is painted with a triangle with its point on the bridge of the nose.

Colors fulfill a much more precise sign function. It is comparatively rare to find the whole face made up with one color, white, black, red, and so forth, these indicating either unambiguous characters or supernatural beings. Black means simplicity, sincerity, courage, and steadfastness; red denotes loyalty, honesty, and patriotism; crimson is used with old men as a sign for the calm of old age and prudence allied to these qualities; blue expresses obstinacy, cruelty, and pride; yellow indicates ruthlessness, slyness, and wiliness; white stands for hypocrisy, irascibility, baseness, and viciousness. The extent of the colored area on the actor's face corresponds to the extent of the moral quality in the character of the dramatis persona. Thus, for example, there are many degrees in the use of white, from a face totally white except for the eyebrows to a mere white spot on the nose. In the first case the spectator is informed that the dramatis persona has no other qualities than those having white as their sign; that is, he is an utter villain (usually of noble birth). In the second case the moral qualities signified by the white color form only a very small part of the character of the dramatis persona; that is, he is an honest man with a few light moral blemishes (usually a simple soldier). Makeup serves also besides costume to set apart supernatural beings; green is reserved for spirits and devils, gold for gods.

The use of false beards and mustaches, of which there are more than a dozen kinds, is also subject to convention. Their shape and mode of wear are nonrealistic; they are fastened with wires behind the ears, and their styles, which are often very bizarre, are signs of the wearer's age, status, and personality.

II   The Action Space

The second type of visual signs are those belonging to the action space. Every motion, gesture, and facial expression of the actor are signs that, as in Western theatre, serve both to expound the character and to indicate its relationship to others. As well as these, however, the Chinese theatre provides abundant examples of signs realized within the action space, which have representative function and stand for referents outside persons; they represent nonexistent components of the scene or scenic articles. Every routine, whatever its particular significance, has been evolved through long tradition into an obligatory convention. Its present shape has been affected not only by the attempt to devise a sign at once simple and comprehensible but also by constant emphasis on aesthetic function. The Chinese player's actions were subjected to precise rules that allow no basic deviation. Perfect mastery of technique is enabled by educating the actor in these rules from a tender age, and by having him play the same part throughout his career. The conventional action signs never aim at imitation of reality. They naturally take this as their starting point, but in most cases they are so constructed as to divorce themselves from realism as much as possible. The player for example suggests the action of drinking tea by raising an imaginary cup to his lips, but in order to avoid being realistic, masks the hand executing the gesture with a special movement of the other hand. To illustrate someone sleeping, he does not lie down but sits leaning the fingers of one hand lightly on his temple. An action sign thus owes its final form to a tension between the aesthetic function and other functions, communicative, expressive, and so on. The relationship of action signs to reality is variable; conventional sequences of movements which relate to the scene even at their most artificial are in fact in closer contact with reality than actions expounding thought processes and character relationships. The Chinese actor evokes the action space with the full gamut of elements of movement, gesture, and facial expression at his disposal. Movements are here taken in the narrower sense of body movements. One special mode of expression is the use of various motions performed by means of pheasants' plumes attached to the player's headgear. These are very long, and the actor may bring them into gyrating or nodding motion by turning or drooping the head or he may move them by hand. The Chinese actor's gestures differ profoundly from those of the Western actor. The primary gestures are made by the hands, which are seldom left free but are generally cloaked in long flowing silken cuffs fastened to the sleeves. The gestures carried out by the actor with these sleeves are rich in signification. Though the facial expressions are not in general distinct from the Western kind, they are more diversified and specific. Movements of the facial muscles are conventionalized; binding stipulations govern which facial expression should be used to express a given emotion relative to character type and age and the nature, intensity, and duration of the feeling. Generally, movements and gestures in the wider sense are conveyors of signs substituting for the scene, while sleeve gestures and facial expressions together express the thoughts and emotions of the dramatis persona.

A great proportion of the actor's routine is devoted to producing signs whose chief function is to stand for components of the scene. An actor's routine must convey all those actions for which the scene provides no appropriate material setup. Using the applicable sequence of conventional moves, the actor performs the surmounting of imaginary obstacles, climbing imaginary stairs, crossing a high threshold, opening a door. The motion signs performed inform the onlooker of the nature of these imaginary objects, tell whether the nonexistent ditch is empty or filled with water, whether the nonexistent door is a main or ordinary double door, single door, and so forth. To show a person entering a dwelling of the poor, the actor carries out the proper motion in a bent position, for the poor live in low-ceilinged basements; if appropriate, the regulations avail him of the opportunity to show himself hitting his forehead on an imaginary lintel. The player's actions are particularly complicated when involving objects or animals; here the actor sometimes bases his routine on residual parts or fragments of the imaginary articles. When speaking about scenic articles, we have mentioned the use of an oar to represent a trip in a boat; if the actor arrives with his oar on an empty stage by the "exit" doorway, this means the whole stage is water; he may receive other persons on board his boat of fantasy and row to the "entrance," which stands for the shore. An unusually involved routine is used by the actor to suggest actions with a horse, mounting, riding, trotting, galloping, dismounting, leading, and so on. The signification of all these movements is so intricately devised that it allows the spectator to imagine even the nature of the imaginary horse. In one play the actor representing a servant has eight imaginary horses on stage; the audience can tell from his behavior that one horse is exceptionally beautiful, another bites, another bucks, another is sick, another worn with age, and so forth. The servant saddles the horses, leads them to his master's residence, and announces to the company that they are in readiness. The knights come out, pretend to mount the imaginary horses, and ride off at a trot. The same degree of detail marks the stipulations governing the representation of diverse types of work and activity: weaving, sewing, thread making, writing, and so on; each dispenses with stage props.

Signs connected with the psychology of the dramatis persona are usually sleeve gestures carefully worked out to fit each individual instance. The "raised sleeve gesture," in which the long sleeve is thrown upwards and hangs out, expresses despair or revolt. Another sleeve gesture signifies a weighty decision; the "decisive sleeve gesture," carried out by the right hand circling slowly upward and quickly downward, signifies that the person has made some fateful decision, sacrificed someone's life, and so forth. To show dejection, for example, frustration of plans, the Chinese actor is not permitted to let his arms dangle by the side of his body, since this gesture does not comply with Chinese aesthetics; the actor lowers only one arm, but this he holds in front of him and presses somewhat to the body, gripping it under the elbow with his other arm, bent. This "gesture of repose," a set position in fact, is observed not merely by actors expressing fatigue but equally by those portraying spirits. Another standard position, to show the poverty or unreality of the dramatis persona, is the "drooping sleeves gesture"; the actor playing a poor man or a spirit allows his sleeves to droop from his arms, held somewhat forward from the body. Gestures performed with the hands alone are also used to signify emotions. If the concept cannot be expressed by a sleeve gesture, the actor tucks up his sleeve in order to have his hand free and covers it again after completion of the gesture. Hand gestures may replace sleeve gestures only in the case of signs representing emotions but some hand gestures cannot be replaced by sleeve gestures. Hand gestures are signs of illness, feelings of heat, cold, powerlessness, disappointment, pain, pity, contemplation, and so on. The gesture of protest may serve to show their complexity. The hand is partially clenched into a fist, the thumb rests on the middle joint of the middle finger, the index finger is curved across the thumb and at the same time the tip of the little finger is made to touch the third finger, to avoid the shape of an ordinary fist. Whereas gestures never signify joyful emotions, body and feather movements have no other function but to express joyful emotions. Military roles contain many motions expressing strength and ardor. A sign of vigor is a movement that the actor performs using his left leg while standing erect on his right; he raises his left thigh and bends his leg at the knee into an obtuse angle. The "dragon's turn" at the waist has the same meaning. Keeping his arms on his hips, the actor rotates his trunk, stretching out deeply in all directions. In one play the actor in this leaning pose uses his teeth to seize a glass of wine from a tray proffered by a servant on his right, leans back, as if to quaff the cup, and returns the glass to the tray, now held by the servant on his left side. The most extreme signs of levity and gaiety are dancing movements with feathers, most often performed by one of the female characters (dàn).

Finally, the last but most important theatrical signs belonging to the concept of action space are those that reveal the relationship of the person performing the routine to another character. Here we have to deal with signs displaying the social relations of individuals, dramatic signs in the true sense of the word, for it is these that express conflict most often. Some have transferred themselves to the Chinese stage straight from the ceremonial of social intercourse, acquiring still greater complexity and lexicality. They concern the salutation and welcome of a guest. The "sleeve gesture of respect" is a sign of a highly courteous greeting; it is performed by a crossing of the arms. If the actor wishes to present his respects or request attention or a hearing, he carries out the "sleeve gesture of address"; he raises his left arm to beneath his chin, letting the sleeve dangle, lightly touches the latter with the fingers of his right hand, leaving out the index finger, and greets the person accosted. This gesture and sign of respect, however, are also performed by the player when uttering the name of a person not present whom he loves or cherishes. An actor acknowledges a greeting or show of respect by performing the "sleeve gesture of attention"; he places his right hand beneath his breast letting the sleeve drop, at the same time bowing. These motions are a sign replacing the verbal wish that the other desist from his greetings. Another series of signs concerns the greeting of a guest. Together with the usual salutations, the actor welcoming a guest performs other gestures; he conveys the dusting down of the chair by a movement of the sleeve right, left, and right again, first with the right arm, then the left, and last the right again. The affectation and significance of this ceremony as carried out on similar lines in everyday life enabled it to be adopted with only minor alterations by the action space. Similar lexicalized routines for greeting a guest, including dusting the chair, are also known in some country districts in Bohemia and had their own importance in a series of cere- monies, for instance matchmaking. The action space of Chinese theatre has also elabor- ated signs expressing disagreeable feelings. Anger, repugnance, or refusal are conveyed by the "sleeve gesture of aversion"; with a circling motion the player hurls his sleeve in the subject's direction and simultaneously twists his head the other way. To send a person away, the actor carries out the "sleeve gesture of refusal." By means of bending movements of the wrists he hurls both sleeves out from the body once, twice, thrice, stepping back at the third gesture. The "sleeve gesture of concealment" indicates that the actor is obscuring his action or words from the other person on stage; its meaning is thus close to the aside of Western theatre. If the player wishes to communicate to the audience some secret that must remain hidden from the other persons, or if he wishes to express a private thought, he raises his right-hand sleeve to the level of his face; this gesture denotes an opaque wall between the other characters and the actor, who then points to them frequently with his other hand. The actor may hide himself behind a still more perfect imaginary wall when in a dilemma or afraid of discovery by using the "sleeve gesture of hiding." Here the arm is bent in an obtuse angle to the brow, and the sleeve flows down across the whole face.

The Acoustic Signs

The second group of Chinese theatrical signs are characterized by the signs of theatrical speech, song, and music. The language in the Chinese theatre has special signs that distinguish it from ordinary speech. The composition of Chinese plays is not in most cases dramatic in the Western sense; it generally lacks the tension reflectable in dialogue. Chinese drama is a structure made up of verse, prose, and music; these elements intermingle and always appear. Theatre speech was formed by an artificial mixing of various dialects and its signification stems also from a special mode of declamation employed. The declaiming of individual words is founded on a strictly adhered to system of four tones which prevents possible errors in comprehension due to the homonymous character of Chinese vocabulary and also serves to heighten the musicality of the speech; at the same time, however, each of the tones is a sign and expresses the speaker's inner state of mind. The spoken word must always blend with the rhythm of movement, whether it be prose or verse. Verse dialogue or monologue is composed of quatrains;

the first two lines are delivered in a monotone, the third line rises and slackens off, and the fourth is delivered slowly and quietly. If, on the other hand, the actor raises his voice on the last line, this announces the imminence of music and dance.

Music in the Chinese theatre follows convention. It is played at the beginning of a play, at actors' entries, and at certain identical situations in the course of the play. The most important instruments of the theatre orchestra are two-string violins, three-string guitars, reed organs, horns, flutes, drums, gongs, cymbals, and clappers. For centuries the music played and written has been based on a five-note scale derived from the ancient Chinese flute, and the classical Chinese theatre remains faithful to this tradition. For the principal situations conventional themes are prescribed which always enter at the reaching of these points in the play; otherwise there is no music or simply improvised music. The themes are stated either by a singer or solo instrument and are then recapitulated in unison by all instruments. Arias are sung in an archaic almost incomprehensible form of language; thus certain features are signaled by the music alone, since the themes are precisely defined, either in conjunction with the action space or in isolation. Occasions where music functions as a sign are, for example, anger, hatred, horror, surprise, anxiety, sadness, meditation, love, joy, drunkenness, the toilette, fray, flight, and so on. Often the circumstance in question is conveyed by the music alone, for instance if drunkenness is to be represented; its realistic imitation, common on the Western stage, is forbidden to the Chinese actor on aesthetic grounds.

By examining the signification of individual elements in the Chinese theatre, we find a structure generally homogeneous, a stock of several systems of lexicalized signs, systems which though autonomous in their own right develop spontaneously one from another. The shaping of these systems, the stability of whose entire structure depends on the maintenance of virtually inviolate lexicons, evidently owed something to external, extra-theatrical influences (religion, traditions of social intercourse, and so forth) but the influence of the scene itself was highly important. Articles on set standing for referents composing the scene grew into special theatrical signs, adopting new functions and bequeathing their original ones to the action space. The latter could discharge only its own role by transferring certain of its sign functions to the remaining elements of the structure, chiefly the music. In Chinese, as opposed to Western theatre, a dramatic work does not envisage realization in some form dependent on numerous chance-shaping factors ranging from a producer's conception to an actor's diction. Production of single established plays in the ancient Chinese theatre are [sic] finalized beforehand down to the last ingredient. They persist in the abstract as uninterrupted series, familiar already to the entire cast in each and every cross-section, and are merely re-evoked from time to time without any serious structural change. The structure is to a certain degree sure in itself, so that there is not even any need for a producer to supervise its unity.

Notes

1   M. Quinn, *The Semiotic Stage: Prague School Theater Theory* (New York: Peter Lang, 1995), 18.
2   K. Elam, *The Semiotics of Theatre and Drama* (London: Routledge, 1980), 13.

Part III

1940–1960

"In the last quarter of a century," wrote scenic designer and theatre critic Robert Edmond Jones in 1941, "we have begun to be interested in the exploration of man's inner life, in the unexpressible and hitherto inexpressible depths of the self."[1] The interest in "depths of the self" owed much to existentialism. Existentialism drew from Edmund Husserl's phenomenology and Martin Heidegger's "questions concerning being" (*Seinfrage*). It emphasized the "here and now" – meaning exists in the present. Enlightenment philosophy, which had been influential to varying degrees right up to the mid-twentieth century, examined humanity in epistemological terms, as a *tabula rasa* fixed in space while registering sense-data and knowledge. Existentialism shifts the ground to a being in motion; we are born, suffer, and die through the course of time. Humanity moves along a spiritual journey of inner truth. "Man is spirit," writes the existentialist Søren Kierkegaard, and "spirit is the self."[2] It is an authentic existence taking into account the self in the here and now. Existentialism and Romanticism had much in common; "The greatest virtue of all," Isaiah Berlin writes, "is what existentialists call authenticity, and what the romantics called sincerity."[3] How to find the inner authenticity was the bread-and-butter of the existentialists, who, as Berlin notes, owed much to Romantic idealism. Heidegger's *Being and Time* (1927) transformed the emphasis on humans from static beings in space to fluid existence in time (*Zeitlichkeit*). Heidegger refers to temporal existence as *Da-sein*, literally "being there." *Da-sein*, he says, "possesses what is past as a property that is still objectively present."[4] The "temporality of being" (*Temporalität des Seins*) illustrates the protean nature of humanity. We are, according to Heidegger, "Beings-in-the-world." In other words, rather than isolated in our own sphere of consciousness, as Leibniz or Descartes would suggest, our consciousness is on the ground – living, breathing, eating, and dying. William Barrett contends that for Heidegger "My Being is not something that takes place inside my skin (or inside an immaterial substance inside that skin); my Being, rather, is spread over a field or region which is the world of its care and concern."[5] Time stops only at death and this terminal awareness, Heidegger says, "is always essentially my own." Death belongs to each of us; it looms over existence as the most extreme of individual possibilities. It is our most personal possession since we endure it alone – nobody else can die for me. In this way death is, Heidegger remarks, "an existential phenomenon" (223) because it forces us to take stock of our existence.

In the aftermath of World War II, the existentialists ruminated on the inscrutability of the war's carnage. As a result, theatre theories of the mid-century turned from the subjective mode (e.g., stream-of-consciousness, which dominates the previous section) to more dynamic paradigms of human interaction and the potential for violence such interactions might instigate. The seminal text of the period was Jean-Paul Sartre's *Being and Nothingness* (1943). It explored the difficulties of existence given the backdrop of two world wars, the Holocaust, and the prospect of a future rife with unprecedented horrors. "Nothingness" for Sartre offers the possibility of reinventing one's life and shaping moral values. No essence of life exists; each of us must forge meaning through active choices and commitment to the world. Sartre centered his philosophy on practical understanding and everyday existence. He attempted to shift its focus from truth as an absolute transcendence to truth as contingency, thereby transforming universal and unchanging structures to context and situatedness. This led to an examination of our social interactions and the way we crave acceptance by others, what Sartre calls "bad faith." Bad faith, he says, is a deliberate surrendering of liberty, the loss of one's individuality and identification through the eyes of others. This deception hides the truth from oneself and allows us to meld into the herd. Bad faith, he says, "implies in essence the unity of a *single* consciousness."[6] Sartre's example is the waiter who nods obsequiously, overacts the role of waiter-ness, and plays "at *being* a waiter in a café" (102). Physical representation itself consumes our behavior and our interiority; the ceremony of role-playing becomes us, eviscerating our individuality and integrity.

In light of Sartre's and other existential critiques, theorists attempted to flesh out the meaning of tragedy. When Sartre says that bad faith "stands forth in the firm resolution *not to demand too much*, to count itself satisfied when it is barely persuaded, to force itself in decisions to adhere to uncertain rules" (113), he influenced dramatists and critics who examined characters unwilling to play the social game. Tragedy means either nonconformity – standing astride the mainstream – or being drawn into the vortex of the status quo. The issues raised by the essayist here convey the existential experience of tragedy and the disappointments that come with conformity. Characters are troubled not by monumental issues but by pettiness and difficulty overcoming the daily grind. This is an era where waiting takes on signification. Albert Camus put it best in *Le Mythe de Sisyphe* (1942, published in English in 1955) when he notes that Sisyphus, condemned to push a rock uphill only to experience its fall again, epitomizes the existential condition. Sisyphus, Camus writes, "is the absurd hero. He *is*, as much through his passions as through his torture. His scion of the gods, his hatred of death, and his passion for life won him that unspeakable penalty in which the whole being is exerted toward accomplishing nothing. This is the price that must be paid for the passion of this earth."[7]

The period was also influenced by an interest in symbols. One of the leading philosopher-critics, Northrop Frye, contributed to a literary theory called "New Criticism," in which the text is perceived as a stand-alone object investigated purely as text rather than historical artifact or biographical reflection of the author. Though Frye was not technically a New Critic, he exerted a strong presence in the field. For him humans organize experience through symbolic systems using language, math, and myth. Symbols for Frye (and for Susanne K. Langer) are alogical and non-discursive; they are, in other words, not representations of reality but rather, like music, artistic symbols creating a coherent unity expressing the artistic experience. The cartographer and the landscape artist, for instance, are dissimilar; the former uses logic and science to create maps, the latter uses aesthetics and harmony to create art. Finally, this section continues where the previous section left off, on the subject of semiotics.

Notes

1   R. E. Jones, *The Dramatic Imagination* (New York: Methuen, 1941), 15.
2   S. Kierkegaard, *Sickness Unto Death*, tr. H. and E. Hong (Princeton: Princeton University Press, 1980), 13.
3   I. Berlin, *The Roots of Romanticism* (Princeton: Princeton University Press, 1999), 139.
4   M. Heidegger, *Being and Time*, tr. J. Stambaugh (Albany: State University of New York Press), 17.
5   W. Barrett, *Irrational Man: A Study in Existential Philosophy* (New York: Doubleday, 1962), 217.
6   J.-P. Sartre, *Being and Nothingness*, tr. H. E. Barnes (New York: Washington Square, 1956), 89.
7   A. Camus, *The Myth of Sisyphus and Other Essays* (New York: Vintage, 1955), 89.

Chapter 30

Jindřich Honzl (1894–1953)

Theorist Jindřich Honzl was a writer, teacher, filmmaker, director, and member of the Prague School of semiotic theory. He directed at the Liberated Theatre in Prague, one of Czechoslovakia's primary pre-World War II theatres. The theatre was closed by the Nazi occupation, but during the early postwar years Honzl was head of Prague's National Theatre. For Honzl theatre is a series of transformable signs. The signs can be suggestive, i.e., objects need only show partials to suggest the whole. For example, a tree can represent a forest, or just a tree. According to Keir Elam, "Honzl's thesis is that any stage vehicle can stand, in principle, for any signified class of phenomena: there are no absolutely fixed representational relations." For Honzl a dramatic scene, Elam contends, "is not always figured analogically through spatial, architectural or pictorial means, but may be indicated gesturally (as in mime), through verbal indications or other acoustic means."[1] Honzl built his theories on the leading Prague School thinkers, including Otakar Zich's *Aesthetics of Dramatic Art* (1931), and shared an interest in semiotics with Jiři Veltrsky's *Man and Object in Theatre* (1940) as well as Peter Bogatyrëc's interest in folk theatre. Their work led the way for other twentieth-century semioticians: Tadeusz Kowzan, Anne Ubersfeld, Patrice Pavis, and Erika Fischer-Lichte, among others.

Dynamics of the Sign in the Theatre (1940)

Everything that makes up reality on the stage – the playwright's text, the actor's acting, the stage lighting – all these things in every case stand for other things. In other words, dramatic performance is a set of signs.

Jindřich Honzl, "Dynamics of the Sign in the Theatre," originally "Pohyb divadelního znaku," *Slovo a slovesnost* (*Word and Poetics*) 6 (1940), tr. I. R. Titunik, from *Semiotics of Art*, ed. Ladislav Matejka and Irwin R. Titunik (Cambridge, MA: MIT Press, 1976), 74–93. © 1976 by The Massachusetts Institute of Technology. Reprinted by permission of The MIT Press.

Otakar Zich expressed such a view in his *Aesthetics of Dramatic Art* when he advanced the notion that "dramatic art is an art of images and is so, moreover, in absolutely every respect."[2] Thus the actor represents a dramatic character [...], the scenery represents the locale where the story unfolds [...], bright lighting represents daytime, dim lighting denotes nighttime, music represents some happening (the noise of battle), and so forth. Zich explains that though the stage certainly involves architectural constructions, still it cannot in his view be consigned to the domain of architecture because architecture does not want to stand for anything and, hence, does not have any image function. The stage has no other function than to stand for something else, and it ceases to be the stage if it does not represent something. To comprehend Zich's assertion better, we may put it into other words and say that it does not matter whether the stage is a construction or not, that is, whether the stage is a place in the Prague National Theatre or a meadow near a forest or a pair of planks supported by barrels or a market square crowded with spectators. What does matter is that the stage of the Prague National Theatre may perfectly well represent a meadow, or the meadow of an outdoor theatre clearly represent a town square. [...]

Moreover, from this instance of the semiotic character of the stage we can draw an analogy to other aspects of the theatrical performance. [...] [A]lthough the stage is usually a construction, it is not its constructional nature that makes it a stage but the fact that it *represents* dramatic place. The same can be said about the actors: the actor is usually a person who speaks and moves about the stage. However, the fundamental nature of an actor does not consist in the fact that he is a person speaking and moving about the stage but that he *represents someone, that he signifies a role in a play.* Hence it does not matter whether he is a human being; an actor could be a piece of wood as well. If the wood moves about and its movements are accompanied by words, then such a piece of wood can represent a character in a play, and the wood becomes an actor. [...]

And if simply a voice, heard from the wings of a stage or over the radio, properly signifies a dramatic character, then such a voice is an actor. Precisely such an acoustic actor appears in Goethe's *Faust*: in the usual performances of this play we perceive the role of God in the prologue merely as a voice. Finally, radio plays, voice, and sound represent not only dramatic characters but also the other facts that make up the reality of the theatre: the stage, scenery, props and lighting. [...]

First of all, let us deal with the stage and those signs that denote it. We may say that the stage can be represented by any real space or, in other words, a stage can equally well be a structure or a town square surrounded by spectators or a meadow or a hall in an inn. But even when a stage is such a space, it need not be denoted solely by its spatial nature. We have already used the example of radio stage (a business office, a coal mine, and so forth) that is denoted acoustically. However, even the conventional theatre can provide us with examples of a nonspatial denotation of a stage, for example, sound representing a stage. In the last act of Chekhov's *The Cherry Orchard* it is precisely the orchard that plays the main role. The cherry orchard is on the stage but in such a way that we cannot see it. It is not represented spatially but acoustically, as the sounds of axes cutting down the orchard are heard in the last act. [...]

[...] Zich's notion has the stage always still in a theatre, in the architecturally denoted place "where plays and operas are performed." It was precisely concrete artistic work that dared to move into the areas where the theory of theatre had not yet entered, even though it had already pointed in that direction. Modern theatre has had the effect precisely of freeing the stage from its previously permanent architectural constants.

Cubo-futuristic theatrical experiments turned our attention to stages and theatres other than those built for the tsarist ballet, the box displays of high society, or for the cultural activity of small-town amateurs. Through these experiments we discovered the theatre of the street, we became fascinated by the theatricality of a sports field and admired the theatrical effects created by the movements of harbor cranes, and so on. Simultaneously we discovered the stage of the primitive theatre, the performances of a barker, children's games, circus pantomimes, the tavern theatre of strolling players, the theatres of masked celebrating villagers. The stage could arise anywhere – any place could lend itself to theatrical fantasy.

With the freeing of the stage, other aspects of theatrical performance were released from their confinements. Scenery of wooden frames and painted canvas awoke from its spell. Stylized theatre from as early as the time of the *Théâtre d'Art* in France, or G. Fuchs and A. Appia in Germany, the Society of New Drama in Russia, and of Kvapil in Bohemia adhered to scenic signs that might be called scenic metonymies. [...] A part represented the whole. But a part could indicate several different wholes: a Venetian column and a flight of stairs sufficed for almost all the scenes in *The Merchant of Venice*, excepting scenes in Portia's or Shylock's rooms or in the garden. The column and the flight of steps were used not only as scenery for the street but also for the harbor, the square, and the court of justice. The attributive scenery of the stylized stage always sought to use devices of one single meaning whenever possible. True, a Venetian column could be placed in a square or in a street or made part of a house. But in each and every case it meant a Venetian building and nothing but a Venetian building, of which it could be a part. With the advent of cubo-futuristic theatre new materials appeared on the stage, and formerly undreamt-of things acquired various representative functions. The theatre of Russian constructivism used a construction made of planks to represent a factory yard, a garden pavilion, a wheat field or a flour mill. The question can be asked, which part or what property of these planks carried the representative function? It was not color or colored shapes, since such constructions were made of raw, unvarnished wood or were uniformly colored. Construction excluded the use of picture or color signs on the stage (at any rate, this is the constructivism of Popova and Meyerhold). However, very often even the arrangement of the construction failed to create an unambiguous theatrical sign. Meyerhold's construction for *The Death of Tarelkin* was simply a crate combined with a cylindrical object of the same material whose circular end faced the audience and could have suggested any number of things, but none of them without ambiguity. Perhaps the most definite idea it conjured up, in this case, was that of a meat grinder. But it could equally well have indicated a circular window or a round cage or a huge mirror, circularity being its most striking feature. [...]

[...] It is only when we see the actor pacing back and forth in the cylindrical structure like a prisoner and clutching its slats like bars that we realize the function of this stage prop: it is a cell. Simultaneously, however, there remain in our minds all the associations of form that originated during our first glance at the said prop. The idea of a "meat grinder" in combination with the idea of a "prison cell" acquires a mutual polarization of new meanings.

If we examine other stage sets used by Meyerhold in his stagings of that period, we frequently see a system of suspended planes, staircases and props whose meaning as a sign is completely indeterminate. The critics of these performances and sets often spoke of abstract scenery. Neither Meyerhold nor any other stage artist was concerned with abstract scenery. His stage sets had very concrete tasks and functions. Indeterminate in shape and color, they became signs only when used for the actor's actions. It can be said that *a representative function was not expressed by means of form or color, but by the actor's actions* on the stage construction, on the bare floor, on the suspended planes, on the staircases, on the slanting surfaces, and so on. [...]

If the constancy of the key points of the structure is assured, transformations in its complex ground plan can be effected without substantial changes. If we remove a single pillar, however, basic changes on the plane of the structure as a whole are necessary. Examples of structural stability are of course theatres with centuries old tradition such as the traditional Japanese Nō theatre, the more recent tradition of Japanese Kabuki theatre, the old Chinese theatre, our puppet theatre, folk theatres, the theatres of primitives, and so on. The consistency of a structure causes theatrical signs to develop complex meanings. The stability of signs promotes a wealth of meanings and associations. [...]

The desire for freedom of expression and technique is a tendency that has constantly had a determining effect on art. The theatre brought about by the cubo-futuristic revolt "for fresh air" introduced new theatrical devices and dispensed with many others. Russian constructivism rid the stage of scenery, wings, borders and backdrops. As a result the stage lost the possibility of localizing an action through the use of painted signs indicating an interior or exterior. That was not all, however. Not only did directors reject scenery, stage front and rear, borders and wings, but they also departed from the bare stage that remained after their revolt. They even rejected the five walls that enclosed the space displayed in front of the auditorium so that every spectator could see it. However, the directors who succeeded them (Okhlopkov,[3] Gropius's theatre design) did away with a stage completely or, more precisely, placed the stage among the spectators so that any free place in front of, above, next to, or behind the audience could be a stage. Thus they consigned to oblivion all those rare and precious stage mechanisms that, in obedience to a single demand by the director, lowered a section of stage or piece of scenery or a prop or even an actor from the height of the fly gallery, rotated the rear part of a stage set to the front, shifted prepared scenery from the wings, raised up whole stage areas with scenery intact through trapdoors and so on. The wizard of the theatre was deprived of all the mechanisms with which he performed his magic. All that was left were his bare hands. To represent or signify the spatial location of a play became problematical with the abandonment of many of the conventions established between stage and auditorium by long-standing tradition. [...]

When the foundations of theatrical structure are shaken in this way, measures must immediately be taken to adapt to new modes of operation. If one of the muscles in the set muscles that move the forearm in a living organism is paralyzed, then that organism is safeguarded by the fact that one of the coordinated muscles will take over the function of the new paralyzed. One theatrical function is to locate a play spatially: to signify a lawn or barroom, to represent a cemetery or a banqueting hall. This is an essential function of the stage which must be implemented just as much by a stage using constructions as by a stage using scenery, and just as much by a stage located in the midst of the spectators as by one that is traditionally located. Signs whose function it is to promote the spectators' understanding always involved the designation of a space. It is precisely this designative function that constitutes the stability of these signs. In all other respects these signs retain the greatest possible dynamics. The fact that the signs are supposed to designate the space in which an action takes place does not mean that they must be spatial signs. We have already shown that space can be designated by an acoustic sign or by means of a light sign. On the centralized stage possibilities are extremely limited for the placing of objects, large pieces of furniture, or scenery signs. While the constructivist stage concentrated on the actor's actions, the centralized stage is often solely dependent on the actor per se. Okhlopkov's theatre has acquainted us with a number of superb instances of the actor becoming a sign for spatial location. Here one found not only actor-scenery and actor-set, but even actor-furniture, actor-props.

Okhlopkov created an *actor-sea* by having a young man dressed in a neutral manner (in blue, that is "invisible," overalls with a blue mask on his face) shake a blue-green sheet attached to the floor in such a way that the rippling of the blue-green sheet expressively replaced the waves of a sea canal. He created *actor-furniture* by having two "invisibly" attired actors kneel opposite each other and stretch between them a tablecloth into the quadrilateral shape of a table. An *actor-prop* originated by placing next to the actor playing the role of the captain another actor dressed in blue overalls who held up the handle of the ship's horn the moment when the captain, pulling the handle, blasts a signal to the sailors. [...]

It would be wrong, however, to think that this changeable method of dramatic expression is a specialty of the Chinese and Japanese theatre or of a Russian innovator from the year 1935. Similar methods of dramatic expression can be found in many Czech dramatic performances. I should like to mention my own production of *The Teacher and the Pupil* (by V. Vančura) in cooperation with the painter Jindřich Štýrský at the Municipal Theatre in Brno in 1930.

The fourth act of the play is situated at the edge of town. In order to indicate this fact we made use of a *dramatic mask*. But we took this dramatic mask from the face of the actor, relocated it, and applied it as a spatial *sign on the stage*. Projected across a wide area of the cyclorama was a face whose lower part was covered with a scarf in the manner of highwaymen. This face, with evil eyes below a forehead covered by a hat, arched above the stage and shaded that area in which the spectator usually sees a sky with floating clouds.

Through relocation, the dramatic mask acquired a new meaning. [...]

In my production of Apollinaire's *The Breasts of Tirésias* (in 1927), the poets words were changed into painter's images. We transformed the actors into fetters which then moved like figures about the stage. The different combinations of letters created different verses.

In the production of Goll's *Methusalem* (1927) *stage props* (bread, a bottle and so on) appeared in the play as characters who rebel against Methusalem. [...]

It is in the changeability of the theatrical sign that the main difficulty of defining theatrical art lies. Definitions of this concept either narrow down theatricality to the manner of expression of our conventional drama and opera theatres or expand it to such an extent that it becomes meaningless.

It is on the basis of changes of the theatrical sign that we explain yet another theoretical confusion that hinders research of the problem of who or what is the central creative element of dramatic expression. If we say that it is the playwright, then we are certainly correct as regards numerous cases and example. However, we still would not grasp the essence of many historical examples of theatre and could not prove that in all cases it is the word of the playwright that presents the axis of theatrical art. The entirely free theme or wholly unthematic characters of improvised Italian comedies and similar forms show that even the playwright and his text are susceptible of the changes we have discussed earlier. Similarly, we cannot regard as completely true the statement that the main bearer of theatrical art is the actor. As a proof of this I have in mind the static positioning of actors on the stage (characteristic of many dramatic styles of both past and present) which converts theatre into a dialogue recital carried out by stationary figures (*Théâtre d'Art*, stylized German theatre, Meyerhold) or anaesthetizes the actor into a puppet with prearranged stilted movements, thus changing the traditional acting function into a function of a stage prop or structure. And should a modern director say that he himself is the centre of dramatic creation, we can agree with his statement only in the instances where he demonstrates this to us. Should he speak of the theatrical art of past times when there was no director, then we cannot but disagree with him.

We do not mean by this to prove that the text, actor, and director are auxiliary or dispensable factors that merely affect the balance of theatrical structure. We wish to show only that every historical period actualizes a different component of dramatic expression and that the creative forces of one factor can replace or suppress others without decreasing the strength of the dramatic effect. We could also prove that certain periods directly demand such shifts in the balance of the dramatic structure. After all, there exist or existed theatres without authors (or without authors of note), there exist or existed theatres without actors or without great actors, and there exist and existed theatres without directors. However, if we go into the matter more deeply, we find that the actor's function is always present even though it may change into, or appear in the guise of, another function. Similarly, we must allow that what we call the organizational force of the director was present in every historical period of the theatre, even when there was no director as such. [. . .]

A number of theories of theatre built around changeability have been advanced in the effort to organize or unify the multiplicity of dramatic material, devices and procedures. The best known of these is undoubtedly Wagner's concept of theatre as "collective art" (*das Gesamtkunstwerk*).

Multiplicity of devices is organized by the "collective art" (*Gesamtkunstwerk*) in such a way that individual components unite in a result, provide a "collective effect." Thus the dramatic character is present not only on the stage but also in the orchestra; we experience its inner state, development and fate not only from words and actions we see on the stage but also from the sounds we hear. Here it is a matter of the parallelism of the musical stream, the dramatic action, the words, scenery, props, lighting and all other factors. [. . .]

This principle of "collective art" (*Gesamtkunstwerk*) assumes that the intensity of dramatic effect, that is, the strength of the spectator's impression, is directly proportional to the *number of perceptions* that synchronically flood the senses and mind of the spectator at any given moment. The task of the dramatic artist (in the Wagnerian sense) is to equalize the effects of various dramatic devices in order to produce impressions of the same impact.

Thus, this theory does not recognize changes of the theatrical sign which can use different materials for its implementation. On the contrary, Wagner's *Gesamtkunstwerk* theory indirectly claims that there is no specific, unitary dramatic material but that there are diverse materials which must be kept apart and treated side by side. Accordingly, there is no dramatic art as such, but there are music, text, actor, scenery, stage props, and lighting, which collectively make up dramatic art. Thus dramatic art cannot exist by itself but only as a collective manifestation of music, poetry, architecture, histrionics, and so on. Dramatic art results as the sum of the other arts.

With regard to the spectator and to the psychology of perception, I am of the opinion that this theory is incorrect. Uppermost is the problem of whether the spectator perceives acoustic and visual signs simultaneously and with the same intensity or whether he concentrates on one aspect only in the course of perception. When trying to solve this question, we must also bear in mind the fact that it is a matter of the perception of *artistic signs* and that this is a special case of perception. If the spectator's mind has to concentrate in order to understand the semiotic value of certain facts, it can certainly be presumed that it also concentrates on perception of a particular kind, visual or acoustic. However, should the concentrated attention of the spectator perceive both visually and acoustically, we cannot speak even in this instance of a *sum* of impressions but only of a special relation of one kind of perception to the other, of the *polarization of these perceptions*.

After all, we encounter among spectators people who visit a theatre to listen to music or to a poet or to see the performance of a certain actor, and so on. However, even persons without special interests find themselves, when attending a theatre, listening only to the music at one moment and captivated by the actor or enchanted by the poetic text at another moment. I would say that nearly all theatregoers fall into this category. At the same time, however, the interest of the spectator does not pass from one device to another merely by chance; it does so deliberately. If we observe the audience at a theatre we see that its members turn their eyes to the same spot on the stage, that they all have the same interest in a single actor at one moment or interest in the observation of the scenery at another moment. The psychology of the spectators' perception thus prevents us from accepting the assumptions of the Wagnerian theory of "collective art." [...]

I commenced my study with a quotation from Zich and I should conclude by returning to Zich's views. [...] According to Zich the specific character of the theatrical unit is the *combination* of "two simultaneous, inseparable but *heterogeneous* components, that is, visual components (optical) and audible components (acoustic)."

However, even this "combination" does not prevent us from seeking and finding a unity in dramatic art, from declaring that it is a single integral art. The binary character of the materials, that is, the visual and acoustic character of dramatic devices, does not negate the unity of the essence of theatre art.

Since the acoustic and the visual can change places on the stage, it may happen that one of the components submerges below the surface of the spectator's conscious attention. [...]

Let us note, furthermore, that the silent film was also once called visual *theatre* and that the radio play could be called acoustic *theatre*. Thus the specific character of theatre art does not lie in the division of its devices into acoustic and visual ones. It is necessary to seek the essence of theatre art elsewhere.

It is my belief that with our analysis of the changeability of the theatrical sign we have undertaken a task that can test the trustworthiness of many definitions of theatrical art and decide whether those definitions make provision for the old and the new types of theatre that have originated in different social structures, in different historical periods, under the influence of different poetic or dramatic personalities, as the result of many technical inventions, and so on. I am also of the opinion that we should restore respect for the old theory of theatrical art which sees its essence in *acting*, in *action*.

In this light, the theatricality of dramatic character and that of place and of plot will not appear to us as things permanently separated from one another. [...]

Action, taken as the essence of dramatic art, unifies word, actor, costume, scenery and music in the sense that we could then recognize them as different conductors of a single current that either passes from one to another or flows through several at one time. Now that we have used this comparison, let us add that this current, that is, dramatic action, is not carried by the conductor that exerts the least resistance (dramatic action is not always concentrated only in the performing actor) but rather theatricality is frequently generated in the overcoming of obstacles caused by certain dramatic devices (special theatrical effects when, for instance, action is concentrated solely in the words or in the actor's motions or in offstage sounds, and so on), in the same way that a filament fibre glows just because it has resistance to an electric current. [...]

Modern theatre begins the very moment scenery is evaluated according to the function it fulfils in the actual dramatic action. The fact that the *Théâtre d'Art* in the nineties restricted its scenery to "a backdrop and a number of movable curtains" has to be explained, from our viewpoint, as a recognition of the real function of stage scenery in plays whose theatricality and action are created verbally (Maeterlinck). If the German Shakespearean stage was limited to a Gothic arch or column against a blue backdrop, it was the result of the awareness that a stage set participates in a Shakespearean play solely as a simple scenic sign informing the spectator of the change of scene.

The new limitations in stage art resulting from Russian constructivism spring from the idea of dramatic performance which is manifested by the player's movements and everything that serves these movements; acrobatic props or contraptions, a moveable wall or floor, and so on. [...]

The examples I have employed show clearly that there are no permanent laws or invariable rules for the unification of dramatic devices via the flow of dramatic action. In its autonomous development, which is an integral feature of the development of every art, the theatre actualizes different aspects of theatricality at different times. For example, Maeterlinck's symbolism actualizes the verbal text as the bearer of dramatic action (Maeterlinck's play *Les Aveugles* [*The Blind*] *is acted out* through the dialogue of immobile actors conversing on stage). Russian constructivism, on the other hand, acts by means of the dance or the "biomechanical" movements of the actor. [...]

The changeability of the hierarchical scale of components of dramatic art corresponds to the changeability of the theatrical sign. I have attempted to throw light on both. I wanted to demonstrate the changeability that makes stage art so varied and all-attractive but at the same time so elusive of definition. Its protean metamorphoses have sometimes even caused the very existence of a theatrical art to be doubted. [...] It was only a combination of separate arts. Theatre had not located either its core or its unity. I have shown that it has both, that it is one and many like the Triune God of Saint Augustine.

Notes

1   K. Elam, *The Semiotics of Theatre and Drama* (London: Routledge, 1980), 13.
2   Otakar Zich, *Estetika dramatického uměni* [*Aesthetics of Dramatic Art*] (Prague, 1931), 35.
3   Nikolai Pavlovich Okhlopkov (1900–67) was an important Soviet actor and director of the Realistic Theatre in the 1930s. – Editor's note.

Chapter 31

Thornton Wilder (1897–1975)

Thornton Wilder was a playwright and novelist. His well-known works include the novel *The Bridge of San Louis Ray* (1927) and the plays *Our Town* (1938) and *The Skin of Our Teeth* (1942). His novels and dramas explore the existential angst of ordinary people caught in extraordinary circumstances. Wilder outlines four fundamental conditions for drama: collaboration, appeal to a group mind, the recognition of stage pretense, and theatre taking place in the present, eliminating the need for exposition required in novels. His prescriptive conditions are in many ways reiterations of nineteenth- and early twentieth-century playwriting books by Gustav Freytag and William Archer. Freytag and Archer, among others, offered formulaic yet nuanced advice on how to structure a drama. Wilder advanced their ideas by utilizing experimental techniques: breaking the fourth wall and imaginatively reframing the linear sequence in his dramas. His advice is enriched by common sense and solid grounding in the art of playmaking.

Some Thoughts on Playwrighting (1941)

Four fundamental conditions of the drama separate it from the other arts. Each of these conditions has its advantages and disadvantages, each requires a particular aptitude from the dramatist, and from each there are a number of instructive consequences to be derived. These conditions are:

1. The theater is an art which reposes upon the work of many collaborators;
2. It is addressed to the group-mind;

Thornton Wilder, "Some Thoughts on Playwrighting," in *Intent of the Artist*, ed. A. Centeno (Princeton: Princeton University Press, 1941), 83–98. © 1941 by The Wilder Family LLC. All rights reserved. Reprinted by permission of The Barbara Hogenson Agency, Inc.

3. It is based upon a pretense and its very nature calls out a m⟩
4. Its action takes place in a perpetual present time.

I   The Theater is an Art which Repo
the Work of Many Collaborat

We have been accustomed to think that a work of art is by
governing selecting will.

A landscape by Cézanne consists of thousands of brushstrokes each con...
one mind. *Paradise Lost* and *Pride and Prejudice,* even in cheap frayed copies, bear the
immediate and exclusive message of one intelligence.

It is true that in musical performance we meet with intervening executants, but
the element of intervention is slight compared to that which takes place in drama.
Illustrations:

1. One of the finest productions of *The Merchant of Venice* in our time showed Sir
Henry Irving as Shylock, a noble, wronged, and indignant being, of such stature that the
Merchants of Venice dwindled before him into irresponsible schoolboys. He was confronted in court by a gracious, even queenly, Portia, Miss Ellen Terry. At the Odéon in
Paris, however, Gémier played Shylock as a vengeful and hysterical buffoon, confronted
in court by a Portia who was a *gamine* from the Paris streets with a lawyer's quill three feet
long over her ear; at the close of the trial scene Shylock was driven screaming about the
auditorium, behind the spectators' back and onto the stage again, in a wild Elizabethan
revel. Yet for all their divergences both were admirable productions of the play.

2. If there were ever a play in which fidelity to the author's requirements were essential
in the representation of the principal role, it would seem to be Ibsen's *Hedda Gabler,*
for the play is primarily an exposition of her character. Ibsen's directions read: "Enter from
the left Hedda Gabler. She is a woman of twenty-nine. Her face and figure show great
refinement and distinction. Her complexion is pale and opaque. Her steel-gray eyes
express an unruffled calm. Her hair is of an attractive medium brown, but is not
particularly abundant; and she is dressed in a flowing loose-fitting morning gown."
I once saw Eleonora Duse in this role. She was a woman of sixty and made no effort
to conceal it. Her complexion was pale and transparent. Her hair was white, and she
was dressed in a gown that suggested some medieval empress in mourning. And the
performance was very fine.

One may well ask: why write for the theatre at all? Why not work in the novel where
such deviations from one's intentions cannot take place?

There are two answers:

1. The theatre presents certain vitalities of its own so inviting and stimulating that the writer
   is willing to receive them in compensation for this inevitable variation from an exact
   image.
2. The dramatist through working in the theatre gradually learns not merely to take
   account of the presence of the collaborators, but to derive advantage from them; and
   he learns, above all, to organize the play in such a way that its strength lies not in
   appearances beyond his control, but in the succession of events and in the unfolding
   of an idea, in narration.

athered audience sits in a darkened room, one end of which is lighted. The nature
transaction at which it is gazing is a succession of events illustrating a general idea –
stirring of the idea; the gradual feeding out of information; the shock and counter-
shock of circumstances; the flow of action; the interruption of action; the moments of
allusion to earlier events; the preparation of surprise, dread, or delight – all that is the
author's and his alone.

For reasons to be discussed later – the expectancy of the group-mind, the problem of
time on the stage, the absence of the narrator, the element of pretense – the theatre carries
the art of narration to a higher power than the novel or the epic poem. The theatre is
unfolding action and in the disposition of events the authors may exercise a governance
so complete that the distortions effected by the physical appearance of actors, by the
fancies of scene painters and the misunderstandings of directors, fall into relative insignificance. It is just because the theatre is an art of many collaborators, with the constant
danger of grave misinterpretation, that the dramatist learns to turn his attention to the
laws of narration, its logic and its deep necessity of presenting a unifying idea stronger
than its mere collection of happenings. The dramatist must be by instinct a storyteller.

There is something mysterious about the endowment of the storyteller. Some very
great writers possessed very little of it, and some others, lightly esteemed, possessed it in
so large a measure that their books survive down the ages, to the confusion of severer
critics. Alexandre Dumas had it to an extraordinary degree; while Melville, for all his
splendid quality, had it barely sufficiently to raise his work from the realm of non-fiction.
It springs, not, as some have said, from an aversion to general ideas, but from an
instinctive coupling of idea and illustration; the idea, for a born storyteller, can only be
expressed imbedded in its circumstantial illustration. The myth, the parable, the fable are
the fountainhead of all fiction and in them is seen most clearly the didactic, moralizing
employment of a story. Modern taste shrinks from emphasizing the central idea that
hides behind the fiction, but it exists there nevertheless, supplying the unity to fantasizing,
and offering a justification to what otherwise we would repudiate as mere arbitrary
contrivance, pretentious lying, or individualistic emotional association spinning. For all
their magnificent intellectual endowment, George Meredith and George Eliot were not
born storytellers; they chose fiction as the vehicle for their reflections, and the passing
of time is revealing their error in that choice. Jane Austen was pure storyteller and her
works are outlasting those of apparently more formidable rivals. The theatre is more
exacting than the novel in regard to this faculty, and its presence constitutes a force
which compensates the dramatist for the deviations which are introduced into his work
by the presence of his collaborators.

The chief of these collaborators are the actors.

The actor's gift is a combination of three separate faculties or endowments. Their
presence to a high degree in any one person is extremely rare, although the ambition
to possess them is common. Those who rise to the height of the profession represent
a selection and a struggle for survival in one of the most difficult and cruel of the artistic
activities. The three endowments that compose the gift are observation, imagination,
and physical coordination.

1. An observant and analyzing eye for all modes of behavior about us, for dress and
    manner, and for the signs of thought and emotion in one's self and in others.

2. The strength of imagination and memory whereby the actor may, at the indication in the author's text, explore his store of observations and represent the details of appearance and the intensity of the emotions – joy, fear, surprise, grief, love, and hatred, and through imagination extend them to intenser degrees and to differing characterizations.

3. A physical coordination whereby the force of these inner realizations may be communicated to voice, face, and body.

An actor must *know* the appearances and the mental states; he must *apply* his knowledge to the role; and he must physically *express* his knowledge. Moreover, his concentration must be so great that he can effect this representation under conditions of peculiar difficulty – in abrupt transition from the non-imaginative conditions behind the stage; and in the presence of fellow-actors who may be momentarily destroying the reality of the action.

A dramatist prepares the characterization of his personages in such a way that it will take advantage of the actor's gift.

Characterization in a novel is presented by the author's dogmatic assertion that the personage was such, and by an analysis of the personage with generally an account of his or her past. Since, in the drama, this is replaced by the actual presence of the personage before us and since there is no occasion for the intervening all-knowing author to instruct us as to his or her inner nature, a far greater share is given in a play to (1) highly characteristic utterances and (2) concrete occasions in which the character defines itself under action and (3) a conscious preparation of the text whereby the actor may build upon the suggestions in the role according to his own abilities.

Characterization in a play is like a blank check which the dramatist accords to the actor for him to fill in – not entirely blank, for a number of indications of individuality are already there, but to a far less definite and absolute degree than in the novel.

The dramatist's principal interest being the movement of the story, he is willing to resign the more detailed aspects of characterization to the actor and is often rewarded beyond his expectation.

The sleepwalking scene from *Macbeth* is a highly compressed selection of words whereby despair and remorse rise to the surface of indirect confession. It is to be assumed that had Shakespeare lived to see what the genius of Sarah Siddons could pour into the scene from that combination of observation, self-knowledge, imagination, and representational skill, even he might have exclaimed, "I never knew I wrote so well!"

II   The Theatre is an Art Addressed to a Group-Mind

Painting, sculpture, and the literature of the book are certainly solitary experiences; and it is likely that most people would agree that the audience seated shoulder to shoulder in a concert hall is not an essential element in musical enjoyment.

But a play presupposes a crowd. The reasons for this go deeper than (1) the economic necessity for the support of the play and (2) the fact that the temperament of actors is proverbially dependent on group attention.

It rests on the fact that (1) the pretense, the fiction, on the stage would fall to pieces and absurdity without the support accorded to it by a crowd, and (2) the excitement induced by pretending a fragment of life is such that it partakes of ritual and festival, and requires a throng.

Similarly the fiction that royal personages are of a mysteriously different nature from other people requires audiences, levees, and processions for its maintenance. Since the beginnings of society, satirists have occupied themselves with the descriptions of kings and queens in their intimacy and delighted in showing how the prerogatives of royalty become absurd when the crowd is not present to extend to them the enhancement of an imaginative awe.

The theatre partakes of the nature of festival. Life imitated is life raised to a higher power. In the case of comedy, the vitality of these pretended surprises, deceptions, and *contretemps* becomes so lively that before a spectator, solitary or regarding himself as solitary, the structure of so much event would inevitably expose the artificiality of the attempt and ring hollow and unjustified; and in the case of tragedy, the accumulation of woe and apprehension would soon fall short of conviction. All actors know the disturbing sensation of playing before a handful of spectators at a dress rehearsal or performance where only their interest in pure craftsmanship can barely sustain them. During the last rehearsals the phrase is often heard: "This play is hungry for an audience."

Since the theatre is directed to a group-mind, a number of consequences follow:

1. A group-mind presupposes, if not a lowering of standards, a broadening of the fields of interest. The other arts may presuppose an audience of connoisseurs trained in leisure and capable of being interested in certain rarefied aspects of life. The dramatist may be prevented from exhibiting, for example, detailed representations of certain moments in history that require specialized knowledge in the audience, or psychological states in the personages which are of insufficient general interest to evoke self-identification in the majority. In the Second Part of Goethe's *Faust* there are long passages dealing with the theory of paper money. The exposition of the nature of misanthropy (so much more drastic than Molière's) in Shakespeare's *Timon of Athens* has never been a success. The dramatist accepts this limitation in subject matter and realizes that the group-mind imposes upon him the necessity of treating material understandable by the larger number.

2. It is the presence of the group-mind that brings another requirement to the theatre – forward movement.

Maeterlinck said that there was more drama in the spectacle of an old man seated by a table than in the majority of plays offered to the public. He was juggling with the various meanings in the word "drama." In the sense whereby drama means the intensified concentration of life's diversity and significance he may well have been right; if he meant drama as a theatrical representation before an audience he was wrong. Drama on the stage is inseparable from forward movement, from action.

Many attempts have been made to present Plato's dialogues, Gobineau's fine series of dialogues, *La Renaissance*, and the *Imaginary Conversations* of Landor; but without success. Through some ingredient in the group-mind, and through the sheer weight of anticipation involved in the dressing up and the assumption of fictional roles, an action is required, and an action that is more than a mere progress in argumentation and debate.

III   The Theatre is a World of Pretense

It lives by conventions: a convention is an agreed-upon falsehood, a permitted lie.

Illustrations: Consider at the first performance of the *Medea*, the passage where Medea meditates the murder of her children. An anecdote from antiquity tells us that the audience was so moved by this passage that considerable disturbance took place.

The following conventions were involved:

1. Medea was played by a man.
2. He wore a large mask on his face. In the lip of the mask was an acoustical device for projecting the voice. On his feet he wore shoes with soles and heels half a foot high.
3. His costume was so designed that it conveyed to the audience, by convention: woman of royal birth and Oriental origin.
4. The passage was in metric speech. All poetry is an "agreed-upon falsehood" in regard to speech.
5. The lines were sung in a kind of recitative. All opera involves this "permitted lie" in regard to speech.

Modern taste would say that the passage would convey much greater pathos if a woman "like Medea" had delivered it – with an uncovered face that exhibited all the emotions she was undergoing. For the Greeks, however, there was no pretense that Medea was on the stage. The mask, the costume, the mode of declamation, were a series of signs which the spectator interpreted and reassembled in his own mind. Medea was being re-created within the imagination of each of the spectators.

The history of the theatre shows us that in its greatest ages the stage employed the greatest number of conventions. The stage is fundamental pretense and it thrives on the acceptance of that fact and in the multiplication of additional pretenses. When it tries to assert that the personages in the action "really are," really inhabit such and such rooms, really suffer such and such emotions, it loses rather than gains credibility. The modern world is inclined to laugh condescendingly at the fact that in the plays of Racine and Corneille the gods and heroes of antiquity were dressed like the courtiers under Louis XIV; that in the Elizabethan age scenery was replaced by placards notifying the audience of the location; and that a whip in the hand and a jogging motion of the body indicated that a man was on horseback in the Chinese theatre; these devices did not spring from naïveté, however, but from the vitality of the public imagination in those days and from an instinctive feeling as to where the essential and where the inessential lay in drama.

The convention has two functions:

1. It provokes the collaborative activity of the spectator's imagination; and
2. It raises the action from the specific to the general.

This second aspect is of even greater importance than the first.

If Juliet is represented as a girl "very like Juliet" – it was not merely a deference to contemporary prejudices that assigned this role to a boy in the Elizabethan age – moving about in a "real" house with marble staircases, rugs, lamps, and furniture, the impression is irresistibly conveyed that these events happened to this one girl, in one place, at one moment in time. When the play is staged as Shakespeare intended it, the bareness of the stage releases the events from the particular and the experience of Juliet partakes of that of all girls in love, in every time, place and language.

The stage continually strains to tell this generalized truth and it is the element of pretense that reinforces it. Out of the lie, the pretense, of the theatre proceeds a truth more compelling than the novel can attain, for the novel by its own laws is constrained to tell of an action that "once happened" – "once upon a time."

IV   The Action on the Stage Takes Place in a Perpetual Present Time

Novels are written in the past tense. The characters in them, it is true, are represented as living moment by moment their present time, but the constant running commentary of the novelist ("Tess slowly descended into the valley"; "Anna Karenina laughed") inevitably conveys to the reader the fact that these events are long since past and over.

The novel is a past reported in the present. On the stage it is always now. This confers upon the action an increased vitality which the novelist longs in vain to incorporate into his work.

This condition in the theatre brings with it another important element:

In the theatre we are not aware of the intervening storyteller. The speeches arise from the characters in an apparently pure spontaneity.

> *A play is what takes place.*
> *A novel is what one person tells us took place.*

A play visibly represents pure existing. A novel is what one mind, claiming to omniscience, asserts to have existed.

Many dramatists have regretted this absence of the narrator from the stage, with his point of view, his powers of analyzing the behavior of the characters, his ability to interfere and supply further facts about the past, about simultaneous actions not visible on the stage, and above *all* his function of pointing the moral and emphasizing the significance of the action. In some periods of the theatre he has been present as chorus, or prologue and epilogue or as *raisonneur*. But surely this absence constitutes an additional force to the form, as well as an additional tax upon the writer's skill. It is the task of the dramatist so to coordinate his play, through the selection of episodes and speeches, that, though he is himself not visible, his point of view and his governing intention will impose themselves on the spectator's attention, not as dogmatic assertion or motto, but as self-evident truth and inevitable deduction.

Imaginative narration – the invention of souls and destinies – is to a philosopher an all but indefensible activity.

Its justification lies in the fact that the communication of ideas from one mind to another inevitably reaches the point where exposition passes into illustration, into parable, metaphor, allegory, and myth.

It is no accident that when Plato arrived at the height of his argument and attempted to convey a theory of knowledge and a theory of the structure of man's nature he passed over into storytelling, into the myths of the Cave and the Charioteer; and that the great religious teachers have constantly had recourse to the parable as a means of imparting their deepest intuitions.

The theatre offers to imaginative narration its highest possibilities. It has many pitfalls and its very vitality betrays it into service as mere diversion and the enhancement of insignificant matter; but it is well to remember that it was the theatre that rose to the highest place during those epochs that aftertime has chosen to call "great ages" and that the Athens of Pericles and the reigns of Elizabeth, Philip II, and Louis XIV were also the ages that gave to the world the greatest dramas it has known.

Chapter 32

Arthur Miller (1915–2005)

Arthur Miller was one of the leading playwrights of the United States. His popular works included *All My Sons* (1947), *The Crucible* (1953), *A View from the Bridge* (1955), *After the Fall* (1964), *Incident at Vichy* (1965), and *The Price* (1968). His most renowned play is *Death of a Salesman* (1949), for which this essay serves as a kind of preface. Miller's antecedents for "Tragedy and the Common Man" can be observed as far back as Gotthold Lessing in the eighteenth century. Lessing, the German dramaturge and critic, wrote in his *Hamburg Dramaturgy* (1767–9) that the "names of princes and heroes can lead pomp and majesty to a play, but they contribute nothing to our emotion. The misfortunes of those whose circumstances most resemble our own, must naturally penetrate most deeply into our hearts, and if we pity kings, we pity them as human beings, not as kings."[1] A century later, the German critic Hermann Hettner said essentially the same thing in his book *The Modern Drama* (1852); tragedy, he writes, "searches for its protagonists not on the throne of kings or from the heights of history; rather, in the lower circles of life, amidst plain and simple relationships. Hence, if the modern era is distinguishable from the Ancients and Middle-Ages chiefly through emancipation which has granted the individual as individual, through the impartial recognition of the purely human in everyone, without consideration of person and rank, then it is altogether in accordance with the nature and necessity of progressive historical development that the so-called middle-class drama must arise together with the beginning of modern history. Hence, in every respect, its origins correspond in time with the origins of modern thinking: each person has his fate, the neediest Bürger as well as the mightiest monarch."[2] Like Lessing and Hettner, Miller challenges the

Arthur Miller, "Tragedy and the Common Man," *New York Times* (February 27, 1949), Sec. 2, pp. 1, 3; reprinted in *The Theater Essays of Arthur Miller*, ed. Robert A. Martin (New York: Viking, 1978), 3–7. © 1949, renewed © 1977 by Arthur Miller. Reprinted by permission of Viking Penguin, a division of Penguin Group (USA) Inc.

Aristotelian notion of tragedy reserved merely for the lofty. The fall of a commoner can be just as tragic, even if the "fall" does not occur from the ruling class.

Tragedy and the Common Man (1949)

In this age few tragedies are written. It has often been held that the lack is due to a paucity of heroes among us, or else that modern man has had the blood drawn out of his organs of belief by the skepticism of science, and the heroic attack on life cannot feed on an attitude of reserve and circumspection. For one reason or another, we are often held to be below tragedy – or tragedy above us. The inevitable conclusion is, of course, that the tragic mode is archaic, fit only for the very highly placed, the kings or the kingly, and where this admission is not made in so many words it is most often implied.

I believe that the common man is as apt a subject for tragedy in its highest sense as kings were. On the face of it this ought to be obvious in the light of modern psychiatry, which bases its analysis upon classic formulations, such as the Oedipus and Orestes complexes, for instance, which were enacted by royal beings, but which apply to everyone in similar emotional situations.

More simply, when the question of tragedy in art is not at issue, we never hesitate to attribute to the well-placed and the exalted the very same mental processes as the lowly. And finally, if the exaltation of tragic action were truly a property of the high-bred character alone, it is inconceivable that the mass of mankind should cherish tragedy above all other forms, let alone be capable of understanding it.

As a general rule, to which there may be exceptions unknown to me, I think the tragic feeling is evoked in us when we are in the presence of a character who is ready to lay down his life, if need be, to secure one thing – his sense of personal dignity. From Orestes to Hamlet, Medea to Macbeth, the underlying struggle is that of the individual attempting to gain his "rightful" position in his society.

Sometimes he is one who has been displaced from it, sometimes one who seeks to attain it for the first time, but the fateful wound from which the inevitable events spiral is the wound of indignity, and its dominant force is indignation. Tragedy, then, is the consequence of a man's total compulsion to evaluate himself justly.

In the sense of having been initiated by the hero himself, the tale always reveals what has been called his "tragic flaw," a failing that is not peculiar to grand or elevated characters. Nor is it necessarily a weakness. The flaw, or crack in the character, is really nothing – and need be nothing – but his inherent unwillingness to remain passive in the face of what he conceives to be a challenge to his dignity, his image of his rightful status. Only the passive, only those who accept their lot without active retaliation, are "flawless." Most of us are in that category.

But there are among us today, as there always have been, those who act against the scheme of things that degrades them, and in the process of action everything we have accepted out of fear or insensitivity or ignorance is shaken before us and examined, and from this total onslaught by an individual against the seemingly stable cosmos surrounding us – from this total examination of the "unchangeable" environment – comes the terror and the fear that is classically associated with tragedy.

More important, from this total questioning of what has previously been unquestioned, we learn. And such a process is not beyond the common man. In revolutions around the world, these past thirty years, he has demonstrated again and again this inner dynamic of all tragedy.

Insistence upon the rank of the tragic hero, or the so-called nobility of his character, is really but a clinging to the outward forms of tragedy. If rank or nobility of character was indispensable, then it would follow that the problems of those with rank were the particular problems of tragedy. But surely the right of one monarch to capture the domain from another no longer raises our passions, nor are our concepts of justice what they were to the mind of an Elizabethan king.

The quality in such plays that does shake us, however, derives from the underlying fear of being displaced, the disaster inherent in being torn away from our chosen image of what and who we are in this world. Among us today this fear is as strong, and perhaps stronger, than it ever was. In fact, it is the common man who knows this fear best.

Now, if it is true that tragedy is the consequence of a man's total compulsion to evaluate himself justly, his destruction in the attempt posits a wrong or an evil in his environment. And this is precisely the morality of tragedy and its lesson. The discovery of the moral law, which is what the enlightenment of tragedy consists of, is not the discovery of some abstract or metaphysical quantity.

The tragic right is a condition of life, a condition in which the human personality is able to flower and realize itself. The wrong is the condition which suppresses man, perverts the flowing out of his love and creative instinct. Tragedy enlightens – and it must, in that it points the heroic finger at the enemy of man's freedom. The thrust for freedom is the quality in tragedy which exalts. The revolutionary questioning of the stable environment is what terrifies. In no way is the common man debarred from such thoughts or such actions.

Seen in this light, our lack of tragedy may be partially accounted for by the turn which modern literature has taken toward the purely psychiatric view of life, or the purely sociological. If all our miseries, our indignities, are born and bred within our minds, then all action, let alone the heroic action, is obviously impossible.

And if society alone is responsible for the cramping of our lives, then the protagonist must needs be so pure and faultless as to force us to deny his validity as a character. From neither of these views can tragedy derive, simply because neither represents a balanced concept of life. Above all else, tragedy requires the finest appreciation by the writer of cause and effect.

No tragedy can therefore come about when its author fears to question absolutely everything, when he regards any institution, habit or custom as being either everlasting, immutable or inevitable. In the tragic view the need of man to wholly realize himself is the only fixed star, and whatever it is that hedges his nature and lowers it is ripe for attack and examination. Which is not to say that tragedy must preach revolution.

The Greeks could probe the very heavenly origin of their ways and return to confirm the rightness of laws. And Job could face God in anger, demanding his right and end in submission. But for a moment everything is in suspension, nothing is accepted, and in this stretching and tearing apart of the cosmos, in the very action of so doing, the character gains "size," the tragic stature which is spuriously attached to the royal or the highborn in our minds. The commonest of men may take on that stature to the extent of his willingness to throw all he has into the contest, the battle to secure his rightful place in his world.

There is a misconception of tragedy with which I have been struck in review after review, and in many conversations with writers and readers alike. It is the idea that tragedy is of necessity allied to pessimism. Even the dictionary says nothing more about the word than that it means a story with a sad or unhappy ending. This impression is so firmly fixed that I almost hesitate to claim that in truth tragedy implies more optimism in its author than does comedy, and that its final result ought to be the reinforcement of the onlooker's brightest opinions of the human animal.

For, if it is true to say that in essence the tragic hero is intent upon claiming his whole due as a personality, and if this struggle must be total and without reservation, then it automatically demonstrates the indestructible will of man to achieve his humanity.

The possibility of victory must be there in tragedy. Where pathos rules, where pathos is finally derived, a character has fought a battle he could not possibly have won. The pathetic is achieved when the protagonist is, by virtue of his witlessness, his insensitivity or the very air he gives off, incapable of grappling with a much superior force.

Pathos truly is the mode for the pessimist. But tragedy requires a nicer balance between what is possible and what is impossible. And it is curious, although edifying, that the plays we revere, century after century, are the tragedies. In them, and in them alone, lies the belief – optimistic, if you will – in the perfectibility of man.

It is time, I think, that we who are without kings, took up this bright thread of our history and followed it to the only place it can possibly lead in our time – the heart and spirit of the average man.

Notes

1   G. E. Lessing, *Hamburg Dramaturgy*, tr. H. Zimmern (New York: Dover, 1962), 38–9.
2   H. Hettner, *Das moderne Drama* (Braunschweig: Bieweg & Sons, 1852), 75–6, editor's translation.

Chapter 33

T. S. Eliot (1888–1965)

Thomas Sterns (T. S.) Eliot was a poet, playwright, and critic. From 1925 until his death he was a director of the English publishing firm Faber and Gwyer. His poetry and essays are considered the gateway to modernist literature and the beginnings of American New Criticism. His verse plays, *Sweeney Agonistes* (1925), *Murder in the Cathedral* (1935), and *The Cocktail Party* (1950), were experimental in form and content. Among his ideas was the concept of "objective correlative." In his 1919 essay "Hamlet and His Problems," he defined the term as "a set of objects, a situation, a chain of events which shall be the formula of that *particular* emotion; such that when the external facts, which must terminate in sensory experience, are given, the emotion is immediately evoked."[1] For Eliot, emotions and thoughts derived from art are not merely elements in themselves but enter into a correlative with other emotions and thoughts. He argues that when art expresses a set of objects or words a particular emotion corresponding to the art object is stimulated. Eliot was a modernist in that he believed in the separation of art and the everyday. This separation partly explains why Eliot, in this essay, justifies his notion of verse drama. "The ideal medium for poetry," he wrote, "is the theatre."[2] Eliot examines the mode of poetic drama, marked by his turn from poetry to drama in the 1950s.

Poetry and Drama (1950)

As I have gradually learned more about the problems of poetic drama, and the conditions which it must fulfill if it is to justify itself, I have made a little clearer to myself, not only my own reasons for wanting to write in this form, but the more general reasons for

Excerpts from T. S. Eliot, *Poetry and Drama* (Cambridge, MA: Harvard University Press, 1951), 10–17. © 1951 T. S. Eliot. Reprinted by permission of Faber and Faber Ltd and Farrar, Straus, and Giroux, LLC. Originally delivered as Eliot's Theodore Spencer Memorial Lecture, November 21, 1950.

wanting to see it restored to its place. And I think that if I say something about these problems and conditions, it should make clearer to other people whether and, if so, why poetic drama has anything potentially to offer the playgoer that prose drama cannot. For I start with the assumption that if poetry is merely a decoration, an added embellishment, if it merely gives people of literary tastes the pleasure of listening to poetry at the same time that they are witnessing a play, then it is superfluous. It must justify itself dramatically, and not merely be fine poetry shaped into a dramatic form. From this it follows that no play should be written in verse for which prose is *dramatically* adequate. And from this it follows, again, that the audience, its attention held by the dramatic action, its emotions stirred by the situation between the characters, should be too intent upon the play to be wholly conscious of the medium.

Whether we use prose or verse on the stage, they are both but means to an end. The difference, from one point of view, is not so great as we might think. In those prose plays which survive, which are read and produced on the stage by later generations, the prose in which the characters speak is as remote, for the best part, from the vocabulary, syntax, and rhythm of our ordinary speech – with its fumbling for words, its constant recourse to approximation, its disorder and its unfinished sentences – as verse is. Like verse, it has been written, and rewritten. Our two greatest prose stylists in the drama – apart from Shakespeare and the other Elizabethans who mixed prose and verse in the same play – are, I believe, Congreve and Bernard Shaw. A speech by a character of Congreve or of Shaw has – however clearly the characters may be differentiated – that unmistakable personal rhythm which is the mark of a prose style, and of which only the most accomplished conversationalists – who are for that matter usually monologuists – show any trace in their talk. We have all heard (too often!) of Molière's character who expressed surprise when told that he spoke prose. But it was M. Jourdain who was right, and not his mentor or his creator: he did not speak prose – he only talked. For I mean to draw a triple distinction between prose, and verse, and our ordinary speech which is mostly below the level of either verse or prose. So if you look at it in this way, it will appear that prose, on the stage, is as artificial as verse: or alternatively, that verse can be as natural as prose. But while the sensitive member of the audience will appreciate, when he hears fine prose spoken in a play, that this is something better than ordinary conversation, he does not regard it as a wholly different language from that which he himself speaks, for that would interpose a barrier between himself and the imaginary characters on the stage. Too many people, on the other hand, approach a play which they know to be in verse, with the consciousness of the difference. It is unfortunate when they are repelled by verse, but it can also be deplorable when they are attracted by verse – if that means that they are prepared to enjoy the play and the language of the play as two separate things. The chief effect and style and rhythm in dramatic speech, whether it be in prose or verse, should be unconscious.

From this it follows that a mixture of prose and verse in the same play is generally to be avoided: each transition makes the auditor aware, with a jolt, of the medium. It is, we may say, justifiable when the author wishes to produce this jolt: when, that is, he wishes to transport the audience violently from one plane of reality to another. I suspect that this kind of transition was easily acceptable to an Elizabethan audience, to whose ears both prose and verse came naturally; who liked highfalutin and low comedy in the same play; and to whom it seemed perhaps proper, that the more humble and rustic characters should speak in a homely language, and that those of more exalted rank should rant in verse. But even in the plays of Shakespeare some of the prose passages seem to be designed for an effect of contrast which, when achieved, is something that can never become old-fashioned. The knocking at the gate in *Macbeth* is an example that comes to everyone's mind; but it has long seemed to me that the alternation of scenes in prose with scenes in verse in *Henry IV* points an ironic contrast between the world of high politics and the world of common life. The audience probably thought they were getting their accustomed chronicle play garnished with amusing scenes of low life; yet the prose scenes of both Part I and Part II provide a sardonic comment upon the bustling ambitions of the chiefs of the parties in the insurrection of the Percys.

Today, however, because of the handicap under which verse drama suffers, I believe that prose should be used very sparingly indeed; that we should aim at a form of verse in which everything can be said that has to be said; and that when we find some situation which is intractable in verse, it is merely that our form of verse is inelastic. And if there prove to be scenes which we cannot put in verse, we must either develop our verse, or avoid having to introduce scenes. For we have to accustom our audiences to verse to the point which they will cease to be conscious of it; and to introduce prose dialogue would only be to distract their attention from the play itself to the medium of its expression. But if our verse is to have so wide a range that it can say anything that has to be said, it follows that it will not be "poetry" all the time. It will only be "poetry" when the dramatic situation has reached such a point of intensity that poetry becomes the natural utterance, because then it is the only language in which the emotions can be expressed at all.

It is indeed necessary for any long poem, if it is to escape monotony, to be able to say homely things without bathos, as well as to take the highest flights without sounding exaggerated. And it is still more important in a play, especially if it is concerned with contemporary life. The reason for writing even the more pedestrian parts of a verse play in verse instead of prose is, however, not only to avoid calling the audience's attention to the fact that it is at other moments listening to poetry. It is also that the verse rhythm should have its effect upon the hearers, without their being conscious of it. A brief analysis of one scene of Shakespeare's may illustrate this point. The opening scene of *Hamlet* – as well constructed an opening scene as that of any play ever written – has the advantage of being one that everybody knows.

What we do not notice, when we witness this scene in the theatre, is the great variation of style. Nothing is superfluous, and there is no line of poetry which is not justified by its dramatic value. The first twenty-two lines are built of the simplest words in the most homely idiom. Shakespeare had worked for a long time in the theatre, and written a good many plays, before reaching the point at which he could write those twenty-two lines. There is nothing quite so simplified and sure in his previous work. He first developed conversational, colloquial verse in the monologue of the character part – Faulconbridge in *King John,* and later the Nurse in *Romeo and Juliet.* It was a much further step to carry it unobtrusively into the dialogue of brief replies. No poet has begun to master dramatic verse until he can write lines which, like these in *Hamlet,* are *transparent.* You are consciously attending, not to the poetry, but to the meaning of the poetry. If you were hearing *Hamlet* for the first time, without knowing anything about the play, I do not think that it would occur to you to ask whether the speakers were speaking in verse or prose. The verse is having a different effect upon us from prose; but, at the moment, what we are aware of is the frosty night, the officers keeping watch on the battlements, and the foreboding of an ominous action. I do not say that there is no place for the situation in which part of one's pleasure will be the enjoyment of hearing beautiful poetry – providing that the author gives it, in that place, dramatic inevitability. And of course, when we have both seen a play several times and read it between performances, we begin to analyze the means by which the author has produced his effects. But in the immediate impact of this scene we are unconscious of the medium of its expression.

From the short, brusque ejaculations at the beginning, suitable to the situation and to the character of the guards – but not expressing more character than is required for their function in the play – the verse glides into a slower movement with the appearance of the courtiers Horatio and Marcellus.

Notes

1   T. S. Eliot, *Selected Essays* (London: Faber & Faber, 1951), 145.
2   T. S. Eliot, *The Uses of Poetry and the Uses of Criticism* (1933; Cambridge, MA: Harvard University Press, 1961), 146.

Chapter 34

Tennessee Williams (1911–1983)

The ebullient playwriting career of Thomas Lanier "Tennessee" Williams ran from 1935 to his death. His large body of plays includes *The Glass Menagerie* (1945), *A Streetcar Named Desire* (1947), *Cat on a Hot Tin Roof* (1955), and *Sweet Bird of Youth* (1959). He was part of a Golden Age of American drama from the end of World War II to 1960. Like Miller, Tennessee Williams is interested in the difficulty of conveying tragedy in a modern idiom. His dramas are concerned with fate and the struggle of the individual to assert his or her identity in the face of crushing conformity. Theatre for Williams condenses time so that we might intensely observe the clash of individual will and the forces that restrict freedom. Williams was also concerned with those discarded by capitalism. He wrote about figures unable to keep pace with the get-up-and-go consumer economy. Williams empathized with characters like Laura in *Glass Menagerie* or Blanche in *A Streetcar Named Desire* who, either through age, physical disability, heightened sensitivity, or lack of empowerment, fall through the cracks of society.

The Timeless World of the Play (1951)

Carson McCullers concludes one of her lyric poems with the line: "Time, the endless idiot, runs screaming 'round the world." It is this continual rush of time, so violent that it appears to be screaming, that deprives our actual lives of so much dignity and meaning, and it is, perhaps more than anything else, the *arrest of time* which has taken place in a

Tennessee Williams, "The Timeless World of the Play," in *The Rose Tattoo* (New York: New Directions, 1951), vi–xi. © 1951 by The University of the South. Reprinted by permission of New Directions Publishing Corp. and Methuen Publishing Ltd.

completed work of art that gives to certain plays their feeling of depth and significance. In the London notices of *Death of a Salesman* a certain notoriously skeptical critic made the remark that Willy Loman was the sort of man that almost any member of the audience would have kicked out of an office had he applied for a job or detained one for conversation about his troubles. The remark itself possibly holds some truth. But the implication that Willy Loman is consequently a character with whom we have no reason to concern ourselves in drama, reveals a strikingly false conception of what plays are. Contemplation is something that exists outside of time, and so is the tragic sense. Even in the actual world of commerce, there exists in some persons a sensibility to the unfortunate situations of others, a capacity for concern and compassion, surviving from a more tender period of life outside the present whirling wire-cage of business activity. Facing Willy Loman across an office desk, meeting his nervous glance and hearing his querulous voice, we would be very likely to glance at our wrist watch and our schedule of other appointments. We would not kick him out of the office, no, but we would certainly *ease* him out with more expedition than Willy had feebly hoped for. But suppose there had been no wrist watch or office clock and suppose there had *not* been the schedule of pressing appointments, and suppose that we were not actually facing Willy across a desk – and facing a person is *not* the best way to see him! – suppose, in other words, that the meeting with Willy Loman had somehow occurred in a world *outside* of time. Then I think we would receive him with concern and kindness and even with respect. If the world of a play did not offer us this occasion to view its characters under that special condition of a *world without time*, then, indeed, the characters and occurrences of drama would become equally pointless, equally trivial, as corresponding meetings and happenings in life.

The classic tragedies of Greece had tremendous nobility. The actors wore great masks, movements were formal, dance-like, and the speeches had an epic quality which doubtless were as removed from the normal conversation of their contemporary society as they seem today. Yet they did not seem false to the Greek audiences: the magnitude of the events and the passions aroused by them did not seem ridiculously out of proportion to common experience. And I wonder if this was not because the Greek audiences knew, instinctively or by training, that the created world of a play is removed from that element which makes people little and their emotions fairly inconsequential.

Great sculpture often follows the lines of the human body: yet the repose of great sculpture suddenly transmutes those human lines to something that has an absoluteness, a purity, a beauty, which would not be possible in a living mobile form.

A play may be violent, full of motion: yet it has that special kind of repose which allows contemplation and produces the climate in which tragic importance is a possible thing, provided that certain modern conditions are met.

In actual existence the moments of love are succeeded by the moments of satiety and sleep. The sincere remark is followed by a cynical distrust. Truth is fragmentary, at best: we love and betray each other not in quite the same breath but in two breaths that occur in fairly close sequence. But the fact that passion occurred in passing, that it then declined into a more familiar sense of difference, should not be regarded as proof of its inconsequence. And this is the very truth that drama wishes to bring us. . . .

Whether or not we admit it to ourselves, we are all haunted by a truly awful sense of impermanence. I have always had a particularly keen sense of this at New York cocktail parties, and perhaps that is why I drink the martinis almost as fast as I can snatch them from the tray. This sense is the febrile thing that hangs in the air. Horror of insincerity, of *not meaning*, overhangs these affairs like the cloud of cigarette smoke and the hectic chatter. This horror is the only thing, almost, that is left unsaid at such functions. All social functions involving a group of people not intimately known to each other are always under this shadow. They are almost always (in an unconscious way) like that last dinner of the condemned: where steak or turkey, whatever the doomed man wants, is served in his cell as a mockingly cruel reminder of what the great-big-little-transitory world had to offer.

In a play, time is arrested in the sense of being confined. By a sort of legerdemain, events are made to remain *events*, rather than being reduced so quickly to mere *occurrences*. The audience can sit back in a comforting dusk to watch a world which is flooded with light and in which emotion and action have a dimension and dignity that they would likewise have in real existence, if only the shattering intrusion of time could be locked out.

About their lives people ought to remember that when they are finished, everything in them will be contained in a marvelous state of repose which is the same as that which they unconsciously admired in drama. The rush is temporary. The great and only possible dignity of man lies in his power deliberately to choose certain moral values by which to live as steadfastly as if he, too, like a character in a play, were immured against the corrupting rush of time. Snatching the eternal out of the desperately fleeting is the great magic trick of human existence. As far as we know, as far as there exists any kind of empiric evidence, there is no way to beat the game of *being* against *non-being*, in which non-being is the predestined victor on realistic levels.

Yet plays in the tragic tradition offer us a view of certain moral values in violent juxtaposition. Because we do not participate, except as spectators, we can view them clearly, within the limits of our emotional equipment. These people on the stage do not return our looks. We do not have to answer their questions nor make any sign of being in company with them, nor do we have to compete with their virtues nor resist their offences. All at once, for this reason, we are able to *see* them! Our hearts are wrung by recognition and pity, so that the dusky shell of the auditorium where we are gathered anonymously together is flooded with an almost liquid warmth of unchecked human sympathies, relieved of self-consciousness, allowed to function....

Men pity and love each other more deeply than they permit themselves to know. The moment after the phone has been hung up, the hand reaches for a scratch pad and scrawls a notation: "Funeral Tuesday at five, Church of the Holy Redeemer, don't forget flowers." And the same hand is only a little shakier than usual as it reaches, some minutes later, for a highball glass that will pour a stupefaction over the kindled nerves. Fear and evasion are the two little beasts that chase each other's tails in the revolving wire-cage of our nervous world. They distract us from feeling too much about things. Time rushes toward us with its hospital tray of infinitely varied narcotics, even while it is preparing us for its inevitably fatal operation....

So successfully have we disguised from ourselves the intensity of our own feelings, the sensibility of our own hearts, that plays in the tragic tradition have begun to seem untrue. For a couple of hours we may surrender ourselves to a world of fiercely illuminated values in conflict, but when the stage is covered and the auditorium lighter, almost immediately there is a recoil of disbelief. "Well, well!" we say as we shuffle back up the aisle, while the play dwindles behind us with the sudden perspective of an early Chirico painting. By the time we have arrived at [the popular Broadway restaurant] Sardi's, if not as soon as we pass beneath the marquee, we have convinced ourselves once more that life has as little resemblance to the curiously stirring and meaningful occurrences on the stage as a jingle has to an elegy of Rilke.

This modern condition of the theatre audience is something that an author must know in advance. The diminishing influence of life's destroyer, time, must be somehow worked into the context of his play. Perhaps it is a certain foolery, a certain distortion toward the grotesque, which will solve the problem for him. Perhaps it is only restraint, putting a mute on the strings that would like to break all bounds. But almost surely, unless he contrives in some way to relate the dimensions of his tragedy to the dimensions of a world in which time is included, he will be left among his magnificent debris on a dark stage, muttering to himself: "Those fools..."

And if they could hear him above the clatter of tongues, glasses, chinaware and silver, they would give him this answer: "But you have shown us a world not ravaged by time. We admire your innocence. But we have seen our photographs, past and present. Yesterday evening we passed our first wife on the street. We smiled as we spoke but we didn't really see her! It's too bad, but we know what is true and not true, and at 3 A.M. your disgrace will be in print!"

Chapter 35

John Gassner (1903–1967)

The critic John Gassner published numerous anthologies and books on dramatic criticism. His major works were *Masters of the Drama* (1940), *The Theatre in Our Time* (1954, excerpts selected here), *Form and Idea in Modern Theatre* (1956), *Directions in Modern Theatre and Drama* (1965), and the posthumously published *Drama Was a Weapon: The Left-Wing Theatre in New York, 1929–1941* (1976). Gassner was, like his contemporaries, searching for a mode to express the tragic form. His efforts reflected the era's attempt to create a drama reflective of both existential angst and realistic tragedy.

"Enlightenment" and Modern Drama (1954)

When I first considered the tragic principle of Enlightenment in 1937, in a piece written for the now defunct *One-Act Play Magazine and Theatre Review* (it gained some currency, and a revised statement of my views subsequently appeared in the American supplement of the 1947 Crown Publishers edition of Barrett H. Clark's *European Theories of the Drama*) I intended to propound a view, perhaps naïvely, that could support the efforts of playwrights to present contemporary realities without feeling that they were for that reason hopelessly excluded from the exalted company of the tragedians. And I wanted them to be more aware of the rich possibilities of tragic art than they appeared to be while they were engaged in writing about these realities.

Willing though I had been to extend patience and the best of my understanding to them, I had to consider that they were in danger of reaching an impasse, if they

Excerpts from John Gassner, "'Enlightenment' and Modern Drama," from *The Theatre in Our Times* (New York: Crown, 1954), 56–66.

had not already reached it, in presenting contemporary issues solely on the levels of problem drama. On one hand, the social theatre of the nineteen-thirties had begun to slump into a state of moribund repetitiousness, and few of its playwrights were fulfilling the promise we had found in their early strivings. On the other hand, those few had given enough indications of a bent for so much more than topicality that the effort to make them aware of a larger reach might not be wasted. Clifford Odets had certainly given such evidence ever since writing *Awake and Sing!* And among members of an older generation, Maxwell Anderson was manifestly, perhaps even too obviously, reaching for the tragic crown after having had his bout with the immediate political scene in his 1933 Pulitzer Prize satire *Both Your Houses*. Two years later in *Winterset*, in fact, he had attempted to perform the very thing I had in mind, namely, represent and express contemporary life and, at the same time, achieve tragic power. I did not believe he had entirely succeeded in *Winterset*, however. He had no sooner faced the substance of his subject, the subversion of justice, in his generally excellent second act than he flew away from it into a world of reminiscent romanticism. *Winterset* became a tragedy less by logic of characterization and theme than by the imposed rhetoric of Anderson's definition of tragedy. The reality of young Mio's pursuit of justice for his victimized father underwent a false transfiguration into grandiloquent assertions concerning the power of love and of the dignity of man by the tragic lovers Mio and Miriamne and by an extremely voluble member of the rabbinate. And in noting this danger of misconceiving tragedy as an expedient for flight and as a springboard for evasion, I felt a further need of extending my views on tragic drama. I intended my concept of Enlightenment to assert the possibility of facing reality in the context of a real, rather than legendary or romanticized and sentimentalized, world. I wanted to say in so many words that a play can be, *in its time*, both social drama and tragedy.

I did not know in 1937 that Maxwell Anderson had also begun to struggle with the concept of Enlightenment, although I never, of course, believed that my view that tragedy had to have meaning had been foreign to playwrights ever since Aeschylus entered the theatre. Anderson, following the "tragic gleam" in 1938 with a "compass," as he put it, arrived at a theory similar to mine, proving that my concern with catharsis and its implications did not begin and end with critics. Aristotle had noted the powerful dramatic effect of a "recognition scene" – that is, the recognition (*anagnorisis*) of one character by another, in Greek tragedies. Some of these scenes (the meeting of Orestes and his sister Electra in Mycenae and that of Orestes and his other sister, Iphigenia, in Tauris) are known to every educated playwright. But the idea of *anagnorisis*, or recognition, can be legitimately extended to the discovery of hidden facts as well as disguised or hitherto unidentified persons. The discovery that Oedipus makes about himself in Sophocles' tragedy gives us perhaps the greatest tragic scene in all literature. With this fact in mind, Anderson came to realize that "recognition scenes" were also present in post-classic drama. He arrived at the conclusion in his essay *The Essence of Tragedy* that the mechanism in modern tragedy is "a discovery by the hero of some element in the environment or in his own personality of which he has not been aware – or which he has not taken sufficiently into account." And seeking to translate this observation into a working principle of playwriting, Anderson proposed the following formulation: "A play should lead up to and away from a central crisis, and this crisis should consist in a discovery by the leading character which has an indelible effect on his thought and emotion and completely alters his course or action."

Anderson refers further on in his essay to the "spiritual awakening or regeneration" of his hero; and John Mason Brown, amplifying Anderson's views in *The Tragic Blueprint*, further exalts this "fulfillment of self" as a spiritual process so purifying that tragic heroes are "fated to leave this earth spiritually cross-ventilated." It is plain, then, that this view of tragic recognition concerns something else and something more than a boy's discovery of the class struggle and recognition of the need to fight for better warehouse conditions in Odets' *Awake and Sing!*

Maxwell Anderson's stimulating theory of "recognition," however, has dangers and limitations. It might be mistaken for the Victorian Sunday School notion of art as a moral lesson. Enlightenment is dramatically ineffective without the collaboration of "pity" and "fear" in an intense complication of dramatic events, and should not be confused with a simple prescription for action, or a mere realization on the part of the tragic character that he was right or wrong. Tragic enlightenment is an *experience*, not a moral tag such as schoolteachers once looked for when teaching Shakespeare's plays to their charges.

Enlightenment is certainly not knowledge imposed, but knowledge *won*. And this is the case even when the tragedy makes some opinion explicit, whether by the characters, as altogether too insistently in the third act of *Winterset*, or by a Greek chorus. When some judgment is explicit in a successful tragedy, it reflects character; as when Othello sums up the error of his life before stabbing himself, or when Macbeth succumbs to despair on receiving the news of Lady Macbeth's death – which does not, however, prevent him from sallying forth to fight his enemies. Or the moral comment is tragically irrelevant and therefore ironic, as it is when the chorus of Theban senators mouths platitudes while Sophocles' Antigone goes to her death.

The most dangerous assumptions concerning tragic art, however, are those that recommend "ennoblement," "enlightenment," or, in Anderson's case, "recognition" as a spiritual exercise of the highest order. Four assumptions bolster this climactic assumption. They are as follows:

1. Tragedy is an emotional orgy of "pity" and "fear" – an ecstasy, so to speak.
2. Tragedy achieves a cleansing of the soul, a *katharsis*.
3. Tragedy must have universality.
4. Man possesses or attains stature in tragedy, or possesses stature initially and becomes even more exalted in the course of the drama. (With respect to this view, too, it must be noted that Aristotle spoke more moderately than his successors, writing that "tragedy is an imitation of persons who are above the common level" and should "preserve the type and yet ennoble it.")

Since some validity can easily be found in each of these principles, they add up to a considerable claim for tragic art. And when it is pressed forcefully enough, it establishes a formidable standard to which the modern drama that concerns itself directly with the modern world and employs the idioms of our time cannot measure up. It is not certain that even the classics of tragedy actually meet the expectations that can be aroused by the altogether too romantic wording of these claims in our time.

For Edith Hamilton, who does not actually lose herself in beatitudes, tragedy deals with "the only true aristocracy, that of passionate souls." Essential in the opinion of Joseph Wood Krutch is the playwright's belief in "the greatness and importance of men." The tragedian must make "a profession of faith"; he may "not believe in God, but must believe in man." For Maxwell Anderson, the playwright must so arrange his story that it will prove that men pass through suffering purified, "that animal though we are in some ways, there is in us all some divine, incalculable fire that urges us to be better than we are." And for John Mason Brown, "death, not life" ultimately becomes the "high concern" of tragic heroes "made whole by their suffering" who are "fated to leave this earth spiritually cross-ventilated." Such are the requirements of a school of criticism that, in compensating for diminished views of humanity by modern realism and modern life alike, departs from Aristotle's plainer humanism and may be denominated Romantic Aristotelianism.

An *ersatz*-mystique, suspect alike to social and to religious realists, can be charged against a fetishist overemphasis of "spiritual awakening" and other towering flights romantically predicated for tragedy. The gospel of salvation by tragic art, which makes catharsis an equivalent or substitute for the "dark night of the soul" described by Spain's mystic poet St. John of the Cross, presses too large a claim for the worldly art of the theatre.

Tragedy, in my view, has its own more modest, if sufficient, place in any hierarchy of values, as we may readily realize the moment we ask whether the writing or witnessing of a play ever changed the moral character of anybody and altered the pattern of his behavior. And that place must certainly be defined in less elevated terms if modern playwrights are to bring the freight of their world with them into the theatre. If they fly too high on Icarian wings, the wings of literary ambition, they will drop into a sea of banality in the course of their rhetorical aspirations toward spiritual significance. They would do better to find support in a strongly grounded religion, as the Catholic poet Paul Claudel realized, or in a simple faith, as Tolstoy realized. Otherwise they may give an impression of self-inflation, such as can be charged against Anderson at the conclusion of *Winterset* and not against Tolstoy in the dénouement of *The Power of Darkness*, O'Casey in the last act of *The Plough and the Stars*, Shaw in the trial and execution scenes of *Saint Joan*, or O'Neill in the resolution of *Desire Under the Elms*. Scorn of earth is a *hybris* as dangerous to playwrights as to other persons.

A major confusion is caused, I believe, by extreme, romantic interpretations of the idea that a tragedy must have "universality." The assumption is made that this can be achieved only by escaping from the actual action or substance of a play, from a specific context of reality, into the most inane of generalizations about life and spirituality. Ibsen and all later realists are accused of a crime against tragic drama for minimizing this view of universality – a view patently flamboyant by comparison with that of Aristotle, who introduced the concept of universality into criticism. "By the universal," Aristotle explained unpretentiously, "I mean how a person or a certain type will on occasion speak or act according to the law of probability or necessity."

Proponents of "universality" have tended to draw up an indictment of modern realistic drama on the grounds of its relevancy. This view encourages confusion and error both in theory and practice. It sometimes leads to the extravagant conclusion that virtually all modern drama that has had any claim to social reality has been unworthy. It has led idealists of the Gordon Craig and "art theatre" school to legitimize only misty dramatic literature such as the plays of Maeterlinck, cultivated naïveté, the masterpiece of which is André Obey's *Noah*, and at best sophisticated versions of myth, such as Cocteau's Oedipus tragedy, *The Infernal Machine*. Only irony, at which Europeans are more adept than Americans, secures some of these plays against banality, for irony takes into account reality by noting contradictions in human behavior and fate. In generalizations, the result is too frequently an academic kind of playwriting that no one can produce, hieratic art which snuggles under the shadow of some great cathedral, or more or less sophomoric theatricality parading as profundity. To different degrees, O'Neill succumbed to the latter in *The Fountain*, *Dynamo*, *Lazarus Laughed*, and other plays. Some of the "universalist" efforts – those that are clever if rather less than tragic, those that possess simplicity, and the very few that, like Claudel's *The Tidings Brought to Mary* or Eliot's *Murder in the Cathedral*, are founded on traditional faith – deserve a place in our theatre. But even the best of these cannot ensure its vitality. By comparison with the major plays of Ibsen, Strindberg, Chekhov, Shaw, and O'Casey, for example, they seem either attenuated or remote – or strained.

Surely the theatre in our time cannot subsist on a diet of "universals" untranslated into recognizably contemporary manners, sensibility, and events. Plays such as *The Infernal Machine*, *Noah*, Fry's *The Boy with a Cart*, and even *Murder in the Cathedral* can be the dessert, but not the main course, in contemporary theatre. Eliot, himself, realized this when he resolved to make the theatre a vocation rather than an avocation. He deliberately turned from *Murder in the Cathedral* to *Family Reunion* and *The Cocktail Party*, in which he tried to steep theology in quotidian reality and to express his Anglo-Catholic philosophy in the familiar terms of English comedy of manners. He arranged a partnership, so to speak, between St. Augustine and Noel Coward in *The Cocktail Party*. His new play *The Confidential Clerk*, which I have neither seen nor read as yet, gives every indication of carrying this austere poet further into the not necessarily inglorious marketplace.

In stage production, moreover, even the older "universal" drama has suffered at the hands of artists whose predilection for universality becomes a case of moral and spiritual elephantiasis. Grandeur becomes the first mark of such universalization of the classics by production art. We see this in the fashionable overproduction of Shakespeare's drama, in which the settings, born of the misty universalism of Gordon Craig, tower over the actors and swathe Shakespeare's intensely immediate human drama in a universal fog. And in acting, the results tend to be the kind of attitudinizing and overprecise elocutionary delivery of Shakespeare's lines that vitiate performances by Maurice Evans and by many German actors who play "*unser* [our] *Shakespeare*" as though he were Schiller.

I have nothing against "universals," but it seems to me that the only universals favored by those who criticize modern drama and try to flee from its realism into "Art" are *dead* ones. They are "dead" in the sense that the so-called universal recognitions are presented with little or no relation to substantial pressures of contemporary reality. Universals are conveniently removed from contemporary tensions, especially if they are social in character; conveniently, because the generalizations are made without reference to verifiable fact or after observable facts have been discarded. It seems to me, on the contrary, that our theatre has been made more vital by an *All My Sons*, for all its rough texture, than by an *Elizabeth the Queen*, for all its glossy one, just as the theatre of half a century ago was more vitalized by *Hedda Gabler* than by *Francesca di Rimini*.

Universals for universals, moreover, there is for me a greater, intenser realization of humanity's eternal urgencies in Lorca's *House of Bernarda Alba* (in the context of Spanish country life) or in Odets' *Awake and Sing!* (in the context of metropolitan American life) than in *The Cocktail Party* (in the context of English life). The conflict between the arid family pride of Bernarda Alba and her daughters' desire for love has more substantial universality than the conflict that leads to an off-stage martyrdom in *The Cocktail Party*. An indigent Bronx family's struggles in *Awake and Sing!* bring us closer to universality than Eliot's domestic squabbles in "polite" society. Eliot, moreover, resolves these with far less universality of principle than Odets resolves conflict in *Awake and Sing!* in noting the failure of compromise for the sake of security and the renunciation of narrow values by the son of the family. When young Ralph starts reading his grandfather's books, turns his inheritance over to his mother, and decides to demand "steam in the warehouse" – flat as these decisions may be – he asserts something just as relevant to human life as Eliot's recognition of the power of Grace – namely, ordinary humanity's capacity for selfless idealism or, at least, rebellion against a narrow, grubbing existence. Everything we have called civilization and much that we have called the life of the spirit have emanated from that restlessness and revolt.

As an incipient Marxist, Ralph is little more than a pipsqueak, and the logic of his cheering his sister Hennie on when she walks out on her husband and child is highly vulnerable. Ralph remains on too low a level of awakening for tragedy when he translates his conversion into specifications within the limits of his mentality and of the situations in the play. But in so far as Odets focuses attention on the boy's capacity for spiritual awakening, his vision draws close to that of Isaiah, from whom he derived the title of his play, a gospel much more universal, as well as reliable, than any gospel according to the garden variety of Marxists whom Odets may have followed in 1935. The most serious limitations of *Awake and Sing!* are that the enlightenment of Hennie, when she runs away with her racketeer-lover, is rather spurious, and that Ralph's enlightenment has not been directly worked out by him for us through any action on his part before he arrives at his conclusions and decisions. These seem tagged on to the play as a lesson, as though they were an afterthought or imposed by the requirements of "social significance" for a playwright of the nineteen-thirties, who was expected to provide a "conversion-ending." Ralph has achieved "recognition," to use Anderson's term, more as an onlooker than as the active agent of the drama, and anything that an observer concludes in a play is a moral tag. If this view of *Awake and Sing!* is unjust to the play as a whole, this is because the action of the play as a family study does involve us in an experience from which insight can be gained dramatically rather than by merely subscribing to a conversion ending. And that insight can be greater than that achieved by Ralph and Hennie. It can be the larger vision of their grandfather, who has rejected materialism, whereas they only rejected compromise; or it can be a view of life enforced by the play which demonstrates man's rebellion remains: pettiness. That the vision or experience is not of the highest order of intensity and comprehensiveness is merely a concomitant of the nature of the play as *drama* rather than tragedy – that is, of a work that mixes modes of drama in order to carry us beyond tragic acquiescence into mundane activism. In the social context used by Odets, that activism tracks the dust of thoroughfares into the tragic theatre.

An absolute distinction between the particular and the universal experience is, in fact, impossible. Immediate realities contain and imply universal ones. Even our most unvarnished economic and political struggles can be related to the universals of desire, anxiety, suffering, and fear of deprivation, pain, and extinction; they can, in the work of a genuine creation, rather than a disguised tract, involve love and hate, loyalty and treason, selfishness and self-sacrifice, honor and dishonor, falsehood and truth, good and evil. And this is only another way of saying that anything we call universal is only a generalization of immediate and specific concerns. Of even "topical" concerns: If we could put ourselves in the place of an Athenian spectator at the first performance of *The Trojan Women*, the Oresteian trilogy, or any other effective tragedy, we would not speak so glibly of universals as though they had no social – or, for that matter, concrete political – relevance whatsoever. In *The Trojan Women*, for example, the issues of "imperialistic aggression" were comparable to the "rape of Belgium" in the First World War, and were just as "topical" – and, of course, just as relevant to personal experience for Athenians. *Richard II*, with its theme of the deposition of a medieval monarch, was "topical" during the Essex Rebellion, and was considered to be such by Elizabeth's government. Universality should not be construed as vacuity in a play. Everything we designate as universal was at one time, and in one sense or another, immediate – socially *and* personally. It couldn't have been universal, indeed, if it couldn't possibly have any immediacy for the playgoer.

The failure of modern plays as tragic art must have other causes than contemporaneity of substance. I would venture the view that a reason for failure will be found in the social dramatist's, let alone the propagandist's, failure to achieve a real tragic catharsis. He fails chiefly because in striving so arduously for an element of "enlightenment," or for the conversion of his characters and the audience to his point of view, he so often substitutes statement for dramatic process. He neglects to effectuate the "pity" and the "fear" – that is, the tensions and the empathy implicit in these Aristotelian terms. Although it is the combination of "pity," "fear," and "enlightenment" that produces tragic catharsis, his assault-strategy makes the frontal attack with "enlightenment" or "conversion" but forgets about the flanks. The unsupported frontal assault soon crumbles, since there is no effective tragic enlightenment when the play lacks compelling human reality. Emotions deeply rooted in character being absent, no rapport has been established between the observer in the auditorium and the actor on the stage except on a basis of superficial agreement or partisanship more or less extraneous to art. That rapport may be lacking for one of several reasons, such as the case-history character of a "problem play" situation, which instantly makes us the observer instead of the participant in an action. This can be the case even when we sympathize with the victim of social circumstance, as we do in Galsworthy's *Justice*. Another reason is the human insignificance of the characters, which is the case when they are insufficiently individualized or used directly for the purpose of demonstrating a point or mouthing a precept. Such characters make only superficial claims on us. They are not compelling enough to draw a response from the depths in us.

We may sum up the case against many realistic treatments of the problems of our time by saying that the plays have moved us a little and informed us a little but have not moved us sufficiently, because they have merely stirred our sentiments, and have not informed us sufficiently, because they have beclouded their argument with these same sentiments. The result has been middling drama that rests on low levels of emotionalism and intellectuality alike. Universality-worship will certainly not remove this deficiency any more than mere inebriation with tragic grandeur will. Only a sufficiently comprehensive view of the dramatic factor of "enlightenment" can help the modern playwright who does not propose to sever his relationship to his times or renounce his intention to have his say about them, and yet aspires to produce tragic art.

Shall we say with one school of literary critics that we have had no tragedies because playwrights stopped writing poetry? This cannot be the case, since there is no evidence whatsoever that catharsis is directly dependent upon poetry. The experience of catharsis with which we are concerned is an experience of theatre or action. It is the result of our observing the doing and the suffering of a thing. It is not primarily a matter of language (surely Martha Graham can effect a catharsis without uttering a word), and Aristotle, in his clear, if somewhat pedestrian or mechanical, fashion, was surely more sensible in treating the language of tragedy separately, almost as an embellishment, than some "New Critics" who consider language in the drama as an end in itself, as though it were lyric poetry, and interpret a play by explicating the lines of verse. Aristotle, who considered the plot, or *mythos*, paramount and the language of a play secondary, had more theatre in his bones than all critics who treat tragedy exclusively as poetry. Besides, it should be evident that the exalted language must come from *something* in the play, from the characters. That is, from incentives to great poetry in their circumstances and frame of mind. Shakespeare, not to mention Sophocles, can instruct us on this subject.

Next, we may consider whether we can concede the point made by Joseph Wood Krutch, and by those who have borrowed from his book *The Modern Temper*, that tragic art has been virtually extinct because the modern skeptical and scientific outlook has reduced man's stature. Mr. Krutch argued ably and eloquently. But it is not clear that his argument applies ineluctably to the dynamics of catharsis. I fail to comprehend why a character's failure to measure up to the "stature" of Hamlet or Lear must be a deterrent to "pity" and "fear." The case of Willy Loman in the successful American production of *Death of a Salesman* would disprove this assumption. It is precisely because Willy was a common man that American audiences felt *pity* for him and *feared* for themselves. Willy was a sort of suburban Everyman with whom audiences readily established a connection, if not indeed an actual identification.

It does not, however, follow that tragedy itself has been well served by a reduction in the stature of dramatic characters, and Joseph Wood Krutch is not refuted when we maintain that "pity" and "fear" have not been banished from the modern theatre. For the purposes of tragedy, "pity and fear," according to my view, are unavailing unless they form a triad with *enlightenment*, and unless this marriage of emotion and understanding lifts us above the perturbing events of a play. The neurotic is cured only when he is brought out of the nightmare world of his inner conflicts by his recognition and understanding of their nature and source. The sinner is redeemed only after he has understood the true nature of his situation. The neurotic's experience and the sinner's parallel the experience of the tragic catharsis. When a dramatic character lacks the stature to understand reality (and in this respect, the language of the character is, of course, decidedly revealing), *to understand after he has had experiences that compel understanding*, we are deprived of the possibility of achieving identification on a sufficiently high level of enlightenment.

We may understand the nature of his plight; we may understand why he failed in his human career. But our view becomes too clinical or sociological to provide a sense of exaltation. A physician or a social worker is not exalted in making a proper diagnosis. (And diagnoses in carefully written realistic drama are fairly obvious, too.) The relationship which becomes, then, too much like that of patient and diagnostician prevents sufficiently identification for us to make a sufficient ascent for or with the character. We can pity him, as we pity the Willy Loman of *Death of a Salesman*, just as we can make obvious deductions concerning his situation, but we cannot attain sufficient enlightenment through the agency of his person.

Inevitably, I believe, we are driven to the conclusion that there are actually *two* species of enlightenment – one fundamentally *tragic*, and the other fundamentally *non-tragic*. Non-tragic enlightenment may have many values but lacks the decisive value for tragedy of ensuring a true catharsis. We cannot have truly tragic enlightenment when the character's mental and spiritual endowment is so low that he cannot give us a proper cue for vision, or cannot set us an example of how high humanity can vault. In true tragedy, we witness the leap of a human being above the level of victim, villain, fool, or erring man in spite of the individual's being "accident-prone," "evil-prone," or "error-prone," as the case may be in the particular play.

There is reason, then, for stressing the value of tragic stature, for such stature is, of course, a matter of mind or spirit. We must be on guard only against assuming that there is an absolute measure of stature that we can apply categorically to every character. Concerning Miller's Willy Loman, I have been inclined to say that Willy the victim of economics or victim of his own fatuous view of life lacks tragic stature, but that Willy the impassioned man, who is loyal to an ideal of himself and of his son Biff, possesses it. The question is simply whether we find in this second Willy an instance of tragic will or an example of merely pathetic self-delusion.

Chapter 36

Friedrich Dürrenmatt (1921–1990)

Friedrich Dürrenmatt was a dramatist and illustrator. His successful plays included *The Marriage of Mr. Mississippi* (1952, produced in the United States as *Fools are Passing Through*), *The Judge and the Hangman* (1952), *The Visit* (1956), and *The Physicist* (1962). Dürrenmatt's *The Pledge* (1958) was made into a film with Jack Nicholson and directed by Sean Penn in 2001. Along with playwright Max Frisch, Dürrenmatt's work investigated hypocrisy and despair. Like Brecht he was interested in epic theatre, and his plays reflect Brecht's concern for political action. But his plays were more pessimistic than Brecht's; he considered the world chaotic and was less inclined towards political solutions. His plays folded into the theatre of the absurd, closer to Beckett than Brecht, and emphasized comedy. The only meaningful response to an absurd world is laughter. This essay, based on Dürrenmatt's lectures in 1954, is a straightforward account of what theatre is and how it should be executed. He takes a dim view of the swirling theories of his time, seeking instead practical solutions to the construction of playmaking and the function of theatre practice.

Problems of the Theatre (1955)

Behold the drive for purity in art as art is practiced these days. Behold this writer striving for the purely poetic, another for the purely lyrical, the purely epic, the purely dramatic. The painter ardently seeks to create the pure painting, the musician pure music, and someone even told me pure radio represents the synthesis between Dionysus

Excerpts from Friedrich Dürrenmatt, "Problems of the Theatre" (1955), tr. Gerhard Nellhaus, *Tulane Drama Review* 3.1 (October 1958), 3–26. © 1955 by Tulane Drama Review. Reprinted by permission of TDR/The Drama Review. This version was prepared for publication from a lecture delivered by Dürrenmatt in the fall of 1954 and the spring of 1955 in Switzerland and West Germany.

and Logos. Even more remarkable for our time, not otherwise renowned for its purity, is that each and everyone believes he has found his unique and the only true purity. Each vestal of the arts has, if you think of it, her own kind of chastity. Likewise, too numerous to count, are all the theories of the theatre, of what is pure theatre, pure tragedy, pure comedy. There are so many modern theories of the drama, what with each playwright keeping three or four at hand, that for this reason, if no other, I am a bit embarrassed to come along now with my theories of the problems of the theatre.

Furthermore, I would ask you not to look upon me as the spokesman of some specific movement in the theatre or of a certain dramatic technique, nor to believe that I knock at your door as the traveling salesman of one of the philosophies current on our stages today, whether as existentialist, nihilist, expressionist, or satirist, or any other label put on the compote dished up by literary criticism. For me, the stage is not a battlefield for theories, philosophies, and manifestos, but rather an instrument whose possibilities I seek to know by playing with it. Of course, in my plays there are people and they hold to some belief or philosophy – a lot of blockheads would make for a dull piece – but my plays are not for what people have to say: what is said is there because my plays deal with people, and thinking and believing and philosophizing are all, to some extent at least, a part of human behavior. The problems I face as playwright are practical, working problems, problems I face not before, but during the writing. To be quite accurate about it, these problems usually come up after the writing is done, arising out of a certain curiosity to know how I did it. So what I would like to talk about now are these problems, even though I risk disappointing the general longing for something profound and creating the impression that an amateur is talking. I haven't the faintest notion of how else I should go about it, of how not to talk about art like an amateur. Consequently I speak only to those who fall asleep listening to Heidegger.

What I am concerned with are empirical rules, the possibilities of the theatre. But since we live in an age when literary scholarship and criticism flourish, I can not quite resist the temptation of casting a few side glances at some of the theories of the art and practice of the theatre. The artist indeed has no need of scholarship. Scholarship derives laws from what exists already; otherwise it would not be scholarship. But the laws thus established have no value for the artist, even when they are true. The artist can not accept a law he has not discovered for himself. If he can not find such a law, scholarship can not help him with one it has established; and when the artist does find one, then it does not matter that the same law was also discovered by scholarship. But scholarship, thus denied, stands behind the artist like a threatening ogre, ready to leap forth whenever the artist wants to talk about art. And so it is here. To talk about problems of the theatre is to enter into competition with literary scholarship. I undertake this with some misgivings. Literary scholarship looks on the theatre as an object; for the dramatist it is never something purely objective, something separate from him. He participates in it. It is true that the playwright's activity makes drama into something objective (that is exactly his job), but he destroys the object he has created again and again, forgets it, rejects it, scorns it, reevaluates it, all in order to make room for something new. Scholarship sees only the result; the process, which led to this result, is what the playwright can not forget. What he says has to be taken with a grain of salt. What he thinks about his art changes as he creates his art; his thoughts are always subject to his mood and the moment. What alone really counts for him is what he is doing at a given moment; for its sake he can betray what he did just a little while ago. Perhaps a writer should never talk about his art, but once he starts, then it is not altogether a waste of time to listen to him. Literary scholars who have not the faintest notion of the difficulties of writing and of the hidden rocks that force the stream of art into oft unsuspected channels run the danger of merely asserting and stupidly proclaiming laws that do not exist.

Doubtless the unities of time, place, and action which Aristotle – so it was supposed for a long time – derived from Greek tragedy constitute the ideal of drama. From a logical and hence also aesthetic point of view, this thesis is incontestable, so incontestable indeed, that the question arises if it does not set up the framework once and for all within which each dramatist must work. Aristotle's three unities demand the greatest precision, the greatest economy, and the greatest simplicity in the handling of the dramatic material. The unities of time, place, and action ought to be a basic dictate put to the dramatist by literary scholarship, and the only reason scholarship does not hold the artist to them is that Aristotle's unities have not been obeyed by anyone for ages. Nor can they be obeyed, for reasons which best illustrate the relationship of the art of writing plays to the theories about that art.

The unities of time, place, and action in essence presuppose Greek tragedy. Aristotle's unities do not make Greek tragedy possible; rather, Greek tragedy allows his unities. No matter how abstract an aesthetic law may appear to be, the work of art from which it was derived is contained in that law. If I want to set about writing a dramatic action which is to unfold and run its course in the same place inside of two hours, for instance, then this action must have a history behind it, and that history is the story which took place before the stage action commenced, a story which alone makes the action on the stage possible. Thus the history behind Hamlet is, of course, the murder of his father; the drama lies in the discovery of that murder. As a rule, too, the stage action is much shorter in time than the event depicted; it often starts out right in the middle of the event, or indeed toward the end of it. Before Sophocles' tragedy could begin, Oedipus had to have killed his father and married his mother. The stage action condenses an event to the extent to which Aristotle's unities are fulfilled; the closer a playwright adheres to the three unities, the more important is the background history of the action.

It is, of course, possible to invent a history and hence a dramatic action that would seem particularly favorable for keeping to Aristotle's unities. But this brings into force the rule that the more invented a story is and the more unknown it is to the audience, the more careful must its exposition, the unfolding of the background, be. Greek tragedy was possible only because it did not have to invent its historical background, because it already possessed one. The spectators knew the myths with which each drama dealt; and because these myths were public, ready coin, part of religion, they made the feats of the Greek tragedians possible, feats never to be attained again; they made possible their abbreviations, their straightforwardness, their stichomythy and choruses, and hence also Aristotle's unities. The audience knew what the play was all about; its curiosity was not focused on the story so much as on its treatment. Aristotle's unities presupposed the general appreciation of the subject matter – a genial exception in more recent times is Kleist's *The Broken Jug* – presupposed a religious theatre based on myths. Therefore as soon as the theatre lost its religious, its mythical significance, the unities had to be reinterpreted or discarded. An audience facing an unknown story will pay more attention to the story than to its treatment, and by necessity then such a play has to be richer in detail and circumstances than one with a known action. The feats of one playwright can not be the feats of another. Each art exploits the chances offered by its time, and it is hard to imagine a time without chances. Like every other form of art, drama creates its world; but not every world can be created in the same fashion. This is the natural limitation of every aesthetic rule, no matter how self-evident such a rule may be. This does not mean that Aristotle's unities are obsolete; what was once a rule has become an exception, a case that may occur again at any time. The one-act play obeys the unities still, even though under a different condition. The plot is dominated by a situation instead of by history, and thus unity is once again achieved.

But what is true for Aristotle's theory of drama, namely its dependency upon a certain world and hence its validity relative to that world, is also true of every other theory of drama. Brecht is consistent only when he incorporates into his dramaturgy that *Weltanschauung*, the communist philosophy, to which he – so he seems to think – is committed; but in doing so he often cuts off his own nose. Sometimes his plays say the very opposite of what they claim they say, but this lack of agreement can not always be blamed on the capitalistic audience. Often it is simply a case where Brecht, the poet, gets the better of Brecht, the dramatic theorist, a situation that is wholly legitimate and ominous only were it not to happen again. [...]

The task of art, insofar as art can have a task at all, and hence also the task of drama today, is to create something concrete, something that has form. This can be accomplished best by comedy. Tragedy, the strictest genre in art, presupposes a formed world. Comedy – insofar as it is not just satire of a particular society as in Molière – supposes an unformed world, a world being made and turned upside down, a world about to fold like ours. Tragedy overcomes distance; it can make myths originating in times immemorial seem like the present to the Athenians. But comedy creates distance; the attempt of the Athenians to gain a foothold in Sicily is translated by comedy into the birds undertaking to create their own empire before which the gods and men will have to capitulate. How comedy works can be seen in the most primitive kind of joke, in the dirty story, which, though it is of very dubious value, I bring up only because it is the best illustration of what I mean by creating distance. The subject of the dirty story is the purely sexual, and, because it is purely sexual, it is formless and without objective distance. To achieve form the purely sexual is transmuted, as I have already mentioned, into the dirty joke. Therefore this type of joke is a kind of original comedy, a transposition of the sexual onto the plain of the comical. In this way it is possible today in a society dominated by John Doe, to talk in an accepted way about the purely sexual. Thus the dirty story demonstrates that the comical exists in forming what is formless, in creating order out of chaos.

The means by which comedy creates distance is the conceit. Tragedy is without conceit. Hence there are few tragedies whose subjects were invented. By this I do not mean to imply that the ancient tragedians lacked inventive ideas of the sort that are written today, but the marvel of their art was that they had no need of these inventions or conceits. That makes all the difference. Aristophanes, on the other hand, lives by conceits. The stuff of his plays are [*sic*] not myths but inventions, which take place not in the past but the present. They drop into their world like bombshells which, by poking holes into the landscape, change the present into the comic and thus scatter the dirt for everyone to see. This, of course, does not mean that drama today can only be comical.

Tragedy and comedy are but formal concepts, dramatic attitudes, figments of the aesthetic imagination which can embrace one and the same thing. Only the conditions under which each is created are different, and these conditions have their basis only in small part in art.

Tragedy presupposes guilt, despair, moderation, lucidity, vision, a sense of responsibility. In the Punch-and-Judy show of our century, in this backsliding of the white race, guilty and, hence, responsible men no longer exist. On all sides we hear: "We couldn't help it," "We didn't really want that to happen." And indeed, things happen without anyone in particular being responsible for them. Everything is swept along and everyone gets caught up somehow in the current of events. We are all collectively guilty, collectively bogged down in the sins of our fathers and of our forefathers. We are the offspring of children. That is our misfortune, but not our guilt; guilt can exist only as a personal achievement, as a religious deed. What is right for us is comedy. Our world has led to the grotesque as well as to the atom bomb, and Jeronimo's madness is with us again, the apocalyptic vision has become the grotesquely real. But the grotesque is only a way of expressing in a tangible manner, of making us perceive physically the paradoxical, the form of the unformed, the face of a world without face; and just as in our thinking today we seem to be unable to do without the concept of the paradox, so also in art, and in our world which at times seems still to exist only because the atom bomb exists, out of fear of the bomb.

But the tragic is still possible even if pure tragedy is not. We can achieve the tragic out of comedy. We can bring it forth as a frightening moment, as an abyss that opens suddenly; indeed many of Shakespeare's tragedies are already really comedies out of which the tragic arises.

All this then might easily lead to the conclusion that comedy is the expression of despair, but this conclusion is not inevitable. To be sure, whoever realizes the senselessness, the hopelessness of this world might well despair, but this despair is not a result of this world. Rather it is an answer given by an individual to this world; another answer would be not to despair, would be an individual's decision to endure this world in which we live like Gulliver among the giants. He also achieves distance, he also steps back a pace or two who takes measure of his opponent, who prepares himself to fight his opponent or to escape him. It is still possible to show man as a courageous being.

In truth this is a principal concern of mine. The blind men, Romulus, Uebelohe, Akki, are all men of courage. The lost world order is restored within them; the universal escapes my grasp. I refuse to find the universal in a doctrine. The universal for me is chaos. The world (hence the stage which represents this world) is for me something monstrous, a riddle of misfortunes which must be accepted but before which one must not capitulate. The world is far bigger than any man, and perforce threatens him constantly. If one could but stand outside the world, it would no longer be threatening. But I have neither the right nor the ability to be an outsider to this world. To find solace in poetry can also be all too cheap; it is more honest to retain one's human point of view. Brecht's thesis, that the world is an accident, which he developed in his *Street Scene* where he shows how this accident happened, may yield – as it in fact did – some magnificent theatre; but he did it by concealing most of the evidence! Brecht's thinking is inexorable, because inexorably there are many things he will not think about.

And lastly it is through the conceit, through comedy that the anonymous audience becomes possible as an audience, becomes a reality to be counted on, and, also, one to be taken into account. The conceit easily transforms the crowd of theatregoers into a mass which can be attacked, deceived, outsmarted into listening to things it would otherwise not so readily listen to. Comedy is a mousetrap in which the public is easily caught and in which it will get caught over and over again. Tragedy, on the other hand, predicates a true community, a kind of community whose existence in our day is but an embarrassing fiction. Nothing is more ludicrous, for instance, than to sit and watch the mystery plays of the Anthroposophists when one is not a participant.[1]

Granting all this there is still one more question to be asked: is it permissible to go from a generality to a particular form of art, to do what I just did when I went from my assertion that the world was formless to the particular possibility for writing comedies today? I doubt that this is permissible. Art is something personal, and something personal should never be explained in generalities. The value of a work of art does not depend on whether more or less good reasons for its existence can be found. Hence I have also tried to avoid certain problems, as, for example, the argument which is very lively today, whether or not plays ought to be written in verse or in prose. My own answer lies simply in writing prose, without any intentions of thereby deciding the issue. A man has to choose to go one way, after all, and why should one way always be worse than another? As far as my concepts of comedy are concerned, I believe that here, too, personal reasons are more important than more general ones that are always open to argument. What logic in matters of art could not be refuted! One talks best about art when one talks of one's own art. The art one chooses is an expression of freedom without which no art can exist, and at the same time also of necessity without which art can not exist either. The artist always represents his world and himself. If at one time philosophy taught men to arrive at the particular from the general, then unlike Schiller, who started out believing in general conclusions, I can not construct a play as he did when I doubt that the particular can ever be reached from the general. But my doubt is mine and only mine, and not the doubt and problems of a Catholic for whom drama holds possibilities non-Catholics do not share. This is so even if, on the other hand, a Catholic who takes his religion seriously is denied those possibilities which other men possess. The danger inherent in this thesis lies in the fact that there are always those artists who for the sake of finding some generalities to believe in accept conversion, taking a step which is the more to be wondered at for the sad fact that it really will not help them. The difficulties experienced by a Protestant in writing a drama are just the same difficulties he has with his faith. Thus it is my way to mistrust what is ordinarily called the building of the drama, and to arrive at my plays from the unique, the sudden idea or conceit, rather than from some general concept or plan. Speaking for myself, I need to write off into the blue, as I like to put it so that I might give critics a catchword to hang onto. They use it often enough, too, without really understanding what I mean by it.

But these matters are my own concerns and hence it is not necessary to invoke the whole world and to make out as if what are my concerns are the concerns of art in general (lest I be like the drunk who goes back to Noah, the Flood, original sin, and the beginning of the world to explain what is, after all, only his own weakness). As in everything and everywhere, and not just in the field of art, the rule is: No excuses, please! [. . .]

Note

1   The Anthroposophists were spiritual followers of Rudolf Steiner (1861–1925). – Editor's note.

Chapter 37

Sean O'Casey (1880–1964)

Sean O'Casey was Ireland's leading dramatist. His works, among them *Shadow of a Gunman* (1923), *Juno and the Paycock* (1924), *The Plough and the Stars* (1926), *The Silver Tassie* (1929), *Within the Gates* (1934), *Purple Dust* (1940), and *Red Roses for Me* (1943), demonstrated his affinity for the working class. His anti-war stance aroused the antipathy of Irish Nationalists. Some of his plays, like those of John M. Synge, instigated violent reaction from the Abbey Theatre crowds. O'Casey was noted for setting the standard of realism on the world stage. In this essay he takes umbrage at the idea of realism, suggesting that authors and dramatists hardly reproduce reality, but cherry-pick situations they present. The theatre is not for O'Casey the locus of real life but an artistic presentation of stories that serve the narrator's purpose.

Green Goddess of Realism (1956)

In the theatre of today, realism is the totem pole of the dramatic critics.

Matter-of-fact plays, true true-to-life arrangement, and real, live characters are the three gods the critics adore and saturate with the incense of their commonplace praise once a day and twice on Sundays in their trimly dressed little articles. What the dramatic critics mean by the various terms they use for Realism is the yearly ton of rubbish that falls on the English stage and is swiftly swept away into the dustbins. The critics give a cordial welcome to the trivial plays because, in my opinion, they are, oh, so easy to understand, and gorge the critics with the ease of an easy explanation. It is very dangerous for a dramatist to be superior to the critics, to be a greater dramatist than the critic is

Sean O'Casey, "Green Goddess of Realism," in *The Green Crow* (New York: George Braziller, 1956), 73–86. © 1956 by Sean O'Casey. Reprinted by permission of the Estate of Sean O'Casey.

a critic. They don't like it, and so most of them do all they can to discourage any attempt in the theatre towards an imagination fancy-free, or an attempt to look on life and mold it into a form fit for the higher feeling and intelligence of the stage. They are those who compare Beaumont and Fletcher's *Philaster* with *Charley's Aunt*, and in their heart of hearts vote for the farce and shove the poetic play out of their way (a few spit the preference in our face, as Archer did). *Charley's Aunt* is loved by Charley's uncles. They have grown fat and lazy on triviality, so fat and so lazy that they are hardly able to move. The curse is that these critics do their best to prevent anyone else from moving either. They will have simply to be roughly shunted out of the way, and these few words are one of the first sharp prods to get them to buzz off and do their sleeping some-where else. Realism, or what the critics childishly believe to be Realism, has had its day, and has earned a rest. It began on a sunny autumn evening in 1886, or thereabouts, as the lawyers say, at the first production of *Ours* by Robertson, when the miracle took place. "In reading the play today," says William Archer, the world-famous dramatic critic, "we recognize in Robertson – just what the stage wanted in its progress towards veri-similitude – the genius of the commonplace. The first act of *Ours* was, in intention at any rate, steeped in an atmosphere quite new to the theatre. The scene was an avenue in Shendryn Park which Robertson describes in the abhorrent prompt-book jargon of the time. But one line had, I venture to say, as yet appeared in no prompt-book in the world: '*Throughout the act the autumn leaves fall from the trees.*' How this effect was produced and whether it was successful, I cannot say. Nor can I discuss the question whether it was a desirable effect, or a mere trick of mechanical realism which the true artist would despise." Now the falling of the leaves from the trees was and could have been nothing but "a mere trick of mechanical realism," because the trees couldn't have been true-to-life trees, and, even if they were, the autumnal leaves couldn't have fallen with the regularity and rhythm required to create the desirable effect. And no true artist of the theatre would despise "a mere trick of mechanical realism" by which to get a scenic or an emotional effect out of his play and over to his audience. We remember the fine effect that the first sound of the first fall of rain had as it fell in the first act of [André] Obey's *Noah*; and this fall of rain was a mere trick of mechanical realism as it was also the opening of the floodgates of Heaven, swelling into a flood that destroyed all life that was in the world save only those who found safe shelter in the faith of Noah; or the sudden change in the wind in *Saint Joan* that set the pennon streaming eastward, and sent Dunois and Saint Joan hurrying out to make for the flash of the guns, and drive the English out of France. You see the artist in the theatre never despises a mere trick of mechanical realism; but he knows how to keep it in its proper place. [...]

Although the bone of realism in the theatre has been picked pretty clean, the critics keep gnawing away at it so that if a playwright as much as gets a character to blow his nose (preferably when "the autumn leaves are falling from the trees"), the critics delight-edly nod to each other, and murmur, "An exact imitation of life, brothers." Commenting on *Call It a Day*, a play in which everything is attempted and nothing done, Mr. Agate tells us that "Miss Jodie Smith is never concerned whether 'it' is a play or not, but whether she has assembled on her stage characters so real that she might have gone into the street and compelled them into the theatre," though these characters that might have been pulled in off the street are as tender and delicate and true as the tenderest and most delicate characters wistfully wandering about in the most wistful Barrie play.

J. G. B. [George Bernard Shaw], commenting on *Love from a Stranger*, tells us that "it is written with brilliant matter-of-factness, and is a real play about real people." Here our noses are shoved up against the image of realism in the theatre. A real play about real people: here's a sentence that apparently punches home; but look well into it, and you'll find it empty of any real meaning. Week in and week out these commonplace plays are reducing the poor critics into more and more vague and vapid expressions that would give a sparkle to the mouth of a politician trying to cod his constituents – and very often succeeding. A real play about real people – what does it mean? This is something of a triumph – a real play with real people in a real theatre before a real audience. But every play is a real play whether it be good or bad, just as a real lion is a real lion and a real mouse is a real mouse, and both are animals. But the real mouse isn't a real lion, nor is the real lion a real mouse, though both are animals. I wonder do the critics get this? There is a big difference between a lion and a mouse, though both are animals, and there is a bigger difference between a good and a bad play, though both are plays just the same. What is a "real play"? Answer, according to J. G. B., *Love from a Stranger* is a real play, therefore the nearer we get to this praised play, the nearer we get to a real play. Now is *The Dream Play by* Strindberg a real play? It certainly bears no resemblance to *Love from a Stranger*, but the imagination can handle *The Dream Play* just as well and with far fuller satisfaction. Apparently the critics think that a play to be a real play must have real people in it, though they never take breath to tell us what they mean by real people. Take people off the street or carry them out of a drawing-room, plonk them on the stage and make them speak as they speak in real, real life, and you will have the dullest thing imaginable. I suppose the critics will be shocked to hear that no real character can be put in a play unless some of the reality is taken out of him through the heightening, widening, and deepening of the character by the dramatist who creates him. Would the dramatic critics call the characters in *Hamlet* real people, or only the creations out of the mind of a poet, and isn't *Hamlet* all the better for its want of reality? Isn't it more of a play, and what has the word "play" got to do with reality? Is Caliban a real person, found in the street and compelled into the theatre? If he isn't, then, isn't the character just as powerful as if he were? What peculiar quality does this term of "real people in a real play" give to a play, seeing that many plays, some of them in step with the greatest, have in them characters far removed from this critic-quality of matter-of-factness? Isn't Caliban as real a character as Gustav Bergmann in *Close Quarters*, or the ladies and gents in *Fallen Angels*, or *Night Must Fall*, or *Call It a Day*, the author of which, as Mr. Agate tells us, assembles on her stage characters so real (again this word "real" – the spyhole through which the critics view the stage) that she might have gone into the street and compelled them into the theatre. (Though how a critic couples a play dealing with sex almost from the word "go" to the last lap, a play in which an accountant goes to the flat of an actress-client and nothing happens; in which the accountant's wife is entertained by a friend, and then entertains the friend alone in her house, and nothing happens; in which their daughter flings herself at an artist, and nothing happens; in which her brother falls for a young lassie that climbs over the garden wall to him, and nothing happens; in which the maid falls for the manservant of the family a few doors down, and nothing happens; and the bitch brought out for a walk by the manservant rubs noses with the dog taken out by the maid, and nothing happens – how a critic couples all this sort of thing with characters hustled in off the streets, only a critic could know, and only a critic can tell.) If all that is in this play be life, then life is a mass of sentimentally holy hokum.

As a matter-of-factness no one, least of all a playwright, can go out into the streets and lanes of the city and compel the people to come on to the stage, for the people on the stage must be of the stage and not of the streets and lanes of the city or of the highways and hedges of the country. The most realistic characters in the most realistic play cannot be true to life. Perhaps the most real character in any play we know of is the character of Falstaff done by Shakespeare. Here is realism as large as life; but it is realism larger, and a lot larger, than life. Falstaff was never pulled off the streets into the theatre by Shakespeare. God never created Falstaff – he sprang from Shakespeare's brain. God, if you like, created Shakespeare, but Shakespeare created Falstaff. Falstaff is no more real, there is no more matter-of-factness in the character of Falstaff, than there is in Caliban or Puck or Ariel. He is a bigger creation than any of these three, and that is all. A play, says Dryden, ought to be a just image of human nature, and this is true of *Hamlet*, of *John Bull's Other Island*, of *Strange Interlude*, of *Six Characters in Search of an Author*, of *Peer Gynt*, of *The Dream Play*; but it is not true of the trivial tomtit-realism in the thousand and one entertainment plays patted and praised by the dramatic critics. Why, even the sawdust characters of the Moor, Petroushka, and the Ballerina are a more just image of human nature than the characters in the matter-of-fact, exact-imitation-of-life plays that flit about on the English stage.

As it is with the play, so it is with the dressed-up stage – the critics want to be doped into the belief that the scene on the stage is as real as life itself. The stirring of the hair is more to them than the stirring of the heart. But things as real as life itself on the stage they can never have; a room can never be a room, a tree a tree, or a death a death. These must take the nature of a child's toys and a child's play. [. . .]

This rage for real, real life on the stage has taken all the life out of the drama. If everything on the stage is to be a fake exact imitation (for fake realism it can only be), where is the chance for the original and imaginative artist? Less chance for him than there was for Jonah in the whale's belly. The beauty, fire, and poetry of drama have perished in the storm of fake realism. Let real birds fly through the air (not like [director] Basil Dean's butterflies in *Midsummer Night's Dream*, fluttering over the stage and pinning themselves to trees), real animals roam through the jungle, real fish swim in the sea; but let us have the make-believe of the artist and the child in the theatre. Less of what the critics call "life," and more of symbolism; for even in the most commonplace of realistic plays the symbol can never be absent. A house on a stage can never be a house, and that which represents it must always be a symbol. A room in a realistic play must always be a symbol for a room. There can never be any important actuality on the stage, except an actuality that is unnecessary and out of place. An actor representing a cavalier may come on the stage mounted on a real horse, but the horse will always look only a little less ridiculous than the "cavalier." The horse can have nothing to do with the drama. I remember a play written round Mr. [Samuel] Pepys, and in this play was used "the identical snuff-box used by him when he was head of the Admiralty in the reign of Charles the Second." So much was said about the snuff-box that I expected it to be carried in on a cushion preceded by a brass band, and hawked around for all to admire before the play began. Now this snuff-box added nothing to the play, and because of this commonplace spirit in the play, the play added nothing to the drama. It seems that the closer we move to actual life, the further we move away from the drama. Drama purely imitative of life isn't drama at all. Now the critics are beginning to use the word "theatre" when they find themselves in a bit of a tangle over what they should say about a play that has a bad whiff of staleness in its theme, character, and form. For instance, [drama critic] Mr. Ivor Brown, writing of a recent play, said that "the play is not life, it is theatre and might be allowed to wear its flamboyant colors"; "might be allowed," mind you – he, too, isn't sure. He doesn't tell us to what theatre the play belonged. He left his readers to find that out for themselves. Was it the theatre of Shakespeare, of Shaw, of Strindberg, of Ibsen, of Goldsmith, of O'Neill, of Pirandello, or of Toiler? Or the theatre of Dan Leno, Marie Lloyd, George Robey, Charlie Chaplin, Sidney Howard, or Will Hay? These are all good theatre and so they are all good life. But it is not the life that they imitate in their plays or in their actions that makes them good theatre, but the unique and original life that is in themselves. They have the life that the present dramatic critics lack, for the critics cannot, or are afraid to, be lively. They wouldn't venture to give the plays they call "theatre" their baptismal name of rubbish. [...]

Chapter 38

Eric Bentley (b. 1916)

Eric Russell Bentley was a leading theatre critic, translator, scholar, and playwright. His influential works on the theatre include *The Playwright as Thinker* (1946), *What is Theatre?* (1956, excerpt reprinted here), *The Life of the Drama* (1964), *Brecht Commentaries* (1981), and *Thinking About the Playwright* (1987). He was a major translator of playwrights Brecht, Pirandello, and Schnitzler into English, and a controversial critic for the *New Republic* from 1952 to 1956. His footnoted remarks in this essay stem from contretemps with Arthur Miller and Tennessee Williams. Bentley consistently probed the meaning of theatre, challenging its aims and reactions. He was fiercely independent, gaining the respect and admiration, if not always the approval, of the theatre community.

What is Theatre? A Point of View (1956)

[...] I have been maintaining that the "serious" modern playwright is, or should be, engaged, along with other modern writers, in the search for the human essence. If it is possible to state in a word what moral quality the artist engaged in this quest needs above all others, I should say that it is audacity. Conversely, artists who are not searching, not reaching out for anything, but working comfortably within their established resources, and who are completely lacking in daring, who never "cock a snoot," "take a crack" at anything, "stick their necks out" – for them should be reserved the harshest adjective in the critical vocabulary: innocuous. In life there are worse things than innocuousness – forms of rampant evil which render innocuousness praiseworthy by comparison. But the Devil doesn't write plays. And when Mussolini wrote them he didn't succeed in projecting anything of the force of his iniquity. Like many a better man, he only succeeded in writing innocuously. But that is the worst type of writing there is.

With the two conceptions of work – art and pastime, exploration and craft – go two conceptions of the worker. The master of pastime is the well-adjusted person, happily holding hands with the audiences.[1] The artist, if not maladjusted, and I believe he is not, is not well-adjusted either; perhaps we should follow [poet] Peter Viereck's suggestion and invent a third category, that of the unadjusted man, the healthy rebel. At any rate, it has been known, at least since Plato, that the artist is a dangerous character, and consequently that art is a subversive activity. I am not speaking of the philosophy, much less of the politics, of artists. Artists are disturbing, unsettling people, not by what they preach but by what they are, conservatives like Dante and Shakespeare being far more disturbing and unsettling than our little revolutionaries. The greater the artist the greater the upset.

In the voice of every artist, however full-throated and mellow, there is an undertone of something very like insolence. The small boy who said to Mme. de Pompadour: "*Why* can't you kiss me? The queen kisses me," was not the devastating Voltaire but the "mild" Mozart. "To kindle art to the whitest heat, there must always be some fanaticism behind it": Bernard Shaw was inspired to write this by seeing, not Ibsen's *Ghosts*, but the music-hall sketches and cabaret songs of Yvette Guilbert. The famous Tramp of Charlie Chaplin was gentle, and beloved by all the world, yet when I heard a candid spectator say of Charlie: "I can't stand the man," I realized how many others would say the same if they rigorously examined their responses; because, for all the charm and the high spirits, Chaplin is an alarming artist. Again, I am not referring to politics (though doubtless Chaplin took up Stalinism because he *thought* it was radical; there, history's joke was on Charlie). About any film of his, however slight, there is an air of menace; whereas most other comedians, for all that they make a lot more noise, are quite harmless.

[Essayist and theorist] Henri de Montherlant devoted an essay to the analogy of playwriting and bullfighting; and I have heard Martha Graham compare the dancer to the matador, and that, not in point of similarity of movement, but similarity of psychology: the dancer will attain to that razor-edge keenness when each move, each fall, each leap has that degree of urgency, that heightened sense of hazard.

"Live dangerously!" The artist follows Nietzsche's recommendation. Ortega y Gasset says there is some vulgarity in it because life is of its nature dangerous. True; but, as the fact is ignored and implicitly denied by modern culture as such, Nietzsche was fully justified in shouting it from the housetops. Even now, though editorials can be uselessly shrill about hydrogen bombs, though facts like the murder of 6,000,000 Jews are common knowledge, that fundamental complacency of middle-class culture – the most imperturbable of all imperturbabilities – is still with us. The works of Nietzsche have not "dated." Nor has the artist's sense of danger: precisely from his "subversiveness" stems his utility to society.

And the theatre could make a special contribution. For though it has sometimes chosen to be the most unenterprising of the arts, the genius, and even the very technics, of the medium tend all the other way. Theatricality is, *by definition*, audacious. A comedian is, *by definition*, a zany. The impertinence, insolence, effrontery that I have speculatively attributed to the artist in general, none would deny to the clown in particular. But have we begun to draw the logical inferences? We have been told often enough of all the gradual, thorough, and fine-spun things that the novel can do and that the stage fails to do, but have we explored the possibilities of theatre in the opposite direction – the realm of the sudden, the astonishing, the extravagant? The theatre is the place for the anarchist to throw his bomb.

Or perhaps for anyone *but* the anarchist to throw his bomb. For while theatre is the art of explosions, the trick is to have them go off at the right time in the right spot. Audacity has no place in the arts until it is brought under iron control. The rhythm of theatre derives from an alternation of explosion and silence; more precisely, there is preparation, explosion, and subsiding. The man of the theatre must not merely bring explosives in his bag; he must know exactly how to prepare the explosions and how to handle their subsidence. For the interplay between audacity and control produces the supreme artistic effects; the work of the masters of dramatic literature abounds in examples. And stage directing calls for the same combination of powers, though usually, even from the expert, we get either audacity without control, or control without audacity. The only man I know of who is endowed with both gifts to the greatest possible extent – and in both fields, playwriting and directing – is Bertolt Brecht. In that fact – and not in the theory and practice of propaganda – lies the secret of his unique importance in the theatre today.

But I am not coming forward with a messiah. No one man will provide the answer to our problem, and to part of it Brecht provides, in my opinion, the wrong answer. He is one of those writers who search less and less after what I have been calling the human essence, because they are more and more convinced that they have already found it. Even supposing that Brecht *has* found it, that fact would not augur well for him as an artist. The only artists today who remain artists after conversion to causes which claim a monopoly of the truth are those who are not wholly convinced. Graham Greene's work derives its vitality now from the fact that he is always fighting his own Catholicism. The minute he says to himself, "I am a Catholic writer," begins to ask the alleged truth of his beliefs to do duty for his personal grasp of truth, however tentative and unsure, he is through. I am not objecting here either to Communism or Catholicism but, rather, pointing out what kind of adherence to these causes, or any other that makes comparable claims for itself, is damaging to an artist. The audacity for which I have praised Brecht was not the product of such an adherence but, on the contrary, of that bourgeois freedom in which Brecht gradually came to disbelieve. As he was an artist by virtue of his subversive activities, and socially and overtly subversive activities at that, absolutely necessary to his art was a society which, first, he wished to subvert and which, second, would permit him to try and subvert it. Bourgeois capitalism met both conditions; Soviet communism neither. And so the *enfant terrible* of the Weimar Republic tried to convert himself into the yes-man of the Soviet bureaucracy and the DDR (Deutsche Demokratische Republik). Only in relation to the West could this political writer even try to remain audacious, and this is that easy audacity (common also among anti-communists) which is no audacity at all.[2] Meanwhile, those larger works which Brecht hopes will have some lasting value are most alive where some unresolved inner conflict forces its way in despite the author and the watching bureaucrats. Into both Galileo and Mother Courage have been smuggled elements which are as subversive to Communism as *The Threepenny Opera* is to capitalism. The Communist press has not been entirely happy about either play.

It is a mistake even to hope that an ideal will find its realization in a single man. It is a mistake to expect that the ideal situation will ever be realized at all. And it is above all a mistake to think that ages of great theatre come about through the critics' explaining how to write plays, or even how not to write them. The critic's influence is not directly on the creative act but on public opinion (the playwright being, however, a member of the public). What the critic influences is morale.

The theatre today is demoralized. It suffers from hysterical oscillation between cheap cynicism and idealistic euphoria. This could be because dramatic art nowadays attracts chiefly manic depressives, though to say so only provokes the query: how has this come to be so? Between flat despair and yeasty zeal, why is there nothing but a vacuum? The question puts the cart before the horse: it is precisely because of this vacuum, this void, this *néant*, that men can only admit defeat or simulate success, descend to cynicism or rise to feverish and showy enthusiasm. Which is to repeat that they are demoralized.

Now, if it isn't too late, what do we do about demoralization in any institution – the church, the army, the nation – but try to recall people to a sense of the past, the glorious origin of the institution, its great men, its highest moments? And this is what I have been doing in the course of this brief attempt to answer the question: What Is Theatre? (or rather, this lengthy attempt to ask that question). We of the theatre need the inspiration and the discipline of Shakespeare and Molière exactly as a musician needs the inspiration and discipline of Bach and Mozart. And we need a sense of where it all came from, this theatre of ours, and where it has been going, and where it seems to be going now. For the task that inexorably confronts us – the task of continuing – we need, also, to assign ourselves a master objective. I have been suggesting that it is to search for our lost humanity. And, as weapons in this quest, I have been commending two that have been there from the beginning without losing any of their efficacity with the passage of time – the audacity of Dionysos and the controlling hand of Apollo.

Notes

1 "The secret of your theatrical prosperity," Scribe was told in a speech that welcomed him into the Academy, "is to have happily seized upon the spirit of your century and to have made the kind of play which it takes to most readily and which most closely corresponds to its nature." Allowing for differences in vocabulary, isn't this what a Broadway critic would say when conferring an award on a Broadway playwright?

2 My comment on Tennessee Williams and Arthur Miller in this book and *The Dramatic Event* are an attempt to describe the phenomenon of easy, of false, audacity in current American drama. This is not to deny that both these authors are capable of real audacity; their superiority to most of their colleagues derives to a large extent from their greater daring.

Chapter 39

Northrop Frye (1912–1991)

Herman Northrop Frye was a leading mid-twentieth-century literary critic. *Fearful Symmetry* (1947) was his first major work, but his most profound contribution to literary history was *Anatomy of Criticism* (1957). Frye's influence spread far and wide, including Harold Bloom and other notables. His interests were largely concerned with myth, which he terms "a structural organizing principle of literary form."[1] Myth for Frye was similar to Aristotle's concept of plot, only for Frye the plot serves as an archetype and guiding motif over the entire work. He used the symbols of the seasons to frame literary genres. Winter, spring, summer, and fall incorporate types of literature and drama. Like the structuralists, Frye relates literary objects to other objects, finding patterns, motifs, taxonomies, and reoccurrences. Although never "formally" a member of structuralism or literary New Criticism, his work profoundly influenced both groups.

Specific Forms of Drama (1957)

[...] The division of dramas into tragedies and comedies [...] is a conception based entirely on verbal drama, and does not include or account for types of drama, such as the opera or masque, in which music and scenery have a more organic place. Yet verbal drama, whether tragic or comic, has clearly developed a long way from the primitive idea of drama, which is to present a powerful sensational focus for a community. The scriptural plays of the Middle Ages are primitive in this sense: they present to the audience

Northrop Frye, "Specific Forms of Drama," reproduced from the fourth essay, "Rhetorical Criticism: Theory of Genres," in *Anatomy of Criticism: Four Essays* (Princeton: Princeton University Press), 282–93. © 1957 by Princeton University Press, 1985 renewed PUP, 2000 paperback edition. Reprinted by permission of Princeton University Press.

a myth already familiar to and significant for that audience, and they are designed to remind the audience of their communal possession of this myth.

The scriptural play is a form of a spectacular dramatic genre which we may provisionally call a "myth-play." It is a somewhat negative and receptive form, and takes on the mood of the myth it represents. The crucifixion play in the Towneley cycle is tragic because the Crucifixion is; but it is not a tragedy in the sense that Othello is a tragedy.[2] It does not, that is, make a tragic *point*; it simply presents the story because it is familiar and significant. It would be nonsense to apply such tragic conceptions as hybris to the figure of Christ in that play, and while pity and terror are raised, they remain attached to the subject, and there is no catharsis of them. The characteristic mood and resolution of the myth-play are pensive, and pensiveness, in this context, implies a continuing imaginative subjection to the story. The myth-play emphasizes dramatically the symbol of spiritual and corporeal communion. The scriptural plays themselves were associated with the festival of Corpus Christi, and Calderón's religious plays are explicitly *autos sacramentales* or Eucharist plays. The appeal of the myth-play is a curious mixture of the popular and the esoteric; it is popular for its immediate audience, but those outside its circle have to make a conscious effort to appreciate it. In a controversial atmosphere it disappears, as it cannot deal with controversial issues unless it selects its audience. In view of the ambiguities attaching to the word myth, we shall speak of this genre as the *auto*.

When there is no clear-cut distinction between gods and heroes in a society's mythology, or between the ideals of the nobility and the priesthood, the *auto* may present a legend which is secular and sacred at once. An example is the No drama of Japan, which with its unification of chivalric and otherworldly symbols and its dreamy un-tragic, un-comic mood so strongly attracted Yeats. It is interesting to see how Yeats, both in his theory of the *anima mundi* and in his desire to get his play as physically close to the audience as possible, reverts to the archaic idea of corporeal communion. In Greek drama, too, there is no sharp boundary line between the divine and the heroic protagonist. But in Christian societies we can see glimpses of a secular *auto*, a romantic drama presenting the exploits of a hero, which is closely related to tragedy, the end of a hero's exploit being eventually his death, but which in itself is neither tragic nor comic, being primarily spectacular.

Tamburlaine is such a play: there the relation between the hero's hybris and his death is more casual than causal. This genre has had varying luck: more in Spain, for instance, than in France, where the establishing of tragedy was part of an intellectual revolution. The two attempts in France to move tragedy back towards heroic romance, *Le Cid* and *Hernani*, each precipitated a big row. In Germany, on the other hand, it is clear that the actual genre of many plays by Goethe and Schiller is the heroic romance, however much affected they have been by the prestige of tragedy. In Wagner, who expands the heroic form all the way back to a sacramental drama of gods, the symbol of communion again occupies a conspicuous place, negatively in *Tristan*, positively in *Parsifal*. In proportion as it moves closer to tragedy and further from the sacred *auto*, drama tends to make less use of music. If we look at the earliest extant play of Aeschylus, *The Suppliants*, we can see that close behind it is a predominantly musical structure of which the modern counterpart would normally be the oratorio – it is perhaps possible to describe Wagner's operas as fermented oratorios.

In Renaissance England the audience was too bourgeois for a chivalric drama to get firmly established, and the Elizabethan secular *auto* eventually became the history-play.

With the history-play we move from spectacle to a more purely verbal drama, and the symbols of communion become much attenuated, although they are still there. The central theme of Elizabethan history is the unifying of the nation and the binding of the audience into the myth as the inheritors of that unity, set over against the disasters of civil war and weak leadership. One may even recognize a secular Eucharist symbol in the red and white rose, just as one may recognize in the plays that end by pointing to Elizabeth, like Peeler's *Arraignment of Paris*, a secular counterpart of a mystery play of the Virgin. But the emphasis and characteristic resolution of the history-play are in terms of continuity and the closing up both of tragic catastrophe and (as in the case of Falstaff) of the comic festival. One may compare Shaw's "chronicle play" of Saint Joan, where the end of the play is a tragedy, followed by an epilogue in which the rejection of Joan is, like the rejection of Falstaff, historical, suggesting continuity rather than a rounded finish.

The history merges so gradually into tragedy that we often cannot be sure when communion has turned into catharsis. *Richard II* and *Richard III* are tragedies insofar as they resolve on those defeated kings; they are histories insofar as they resolve on Boling-broke and Richmond, and the most one can say is that they lean toward history. *Hamlet* and *Macbeth* lean toward tragedy, but Fortinbras and Malcolm, the continuing characters, indicate the historical element in the tragic resolution. There seems to be a far less direct connection between history and comedy: the comic scenes in the histories are, so to speak, subversive. *Henry V* ends in triumph and marriage, but an action that kills Falstaff, hangs Bardolph and debases Pistol is not related to comedy in the way that *Richard II* is related to tragedy.

We are here concerned only with tragedy as a species of drama. Tragic drama derives from the *auto* its central heroic figure, but the association of heroism with downfall is due to the simultaneous presence of irony. The nearer the tragedy is to *auto*, the more closely associated the hero is with divinity; the nearer to irony, the more human the hero is, and the more the catastrophe appears to be a social rather than a cosmological event. Elizabethan tragedy shows a historical development from Marlowe, who presents his heroes more or less as demigods moving in a kind of social ether, to Webster, whose tragedies are almost clinical analyses of a sick society. Greek tragedy never broke completely from the *auto*, and so never developed a social form, though there are tendencies to it in Euripides. But whatever the proportions of heroism and irony, tragedy shows itself to be primarily a vision of the supremacy of the event or *mythos*. The response to tragedy is "this must be," or, perhaps more accurately, "this does happen": the event is primary, the explanation of it secondary and variable.

As tragedy moves over towards irony, the sense of inevitable event begins to fade out, and the sources of catastrophe come into view. In irony catastrophe is either arbitrary and meaningless, the impact of an unconscious (or, in the pathetic fallacy, malignant) world on conscious man, or the result of more or less definable social and psychological forces. Tragedy's "this must be" becomes irony's "this at least is," a concentration on foreground facts and a rejection of mythical superstructures. Thus the ironic drama is a vision of what in theology is called the fallen world, of simple humanity, man as natural man and in conflict with both human and non-human nature. In nineteenth-century drama the tragic vision is often identical with the ironic one, hence nineteenth-century tragedies tend to be either *Schicksal* dramas dealing with the arbitrary ironies of fate, or (clearly the more rewarding form) studies of the frustrating and smothering of human activity by the combined pressure of a reactionary society without and a disorganized soul within. Such irony is difficult to sustain in the theatre because it tends toward a stasis of action. In those parts of Chekhov, notably the last act of *The Three Sisters*, where the characters one by one withdraw from each other into their subjective prison-cells, we are coming about as close to pure irony as the stage can get.

The ironic play passes through the dead center of complete realism, a pure mime representing human life without comment and without imposing any sort of dramatic form beyond what is required for simple exhibition. [...]

Ironic comedy presents us of course with "the way of the world," but as soon as we find sympathetic or even neutral characters in a comedy, we move into the more familiar comic area where we have a group of humors outwitted by the opposing group. Just as tragedy is a vision of the supremacy of *mythos* or thing done, and just as irony is vision of *ethos*, or character individualized against environment, so comedy is a vision of *dianoia*, a significance which is ultimately social significance, the establishing of a desirable society. As an imitation of life, drama is, in terms of *mythos*, conflict; in terms of *ethos*, a representative image; in terms of *dianoia*, the final harmonic chord revealing the tonality under the narrative movement, it is community. The further comedy moves from irony, the more it becomes what we here call ideal comedy, the vision not of the way of the world, but of what you will, life as you like it. Shakespeare's main interest is in getting away from the son–father conflict of ironic comedy towards a vision of a serene community, a vision most prominent in *The Tempest*. Here the action is polarized around a younger and an older man working in harmony together, a lover and a benevolent teacher.

The next step brings us to the extreme limit of social comedy, the symposium, the structure of which is, as we should expect, clearest in Plato, whose Socrates is both teacher and lover, and whose vision moves toward an integration of society in a form like that of the symposium itself, the dialectic festivity which, as is explained in the opening of the *Laws*, is the controlling force that holds society together. It is easy to see that Plato's dialogue form is dramatic and has affinities with comedy and mime; and while there is much in Plato's thought that contradicts the spirit of comedy as we have outlined it, it is significant that he contradicts it directly, tries to kidnap it, so to speak. It seems almost a rule that the more he does this, the further he moves into pure exposition or dictatorial monologue and away from drama. The most dramatic of his dialogues, such as *Euthydemus*, are regularly the most indecisive in philosophical "position."

In our own day Bernard Shaw has tried hard to keep the symposium in the theatre. His early manifesto, *The Quintessence of Ibsenism*, states that a play should be an intelligent discussion of a serious problem, and in his preface to *Getting Married* he remarks approvingly on the fact that it observes the unities of time and place. For comedy of Shaw's type tends to a symposium form which occupies the same amount of time in its action that the audience consumes in watching it. However, Shaw discovered in practice that what emerges from the theatrical symposium is not a dialectic that compels to a course of action or thought, but one that emancipates from formulated principles of conduct. The shape of such a comedy is very clear in the bright little sketch *In Good King Charles's Golden Days*, where even the most highly developed human types, the saintly Fox and the philosophical Newton, are shown to be comic humors by the mere presence of other types of people. Yet the central symposium figure of the haranguing lover bulks formidably in *Man and Superman,* and even the renunciation of love for mathematics at the end of *Back to Methusaleh* is consistent with the symposium spirit. [...]

The further comedy moves from irony, and the more it rejoices in the free movement of its happy society, the more readily it takes to music and dancing. As music and scenery increase in importance, the ideal comedy crosses the boundary line of spectacular drama and becomes the masque. In Shakespeare's ideal comedies, especially *A Midsummer Night's Dream* and *The Tempest,* the close affinity with the masque is not hard to see. The masque – or at least the kind of masque that is nearest to comedy, and which we shall here call the ideal masque – is still in the area of *dianoia*: it is usually a compliment to the audience, or an important member of it, and leads up to an idealization of the society represented by that audience. Its plots and characters are fairly stock, as they exist only in relation to the significance of the occasion.

It thus differs from comedy in its more intimate attitude to the audience: there is more insistence on the connection between the audience and the community on the stage. The members of a masque are ordinarily disguised members of the audience, and there is a final gesture of surrender when the actors unmask and join the audience in a dance. The ideal masque is in fact a myth-play like the *auto,* to which it is related much as comedy is to tragedy. It is designed to emphasize, not the ideals to be achieved by discipline or faith, but ideals which are desired or considered to be already possessed. Its settings are seldom remote from magic and fairyland, from Arcadian and visions of earthly Paradise. It uses gods freely, like the *auto,* but possessively, and without imaginative subjection. In Western drama, from the Renaissance to the end of the eighteenth century, masque and ideal comedy make great use of Classical mythology, which the audience is not obliged to accept as "true."

The rather limited masque throws some light on the structure and characteristics of its two far more important and versatile neighbors. For the masque is flanked on one side by the musically organized drama which we call opera, and on the other by a scenically organized drama, which has now settled in the movie. Puppet-plays and the vast Chinese romances where, as in the movie, the audience enters and leaves unpredictably, are examples of pre-camera scenic masques. Both opera and movie are, like the masque, proverbial for lavish display, and part or the reason for it in the movie is that many movies are actually bourgeois myth-plays, as half a dozen critics suddenly and almost simultaneously discovered a few years ago. The predominance of the private life of the actor in the imaginations of many moviegoers may perhaps have some analogy with the consciously assumed disguise of the masque. [...]

For our next step we must return to the masque proper. The further comedy moves from irony, the less social power is allowed to the humors. In the masque, where the ideal society is still more in the ascendant, the humors become degraded into the uncouth figures of the Jonsonian antimasque, who are said to be descended from a dramatic form far older than the rest of the masque. Farce, being a non-mimetic form of comedy, has a natural place in the masque, though in the ideal masque its natural place is that of a rigorously controlled interlude. In *The Tempest,* a comedy so profound that it seems to draw the whole masque into itself, Stephano and Trinculo are comic humors and Caliban an antimasque figure, and the group shows the transition very clearly. The main theme of the masque involves gods, fairies, and personifications of virtues; the figures of the antimasque thus tend to become demonic, and dramatic characterization begins to split into an antithesis of virtue and vice, god and devil, fairy and monster. The tension between them partly accounts for the importance of the theme of magic in the masque. At the comic end this magic is held by the benevolent side, as in *The Tempest*; but as we move further away from comedy, the conflict becomes increasingly serious, and the antimasque figures less ridiculous and more sinister, possessed in their turn of powers of enchantment. This is the stage represented by *Comus*, which is very close to the open conflict of good and evil in the morality play. With the morality play we pass into another area of masque which we shall here call the archetypal masque, the prevailing form of most twentieth-century highbrow drama, at least in continental Europe, as well as of many experimental operas and unpopular movies.

The ideal masque tends to individualize its audience by pointing to the central member of it: even the movie audience, sitting in the dark in small units (usually of two), is a relatively individualized one. A growing sense of loneliness is noticeable as we move away from comedy. The archetypal masque, like all forms of spectacular drama, tends to detach its settings from time and space, but instead of the Arcadias of the ideal masque, we find ourselves frequently in a sinister limbo, like the threshold of death in *Everyman*, the sealed underworld crypts of Maeterlinck, or the nightmares of the future in expressionist plays. As we get nearer the rationale of the form, we see that the *auto* symbol of communion in one body is reappearing, but in a psychological and subjective form, and without gods. The action of the archetypal masque takes place in a world of human types, which at its most concentrated becomes the interior of the human mind. This is explicit even in the old moralities, like *Mankynd* and *The Castle of Perseverance*, and at least implicit in a good deal of Maeterlinck, Pirandello, Andreyev, and Strindberg.

Naturally, with such a setting, characterization has to break down into elements and fragments of personality. This is why I call the form the archetypal masque, the word archetype being in this context used in Jung's sense of an aspect of the personality capable of dramatic projection. Jung's persona and anima and counsellor and shadow throw a great deal of light on the characterization of modern allegorical, psychic, and expressionist dramas, with their circus barkers and wraith-like females and inscrutable sages and obsessed demons. The abstract entities of the morality play and the stock types of the commedia dell' arte (this latter representing one of the primitive roots of the genre) are similar constructions.

A sense of confusion and fear accompanies the sense of loneliness: Maeterlinck's early plays are almost dedicated to fear, and the constant undermining of the distinction between illusion and reality, as mental projections become physical bodies and vice versa, splits the action up into a kaleidoscopic chaos of reflecting mirrors. The mob scenes of German expressionist plays and the mechanical fantasies of the Capeks show the same disintegration at work in a social context. From the generic point of view, one of the most interesting archetypal plays is Andreyev's powerful *The Black Maskers*, in which its author saw reflected not only the destruction of an individual's *nobile castello*, which is its explicit theme, but the whole social collapse of modern Russia. This play distinguishes two groups of dissociative elements of personality, one group connected with self-accusation and the other with the death-wish, and it exhibits the human soul as a castle possessed by a legion of demons. It is evident that the further the archetypal masque gets from the ideal masque, the more clearly it reveals itself as the emancipated antimasque, a revel of satyrs who have got out of control. The progress of sophisticated drama appears to be towards an *anagnorisis* or recognition of the most primitive of all dramatic forms.

At the far end of the archetypal masque, where it joins the *auto*, we reach the point indicated by Nietzsche as the point of the birth of tragedy, where the revel of satyrs impinges on the appearance of a commanding god, and Dionysos is brought into line with Apollo. We may call this fourth cardinal point of drama the epiphany, the dramatic apocalypse or separation of the divine and the demonic, a point directly opposite the mime, which presents the simply human mixture. This point is the dramatic form of the point of epiphany, most familiar as the point at which the Book of Job, after describing a complete circuit from tragedy through symposium, finally ends. Here the two monsters behemoth and leviathan replace the more frequent demonic animals.

The Classical critics, from Aristotle to Horace, were puzzled to understand why a disorganized ribald farce like the satyr-play should be the source of tragedy, though they were clear that it was. In medieval drama, where the progression through sacred and heroic *auto* to tragedy is so much less foreshortened, the development is plainer. The most clearly epiphanic form of scriptural drama is the Harrowing of Hell play, which depicts the triumph of a divine redeemer over demonic resistance. The devils of that play are the Christian forms of figures very like the Greek satyrs, and dramatic groups generically very close to the satyrs are never far from any scriptural play that deals directly with Christ, whether tamed and awed as in the *Secunda Pastorum*, or triumphantly villainous, as in the crucifixion and Herod plays. And just as Greek tragedy retained and developed the satyr-play, so Elizabethan tragedy retains a satyric counterpoint in its clown scenes and the farcical underplots of *Faustus* and many later tragedies. The same element provides those superb episodes of the porter in *Macbeth*, the grave-diggers in *Hamlet*, and the serpent-bearer in *Antony and Cleopatra*, which so baffled Classically-minded critics who had forgotten about the satyr-play. Perhaps we could make more dramatic sense out of *Titus Andronicus* if we could see it as an unharrowed hell, a satyr-play of obscene and gibbering demons.

The two nodes of the scriptural play are Christmas and Easter: the latter presents the triumphant god, the former the quiet virgin mother who gathers to herself the processional masque of the kings and shepherds. This figure is at the opposite end of the masque from the watching queen or peeress of an ideal masque, with the virtuous but paralyzed Lady of *Comus* halfway between. A female figure symbolizing some kind of reconciling unity and order appears dimly at the end of the great panoramic masques of *Faust* and *Peer Gynt*, the "eternal feminine" of the former having some of its traditional links. Modern examples of the same epiphanic form range from Claudel's Annunciation play to Yeats's *Countess Cathleen*, where the heroine is really a female and Irish Jesus, sacrificing herself for her people and then cheating the devils by the purity of her nature, very much as in the pre-Anselm theory of the atonement. As Yeats remarks, in a note, the story represents one of the supreme parables of the world.

Notes

1   N. Frye, *Anatomy of Criticism* (Princeton: Princeton University Press, 1957), 342.
2   The medieval Towneley cycle consisted of 32 plays performed during Corpus Christi Day. – Editor's note.

Chapter 40

Eugène Ionesco (1909–1994)

Eugène Ionesco was one of the leading playwrights of the Theatre of the Absurd. Along with Samuel Beckett he emblazoned the spirit of the European avant-garde with his dramas of absurdity, comedy, and the irrational. His most famous plays were *The Lesson* (1951), *The Chairs* (1952), *Rhinoceros* (1960), and *Exit the King* (1962), which build on comic implausibility and absurd situations. In this essay he articulates the concepts of the avant-garde, a genre in which he belonged. Although reluctant to be pigeonholed, Ionesco nonetheless clarifies many of the nuances of the avant-garde that would influence the remainder of the century.

The Avant-Garde Theatre (1960)

I am, it seems, an avant-garde dramatist. It would even seem obvious since I am present here at discussions on the avant-garde theatre as a representative of this avant-garde. It is all entirely official.

But what does the term avant-garde mean? I am not a Doctor of Theatrology, nor Philosophy, nor Art: nor am I what is commonly called a "man-of-the-theatre." Perhaps I am a kind of mason, knowing certain laws of dramatic construction, but in an empirical or instinctive manner.

If I have formed certain ideas about the theatre, they refer above all to my theatre for they have sprung from my own creative experience: they are hardly normative, but rather descriptive. I hope, of course, that rules which apply to me will also apply to others, for the others are all contained in each one of us.

Eugène Ionesco, "The Avant-Garde Theatre," *Tulane Drama Review* 5.2 (1960), 44–53. © 1960 by Tulane Drama Review. Reprinted by permission of TDR/The Drama Review.

In any case, any laws of theatre which I may discover are provisional and mobile; they come after, not before, artistic creation. If I write a new play, my point of view may be profoundly modified. I may be obliged to contradict myself and I may no longer know whether I still think what I think.

I hope, nevertheless, that some fundamental principles may remain upon which I can lean consciously and instinctively. And here again I can only share with you a purely personal experience.

However, so that I would not make any serious blunders, I looked up the word "avant-garde" in my Larousse dictionary before I came. I found that the avant-garde, or the van-guard, "are the troops which precede an armed land, sea or air force and prepare the way for its entry into action."

Thus, by analogy, in the theatre, the avant-garde would consist of a small shock force of dramatists and sometimes directors, followed at a certain distance by the main body of actors, playwrights and producers. This analogy is perhaps valid when we see what Alberes has stated in his book, *L'Aventure intellectuelle du XXe Siècle:* "by a phenomenon which no one has troubled to explain (and which indeed would seem difficult) literary sensibility (and artistic of course) has always, in our century, preceded the historic events which were later to corroborate them." Indeed Baudelaire, Kafka, Pirandello ("who took apart the machinery of lofty family sentiments, etc. . . ."), and Dostoyevsky were regarded with good reason as writer-prophets.

Thus the avant-garde would seem to be an artistic and cultural phenomenon of a precursory nature, which tallies with its literal meaning. It would be a kind of "pre-style" indicating and pointing the direction of a change which will triumph in the end, a change which will truly change everything. This amounts to saying that the avant-garde cannot generally be recognized until after the event, when they have succeeded, when the avant-garde writers and artists have acquired a following, when they have founded a prevailing school, a cultural style which is recognized and will conquer an age. Consequently, one can only see that there has been an avant-garde when it no longer exists as such, when it has in fact become a rear guard, when it has been joined and even outstripped by the main army. But an army marching towards what?

I prefer to define the avant-garde in terms of opposition and rupture. While most writers, artists and thinkers believe they belong to their time, the revolutionary playwright feels he is running counter to his time. As a matter of fact, thinkers, artists and so on, after a certain time only make use of ossified forms; they feel they are becoming more and more firmly established in some ideological, artistic, or social order which to them seems up to date but which in fact is already tottering and yawning with unsuspected cracks. By the very force of circumstances any system, the moment it is established, is already outworn. As soon as a form of expression becomes recognized, it is already out of date. A thing once spoken is already dead, reality lies somewhere beyond it and the thought has become petrified, so to speak. A manner of speaking – and therefore a manner of being – once accepted is already unacceptable. An avant-garde man is like an enemy inside a city which he is bent on destroying, against which he rebels; for like any system of government, an established form of expression is also a form of oppression. The avant-garde man is the opponent of an existing system. He is a critic of, and not an apologist for, what exists now. It is easy to criticize the past particularly when the prevailing regime encourages you to do so; but this is only to sanctify ossification and kowtow to tyranny or convention.

I am well aware that I have not thrown any light on the problem. The word avant-garde in fact is used with various meanings. It can quite simply be identified with the "art theatre," that is the theatre which is more literary, exacting and daring than the kind known in France as the "théâtre de boulevard." This, it seems, is what Georges Pillement meant when, in his theatre anthology published in 1946, he divided dramatists into two categories: the writers of the "comédie de boulevard" among whom Robert de Flers ranked with François de Curel; and those of the avant-garde which included Claude-André Puget as well as Passeur, Jean Anouilh, and Giraudoux. This seems rather strange today for the works of these writers are now practically classics. But Maurice Donnay, in his time, as well as [Georges] Bataille were avant-garde writers since they expressed a rupture, a new departure and an opposing force. They finally merged into the theatrical tradition and that is what must happen to every good avant-gardist. In any case they represented a protest and the proof of this was that at the outset these authors were given a bad reception by the critics, who protested at their protestations. The protestation of an avant-garde dramatist can be a reaction against Realism when that is the most prevalent and abused form of expression in the theatre; it can be a protest against a certain Symbolism when that Symbolism has become abused, arbitrary, and no longer captures reality. In any case what we call the avant-garde theatre, which coexists with the conventional theatre, seems by its expression, its questing nature and difficulty to be of greater value. For the very reason that it is exacting and difficult to follow, it is obvious that before it becomes generally accepted it can only be the theatre of a minority. The avant-garde theatre, and indeed all new arts and theatre, must be unpopular.

It is certain that any attempt to introduce new ideas will be met on all sides by conformities and mental apathy. Obviously it is not essential that a dramatist should wish to be unpopular, but neither is it essential that he should wish to be popular. His efforts, his creative work are above such considerations. Either this theatre will always remain unpopular, will never be recognized and so will never exist as theatre or it will in time, naturally and by the force of circumstances, become popular and generally recognized.

Today everyone understands the elementary laws of physics or geometry which must certainly have been at first only understood by learned men who never thought of offering the public popular geometry or physics. They did not express the truth of a certain narrow caste but truths which were undeniably objective. The question of the similarities which may exist between science and art does not fall within my province. We all know that the differences between these two domains of the mind are far greater than the similarities. However, each new author seeks to fight in the name of truth. Boileau wished to express truth. In his foreword to *Cromwell*, Victor Hugo considered that Romantic Art rather than Classical contained more truth and was more complex. The aim of Realism and Naturalism was also to extend the realms of reality or reveal new and still unknown aspects of it. Symbolism and later Surrealism were further attempts to reveal and express hidden realities.

The question then is simply for an author to discover truths and to state them. And the manner of stating them is naturally unfamiliar for this statement itself is the truth for him. He can only speak it for himself. It is by speaking it for himself that he speaks it for others. Not the other way round.

If I should consider the popular theatre, I run the risk of imparting truths which have not been discovered by myself, but which have already been imparted to me by others and which I would only be passing on at second hand. The artist is not a pedagogue, neither is he a demagogue. Dramatic creation satisfies a mental need, this need must be sufficient in itself. A tree is a tree, it does not need my permission to be a tree, the tree is not faced with the problem of being a certain kind of tree in order to be recognized, as a tree. It does not make itself explicit. It exists and is made manifest by its very existence. It does not seek to make itself understood. It does not assume a more understandable form; otherwise it would no longer be a tree but only the explanation of a tree. In the same way, a work of art is sufficient in itself and I can easily imagine theatre without a public. The public will come by itself, and will recognize this theatre as it recognizes a tree as a tree.

The songs of Béranger were far more popular than the poems of Rimbaud, who was quite incomprehensible in his day. Should one for that reason exclude Rimbaud's poetry? Eugène Sue was extremely popular. Proust was not. He was not understood. He did not speak to everyone. He simply contributed his kind of truth towards the development of literature and the mind. Should one debar Proust and recommend Sue? Today it is Proust who offers a wealth of truth, it is Eugène Sue who seems empty. How fortunate that the authorities did not forbid Proust to write in Proustian language!

A creative idea can only be expressed by a means of expression which is suited to it, so much so that idea and means of expression are one and the same.

There is popular theatre and popular theatre. We think, erroneously, that popular theatre must be theatre for those who are lacking in intellect: but there is the kind which is intended to instruct, a theatre for our edification, the tool of a political creed, of some ideology of which it is the duplicate – a useless and "conformist" repetition.

A work of art and a dramatic work too, therefore, must be a primary instinct, profound or vast according to the talent or genius of the artist, but a truly primary instinct which owes nothing to anything but itself. But in order that it may rise up and take shape, one must let the imagination run free above external and secondary considerations such as those of its future, its popularity or its need to express an ideology. In this flowering of the imagination, meanings emerge by themselves and they are eloquent for some and less so for others. For my part I cannot understand how anyone can have the ambition to speak for everybody, to possess the unanimous support of the public while, within one class of people for instance, some prefer strawberries, others cheese, some prefer aspirin for their headaches, others bismuth for their stomach-aches. In any case, I don't worry about the support of the public. Or perhaps I do, but only when the play has been written and I am considering the question of how to place it. Support comes or doesn't come, quite naturally. It is quite certain that one can never speak for everybody. At the most, one can speak on behalf of a large majority and in this case one can only produce demagogic or ready-made drama. If you wish to speak to everybody, you will really speak to no one: the things which interest everybody in general have very little interest for each man in particular. Besides which, a creative work of art is, by its very novelty, aggressive, spontaneously aggressive, it strikes out at the public, against the vast majority; it rouses indignation by its nonconformity which is, in itself, a form of indignation. This is inevitable for it does not keep to the beaten track but opens up a new one, cutting across country, alone. This is the sense in which a work of art is unpopular, as I have already said. But new art is only apparently unpopular; it is not so in essence, it is unpopular only because of its unfamiliarity. The so-called popular theatre is actually far more unpopular. It is a theatre which is arrogantly imposed throughout by a ruling aristocracy, a special class of initiates who know or think they know in advance what the public needs. They even say to the public: "You must only need what we want you to need and you must only think in the way we think." Paradoxically, the free work of art, by its individualistic character, despite its unusual appearance, alone springs from men's hearts, through a man's heart; it is the only thing which really expresses the people.

It is said that the theatre is in danger and in a critical state. This is due to many reasons. Very soon dramatists will be made apostles of all kinds of theologies, they will not be free, they will be told only to defend, attack or praise this or that. If they are not apostles then they are pawns. Elsewhere the theatre is the prisoner not of ideologies but conventions, taboos, hardened mental habits, fixations. When the theatre could be the place of the greatest freedom, of the wildest imaginings, it has become that of the greatest constraint, of a rigid and set system of conventions which may be called "realist" or otherwise. We are afraid of too much humor (and humor is freedom). We are afraid of freedom of thought, of a play which is too tragic or too despairing. Optimism and hope are compulsory under pain of death. And what is sometimes labeled the absurd is only the denunciation of the ridiculous nature of a language which is empty of substance, sterile, made up of clichés and slogans; of theatre-that-is-known in-advance. I personally would like to bring a tortoise onto the stage, turn it into a racehorse, then into a hat, a song, a dragoon and a fountain of water. One can dare anything in the theatre and it is the place where one dares the least.

I want no other limits than the technical limits of the stage machinery. People will say that my plays are music-hall or circus. So much the better: let's bring in the circus! One can accuse the dramatist of being arbitrary, but the theatre is the place where one can be arbitrary. As a matter of fact, it is not arbitrary. The imagination is not arbitrary, it is revealing. Without the guarantee of total freedom, the dramatist will never be himself, he will say nothing except what has already been formulated: my own intention was not to recognize any laws except those of my imagination and since the imagination has laws that is a further proof that finally it is not arbitrary.

It has been said that what distinguishes man from the other animals is that he is the animal that laughs; he is above all else the animal that creates. He introduces into the world things which were not there before: temples and rabbit-hutches, wheelbarrows, locomotives, symphonies, poems, cathedrals and cigarettes. The usefulness of all these things is often only a pretext. What is the use of existing? – to exist. What is the use of a flower? – to be a flower. Of what use is a temple or a cathedral? To house the faithful? I doubt it, since the temples are no longer used and we still admire them. They serve to reveal to us the laws of architecture and perhaps of universal construction which are apparently reflected in our mind since the mind discovers these laws within itself. But the theatre is dying for lack of courage. We seem no longer to realize that a world we invent cannot be false. It can only be false if I want to fabricate a truth and imitate truth, for in so doing I fabricate a false truth. I am conscious of being true when I invent and imagine. Nothing is more rational than the imagination. I could even go so far as to say that to me it is the world which seems irrational, which is growing irrational and which baffles my understanding. The laws to which I try continually to adapt and submit it, I find in my own mind. But this again lies outside our province.

When an author writes something, a play for instance, he has, as I have said, the clear or confused impression that he is fighting a battle, that if he has something to say, it is because others have not said that thing properly, or that they no longer know how to say it. He wishes to say something new, otherwise why would he write? To say what he has to say, to impose his world is itself the battle. A tree in order to grow must overcome the resistance of matter. For an author, this matter is the already-done, the already-said. He writes not for or against something but in spite of something: In this sense, each artist is to varying degrees and according to his powers, a rebel. If he copies, if he reproduces, if he exemplifies, he is nothing. It therefore seems that a poet is fighting against a tradition, but in most cases involuntarily, by the very fact of his existence.

To the extent that a poet feels that the language no longer corresponds to reality, no longer expresses a truth, he must endeavor to capture reality, to express it better, in a way which is more pungent, more eloquent, clearer, more precise and adequate. By this means, he overtakes and modernizes a living tradition which had got lost. An avant-garde dramatist can feel, and in any case this is his wish, that he is making a better attempt than others around him. He is making a real attempt to return to the source. But what source? That of the theatre. A return to an inner ideal of the theatre; for it is in oneself that one discovers the deep and permanent foundations of theatre.

Pascal discovered within himself the principles of geometry, Mozart as a child discovered in himself the rudiments of his music. Very few artists, of course, can measure up to the stature of these two giants. Nevertheless, it seems certain to me that one hasn't got what is so aptly called "theatre in the blood" if one cannot reinvent a little oneself. I am also quite certain that if all libraries were swallowed up in some great cataclysm together with all museums, those who escaped would sooner or later rediscover for themselves painting, music, and theatre which, like bodily functions, are as natural, necessary and instinctive as breathing. He who does not possess even to a slight degree the function of theatre is not a man of the theatre. To discover it one must perhaps have a certain ignorance, a certain naïveté, a boldness which springs from this naïveté, but a naïveté which is not simplicity of mind, and an ignorance which does not rule out knowledge but which assimilates and rejuvenates it. A work of art is not devoid of ideas. Since it is life or the expression of life, ideas are emanated from it: the work of art does not emanate from an ideology. The new dramatist is one who, contradictorily, endeavors to overtake what is most ancient: new language and subject matter in a dramatic structure which aims at being clearer, more stripped of inessentials and more purely theatrical; the rejection of traditionalism to rediscover tradition; a synthesis of knowledge and invention, of the real and the imaginary, of the particular and the universal or as they say now, of the individual and the collective; the expression, over and above classes of that which transcends them. By expressing my deepest feelings, I express my deepest humanity. I become one with all others, spontaneously, over and above all the barriers of cast and different psychologies. I express my solitude and become one with all other solitudes; my joy at existing or my surprise at being are those of everyone even if, for the moment, everyone refuses to recognize it. A play such as *The Quare Fellow* by the Irish writer Brendan Behan was the fruit of his own experiences: prison. Nevertheless I feel concerned, for this prison becomes all prisons, it becomes the world and all its classes of people. Inside this English prison there are of course prisoners and there are warders. That is slaves and masters, the rulers and the ruled. They are all enclosed within the same walls. The prisoners hate their warders, the warders scorn their prisoners. But the prisoners also loathe each other, and neither do the warders agree amongst themselves. If there were just the simple conflict between the warders on the one hand and the prisoners on the other; if the play were limited to this obvious conflict, there would be nothing new, profound, or revealing, but a coarse and crudely sketched reality. But this play shows that reality is far more complex. A man in this prison is to be executed. The condemned man does not appear on the stage. He is, however, present in our consciousness and continually haunts us. He has the leading role. Or rather death has the leading role. Warders and prisoners feel together this presence of death. The play's deep humanity dwells in the terrible communion of this haunting thought, this agony which is that of all, above the category of warders or prisoners. It is a communion beyond differences, an almost unconscious feeling of fellowship of which the dramatist makes us conscious. The common identity of all men is revealed to us. This could help to draw the enemy camps together. Indeed the prisoners and warders suddenly appear to us as mortals, united and governed by the same problem which surpasses all others. Here is popular theatre indeed; one of communion in the same agony. It is an old play for it deals with a fundamental and age-old problem. It is a new and localized play for it deals with a prison at a certain moment in time in a particular country.

At the beginning of this century and in the 1920's in particular, a vast universal avant-garde movement was felt in all domains of the mind and human activity. An overthrowing of our mental habits. Modern painting from Klee to Picasso, from Matisse to Mondrian, from Cubism to Abstractionism expresses this overthrow, this revolution. It emerged in music and films and it affected architecture. Philosophy and psychology were transformed. Science (but I am not competent to speak on this subject) gave us a new vision of the world. A new style emerged and continues to emerge. An age is distinguished by its unity of style, a synthesis of various styles and so there are obvious similarities between architecture and poetry, mathematics and music. There is an essential unity between the Palace of Versailles and Cartesian thought, for instance. Literature and drama from André Breton to Maïakovski, from Marinetti to Tristan Tzara or Apollinaire, from the Expressionist drama to Surrealism, down to the most recent novels by Faulkner and Dos Passos and quite recently those of Nathalie Sarraute and Michel Butor, have all shared in this surge of this new life. But all literature did not follow this movement and in the theatre it seems to have been arrested in 1930. The theatre is the most behindhand. The avant-garde were halted at the theatre if not in literature. Wars, revolutions, Nazism and other forms of tyranny, dogmatism, and in some countries bourgeois inertia too, have prevented it developing for the moment. But it must be resumed. I myself hope to be one of the modest artisans who may restart this movement. Indeed, this abandoned avant-garde movement has not been outstripped but buried by the reactionary return of old dramatic formulas which sometimes dare to pretend they are new ones. The theatre is not of our age: it manifests a limited psychology, the light comedy style, bourgeois prudence and a realism which refuses to be called conventional but which really is a submission to dogmatism which is a menace to the artist.

The young generation of French film production is far more advanced than that of the theatre. Young film producers have been trained in film libraries and film clubs. This is where they have received their instruction. There they have seen art films; the great classics of the cinema, avant-garde films, uncommercial and nonpopular, many of which have never been shown in big cinemas or have only been shown for a short time because of their uncommercial nature. Although it is far more difficult for the theatre, it also needs these places for experiment, these laboratories protected from the superficiality of the general public. A danger in some countries, and still a necessary evil unfortunately, is the manager. He is a tyrant in this domain. The theatre must show a profit; to do so all boldness and creativeness must be eliminated so as not to upset anyone. A manager who is also a friend of mine once asked me to change everything in my plays and make them comprehensible. I asked him by what right he interfered with matters of dramatic construction which should only concern myself and my director: for it seemed to me that to pay money to produce a play was not sufficient reason to dictate conditions and alter my work. He replied that he represented the public. I replied that we had to wage war against the public and upon him, the manager. To wage war against or else to ignore.

We need a liberal State, befriending thought and art, believing in their necessity and the necessity for laboratories. Before an invention or a scientific theory is made known, it has been long prepared, tested out and thought out in the laboratories. I demand that dramatists should have the same opportunities as scientists for making experiments. One cannot say that a scientific discovery is, for that reason, unpopular. I do not think that the realities of the mind, welling up from the deepest part of my being, are unpopular. To have a following is not always to be popular. The aristocracy of a poet is not a false aristocracy as the aristocracy of a class is false. In France we have some exciting new dramatists: Jean Genet, Beckett, Vauthier, Pichette, Schéhadé, Audiberti, Ghelderode, who carry on the tradition, while opposing it, of Giraudoux, Anouilh, Jean-Jacques Bernard and many others. They are only points of departure for a possible development of a free and living theatre.

For the avant-garde stands for freedom.

Chapter 41

Jean-Paul Sartre (1905–1980)

Among the leading French philosophers, Jean-Paul Sartre must be considered existentialism's greatest advocate. Sartre was also a playwright whose works, like Ionesco's, influenced the avant-garde. He received the Nobel Prize for Literature in 1964. His major plays were *The Flies* (1943) and *No Exit* (1944). His philosophical work, *Being and Nothingness*, was widely read and disseminated. His first novel, *Nausea* (1938), examines the emptiness of living. In the absence of absolute values, one must look inward and engage in acts of creation to find fulfillment. During World War II, Sartre wrote *The Flies*, a revision of Euripides' *Orestes*, as an act of defiance against French occupation. In perhaps his most produced play, *No Exit* (*Huis clos* in French, meaning "behind closed doors," or "in camera" as it is used in legal terms), Sartre reiterates his existential philosophy. Inez, one of three characters locked in a room – their metaphoric hell – remarks: "One always dies too soon – or too late. And yet one's whole life is complete at that moment, with a line drawn neatly under it, ready for the summing up. You are – your life, and nothing more."[1] Sartre's works examine freedom and moral activism. In this essay Sartre was concerned with reversing the course of modern drama, which he perceived to have become the domain of the bourgeoisie. He considered the bourgeois life an entrapment, which, likewise Ibsen's dramas, caused a Faustian bargain: success and stability in exchange for passion.

Jean-Paul Sartre, "Beyond Bourgeois Theatre" (1960), tr. R. D. Reck, *Tulane Drama Review* 5.3 (March 1961), 3–11. © 1961 by Tulane Drama Review. Reprinted by permission of TDR/The Drama Review. From a lecture given at the Sorbonne, March 29, 1960. The full version of this lecture, titled "Epic Theater and Dramatic Theater," is contained in *Sartre on Theater*, ed. M. Contat and M. Rybalka (New York: Pantheon, 1976), 77–120.

Beyond Bourgeois Theatre (1960)

The bourgeoisie has been in control of the theatre for about 150 years now. First of all, it controls it by the price of land, which rose so sharply in the 19th century that, as you know, the workers left the city, resulting in buildings and entire quarters belonging to the bourgeois; the theatres are almost all located in the center of the city. The bourgeoisie controls the theatre by the price of tickets which rose steadily in order to make the theatre a profit-making enterprise. In France it also controls it by centralization, so that in just those cities where contact with a varied audience would be possible, plays do not come or come much later, on tour. Finally, it controls it through the critics. It is an error to contrast the newspaper critic with the public. The critic is the mirror of his public. If he writes nonsense, it is because the public which reads the newspaper will speak nonsense too; therefore, it would be futile to oppose one to the other....

...One deals here with an absolute control, the more because this same bourgeoisie, to scuttle a play, has merely to do one thing – namely, not to come. It is evident then that the dictatorship of the bourgeoisie has created a bourgeois theatre. Is this simply dangerous, this introduction of a too particular content, or has this dictatorship destroyed the very foundations of what the theatre should be? This is what we shall attempt to discover.

...A question immediately arises: why do men live surrounded by their own images? After all, they could very well not have any images. You remember that Baudelaire used to speak of the "tyranny of human passion." Sometimes it is so tiring to submit to this tyranny all day. My God, why must we also have portraits in our room, why must we see representations of ourselves in the theatre, why must we walk in the midst of statues which represent us, why must we go to the movies and always see ourselves again? There is a kind of endless repetition of oneself by people, by all of you and by myself, which is rather surprising. If one reflects on it, however, it is not so difficult to explain. I think that people live in the midst of their own images because they do not succeed in being real objects for themselves. Men are objects for others but they are not completely objects for themselves. Take an individual example, be it in the form of the experiment of the mirror which is so important in all of early childhood, be it in the errors of an animal who looks into a mirror, be it in the mistake of an adult who, in a dark room, suddenly sees someone in a mirror and does not notice that it is he. One comes to oneself as to an object, because one comes to oneself as to another. That is objectivity. As soon as you recognize yourself, you are no longer an object. In fact, one does not see one's own face as one sees that of others. One sees it with privileged elements because one has a profound interest in the one who is there; it is impossible to seize him with this absolutely cold and formal bond which is simple sight. One seizes him by a kind of participation.

...What I say about the individual is valid for any social group as well. Men cannot see themselves from the outside, and the real reason for this is that in order truly to seize a man as object, one would both have, at the same time and contradictorily, to understand and not to understand his actions. For you evidently cannot consider that you have before you a truly objectified man, someone of whom you can say, he's really someone I know, if you don't know him through an understanding of what he seeks, what he wants, beginning with his future, with his most personal efforts to attain his ends. But if you know him by understanding him, this also means that, whatever disapprobations you may feel with regard to his conduct on other levels, you share his aims, you are in a completely closed world or rather, if you wish, not closed but limited, limited by itself and from which you can never escape.... If, on the other hand, you cease to understand his aims and if he becomes, at that moment, a being who is uniquely comprehensible, or at least explicable by the order of things, at that very moment you have lost the man, you have the insect. So that between this understanding of man in which man is never wholly an object but rather a quasi-object for other men, and this refusal to understand, there is no place for men to know one another completely, as objects. One might be a total object for the ants or for the angels, but not as a man for men.

... The theatre being an image, gestures are the image of action, and (here is something never said since the advent of bourgeois theatre and which must nevertheless be said) dramatic action is the action of characters. People always think that dramatic action means great gestures, bustle. No, that's not action; that's noise and tumult. Action, in the true sense of the word, is that of the character; there are no images in the theatre but the image of the act, and if one seeks the definition of theatre, one must ask what an act is, because the theatre can represent nothing but the act. Sculpture represents the form of the body, the theatre the act of this body. Consequently, what we want to recover when we go to the theatre is evidently ourselves, but ourselves not as we are, more or less poor, more or less proud of our youth and our beauty; rather to recover ourselves as we act, as we work, as we meet difficulties, as we are men who have rules and who establish rules for these actions. Unfortunately, as you see, we are very far at this moment from the bourgeois theatre; if what I say to you in no way resembles what has been playing on the stage for the last 150 years, except, of course, for a few exceptions, it is because the bourgeois theatre does not want any dramatic action. It desires, more precisely, neo-dramatic action; but it does not want the action of man to be represented, it wants the action of the author constructing events. In truth the bourgeoisie wants to have an image of itself represented, but – and here one understands why Brecht created his epic theatre, why he went completely in the other direction – an image which is pure participation; it absolutely does not want to be represented as a quasi-object. When it is totally object, that's not very agreeable.... The bourgeois theatre is therefore subjective, not because it shows what is going on inside the head of the character (often one does not see this at all), but because the bourgeoisie wants a representation of itself which is subjective. That is to say, it wants produced in the theatre an image of man according to its own ideology and not man seeking through this sort of world of individuals who see one another, of groups which form judgments about one another, because then, the bourgeoisie would be contested.

One recognizes what is human in the bourgeoisie by what is bad, since the reasoning usually is: it's human when someone has just committed a knavery, a cowardice; therefore, it is necessary that this nature be bad and it is necessary that it be immutable. I don't insist on that point, and you can see why: if man is bad, then that which counts is order, any order at all.... Besides, if human nature is bad and eternal, isn't it evident that no effort is necessary to achieve some progress.... But, to act, which is precisely the object of the theatre, is to change the world and in changing it, of necessity to change oneself. Fine. The bourgeoisie has changed the world profoundly, and now it no longer has any desire to be changed itself, above all from without. If it changes, it is in order to adapt itself, to keep what it has, and in this position what it asks of the theatre is not to be disturbed by the idea of action.... There can be no action, because in these plays the moving element, as in the philosophy of Aristotle, must be a rapid disturbance between two moments of calm.... In effect, in its plays the bourgeois theatre has replaced action with passion, and action such as it is known today in the theatre simply means a practical construction.

... Brecht felt that the distance between actors and audience was not great enough, that one tried much too much to *move* the audience, to touch them, and not enough to *show* them; in other words, too many participational relationships, too many images, not enough objectivity. In my opinion the bourgeois public is foolish not because it participates, but because it participates in an image which is the image of a fool.

... We have a number of plays today which, in good faith, use the expressionist themes again without realizing it. For example, the theme of Beckett, in *Waiting for Godot*, is a very remarkable thing. I find it the best play since 1945, but one must admit that it is expressionist and that it is at the same time pessimist.... But it is a play which, at bottom, has a content pleasing to the bourgeois. In the same way, another recent play, Ionesco's *Rhinoceros*, is an expressionist play, since you have a man who becomes "a rhinoceros...." What does it mean to become a rhinoceros? Is it to become a fascist or a communist, or both? It is evident that if the bourgeois public is delighted with it, it must be both. Do you follow me? It is absolutely impossible to derive any meaning from Ionesco's play except that a great misfortune, a great peril of annihilation menaces the world and that, good heavens, the danger of contagion is very grave. [...] And why is there one man who resists? At least we could learn why, but no, we learn not even that. He resists because he is there. He resists because he is *Ionesco*: he represents Ionesco, he says I resist, and there he remains in the midst of the rhinoceroses, the only one to defend man without our being very sure if it might not be better to be a rhinoceros. Nothing has been proved to the contrary....

... I only mean to say that you always have the right to speak ill of the bourgeois as a man, but not as a bourgeois. That's the heart of the matter. The pessimism must be a total pessimism, a pessimism of inaction, it must be a pessimism which condemns all possibilities, all hopes, individuals. But if it is a moderate pessimism which simply says: the situation is not good, our ruling classes could do better than they do, etc.... Then that's no longer theatre, is it? That's subversion. I don't want you to think that pessimistic theatre is not bourgeois theatre. All the theatre I have just mentioned, of passivity, of permissiveness, of dead end and of evil, is bourgeois theatre.... If, on the contrary, we want to know what true theatre is, we must look in the opposite direction. This means that dramatic action is the narration of an action, is the staging of an action, one or several, of a few individuals or of a whole group – some people find themselves at the point of wanting something and they try to realize this desire. It makes no difference whether they succeed or fail; what is clear is that they must realize an attempt on the stage and that this is what we demand to see.

... From this arises a problem: the accessories are of no use. The settings are never of any use. One can never illuminate a place by some thing. That is not the director's role; these are merely bits of bravura. The only manner in which objects are born is in the gestures: the gesture of stabbing gives birth to the knife.

... The real problem is to know how to create real contradictions and a real dialectic of the object, the act and the man in the theatre. This is one of the most difficult things, precisely because the object comes after the action. In the films the object engenders the action, in the theatre it comes after, is engendered by it. Thus the whole problem of the dialectic of work is a real problem. In a film you can very easily recount the life of a mechanic in a documentary without boring anyone. Can you imagine this in the theatre? With a cardboard locomotive! With fireworks to move it! This is impossible, and yet what is the theatre to speak of if not of work, for in the final analysis action and work are the same thing. Here is the true inner contradiction of the theatre, and here is why it has not yet been resolved; because it is not enough, as the epic theatre shows us, to show contradictions which engender actions, actions which are not quite action because they bear too strongly the mark of their former maledictions. What we must find out is how to convey work in the theatre without having someone say, "Ah! You have worked hard, my friend." This has never been resolved.... There is a language particular to the theatre: it must be as irreversible as action; that is to say, not in a single sentence nor a single piece of dramatic prose spoken by an actor, must one be able to change the order of sentences at will.... The meaning of action is that it always radicalizes itself, unless the person acting dies or there is some brusque interference.... The action itself always goes to the end, it is irreversible, and if it is irreversible, the story too must be irreversible. But then you will ask me, "Is there nothing but action? Aren't there passions? Don't people love, and don't they hate? The theatre you describe is indeed hard and cold!" My answer is that, on the contrary, we will have only characters who are passionate, but only in the good sense of the word and not in the bad. The bad sense of the word passion means: blindly sufficient unto yourself and to others, so that you accomplish only foolishness and finally you wander away from your interests by massacring everyone around you; but you have understood nothing of what is happening to you: a fit of passion, people say, meaning a fit of foolishness. I have never met people who were like that. I have met people who were foolish, but foolishness and passion didn't necessarily go together and usually, when they were passionate, they were less foolish.

... Today it is impossible to distinguish in a general way the individual man from the social man in us, and the social man is, of necessity, at the base of all of our passions. Envy is an exigency, an extremely unfortunate passion but at the same time a feeling of right.... Passion is a way of sensing that one is right, of relating oneself to a social world of exigencies and values. To justify wanting to keep something, to take, destroy, construct something, passionate men do nothing but reason.... They are frequently very tiresome and Pirandello saw this: in Pirandello, every time a man comes to grips with a passion, he speaks endlessly, because the passion expresses itself through words, through calculations, through researches.... Vailland has said, "Italians are jurists," and I think passionate men are also jurists. In these conditions, passion appears when a right is infringed; the passion is a reciprocal phenomenon, in the sense that it is a social claim an individual makes when he decides to go to any length to realize it. From that moment, he must judge himself wronged by another and the other must judge himself wronged by this right. In effect, passion exists only in the form of contradictory demands.

... There is no need for psychology in the theatre. Psychology is a waste of time; because plays are long, the public has only a brief span of attention, and nuances have absolutely no interest. A play is something which hurls people into an undertaking. There is no need for psychology. Instead, there is need of delimiting very precisely what position, what situation each character can take, as a function of the causes and the anterior contradictions produced with respect to the principal action. In this way we will have a certain number of secondary or primary characters who will define themselves in the course of the action itself, and this action must be a common enterprise containing the contradictions of each and of all. For example, the very contradictions of war are marked by the contradictions of *Mother Courage* by Brecht, for she is a woman who detests war but thrives on it. War hurts her in every possible way but she cannot live without it, she is happy when it begins again and she is miserable when it continues – an admirable choice, to have taken the contradictions of war in order to see war.... Up to that point all goes smoothly. We all agree; the real problem arises in a different way, it arises the moment we ask ourselves: is it necessary that the object created thus, which is the play, be represented before the audience *qua* object or *qua* image? I mean: is it really necessary, under the pretext that the bourgeoisie used it as a weapon, to reject participation, which is the profound essence of the theatre? And if one does not suppress, must one at least reduce it so as to give a greater place to application and to understanding? Or must one consider the whole problem from a different angle, by refusing precisely to suppress this participation? The epic theatre aims to show us the individual adventure in the measure that it expresses the social adventure, and it aims at the same time, in a non-didactic way but based on didactic plays, to show us the implications and the reciprocal corrections beginning with a larger system, for example, modern capitalistic society.

There is a choice in Brecht. The proof is that in *The Caucasian Chalk Circle* he distinguishes levels of reality and levels of characters. One may debate whether there are political or moral judgments (or whatever you wish) made about these, but why declare *a priori* that certain characters, namely the bad ones, for example the brutes who are palace guards and who play cards all day and kill people as if they were nothing, why declare that they are to wear masks while the two or three characters from the people are not to wear any? At that moment, therefore, in the name of social contradictions we establish people who are actually empty bodies, who are eaten away inside and whom we need only represent with masks. Then another category which will be further away from the mask but still not quite human, and finally the serving girl and her fiancé who are a true woman and a true man almost without makeup and acting in a natural manner because they have a kind of plenitude. But what gives them more dimension, under the pretext that they do things in the direction of social utility, in the direction of their nature and their reality, than these guards? The latter are people no more or less dimensional, they are men. This way of conceiving things is too simple. It consists in saying that man is transformed into an abstract, it is a way of understanding Marxism which is not the good way. To put various realities into perspective indicates an extremely dubious ideological position. Such a thing must not be accepted. Reality cannot be put into perspective because it is not in perspective. It is, on other levels, but a man is a man, whatever he be, and there are no men who must be conceived more or less fully. If this is an esthetic point of view, it must be based on something and there it is founded on nothing. In my opinion, therefore, hierarchies are constructed and perspectives established which are not suitable. Besides, who proves to us that this way of suppressing the participation we seek is staked on a true philosophy? That Marx is the great philosopher of the 19th century, there is no doubt; that Brecht read Marx and that he knew him well, about this too there is no doubt. But there is also no doubt that there are 500 interpretations of Marx. Therefore, why declare that the theatre will be demonstrative if it is uncertain what is to be demonstrated? And if the theatre must limit itself to a few reflections, to carrying out certain very rudimentary thoughts found in Marx, the simplest, I see no need to create distanciation for this. If the theatre should go further, let it be revealed how, and what is to be shown us. . . . Which proves that there will not be a great number of epic theatres which will have varying meanings, for the difference between the epic and the dramatic theatre is that the author who creates dramatic theatre speaks in his own name, tells a story with his own interpretation, while the other is demonstrative and does not speak in his own words. He effaces himself at the same time that he effaces the audience before the play he presents. At this level, that's fine when it concerns a society which is in the process of disappearing and when one takes the point of view of one of the classes, for example the class which is rising or which wants to rise, and which is doing so on the shoulders of the others. It's fine in a period when, for example, Brecht can consider himself the spokesman of the oppressed classes and "judge-explicator" of the bourgeoisie to those classes. But now let us suppose that in East Germany, for example, Brecht had had the opportunity of speaking of East Germany as well.... Let us suppose that Brecht had wanted to explain, for himself or for his public, in what ways there are also contradictions in socialist society. Would he have used the same method? Would one have seen functionaries guilty of a little negligence or of a total lack of imagination, would they have worn masks? Would one have seen them from outside and in the absurdity of their contradictions or, on the contrary, at that moment *with* their contradictions – for Brecht was honest, but from the inside, in sympathy with them. To explain another way, if we imagine the history of a functionary who has committed faults, errors which manifest the contradictions of socialism, I am convinced that this character would have been treated by Brecht taking his aims into consideration, considering that he is a man who was defined from the outset by aims which must be understood, the same aims as Brecht, to accomplish the Revolution. When one does not share the aims of a social group one is defining, one can create a kind of distanciation and, as a result, show people from the outside. But when one is in a society whose principles one shares, this becomes more difficult and therefore one must say, "Yes, he is guilty, but the poor boy, you don't realize the problems there are.... Here are the contradictions...," etc. At that moment we are dealing with another theatre, a theatre which tries to understand. This is precisely the difference between the epic and the dramatic theatre: that in the dramatic one can try to understand, and in the epic as it now exists, one explains what one doesn't understand. I am not speaking of Brecht himself, but in a general way. Thus, if you wish, we shall say that if there is a clear insufficiency in the epic theatre, this is due to the fact that Brecht never resolved (and he never had any reason to do so), in the framework of Marxism, the problem of subjectivity and objectivity. And therefore he was never able to make a meaningful place in his work for subjectivity as it should be.

...The serious flaw in dramatic theatre is that it has sprung, all the same, from the bourgeois theatre, that it has sprung from means created by its individualism and is still poorly adapted to speaking of work. The other cannot do this either, but it is quite evident that it would be a pity to renounce one or the other of these branches and say that each author may not seek, if he wishes, to create an epic or a truly dramatic drama. In these conditions it seems that all the forces which the young theatre can marshal against the bourgeois plays which we have now must be united, and that there is, in short, no true antagonism between the dramatic form and the epic form, except that one of them draws toward the quasi-objectivity of the object, which is man. The error here lies in believing that one can present a society-object to the audience, while the other form, if uncorrected, would go too far in the direction of sympathy with the aim of objectivity, and thus would risk falling to the bourgeois side. Therefore, I believe that today the problem can be pinpointed between these two forms of theatre.

Note

1   J.-P. Sartre, *No Exit and Three Other Plays*, tr. S. Gilbert (New York: Vintage, 1989), 43.

Part IV

1960–1980

If the essays of the previous section were concerned with the idea of tragedy, existential or otherwise, the essays in this section either abandon the notion of tragedy or consider it as something other than its previous incarnation. The revolutionary ferment of the 1960s influenced playwrights globally, fostering a theatre of the absurd, a term coined by Martin Esslin (see the opening essay in this section). Dance scholar Sally Banes put it best when she said that the "concreteness of existence, the interest in the everyday actions people practice, the question of identity, both individual and collective, that were topics of these philosophical systems ... were appropriate questions for modernist artists after the middle of the twentieth century." In an effort to uncover the core of artistic experimentation, "Poetry, music, theater, and dance stressed performance more than the literary aspect of their forms, aspiring to more immediacy, more 'presentness,' more concrete experience."[1] Absurdist theatre turned to themes of incoherence and the illusion of human agency. Others, however, particularly theorists from oppressed groups, attempted to assert agency, self-determination, and social relevancy (Luis Valdez, for instance; see Chapter 55).

By the 1960s, the first stirrings of the revolt against modernist orthodoxy in theatre had been felt, although it would be several years before postmodernism and poststructuralism became widely accepted. Nevertheless, while poststructuralism was still under the influence of figureheads in linguistics such as Ferdinand de Saussure, Roman Jakobson, and Kenneth Burke (see Chapter 48), and in anthropology (Claude Lévi-Strauss), in other areas, especially psychology (Jacques Lacan), hermeneutics (Paul Ricœur), Marxism (Louis Althusser), and epistemology (Michel Foucault), a transition was underway. Structuralist thinkers emphasized an object in relation to other objects. Unlike the existentialists, New Critics, and other modernists, structuralists focused on analogies and comparisons. Broadly construed, structuralism, writes Robert Scholes, "is a way of looking for reality not in individual things but in relationships among them."[2] Structuralism stressed what Peter Caws calls "an engagement with the world, an active participation in significant activity, which in structuring the world will bring the subject into equilibrium with it."[3] Like semiotics, structuralism analyzes the creation of transforming symbols; the process of structuralism, writes Terence Hawks, "is not static" but "structuring," that is, "the structure must be capable of *transformational* procedures, whereby new material is constantly processed by and through it."[4] In theatre, the process involves the theatrical signs – gesture, costume, design – that can be interpreted from several vantage points: as metaphor, metonymy, symbol, allegory, analogy, and so forth.

During this period binary analysis shifted from a duality to multiplicity. "Poststructuralism," primarily led by Jacques Derrida, derived its meaning from structuralism's comparatives but broke from the binary or one-to-one relationship. François Dosse writes in his *History of Structuralism* that the "various binary couples – signifier/signified, nature/culture, voice/writing, perceptible/intelligible – that compose the very instrument of structural analysis were," under poststructuralism, "put into question, pluralized, disseminated in an infinite game that peeled, disjoined, and dissected the meaning of words, tracking down every master word, every transcendence." This transition resulted in a "whole Derridean language," yielding a "destabilized traditional opposition by bringing undecidables into play as veritable units of simulacrum, organizers of a new, carnivalesque order of reason."[5]

The shift from structuralism to poststructuralism in theatre criticism is evidenced by Jan Kott's signatory book, *Shakespeare Our Contemporary* (1964). This work, which gained importance in the 1960s along with Grotowski's *Towards a Poor Theatre* and Brook's *The Empty Space* (both represented in this collection; see Chapters 50 and 52), influenced Peter Brook's 1971 production of *King Lear* as well as other countercultural productions. In his comparative analysis of two plays, *King Lear* and *Endgame*, Kott brings into view both the theatricality and the philosophy of the clown. The comparison is not merely about binaries, but rather takes into account poststructuralism's wider chiasm. According to Kott, "A fool who has recognized himself for a fool, who has accepted the fact that he is only a jester in the service of the prince, ceases to be a clown." However, Kott adds that the "clown's philosophy is based on the assumption that every one is a fool; and the greatest fool is he who does not know he is a fool: the prince himself. That is why the clown has to make fools of others; otherwise he would not be a clown." The clown is, on the one hand, "subject to alienation because he is a clown," but on the other, the clown "cannot accept the alienation; he rejects it when he becomes aware of it." As a result, the clown "has the social position of the bastard, as described many times by Sartre. The bastard is a bastard for as long as he accepts his bastard position and regards it as inevitable. The bastard ceases to be a bastard when he does not consider himself a bastard any more. But at this point the bastard must abolish the division into bastards and legitimate offspring. He then enters into opposition against the foundations of social order, or at least exposes them. Social pressures want to limit the Clown to his part of a clown, to pin the label 'clown' on him. But he does not accept this part. On the contrary: he constantly pins that label on others."[6] The binary of clown and status quo is, in Kott's astute analysis, subjected to multiple layering, what Dosse, quoted earlier, calls "a new, carnivalesque order of reason." The hierarchy of clown and prince are thrown into disorder, top rail on bottom and bottom on top, with no one able to discern which is which.

The essayists in this section also initiated a new look at the devices of theatre, attempting to invigorate an art form that had relied on illusion, realism, and the fourth wall. Tragedy, which had depended on identification with the protagonist and the illusion of reality, was challenged by thinkers eager to return theatre back to its ritualistic roots. For many of the theorists here, theatre was theatre, not a novel or film, and therefore must avoid operating as a derivative of other arts. Absurdism, metatheatre, and *mise-en-scène* were terms used by philosophers to describe the shifting relationship of theatre in theory.

Notes

1 S. Banes, *Judson Dance Theatre: Democracy's Body, 1962–1964* (Durham, NC: Duke University Press, 1993), xv–xvi.
2 R. Scholes, *Structuralism in Literature* (New Haven: Yale University Press, 1974), 4.
3 P. Caws, *Structuralism: A Philosophy for the Human Sciences* (New Jersey: Humanities Press, 1988), 34.
4 T. Hawkes, *Structuralism and Semiotics* (Berkeley: University of California Press, 1977), 16.
5 F. Dosse, *History of Structuralism*, Vol. 2: *The Sign Sets, 1967–Present*, tr. D. Glassman (Minneapolis: University of Minnesota Press, 1997), 22.
6 J. Kott, *Shakespeare Our Contemporary* (New York: Norton, 1964), 164.

Chapter 42

Martin Esslin (1918–?

Martin Esslin was a critic, translator, scholar, producer, and playwright. His broad knowledge of literature and theatre led to many scholarly contributions. His major work, *The Theatre of the Absurd*, captured the spirit of a radical group of playwrights dissatisfied with the status quo. Esslin used the term "absurd" broadly, encapsulating a wide variety of playwrights. "Absurd" is a musical term meaning out of harmony; Esslin expands on this, using "absurd" to define a theatre out of harmony with reason and propriety, accentuating the incongruous, unreasonable, inscrutable, and illogical. Samuel Beckett's favorable reception at San Quentin prison was a sobering reminder to critics who failed at first to grasp the meaning of *Waiting for Godot*. Whereas critics and audiences were generally baffled by Beckett's ambiguity and esotericism when the play first appeared in the mid-1950s, the prisoners identified with Beckett's existential waiting. Esslin argues that Beckett and others have tapped into a rich vein of dramatic nuance. He brings together a disparate group of dramatists under the rubric of "theatre of the absurd," a poignant phrase that has remained in the social lexicon.

The Theatre of the Absurd (1961)

The reception of *Waiting for Godot* at San Quentin [given by the San Francisco Actors' Workshop in 1957], and the wide acclaim given to plays by Ionesco, Adamov, Pinter, and others, testify that these plays, which are so often superciliously dismissed as nonsense or mystification, *have* something to say and *can* be understood. Most of the incomprehension with which plays of this type are still being received by critics and theatrical reviewers, most of

Excerpts from Martin Esslin, *Theatre of the Absurd* (New York: Anchor Books, 1961; reprinted New York: Penguin, 1980), 19–26. © 1961 by Martin Esslin. Reprinted by permission of Doubleday, a division of Random House, Inc., and Methuen Publishing Ltd.

ewilderment they have caused and to which they still give rise, come from the fact that
y are part of a new, and still developing, stage convention that has not yet been generally
understood and has hardly ever been defined. Inevitably, plays written in this new convention
will, when judged by the standards and criteria of another, be regarded as impertinent and
outrageous impostures. If a good play must have a cleverly constructed story, these have
no story or plot to speak of; if a good play is judged by subtlety of characterization and
motivation, these are often without recognizable characters and present the audience with
almost mechanical puppets; if a good play has to have a fully explained theme, which is neatly
exposed and finally solved, these often have neither a beginning nor an end; if a good play is to
hold the mirror up to nature and portray the manners and mannerisms of the age in finely
observed sketches, these seem often to be reflections of dreams and nightmares; if a good play
relies on witty repartee and pointed dialogue, these often consist of incoherent babblings.

But the plays we are concerned with here pursue ends quite different from those of the
conventional play and therefore use quite different methods. They can be judged only by
the standards of the Theatre of the Absurd. [. . .]

It must be stressed, however, that the dramatists whose work is here discussed do not
form part of any self-proclaimed or self-conscious school or movement. On the contrary,
each of the writers in question is an individual who regards himself as a lone outsider, cut
off and isolated in his private world. Each has his own personal approach to both subject
matter and form; his own roots, sources, and background. If they also, very clearly and in
spite of themselves, have a good deal in common, it is because their work most sensitively
mirrors and reflects the preoccupations and anxieties, the emotions and thinking of many
of their contemporaries in the Western world.

This is not to say that their works are representative of mass attitudes. It is an oversim-
plification to assume that any age presents a homogeneous pattern. Ours being, more than
most others, an age of transition, it displays a bewildering stratified picture: medieval beliefs
still held and overlaid by eighteenth-century rationalism and mid-nineteenth-century
Marxism, rocked by sudden volcanic eruptions of prehistoric fanaticisms and primitive
tribal cults. Each of these components of the cultural pattern of the age finds its own artistic
expression. The Theatre of the Absurd, however, can be seen as the reflection of what seems
to be the attitude most genuinely representative of our own time.

The hallmark of this attitude is its sense that the certitudes and unshakable basic
assumptions of former ages have been swept away, that they have been tested and
found wanting, that they have been discredited as cheap and somewhat childish illusions.
The decline of religious faith was masked until the end of the Second World War by the
substitute religions of faith in progress, nationalism, and various totalitarian fallacies. All
this was shattered by the war. By 1942, Albert Camus was calmly putting the question why,
since life had lost all meaning, man should not seek escape in suicide. In one of the great,
seminal heart-searchings of our time, *The Myth of Sisyphus*, Camus tried to diagnose the
human situation in a world of shattered beliefs:

A world that can be explained by reasoning, however faulty, is a familiar world. But in a
universe that is suddenly deprived of illusions and of light, man feels a stranger. His is an
irremediable exile, because he is deprived of memories of a lost homeland as much as he lacks
the hope of a promised land to come. This divorce between man and his life, the actor and his
setting, truly constitutes the feeling of Absurdity.[1]

"Absurd" originally means "out of harmony," in a musical context. Hence its dictionary definition: "out of harmony with reason or propriety; incongruous, unreasonable, illogical." In common usage, "absurd" may simply mean "ridiculous," but this is not the sense in which Camus uses the word, and in which it is used when we speak of the Theatre of the Absurd. In an essay on Kafka, Ionesco defined his understanding of the term as follows: "Absurd is that which is devoid of purpose. . . . Cut off from his religious, metaphysical, and transcendental roots, man is lost; all his actions become senseless, absurd, useless."[2]

This sense of metaphysical anguish at the absurdity of the human condition is, broadly speaking, the theme of the plays of Beckett, Adamov, Ionesco, Genet, and the other writers [. . .]. But it is not merely the subject matter that defines what is here called the Theatre of the Absurd. A similar sense of the senselessness of life, of the inevitable devaluation of ideals, purity, and purpose, is also the theme of much of the work of dramatists like Giraudoux, Anouilh, Salacrou, Sartre, and Camus himself. Yet these writers differ from the dramatists of the Absurd in an important respect: they present their sense of the irrationality of the human condition in the form of highly lucid and logically constructed reasoning, while the Theatre of the Absurd strives to express its sense of the senselessness of the human condition and the inadequacy of the rational approach by the open abandonment of rational devices and discursive thought. While Sartre or Camus expresses the new content in the old convention, the Theatre of the Absurd goes a step further in trying to achieve a unity between its basic assumptions and the form in which these are expressed. In some senses, the theatre of Sartre and Camus is less adequate as an expression of the *philosophy* of Sartre and Camus – in artistic, as distinct from philosophic, terms – than the Theatre of the Absurd.

If Camus argued that in our disillusioned age the world has ceased to make sense, he did so in the elegantly rationalistic and discursive style of an eighteenth-century moralist, in well-constructed and polished plays. If Sartre argues that existence comes before essence and that human personality can be reduced to pure potentiality and the freedom to choose itself anew at any moment, he presents his ideas in plays based on brilliantly drawn characters who remain wholly consistent and thus reflect the old convention that each human being has a core of immutable, unchanging essence – in fact, an immortal soul. And the beautiful phrasing and argumentative brilliance of both Sartre and Camus in their relentless probing still, by implication, proclaim a tacit conviction that logical discourse can offer valid solutions, that the analysis of language will lead to the uncovering of basic concepts – Platonic ideas.

This is an inner contradiction that the dramatists of the Absurd are trying, by instinct and intuition rather than by conscious effort, to overcome and resolve. The Theatre of the Absurd has renounced arguing *about* the absurdity of the human condition; it merely *presents* it in being – that is, in terms of concrete stage images. This is the difference between the approach of the philosopher and that of the poet; the difference, to take an example from another sphere, between the *idea* of God in the works of Thomas Aquinas or Spinoza and the *intuition* of God in those of St. John of the Cross or Meister Eckhart – the difference between theory and experience.

It is this striving for an integration between the subject matter and the form in which it is expressed that separates the Theatre of the Absurd from the Existentialist theatre.

It must also be distinguished from another important, and parallel, trend in the contemporary French theatre, which is equally preoccupied with the absurdity and uncertainty of the human condition: the "poetic avant-garde" theatre of dramatists like Michel de Ghelderode, Jacques Audiberti, Georges Neveux, and, in the younger generation, Georges Schéhadé, Henri Pichette, and Jean Vauthier, to name only some of its most important exponents. This is an even more difficult dividing line to draw, for the two approaches overlap a good deal. The "poetic avant-garde" relies on fantasy and dream reality as much as the Theatre of the Absurd does; it also disregards such traditional axioms as that of the basic unity and consistency of each character or the need for a plot. Yet basically the "poetic avant-garde" represents a different mood; it is more lyrical, and far less violent and grotesque. Even more important is its different attitude toward language: the "poetic avant-garde" relies to a far greater extent on consciously "poetic" speech; it aspires to plays that are in effect poems, images composed of a rich web of verbal associations.

The Theatre of the Absurd, on the other hand, tends toward a radical devaluation of language, toward a poetry that is to emerge from the concrete and objectified images of the stage itself. The element of language still plays an important part in this conception, but what *happens* on the stage transcends, and often contradicts, the *words* spoken by the characters. In Ionesco's *Chairs*, for example, the poetic content of a powerfully poetic play does not lie in the banal words that are uttered but in the fact that they are spoken to an ever-growing number of empty chairs.

The Theatre of the Absurd is thus part of the "anti-literary" movement of our time, which has found its expression in abstract painting, with its rejection of "literary" elements in pictures; or in the "new novel" in France, with its reliance on description of objects and its rejection of empathy and anthropomorphism. [...]

Notes

1   A. Camus, *Le Mythe de Sisyphe* (Paris: Gallimard, 1942), 18.
2   E. Ionesco, *"Dans les armes de la ville,"* *Cahiers de la Compagnie Madeleine Renaud–Jean-Louis Barrault*, Paris no. 20, October 1957.

Chapter 43

George Steiner (b. 1929)

Francis George Steiner is a critic of comparative literature who has examined the connection between literature, language, and culture. Like many in this period, he takes up tragedy in his book *The Death of Tragedy*, and finds the modern world unsuited for tragedy's strictures. He considers the twin pillars of Western civilization, the Judaic and the Hellenic, finding the former the basis of rationalism and hence untragic, and the latter suited to tragedy because it accepts the unknowable. Tragedy is concerned with fate and humanity's inability to defeat the forces beyond its control. Fate consumes the will, and these are the grounds on which tragedy exists. But in the modern age fate's significance has diminished, rendering tragedy ineffectual. Among Steiner's many works are *Language and Silence* (1967), *After Babel* (1975), *Antigones* (1984), and *What is Comparative Literature?* (1995).

The Death of Tragedy (1961)

All men are aware of tragedy in life. But tragedy as a form of drama is not universal. Oriental art knows violence, grief, and the stroke of natural or contrived disaster; the Japanese theatre is full of ferocity and ceremonial death. But that representation of personal suffering and heroism which we call tragic drama is distinctive of the western tradition. It has become so much a part of our sense of the possibilities of human conduct, the *Oresteia, Hamlet*, and *Phèdre* are so ingrained in our habits of spirit, that we forget what a strange and complex idea it is to re-enact private anguish on a public stage. This idea and the vision of man which it implies are Greek. And nearly till the moment of their decline, the tragic forms are Hellenic.

Excerpts from George Steiner, *The Death of Tragedy* (New York: Oxford University Press, 1961, 1980), 3–10. © 1961, 1980 by George Steiner. Reprinted by permission of Faber and Faber Ltd and Knopf, a division of Random House, Inc.

Tragedy is alien to the Judaic sense of the world. The book of Job is always cited as an instance of tragic vision. But that black fable stands on the outer edge of Judaism, and even here an orthodox hand has asserted the claims of justice against those of tragedy:

> So the Lord blessed the latter end of Job more than the beginning: for he had fourteen thousand sheep, and six thousand camels, and a thousand yoke of oxen, and a thousand she-asses.

God has made good the havoc wrought upon His servant; he has compensated Job for his agonies. But where there is compensation, there is justice, not tragedy. This demand for justice is the pride and burden of the Judaic tradition. Jehovah is just, even in His fury. Often the balance of retribution or reward seems fearfully awry, or the proceedings of God appear unendurably slow. But over the sum of time, there can be no doubt that the ways of God to man are just. Not only are they just, they are rational. The Judaic spirit is vehement in its conviction that the order of the universe and of man's estate is accessible to reason. The ways of the Lord are neither wanton nor absurd. We may fully apprehend them if we give to our inquiries the clear-sightedness of obedience. Marxism is characteristically Jewish in its insistence on justice and reason, and Marx repudiated the entire concept of tragedy. "Necessity" he declared, "is blind only in so far as it is not understood."

Tragic drama arises out of precisely the contrary assertion: necessity is blind and man's encounter with it shall rob him of his eyes, whether it be Thebes or in Gaza. The assertion is Greek, and the tragic sense of life built upon it is the foremost contribution of the Greek genius to our legacy. […]

The Judaic vision sees in disaster a specific moral fault or failure of understanding. The Greek tragic poets assert that the forces which shape or destroy our lives lie outside the governance of reason or justice. Worse than that: there are around us daemonic energies which prey upon the soul and turn it to madness or which poison our will so that we inflict irreparable outrage upon ourselves and those we love. Or to put it in the terms of the tragic design drawn by Thucydides: our fleets shall always sail toward Sicily although everyone is more or less aware that they go to their ruin. Eteocles knows that he will perish at the seventh gate but goes forward nevertheless:

> We are already past the care of gods.
> For them our death is the admirable offering.
> Why then delay, fawning upon our doom?

Antigone is perfectly aware of what will happen to her, and in the wells of his stubborn heart Oedipus knows also. But they stride to their fierce disasters in the grip of truths more intense than knowledge. To the Jew there is a marvellous continuity between knowledge and action; to the Greek an ironic abyss. The legend of Oedipus, in which the Greek sense of tragic unreason is so grimly rendered, served that great Jewish poet Freud as an emblem of rational insight and redemption through healing.

Not that Greek tragedy is wholly without redemption. In the *Eumenides* and in *Oedipus at Colonus*, the tragic action closes on a note of grace. Much has been made of this fact. But we should, I think, interpret it with extreme caution. Both cases are exceptional; there is in them an element of ritual pageant commemorating special aspects of the sanctity of Athens. Moreover, the part of music in Greek tragedy is irrevocably lost to us, and

I suspect that the use of music may have given to the endings of these two plays a solemn distinctness, setting the final moments at some distance from the terrors which went before.

I emphasize this because I believe that any realistic notion of tragic drama must start from the fact of catastrophe. Tragedies end badly. The tragic personage is broken by forces which can neither be fully understood nor overcome by rational prudence. This again is crucial. Where the causes of disaster are temporal, where the conflict can be resolved through technical or social means, we may have serious drama, but not tragedy. More pliant divorce laws could not alter the fate of Agamemnon; social psychiatry is no answer to *Oedipus*. But saner economic relations or better plumbing *can* resolve some of the grave crises in the dramas of Ibsen. The distinction should be borne sharply in mind. Tragedy is irreparable. It cannot lead to just and material compensation for past suffering. Job gets back double the number of she-asses; so he should, for God has enacted upon him a parable of justice. Oedipus does not get back his eyes or his sceptre over Thebes.

Tragic drama tells us that the spheres of reason, order, and justice are terribly limited and that no progress in our science or technical resources will enlarge their relevance. Outside and within man is *l'autre*, the "otherness" of the world. Call it what you will: a hidden or malevolent God, blind fate, the solicitations of hell, or the brute fury of our animal blood. It waits for us in ambush at the crossroads. It mocks us and destroys us. In certain rare instances, it leads us after destruction to some incomprehensible repose.

None of this, I know, is a definition of tragedy. But any neat abstract definition would mean nothing. When we say "tragic drama" we know what we are talking about; not exactly, but well enough to recognize the real thing. In one instance, however, a tragic poet does come very near to giving an explicit summary of the tragic vision of life. Euripides' *Bacchae* stands in some special proximity to the ancient, no longer discernible springs, of tragic feeling. At the end of the play, Dionysus condemns Cadmus, his royal house, and the entire city of Thebes to a savage doom. Cadmus protests: the sentence is far too harsh. It is utterly out of proportion with the guilt of those who fail to recognize or have insulted the god. Dionysus evades the question. He repeats petulantly that he has been greatly affronted; then he asserts that the doom of Thebes was predestined. There is no use asking for rational explanation or mercy. Things are as they are, unrelenting and absurd. We are punished far in excess of our guilt.

It is a terrible, stark insight into human life. Yet in the very excess of his suffering lies man's claim to dignity. Powerless and broken, a blind beggar hounded out of the city, he assumes a new grandeur: Man is ennobled by the vengeful spite or injustice of the gods. It does not make him innocent, but it hallows him as if he had passed through flame. Hence there is in the final moments of great tragedy, whether Greek or Shakespearean or neoclassic, a fusion of grief and joy; of lament over the fall of man and of rejoicing in the resurrection of his spirit. No other poetic form achieves this mysterious effect; it makes of *Oedipus*, *King Lear*, and *Phèdre* the noblest yet wrought by the mind.

From antiquity until the age of Shakespeare and Racine, such accomplishment seemed within the reach of talent. Since then the tragic voice in drama is blurred or still. [. . .]

Chapter 44

Roland Barthes (1915–1980)

Roland Barthes was a literary and cultural critic. His influence ranged wide, covering philosophy, semiotics, structuralism, music, photography, and drama. Among his major works are *Writing Degree Zero* (1953), *Mythologies* (1957), *Criticism and Truth* (1966), *The Pleasure of the Text* (1973), and *Image/Music/Text* (1977). While one of his well-known works, the essay "The Death of the Author" (1968, reproduced in *Image/Music/Text*), would label him a cohort of deconstruction, his body of work was eclectic. In the appreciative essay on Brecht reproduced here, Barthes considers the four methods of criticism: sociological, ideological, semiological, and moral. The second essay demonstrates his interest in semiology, the theory of signs and their referentiality. Barthes's analysis of theatre, Timothy Scheie notes, weaves Brecht's "materialist grasp of history, Sartre's humanism, and Saussure's synchronic and detached analysis of structure over historical events or autonomous subject" into Barthes's "appreciation of Brecht."[1]

The Task of Brechtian Criticism (1956)

There is little risk in prophesying that Brecht's works will become increasingly important, not only because of the extent of his output but also because his work is exemplary. Today at least, Brecht's work shines out with special brilliance across two deserts: the desert of contemporary theatre where, with the exception of Brecht, there are no great names to mention, and the desert of revolutionary art, which has been barren since the start of the Zhadanovian impasse.[2]

Roland Barthes, "The Task of Brechtian Criticism" (1956) and "Theatre and Signification" (1963), from "Barthes on Theatre," tr. Peter W. Mathers, *Theatre Quarterly* 9.33 (Spring 1979), 25–30.

Anyone who wants to consider theatre and revolution will inevitably encounter Brecht. Brecht himself wanted it so, his work opposes itself with all its force to the reactionary myth of unthinking genius and shows the most appropriate kind of greatness for our age, the greatness of responsibility. It is a body of work which happens to be in a state of complicity with the world, our world. A knowledge of Brecht, consideration of Brecht – in short, Brechtian criticism – is by definition to cover the basic issues of our time. It is necessary to repeat this truth unceasingly: to know Brecht is of a different degree of importance than to know Shakespeare or Gogol since it is precisely for us that Brecht wrote his theatre and not for eternity.

Brechtian criticism is therefore thorough criticism by spectators, readers, and consumers and not by the learned scholar. And if I myself had to write the sort of criticism I am outlining here I would not fail to mention, despite the risk of appearing improper, the way in which his works affect me personally as a man. But in order to confine myself to the basic elements of a design for a Brechtian criticism, I will only give the analytical categories within which such a criticism might subsequently be located.

1. Sociology: In a general way we have not yet established adequate modes of questioning for the definition of different theatre audiences. In the meantime, in France at least, Brecht has not yet moved beyond experimental theatres (except for the *Mother Courage* at the TNP [Théâtre National Populaire], a rather unhelpful case because of the contradictions of the *mise-en-scène*). For the moment one can only study the reactions of the press.

It is necessary to distinguish, at this particular time, four types of reaction. On the Extreme Right the work of Brecht is discredited in its entirety because of its political attachments: the theatre of Brecht is a mediocre theatre *because* it is a Communist theatre. On the Right (shrewder Right, which can be identified roughly with the "modernist" bourgeoisie of *L'Express*), Brecht is subjected to a traditional operation of political dismantling: the man is dissociated from his work, the former being abandoned to politics (by underlining successfully and contradictorily his independence of and servility towards the Party), while the latter is placed under the banner of Eternal Theatre. Brecht's works, we are told, are magnificent in spite of him, in contradiction of him.

On the Left there has already been a humanist welcome for Brecht. Brecht is seen as one of the vast creative consciousnesses attached to the humanitarian championing of man – as also might Romain Rolland [see Chapter 5, this volume] or Barbusse. This sympathetic point of view unfortunately exposes a certain anti-intellectual prejudice common in some sections of the Extreme Left: in order better to "humanize" Brecht they minimized. Brecht's work can be great *despite* his systematic views of epic theatre, the actor, distancing technique, etc. In fact one of the fundamental theorems of petit-bourgeois culture is also added: the romantic contrast between heart and mind, intuition and reflection, the ineffable and the rational – an opposition which serves finally to obscure a magic concept of art.

Finally, some reservations have been expressed on the part of the Communist Party (at any rate in France) with regard to Brechtian theatre, where the concern in general is with Brecht's opposition to positive heroes, his epic conception of theatre, and the "formalist" orientation of Brechtian dramaturgy. Leaving aside Roger Vailland's arguments, based on a defense of French tragedy as dialectical art arising from the crisis, these criticisms proceed from a Zhadanovian conception of art.

I am quoting here from memory, and it would be necessary to check this out in detail. However, it would not only be a question of refuting the critics of Brecht, but rather of approaching Brecht through the voices that our society spontaneously employs in order to *swallow* him. Brecht *exposes* anyone who talks about him and this naturally interests Brecht as much as anything.

2. Ideology: Is it necessary to oppose the "swallowing" of Brecht's work with a canonically true Brecht? In a sense and within certain limits, yes. There is in the theatre of Brecht a precise ideological content, a coherent, consistent, remarkably *organized*, one which argues against abusive deformations. And this content must be described.

In order to do this one must consider two sorts of text. First, the theoretical texts, sharply intelligent (it is not a matter of indifference to meet an intelligent man of the theatre) and of tremendous ideological lucidity – texts which it would be puerile to try to underestimate under the pretext that they are nothing but an intellectual appendix to an essentially creative body of work. Certainly, Brecht's theatre is meant to be performed. But before performing it or seeing it performed, there is no law which says it must not be understood.

This intelligence is linked organically to the essential function of the text, which is to change an audience at the very moment when they are enjoying themselves. To a Marxist like Brecht, the connections between theory and practice could not be underestimated or subverted. To separate Brechtian theatre from its theoretical basis would be as mistaken as to want to understand the actions of Marx without reading *The Communist Manifesto*, or Lenin's politics without reading *State and Revolution*. There is no state decree or supernatural intervention which can graciously free theatre from the exigencies of theoretical reflection. Against a whole critical tendency the prime importance of the systematic writings of Brecht must be affirmed. It does not enfeeble the creative worth of his theatre to see it as a theatre that has been thought through.

Moreover, the work itself provides the principal elements of Brechtian ideology. I can only mention the main ones here: the historical character and not the "natural" one of human misfortune, the spiritual contagion of economic alienation, whose final effect is to blind to the causes of their servitude those same people it oppresses, the changeable order of Nature, the manipulability of the world, the necessary equation of means and situations (for example, in a rotten society right can only be reestablished through a flippant judge), the transformation of ancient psychological "conflicts" into historical contradictions, submitted as such to the correcting power of men.

It is important to state here that these terms are never used except as the results of concrete situations, and these situations are infinitely plastic. Contrary to the prejudice of the Right, Brecht's theatre is not a thesis theatre, nor is it a theatre of propaganda. What Brecht took from Marxism was not its words of command or articulation of arguments but a general method of explication. It follows that in Brechtian theatre the Marxist elements always appear recreated.

At bottom the greatness of Brecht (and his solitary position, too) are because he ceaselessly invents Marxism. The ideological theme in Brecht could be defined very exactly as a dynamic of events which combine together evidence and explanation, the ethical and the political. Following the basic teaching of Marxism, each theme is at one and the same time an expression of man's desire to be and of the being of things, yet it is at the same time a protest (because it unmasks) and a reconciling force (because it explains).

3. Semiology: Semiology is the study of signs and significations. I do not want to enter here into a discussion of this science, which was put forward forty years ago by Saussure,

the linguist, and which is, in general, held in great suspicion as being "formalist." Without being intimidated by words, there is an interest in recognizing that Brechtian dramaturgy, epic theory, distancing technique, and all the practice of the Berliner Ensemble with regard to costume and design poses an acknowledged semiological problem. For what all Brechtian dramaturgy postulates is that today at least dramatic art should not so much express the real as signify it.

It is thus necessary for there to be a certain distance between the signified and its signifier. Revolutionary art should allow a certain arbitrariness of signs, it should allow for a certain "formalism," in the sense that it should treat the form according to a proper method, which is the semiological method. All Brechtian art protests against the Zhadanovian confusion between ideology and semiology, for it knows to what aesthetic impasse that led.

Furthermore, it will be clear why it is this aspect of Brechtian thought that is most unattractive to bourgeois and Zhadanovian criticism, for both are committed to an aesthetic of the "natural" expression of reality. Art for them is a false Nature, a *pseudo-Physis*.

For Brecht, on the other hand, art today – this is to say, at the centre of an historical conflict, the resolution of which is human freedom from alienation – must be an anti-Physis. Brecht's formalism is a radical protest against the cloyingness of the false Nature of the bourgeoisie and petit-bourgeoisie. In a society that is still alienated, art must be critical, it must cut out all illusion, even that of "Nature." The sign must be partially arbitrary, for without that one falls back into an art of expression, into an art of essentialist illusion.

4. Morality: Brecht's theatre is a moral theatre – that is to say, a theatre which asks itself and the spectator: what must be done in a given situation? This leads to an examination and definition of the archetypal situations in Brechtian theatre which return, I think, to a single problem: how to be good in a rotten society? It seems to me of great importance to clarify the moral structure of Brecht's theatre. It is clearly understood that Marxism has had other more urgent tasks than focusing on the problems of individual conduct, but capitalist society goes on, Communism itself is changing, revolutionary action must increasingly coexist in an almost institutionalized way with the norms of bourgeois and petit-bourgeois morality. Problems of behaviour and no longer of action arise. Here Brecht can have a great scouring and sharpening function.

Inasmuch as his morality avoids becoming a catechism, it is for the most part strictly interrogative. Certain of his works do finish with a literal interrogation of the audience, to whom the author leaves the responsibility of finding a solution to the problem posed. Brecht's moral role is sharply to pose a question just when something seems clear (this is the motif of the exception and the rule). For what we have here is essentially a morality of discovery.

Brechtian discovery is a tactical process for unifying the correcting process of revolution. That is to say that, for Brecht, the result of any moral impasse depends on a fairer analysis of the concrete situation in which the subject is to be found. It is in acutely presenting oneself again with the historical particularity of that situation – its artificial, mere conformist nature – that the conclusion is forthcoming. The morality of Brecht consists essentially in a correct reading of history and the plasticity of this morality (*change, when necessary, Dominant Custom*) keeps to the very plasticity of history.

Theatre and Signification (1963)

What is theatre? A sort of cybernetic machine. When not working, this machine is hidden behind a curtain; but as soon as it is revealed it begins to transmit a certain number of messages in your direction. These messages are distinctive in that they are simultaneous and yet have different rhythms. At every point in a performance you are receiving (*at the same second*) six or seven items of information (from the scenery, the costuming, the lighting, the position of the actors, their gestures, their mode of playing, their language), but some of these items *remain fixed* (this is true of the scenery) while others *change* (speech, gestures).

We have, therefore, a genuinely polyphonic system of information, which is theatrical; *a density of signs* (this in contrast to literature as monodic, leaving aside the problem of the cinema). What is the relationship between these signs, arranged in counterpoint (that is to say, dense and extended at the same time, simultaneous and successive)? They do not have the same signifiers (by definition), but do they always have the same signified? *Do they all work together* for a single meaning? What is the relationship that brings them across a period of time, often quite long, to this final meaning which is, if one may say it, a retrospective meaning, since it is not in the final representation and is only clear once the play is over? On the other hand, how is the theatrical signifier formed? What are its models?

We know that the linguistic sign is not "analogous" (the word "ox" does not resemble an ox), it is formed with reference to a digital code, but what about other signifiers? For the sake of simplification, what about visual signifiers which hold sway over the stage? All representation is an extremely dense semantic act. Interrelationship between the code and the acting (that is between *langue* and *parole*), the nature (analogous, symbolic, conventional) of the theatrical sign, signifying variations of this sign, constraints of interconnections, denotation and connotation of the message; all these fundamental problems of semiology are present in the theatre. It might even be said that the theatre constitutes a semiotically privileged object, since its system is apparently original (polyphonic) compared to that of language (which is linear).

Brecht has illustrated – and justified – with brilliance the semantic status of theatre. Firstly, he understood that the theatrical act could be dealt with in cognitive terms and not in emotive terms. He accepted the intellectual cognition of theatre, abolishing the mythical distinction (decayed but still extant) between creation and thought, the natural and the systemized, the spontaneous and the rational, the "heart" and the "head." His theatre is neither touching nor cerebral, it is a *justified* theatre.

And then he decided that dramatic form had a political responsibility, that the position of a lantern, the interruption of a scene by a song, the addition of a placard, the extent of wear of a costume, an actor's delivery *signified* that certain decisions had been made, not about art but about man and the world. In short, that the materiality of the performance did not only show an aesthetic or a psychology of emotions, but also, and principally, a technique of signification. In other words, that the meaning of a theatrical work (a tasteless notion ordinarily confused with the "philosophy" of the author) depended not on a summation of intentions and "chance discoveries" but on what might properly be called an intellectual system of signification.

Finally, Brecht had some idea of the variety and relativity of semantic systems: the theatrical sign is *not self-determined*, that which we call *naturalness* in an actor or the *truth* of a style of acting is only one language among many (a language accomplishes its function, which is to communicate, through its validity not through its veracity), and this language is a by-product of a certain mental set – that is, of a certain history in such a way that *to change the signs* (and not just what they say) is to give to the natural *a new deal* (an undertaking that precisely defines art), and to base this deal not on "natural" laws but, on the contrary, to base it on the freedom that men have to make things signify.

But, above all, at the same time as he connected this theatre of signification to a political conception, Brecht (if it may be said) reaffirmed its meaning but did not flesh it out. True, his theatre is ideological, more openly so than many others. It takes sides on nature, work, racism, fascism, history, war, alienation; yet it is a theatre of knowledge, not of action, of problems, not of answers. Like all literary language it serves to "formulate," not to "do." All Brecht's plays conclude implicitly with a *"Find the way out"* addressed to the spectator in the name of that deciphering to which the materiality of the performance should lead.

Consciousness of the unconsciousness, consciousness that the audience should have of the unconsciousness which prevails on stage: this is the theatre of Brecht. It is, without doubt, this that explains why this theatre is so strongly signifying and so far from sermonizing. The function of the system here is not to hand on a positive message (it is not a theatre of signifies), but to make it understood that the world is an object that must be deciphered (it is a theatre of signifiers).

Brecht also examined the tautological status of all literature, which is a message about the signification of things, not about their meaning (by *signification* I mean the process which produces meaning and not meaning itself). What makes Brecht's undertaking exemplary is the fact that it took more risks than any other. Brecht approached the limits of a *certain* meaning (which could be called Marxist in the broadest sense) but at the moment in which it "thickened" (became solid in a positive signified), he left this meaning hanging in the balance (a balance that is met with again in the particular quality of the historical period that he presents in his theatre and which is a time of *not-again*).

This very subtle interaction between a meaning (complete) and a signification (in the balance) is an undertaking which, in its daring, difficulty, and necessity, also leaves the interruption of meaning that the avant-garde believed it could effect by merely subverting ordinary language and theatrical conformism far behind. A vague question (of the kind which a philosophy of the absurd would pose to the world) has much less force (it discards less) than a question to which the reply is imminent but nevertheless held back (like that of Brecht). In literature, which is a system of connotation, there is no mere question. A question is never anything but its own scattered answer, dispersed in fragments between which meaning is extended and shifts ground at the same time.

Notes

1   Timothy Scheie, *Performance Degree Zero: Roland Barthes and Theatre* (Toronto: University of Toronto Press, 2006), 53.

2   Barthes is referring to Andrej Aleksandrovich Zhadanov, Stalinist Soviet supporter of orthodox Socialist Realism. – Editor's note.

Chapter 45

Lionel Abel (1910–2001)

Lionel Abel was a playwright, essayist, and novelist. His book, *Metatheatre: A New View of Dramatic Form,* was part of a theoretical movement that sought to retool the concept of tragedy. Like Roland Barthes, he appreciated Brecht, and like George Steiner, he analyzed the difficulties of writing tragedy for the modern age. Abel popularized the term "metatheatre," a concept used by André Gide during the early twentieth century. It derives from a "play-within-a-play" idea, whereby actors perform the role of actors or there is an internal play commenting on the larger plot. The most famous example is *Hamlet,* in which Hamlet orchestrates a drama in order to observe his uncle. Broadly construed, metatheatre refers to any form of internal reproduction of an outer structure whereby a storyteller tells a story while conscious of the telling. Abel expands the term to anything onstage that reflects back on the notion of performing. Like Esslin's "theatre of the absurd," Abel ushers into view a new way of perceiving theatre theory. But as Martin Puchner writes in his Introduction to the revised edition of *Metatheatre,* Abel's text "is an attempt to come up with a better alternative to 'theatre of the absurd,' to attempt a positive explanation of modernist theatre." Instead of looking backwards to Greek drama as a model – something Ibsen attempted – Abel argued that it was the task of modern drama to "exorcise that specter" of Greek influence. For Abel, "Ibsen was not so much the beginning of modern drama, as a false beginning, and modern metatheatre could emerge only once this false beginning was corrected, once Ibsen's ghosts were banished."[1] Metatheatre was an effort to build a new drama.

Lionel Abel, "Of Bert Brecht – Not Simple but Simplified," excerpted from Abel, *Metatheatre: A New View of Dramatic Form* (New York: Hill & Wang, 1963), 103–7.

Of Bert Brecht – Not Simple but Simplified (1963)

If the judgments I have made are valid – I have based them on the same facts presented by Brecht's critics – then surely it is possible to see, beyond the playwright's ambiguities, not to be explained away, a Brecht rather impressive in his consistency. He began by denying moral experience and the individual – not I think out of indifference, but moved by rage and disappointment by the discovery that in his time the very idea of the European individual was dying, burying itself, in Hofmannsthal's words, "in the grave it dug for itself." It is to be noted that a similar conviction about the individual is discoverable in the works of Western writers before and during Brecht's time. What but the judgment that the individual was dead or dying lies behind Eliot's suspicion of individual insight, Joyce's cult of impersonality, the surrealist's dependence on automatic writing, Lawrence's assertion that he was not interested in describing individuals, but only psychic and biological forces? Brecht of course denied the individual more radically than anyone else and maintained this negation throughout his life. This does not mean, however, that we should judge him a moral cynic.

But if Brecht denied moral experience, can he be called a moralist? This is a more complicated matter; but one point has to be made strongly. Brecht was not, except for a short period in his career, the moralist of commitment to Communist Party authority. It is true that he noted *The Measures Taken*. And Sidney Hook tells this story about Brecht: In New York, during the preparation of one of the Moscow trials, Brecht was asked by Hook if he thought the accused in Moscow were guilty or innocent. Brecht replied cryptically: "If they are innocent they ought to be shot." Hook, telling the story with great moral heat, accuses Brecht of being an antihumanist. But Brecht never claimed to be a humanist. He had never affirmed the individual; I think he never believed the individual in this society could be quite real or that moral experience could be anything but an imposture. Hence, what difference did it make whether the accused in Moscow were innocent or guilty? He was not going to fight against the Soviet State in the name of something he thought an anachronism. If he was a moralist at all, then it was in a stern refusal to regard moral experience positively – and so uncompromising a refusal does have a moral side. (One thinks of Brecht's saying that Azdak has a tragic side.)

What Brecht affirmed was the body, the human body in its warmth, its weakness, its susceptibility, its appetites, the human body in its longing and in its thought. Why did he remain a Communist? He may have thought that even distorted modern Communism, because of its philosophical basis in materialism, was the politics of the human body and hence preferable to Western liberalism based on what he considered a false affirmation of the individual soul.

It may be that his interest in the body extended itself to an interest in the physical details of his own productions, in the material and circumstantial values his plays could have, in their bodies, so to speak, as against their written dialogue, which we may not incorrectly think of as a play's soul. The attention other playwrights have given to the literary form of their plays Brecht devoted indefatigably to the details of his productions. Writers have been honored for their conscientious search for the right word. Brecht was utterly conscientious in his search for the right stage business to bring out the strongest meanings of his plays.

I think of Brecht as somehow the opposite of Webster, with whom the great period of Elizabethan drama came to a close. Webster placed on the stage characters of tremendous will and ruthless energies, aristocrats, marvelously appareled. They live in palaces and plot continuously against each other. Though not noble in the moral sense they are highly spiritual, refined even in their cruelties, and invariably they are betrayed. By what? By their bodies. Under the refined garments the bodies that bear their violent wills are destructible, susceptible to decay and to death. The power of the human will belied by the weakness of the body which is its seat, such is the theme of Webster's meditation, of his grandiose eloquence.

And in Brecht we have the very reverse. The best of his characters are mainly passive, morally inconsequential, or inconsistent. They live by lies, by fraud, and if, on occasion by feats of thought, the thought generally ministers to their bodies. I think Brecht loved the body, in the abstract, of course, with a feeling similar to what each person feels for his own.

To make the body his hero, Brecht of course had to make use of a very particular dramatic method and rely on a special form.

Note

1   M. Puchner, "Introduction," in *Tragedy and Metatheatre: Essays on Dramatic Form* (New York: Holmes & Meier, 2003), 3, 15, 16.

Chapter 46

Francis Fergusson (1904–1986)

Francis Fergusson was a drama critic and theorist. His most important critical work, *The Idea of a Theatre* (1953), examines ten plays in light of the Aristotelian notion of dramatic action. His essays hewed closely to the spirit if not the letter of Aristotle, analyzing drama in terms of dramatic action. A student of Russian émigré acting teachers Richard Boleslavsky and Maria Ouspenskaya, Fergusson absorbed the lessons of action as a complex investigation of character. For Fergusson action was based on Freudian motivation, but it also included sociology and the author's theme. While many of Fergusson's contemporaries abandoned Aristotelian action in favor of Beckett's inaction or Brecht's estrangement, Fergusson remained steadfast in his belief that drama must convey pathos which can only come about through a character's active pursuit of a goal.

The Notion of "Action" (1964)

In my opinion the notion of "action" is the most basic, and potentially the most valuable, part of the Moscow Art Theatre technique. But it is notoriously hard to be sure just what Stanislavski meant by his technical terms. His disciples interpret them in various ways, and he himself seems to have changed his mind, from time to time, about their exact meaning. My own understanding of the Moscow technique is based upon what Richard Boleslavski and Madame Maria Ouspenskaya were teaching at the Laboratory Theatre, from 1926 to 1930, and I don't know whether they were orthodox or not.

Francis Fergusson, "The Notion of 'Action,'" *Tulane Drama Review* 9.1 (Fall 1964), 85–7. © 1964 by Tulane Drama Review. Reprinted by permission of TDR/The Drama Review.

"Action" was certainly the word we heard most frequently from them; from Boleslavski in his rehearsals and informal talks, from Madame [Ouspenskaya] in her classes in the technique of acting. "How t'is about *Ahction*?" Madame would demand in her coldest and hoarsest voice, affixing her monocle and scornfully puffing her little cigar. The actors, who had just done a scene or an improvisation for her, would know that she had found their performance lacking in true feeling and motivation. Boleslavski, when working on a play, would always devote the first couple of weeks to "finding the action"; the main action, or "spine," of each character, and the changes of that action in each situation of the play; the action of the play as a whole which defined *its* life and movement, and which he also called "spine."

In teaching us what they meant by "action" Boley [Boleslavsky] and Madame relied mostly on direct demonstration, for their English was primitive, while their acting was superb. I have seen Madame, who looked like a small withered witch, "get" Juliet's action at some moment in her scene with Romeo, so completely that we perceived the childish spirit of Juliet more clearly than the visible Madame. Or she could frighten us, suddenly, by looking us in the eye with the murderous action of Macbeth. Such performances look magical, but Boley and Madame explained them as simply the result of conscious technique and long practice. They would tell us that they had learned to make, with their own minds and desires, the action of another character, as a violinist makes, with his instrument, the music of the composer.

Like almost all practicing artists, Boley and Madame did not have much faith in theorizing, but they were willing to try to explain "action" in words. Yes, they would say, it is *like* "motive" – provided you understand that a man's real motive is not necessarily what he says it is, or thinks it is, when he tries to rationalize it. They taught us that, in finding the action of a character in a play, the only way to indicate it was by means of an infinitive, for action is the *movement* of the psyche, not a passive state, like a mood. Hence the action of *Three Sisters*: "to get to Moscow," the motive which, in many ways, and more or less consciously, defines the life of all the nostalgic characters. All action, they would say, aims at some "objective," and if you can see what that is, you can understand the action. In this case, of course, the "objective" is the more or less illusory Moscow.

Did the Moscow Art Theatre people get their basic technical concept from Aristotle's *Poetics*? Or was it by mere chance that they used the same word that Aristotle used, as the basis of *his* theory of art? Perhaps some one has investigated this matter, but if so I do not know about it. Knowing no Russian, I have never tried, myself, to find out where their word "action" came from. But I am convinced that Boley and Madame were talking about the same thing as Aristotle was: they too saw the movement of the psyche toward the object of its desire as what the dramatist was imitating in plot, character, and language, and what the actor imitates in the medium of his own feeling and perception.

The *Poetics* certainly makes more sense if one reads it after a long immersion in Boley's and Madame's practical lore of action. Unless one has learned to see action in life, and in the art of actors, the *Poetics* can hardly mean more than a collection of superannuated rules and regulations.

Conversely, the Moscow technique makes more sense when cultivated in the light of Aristotle's doctrine of action. A technique of acting is always in danger of becoming private, "mystical," and cultish. As soon as the adepts begin to understand it, they feel that they are alone with their uniquely marvellous and esoteric jargon in a world of Philistines.

The study of Aristotle helps to clarify and objectify the technique of acting, and to relate it to the long tradition. Aristotle, the "master of those who know," would make a better patron saint for a school of acting than Dr. Freud, the master of modern psychopathology.

The Moscow technique is often supposed to work only for modern realistic drama. It developed in close touch with Chekhov's subtle realism, and its early triumphs in this country – some of Boley's productions, some of the Group Theatre's productions – were more *really* realistic than anything we'd seen before. But after thirty or forty years realism begins to look like a *cul de sac*. The more realistic our plays and our acting become, the narrower and more subjective they seem.

I do not think the Moscow technique is to be blamed for this, but rather the way it has been interpreted and adapted to our theatre. Boley and Madame did not suffer from this "realistic" limitation. Their technique worked for theatre-poetry like *Twelfth Night*, for neoclassic farce like Cervantes' *Interludes*; for dry modern comedy like *Dr. Knock*. I have heard Boleslavski explain the action of a Shaw play, which is a matter not of the yearning of the morose gut, but of the light and agile play of the mind, when particularly pleased with itself. They were very much aware of the distinction between art and direct experience of life; they often preached to us about style. This freedom and sophistication, this easy access to the varied theatre-forms of the tradition, was due, I think, to their emphasis on action, and to the fact that they meant by the word what Aristotle did in his theory of drama and of art in general.

Chapter 47

Peter Szondi (1929–1971)

Peter Szondi was a Romanian critic and philologist whose literary interests focused on hermeneutics, the science of interpretation, as opposed to exegesis, which is a practical explanation of texts. His most important work on drama, *The Theory of the Modern Drama*, focuses on content and form. Unlike Lukács, who argued for the superiority of content over form, Szondi contends that form is the best means of studying literature. For Szondi, form emerges out of culture and the audience–performer relationship. Szondi uses the concept of epic theatre more broadly than Brecht, interpreting what he calls the "epic I" in opposition to Hegelian action. In *Theory of the Modern Drama*, Szondi writes: "According to Hegel, the Drama shows only that which the hero's subjectivity objectifies in action and that which this action retains of the objective world and transfers into subjectivity. In epic theatre, on the other hand, and in line with its scientific-sociological intention, there is a process of reflection on the social 'base' of actions and their reified alienation" (71). This interpretation allows Szondi to incorporate concepts such as expressionism, political theatre, and montage, and playwrights Pirandello, O'Neill, Wilder, and Miller into the category of epic, inclusions which are not necessarily in concert with Brecht's idea. Among Szondi's other important contributions are *On Textual Understanding and Other Essays* (1986) and *An Essay on the Tragic* (2002).

Peter Szondi, "The Drama" (1965), from *Theory of the Modern Drama*, tr. and ed. Michael Hays (Minneapolis: University of Minnesota Press, 1987), 7–10. Original work published in German as *Theorie des modernen Dramas*, copyright © 1965 by Suhrkamp Verlag. English translation © 1987 by the University of Minnesota. Reprinted by permission of Polity and Suhrkamp Verlag.

The Drama (1965)

The Drama of modernity came into being in the Renaissance. It was the result of a bold intellectual effort made by a newly self-conscious being who, after the collapse of the medieval worldview, sought to create an artistic reality within which he could fix and mirror himself on the basis of interpersonal relationships alone.[1] Man entered the drama only as a fellow human being, so to speak. The sphere of the "between" seemed to be the essential part of his being; freedom and obligation, will and decision the most important of his attributes. The "place" at which he achieved dramatic realization was in an act of decision and self-disclosure. By deciding to disclose himself to his contemporary world, man transformed his internal being into a palpable and dramatic presence. The surrounding world, on the other hand, was drawn into a rapport with him because of his disclosure and thereby first achieved dramatic realization. Everything prior to or after this act was, had to remain, foreign to the drama – the inexpressible as well as the expressed, what was hidden in the soul as well as the idea already alienated from its subject. Most radical of all was the exclusion of that which could not express itself – the world of objects – unless it entered the realm of interpersonal relationships.

All dramatic themes were formulated in this sphere of the "between" – for example, the struggle of passion and *devoir* in the Cid's position between his father and his beloved; the comic paradoxes in "crooked" interpersonal situations, such as that of Justice Adam; the tragedy of individuation as it appeared to Hebbel; the tragic conflict between Duke Ernst [in Corneille's *The Cid*], Albrecht [in Kleist's *The Broken Jug*], and Agnes Bernauer [in Hebbel's *Agnes Bernauer*].

The verbal medium for this world of the interpersonal was the dialogue. In the Renaissance, after the exclusion of prologue, chorus, and epilogue, dialogue became, perhaps for the first time in the history of the theater (excluding the monologue, which remained occasional and therefore did not constitute the form of the Drama), the sole constitutive element in the dramatic web. In this respect, the neoclassical Drama distinguishes itself not only from antique tragedy but also from medieval clerical plays, from the baroque world theater, and from Shakespeare's histories. The absolute dominance of dialogue – that is, of interpersonal communication, reflects the fact that the Drama consists only of the reproduction of interpersonal relations, is only cognizant of what shines forth within this sphere.

All this shows that the Drama is a self-contained dialectic but one that is free and redefined from moment to moment. With this in mind, the Drama's major characteristics can now be understood and described.

The Drama is absolute. To be purely relational – that is, to be dramatic – it must break loose from everything external. It can be conscious of nothing outside itself.

The dramatist is absent from the Drama. He does not speak; he institutes discussion. The Drama is not written, it is set. All the lines spoken in the Drama are disclosures. They are spoken in context and remain there. They should in no way be perceived as coming from the author. The Drama belongs to the author only as a whole, and this connection is just an incidental aspect of its reality as a work.

The same absolute quality exists with regard to the spectator. The lines in a play are as little an address to the spectator as they are a declaration by the author. The theatergoer is an observer – silent, with hands tied, lamed by the impact of this other world. This total passivity will, however (and therein lies the dramatic experience), be converted into irrational activity. He who was the spectator is pulled into the dramatic event, becomes the person speaking (through the mouths of all the characters, of course). The spectator–Drama relationship is one of complete separation or complete identity, not one in which the spectator invades the Drama or is addressed through the Drama.

The stage shaped by the Renaissance and the neoclassical period, the much-maligned "picture-frame" stage, is the only one adequate to the absoluteness of the drama and bears witness to it in each of its features. It is no more connected to the house (by steps, for example) than the Drama is connected (stepwise) to the audience. The stage becomes visible, thus exists, only at the beginning of the play – often, in fact, only after the first lines have been spoken. Because of this, it seems to be created by the play itself. At the end of the act, when the curtain falls, the stage is again withdrawn from the spectator's view, taken back as if it were part of the play. The footlights which illuminate it create the impression that the play sheds its own light on stage.

Even the actor's art is subservient to the absoluteness of the Drama. The actor–role relationship should not be visible. Indeed, the actor and the character should unite to create a single personage.

That the Drama is absolute can be expressed in a different manner: the Drama is primary. It is not a (secondary) representation of something else (primary); it presents itself, is itself. Its action, like each of its lines, is "original"; it is accomplished as it occurs. The Drama has no more room for quotation than it does for variation. Such quotation would imply that the Drama referred to whatever was quoted. Variation would call into question the Drama's quality of being primary ("true") and present it as secondary (as a variation of something and as one variation among many). Furthermore, it would be necessary to assume a "quoter" or "varier" on whom the Drama would depend.

The Drama is primary. This also explains why historical plays always strike one as "undramatic." The attempt to stage *Luther the Reformer* requires some reference to history. If it were possible, in the absolute dramatic situation, to show Luther in the process of deciding to reform the faith, the Reformation Drama could be said to exist. But at this point, a second problem arises: the objective conditions which are necessary to motivate the decision demand epic treatment. An interpersonal portrayal of Luther's situation would be the only possible foundation for the Drama, but this account would be understandably alien to the intent of a Reformation play.

Because the Drama is always primary, its internal time is always the present. That in no way means that the Drama is static, only that time passes in a particular manner: the present passes and becomes the past and, as such, can no longer be present on stage. As the present passes away, it produces change, a new present springs from its antithesis. In the Drama, time unfolds as an absolute, linear sequence in the present. Because the Drama is absolute, it is itself responsible for this temporal sequence. It generates its own time. Therefore, every moment must contain the seeds of the future. It must be "pregnant with futurity."[2] This is possible because of the Drama's dialectical structure, which, in turn, is rooted in interpersonal relationships.

From this point of view, the demand that one adhere to the unity of time acquires new meaning. Temporal fragmentation of the scenes in a play would subvert the principle of absolute presence and linearity because every scene would have its own antecedents and results (past and future) external to the play. The individual scenes would thus be relativized. In addition, only when each scene in succession generates the next (the kind of progression necessary to the Drama) can the implicit presence of a *monteur* [editor] be avoided. The (spoken or unspoken) "three years later" presupposes an epic *I*.

A comparable set of conditions leads to the demand for unity of place. As with time, the spectator should not be conscious of a larger spatial context. Only then can an absolute – that is, a dramatic – scene arise. The more frequent the change in scene, the more difficult this is to accomplish. Besides, spatial fragmentation (like temporal) assumes an epic I. (Cliché: Now we will leave the conspirators in the forest and return to the unsuspecting king in his palace.)

It is generally agreed that Shakespeare's plays differ most markedly from the French neoclassical form in these two areas. But his loose and multiplace succession of scenes should be examined in conjunction with the histories (e.g., *Henry V*) in which a narrator, designated "Chorus," presents the individual acts to the audience as chapters in a popular history.

The insistence on motivation and the exclusion of accident are also based in the absoluteness of the Drama. The accidental enters the Drama from outside, but, by motivating it, accident is domesticated; it is rooted in the heart of drama itself.

Ultimately, the whole world of the Drama is dialectical in origin. It does not come into being because of an epic I which permeates the work. It exists because of the always achieved and, from that point, once again disrupted sublation of the interpersonal dialectic, which manifests itself as speech in the dialogue. In this respect as well, the dialogue carries the Drama. The Drama is possible only when dialogue is possible.

Notes

1   In relation to the following discussion see Hegel, *Vorlesungen über die Äesthetik*, in *Werke* 14, p. 479 [G. W. F. Hegel, *Aesthetics: Lectures on Fine Art* 2, tr. T. M. Knox (Oxford, 1975), p. 1158f.].

2   See the discussion of dramatic style in [Emil] Staiger, *Grundbegriffe* [*der Poetik*, 1946] (p. 143ff.).

Chapter 48

Kenneth Burke (1897–1993)

Prolific music theorist, literary critic, and philosopher, Kenneth Burke was known for his work on rhetoric, symbolism, structuralism, and aesthetics. His most well-known books, *Philosophy of Literary Form: Studies in Symbolic Action* (1941), *A Grammar of Motives* (1945), *A Rhetoric of Motives* (1950), *The Rhetoric of Religion* (1961), and *Language as Symbolic Action* (1966), explore, among other things, the structure of language. Burke coined the term "dramatism," by which he meant the act, scene, agent, agency, and purpose of drama. His theory of dramatism, Martin Puchner contends, is based on "the theory of gesture." Gesture, for Burke, "is the category that connects corporeality to linguistic articulation and therefore promises to fill the gap left by theories of language based on the semantic ideal."[1] Burke's work grew out of the Anglo-American school of New Criticism, a literary philosophy that centered on the study of the text as an autonomous object without interest in social context or authorial biography. Like the New Critics, Burke was concerned with symbolism, the manner in which symbols related to other images emanating from the text. However, he diverged from the New Critics, observing literature from a wider perspective than the mere text. Literary work, he said, "is designed to 'do something' for the poet and the reader... and we can make the most relevant observations about it designed by considering the poem as the embodiment of this act."[2] In this essay, Burke analyzes dramatic structure from a temporal and spatial perspective.

Dramatic Form – And: Tracking Down Implications (1966)

In Chicago during the summer of 1961, I offered part of a paper on "Dramatic Form and Human Motivation." I began with the theory of classical form (as the arousing and fulfillment of expectations) which I had originally developed in *Counter-Statement*.

Kenneth Burke, "Dramatic Form – And: Tracking Down Implications," *Tulane Drama Review* 10.4 (Summer 1966), 54–63.
© 1966 by Tulane Drama Review. Reprinted by permission of TDR/The Drama Review.

Form as so conceived was reduced to three principles: progressive, repetitive, and conventional.

"Progressive" form was said to involve the use of situations which led the audience to anticipate or desire certain developments. "Repetitive" form involves the ways in which a work embodies a fixed character or identity, the ways in which a work, however disjunct, manifests some kinds of internal self-consistency. "Conventional" form (or "categorical expectancy") involves the kinds of expectation which an audience brings to the theatre as an established institution. For instance, an audience at an Athenian tragedy expected a Chorus with ritualized speech and movements. A Roman audience at the gladiatorial games expected live victims, whereas in even our most "brutal" plays we expect to witness only an *imitation* of sacrifice. I also listed "minor" or "incidental" forms (as one speech might have a beginning, middle, and end of such a sort that it could be isolated and appreciated in and for itself, over and above its place in the total context). And I tentatively added a category which I had not originally included: "negative expectation." I here had in mind the thought that, if one goes to an *avant-garde* drama, though the opening episode might but vaguely indicate what we should expect, from the start it builds up in us a feeling such that certain kinds of development would *not* be acceptable. For instance, it wouldn't require as much as the first minute of *Who's Afraid of Virginia Woolf?* for an audience to have had "negative expectation" that a serious episode in the style of *The Iliad* would be out of bounds.

I next tried to show how the classical principles of dramatic form are implicit in political, historical, philosophical, metaphysical, and theological systems, and the like (as studied particularly in the theory of "Dramatism" developed in my *Grammar of Motives*). There is no need to review those considerations now, except for one point. This section of my paper terminated in a stress upon the matter of terminology. That is, a work is a structure of interrelated terms, and we experience the work *in terms of* these terms. ("Terms" in this sense need not be exclusively verbal, or even verbal at all. A painting, for instance, may be experienced *in terms of* colors and visual forms.)

This stress upon terms gave me my next step. My first critical speculations had been done in the aesthetic tradition that stressed self-expression. In my theory of classical form, I had made the step from self-expression to communication. But I had since come to feel that it is not enough to deal with form in terms of communication, and of the ways in which self-expression and communication variously re-enforce or correct each other. I had begun to realize that there is another kind of expectation, got *by tracking down the implications of a terminology*. For instance, physicists compulsively tracked down the implications of their terminologies, thereby producing the atom bomb, even though many of them secretly hoped that their experiments would fail.

I submit that this principle (of "consummation") might serve to place certain characteristic aspects of contemporary literature (or art in general). To a large extent, I think that many aspects of form can be identified somewhat "negativistically," as fragments, distortions, or perversions of classical norms. (For wherever there is an expectation there is a corresponding perverse effect to be got by the affronting of that expectation. Comedy traditionally illustrates the norms of propriety by exemplifying them in reverse. Grotesque art in various ways does the same thing, but without the classical propriety of laughter.)

And in the part of my talk which was almost eliminated since time did not permit me to dwell on this matter, I used Ionesco's play, *Victims of Duty*, as test case, and asked how it would look, as analyzed from this point of view. That is, while keeping in mind the likelihood that classical or, Aristotelian tests of formal propriety might show up in spurts or twists, let us ask ourselves whether, on the tentative assumption that the play is accurately entitled, we can "track down the admitted implications of the title," as manifested in the successive details of the play.

(Obviously, in many cases a title cannot be relied on. In such cases, it is the critic's job to say what the title "should be," as viewed from the standpoint of this particular problem. And he should say why. His arguments in no way need mean that *in actuality* the play should have a different title. The title that it has may serve a sufficient purpose in the vague arousing of expectations. We are not here quarrelling with the showmanship of the box office. We are merely reminding ourselves that, when we are tracking down the implications of a work's generative principle, we might be required to give it a different title. On the other hand, there is always the possibility that, whereas one critic has tracked down his implications of the basis of one title, another critic might show why a different title would serve better as *Ausgangspunkt* [starting point].)

Consider the opening stage directions. The setting is: *A petit-bourgeois interior. Choubert is sitting in an arm-chair near the table reading a newspaper. Madeleine, his wife, is sitting at the table darning socks.* Note that here we have a quite standard scene–act ratio. (That is, the nature of the scene, or situation, is "proper," in a quite classical or traditional sense, to the nature of the act that we see imitated.) A petty bourgeois couple, in a petty bourgeois interior; the wife engaging in a typical petty bourgeois duty: darning socks. Her husband, reading a newspaper; he is the typical sage of the headlines; he will be in the role of telling her. To her question, "Any news in the paper?" he answers with the extremes of news, the universal and the over-particularized: "A few comets and a cosmic disturbance somewhere in the universe"... and "The neighbours have been fined for letting their dogs make a mess on the pavement." Here is the subject of duty in burlesqued form, in the sense of the French expression, *faire ses devoirs.* (You can get the point better if you translate the sentence thus: "fined for letting dogs *do their job* on the sidewalk.") You might say that the idea of the wife as "victim" of duty is implicit in her darning of the socks; the theme of victimage is now explicit, though trivially, in the notion that the neighbours have been *fined* for their part in the dutiful conduct of the dogs. The reference to the "cosmic disturbance" would fit well as this play's particular equivalent for the traditional ecclesiastical role of "heaven" in thoughts of duty.

Next, in a half-realistic, half-grotesque way, such topics as "detachment," "renunciation," and "sacrifice" are introduced. All, obviously, are terms that one could "properly" encounter, when tracking down the implications of the idea summed up in the title.

But Choubert, the solemn hardline-thinker, is also entrusted with another job: he is to serve as spokesperson for the formal (or "informal?") tactics employed in this play:

> All the plays that have ever been written, from Ancient Greece to the present day, have never really been anything but thrillers. Drama's always been realistic and there's always been a detective about. Every play's an investigation brought to a successful conclusion. There's a riddle, and it's solved in the final scene. Sometimes earlier. You seek, and then you find. Might as well give the game away at the start.

And a bit later he sums up by defining the classics as "refined detective drama." In sum, the traditional structure of dramatic expectancy involves the kind of form exemplified to perfection in a play so wholly "Aristotelian" as Sophocles' *Oedipus Rex.*

In contrast, this play is not going to follow the traditional form whereby the *complications* of a riddle are first established, then the riddle is resolved in the *denouement.* Rather, this play will "process" its problem somewhat along the lines of the procedure in Samuel Beckett's play, the title of which, for our purposes, we might best translate as *Expecting Godot.*[3]

After Choubert's transformation from the dealer in journalistic clichés to the spokesman for the playwright's "anti-Aristotelian" dramaturgy, the couple fall into one of those embarrassing silences which Ionesco makes the most of. In its perversity, it is precisely the kind of silence that classical form would fear like poison. Then "someone is heard knocking at the door." (In terms of duty, the "knock of conscience?") The knocking is repeated several times, with someone shouting "Concierge! Concierge!" The couple is indignant that the concierge does not answer, and the wife observes quietly: "It's no business of ours. Neither of us is a concierge, you know. Everybody in society has his own special duty to perform!" (Clearly this is another implication drawn perversely from the idea of duty, as conceived *in terms of* the play's setting.) Eventually, after further business, a Detective is admitted – and soon there begins the series of transformations designed to successively reveal the various associated ideas which are, for the playwright, implicit in the ideas of duty and victimage. The Detective, we should recall, is looking for a character with a relevant name: *Mallot,* "evil destiny," a theme clearly on the "victimage" slope of the title, while the Detective's search is clearly on the slope of "duty," the sheerly compulsive nature of which is further suggested by the vagueness of his aim, though his role as a *detective* obviously makes him a proper fit for the theme, even as regards classical tests. This resource will be exploited throughout the play. In going through the sheer *forms* of sacrificial striving, without a corresponding *rationale,* the characters are properly designed to impose somnambulistic connotations upon the idea of all human conscience-laden effort, as though the sum of all our pursuits were like the tangled phantasies of a mosquito-plagued dreamer tossing in his sleep. Here also, of course, would be an implication, or tangle of implications, which the play tracks down.

We need not consider in detail the several steps that follow the entrance of the Detective. For our purposes the main thing is to note a kind of "non-temporal relationship" which the various episodes bear to the generating principle, as summed up in the title. (As we have said, in cases where a title did not happen to be so accurate, the critic would have to supply a working title of his own, along with arguments why it should be used instead of the actual title, to indicate the logic of the generative summarization.)

But I should here pause to make a brief statement about what I mean by a "non-temporal relationship" between the title and the various episodes or transformations which reveal one or another of the associated ideas implicit in the title. In the course of analyzing the myth of the Creation and the Fall in the first three chapters of Genesis, I found it necessary to work out what I have called a "Cycle of Terms Implicit in the Idea of 'Order.'" The most obvious of such implications, for instance, is the contrary term, "disorder." Other implications would be: the idea of "obedience" to the order, or "disobedience"; of "reward" for obedience, or "punishment" for disobedience; of "humility" as the attitude that leads into obedience, or of "pride" as the attitude that leads into disobedience; of some "author" or "authority" who gave the order or set up the order; of "reason" or "faith" as principles of rule that help enforce the order; or sensations and imaginings that function as temptations to resist the order, and so on. (The essay is reprinted in my book, *The Rhetoric of Religion.*)

The point is: in such a cycle of terms that imply one another, there is no one temporal succession. You can go from any of the terms to any of the others. For instance, you can with as much justice say either that the term "order" implies the contrary term "disorder," or that the term "disorder" implies the term "order."

However, when one turns to the mythic narrative in the opening chapters of Genesis, one finds a quite different situation. First, there is the Author and Authority who sets up the natural order; later in the Creation the creature is introduced to whom He explicitly gives a moral order (a thou-shalt-not); later comes the serpent who has the role of tempting against the order; then the disobedience; then the punishment, etc. In brief, as contrasted with a cycle of terministic implications such as I lined up in my chart, here everything proceeds in one irreversibly fixed direction.

In the Ionesco play, the various episodes occur in the one irreversible narrative direction in which they are printed. But so far as their relation to the title is concerned, each is analyzable directly as an implication of the seminal title. We might use the analogy of points along the arc of a circle.

I here have in mind a design of this sort:

Any narrative form (such as a play) in its necessary progression from one episode to the next is like the stages from A to I along the arc. But as regards the principle of internal consistency, *any* point along the arc is as though generated from Center O. And the various steps from A to I can be considered as *radiating* from generative principle O, regardless of their *particular* position along the arc of the narrative sequence.

For present purposes, then, our task is simply to examine this *radial* relation to and from the center, itself aptly indicated by the title, *Victims of Duty*. To list some of the more obvious points along the arc (our purpose now being not to work out the problem in detail but to illustrate it in principle):

A first transformation concerns the Detective. At the start, he is tentative, timid, deferential. But he soon moves in on the situation, and starts ordering the couple around. Surely here, too, is one of the ways in which duty is found to imply victimization. The pattern will get a sturdy variant near the end of the play when a fourth character, Nicolas, first rescues the husband from the Detective's tyranny, and then himself does the tyrannizing.

Among the other implications there are:

A. The episode, or transformation, in which the wife has become young, and the husband is impelled by his duties as a young lover. Let us, for convenience, henceforth call them, as in the play, "Madeleine" and "Choubert." In this scene, where Choubert is encouraged to keep going down (vaguely in search of Mallot), the action is marked by erotic double-meanings. And these in turn become transformed into connotations of filth (as Choubert affirms that he is walking in mud).

B. Next, by contrast, Madeleine is very old and Choubert's duties now are correspondingly transformed (along the lines, we might say, of the popular song: "Will you love me in December as you did in May?"). The theme of descent into the mud continues throughout this episode.

Note that, although these sudden shifts of identity might at first glance seem simply to violate the classical principles of form, a closer look helps us to realize how they but embody *the same principle of consistency* in a more recondite or "sophisticated" way. When the two are young, they act young; when they are old, they act old. Such *ad interim* consistency would be a perfect instance of what in my *Grammar of Motives* I call an "agent–act ratio" (which is to say, a kind of formal propriety whereby old people establish their identity for the audience by acting old and young people establish their identity by acting young; in brief, they exemplify the classical principle of acting in character). You might complicate such correlations, but in the last analysis you can't have anything unless you have expectations based upon *uniformity* of some sort. Trick it out as you will, you can't get a work of art without some measure of internal consistency. Man is of such a nature that, if you throw down pebbles at random, he will necessarily see them as falling into some kind of order. At its extreme, even the sheer word "chaos" imposes an order. A total violation of classical propriety is simply impossible, even on a box-office basis. For if a work did not embody classical principles of consistency and development at least in fragmentary ways, it could not even contrive to be.

C. The search next leads to Choubert's complete immersion, a fantastic equivalent, perhaps, of Hercules' dutiful labor in cleansing the Augean stables. (Also, it is a burlesque of baptism.)

D. Next, Madeleine and the Detective become Choubert's mother and father, with variations of maternal duty to son and son's filial duty to father (further complicated by Choubert's inability to make actual contact with the figures he is observing).

E. Episode detailing father's recital of his own conscience-ridden career, with correspondingly complicated relations to his son.

F. Choubert as actor, Madeleine and Detective as theatre-goers, witnessing his performance, critically. An episode in which the dutiful motives of the playwright's calling are fancifully touched upon.

G. Choubert transformed into Alpinist. The duty of *descent* now transformed into the duty of *ascent*. (Still, of course, the sheer *formality* of search, accentuated by the pointless references to Mallot.)

H. A passing moment during which Madeleine is a beggar woman. (This episode would touch upon problems of duty conceived in terms of a money economy viewed as the norm.)

I. The complexity of final transformations that might, for present purposes, be summed up as the completion of the search for essence or beginnings whereby Choubert becomes a sulky child being forcibly fed ("Chew! Swallow!"). During this infantile search for beginnings, the Detective has an accident: in a paroxysm of fear, he befouls himself, a form of purgation that, whatever its misfit with "Aristotelian" tragedy, would have gone well with Aristophanic comedy, and thus fits the "proprieties" of Ionesco's grotesque. And finally, there is the total socialization of duty as so conceived: "While all the characters are ordering one another to chew and swallow, the curtain falls."

In sum, note that all these episodes, or transformations, are placeable as various implications of the same title. In this sense, they could be described as "deducible from" the title, when viewed *in terms of* the conditions indicated in the opening petty bourgeois stage-set (scene), which immediately begins to form our expectancies, at least negatively, in the sense that we should not expect to see the play unfold, say, in the style of *King Lear*.

Ideally, these episodes should be so arranged that the unfolding of each transformation prepares for the next, as the removal of one card from a deck reveals the next one immediately beneath it. And the critic would complete his particular task with regard to the play by analyzing such a series of steps as an irreversible, temporal sequence. That is, he should discuss not only their relationship to the central idea from which they all radiate, but also their order with relation to one another along the arc of their development, though we might well take it for granted that works of this sort are more likely to meet in fragmentary and distorted ways the tests of internal consistency ("repetitive" form) than to show up as Sophoclean examples of "progressive" form. And we should always keep ourselves reminded that, in violating any particular brand of conventional form, a work can set up its own conventions. In all probability such improvising is aided these days by the experimental nature of contemporary science. The formal *artistic* equivalent of such scientific tentatives might well be the *tour de force*, a use-once-and-throw-away kind of "hygienic" inventiveness. And for a complete analysis, along with the theme of duty and victimage, the critic should also have to trace the series of releases by which the play unfolds its secondary theme, the rationale for the so-called anti-Aristotelian theatre, which is sporadically developed at strategic spots along the way. (In its way, the drama is as "doctrinal" as Ibsen's *Enemy of the People* or James Joyce's *Portrait of the Artist as a Young Man*; on this score, it is not much different from the Christian gospels, so far as the interweaving of "story" and "message" is concerned.)

In sum: at a close look we find that the classical principles of consistency are here being soundly exploited. Though the many abrupt transformations which the characters undergo might at first glance seem to outrage the norms of classical dramaturgy, within the limits of each episode the scene–act and agent–act ratios proper to that particular episode are maintained, usually with total uniformity, sometimes with minor momentary incursions of transformation-within-transformation. It is only by some measure of *uniformity* that a structure of expectation can arise at all. And seen from this point of view, the sudden transformations of role are hardly other than a new bit of conventional form which the audience quickly learns to *expect*, a trick way of juxtaposing changes by sheer elision, or without the use of another convention, the curtain, which might be used only at the *end* of the play, or not at all.

Even the most traditional of dramas can also lend themselves to this kind of analysis, and perhaps critics should always add this dimension when inquiring into the internal structure of a work. In brief, the attempt to work out a calculus for studying the internal consistency (repetitive form) of contemporary plays (that on their face are quite loose in structure) may also involve lines of inquiry that fit *all* plays. But such an approach is made more necessary in the case of modern works which have abandoned the traditional classical criteria of form, except in such perverse and fragmentary manifestations as we have been considering. The *tour de force* kind of conventions typical of contemporary "experimental" form (form that in this sense is analogous to "laboratory method") may involve abrupt associative leaps, whereas in classical forms such a way of ticking things off step by step might be hidden by transitions and modulations.

Notes

1 M. Puchner, "Kenneth Burke: Theater, Philosophy, and the Limits of Performance," in *Staging Philosophy: Intersections of Theater, Performance, and Philosophy*, ed. D. Krasner and D. Z. Saltz (Ann Arbor: University of Michigan Press, 2006), 46.

2 K. Burke, *The Philosophy of Literary Form* (Berkeley: University of California Press, 1973), 89.

3 In effect, the *formal principle* of dramatic expectation becomes the *theme* of the drama. And notable among its implications is the burlesque of religious vigil (a frustrated awaiting of the savior).

Chapter 49

Jacques Derrida (1930–2004)

One of the most influential and controversial critics of the last quarter of the twentieth century, Jacques Derrida is known for literary and cultural "deconstruction." Deconstruction challenges (among other ideas) Enlightenment Western rationalism (logocentrism), Lévi-Strauss's structuralism, Husserl's phenomenology, Saussure's language as a singular signifying system, and Hegel's dialectic. It emphasizes instead a radical subversion of these sacrosanct ideas. Derrida's deconstruction situates texts and their interpretation in a fungible context. He critiques Husserl's phenomenology, calling it a "metaphysics of presence" that suppresses or avoids what is absent, and challenges representational certainty. He writes that theory "ought to suspend or at any rate to complicate, with great caution, the naïve opening that once linked the text to its thing, referent, or reality, or even to some last conceptual of semantic instance."[1] He mistrusted the accepted relationship of reality and representation, as if representation can unequivocally stand in for reality. Such one-to-one relationship of the thing and its representation is for Derrida (as well as for Foucault and other poststructuralists) marked by "*différance*," a term he coined to describe a fluid interpretation. Derrida notes that in highlighting *différance* (a combination of "to differ" and "to defer"), "everything is a matter of strategy and risk. It is a question of strategy because no transcendent truth present outside the sphere of writing can theologically command the totality of this field." Reading (and observing theatre) is a "strategy without finality."[2] Texts and plays for Derrida interface with other texts and plays, other realities and rhetoric, ceaselessly absorbing, interfacing with, and reinventing these "other" forms

Jacques Derrida, "Theatre of Cruelty and the Closure of Representation" (1966). Lecture originally delivered as "Le théâtre de la cruauté et la clôture de la représentation" at the Artaud colloquium, International Festival of University Theater, Parma, April 1966, and published in *Critique* 230 (July 1966). Excerpted here from Derrida, *Writing and Difference*, tr. Alan Bass (Chicago: University of Chicago Press, 1978), 232–9. © 1978 by The University of Chicago. Reprinted by permission of The University of Chicago Press and Taylor and Francis Books UK.

and concepts. In the act of creating – actually "re-creating" – what remains is merely a "trace" of the original idea, "the simulacrum of a presence that dislocates, displaces, and refers beyond itself."[3] Derrida's intellectual models were Bataille and Artaud, rebel thinkers determined to undermine certainties and strip the scaffolding of values. For Derrida texts are open to interpretations, and then reopened, challenging even the very critique that first called the status quo into question. In this way a text is, to follow Nietzsche, rhetoric (the term used by poststructuralists is "discourse"), a series of words whose meaning is thrown open to various interpretations. Along with Derrida's friend and colleague Paul de Man, poststructuralists inaugurated schools of thought throughout the Anglo-European world that were as prolific as they were controversial.

In the following essay Derrida considers Artaud's theatre of cruelty as a form of deconstruction of the theatre. Representation, which even Artaud depended on, must be undermined in the theatre of cruelty. Yet herein is Artaud's paradox: the collapse of meaning and representation will nullify theatre even as it attempts to liberate it from the confines of representation. To create a theatre without representation is to situate the theatre outside of consciousness. Representation is the doubling (reflecting, mimesis, repetition) that Artaud seeks to overcome. Yet, in circumventing representation, theatre loses its moorings as a spatial-temporal event, becoming a concept solely of the mind. Derrida's analysis of what Shannon Jackson calls Artaud's "irreconcilable hopes" and "metaphysical yearnings" acknowledges that Artaud was aware of the paradox between an embodied immediacy and the nature of theatrical mimesis.[4] Artaud's dilemma is also Derrida's (and Plato's, Aristotle's, and Nietzsche's): if writing is deconstructing by the very act of writing, what meaning can be construed by Derrida's own words? Derrida's important essay finds in Artaud a kindred scholar wrestling with the contradictions of a theory that Derrida would examine throughout his life.

Theatre of Cruelty and the Closure of Representation (1966)

[…] If throughout the world today – and so many examples bear witness to this in the most striking fashion – all theatrical audacity declares its fidelity to Artaud (correctly or incorrectly, but with increasing insistency), then the question of the theatre of cruelty, of its present inexistence and its implacable necessity, has the value of a *historic* question. A historic question not because it could be inscribed within what is called the history of theatre, not because it would be epoch-making within the becoming of theatrical forms, or because it would occupy a position within the succession of models of theatrical representation. This question is historic in an absolute and radical sense. It announces the limit of representation.

The theatre of cruelty is not *a representation*. It is life itself, in the extent to which life is unrepresentable. Life is the nonrepresentable origin of representation. "I have therefore said 'cruelty' as I might have said 'life.'"[5] This life carries man along with it, but is not primarily the life of man. The latter is only a representation of life, and such is the limit – the humanist limit – of the metaphysics of classical theatre. "The theatre as we practice it can therefore be reproached with a terrible lack of imagination. The theatre must make itself the equal of life – not an individual life, that individual aspect of life in which CHARACTERS triumph, but the sort of liberated life which sweeps away human individuality and in which man is only a reflection" (*TD*, 116).

Is not the most naïve form of representation *mimesis*? Like Nietzsche – and the affinities do not end there – Artaud wants to have done with the *imitative* concept of art, with the Aristotelian aesthetics[6] in which the metaphysics of Western art comes into its own. "Art is not the imitation of life, but life is the imitation of a transcendental principle which art puts us into communication with once again."[7]

Theatrical art should be the primordial and privileged site of this destruction of imitation: more than any other art, it has been marked by the labor of total representation in which the affirmation of life lets itself be doubled and emptied by negation. This representation, whose structure is imprinted not only on the art, but on the entire culture of the West (its religions, philosophies, politics), therefore designates more than just a particular type of theatrical construction. This is why the question put to us today by far exceeds the bounds of theatrical technology. Such is Artaud's most obstinate affirmation: technical or theatrological reflection is not to be treated marginally. The decline of the theatre doubtless begins with the possibility of such a dissociation. This can be emphasized without weakening the importance or interest of theatrological problems, or of the revolutions which may occur within the limits of theatrological problems, or of the revolutions which may occur within the limits of theatrical technique. But Artaud's intention indicates these limits. For as long as these technical and intratheatrical revolutions do not penetrate the very foundations of Western theatre, they will belong to the history and to the stage that Antonin Artaud wanted to explode.

What does it mean to break this structure of belonging? Is it possible to do so? Under what conditions can a theatre today legitimately invoke Artaud's name? It is only a fact that so many directors wish to be acknowledged as Artaud's heirs, that is (as has been written), his "illegitimate sons." The question of justification and legality must also be raised. With what criteria can such a claim be recognized as unfounded? Under what conditions could an authentic "theatre of cruelty" "begin to exist?" These simultaneously technical and "metaphysical" questions (metaphysical in the sense understood by Artaud), arise spontaneously from the reading of all the texts in *The Theatre and Its Double*, for these texts are more *solicitations* than a sum of precepts, more a system of critiques *shaking the entirety* of Occidental history than a treatise on theatrical practice.

The theatre of cruelty expulses God from the stage. It does not put a new atheist discourse on stage, or give atheism a platform, or give over theatrical space to a philosophizing logic that would once more, to our greater lassitude, proclaim the death of God. The theatrical practice of cruelty, in its action and structure, inhabits or rather *produces* a nontheological space.

The stage is theological for as long as it is dominated by speech, by a will to speech, by the layout of a primary logos which does not belong to the theatrical site and governs it from a distance. The stage is theological for as long as its structure, following the entirety of tradition, comports the following elements: an author-creator who, absent and from afar, is armed with a text and keeps watch over, assembles, regulates the time or the meaning of representation, letting this latter *represent* him as concerns what is called the content of his thoughts, his intentions, his ideas. He lets representation represent him through representatives, directors or actors, enslaved interpreters who represent characters who, primarily through what they say, more or less directly represent the thought of the "creator." Interpretive slaves who faithfully execute the providential designs of the "master." Who moreover – and this is the ironic rule of the representative structure which organizes all these relationships – creates nothing, has only the illusion of having created, because he only transcribes and makes available for reading a text whose nature is itself necessarily representative; and this representative text maintains with what is called the "real" (the existing real, the "reality" about which Artaud said, in the "Avertissement" to *Le moine*, that it is an "excrement of the mind") an imitative and reproductive relationship. Finally, the theological stage comports a passive, seated public, a public of spectators, of consumers, of "enjoyers" – as Nietzsche and Artaud both say – attending a production that lacks true volume or depth, a production that is level, offered to their voyeuristic scrutiny. (In the theatre of cruelty, pure visibility is not exposed to voyeurism.) This general structure in which each agency is linked to all the others by representation, in which the irrepresentability of the living present is dissimulated or dissolved, suppressed or deported within the infinite chain of representations – this structure has never been modified. All revolutions have maintained it intact, and most often have tended to protect or restore it. And it is the phonetic text, speech, transmitted discourse – eventually transmitted by the prompter whose hole is the hidden but indispensable center of representative structure – which ensures the movement of representation. Whatever their importance, all the pictorial, musical and even gesticular forms introduced into Western theatre can only, in the best of cases, illustrate, accompany, serve, or decorate a text, a verbal fabric, a logos which *is said* in the beginning. "If then, the author is the man who arranges the language of speech and the director is his slave, there is merely a question of words. There is here a confusion over terms, stemming from the fact that, for us, and according to the sense generally attributed to the word *director*, this man is merely an artisan, an adapter, a kind of translator eternally devoted to making a dramatic work pass from one language into another; this confusion will be possible and the director will be forced to play second fiddle to the author, only so long as there is a tacit agreement that the language of words is superior to others and that the theater admits none other than this one language" (*TD*, 119). This does not imply, of course, that to be faithful to Artaud it suffices to give a great deal of importance and responsibility to the "director" while maintaining the classical structure.

By virtue of the word (or rather the unity of the word and the concept, as we will say later – and this specification will be important) and beneath the theological ascendancy both of the "verb [which] is the measure of our impotency" (*OC* 4: 277) and of our fear, it is indeed the stage which finds itself threatened throughout the Western tradition. The Occident – and such is the energy of its essence – has worked only for the erasure of the stage. For a stage which does nothing but illustrate a discourse is no longer entirely a stage. Its relation to speech is its malady, and "we repeat that the epoch is sick" (*OC* 4: 280). To reconstitute the stage, finally to put on stage and to overthrow the tyranny of the text is thus one and the same gesture. "The triumph of pure mise en scène" (*OC* 4: 305).

This classical forgetting of the stage is then confused with the history of theatre and with all of Western culture; indeed, it even guaranteed their unfolding. And yet, despite this "forgetting," the theatre and its arts have lived richly for over twenty-five centuries: an experience of mutations and perturbations which cannot be set aside, despite the peaceful and impassive immobility of the fundamental structures. Thus, in question is not only a forgetting or a simple surface concealment. A certain stage has maintained with the "forgotten," but, in truth, violently erased, stage a secret communication, a certain relationship of *betrayal*, if to betray is at once to denature through infidelity, but also to let oneself be evinced despite oneself, and to manifest the foundation of force. This explains why classical theatre, in Artaud's eyes, is not simply the absence, negation, or forgetting of theatre, is not a nontheatre: it is a mark of cancellation that lets what it covers be read; and it is corruption also, a "perversion," a *seduction*, the margin of an aberration whose meaning and measure are visible only beyond birth, at the eve of theatrical representation, at the origin of tragedy. Or, for example, in the realm of the "Orphic Mysteries which subjugated Plato," or the "Mysteries of Eleusis" stripped of the interpretations with which they have been covered, or the "pure beauty of which Plato, at least once in this world, must have found the complete, sonorous, streaming naked realization" (*TD*, 52). Artaud is indeed speaking of perversion and not of forgetting, for example, in this letter to Benjamin Crémieux:

> The theatre, an independent and autonomous art, must, in order to *revive or simply to live*, realize what differentiates it from text, pure speech, literature, and all other fixed and written means. We can perfectly well continue to conceive of a theater based upon the authority of the text, and on a text more and more wordy, diffuse, and boring, to which the esthetics of the stage would be subject. But this conception of theatre, which consists of having people sit on a certain number of straight-backed or overstuffed chairs placed in a row and tell each other stories, however marvelous, is, if not the absolute negation of theatre – which does not absolutely require movement in order to be what it should – certainly its *perversion* (*TD*, 106; my italics).

Released from the text and the author-god, mise en scène would be returned to its creative and founding freedom. The director and the participants (who would no longer be actors or spectators) would cease to be the instruments and organs of representation. Is this to say that Artaud would have refused the name *representation* for the theatre of cruelty? No, provided that we clarify the difficult and equivocal meaning of this notion. Here, we would have to be able to play upon all the German words that we indistinctly translate with the unique word representation. The stage, certainly, *will no longer represent*, since it will not operate as an addition, as the sensory illustration of a text already written, thought, or lived outside the stage, which the stage would then only repeat but whose fabric it would not constitute. The stage will no longer operate as the repetition of a *present*, will no longer *re*-present a present that would exist elsewhere and prior to it, a present that would exist elsewhere and prior to it, a present whose plenitude would be older than it, absent from it, and rightfully capable of doing without it: the being-present-to-itself of the absolute Logos, the living present of God. Nor will the stage be a representation, if representation means the surface of a spectacle displayed for spectators. It will not even offer the presentation of a present, if present signifies that which is maintained *in front* of me. Cruel representation must permeate me. And nonrepresentation is, thus, original representation, if representation signifies, also, the unfolding of a volume, a multidimensional milieu, an experience which produces its own space. *Spacing* [*espacement*], that is to say, the production of a space that no speech could condense or comprehend (since speech primarily presupposes this spacing), thereby appeals to a time that is no longer that of so-called phonic linearity, appeals to "a new notion of space" and "a specific idea of time" (*TD*, 124). "We intend to base the theatre upon spectacle before everything else, and we shall introduce into the spectacle a new notion of space utilized on all possible levels and in all degrees of perspective in depth and height, and within this notion a specific idea of time will be added to that of movement... Thus, theatre space will be utilized not only in its dimensions and volume but, so to speak, in its undersides (*dans ses dessous*)" (*TD*, 124).

Thus, the closure of classical representation, but also the reconstitution of a closed space of original representation, the archi-manifestation of force or of life. A closed space, that is to say a space produced from within itself and no longer organized from the vantage of an other absent site, an illocality, an alibi or invisible utopia. The end of representation, but also original representation; the end of interpretation, but also an original interpretation that no master-speech, no project of mastery will have permeated and leveled in advance. A visible representation, certainly, directed against the speech which eludes sight – and Artaud insists upon the productive images without which there would be no theatre (*theaomai*) – but whose visibility does not consist of a spectacle mounted by the discourse of the master. Representation, then, as the autopresentation of pure visibility and even pure sensibility.[8] [...]

Notes

1   J. Derrida, *Dissemination*, tr. B. Johnson (Chicago: University of Chicago Press, 1981), 43.

2   J. Derrida, "Différance," in *Speech and Phenomena, And Other Essays on Husserl's Theory of Signs*, tr. D. B. Allison (1968; Evanston: Northwestern University Press, 1973), 135.

3   Ibid., 156.

4   S. Jackson, *Professing Performance: Theatre in the Academy from Philology to Performativity* (Cambridge: Cambridge University Press, 2004), 118.

5   Artaud, *The Theatre and its Double*, tr. M. C. Richards (New York: Grove, 1958), 114. Hereafter cited as *TD* with page numbers in the text. See Chapter 26, this volume. – Editor's note.

6   "The psychology of orgiasm conceived as the feeling of a superabundance of vitality and strength, within the scope of which even pain acts as a *stimulus*, gave me the key to the concept of *tragic* feeling, which has been misunderstood not only by Aristotle, but also even more by our pessimists." (Friedrich Nietzsche, *The Twilight of the Idols*, tr. A. Ludovici [New York: Russell & Russell, 1964], 119). Art, as the imitation of nature, communicates in an essential way with the theme of catharsis. "Not in order to escape from terror and pity, not to purify one's self of a dangerous passion by discharging it with vehemence – this is how Aristotle understood it – but to be far beyond terror and pity and to be the eternal lust of becoming itself – that lust which also involves the *lust of destruction*. And with this I once more come into touch with the spot from which I once set out – the 'Birth of Tragedy' was my first transvaluation of all values: with this again I take my stand upon the soil from out of which my will and my capacity spring – I, the last disciple of the philosopher Dionysus – I, the prophet of eternal recurrence." (Ibid., 120).

7   Artaud, *Oeuvres complètes* 4 (Paris: Gallimard, 1970), 310. Further references to this text are cited as *OC* with page numbers. – Editor's note.

8   Nietzsche, *Twilight of the Idols*, 6.

Chapter 50

Jerzy Grotowski (1933–1999)

Jerzy Grotowski was a director and theorist. His work in the Polish Laboratory theatre (*Laboratorium*) during the 1960s revolutionized theatre training. His concept of "poor theatre" stripped the theatre of its showiness, emphasizing instead the actor's voice and body as theatre's essential features. His co-authored book, *Towards a Poor Theatre* (1968), conveys his idea of *via negativa*, meaning the eradication of the actor's bourgeois mannerism and clichés. Grotowski wanted to excavate the root of the performing arts; he found that the shallowness of commercial theatre inhibited the direct link between performer and audience. He was influenced by early twentieth-century directors Stanislavsky, Vakhtanghov, and Meyerhold; but for Grotowski their ideas had been polluted by embellished razzle-dazzle. He wanted to find the essence of their thoughts on physical theatre, privileging the actor over sets, lights, costume, props, and primarily theatre's commercialization. He rejected the actor's "bag of tricks," gestures or behaviors that showcased the actor's ostentatious charm or stale recreation of previous successes. Instead he challenged actors to reinvent themselves every time they appeared on stage by exposing their vulnerability and physical dexterity. The theatre should be a sacred location, he believed, akin to religious ritual but enjoying its uniqueness separate from the pulpit. His major directorial works were Mayakovsky's *Mystery-Bouffe* (1960), Kalidasa's *Shukuntula* (1960), Wyspiański's *Acropolis* (1962), Marlowe's *Faust* (1963), and Calderón's *The Constant Prince* (1973).

Jerzy Grotowski, "Towards the Poor Theatre," tr. T. K. Wiewiorowski, *Tulane Drama Review* 11.3 (Spring 1967), 60–5. © 1967 by Tulane Drama Review. Reprinted by permission of TDR/The Drama Review.

Towards the Poor Theatre (1967)

The Spiritual Process Through Signs

I am a bit impatient when asked, "What is the origin of your experimental theatre productions?" The assumption seems to be that "experimental" work is tangential (toying with some "new" technique each time) and tributary. The result is supposed to be a contribution to modern staging – scenography using current sculptural or electronic ideas, contemporary music, actors independently projecting clownish or cabaret stereotypes. I know that scene: I used to be part of it. Our Theatre Lab productions are going in another direction. In the first place, we are trying to avoid eclecticism, trying to resist thinking of theatre as a composite of disciplines. We are seeking to define what is distinctively theatre, what separates this activity from other categories of performance and spectacle. Secondly, our productions are detailed investigations of the actor–audience relationship. That is, *we consider the spiritual and scenic technique of the actor as the core of theatre art*.

It is difficult to locate the exact sources of this approach, but I can speak of its tradition. I was brought up on Stanislavski; his persistent study, his systematic renewal of the methods of observation, and his dialectical relationship to his own earlier work make him my personal ideal. Stanislavski asked the key methodological questions. Our solutions, however, differ widely from his – sometimes we reach opposite conclusions.

I have studied all the major actor-training methods of Europe and beyond. Most important for my purposes are: Dullin's rhythm exercises, Delsarte's investigations of centrifugal reactions, Stanislavski's work on "physical actions," Meyerhold's biomechanical training, Vakhtanghov's synthesis. Also particularly stimulating to me are the training techniques of oriental theatre – specifically the Peking Opera, Indian Kathakali, and Japanese No theatre. I could cite other theatrical systems, but the method which we are developing is not a combination of techniques borrowed from these sources (although we sometimes adapt elements for our use). We do not want to teach the actor a predetermined set of skills or give him a "bag of tricks." Ours is not a deductive method of collecting skills. *Our goal is to expose totally the spiritual process of the actor*. This is not an egoistic technique based on the actor's enjoyment of his own emotional experience, but rather the revealing technique of trance, an integration of spiritual, psychic, and physical faculties climaxing in a "penetration" from and by the actor's intimate instinctive psyche: the actor in the act of giving himself.

The education of an actor in our theatre is not a matter of teaching him something; we attempt to eliminate his organism's resistance to this spiritual process. The result is freedom from the time-lapse between inner impulse and outer reaction. Impulse and action are concurrent: *the body vanishes, burns*. The spectator sees only the visible reflection of spiritual impulses.

Ours then is *via negativa* – not a collection of skills but an eradication of blocks. One may object that the actor's spiritual process is itself a skill. This is not so: the process cannot be taught. The specially designed exercises are essentially only a means to proper concentration and only partially related to physico-plastic or verbal training. Sometimes, after years of work, the actor is able to discover in himself the beginning of this process. Then it is possible to carefully cultivate what has been awakened. The process itself, though to some extent dependent upon concentration, confidence, exposure, and almost disappearance into (acting) the role, is not voluntary. The requisite state of mind is a passive readiness to realize an active role, a state in which one does not "want to do that" but rather "resigns from not doing it."

Most of the actors at the Theatre Lab are just beginning to work toward the possibility of making such a process visible. In their daily work they do not concentrate on the spiritual technique but on the composition of the role, on the construction of form, on the expression of signs – i.e., on artifice. There is no contradiction between inner technique and artifice (articulation of a role by signs). We believe that a spiritual process which is not supported and expressed by a formal articulation and disciplined structuring of the role will collapse in shapelessness. And we find that artificial composition not only does not limit the spiritual but actually leads to it. (The tropistic tension between the inner process and the form strengthens both. The form is like a baited trap, to which the spiritual process responds spontaneously and against which it struggles.) The forms of common "natural" behavior obscure the truth; we compose a role as a system of signs which demonstrate what is behind the mask of common vision: the dialectics of human behavior. At a moment of psychic shock, a moment of terror, of mortal danger or tremendous joy, a man does not behave "naturally." A man in an elevated spiritual state uses rhythmically articulated signs, begins to dance, to sing. *A sign*, not a common gesture, is the elementary integer of expression for us.

In terms of formal technique, we do not work by proliferation of signs, or by accumulation of signs (as in the formal repetitions of oriental theatre). Rather, we subtract, seeking *distillation* of signs by eliminating those elements of "natural" behavior which obscure pure impulse. Another technique which illuminates the hidden structure of signs is *contradiction* (between gesture and voice, voice and word, word and thought, will and action, etc.) – here, too, we take the *via negativa*.

The Poor Theatre

It is difficult to say precisely what elements in our productions result from a consciously formulated program and what derive from the structure of our imagination. I am frequently asked whether certain "medieval" effects indicate an intentional return to "ritual roots." There is no single answer. At our present point of artistic awareness, the problem of mythic "roots," of the elementary human situation, has definite meaning. However, this is not a product of a "philosophy of art" but comes from the practical discovery and use of the rules of theatre. That is, the productions do not spring from *a priori* aesthetic postulates; rather, as Sartre has said: "Each technique leads to metaphysics."

For several years, I vacillated between practice-born impulses and the application of *a priori* principles, without seeing the contradiction. My friend and colleague Ludwik Flaszen was the first to point out this confusion in my work: the material and techniques which came spontaneously in preparing the production, from the very nature of the work, were revealing and promising; but what I had taken to be applications of theoretical assumptions were actually more functions of my personality than of my intellect. I realized that the production led to awareness rather than being the product of awareness. Since 1960, my emphasis has been on methodology. Through practical experimentation I sought to answer the questions with which I had begun: What is the theatre? What is unique about it? What can it do that film and television cannot? Two concrete conceptions crystallized: the poor theatre, and performance as an act of transgression.

By gradually eliminating whatever proved superfluous, we found that theatre can exist without make-up, without autonomic costume and scenography, without a separate performance area (stage), without lighting and sound effects, etc. It cannot exist without the actor–spectator relationship of perceptual, direct, "live" communion. This is an ancient theoretical truth, of course, but when rigorously tested in practice it undermines most of our usual ideas about theatre. It challenges the notion of theatre as a synthesis of disparate creative disciplines – literature, sculpture, painting, architecture, lighting, acting (under the direction of a *metteur-en-scène*). This "synthetic theatre" is the contemporary theatre, which we readily call the "Rich Theatre" – rich in flaws.

The Rich Theatre depends on artistic kleptomania, drawing from other disciplines, constructing hybrid-spectacles, conglomerates without backbone or integrity, yet presented as an organic art-work. By multiplying assimilated elements, the Rich Theatre tries to escape the impasse presented by movies and television. Since film and TV excel in the area of mechanical functions (montage, instantaneous change of place, etc.), the Rich Theatre countered with a blatantly compensatory call for "total theatre." The integration of borrowed mechanisms (movie screens onstage, for example) means a sophisticated technical plant, permitting great mobility and dynamism. And if the stage and/or auditorium were mobile, constantly changing perspective would be possible. This is all nonsense.

No matter how much theatre expands and exploits its mechanical resources, it will remain technologically inferior to film and television. Consequently, the Theatre Lab proposes to accept the poverty of the theatre. We have resigned from the stage and auditorium plant: for each production, a new space is designed for the actors and spectators. Thus, infinite variation of performer–audience relationships is possible. The actors can play among the spectators, directly contacting the audience and giving it a passive role in the drama [e.g., the Lab's productions of Byron's *Cain* and Kalidasa's *Shukuntula*]. Or the actors may build structures among the spectators and thus include them in the architecture of action, subjecting them to a sense of the pressure and congestion and limitation of space [Wyspiański's *Acropolis*]. Or the actors may play among the spectators and ignore them, looking through them. The spectators may be separated from the actors – for example, by a high fence, over which only their heads protrude [*The Constant Prince*, by Calderón]; from this radically slanted perspective, they look down on the actors as if watching animals in a ring, or like medical students watching an operation (also, this detached, downward viewing gives the action a sense of moral transgression). Or the entire hall is used as a concrete place: Faust's "last supper" in a monastery refectory, where Faust entertains the spectators, who are guests at a baroque feast served on huge tables, offering episodes from his life. The elimination of stage–auditorium dichotomy is not the important thing – that simply creates a bare laboratory situation, an appropriate area for investigation. The essential concern is finding the proper spectator–actor relationship for each type of show and embodying the decision in physical arrangements.

We forsook lighting effects, and this revealed a wide range of possibilities for the actor's use of stationary light-sources by deliberate work with shadows, bright spots, etc. This led us to the illuminated spectator as a functional part of the performance. It also became evident that the actors, like figures in El Greco's paintings, can "illuminate" through spiritual technique, becoming a source of "psychic light." We abandoned make-up, fake noses, pillow-stuffed bellies – everything that the actor puts on in the dressing room before performance. We found that it was consummately theatrical for the actor to transform from type to type, character to character, silhouette to silhouette – while the audience watched – in a *poor* manner, using only his own body and craft. The composition of a fixed facial expression by using the actor's own muscles and inner impulses achieves the effect of a strikingly theatrical transubstantiation, while the mask prepared by a make-up artist is only a trick.

Similarly, a costume with no autonomous value, existing only in connection with a particular character and his activities, can be transformed before the audience, contrasted with the actor's functions, etc. Elimination of plastic elements which have a life of their own (i.e., represent something independent of the actor's activities) led to the creation by the actor of the most elementary and obvious objects. By his controlled use of gesture the actor transforms the floor into a sea, a table into a confessional, a piece of iron into an animate partner, etc. Elimination of music (live or recorded) not produced by the actors enables the performance itself to become music through the orchestration of voices and clashing objects. We know that the text *per se* is not theatre, that it becomes theatre only through the actors' use of it – as an intonation, as a combination of sounds, as a musical unit.

The acceptance of the poverty of theatre, stripped of all that is not essential to it, revealed to us not only the backbone of the medium, but also the deep riches which lie in the very nature of the art-form.

The Spectacle as Act of Transgression

Why are we concerned with art? To cross our frontiers, exceed our limitations, fill our emptiness – fulfill ourselves. This is not a condition but a process in which what is dark in us slowly becomes transparent. In this struggle with one's own truth, this effort to peel off the life-mask, the theatre, with its full-fleshed perceptivity, has always seemed to me a place of provocation. It is capable of challenging itself and its audience by violating accepted stereotypes of vision, feeling, and judgment – more jarring because it is imaged in the human organism's breath, body, and inner impulses. This defiance of taboo, this transgression, provides the shock which rips off the mask, enabling us to give ourselves nakedly to something which is impossible to define but which contains Eros and Caritas.

I am tempted by elementary and archaic religious and national taboos. Fascinated and tremulous, I feel the need to collide with these values, I want to blaspheme, to free my impulses and provoke a confrontation between personal experience and epochal experience and prejudice. This element of our productions has been variously called "collision with the roots," "the dialectics of mockery and apotheosis," or even "religion expressed through blasphemy; love speaking out through hate."

As soon as my practical awareness became conscious and when experiment led to a method, I was compelled to take a fresh look at the history of theatre in relation to other branches of knowledge, especially cultural and psychological anthropology. A rational review of the problem of myth was called for. Then I clearly saw that myth was both a primeval situation and a complex model with an independent existence in the psychology of social groups, inspiring group behavior and tendencies.

The theatre, when it was still part of religion, was already theatre: it liberated the spiritual energy of the congregation or tribe by incorporating myth. The spectator thus had a renewed awareness of his personal truth in the truth of the myth, and through fright he came to catharsis. It was not by chance that the Middle Ages produced the idea of "sacral parody." But today's situation is much different. As social groupings are less and less defined by religion, traditional mythic forms are in flux, disappearing and being reincarnated. The spectators are more and more individuated in their relation to the myth as corporate truth or group model, and belief is often a matter of intellectual conviction. This means that it is much more difficult to elicit the sort of shock needed to get at those psychic layers behind the life-mask. Group identification with myth – the equation of personal, individual truth with universal truth – is virtually impossible today.

What is possible? First, *confrontation* with myth rather than identification. In other words, while retaining our private experiences, we can attempt to incarnate myth, putting on its ill-fitting skin to perceive the relativity of our problems, their connection to the "roots," and the relativity of the "roots" in the light of today's experience. If the situation is brutal, if we strip ourselves and touch an extraordinarily intimate layer, exposing it, the life-mask cracks and falls away. Secondly, even with the loss of a "common sky" of belief and the loss of impregnable boundaries, the perceptivity of the human organism remains. Only myth – incarnate in the fact of the actor, in his living organism – can function as a taboo. The violation of the living organism, the exposure carried to outrageous excess, returns us to a concrete mythical situation, an experience of common human truth.

Originality and Humility

Again, the rational sources of our terminology cannot be cited precisely. I am often asked about Artaud when I speak of "brutality," although his formulations were based on different premises and took a different tack. Artaud was an extraordinary visionary, but his writings have little methodological meaning because they are not the product of long-term practical investigations. They are an astounding prophecy, not a program. When I speak of "roots" or "mythical soul," I am asked about Nietzsche; if I call it "group imagination," Durkheim comes up; if I call it "archetypes," Jung. But my formulations are not derived from humanistic disciplines, though I may use them for analysis. When I speak of the actor's expression of signs, I am asked about oriental theatre, particularly classical Chinese theatre (especially when it is known that I studied there). But the hieroglyphic signs of the oriental theatre are inflexible, like an alphabet, whereas the signs we use are the skeletal forms of human action, a crystallization of a role, an articulation of the particular psycho-physiology of the actor.

I am not claiming absolute originality. We are of course influenced osmotically by our culture; just by living when and where we do, our deeds and needs reflect a whole bundle of traditional knowledge about man and art, reflect tacitly accepted prejudices, forecasts, and expectations. When we confront the general tradition of the Great Reform of the theatre from Stanislavski to Dullin and from Meyerhold to Artaud, we realize that we have not started from scratch but are operating in a defined and special atmosphere. When our investigation reveals and confirms someone else's flash of intuition, we are filled with humility. We realize that theatre has certain objective laws and that fulfillment is possible only within them, or, as Thomas Mann said, through a kind of "higher obedience," to which we give our "dignified attention."

Leadership in Rebirth

I hold a peculiar position of leadership in the Polish Theatre Laboratory. I am not simply the director or producer or "spiritual instructor." In the first place, my relation to the work is certainly not one-way or didactic. If my suggestions are reflected in the spatial compositions of our architect Gurawski, it must be understood that my vision has been formed by years of collaboration with him.

There is something incomparably intimate and productive in the work with the actor entrusted to me. He must be attentive and confident and free, for our labor is to explore his possibilities to the utmost. His growth is attended by observation, astonishment, and desire to help; my growth is projected onto him, or, rather, is *found in him* – and our common growth becomes revelation. This is not instruction of a pupil but utter opening to another person, in which the phenomenon of "shared or double birth" becomes possible. The actor is reborn – not only as an actor but as a man – and with him, I am reborn. It is a clumsy way of expressing it, but what is achieved is a total acceptance of one human being by another.

Chapter 51

Raymond Williams (1921–1988)

Raymond Williams was a Marxist literary critic, novelist, and social theorist. He investigated "culture," challenging the general trend of mid-twentieth-century New Critics who emphasized literature as stand-alone objects devoid of social references. In his other major work on drama, *Modern Tragedy* (1966), he defends the tragic genre in light of critics who dismiss it as a relic of the past. Contemporary life may not hold fate in the same regard, but our fears warrant tragic consequences. Ancient tragedy depended on order and the disarray occurring within the purview of the tragic hero. In modern tragedy the issue of stability remains since violence and catastrophe are still the main currents of tragedy. These concerns may no longer be accountable to a single institutional idea (state, religion, etc.), but they are concerns nonetheless. Even when a solution to instability fails to surface, drama can attain tragic dimensions because what happens is not necessarily what is done to the hero, but what actions occur "through the hero." Tragedy can transcend the hero's milieu, forcing us to observe the consequences that change from era to era. In the portion selected here, Williams focuses on the "horizon of feeling" that one experiences in modern drama.

Drama from Ibsen to Brecht (1968)

It is now just over a hundred years since Ibsen published *Brand* and *Peer Gynt*. The drama written and performed in the intervening century is by any standards a major achievement. There has never been, in any comparable period, so much innovation and experiment, and

Raymond Williams, "Drama from Ibsen to Brecht," excerpted from his "Introduction" to *Drama from Ibsen to Brecht* (New York: Penguin, 1968), 1–12. © 1952, 1964, 1968 by Raymond Williams. Reprinted by permission of The Random House Group Ltd.

this has been related, throughout, to a growth and crisis of civilization which the drama has embodied, in some remarkable ways. For much of the century, and especially for its first seventy-five years, the play was overshadowed by the novel, as a major form. Yet it is still impossible to understand modern literature without the work of at least eight or ten dramatists, or, in another way of putting it, without a critical understanding of dramatic naturalism, dramatic expressionism, and certain related movements. At the same time, since Ibsen published *Brand* and *Peer Gynt* rather than submitting them for performance, there has been a very complicated and difficult relationship between literature and the theatre: a relationship which at times obscures and always affects the achievement of this drama. The crisis of performance, and of the theatre as an institution, itself affected by new means of dramatic performance in the cinema, in radio, and in television, has made the continuing problem of dramatic form especially acute. Certain orthodoxies have hardened, and many damaging gaps have appeared, and continue to appear. But also, through and within these difficulties, the energy and power of dramatic imagination have continued to create some of the essential consciousness of our world. Without this drama, we would all lack a dimension, and to study and understand it is the major critical challenge. [...]

In a period as various, as experimental and innovating, as modern drama, the problem of conventions is necessarily central. Indeed the idea of convention is basic to any understanding of drama as a form. Yet it is always a difficult idea, and especially so in a period in which certain basic conventions are changing. It is worth, then, looking at the idea of convention directly.

The ordinary dictionary senses provide a useful starting point. Thus, *convention* is the act of coming together; an assembly, union, coalition, especially of representatives, for some definite purpose; an agreement previous to a definitive treaty; a custom. *Conventional*, similarly, is: settled by stipulation or by tacit consent; as sanctioned and currently accepted by tacit agreement; agreeable to accepted standards; agreeable to contract. As we go through these senses, and through those of the various derived words, we see an ambiguity which is important both because it indicates a possible source of confusion which requires discussion and because it indicates an important point of entry for an analysis of the place of conventions in drama.

The possible source of confusion is the fact that convention covers both *tacit consent* and *accepted standards*, and it is easy to see that the latter has often been understood as a set of formal rules. Thus it is common in adverse comment to say that a work is just *conventional, a familiar routine, old stuff, the mixture as before.* We use the word in the same way in adverse comment on people and actions that we find dull, or narrow, or old-fashioned, or unoriginal, or unreceptive to new ideas. To explain the development of *conventional* as an adverse term in criticism would take us a long way into cultural history. Briefly, it is the result of the controversy that was part of the Romantic Movement, in which emphasis fell heavily on the right of the artist to disregard, where he saw fit, the rules that had been laid down by others for the practice of his art. This was an essential emphasis, from which we have all gained. But it is then unfortunate that *convention* and *conventional* should have been so heavily compromised. For an artist only leaves one convention to follow or create another; this is the whole basis of communication. [...]

Ultimately, however, we judge a convention, not by its abstract usefulness, and not by referring it to some ultimate criterion of probability, but rather by what it manages, in an actual work of art, to get done. If in fact it were not historically true that certain works have been able, by their own strength, to modify old conventions and to introduce new ones, we should have had no change at all, short of some absolutist decree. We accept, with a common and easy sentiment, such triumphs of the past. We read, sympathetically, the biographies of an Ibsen or a Stanislavsky. But the sympathy is merely sentimental unless it can be made active, and creative, at our own point in time.

Ibsen and Stanislavsky have won, as Æschylus won when he introduced the second actor, or Shakespeare when he transformed the tragedy of blood. Yet the history of art is not one of continual evolution into higher and better forms; there is debasement as well as refinement, and a novelty, even a transformation, may be bad as well as good. It would be absurd to imagine that our own contemporary segment from the great arc of dramatic possibility is, because the latest, necessarily the best. Yet, because of the nature of convention, because of the dependence of any dramatic method upon this particular type of agreement, it is not possible, in any age, to go very far from the segment which is that age's living tradition, or to begin from anywhere but within or on its borders.

Thus we have the necessity of tradition – convention as tacit consent – and at times the equal necessity of experiment, from the development of new modes of feeling, and from the perception of new or rediscovered technical means – convention as dramatic method. It is to the interplay of these two senses of convention that we must now turn.

If we think of a dramatic convention as a technical means in an acted performance, it is clear that there is no absolute reason why any means should not be employed, and judged by its dramatic result. But we have seen that, in practice, this absolute freedom of choice is not available: a dramatist must win the consent of his audience to any particular means that he wishes to employ, and while he may often be able to do this in the course of a work itself, by the power of the effect which the method makes possible, he cannot entirely rely on this, for even if the audience is sympathetic, too great a consciousness of the novelty or strangeness of the means may as effectively hamper the full communication of a play as would open hostility. It seems probable, when we look back into the history of drama, that the effective changes took place when there was already a latent willingness to accept them, at least among certain groups in society, from whom the artist drew his support. But while it is possible to see this in retrospect, it could never have been easy, and it is not easy now, to see such a situation, with sufficient clarity, in the flux of present experience. It is here that we find ourselves considering the very difficult relations between conventions and structures of feeling.

All serious thinking about art must begin from the recognition of two apparently contradictory facts: that an important work is always, in an irreducible sense, individual; and, yet that there are authentic communities of works of art, in kinds, periods and styles. In everyday discussion, we succeed in maintaining both ideas at the same time, without real consideration of the relations between them. We see a particular play, and say, often genuinely, that in this speech, this character, this action, a particular dramatist makes himself known; it is for this specific achievement that we value his work. But then, sometimes in the next breath, we look at the speech, the character or the action and say: this is characteristic of a particular kind of drama, in a particular period. Each kind of observation is important; each helps us, every day, to understand drama better. But the difficulty, raised by their apparent contradiction – here pointing to a single hand, there to a group or period – must in the end be faced. For the contradiction cannot be resolved by saying that we are in each case pointing at a different kind of fact. It is true that in some works it is possible to separate out different elements, and to say: here the dramatist is simply following the conventions of his genre or period, but here he is contributing something entirely his own. Yet in many important works it is not possible to do this: the individual genius and the particular conventions through which it is expressed are or seem inseparable. In pointing to what a particular man has done, in a particular style, we are often in the position of learning what that style is, what it is capable of doing. The individual dramatist has done this, yet what he has done is part of what we then know about a general period or style.

It is to explore this essential relationship that I use the term "structure of feeling." What I am seeking to describe is the continuity of experience from a particular work, through its particular form, to its recognition as a general form, and then the relation of this general form to a period. We can look at this continuity, first, in the most general way. All that is lived and made, by a given community in a given period, is, we now commonly believe, essentially related, although in practice, and in detail, this is not always easy to see. In the study of a period, we may be able to reconstruct, with more or less accuracy, the material life, the general social organization, and, to a large extent, the dominant ideas. It is often difficult to decide which, if any, of these aspects is in the whole complex, determining; their separation is, in a way, arbitrary, and an important institution like the drama will, in all probability, take its colour in varying degrees from them all. But while we may, in the study of a past period, separate out particular aspects of life, and treat them as if they were self-contained, it is obvious that this is only how they may be studied, not how they were experienced. We examine each element as a precipitate, but in the living experience of the time every element was in solution, an inseparable part of a complex whole. And it seems to be true from the nature of art that it is from such a totality that the artist draws; it is in art, primarily, that the effect of a whole lived experience is expressed and embodied. To relate a work of art to any part of that whole may, in varying degrees, be useful; but it is common experience, in analysis, to realize that when one has measured the work against the separable parts, there yet remains some element for which there is no external counterpart. It is this, in the first instance, that I mean by the structure of feeling. It is as firm and definite as "structure" suggests, yet it is based in the deepest and often least tangible elements of our experience. It is a way of responding to a particular world which in practice is not felt as one way among others – a conscious "way" – but is, in experience, the only way possible. Its means, its elements, are not propositions or techniques; they are embodied, related feelings. In the same sense, it is accessible to others – not by formal argument or by professional skills, on their own, but by direct experience – a form and a meaning, a feeling and a rhythm – in the work of art, the play, as a whole.

We can often see this structure in the dramas of the past. But then it follows, from the whole emphasis of the term, that it is precisely the structure of feeling which is most difficult to distinguish while it is still being lived. Just because it has then not passed, or wholly passed, into distinguishable formations and beliefs and institutions, it is known primarily as a deep *personal* feeling; indeed it often seems, to a particular writer, unique, almost incommunicable, and lonely. We can see this most clearly in the art and thought of past periods, when, while it was being made, its creators seemed often, to themselves and others, isolated, cut off, difficult to understand. Yet again and again, when that structure of feeling has been absorbed, it is the connections, the correspondences, even the period similarities, which spring most readily to the eye. What was then a living structure, not yet known to be shared, is now a recorded structure, which can be examined and identified and even generalized. In one's own time, before this has happened, it is probable that those to whom the new structure is most accessible, in whom indeed it is most clearly forming, will know their experience primarily as their own: as what cuts them off from other men, though what they are actually cut off from is the set of received informations and conventions and institutions which no longer express or satisfy their own most essential life. When such a man speaks, in his work, often against what is felt to be the grain of the time, it is surprising to him and to others that there can be recognition of what had seemed this most difficult, inaccessible, unshared life. Established formations will criticize or reject him, but to an increasing number of people he will seem to be speaking for them, for their own deepest sense of life, just because he was speaking for himself. A new structure of feeling is then becoming articulate. It is even possible, though very difficult even by comparison with the analysis of past structures, to begin to see this contemporary structure directly, rather than only in the power of particular works. Many such expositions are too early, too superficial, or too rigid, but it remains true that discovery of actual contemporary structures of feeling (usually masked by their immediate and better recognized predecessors) is the most important kind of attention to the art and society of one's own time.

The artist's importance, in relation to the structure of feeling, has to do above all with the fact that it is a *structure*: not an unformed flux of new responses, interests and perceptions but a formation of these into a new way of seeing ourselves and our world. Such a formation is the purpose of all authentic contemporary activity, and its successes occur in fields other than art. But the artist, by the character of his work, is directly involved with just this process, from the beginning. He can only work at all as such formations become available, usually as a personal discovery and then a scatter of personal discoveries and then the manner of work of a generation. What this means, in practice, is the making of new conventions, new forms.

It is in this respect, finally, that I see the usefulness of "structure of feeling" as a critical term. [. . .] As we collect our experience of particular plays, we see the structure of feeling at once extending and changing: important elements in common, as experience and as method, between particular plays and dramatists; important elements changing, as the experience and the conventions change together, or as the experience is found to be in tension with existing conventions, and either succeeds or fails in altering them. Slowly, what emerges is much wider than a particular work: it is a problem of form, but also, crucially, a problem of experience for many dramatists, and in effect for a period and for successive periods. In any real analysis, the relationships are usually very difficult to sustain; but there is the possibility, which I am especially testing in this study of modern drama, of substantial connections between the most particular and the most general forms. What the analysis often shows is a change in dramatic method, but the point of my argument, through the relation of conventions and structures of feelings, is that we can look at dramatic methods with a clear technical definition, and yet know, in detail, that what is being defined is more than technique: is indeed the practical way of describing those changes in experience the responses and their communication; the "subjects" and the "forms" – which make the drama in itself and as a history important. [. . .]

Chapter 52

Peter Brook (b. 1925)

One of the most important directors of the twentieth century, Peter Brook revolutionized the theatre with his groundbreaking productions. Influenced by Meyerhold, Grotowski, Brecht, and Artaud, he epitomized the avant-garde theatre with his Beckettian *King Lear* (1962), his absurdist, Grotowski-style *Marat/Sade* (1964), the circus and rock-n-roll production of *A Midsummer Night's Dream* (1970), *The Conference of the Birds* (1976), and the Indian epic *The Mahabharata* (1985). His book *The Empty Space* (1968, excerpted here) emerged from a series of lectures and attained near biblical status for the avant-garde. One of his most memorable remarks occurs in this text: "I can take any empty space and call it a bare stage. A man walks across this empty space whilst someone else is watching him, and this is all that is needed for an act of theatre to be engaged" (9). Brook was interested in the immediacy of theatre; like Artaud he wanted to eliminate the intermediary of representation – the experience of actors doubling or recreating a role that eventuates in *rigor mortis* and nullifies spontaneity. His life's work involved a constant reinvention of forms and exploration of various styles of theatre outside the Western canon.

The Immediate Theatre (1968)

There is no doubt that a theatre can be a very special place. It is like a magnifying glass, and also like a reducing lens. It is a small world, so it can easily be a petty one. It is different from everyday life so it can easily be divorced from life. On the other hand, while we live less and less in villages or neighbourhoods, and more and more in open-ended global communities, the theatre community stays the same: the cast of a play is still the size that it has always been. The theatre narrows life down: It narrows it down in many ways. It is always hard for anyone to have one single aim in life – in the theatre, however, the goal is clear. From the first rehearsal, the aim is always visible, not too far away, and it involves everyone. We can see many model social patterns at work: the pressure of a first night, with its unmistakable demands, produces that working-together, that dedication, that energy and that consideration of each other's needs that government despair of ever evoking outside wars.

Furthermore, in society in general the role of art is nebulous. Most people could live perfectly well without any art at all – and even if they regretted its absence it would not hamper their functioning in any way. But in the theatre there is no such separation: at every instant the practical question is an artistic one: the most incoherent, uncouth player is as much involved in matters of pitch and pace, intonation and rhythm, position, distance, colour and shape as the most sophisticated. In rehearsal, the height of the chair, the texture of the costume, the brightness of the light, the quality of emotion, matter all the time: the aesthetics are practical. One would be wrong to say that this is because the theatre is an art. The stage is a reflection of life, but this life cannot be relived for a moment without a working system based on observing certain values and making value-judgements. A chair is moved up or down stage, because it's "better so." Two columns are wrong – but adding a third makes them "right" – the words "better," "worse," "not so good," "bad" are day after day, but these words which rule decisions carry no moral sense whatsoever.

Anyone interested in processes in the natural world would be very rewarded by a study of theatre conditions. His discoveries would be far more applicable to general society than the study of bees or ants. Under the magnifying glass he would see a group of people living all the time according to precise, shared, but unnamed standards. He would see that in any community a theatre has either no particular function – or a unique one. The uniqueness of the function is that it offers something that cannot be found in the street, at home, in the pub, with friends, or on a psychiatrist's couch, in a church or at the movies. There is only one interesting difference between the cinema and the theatre. The cinema flashes on to a screen images from the past. As this is what the mind does to itself all through life, the cinema seems intimately real. Of course, it is nothing of the sort – it is a satisfying and enjoyable extension of the unreality of everyday perception. The theatre, on the other hand, always asserts itself in the present. This is what can make it more real than the normal stream of consciousness. This also is what can make it so disturbing.

No tribute to the latent power of the theatre is as telling as that paid to it by censorship. In most régimes, even when the written word is free, the image free, it is still the stage that is liberated last. Instinctively, governments know that the living event could create a dangerous electricity – even if we see this happen all too seldom. But this ancient fear is a recognition of an ancient potential. The theatre is the arena where a living confrontation can take place. The focus of a large group of people creates a unique intensity – owing to this forces that operate at all times and rule each person's daily life can be isolated and perceived more clearly.

Now, I must become unashamedly personal. In the three preceding chapters I have dealt with different forms of theatre, in general, as they occur all over the world, and naturally as they occur to me.[1] If this final section, which inevitably is a sort of conclusion, takes the form of a theatre I appear to recommend, this is because I can only speak of the theatre I know. I must narrow my sights and talk about theatre as I understand it, autobiographically. I will endeavour to speak of actions and conclusions from within my field of work: this is what constitutes my experience and my point of view. In turn, the reader must observe that it is inseparable from all the things on my passport – nationality, date of birth, place of birth, physical characteristics, colour of eyes, signature. Also, it is inseparable from today's date. This is a picture of the author at the moment of writing: searching within a decaying and evolving theatre. As I continue to work, each experience will make these conclusions inconclusive again. It is impossible to assess the function of a book – but I hope this one may perhaps be of use somewhere, to someone else wrestling with his own problems in relation to another time and place. But if anyone were to try to use it as a handbook, then I can definitely warn him – there are no formulas: there are no methods. I can describe an exercise or a technique, but anyone who attempts to reproduce them from my description is certain to be disappointed. I would undertake to teach anyone all that I know about theatre rules and technique in a few hours. The rest is practice – and that cannot be done alone. We can just attempt to follow this to a limited degree if we examine the preparation of a play towards performance.

Note

1   Brook is referring to the Deadly, Holy, and Rough Theatres. This excerpt is from the chapter Immediate Theatre. – Editor's note.

Chapter 53

Peter Weiss (1916–1982)

Peter Weiss was a playwright and painter whose best-known work, the play *Marat/Sade* (1964), was directed by Peter Brook in 1965 (see Chapter 52). In this essay Weiss considers the problems of documentary theatre. Journalistic theatre, ripped from the pages of the press, creates certain problems but also establishes criteria that make documentary theatre noteworthy. Weiss explores similar problems raised by Artaud: how does the doubling of representation undermine the immediacy of a performance? His other major works were *The Song of the Lusitanian Bogey* (1967) and *Trotsky in Exile* (1970). His interests lay in exploring the possibilities for social change.

Notes on the Contemporary Theatre (1971)

Realistic topical theatre, which has gone through numerous transformations since the time of the *Proletkult* movement and agitprop, Piscator's experiments and Brecht's didactic plays, can now be found under various labels such as Political Theatre, Theatre of Protest, Anti-Theatre, etc. Beginning with the difficulty of finding a classification for this kind of theatre's various forms of expression, we shall attempt here to examine one of its variants, the one that exclusively deals with the documentation of a particular subject-matter and which might therefore be called Documentary Theatre.

Peter Weiss, "Notes on the Contemporary Theatre," tr. Joel Agee, in *Essays on German Theater*, ed. Margaret Herzfeld-Sander (New York: Continuum, 1985), 294–301. © 1985 by the Continuum Publishing Company. Reprinted by permission of The Copyright Clearance Center on behalf of The Continuum Publishing Company. Originally published as "Notizen zum dokumentarischen Theater," *Rapporte* 2 (Frankfurt am Main: Suhrkamp Verlag, 1971).

1

Documentary theatre is a theatre of reportage. Trial records, dossiers, letters, statistical tabulations, stock market bulletins, closing reports of banking corporations and industrial concerns, government declarations, speeches, interviews, statements by public personalities, newspaper and radio reports, photographs, journalistic movies and other documents of contemporary life provide the foundation of the performance. Documentary theatre abstains from any kind of invention, it adopts authentic material and presents it on the stage without any modification of its content, but with definite formal modifications. In contrast to the random character of the news material that flows in upon us from all sides every day, a selection is presented on the stage which concentrates on a particular subject, usually of a social or political nature. It is this critical selection, and the principle determining the assemblage of the excerpts from reality, that make up the quality of documentary drama.

2

Documentary theatre is a component of public life as it is brought to our attention by the mass media, and its distinguishing characteristic is the criticism it performs in various degrees.

a. A critique of cover-ups. Are the reports of the press, the radio, and television being manipulated by dominant interest groups? What information is being withheld from us? Whose interests are served by these expurgations? Which circles are benefited when certain social phenomena are hushed up, altered, idealized?

b. A critique of falsifications of reality. Why is a historical figure, a period or epoch erased from our consciousness? Whose position is strengthened by the elimination of historical facts? Who profits from a deliberate distortion of trenchant and significant events? What social strata are interested in hiding the past? How are these falsifications expressed? How are they received?

c. A critique of lies. What are the effects of a historical deception? What is the appearance of a contemporary situation that has been built on lies? What difficulties are likely to arise when the truth is discovered? Which influential organs and power groups will do everything they can to prevent the truth from being known?

3

Although the means of communications have been distributed to a maximal degree and provide us with news from all parts of the world, the most important events that determine our present and our future remain concealed from us in their causes and their interconnections. The information banks of the responsible parties, material that could provide us with insight into activities of which we only see the results, are made unavailable to us. A documentary theatre that wants to treat subjects like the murders of Lumumba, Kennedy, Che Guevara, the massacre in Indonesia, the secret agreements during the negotiations on Indochina in Geneva, the latest conflict in the Middle East, and the preparations of the government of the United States to wage war against Vietnam finds itself faced at the outset with the artificial obscurity behind which the powerful conceal their manipulations.

4

A documentary theatre that opposes those groups that have an interest in pursuing a policy of obscuring and obliterating the truth, that opposes the tendency of the mass media to keep the population subject by enclosing it in a vacuum of narcotization and stupefaction, such a theatre finds itself at the same point of departure as any citizen who wishes to conduct his own research, has his hands tied, and finally resorts to the only means available to him: public protest. Like the spontaneous rally with posters, banners, and chants, the documentary theatre demonstrates a reaction to contemporary conditions and a demand that they be revealed to the public.

5

Demonstrating in the streets, distributing leaflets, marching in rows, interacting with a broad public – these are concrete and immediately effective actions. They are strongly dramatic in their improvisation, their course is unpredictable, at any moment they might be intensified by a clash with the police and thereby bring out the contradiction in the social conditions. A documentary theatre offering a summing up of latent tendencies in society tries to present its material in such a way that it doesn't lose any of its topical import. But the very process of putting together the material for a closed performance on a predetermined date in a limited space involving actors and audience confronts the documentary theatre with conditions that are different from those that apply to direct political action. Instead of showing reality in its immediacy, the documentary theatre presents an image of a piece of reality torn out of its living context.

6

Documentary theatre, insofar as it does not choose to perform its spectacles in the street, cannot achieve the same degree of reality as an authentic, political manifestation. It can never be as dynamic as the opinions expressed in the public arena. Confined to the stage and the auditorium, it cannot challenge the authorities of state and government in the same way that a protest march to government buildings and military and industrial centers does. Even when it tries to free itself from the framework that defines it as an artistic medium, even when it renounces all aesthetic categories, when it refuses to be anything fixed and finished, so as to present nothing more than clear opposition and militant action, even when it pretends to have been born of the moment and to have acted spontaneously, it will be an art product, and it must become an art product if it is to have any justification.

7

For a documentary theatre that wants primarily to be a political forum and renounces artistic achievement, calls itself into question. In such a case, practical political action in the outside world would be more effective. Not until the factual material gathered by probing, examining, scrutinizing reality has been transformed into an artistic tool can the documentary theatre attain full validity in its struggle with reality. Such a theatre makes it possible for a dramatic work to become an instrument of political persuasion. But close attention must be given to the documentary theatre's special forms of expression, which differ from traditional aesthetic concepts.

8

The strength of the documentary theatre resides in its ability to arrange fragments of reality into a usable model, a sample of real processes as they actually occur. It is not situated at the center of the event but assumes the position of the observer and analyst. With its cinematic cutting technique it isolates perceptible details from the chaotic materials of external reality. By juxtaposing contradictory details, it focuses attention on an actual conflict and then, on the basis of the data it has collected, offers a recommendation for solving that conflict, or issues a call to action, or poses a radical question. Unlike open improvisation and unlike the politically coloured Happening, which produce a diffusion of tension, emotional participation, and an illusion of political involvement, documentary theatre treats its subject in a conscious, attentive, and reflective manner.

9

Documentary theatre submits facts for the audience's appraisal. It shows the various ways in which an event or a statement is received. It shows the motives of that reception. One side is benefited by an event, the other is damaged by it. These two parties stand opposed to one another. A light is cast on their mutual dependence, and on the bribery and blackmail that are supposed to keep this dependence intact. Losses are tabulated next to lists showing gains. The ones who are winning defend themselves. They present themselves as the keepers of public order. They show how they administer their possessions. In contrast to them, the ones who are losing. The traitors in the ranks of the losers who hope for a chance to rise. The others who are trying to avoid losing more than they already have. A constant collision of inequalities. Glimpses of inequality shown so concretely that it becomes intolerable. Injustices so convincing they cry out for immediate redress. Situations so twisted they can only be changed by force. Controversial views of the same subject are aired. Assertions are compared with actual conditions. Avowals and promises followed by actions that contradict them. The results of actions initiated in secret planning centers are examined. Whose position was this meant to strengthen, who was affected by it? The silence, the evasions of those involved are documented. Circumstantial evidence is submitted. Corollaries are drawn from a recognizable pattern. The representatives of certain social interests are identified by name, but the point is not to depict individual conflicts, but patterns of socio-economic behavior. Documentary theatre is only concerned with what is exemplary, in contrast to the quickly exhausted external constellation; it does not work with stage characters and depictions of milieux, but with groups, force-fields, trends.

10

Documentary theatre is partisan. Many of its themes cannot be treated in any way other than as an indictment. For such a theatre, objectivity is a concept that under certain circumstances can serve to justify the activities of a power group. The appeal for moderation and understanding is shown to be the appeal of those who don't want to lose their advantages. The aggressions of the Portuguese colonists against Angola and Mozambique, the South African government's assaults on the African population, the aggression of the United States of America against Cuba, the Dominican Republic, and Vietnam, cannot be presented as anything other than unilateral crimes. There is nothing wrong with depicting genocide and predatory war in black-and-white terms, denying the butchers any endearing traits whatsoever and resolutely siding with their victims in every possible way.

11

Documentary theatre can take the form of a tribunal. Here, too, it does not pretend to approach the authenticity of a Nuremberg trial, an Auschwitz trial in Frankfurt, a hearing in the American Senate, a session of the Russell tribunal; but it can make a new kind of testimony out of those questions and points of attack that were voiced in the context of a real inquest. Having gained some distance, it can look back on the proceedings from a point of view that did not present itself at the time. The original protagonists are transposed into a new historical context. At the same time that their actions are portrayed, we are shown the development of which they are the product, and attention is directed to those repercussions and consequences which are still with us. By showing their activities, the performance reveals the mechanism that continues to impinge on reality. Everything tangential, every kind of digression, can be cut in favor of a clear statement of the problem itself. This entails a loss of surprise value, local color, sensationalism; what is gained is universality. Documentary theatre, unlike an actual trial court, can include the audience in the proceedings, put the audience in the position of the accused or the prosecution, invite it to collaborate with an investigatory commission; it can contribute to the understanding of a complex issue or challenge a resistant attitude to the point of extreme provocation.

12

Some more examples of the formal use of documentary material.

a. Reports and parts of reports, rhythmically arranged in precise intervals. Brief moments consisting of a single fact or exclamation followed by longer, complicated units. A quotation followed by the portrayal of a situation. The situation abruptly changes into another, opposite one. Individual speakers stand opposite a majority of speakers. The composition consists of antithetical pieces, of related examples in sequential order, of contrasting forms, of alternating scales of dimension. Variations on a theme. Intensification of a process. Introduction of disturbances, dissonances.

b. Linguistic elaboration of the factual material. Stressing what is typical in a quotation. Making caricatures of certain personages, drastically simplifying situations. Speeches, commentaries, summaries are delivered in the form of songs. Introduction of chorus and pantomime. Use of gesture to indicate action. Parodies, use of masks and decorative attributes. Instrumental accompaniment. Sound effects.

c. Interrupting the report by reflections, monologues, dreams, retrospections, contradictory behavior. These breaks in the action, which produce an insecurity that can have the effect of a shock, show how an individual or a group is affected by the events. Portrayal of inner reality as a response to outer events. However, such brusque displacements should not produce confusion but should draw attention to the many-layered complexity of the event; the means employed, instead of being ends in themselves, should always provide a verifiable experience.

d. Dissolving the structure. Not a calculated rhythm, but raw material, compact or else flowing without restraint, to show social struggles, to depict revolutionary situations, to report on a war. Conveying violence in the clash of opposing forces. But here, too, the upheaval on the stage, the expression of fear and outrage, must not remain unexplained and unresolved. The more urgent the implications of the material, the greater the need for an overview, a synthesis.

13

A documentary theatre's effort to find a persuasive form of expression is closely related to the need to find an adequate place to perform in. If the performance takes place in a commercial theatre with its high price of admission, it will be caught in the system it wants to attack. If it sets itself up outside the establishment, it will be limited to locations that are usually visited only by a small and like-minded crowd. Instead of having an impact on society, it often merely succeeds in showing its impotence with regard to the status quo. Documentary theatre must gain access to factories, schools, stadiums, meeting houses. Just as it detaches itself from the aesthetic canons of traditional theatre, it must put its own methods in question again and again and develop new techniques that are adequate to new situations.

14

Documentary theatre can only be sustained by a firm, politically and sociologically educated group of collaborators who are supported by an extensive archive and are capable of scientific investigation. A documentary dramaturgy that shrinks back from defining a condition, that only shows a condition without revealing its causes and pointing out the necessity and the possibility of its removal, a documentary dramaturgy that freezes in a gesture of desperate attack without ever striking the enemy, devalues itself. For this reason, documentary theatre opposes the kind of drama that uses its own rage and despair as its main theme and clings to the notion of a hopeless and absurd world. Documentary theatre argues for the alternative view, according to which reality, however impenetrable it tries to be, can be explained in all its details.

Chapter 54

Joyce Carol Oates (b. 1938)

Joyce Carol Oates is a prolific novelist, critic, playwright, poet, and essayist. Her interests range from film and photography to culture and prize fighting. Among her collections of essays are *The Profane Art* (1983), *On Boxing* (1987), *(Woman) Writer* (1988), *Where I've Been, And Where I'm Going* (1999), and *Uncensored* (2005). This essay from *The Edge of Impossibility* takes up issues that were raised by George Steiner and Lionel Abel (see Chapters 43 and 45) that tragedy is no longer viable. She considers fear and violence as requisites for tragic literature. Isolation and alienation are tragic. Oates defends the emotional and existential break from the community (the outré person) of the tragic figure.

The Edge of Impossibility: Tragic Forms in Literature (1972)

We seek the absolute dream. We are forced back continually to an acquiescence in all that is hallucinatory and wasteful, to a rejection of all norms and gods and dreams of "tragedy" followed by the violent loss of self that signals the start of artistic effort: an appropriation by destruction, or an assimilation into the self of a reality that cannot be named. The art of tragedy grows out of a break between self and community, a sense of isolation. At its base is fear. If it is not always true that human life possesses value, it is at least true that some human life, or the abstract parody of human life as acted out by gods, has a profound and magical value, inexplicable. The drama begins only when a unique human reality asserts its passion against the totality of passion, "arranging the same materials in a unique pattern," risking loss of self in an attempt to realize self – there

Excerpts from Joyce Carol Oates, *The Edge of Impossibility: Tragic Forms in Literature* (Greenwich, CT: Fawcett Premier Books, 1972), 8–12. © 1972 by Joyce Carol Oates. Reprinted by permission of the author.

steps forward out of the world an Oedipus, an Antigone. The making of domestic landscapes into wilderness is the aspect of tragedy that always shocks us, for in our wholesome terror we cannot conceive of the justification of our lives calling forth a death of passion, an annihilation of passion, – what are we except passion, and how are we to survive when this passion breaks its dikes and flows out to nature?

The hero at the center of tragedy exists so that we may witness, in his destruction, the reversal of our private lives. We adjust ourselves to the spectacle of an art form, we paralyze our skepticism in order to see beyond the artifice of print or stage, and we share in a mysterious dream necessary loss of self, even as this self reads or watches, losing ourselves in the witnessing of someone's death that, in our human world, this hero may be reborn. The tragic hero dies but is reborn eternally in our dreams; the crudity of our desire for an absolute – an absolute dream, an absolute key – is redeemed by the beauty that so often surrounds this dream. One can explain the dream but never its beauty.

The hero dies into our imaginations as we, helpless, live out lives that are never works of art – even the helpless lives of "artists"! – and are never understood. Suffering is articulated in tragic literature, and so this literature is irresistible, a therapy of the soul. We witness in art the reversal of our commonplace loss of passion, our steady loss of consciousness that is never beautiful but only biological. Therefore our love for art, and our resentment of it. We consume ourselves into a present without horizon, and without value; the creations of our imagination consume themselves into a marvelous future, a universal future in which we somehow share. The object of our fascination, in Husserl's words, *gives itself as having been there before reflection*, and we feel that the triumph over nothing that art represents is assured of a future beyond even our ability to imagine. We acclaim the marvelous in ourselves.

Of the many contemporary critics who have written tragedy, George Steiner and Lionel Abel are among the most provocative [see Chapters 43 and 45, this volume]. Steiner's thesis, like that of Joseph Wood Krutch before him, is that tragedy is dead. We have heard this often, we will be hearing it often: "Tragedy is that form of art which requires the intolerable burden of God's presence. It is dead now because His shadow is no longer upon us as it fell upon Agamemnon or Macbeth or Athalie." If it returns it will be in a new form, and Steiner implies that it will be a form perhaps unintelligible to the West. In his brief, strange book, *Metatheater*, Abel tries to solve the critical problem of the relationship between "tragedy" and less pure forms of drama by denying that tragedy is a natural Western art form at all. According to Abel, Shakespeare wrote no tragedies, with the possible exception of *Macbeth*. The dominant dramatic form is not tragedy but "metatheater" – the kind of drama that assumes the total subjectivity of the world and its metamorphosis, by way of a mysterious psychological process, into theater. Theater as *theater*, as self-conscious and ironic subjectivity – this is "metatheater."

What are we to make of such assumptions? Does the frequent appearance in dramatic literature of the world-as-stage and life-as-dream bring along with it the actual valuelessness of the contextual world? Where is history? Where is personal history? Certain critics are always convinced that an epoch creates art, but a great work always tells us that it is isolated, unique, accidental, and inexplicable – not even the possession of the creator himself – and that its true context is not history but dreams, ahistorical dreams. Like a personality, a work of art occurs once, and, re-experienced, is redefined; it has no "existence" at all. But to argue backward from this insight, to argue that the dreamlike quality of a work of art indicates a dreamlike, nihilistic culture beyond it, is irresponsible. If Hamlet represents the most developed figure of Western "metatheater," then he is a prince of nihilism and nothing more. According to Abel, "One cannot create tragedy without accepting some implacable values as true. Now, the Western imagination has, on the whole, been liberal and skeptical; it has tended to regard *all* implacable values as false." But from what ground does the play arise? What is its fundamental delusion? If the play is Hamlet, the hero's delusion is certainly not that he cannot locate truth, but rather that he cannot reject it powerfully enough; though appearances argue that all values are false, Hamlet's tragedy is that he cannot accept appearances. Out of his faith comes the tragedy.

Nothing can come from nothing, no energy from a bodiless spirit; thus, there can be no violence out of a sense of nothing, for violence is always an affirmation. Abel claims that the West has always been nihilistic in its imaginative literature, but how can such an assumption account for its very shape, the structural consummation of violent action? Art is built around violence, around death; at its base is fear. The absolute dream, if dreamed, must deal with death, and the only way toward death we understand is the way of violence. In the various works examined in this collection of essays, as well as in *Hamlet*, nihilism is overcome by the breaking-down of the dikes between human beings, the flowing forth of passion; Melville alone, with his essentially religious and superstitious imagination, can create a tragedy of "nihilism." In our ingenious theater of the absurd, and to some extent in Chekhov, the dramatic structure itself becomes equated with the sense of loss and inertia of the fictional characters, who are incapable of violence except as victims. And yet they perpetuate acts of violence, by being victims. Here human life is microscopic, imagined as magical and reductive to an instant in time, as in *Waiting for Godot*: "One day we were born, one day we'll die, the same day, the same second.... They give birth astride of a grave, the light gleams an instant, then it's night once more." In Beckett we have a true delight in boredom and in the boring of others, a powerful substitute for ancient types of aggression.

Parody is an act of aggression. Twentieth-century literature is never far from parody, sensing itself anticipated, overdone, exhausted. But its power lies in the authenticity of its anger, its parodistic instinct, the kind of art in which Mann's Adrian Leverkühn and Dostoevski's Ivan Karamazov excel: "the playing of forms out of which life has disappeared." If it is true, as George Steiner argues, that the death of God means the death of tragedy, then we need to ask what tragedy has dealt with all along – has it not been the limitations of the human world? What is negotiable, accessible, what can be given proper incantatory names, what is, in Nietzsche's phrasing, "thinkable" – this is the domestic landscape out of which the wilderness will be shaped. If communal belief in God has diminished so that, as writers, we can no longer presume upon it, then a redefinition of God in terms of the furthest reaches of man's hallucinations can provide us with a new basis for tragedy. The abyss will always open for us, though it begins as a pencil mark, the parody of a crack; the shapes of human beasts – centaurs and satyrs and their remarkable companions – will always be returning with nostalgia to our great cities.

Chapter 55

Luis Valdez (b. 1940)

Luis Valdez, playwright, director, and filmmaker, founded El Teatro Campesino (The Peasant Theatre) in 1965. This theatre spoke for and to Latino/a migrant workers in California. Valdez joined unionizer and political activist César Chávez to create theatre representing disenfranchised workers of the United Farm Workers' Association (UFWA). Often working without props, their one-act plays (*actos*) were meant to educate and entertain through *commedia dell'arte* style and Brechtian methods. Valdez's best-known play was *Zoot Suit* (1978, later made into a movie). It concerned the 1942 Sleepy Lagoon murder which sparked an uprising in California. He also directed the film *La Bamba* (1987). Valdez examines cultural identity and self-determination. His essay runs counter to the absurdist movement of the time. Instead of jettisoning identity and questioning representation, Valdez affirms Chicano/a presence in society and fleshes out its culture in theatre through ritual and social protest. As Harry Elam astutely observes, social protest performances of El Teatro Campesino "transformed spectators into active participants, and their participatory activity inside the theater was an indicator of or precursor to revolutionary activity outside of the theater."[1]

Notes on Chicano Theater (1973)

What is Chicano theater? It is theater as beautiful, rasquachi, human, cosmic, broad, deep, tragic, comic, as the life of the Raza[2] itself. At its high point Chicano theater is religion – the huelguistas de Delano praying at the shrine of the Virgin de Guadelupe, located in the

Luis Valdez, "Notes on Chicano Theater," excerpted from *Guerrilla Theater: Scenarios for a Revolution*, ed. John Weisman (Garden City, NY: Anchor, 1973), 55–8.

rear of an old station wagon parked across the road from DiGiorgio's camp No. 4; at its low point, it is a cuento or a chiste told somewhere in the recesses of the barrio, puro pedo.

Chicano theater then is first a reaffirmation of *life*. That is what all theater is supposed to do, of course; but the limp, superficial gringo seco productions in the "professional" American theater (and the college and university drama departments that serve it) are so antiseptic, they are anti-biotic (anti-life). The characters and life situations emerging from our little teatros are too real, too full of sudor, sangre, and body smells to be boxed in. Audience participation is no cute trick with us; it is a pre-established, pre-assumed privilege. "Qué le suene la campanita!"

Defining Chicano theater is a little like defining a Chicano car. We can start with a low-rider's cool Merc, or a campesino's banged-up Chevy, and describe the various paint jobs, hub caps, dents, taped windows, Virgin on the dashboard, etc., that define the car as particularly Raza: Underneath all the trimmings, however, is an unmistakable Detroit production, an extension of General Motors. Consider now a theater that uses the basic form, the vehicle, created by Broadway or Hollywood: that is, the "realistic" play. Actually, this type of play was created in Europe, but where French, German, and Scandinavian playwrights went beyond realism and naturalism long ago, commercial gabacho theater refuses to let go.

It reflects a characteristic "American" hangup on the material aspect of human existence. European theater, by contrast, has been influenced since around 1900 by the unrealistic, formal rituals of Oriental theater.

What do Oriental and European theater have to do with teatros Chicanos? Nothing, except we are talking about a theater that is particularly our own, not another imitation of the gabacho. If we consider our origins, say the theater of the Mayans or the Aztecs, we are talking about something totally unlike the realistic play, and something more Chinese or Japanese in spirit. Kabuki, as a matter of fact, started some time ago as something like our actos and evolved over the centuries into the highly exciting art form it is today; but it still contains pleberias. It evolved from and still belongs to el pueblo japonés.

In Mexico, before the coming of the white man, the greatest examples of total theater were, of course, human sacrifices. *El Rabinal Achi*, one of the few surviving pieces of indigenous theater, describes the sacrifice of a courageous guerrillero who, rather than dying passively on the block, is granted the right to fight until he is killed. It is a tragedy, naturally, but it is all the more transcendent because of the guerrillero's identification, through sacrifice, with God. The only "set" such a drama-ritual needed was a stone block. Nature took care of the rest.

But since the conquest, Mexico's theater, like its society, has had to imitate Europe and, in recent times, the United States. In this same vein, Chicanos in Spanish classes are frequently involved in productions of plays by Lope de Vega, Calderón de la Barca, Tirso de Molina, and other classic playwrights. Nothing is wrong with this, but it does obscure the Indio foundations of Chicano culture. Is Chicano theater, in turn, to be nothing but an imitation of gabacho playwrights, with barrio productions of racist works by Eugene O'Neill and Tennessee Williams? Will Broadway produce a Chicano version of *Hello Dolly* now that it has produced a black one?

The nature of Chicanismo calls for a revolutionary turn in the arts as well as in society. Chicano theater must be revolutionary in technique as well as content. It must be popular, subject to no other critics except the pueblo itself; but it must also educate the pueblo toward an appreciation of *social change*, on and off the stage.

It is particularly important for teatro Chicano to draw a distinction between what is theater and what is reality. A demonstration with a thousand Chicanos, all carrying flags and picket signs, shouting CHICANO POWER! is not the revolution. It is theater about revolution. The people must act in *reality*, not on stage (which could be anywhere, even on a sidewalk) in order to achieve real change. The Raza gets excited, but unless the demonstration evolves into a street battle (which has not happened yet but is possible), it is basically a lot of emotion with very little political power, as Chicanos have discovered by picketing, demonstrating, and shouting before school boards, police departments, and stores to no avail.

Such guerrilla theater passing as a demonstration has its uses, of course. It is agitprop theater, as the gabachos used to call it in the thirties: agitation and propaganda. It helps stimulate and sustain the mass strength of a crowd. Hitler was very effective with this kind of theater, from the swastika to the Wagneresque stadium at Nuremberg. On the other end of the political spectrum, the huelga march to Sacramento in 1966 was pure guerrilla theater. The red-and-black thunderbird flags of the UFWOC (then NFWA) and the standards of the Virgin de Guadelupe challenged the bleak sterility of Highway 99. Its emotional impact was irrefutable. Its actual political impact was somewhat less. Governor Brown was not at the state Capitol, and only one grower, Schenley Industries, signed a contract. Later contracts have been won through a brilliant balance between highly publicized events that gained public support (marches, Cesar's fast, visits by Reuther, Robert and Ted Kennedy, etc.) and actual hard-ass door-to-door, worker-to-worker, organizing. Like Delano, other aspects of the Chicano movement must remember what is teatro and what is reality.

But beyond the mass struggle of La Raza in the fields and barrios of America, there is an internal struggle in the very corazón of our people. That struggle, too, calls for revolutionary change. Our belief in God, the Church, the social role of women – these must be subject to examination and redefinition on some kind of public forum. And that again means teatro. Not a teatro composed of actos or agitprop but a teatro of ritual, of music, of beauty, and of spiritual sensitivity. A teatro of legends and myths. A teatro of religious strength. This type of theater will require real dedication; it may, indeed, require a couple of generations of Chicanos devoted to the use of the theater as an instrument in the evolution of our people.

The teatros in existence today reflect the most intimate understanding of everyday events in the barrios from which they have emerged. But, if Aztlan is to become reality, then we as Chicanos must not be reluctant to act nationally – to think in national terms, politically, economically, spiritually. We must destroy the deadly regionalism that keeps us apart. The concept of a national theater for La Raza is intimately related to our evolving nationalism in Aztlan.

Consider a Teatro Nacional de Aztlan that performs with the same skill and prestige as the Ballet Folklórico de México (not for gabachos, however, but for the Raza). Such a teatro could carry the message of La Raza into Latin America, Europe, Japan, Africa – in short, all over the world. It would draw its strength from all the small teatros in the barrios, in terms of people and their plays, songs, designs; and it would give back funds, training, and augmenting strength of national unity. One season the teatro members would be on tour with the Teatro Nacional; the next season they would be back in the barrio sharing their skills and experience. It would accommodate about 150 people altogether, with 20 to 25 in the Nacional and the rest spread out in various parts of Aztlan, working with the campesino, the urbano, the mestizo, the piojo, etc.

Above all, the national organization of teatros would be self-supporting and independent, meaning no government grants. The corazón de la Raza cannot be revolutionized on a grant from Uncle Sam. Though many of the teatros, including El Campesino, have been born out of pre-established political groups – thus making them harbingers of that particular group's viewpoint, news, and political prejudices – there is yet a need for independence for the following reasons: objectivity, artistic competence, survival. El Teatro Campesino was born in the huelga, but the very huelga would have killed it if we had not moved sixty miles to the north of Delano. A struggle like the huelga needs every person it can get to serve its immediate goals in order to survive; the Teatro, as well as the clinic, service center, and newspaper being less important at the moment than the survival of the union, were always losing people to the grape boycott. When it became clear to us that the UFWOC (United Farm Workers of California, formerly Farm Workers' Association) would succeed and continue to grow, we felt it was time for us to move and begin speaking about things beyond the huelga: Vietnam, the barrio, racial discrimination, etc.

The teatros must never get away from the Raza. Without the palomia [the people] sitting there, laughing, crying, and sharing whatever is onstage, the teatros will dry up and die.[3] If the Raza will not come to theater, then the theater must go to the Raza. This, in the long run, will determine the shape, style, content, spirit, and form of el teatro Chicano.

Pachucos, campesinos, low-riders, pintos, chavalonas, familias, cuñados, tíos, primos, Mexican-Americans, all the human essence of the barrio is starting to appear in the mirror of our theater. With them come the joys, sufferings, disappointments, and aspirations of our gente. We challenge Chicanos to become involved in the art, the lifestyle, the political and religious act of doing teatro.

Notes

1   H. J. Elam, Jr., *Taking It to the Streets: The Social Protest Theater of Luis Valdez and Amiri Baraka* (Ann Arbor: University of Michigan Press, 1997), 11.

2   The "race" of Mexican people. Other Spanish or Mexican words: *Chicano*, Mexican (in US); *rasquachi*, of the underdog; *huelgistas*, strikers; *cuento* or *chiste*, tale or joke; *puro pedo*, unadulterated fart; *gringo seco*, dried up (white) foreigner; *teatros*, theatres; *sudor*, sweat; *sangre*, blood; *Qué le suene la campanita!* May the bell ring for him; *campesino*, peasant, fieldworker; *gabacho*, yankee; *pleberias*, plebs; *el pueblo japonés*, the Japanese people; *guerrillero*, guerrilla; *barrio*, neighborhood; *corazón*, heart; *actos*, acts; *Aztlan*, greater Mexico (including US-annexed territory); the *campesino*, the *urbano*, the *mestizo*, the *piojo*, the farm-worker, city dweller, person of mixed race, the louse or dregs; *huelga*, strike; *carpa*, itinerant tent show, form of Mexican popular theatre, employing oral performance and improvisation; *pachucos, pintos, chavalonas, familias, cuñados, tíos, primos*, snazzy dresser, sharp lads, guttersnipes, families, brother-in-law, uncles, cousins; *gente*, people.

3   "La palomia" means the class-based working class, including children to grandparents, all sitting in the audience and enjoying their reflections on stage. – Editor's note.

Chapter 56

Augusto Boal (b. 1931)

Augusto Boal is an influential theatre director, political activist, and founder of the Theatre of the Oppressed. His Brazilian-based theatre (Boal's political exile forced the theatre to relocate to Paris for a time) is an anti-Aristotelian concept. Rather than proposing a theatre rehearsed and pre-conditioned by actors and brought fully formed to the community, Boal incorporates the community into the function of theatre through audience participation. His major works, *Theatre of the Oppressed* (1979), *Games for Actors and Non-Actors* (1992), and *The Rainbow of Desire* (1995), outline tasks and exercises for theatre groups wishing to address the needs of local participants. Influenced by Brecht, Boal creates a ''forum'' theatre in which scenes enacting oppression or inequity are played out and then reflected upon by the actors and the audience. The work is improvisational and outcomes of the performances are often orchestrated by the audience. Boal's Marxist political theatre has often stirred controversy, and his exile attests to his challenge of the status quo. In *Theatre of the Oppressed*, Boal reframes the notion of empathy to embrace a more inclusive concept than Brecht demanded.

"Empathy or What? Emotion or Reason?" and "Experiments with the People's Theatre in Peru" (1974)

As we have seen in "Aristotle's Coercive System to Tragedy," *empathy* is the emotional relationship which is established between the character and spectator and which provokes, fundamentally, a delegation of power on the part of the spectator, who becomes

Augusto Boal, "Empathy or What? Emotion or Reason?" and excerpt from "Experiments with the People's Theatre in Peru," from *Theatre of the Oppressed*, tr. Charles A. and Maria-Odilia Leal McBride (1979; New York: TCG, 1985), 102–4, 122; originally published in Spanish as *Teatro de Oprimido* (1974). Translation © 1979 by Charles A. and Maria-Odilia Leal McBride. Reprinted by permission of Theatre Communications Group.

an object in relation to the character: whatever happens to the latter, happens vicariously to the spectator.

In the case of Aristotle, the empathy he recommends consists in the emotional tie which involves two basic emotions: pity and fear. The first binds us (the spectators) to a character who suffers a tragic fate that is undeserved, given his great virtues, and the second refers to the fact that that character suffers the consequences of possessing some fault which we also possess.

But empathy does not necessarily refer only to those two emotions – it can be realized through many other emotions, too. The only indispensable element in empathy is that the spectator assumes a "passive" attitude, delegating his ability to act. But the emotion or emotions which provoke that phenomenon can be any – fear (e.g., seeing films about vampires), sadism, sexual desire for the star, or whatever.

We should note, furthermore, that already in Aristotle empathy did not appear alone, but simultaneously with another type of relation: dianoia (character's thought–spectator's thought). That is, empathy was the result of the ethos, but the action of dianoia also provoked the action of a relation which John Gassner called "enlightenment."[1]

What Brecht asserts is that in idealist works the emotion acts by and for itself, producing what he calls "emotional orgies," while a materialist poetics – whose objective is not only that of interpreting the world but also of transforming it and making this earth finally habitable – has the obligation of showing how the world can be transformed.

A good empathy does not prevent understanding and, on the contrary, needs understanding precisely in order to avoid the spectacle's turning into an emotional orgy and the spectator's purging of his social sin. What Brecht does, fundamentally, is to place the emphasis on understanding (enlightenment), on dianoia [understanding].

At no time does Brecht speak against emotion, though he always speaks against the emotional orgy. He says that it would be absurd to deny emotion to modern science, thus clearly indicating that his position is entirely favorable to that emotion which is born of pure knowledge, as opposed to the emotion which is born out of ignorance. Before a dark room from which a scream is heard, a child becomes frightened: Brecht is against any attempts to move the spectator with scenes of this type. But if Einstein discovers that $E = mc^2$, the formula of the transformation of matter into energy, what an extraordinary emotion! Brecht is totally in favor of this type of emotion. Learning is an emotional experience, and there is no reason to avoid such emotions. But at the same time, ignorance causes emotions, and one must oppose emotions of this kind!

How can one fail to be moved when Mother Courage loses her sons, one by one, in the war? Inevitably, the spectator is moved to tears. But the emotion caused by ignorance must be avoided: let no one weep over the "fate" that took Mother Courage's sons from her! Let one cry rather with anger against war and against the commerce of war, because it is this commerce that takes away the sons of Mother Courage.

Another comparison may help to clarify the distinction: there is a remarkable parallel between *Riders to the Sea*, by the Irishman J. M. Synge, and *Señora Carrar's Rifles*. The two works are tremendously moving. The stories are very similar: two mothers whose sons are lost at sea. In Synge's work the sea itself is the murderer; the waves, fate. In Brecht, it is the soldiers who shoot innocent fishermen. Synge's work produced a violent emotion, caused by the sea – unknown, impenetrable, fateful.

Brecht's work arouses a deep emotion of hatred against Franco and his fascist followers! In both cases emotion is produced, but of different colors, for different reasons, and with different results.

We must emphasize: What Brecht does *not* want is that the spectators continue to leave their brains with their hats upon entering the theater, as do bourgeois spectators. [...]

In order to understand this *poetics of the oppressed* one must keep in mind its main objective: to change the people – "spectators," passive beings in the theatrical phenomenon – into subjects, into actors, transformers of the dramatic action. I hope that the differences remain clear. Aristotle proposes a poetics in which the spectator delegates power to the dramatic character so that the latter may act and think for him. Brecht proposes a poetics in which the spectator delegates power to the character who thus acts in his place but the spectator reserves the right to think for himself, often in opposition to the character. In the first case, a "catharsis" occurs; in the second, an awakening of critical consciousness. But the *poetics of the oppressed* focuses on the action itself: the spectator delegates no power to the character (or actor) either to act or to think in his place; on the contrary, he himself assumes the protagonic role, changes the dramatic action, tries out solutions, discusses plans for change – in short, trains himself for real action. In this case, perhaps the theater is not revolutionary in itself, but it is surely a rehearsal for the revolution. The liberated spectator, as a whole person, launches into action. No matter that the action is fictional; what matters is that it is action!

I believe that all the truly revolutionary theatrical groups should transfer to the people the means of production in the theater so that the people themselves may utilize them. The theater is a weapon, and it is the people who should wield it.

Note

1   See Chapter 35, this volume. – Editor's note.

Chapter 57

Charles Ludlam (1943–1987)

Charles Ludlam was an actor, playwright, director, and founder of the Ridiculous Theatre Company in 1967. Among his plays produced by the Ridiculous Company were *Bluebeard* (1970), *Camille* (1973), *Stageblood* (1975), *Le Bourgeois Avant-Garde* (1982), and his most well-known work, *The Mystery of Irma Vep* (1984). His work epitomizes ''camp,'' an art form combining kitsch, melodrama, drag, and plots parodically and unabashedly drawn from other sources. His ideas of spoofing also contained emulation. Ludlam often performed in drag, making his female impersonations one of the most inspiring actions of the gay liberation movement. In 1984 he played Hedda Gabler, marking his excellence not only as an actor but also as a political activist.

Ridiculous Theatre, Scourge of Human Folly (1975)

Aim: To get beyond nihilism by revaluing combat. Axioms to a theatre for ridicule:

1 You are a living mockery of your own ideals. If not, you have set your ideals too low.
2 The things one takes seriously are one's weaknesses.
3 Just as many people who claim a belief in God disprove it with their every act, so too there are those whose every deed, though they say there is no God, is an act of faith.
4 Evolution is a conscious process.
5 Bathos is that which is intended to be sorrowful but because of the extremity of its expression becomes comic. Pathos is that which is meant to be comic but because of

Charles Ludlam, "Ridiculous Theatre, Scourge of Human Folly," *The Drama Review* 19.4 (December 1975), 70. © Charles Ludlam.

the extremity of its expression becomes sorrowful. Some things which seem to be opposites are actually different degrees of the same thing.

6   The comic hero thrives by his vices. The tragic hero is destroyed by his virtue. Moral paradox is the crux of the drama.

7   The theatre is a humble materialist enterprise which seeks to produce riches of the imagination, not the other way around. The theatre is an event and not an object. Theatre workers need not blush and conceal their desperate struggle to pay the landlords their rents. Theatre without the stink of art.

Instructions for use:

This is farce not Sunday school. Illustrate hedonistic calculus. Test out a dangerous idea, a theme that threatens to destroy one's whole value system. Treat the material in a madly farcical manner without losing the seriousness of the theme. Show how paradoxes arrest the mind. Scare yourself a bit along the way.

Chapter 58

Michael Kirby (b. 1931)

Editor, theorist, and academic, Michael Kirby's major works include *Happenings* (1965), *Futurist Performance* (1986), and *Formalist Theatre* (1987). Kirby was concerned with defining the structures of theatre. He was influenced by semiotics and the desire to comprehend the language of performance. His groundbreaking works, along with those of Victor Turner and Richard Schechner (see Chapters 67 and 78, this volume), established the study of performance in the academy. For Kirby and others, "performance studies" draws from anthropology, ethnography, and culture, but it is also a unique form of research answerable to its own inquiry. He defined performance as "non-matrixed" – where the performer "never behaves as if he were anyone other than himself. He never represents elements of character. He merely carries out certain actions" – and its opposite, "matrixed" – where the actor incorporates a representational aspect of a character and, depending on the degree of incorporation, is said to embody referentiality.[1] Along a sliding scale, the more the performer incorporates that which he or she is not, the more the actor is said to be "matrixed acting." The non-matrixed performance is best exemplified by a circus, which for Kirby also defines a "Happening." Except for the clowns, he says, the "acrobats, jugglers, and animal trainers are merely carrying out their activities. The grips or stagehands become performers, too, as they dismantle and rig the equipment – demonstrating that non-matrixed performing exists at all levels of difficulty."[2] In the following extract, Kirby lays the foundation of performance studies by examining the structures of theatre. He oscillates his description of theatre from formalist to structuralist, but ultimately his aim in either definition, Martin Puchner explains, is "to downplay historical change." Kirby seeks "to evade the kind of historiography that would declare the avant-garde

Michael Kirby, "Manifesto of Structuralism," *The Drama Review* 19.4 (December 1975), 82–3. © 1975 by Tulane Drama Review. Reprinted by permission of TDR/The Drama Review.

to be over."[3] He examines, like Peter Brook and Artaud before him, the immediacy of theatre – theatre not so much as a representation but as an event that recreates itself anew in each theatrical moment.

Manifesto of Structuralism (1975)

Nothing exists without structure. Every atom, every action has structure. Every play, every performance, every presentation has structure. There is no such thing as "structureless" theatre. There are only people who are not aware of perceiving structure.

Structuralism, in all art and in performance, makes structure the most important element. Structuralist theatre relegates any and all other aspects of a performance to lesser positions. In structuralism, structure dominates.

In most theatre, structure is subservient. It exists as an armature upon which incidents hang. It serves as a display rack for characters and scenes. It is subservient to the message, to the moment of song and dance, to visual effects.

What is structure? What is it that the structuralist wishes to make most important in the performance? And what is its effect?

"Structure," Webster [dictionary] says, is the "arrangement or interrelation of all the parts of the whole." Thus, while the total structure of performance involves space, it is primarily a structuring of time.

It is the unusual theatre piece that exists entirely in the present moment, only the instantaneous performance is here-and-now. The "thing" that is the performance is expectation, is a mixture of memory and expectation, is (finally) only memory.

The structuralist knows how the mind reaches out in both directions along the continuum in time. He knows how time is crossed by mental connections. He knows about memory and expectancy and how these mechanisms work. He knows that anything that is remembered or expected – a phrase, a gesture, an action, an attitude, a thing, a color, a shape – indicates structure. He knows that structure becomes manifest in the workings of the mind.

Must structure, then, be always conscious? Does it register only at the conscious levels of the mind? Of course not. We may consciously recognize structure; we may have a heightened awareness of its presence. But we also may merely be aware of certain reflections, certain echoes, certain commotions, certain answers, certain frustrations, certain fulfillments, the working of structure need not be obvious.

This does not mean that structuralism as an artistic phenomenon is the same as structuralism in philosophy or that it has any relationship to structural anthropology. It is not concerned with theory of the unconscious, whether Freudian, Jungian, or Lévi-Straussian. It is concerned primarily with making works of art – according to certain structural principles, concepts, hypotheses, ideas.

Does structure function in a purely formal and intellectual way or does it involve the emotions? The structuralist refuses to make the distinction, he makes it only for purposes of analysis and activity. The structuralist knows that arrangements and interrelationships in time, however formal or informal, have their emotional dimensions. He knows that structure creates, gives rise to, is fused with, very particular and subtle emotions. These are not necessarily the emotions of everyday life: love, hate, joy, fear, etc. They are the emotions of structure.

The structuralist does not say that a structuralist play is better (or worse) than any other kind of play. It is merely different. Yet these differences have great significance to the structuralist. He sees structuralism as having, at this moment, great potential. There is much work to be done; much exploration is needed in the area. We have much to learn about the ways in which the structure of performance affects the mind. Someday, the importance of structuralism will fade away. But that time is far in the future.

Notes

1   M. Kirby, *A Formalist Theatre* (Philadelphia: University of Pennsylvania Press, 1987), 5.
2   M. Kirby, *Happenings: An Illustrated Anthology* (London: Sidgwick and Jackson, 1965), 30.
3   M. Puchner, *Poetry of the Revolution: Marx, Manifestos, and the Avant-Gardes* (Princeton: Princeton University Press, 2006), 249.

Chapter 59

Wole Soyinka (b. 1934)

The prolific Nigerian playwright, author, theorist, and political activist Wole Soyinka (awarded the Nobel Prize in 1986) examines myth, ritual, and human freedom in light of political oppression. His plays are widely produced, among them *The Lion and the Jewel* (1963), *The Bacchae of Euripides* (1973), *Death and the King's Horseman* (1975), and *The Beautification of Area Boys* (1995). They examine the tension of African and Western influences, especially regarding the spiritual and mythic interconnection of Christian and Yoruba religions. His works connect past, present, and future in conflict, as well as the role of the artist's vision in a conforming society. His activism and creativity have received international acclaim. He was incarcerated from 1967 to 1969 for his outspoken criticisms of oppression. His significant work, *Myth, Literature, and the African World* (1976, portions reproduced here), takes up the Nietzschean idea of ritual empowerment.

Drama and the African World-View (1976)[1]

Let us, by way of a paradigmatic example, take a common theme in traditional mask-drama: a symbolic struggle with chthonic presences, the goal of the conflict being a harmonious resolution for plenitude and the well-being of the community. Any individual within the "audience" knows better than to add his voice *arbitrarily* even to the most seductive passages of an invocatory song, or to contribute a refrain to the familiar sequence of liturgical exchanges among the protagonists. The moment for choric participation is

Wole Soyinka, "Drama and the African World-View," excerpted from *Myth, Literature, and the African World* (Cambridge: Cambridge University Press, 1976), 37–44, 142–7 (appendix). © 1976 by Cambridge University Press. Reprinted by permission of the author and publisher.

well-defined, but this does not imply that until such a moment, participation ceases. The so-called audience is itself an integral part of that arena of conflict; it contributes spiritual strength to the protagonist through its choric reality which must first be conjured up and established, defining and investing the arena through offerings and incantations. The drama would be non-existent except within and against this symbolic representation of earth and cosmos, except within this communal compact whose choric essence supplies the collective energy for the challenger of chthonic realms. Overt participation when it comes is channeled through a formalized repertoire of gestures and liturgical responses. The "spontaneous" participant from within the audience does not permit himself to give vent to a bare impulse or a euphoria which might bring him out as a dissociated entity from within the choric mass. If it does happen, as of course it can, the event is an aberration which may imperil the eudaemonic [happiness] goals of that representation. The interjector – whose balance of mind is regarded as being temporarily disturbed – is quietly led out and the appropriate (usually unobtrusive) spells are cast to counter the risks of the abnormal event.

I would like to go a little deeper into this ritualistic sense of space since it is so intimately linked with the comprehensive world-view of the society that gave it birth. We shall treat it first as a medium in the communicative sense and, like any other medium, it is one that is best defined through the process of interruption. In theatrical terms, this interruption is effected principally by the human apparatus. Sound, light, motion, even smell, can all be used just as validly to define space, and ritual theatre uses all these instruments of definition to control and render concrete, to parallel (this is perhaps the best description of the process) the experiences or intuitions of man in that far more disturbing environment which he defines variously as void, emptiness or infinity. The concern of ritual theatre in this process of spatial definition which precedes, as we shall discover, the actual enactment must therefore be seen as an integral part of man's constant efforts to master the immensity of the cosmos with his minuscule self. The actual events which make up the enactment are themselves, in ritual theatre, a materialization of this basic adventure of man's metaphysical self.

Theatre then is one arena, one of the earliest that we know of, in which man has attempted to come to terms with the spatial phenomenon of his being. Again, in speaking of space, let us recognize first of all that with the advancement of technology and the evolution – some would prefer to call it a counter-evolution – of the technical sensibility, the spatial vision of theatre has become steadily contracted into purely physical acting areas on a stage as opposed to a symbolic arena for metaphysical contests. The pagan beginnings of Greek theatre retained their symbolic validity to dramaturgists for centuries after the event, so that the relative positions of suppliant, tyrant or *deus ex machina*, as well as the offertory or altar, were constantly impressed on their audience and created immediate emotional overtones both when they were used and by their very act of being. (I do not, for the purpose of this essay, wish to debate whether the fixity of these positions did not, contrasted with the fluid approach of African ritual space, detract from the audience's experience of cosmic relations.) Medieval European theatre in its turn, corresponding to the religious mythology of its period, created a constant *microcosmos* by its spatial correspondences of good and evil, angels and demons, paradise, purgatory and hell. The protagonists of earth, heaven and hell enacted their various trials and conflicts in relation to these traditional positions, and the automatic recognition of three hierarchical situations of man created spiritual anxieties and hopes in the breasts of the audience. But observe, the apprehended territory of man has already begun to contract! Cosmic representation has shrunk into a purely moral one, a summation in terms of penalties and rewards. The process continued through successive periods of European partial explorations of what was once a medium of totality, achieving such analytical aberrations as in this sample of compartmentalization which claims that the right (actor's) wing of the stage is "stronger" than the left. We shall not encounter any proofs of this ludicrous assertion in the beginnings of theatre, Greek or African.

Ritual theatre, let it be recalled, establishes the spatial medium not merely as a physical area for simulated events but as a manageable contraction of the cosmic envelope within which man – no matter how deeply buried such a consciousness has latterly become – fearfully exists. And this attempt to manage the immensity of his spatial awareness makes every manifestation in ritual theatre a paradigm for the cosmic human condition. There are transient parallels, brief visual moments of this experience in modern European theatre. The spectacle of a lone human figure under a spotlight on a darkened stage is, unlike a painting, a breathing, living, pulsating, threateningly fragile example of this paradigm. It is threatening because, unlike a similar parable on canvas, its fragility is experienced both at the level of its symbolism and in terms of sympathetic concern for the well-being of that immediate human medium. Let us say he is a tragic character: at the first sign of a check in the momentum of a tragic declamation, his audience becomes nervous for him, wondering – has he forgotten his line? has he blacked out? Or in the case of opera – will she make that upper register? Well, ritual theatre has an additional, far more fundamental anxiety. Indeed, it is correct to say that the technical anxiety even where it exists – after all it does exist; the element of creative form is never absent even in the most so-called primitive consciousness – so, where it does exist, it is never so profoundly engaged as with a modern manifestation. The real unvoiced fear is: will this protagonist survive confrontation with forces that exist within the dangerous area of transformation? Entering that *microcosmos* involves a loss of individuation, a self-submergence in universal essence. It is an act undertaken on behalf of the community, and the welfare of that protagonist is inseparable from that of the total community.[2]

This ritual understanding is essential to a profound participation in the cathartic processes of the great tragedies. To attempt to define it even more clearly I would like to refer once again to painting, that essentially individualistic art. In surmounting the challenge of space and cosmos, a Turner, a Wyeth or a van Gogh utilizes endless permutations of color, shapes and lines to extract truly harrowing or consoling metaphysical statements from natural phenomena. There is, however, no engagement of the communal experience in this particular medium. The transmission is individual. It is no less essential to the sum of human experience but it is, even when viewed by a thousand people simultaneously, a mere sum of fragmented experiences, individual and vicarious. The singularity of theatre is its simultaneity in the forging of a single human experience – at its most successful. That it does not often succeed is true enough, but that does not invalidate the truth that, at the very roots of the dramatic phenomenon, this affirmation of the communal self was the experiential goal. The search, even by modern European dramatists for ritualist roots from which to draw out visions of modern experience, is a clue to the deep-seated need of creative man to recover this archetypal consciousness in the origins of the dramatic medium.

Ritual theatre, viewed from the spatial perspective, aims to reflect through physical and symbolic means the archetypal struggle of the mortal being against exterior forces. A tragic view of the theatre goes further and suggests that even the so-called realistic or literary drama can be interpreted as a mundane reflection of this essential struggle. Poetic drama especially may be regarded as a repository of this essential aspect of theatre; being largely metaphorical, it expands the immediate meaning and action of the protagonists into a world of nature forces and metaphysical conceptions. Or, to put it the other way round, powerful natural or cosmic influences are internalized within the protagonists and this implosive factor creates the titanic scale of their passions even when the basis of the conflict seems hardly to warrant it. (Shakespeare's *Lear* is the greatest exemplar of this.) Indeed, this view of theatre sees the stage as a constant battleground for forces larger than the petty infractions of habitual communal norms or patterns of human relationships and expectations, beyond the actual twists and incidents of action and their resolutions. The stage is created for the purpose of that communal presence which alone defines it (and this is the fundamental defining concept, that the stage is brought into being by a communal presence); so, for this purpose, the stage becomes the affective, rational and intuitive milieu of the total communal experience, historic, race-formative, cosmogonic. Where such theatre is encountered in its purest form, not as re-created metaphors for the later tragic stage, we will find no compass points, no horizontal or vertical definitions. There are no reserved spaces for the protagonists, for his very act of representational being is defined in turn by nothing less than the infinite cosmos within which the origin of the community and its contemporaneous experience of being is firmly embedded. Drama, however, exists on the boards; in the improvised space among stalls in the deserted or teeming market, on the raised platform in a school or community hall, in the secretive recesses of a nature-fringed shrine, among the push-buttons of the modern European stage or its equivalents in Africa – those elegant monstrosities raised to enshrine the spirit of misconceived prestigiousness. It is necessary always to look for the essence of the play among these roofs and spaces, not confine it to the printed text as an autonomous entity. [...]

Appendix

Yoruba tragedy plunges straight into the "chthonic realm," the seething cauldron of the dark world of will and psyche, the transitional yet inchoate matrix of death and becoming. Into this universal womb once plunged and emerged Ogun, the first actor, disintegrating within the abyss. His spiritual re-assemblage does not require a copying of actuality in the ritual re-enactment of his devotees, any more than Obatala does in plastic representation, in the art of Obatala. The actors in Ogun Mysteries are the communicant chorus, containing within their collective being the essence of that transitional abyss. But only as essence, held, contained and mystically expressed. Within the mystic summons of the chasm the protagonist actor (and every god-suffering choric individual) resists, like Ogun before him, the final step towards complete annihilation. From this alone steps forward the eternal actor of the tragic rites, first as the unresisting mouthpiece of the god, uttering visions symbolic of the transitional gulf, interpreting the dread power within whose essence he is immersed as agent of the choric will. Only later, in the evenness of release from the tragic climax, does the serene self-awareness of Obatala reassert its creative control. He, the actor, emerges still as the mediant voice of the gods, but stands now as it were beside himself, observing, understanding, creating. At this stage is known to him the sublime *aesthetic* joy, not within Nietzsche's heart of original oneness but in the distanced celebration of the cosmic struggle. This resolved aesthetic serenity is the link between Ogun's tragic art and Obatala's plastic beauty. The unblemished god, Obatala, is the serene womb of chthonic reflection (or memory), a passive strength awaiting and celebrating each act of vicarious restoration of his primordial being. [. . .]

Tragedy, in Yoruba traditional drama, is the anguish of this severance, the fragmentation of essence from self. Its music is the stricken cry of man's blind soul as he flounders in the void and crashes through a deep abyss of a-spirituality and cosmic rejection. Tragic music is an echo from that void; the celebrant speaks, sings and dances in authentic archetypal images from within the abyss. All understand and respond, for it is the language of the world.

It is necessary to emphasize that the gods were coming down to be reunited with man, for this tragedy could not be, the anguish of severance would not attain such tragic proportions, if the gods' position on earth (i.e. in man's conception) was to be one of divine remoteness. This is again testified to by the form of worship, which is marked by camaraderie and irreverence just as departure to ancestorhood is marked by bawdiness in the midst of grief. The anthropomorphic origin of uncountable deities is one more leveler of divine class-consciousness but, finally, it is the innate humanity of the gods themselves, their bond with man through a common animist relation with nature and phenomena. Continuity for the Yoruba operates both through the cyclic concept of time and the animist interfusion of all matter and consciousness.

The first actor – for he led the others – was Ogun, first suffering deity, first creative energy, the first challenger, and conqueror of transition. And his, the first art, was tragic art, for the complementary drama of the syncretic successor to Orisa-nla, Obatala's "Passion" play, is only the plastic resolution of Ogun's tragic engagement. The Yoruba metaphysics of accommodation and resolution could only come after the passage of the gods through the transitional gulf, after the demonic test of the self-will of Ogun the explorer-god in the creative cauldron of cosmic powers. Only after such testing could the harmonious Yoruba world be born, a harmonious will which accommodates every alien material or abstract phenomenon within its infinitely stressed spirituality. The artifact of Ogun's conquest of separation, the "fetish" was iron ore, symbol of earth's womb-energies, cleaver and welder of life. Ogun, through his redemptive action, became the first symbol of the alliance of disparities when, from earth itself, he extracted elements for the subjugation of chthonic chaos. In tragic consciousness the votary's psyche reaches out beyond the realm of nothingness (or spiritual chaos) which is potentially destructive of human awareness, through areas of terror and blind energies into a ritual empathy with the gods, the eternal presence, who once preceded him in parallel awareness of their own incompletion. Ritual anguish is therefore experienced as that primal transmission of the god's despair – vast, numinous, always incomprehensible. In vain we seek to capture it in words; there is only for the protagonist the certainty of the experience of this abyss – the tragic victim plunges into it in spite of ritualistic earthing and is redeemed only by action. Without acting, and yet in spite of it he is forever lost in the maul of tragic tyranny.

Acting is therefore a contradiction of the tragic spirit, yet it is also its natural complement. To act, the Promethean instinct of rebellion channels anguish into a creative purpose which releases man from a totally destructive despair, releasing from within him the most energetic, deeply combative inventions which, without usurping the territory of the infernal gulf, bridges it with visionary hopes. Only the battle of the will is thus primally creative; from its spiritual stress springs the soul's despairing cry which proves its own solace, which alone reverberating within the cosmic vaults usurps (at least, and however briefly) the powers of the abyss. At the charged climactic moments of the tragic rites we understand how music came to be the sole art form which can contain tragic reality. The votary is led by no other guide into the pristine heart of tragedy. Music as the embodiment of the tragic spirit has been more than perceptively exhausted in the philosophy of Europe; there is little to add, much to qualify. And the function and nature of music in Yoruba tragedy is peculiarly revealing of the shortcomings of long accepted conclusions of European intuition. [. . .]

Notes

1 The remarks which follow are based on plays observed in situ, that is, on the spot where the performance originates and ends, and at its appropriate time of year, not itinerant variations on the same theme. The specific play referred to here was a harvest play which took place on a farm-clearing some three miles south of Ihiala in the then Eastern Regions of Nigeria, 1961.
2 Kola Ogunmola, in his stage adaptations of Amos Tutuola's *Palmwine Drunkard*, built on this tradition, one that is still manifested in ancestral mask comedies.

Chapter 60

Robert Wilson (b. 1941)

Robert Wilson is an international theatre director, painter, and installation artist whose stylized works seek to expand the boundaries of theatre. His work with children with disabilities informs his investigation of time and space onstage. His well-known directorial works include *Deafman Glance* (1970), *Overture to Ka Mountain* (1972, a performance staged on an Iranian mountaintop and lasting over a week), *Einstein on the Beach* (1976), *Civil Wars* (1983), Wagner's *Parsifal* (1991) and *Lohengrin* (1998), and Ibsen's *Peer Gynt* (2005, in Norway). Often working with composer Philip Glass, Wilson stages slow motion, spatial collage, visual splendor, aural texture (sound, music, opera), and juxtaposed images that demand an intense viewing experience. Laurence Shyer notes that Wilson's prolonged duration in his productions provides ''a means of opening up channels of perception and communication and overcoming sensory overload. Slowing down and extending performances over greater periods would enable the spectator to both enter Wilson's private world and view each image clearly; time would provide the space in which to more fully see, hear and experience.''[1]

"... I thought I was hallucinating hallucinating" (1977)

I began writing *I was sitting on my patio this guy appeared I thought I was hallucinating* a few days after the final performance of *Einstein on the Beach* in November of 1976.

I wrote a few pages of dialog at a time in a large notebook with blank pages that I often write and draw in when working on a piece. The language I wrote was more a reflection of the way we think than of the way we normally speak. My head became like a TV, switching

Robert Wilson, "... I thought I was hallucinating hallucinating," *The Drama Review* 21.4 (December 1977), 76–8. © 1977 by Tulane Drama Review. Reprinted by permission of TDR/The Drama Review.

from thought to thought (and in writing from phrase to phrase) like flipping a dial from channel to channel.

I write when I am alone and work best when there are no interruptions. I sometimes keep a television on at low volume and incorporate phrases I hear into my text, which I write quickly, usually leaving it untouched and in its original order once the words are on the page. Every few days I had a few pages of writing typed up.

A few weeks later I began making sketches, often on long rolls of paper (as well as in my notebook), of the image I was thinking of using for a basic stage set. I made about twenty-five drawings a day for two weeks, sometimes making slight alterations in them. I often follow a similar procedure before arriving at a final image used as a model for scenery. Christina Giannini and I worked together on translating the image into actual scenery, which she then built.

I continued to write dialog while making the set designs. Film and sound cues were written in as I wrote. The play was structured in two acts of equal length for which the material was very similar but treated in a very unlike manner by two performers, each to direct his or her respective act. When the last few pages of the verbal script had been typed up, the two cast members, Lucinda Childs and myself, were each given a copy for memorization. (The play was not necessarily written for a man, Act I, and a woman Act II. It could just as well be performed by a woman, Act I, and a man, Act II, as by two women or two men.)

I knew at the outset that the play was intended to be performed on a small proscenium stage and that the basic image for both acts would be the interior of a room having three tall narrow windows in its black back wall. For the short prolog to each act the windows would be "open" with bright "daylight" behind them casting long diagonal shadows and shafts of light across the room, silhouetting the performers and tracing the parts of the body with light. In contrast to this, for the main part of each act, the windows would be filled in with bookshelves, making the room much darker.

Shortly after Lucinda was given her script, she memorized a good part of it and began blocking her movements. I watched her develop the material for a month before I began blocking my own movements. My part was then fashioned in complementary contrast to hers.

During that first month of rehearsal I memorized my lines and finalized the set drawings. Originally I had considered having a backdrop of a wave behind the windows. I later decided on a solid white backdrop, giving the illusion of vast space, accompanied during the Act I prolog by silence and the Act II prolog by an audiotape of waves. I decided to have the last few lines of dialog repeated at the end of Act II. These lines, in conjunction with movements, would become an epilog, during which the room would become light-filled again, the bookcases and back wall having each slowly disappeared. The sequence of the prologs, acts, and epilog thus became the following:

1   *Black/White*
2   *Black*
3   *Black/White*
4   *Black*
5   *White*

We rehearsed in a loft using makeshift furniture the same dimensions as the chaise longue, shelf, and telephone table that I was designing at the time and which were to be the only set pieces on stage. The only two props were a wineglass and a telephone. Shortly after I began blocking movements and gestures for my act (Act I), we began holding weekly open rehearsals.

During the earlier rehearsals Alan Lloyd, who had read the script a number of times, began composing the score. About halfway through I suggested he might write the rest from the end to the middle, which is what happened. By the time open rehearsals started, we were using a cassette tape that was cued to the dialog and played very softly. The music for Act I was piano, and that for Act II, clavichord. James Neu, who also did the voice-overs, was largely responsible for the coordination between dialog and music.

I am always concerned with how the total stage picture looks at any given moment. The placement and design (shape, proportion, materials) of furniture, the color, fabric, and design of costumes, placement and content of film, paths and gestures of performers, and lighting were all major considerations, no less important than the dialog or music. The details of the furniture, costumes, and film content were arrived at after the overall image had been finalized, their selection being based, in part, on the mood and architecture of the setting (stage set, dialog, music and characters) we had begun to establish.

Note

1   L. Shyer, *Robert Wilson and His Collaborators* (New York: Theatre Communications Group, 1989), xvi.

Chapter 61

Patrice Pavis (b. 1947)

Patrice Pavis is an influential theatre scholar, critic, and Professor of Theatre at the University of Paris VIII-Saint-Denis. His principal concerns are theatrical sign systems (semiotics). He investigates the ways in which gesture, costume, design, relationships, and mood are communicated to an audience. Pavis is among the semioticians who began to take into account the impact of interpretation (director, actor, designer) on the creation of theatrical meanings. The *mise en scène*, a term he frequently employs, examines interpretation: how, he asks, is the language of the stage read, translated, and absorbed at the moment of performance? The *mise en scène* is the result of artistic choices, but these choices fluctuate from performance to performance, and each performance is responsible for a new ideology, meaning, and signatory system. Pavis designs several ways of interpreting the moment of performance: as closed moments having no outside reference (auto-textual), or as signs that open up as references to outside the world of the stage (ideo-textual). His major works, *Voix et images de la scène: Vers une sémiologie de la réception* (*Sounds and Images of the Stage: Towards a Semiotics of Reception*, 1985), *Dictionnaire du théâtre* (1987), and *Le Théâtre aux croisements des cultures* (1990), examine the relationship of word, text, gesture, and narrative.

Languages of the Stage (1978)

It would be a great imp(r)udence to turn to Brecht's theoretical writings in order to extract from them certain concepts, to comment on them and to link them with other commentaries or to propose new definitions in the meta-language of semiology. Brecht's

Patrice Pavis, "Languages of the Stage" (1978), in *Languages of the Stage: Essays in the Semiology of Theatre*, tr. Susan Melrose (New York: PAJ, 1982), 39–49. First published in *Silex* 7 (1978). © 1978. Reprinted by permission of Susan Melrose.

way of posing problems is extremely clear. He carefully illustrates them by reference to his theatre practice. He never hesitates – in the *Short Organum for the Theatre*, for example – to make those corrections necessitated by the evolution of his thinking, and the new demands of his aesthetic and political battles.

It would be highly dangerous, moreover, to isolate a concept for the sole purpose of clarifying it only in the context of written works of theory, without verifying what use Brecht makes of it in his writings or productions, and without comparing it dialectically with other notions of his system. This is precisely what has happened frequently with the concept of epic drama ("epische Spielweise"). "The contradiction between acting (demonstration) and experience (empathy) often leads the uninstructed to suppose that only one or the other can be manifest in the work of the actor, as if the *Short Organum* concentrated only entirely on acting and the old tradition entirely on experience."[1] So we stand forewarned; and if we insist on making an excursion (incursion) into the unknown land of the *Gestus*, we do so at our own risk, justified solely by the fact that the term itself, although in abundant use in Brecht's "theoretical writings," remains very vaguely and contradictorily defined.

In the vast mass of his writing on the theatre[2] which has appeared since "Non-Aristotelian Drama" (1932–1941) from *The Messingkauf Dialogues* up through the "Short Organum for the Theatre" (1948–1954), the center of gravity is constantly shifting. Brecht formulates his critique of the "Aristotelian" dramatic form in reaction to the notion of identification and catharsis; then he shows his interest in the possibility of imitation and of critical realism; finally, "theatre dialectics" gives him the chance to propose a method of analysis of reality, and to go beyond the overly stressed oppositions between epic/dramatic, formalism/realism, showing/incarnating, etc.

However, in this journey towards a theory of dialectical theatre two key notions are particularly resistant to thematic and terminological variations: that of the *Gestus*, and that of the Story (*die Fabel*). They are veritable pillars of the theoretical structure, which is massive and solid, but whose foundations need to be examined. Brecht himself comes ever closer to a definition of *Gestus* and Story, without reducing them to an unequivocal meaning, as though he wanted to preserve their richness and their productive contradictions. But it is only at the end of his "demonstration" that he introduces them into the *Short Organum* (*BT, S* 61–76); following the thread of Aristotelian demonstration he sets out from the concept of imitation and the spectator's pleasure at that imitation, ending up at the "*Gestus* of delivery" of the performance (*BT, S* 76).

The itinerary to be followed by the author, the theoretician and the spectator is perfectly described in two sentences: "Splitting such material into one gest after the other, the actor masters his character by first mastering the 'story'" (*BT, S* 64, p. 200). "The exposition of the story and its communication by suitable means of alienation constitute the main business of the theatre" (*BT, S* 70, p. 202). According to these definitions it seems rather difficult to tell which element, *Gestus* or Story, is logically and temporally anterior to the other; it appears at any rate that Story and *Gestus* are closely linked, and constitute the play and its *mise en scène*. Theatre, in fact, always does tell a story (even if it is illogical) by means of gesture (in the widest meaning of the term): the actors' bodies, stage configurations, "illustrations" of the social body. [...]

Social *Gestus* and Basic Gestures

Faced with the multiple forms of *Gestus*, Brecht is led to distinguish between the simple incidental social *Gestus*, characteristic of an actor or a particular stage business, and the basic *Gestus* ("*Grundgestus*"), which is characteristic of the play or of a particular action. [...]

The basic *Gestus* describes a condensed version of the story; it constitutes the inalienable substratum of the gestural relationship between at least two people, a relationship which must always be readable whatever the options of the *mise en scène*. This *Gestus* (close to enunciation, a linguistic term which describes the attitude of the speaker to his utterance) gives us the key to the relationship between the play being performed and the public. The author's attitude to the public, that of the era represented and of the time in which the play is performed, the collective style of acting of the characters, etc., are a few of the parameters of the basic *Gestus*. Today we would also call it the "discourse" of the *mise en scène* or of the "performance structure" without, however, insisting as Brecht does on the physical character (gesture and attitude) of this relationship with the public.

Once this general context of the *Gestus* is outlined, it becomes possible, through a series of approximations, to indicate its properties and its importance for the theory of theatre. *Gestus* appears to be a remarkable instrument for unlocking the contradictions of action and character, of the individual and the social body, of logos and gesture, of distance and identification.

Between Action and Character

The discussion about the link between action and characters, and the way in which one is determined by the other, is one of the oldest in theatrical aesthetics. Like Aristotle in his *Poetics*, Brecht conceives of theatre as a succession of actions from which the characterization flows. In the early Brecht, in *Man is Man* for example, the conception of man is quasi-behavioristic and mechanistic. (It is well known how the clownish characters of [Karl] Valentin and Chaplin fascinated Brecht.) For the mature Brecht, man is no longer pure gesticulation; he cannot be reduced to a single exterior behavior-pattern; he is no longer an "activist" but a dialectical strategist. His way of acting influences and modifies the deepest elements of his nature.

Gestus can therefore assure the mediation between bodily action and character behavior; it is situated midway between the character and the determination of his possible actions (of his "spheres of action" in the functionalist terminology of Propp).[3] As an object of the actor's research, it becomes more and more specific in defining what the character does, and, consequently, what he is: way of being and way of behaving become complementary. The importance to the actor of this way of approaching the *Gestus* and the character is not difficult to imagine. Running through the opening scenes of his *Galileo*, Brecht analyzes Galileo's "stage business": his pleasure in drinking his milk, in washing himself, and in thinking form a *Gestus* which informs us as much about the person of the character (that is, about his possible weaknesses, which are confirmed in what follows) as about his activities as milk-drinker and thinker.

In practice, it is often very difficult to observe the dialectical mobility of *Gestus*, between a way of behaving and a gestuality which are fixed, on the one hand, and a spontaneous and creative activity on the other. It is, however, only at this price that the Brechtian notion retains its efficacy in going beyond the alternatives of action/character. The assembling of different *Gestus* by the actor will then allow him to reconstitute the Story. In the Brechtian concept the Story is not simply (as it is in *Poetics*) the "principle and the soul of the tragedy, with the characters in second place only" (1450a); it is principally the sum total of the *Gestus* and the relationships between the characters, "the realm of attitudes adopted by the characters towards one another" (*BT, S* 61, p. 198), "the groupings and the movements of the characters" (*GW* 17, 1218).

This integration of particular *Gestus* in the story explains its fragmented and non-continuous nature: "He [the actor] must be able to space his gestures as the compositor produces spaced type."[4] The "story-maker" spaces the narrative episodes. The development of the story occurs by leaps and not by a sliding of scenes one into the other. The fragmentation of the story corresponds to the "shifting" gesture (which always implies more than it actually shows). This shifting movement and the fragmentation are, in fact, iconically, musically, reproducing the contradictions of social processes. The Story does not mask (as does the traditional dramatic form) the illogical nature of the linking of the scenes but lets us become aware of it. Thus, for example, the dual attitude of Mother Courage: living off the war *and* sacrificing nothing to it; loving her children *and* making use of them in her business, etc.

If the *Gestus* refers directly to a position in the social reality represented, the story does not have to mold itself to the undulatory and contradictory movement of history, to follow faithfully the same logico-temporal presentation. There is never a perfect parallelism between social processes and the arrangement of the *Gestus* within the plot. The spectator's pleasure lies in rectifying the proportions between Story and history, in perceiving the disconnections between these two levels: thus in *Galileo* we wait in vain for a dramatic scene of retraction. In *The Resistible Rise of Arturo Ui*, the life of the gangster does not follow that of his historical model.

Individual and Social

The distinction between an *individual* gesture and a *socially* encoded one is also quite irrelevant to *Gestus*. For Brecht, gesture is not the free and individual part of man in opposition to the collective domination of language and ideology (and for the actor, of the "text to be said"). He does not own it personally; it belongs and refers to a group, a class, a milieu. He always quotes a particular gestuality of these groups, even one of his own previous gestures, as "the rough sketching which indicates traces of other movements and features all around the fully-worked-out figure" (*BT, S* 39, p. 191). Man's gesture, as Brecht tries to reflect it in the *Gestus*, is neither conventional (of the type "capitalists walk like this"), nor entirely invented (spontaneous, expressive or aestheticizing gesture). He uses materials from the code of gestural conventions for his own purposes, and to express one or another individual variant corresponding to the specific situation of man, which is never twice repeated in identical form. The *Gestus* does not lead to a puppet-like use of gesture, where the slightest indication of behavior immediately takes on the function of a signal: the spectator (and the actor) is constantly invited to select a few details from the gesture in order to have them reveal a social conduct which is not delivered in its definitive form but remains the object of critical appraisal. So the *Gestus* is in no sense the "cheap imitation" of a fixed sociological vision of human behavior. The creators of *mises en scène* where socially marked figures appear (workers, exploiters, soldiers) have sometimes forgotten this aspect of *Gestus*.

Logos and Gestuality

The role of *Gestus* is also very important when it comes to understanding the relationship between logos and gestuality in epic theatre. In a dramatic form where the text is staged, the actors' gestures often only illustrate or punctuate the spoken word by creating the illusion that it is a perfectly integrated part of the enunciator, thus of his gestural universe. *Gestus*, on the contrary, approaches the text/gesture ensemble so as not to eliminate either of the two terms of the dichotomy. It reveals how gestural a discourse may be (see below on the "gestuality" of discourse) by stressing the rhythm of the diction, and the actor's effort in the production and ostension of the text. The stage and the speaking body (the actor) are made "readable" for the audience (if necessary by means of printed banners).

So instead of fusing logos and gestuality in an illusion of reality, the *Gestus* radically cleaves the performance into two blocks: the shown (the said) and the showing (the saying). Discourse no longer has the form of a homogenous block; it threatens at any moment to break away from its enunciator. Far from assuring the construction and the continuity of the action, it intervenes to stop the movement and to comment on what might have been acted on stage. *Gestus* thus displaces the dialectic between ideas and actions; the dialectic no longer operates within the system of these ideas and actions, but at the point of intersection of the enunciating gesture and the enunciated discourse: "... in epic theatre, the dialectic is not born of the contradiction between successive statements or ways of behaving, but of the gesture itself."[5]

Alienation

This phenomenon of the "cleaving" of the performance by *Gestus* is, in fact, the principle of the alienation effect. By making visible the class behind the individual, the critique behind the naïve object, the commentary behind the affirmation, the attitude of demonstration behind the demonstrated thing, the *Gestus* lies at the core of the alienation effect where the thing is simultaneously recognized and made strange, where gesture invites us to reflect on the text and the text contradicts the gesture. This device, which Brecht did not invent but which he had reinvested with a social (and not simply aesthetic) content, is as applicable to social gesture as to stage signs or the arrangement of events in the story. The same signifier (gesture, stage sign, narrative episode) takes on a "double appearance," splits itself into two signifieds: a concrete object, naïvely "delivered" and an abstract object of knowledge, criticized and "alienated."

Gestus, stage sign and Story reveal at the same time materiality and abstraction, historical exactitude and philosophical meaning, the particular and the general.[6] The dose of these two contradictory ingredients runs the risk of being rather "explosive," since, according to Brecht, the art of abstraction must be mastered by realists. The thankless task of gathering together these contradictory demands falls to *Gestus*, since it always allows for the passage from actor to character, from the body to the reading of it, from the reconstituted event to its fiction, from theory to theatrical and social praxis.

Subject-Matter and Point of View

The way in which the *Gestus* is determined by the actor and the director poses a difficult theoretical problem: the director, Brecht tells us, must gather information about the era in which the gestures originated, as much as about his own social reality. [. . .]

In fact, *Gestus* and Story are tools which are constantly being elaborated. They are located at the precise point of intersection of the real object to be imitated (to be shown and told) and the subject perceiving and criticizing this reality. *Gestus* concentrates within it a certain gestuality (given by the ideological code of a certain time) and the personal and demonstrative gestuality of the actor. In the same way, the story designates for Brecht the logic of the represented reality (the signified of the narrative), the Story (*histoire* for Benveniste) and the specific narration of these events from the critical point of view of the story-maker (the signifier of the narrative or *discourse* for Benveniste).

Extracting the Story or conveying the appropriate *Gestus* will never mean discovering a universally decipherable Story once and for all inscribed within the text. In seeking out the Story, the reader and the director express their own views on the reality they want to represent. This work of exposition has always to be complemented by the spectator's own work, the spectator having the last word, i.e., the right to watch/control the playwright's "view." In the same way, in the case of the *Gestus* shown by the actor, we should not be content to receive it as is (i.e., as a "compact signified" wherein the split between the thing and its critique does not appear). We have to seize the *Gestus* on the rebound, to see in it and to inscribe in it its constitutive contradiction, to understand it as a gesture which is internal to the fiction (gestuality) and as the "*Gestus* of handing over a finished article" (*BT, S* 76, p. 204). What could be more efficacious for the manipulations of a dialectical theatre than the *Gestus*?

Semiosis of *Gestus*

The most extreme formulation of the enormous resources of *Gestus* is to be found in "On Gestic Music" (1932) and "On Rhymeless Verse with Irregular Rhythms" (1939). In these Brecht expands the notion of *Gestus* to music and to the text: "A language is gestic when it is grounded in a *Gestus* and conveys particular attitudes adopted by the speaker towards other men. The sentence 'pluck the eye that offends thee out' is less effective from the gestic point of view than 'if thine eye offend thee, pluck it out.' The latter starts by presenting the eye, and the first clause has the definite gest of making an assumption; the main clause then comes as a surprise, a piece of advice, and a relief" (*BT*, p. 104). With this metaphor, Brecht describes one of the key problems of theatre semiology: the link between *iconic* system (gesture) based on the resemblance between the sign and its object, and the *symbolic* system which is based on the arbitrariness of the sign.

In this context, the Brechtian *Gestus* is not necessarily translatable into a movement or an attitude. It may be entirely constituted by words (as, for instance, in a radio broadcast). In this case, gestuality and mimic expression, which are quite precise and easy to visualize, "impregnate," these words (a humble bending of the knee, a hand tapping a shoulder). In the same way, gestures and mimic expression (in the silent film) or simple gestures (in shadow theatre) can contain words. Words and gestures can be replaced by other words and gestures, without the *Gestus* being modified. The *Gestus* here plays the role of the *interpreter* in Peirce's semiotics. The sign meaning (gestural or prosodic) helps us to associate it with certain equivalents, to constitute the paradigms of possible variations, to establish series and networks of correspondences between voice and gesture.

To a certain extent, every *mise en scène* is a search for an adequate *interpreter* which connects the *mise en place* (placement) of the enunciators and the text to be acted. But such a rich theoretical perspective should not remain, as in Brecht's theoretical writing, at the stage of a declaration of principle. This "gestic music," this "iconic discourse" specific to the theatre should seek to define its own units, and to explicate the laws of its own functioning. This aspect of *Gestus* exists mostly in the case of motivated or poetic signs and of onomatopoeia, a marginal area where the sign and its referent are reunited under the patronage of *Gestus*. Unfortunately, this type of *Gestus* remains too global a notion and Brecht possibly limits it too much to syntax and to the rhetorics of the sentence; he only examines the "(shifting, syncopated, gestic) Rhythm" (*BT*, p. 115), to which the idea of a knocked-about and fractured world must correspond in the meaning of the text.

In his "On Rhymeless Verse with Irregular Rhythms" he reports how, at the beginning of his career, despite his "disgracefully meager" political knowledge, he was aware of the lack of harmony in social relationships and refused to "... iron out all the discordances and interferences of which (he) was strongly conscious" (*BT*, p. 116). He then decided "to show human dealings as contradictory, fiercely fought over, full of violence" (*BT*, p. 116). This *Gestus* of syncopation characterizes the speaker's attitude towards the world, and what he has to say about it. It serves as a hermeneutic tool which helps constitute the meaning of the text. It is in the form of the text that one can read the *Gestus* and thus the attitude of the speaker towards the enunciation.

Once again, *Gestus* here fills the breach between utterance and enunciation (*énoncé/énonciation*). It recalls for us the basic truth that a theatre text only finds its full volume and its meaning in the choice of the situation of enunciation. Brecht, who carefully chose a tonality for each play according to the nature of the language used, knew this well: for instance, the German spoken in Prague for *Schweik*, the parody of classical verse for *Saint Joan*, the popular style and the poetic prose for *Puntila*, etc.

Gestus and the Body

One cannot help regretting that Brecht was not more explicit on "gestic music" and that he did not give any formulas on how to find the *Gestus*, which is best understood intuitively, and by the methodological application of different readings of the text on the basis of different subjective attitudes. It has nothing to do with the "writing of the body" as it has sometimes been referred to in the context of Artaud, Céline, or Bataille. *Gestus* never deals exclusively with the problem of the materiality of the textual signifier; it exists at the level of prosodic and textual signifieds. It is a tool which remains exterior to the text, just as a seismograph is capable of recording the shakings of the earth without being a part of that shaking. The *Gestus* at best is only – but this is not negligible – a meaning "detector," a way of "accompanying the reading with certain appropriate body movements, signifying politeness, anger, the desire to persuade, goading, the effort to fix in one's memory, the effort to surprise an adversary; the fear that one feels or fear that one wants to inspire..." (cf. Brecht's comments on the Chinese poet Kin-Yem).

Is it legitimate, though, to understand *Gestus* as a "simple mimed expression" excluding everything that the signifying work of the body can produce outside of the representation/performance?[7]

It seems quite contrary to the spirit of *Gestus* to conceive of it as the mimetic production of eternally fixed social gestuality. There still remains in it the material "traces of other movements and features all around the fully-worked-out figure" (*BT*, p. 191), and if it is obviously never like the ideograms of Grotowskian gestures, "a living form possessing its own logic," neither is it the reified image of a social relationship.

These brief remarks on *Gestus* are far from exhausting the substance of the notion, and only sketch out a few possible developments. At least, it should be clear how central the concept of *Gestus* is to all of the different theoretical Brechtian paths. And is it not in the nature of the *Gestus*, after all, that it can only be grasped by the actor and the critic in approximate form?

Notes

1   Brecht, Section 53, *Brecht on Theatre*, ed. and tr. John Willett (New York: Hill & Wang, 1964, 2000), 277–8. Further references are cited in the text as *BT*, section (*S*) of *Short Organum*, with page numbers. – Editor's note.

2   My quotations of Brecht come from the English translation of John Willett [see note 1]. For the German texts, not included in Willett's anthology, I have used *Gesammelte Werke in 20 Minden* (*GW*), Suhrkamp Verlag, Frankfurt am Main, 1967. I chose to keep *Gestus* in English, although Willett used *gest*. I had to introduce the terms of *gestuality* (*gestualité*) and *gestural* (*gestuel*).

3   V. Propp, *Morphology of the Folktale*, Indiana Research Centre in Anthropology, Bloomington, 1958.

4   Benjamin, *Understanding Brecht*, London, NLB, 1973, p. 11.

5   Benjamin, op. cit., p. 12.

6   Cf. Bernard Dort, "Le général et le particulier," in *L'Arc*, no. 55, pp. 3–8 and the *Modellbuch*: "Unearth the truth from the debris of the evidence, tie together in a visible manner the individual and the general, retain the particular in the overall process, this is the art of the realist" (*Theaterarbeit*, op. cit., p. 264).

7   Guy Scarpetta, "Brecht et la Chine," in *La Nouvelle Critique*, no. 39 bis, 1971.

Chapter 62

Heiner Müller (1929–1995)

Heiner Müller was an experimental dramatist and East German political activist. His major works are *Tractor* (1961) and *Cement* (1972), and fragmentary reworking of classics, *Hamlet-Machine* (1977) and *Depraved Shore* (a reworking of *Medea*, 1982). Although his plays were censored by the East German authorities, Müller maintained his allegiance to socialism. He had, however, an uneasy relationship to revolutionary dogma. Müller's play *Mauser* (1976) is a response to Brecht's learning plays (*Lehrstücke*), specifically Brecht's *Maβnahme* (*The Measures Taken*, 1930). In Brecht's play the collective's commitment to communism is challenged by an individual whose actions jeopardize the unit. The individual must be sacrificed for the common good. *Mauser*, too, investigates the necessity of killing for revolutionary goals. But rather than situating the problem in an either/or context – either killing for the good of the whole or no killing at all – Müller, like Brecht, focuses on consciousness and necessity. The Marxist-Leninist ideology asserts that an action now will later become obsolete once utopian socialism is in place. Müller's *Mauser*, writes Andreas Huyssen, "obstructs any facile glorification of revolution or violence" by going to the core of consciousness – how do we think about revolution?[1] Müller's essay here is similarly a challenge to postmodern theatre: how should we think through its political efficacy?

Reflections on Post-Modernism (1979)

1

Orpheus the singer was a man who could not wait. He had his wife by sleeping with her too soon after she gave birth to a child, or by giving her a forbidden glance too soon during their return from the underworld after his song had liberated her from death. Thus

Heiner Müller, "Reflections on Post-Modernism," tr. Jack Zipes, with B. N. Weber, in *New German Critique* 16 (Winter 1979), reprinted in *Essays on German Theater*, ed. Margaret Herzfeld-Sander (New York: Continuum, 1985), 345–48. © 1979. Reprinted by permission of Jack Zipes.

she was turned back into dust before becoming anew whereupon Orpheus invented pederasty which excluded childbirth and is closer to death than is the love for women. Those he scorned hunted him with the weapons of their bodies, bran and stones. But the song protects the singer: what he had praised with his song could not scratch his skin. Farmers, scared by noise of the hunt, ran away from their plows for which there been no place in his song. So his place was under the plows.

2

Literature is an affair of the people. (Kafka)

3

Writing under conditions in which the consciousness of a social character of writing can no longer be repressed. Just talent in itself is a privilege, but privileges have their price: the way one contributes to one's own expropriation is one of the criteria of talent. With the rise of free enterprise the illusion about autonomy of art, a prerequisite for modernism, begins to fall. The planned economy does not exclude art. It endows art with a social function again. Until art ceases to be art (that is, a narrow-minded activity in the way Marx described it) it cannot be relieved of this function. In the meantime this activity is practiced in my country as well – by specialists who are more or less qualified for this. The level of culture cannot be raised if it is not expanded. This expansion occurs at the expense of the cultural quality – in my country as well – and this is due to the smog of the media which prevents the masses from seeing the real situation, blots out their memory, and makes their imagination sterile. In the *realm of necessity*, realism and popular culture (*Volkstümlichkeit*) are two separate things. The split goes through the author.

In regard to the conditions under which I work, I find myself at odds with the notion of post-modernism. My role is not that of Polonius, the first comparatist in dramatic literature, least of all in his dialogue with Hamlet about the shape of a certain cloud which demonstrates the real misery of power structures in the very misery of comparison. Nor is my role unfortunately that of the gypsy in Lorca's one-act play who turns a police investigator into a screaming bundle of nerves by giving senseless, surrealistic answers to official questions about birthplace, date, name, family, etc.

I cannot keep politics out of the question of post-modernism. Periodization is the politics of colonialism as long as history has as its prerequisite the domination of elites through money or power and does not become universal history which has as its prerequisite real equal opportunity. Perhaps that which predated modernism will reappear in other cultures in a different way, albeit enhanced by the technological progress of modernism influenced by Europe: a social realism which helps close the gap between art and reality, *art without strain addressing humankind intimately* – Leverkühn's dream before the devil comes to fetch him, a new magic for healing the rift between humankind and nature. The literature of Latin America could stand for this hope. Yet, hope guarantees nothing: the literature of Arlt, Cortázar, Marquez, Neruda, Onetti does not amount to a plea in defense of the conditions on their continent. Good writing still grows from tainted soil. A better world will not be achieved without bloodshed; the duel between industry and the future will not be fought with songs which allow one to feel at ease. Its music is the cry of Marayas springing the strings of his divine torturer's lyre.

4

The seven major characteristics of modernism or their post-modernistic variation as formulated by Ihab Hassan described New York just as well as the Orpheus myth in Ovid or Beckett's prose. New York constitutes itself out of its decay. A system which is composed from its own explosion. The metropolis of dilettantism: art is what one wants, not what one can do. An Elizabethan city: the impression of free choice is an illusion of freedom.

Warhol in Basle, Rauschenberg in Cologne are major events. In the context of New York they dwindle to symptoms. Robert Wilson's theater – as naïve as it is elitist, infantile toe-dance and mathematical child's play – does not distinguish between amateur and professional actors [see Chapter 60, this volume]. A prospect of epic theater as Brecht conceived it but never realized it, making a profession out of the luxury. The murals painted by minority groups and the proletarian art of the subway, anonymously created with stolen paints, occupy an area beyond the commercial market. Here the underprivileged reach out of their misery and encroach upon the *realm of freedom* which lies beyond privileges. A parody of the Marxist vision where art assumes a new function in a society whose members are all artists and have other vocations as well.

5

As long as freedom is based on violence and the practice of art on privileges, works of art will tend to be prisons; the great works, accomplices of power. The outstanding literary products of the century work toward the liquidation of their autonomy (autonomy = product of incest with private property), toward the expropriation and finally the disappearance of the author. That which is lasting is fleeting. Whatever is in flight remains. Rimbaud and his escape to Africa, out of literature into the desert. Lautréamont, the anonymous catastrophe. Kafka, who wrote to burn his works because he did not want to keep his soul as Marlowe's Faust did. And he was denied the ashes. Joyce, a voice beyond literature, Mayakovsky and his crash-dive *out of the Heavens of poetry* into the arena of class struggle. His poem *150 Million* bears the name of the author: *150 Million*. Suicide was his response to the signature which never came. Artaud, the language of torment under the sun of torture, the only one which illuminates all continents of this planet simultaneously. Brecht, who saw the new creature which was to replace humankind. Beckett, a life-long attempt to silence his own voice. Two figures of poetry who fuse into one in the hour of incandescence. Orpheus singing under the plows, Daedalus lying through the labyrinthic intestines of Minotauros.

6

Literature participates in history by participating in the movement of language first evident in common language and not on paper. In this sense literature is *an affair of the people* and the illiterates are the hope of literature. Work toward the disappearance of the author is resistance against the disappearance of humankind. The movement of language shows two alternatives: the silence of entropy or the universal discourse which omits nothing and excludes no one. *The first shape of hope is fear, the first appearance of the new arouses a feeling of horror.*

Note

1	A. Huyssen, *After the Great Divide: Modernism, Mass Culture, Postmodernism* (Bloomington: Indiana University Press, 1986), 92.

Chapter 63

Ntozake Shange (b. 1948)

Ntozake Shange (Pauline Williams) is a playwright and political activist. Her first play, *for colored girls who have considered suicide when the rainbow is enuf* (1976), was a radical departure from traditional narrative drama. It consisted of seven women, each representing the colors of a rainbow, celebrating their lives and interactions. Shange considered herself a playwright, poet, and choreographer. With one exception, the conventional narrative play *A Photograph* (1977), her works consist of a combination of dramatist-poetess-choreographer elements in order to create a total theatrical experience. Her other well-known works are *Spell #7* (1978) and *Boogie Woogie Landscapes* (1980).

unrecovered losses/black theater traditions (1979)

as a poet in american theater/i find most activity that takes place on our stages over-whelmingly shallow/stilted & imitative. that is probably one of the reasons i insist on calling myself a poet or writer/rather than a playwright/i am interested solely in the poetry of a moment/the emotional & aesthetic impact of a character or a line. for too long now afro-americans in theater have been duped by the same artificial aesthetics that plague our white counterparts/"the perfect play," as we know it to be/a truly european framework for european psychology/cannot function efficiently for those of us from this hemisphere.

furthermore/with the advent of at least 6 musicals about the lives of black musicians & singers/(EUBIE, BUBBLING BROWN SUGAR, AIN'T MISBEHAVIN', MAHALIA, etc.)/the lives of millions of black people who don't sing & dance for a living/are left

Ntozake Shange, "Unrecovered losses/black theater traditions," from *Three Pieces* (New York: St. Martin's Press, 1981), ix–xi. © 1981 by Ntozake Shange. Reprinted by permission of St. Martin's Press, LLC.

unattended to in our theatrical literature. not that the lives of Eubie Blake or Fats Waller are well served in productions lacking any significant book/but if the lives of our geniuses aren't artfully rendered/& the lives of our regular & precious are ignored/we have a double loss to reckon with.

if we are drawn for a number of reasons/to the lives & times of black people who conquered their environments/or at least their pain with their art, & if these people are mostly musicians & singers & dancers/then what is a writer to do to draw the most human & revealing moments from lives spent in nonverbal activity. first of all we should reconsider our choices/we are centering ourselves around these artists for what reasons/ because their lives were richer than ours/because they did something white people are still having a hard time duplicating/because they proved something to the world like Jesse Owens did/like Billie Holiday did. i think/all the above contributes to the proliferation of musicals abt our musicians/without forcing us to confront the real implications of the dynamic itself. we are compelled to examine these giants in order to give ourselves what we think they gave the worlds they lived in/which is an independently created afro-american aesthetic. but we are going abt this process backwards/by isolating the art forms & assuming a very narrow perspective vis-a-vis our own history.

if Fats Waller & Eubie Blake & Charlie Parker & Savilla Fort & Katherine Dunham moved the world outta their way/how did they do it/certainly not by mimicking the weakest area in american art/the american theater. we must move our theater into the drama of our lives/which appeals to us because it is directly related to lives of those then living & the lives of the art forms.

in other words/we are selling ourselves & our legacy quite cheaply/since we are trying to make our primary statements with somebody else's life/and somebody else's idea of what theater is. i wd suggest that: we demolish the notion of straight theater for a decade or so, refuse to allow playwrights to work without dancers & musicians. "coon shows" were somebody else's idea. we have integrated the notion that a drama must be words/with no music & no dance/cuz that wd take away the seriousness of the event/cuz we all remember too well/the chuckles & scoffs at the notion that all niggers cd sing & dance/& most of us can sing & dance/& the reason that so many plays written to silence & stasis fail/is cuz most black people have some music & movement in our lives. we do sing & dance. this is a cultural reality. this is why i find the most inspiring theater among us to be in the realms of music & dance.

i think of my collaboration with David Murray on A PHOTOGRAPH/& on WHERE THE MISSISSIPPI MEETS THE AMAZON/& on SPELL #7/in which music functions as another character. Teddy & his Sizzling Romancers (David Murray, sax.; Anthony Davis, piano; Fred Hopkins, bass; Paul Maddox, drums; Michael Gregory Jackson, guitar, harmonica & vocals) were as important as The Satin Sisters/though the thirties motif served as a vehicle to introduce the dilemmas of our times. in A PHOTOGRAPH the cello (Abdul Wadud) & synthesizer (Michael Gregory Jackson) solos/allowed Sean to break into parts of himself that wd have been unavailable had he been unable to "hear." one of the bounties of black culture is our ability to "hear"/if we were to throw this away in search of less (just language) we wd be damning ourselves. in slave narratives there are numerous references to instruments/specifically violins, fifes & flutes/"talking" to the folks. when working with Oliver Lake (sax.) or Baikida Carroll (tr.) in FROM OKRA TO GREENS/or Jay Hoggard (vibes) in FIVE NOSE RINGS & SOWETO SUITE/i am terribly aware of a conversation. in the company of Dianne McIntyre/or Dyanne Harvey's work with the Eleo Pomare Dance Company/one is continually aroused by the immediacy of their movements/"do this movement like yr life depends on it"/as McIntyre says.

the fact that we are an interdisciplinary culture/that we understand more than verbal communication/lays a weight on afro-american writers that few others are lucky enough to have been born into. we can use with some skill virtually all our physical senses/as writers committed to bringing the world as we remember it/imagine it/& know it to be to the stage/we must use everything we've got. i suggest that everyone shd cue from Julius Hemphill's wonderful persona, Roi Boye/who ruminates & dances/sings & plays a saxophone/shd cue from Cecil Taylor & Dianne McIntyre's collaboration on SHADOWS/shd cue from Joseph Jarman & Don Moye (of The Art Ensemble of Chicago) who are able to move/to speak/to sing & dance & play a myriad of instruments in EGWU-ANWU. look at Malinke who is an actor/look at Amina Myers/Paula Moss/Aku Kadogo/Michele Shay/Laurie Carlos/Ifa Iyaun Baeza & myself in NEGRESS/a collective piece which allowed singers, dancers, musicians & writers to pass through the barriers & do more than 1 thing. dance to Hemphill or the B.A.G. (Black Artist Group)/violinist Ramsey Amin lets his instrument make his body dance & my poems shout. i find that our contemporaries who are musicians are exhibiting more courage than we as writers might like to admit.

in the first version of BOOGIE WOOGIE LANDSCAPES i presented myself with the problem of having my person/body, voice & language/address the space as if i were a band/a dance company & a theater group all at once. cuz a poet shd do that/create an emotional environment/felt architecture.

to paraphrase Lester Bowie/on the night of the World Saxophone Quartet's (David Murray, Julius Hemphill, Hamiett Bluiett & Oliver Lake) performance at the Public Theater/"those guys are the greatest comedy team since the Marx Brothers." in other words/they are theater. theater which is an all encompassing moment/a moment of poetry/the opportunity to make something happen. We shd think of George Clinton/ a.k.a. Dr. Funkenstein/as he sings/"here's a chance to dance our way out of our constrictions." as writers we might think more often of the implications of an Ayler solo/the meaning of a contraction in anybody's body. we are responsible for saying how we feel. we "ourselves" are high art. our world is honesty & primal response.

Part V

1980–2000

The final decades of the twentieth century experience a shift in the relationship of art and everyday life. The eradication of a distinction between commercial and fine art, made evident by the influence of Andy Warhol and other postmodern artists, takes root in theatre. Warhol's *Brillo Box* sculpture and *Campbell Soup Can* painting, combined with postmodern architecture's playful designs, blur the distinctions of highbrow and lowbrow. As a result of these changes, classical designs of modernism – steel, glass, and concrete – mix seamlessly with Las Vegas kitsch or other parodic elements. Whereas modernism distinguishes between (and largely divides) art and fashion – deco and advertisements, for example – postmodernism maximizes collage, interconnections, and pastiche. Postmodernism also challenges objective truth: reality is rhetoric ("discourse"), something reformulated from previous ideas. As Nick Kaye notes, to be postmodern is to "doubt the very 'decidability' of meaning" and to emphasize signification as "a function not of presence but of absence and difference."[1] Meaning is defined by what is present and also what (and who) is absent. Additionally there occurred an ontological shift: for mid-twentieth-century existentialists, to employ Sartre's phrase, "existence precedes essence"; for late twentieth-century postmodernists, identity is a performance that precedes both essence and existence.

With the entrance of postmodernism (or poststructuralism),[2] the argument over dramatic theory shifts literally from the ground up. Postmodernism initiates a series of challenges to the certainty of art's autonomy. Postmodern drama emphasizes baroque word play, disassociative images, and semantics over narrative development, character delineation, and pictorial representation. Modernist conventions of representation, either realist or avant-garde, maintain a hierarchal divide between everyday life and art. Instead of mimesis as separate from reality and held "above" by virtue of being "art," postmodern theatre followed art's lead by conflating the everyday with formalized theatrical structure. According to Jon McKenzie, "the presentational forms associated with theatrical performance have been transformed into analytical tools, generalized across disciplinary fields, and reinstalled in diverse locations. Anthropologists and folklorists have studied the rituals of both indigenous and diasporic groups as performance, sociologists and communication researchers have analyzed the performance of social interactions and nonverbal communication, while cultural theorists have researched the everyday workings of race, gender, and sexual politics in terms of performance."[3] Performance, in other words, became a buzzword for more than theatre.

The notion of "presence" – the actor's charismatic power – was called into question by what Philip Auslander refers to as the postmodern "anxiety created by historical demonstrations of collusion between presence as charisma or salesmanship and repressive power structures."[4] As Brecht, Benjamin, and others had warned (and Plato had cautioned even before them), the actor's conviction and authority can veil ideological intent and hypnotize an audience into assuming a reality that is, in fact, manipulated, constructed, and falsified. In reaction to this, artists such as Anna Deavere Smith and Moisés Kaufman consider representation and reality as overlapping and indeterminate rather than fixed and sequential. In *Fires in the Mirror* (1992) and *The Laramie Project* (2000), for example, performers record people speaking about real events and then recreate the recordings. Although the artists distill the recordings, they assert minimal intervention, letting the words themselves circulate. The replications create an illusion of the real, but in fact reality merely mirrors a sequence of previous expressions, what Jean-François Lyotard calls "Return upon the Return."[5] The tape recorder is merely one sequence of an "eternal reoccurrence," to borrow Nietzsche's phrase. Reality is simulacrum – a Jean Baudrillard coinage stressing that nothing is truly original. "All of Western faith and good faith," Baudrillard contends, "was engaged on this wager of representation: that a sign could exchange for meaning." But if there is no essential origination, then, he says, "the whole system becomes weightless, it is no longer anything but a gigantic simulacrum – not unreal, but a simulacrum, never again exchanging for what is real, but exchanging in itself, in an uninterrupted circuit without reference or circumference."[6] Given a world of repeatability and imitation, the very idea of originality diminishes. The sign or representation can find no certainty because the object it imitates is itself an imitation. Psychoanalyst and literary scholar Julia Kristeva observes that "any text is constructed as a mosaic of quotations; any text is the absorption and transformation of another." In this way the "notion of *intertextuality* replaces that of intersubjectivity, and poetic language is read as at least *double*."[7] Postmodernism, rather than ceding authority to originality, concentrates on repeatability by investigating a bricolage of meaning. Meaning is not only constructed, it is continually "deconstructed"; mutability overtakes certainty as shifting images and ideas supersede fixed representation and conventional wisdom. Referential polyvalence creates a theatrical montage of dreams, images, illusions, perceptions, and interactions.

Postmodernism also reduces the role of human intention and free agency. If the theories of existential modernism found human will essential yet futile (the plays of Beckett and Pinter, for instance), poststructuralism undermines all semblance of human agency. Human action, according to poststructural anthropologists, was determined not by biology or physical laws but by different systems. This led to the belief in "social construction," the idea that beings are shaped by environment and ideas derived from the interaction of power and rhetoric. It is up to theorists to see through the veil of rhetorical deception, or, as Michel Foucault put it, "we must reconstitute another discourse, rediscover the silent murmuring, the inexhaustible speech that animates from within the voice that one hears, re-establish the tiny, invisible text that runs between and sometimes collides with them." Analyzing ideas is "always *allegorical* in relation to the discourse that it employs."[8]

The essayists in this section are indebted to postmodernism, but three other ideas surface. Performance studies is the field of inquiry that combines established disciplines such as anthropology, ethnography, and sociology with new concerns of race, postcolonialism, gender, and queer theory. It examines theatre in the traditional sense – the dramatic texts as the source of understanding – but adds non-traditional venues such as parades, rituals, ceremonies, funerals, storytelling, and other events that reconfigure the traditional design of audience and actor. Although performance studies, Marvin Carlson has observed, "is both historically and theoretically a primarily American phenomenon,"[9] it has made influential inroads. Performance studies questions the hierarchy of the text over the performance, seeking to credit the performance as the nodal point of inquiry. Non-Western societies that celebrate oral traditions (Yoruba rituals, for instance) and sustained traditions (Japanese Nōh theatre, for example) are examined as models of a new kind of hierarchy. These new modes of inquiry highlight gesture, costume, behavior, stage history, physical relationships, social moorings, and the passing down of performative traditions. Diana Taylor, one of the leading scholars of performance studies, notes that performances "function as vital acts of transfer, transmitting social knowledge, memory and a sense of identity." Performance, she maintains, "constitutes the object/process of analysis" in "the many practices and events – dance, theatre, ritual, political rallies, funerals – that involve theatrical, rehearsed, or conventional/event-appropriate behaviors" and also "constitutes the methodological lens that enables scholars to analyze events *as* performance." Because "civic disobedience, resistance, citizenship, gender, ethnicity, and sexual identity" are "rehearsed and performed daily in the public sphere," performance studies functions epistemologically.[10] Performance studies began during the early 1980s in United States universities, and several essays represent key thinkers of the field.[11]

The essays here also reflect the significance of feminism in dramatic theory. Around 1980 second-wave feminism appeared. First-wave feminism emphasized equal rights. The advances made by this movement cannot be underestimated: activists gained ground for equal pay and representation. Still, the first wave generally avoided the difficult questions of self – how women might fulfill themselves not only as equals but also as women. In theatre, it was not enough that more female directors, designers, and producers worked; the theories of second-wave feminists challenged the foundation of theatre itself, the voyeuristic proclivity of exhibitionism and the countermanding role of gender and queer theory to the status quo. The act of framing the body onstage – placing it before an audience – is tied to the "gaze" that has offended censors for centuries. For feminists, theatre's framing process is both binding and liberating. Barbara Freedman observes that this process is "the extent to which theatre is always already determined by frames put onstage, and the extent to which theatre provides a means for reframing. Given the longstanding debt of psychoanalysis to classical drama and the centrality of the Oedipus to both disciplines, is a feminist, anoedipal theatre possible, or possibly a contradiction in terms?" Many essays in this section consider what Freedman posits: "the potential of feminism, psychoanalysis, and theatre to reflect and effect change – to insert a difference in our construction of the subject and so to make a difference."[12]

Finally, essays in this section represent voices outside the Western canon. The importance of these new ideas cannot be overstated: concepts of global theatre have influenced non-canonical theatre theory, paving the way towards more inclusivity. Many of the thinkers outside the Western canon have successfully incorporated Western traditions but have reinvented them alongside their indigenous traditions. The process of adaptation, moreover, is not a one-way street: non-Western theories have informed Western ideas as well. This interaction has produced a dynamic mixture and iridescent quality of theatre that changes in appearance depending on the angle of interrogation.

Notes

1   N. Kaye, *Postmodernism and Performance* (London: Macmillan, 1994), 16.
2   If postmodernism undermines the certainty of modernism's binary division of high and low, then poststructuralism follows suit in undermining structuralism's dual-relational world.
3   J. McKenzie, *Perform or Else: From Discipline to Performance* (London: Routledge, 2001), 8.
4   P. Auslander, *From Acting to Performance: Essays in Modernism and Postmodernism* (London: Routledge, 1997), 63.
5   J.-F. Lyotard, "Return upon the Return," in *Toward the Post-Modern*, ed. R. Harvey and M. Roberts (New Jersey: Humanities Press, 1993), 192–206.
6   J. Baudrillard, *Simulations*, tr. P. Foss et al. (New York: Semiotext[e], 1983), 10, 11.
7   J. Kristeva, "Word, Dialogue, and Novel," tr. A. Jardin et al., in *The Kristeva Reader*, ed. T. Moi (Oxford: Blackwell, 1986), 37.
8   M. Foucault, *The Archaeology of Knowledge and The Discourse of Language*, tr. A. M. S. Smith (New York: Pantheon, 1972), 27.
9   M. Carlson, *Performance: A Critical Introduction* (London: Routledge, 1996), 2.
10 D. Taylor, *The Archive and the Repertoire: Performing Cultural Memory in the Americas* (Durham, NC: Duke University Press, 2003), 2, 3.
11 For a history of its development, see S. Jackson, *Professing Performance: Theatre in the Academy from Philology to Performativity* (Cambridge: Cambridge University Press, 2004).
12 B. Freedman, "Frame-Up: Feminism, Psychoanalysis, Theatre," in *Feminist Theatre and Theory*, ed. H. Keyssar (New York: St. Martin's Press, 1996), 81.

Chapter 64

Tadeusz Kantor (1915–1990)

Tadeusz Kantor was an eclectic director, scene designer, and visual artist. His directing is primarily associated with Stanislaw Witkiewicz (see Chapter 16) and the institution of "Happenings" (see Michael Kirby, Chapter 58). In 1938 he founded the Ephemeric (Mechanic) Theatre, and in 1942 he organized underground theatres during the Nazi occupation of Poland. Kantor was affected by the war and its atrocities; he attempted to find the right expression for carnage and chaos. He was also influenced by early twentieth-century avant-garde movements such as Dada and Duchamp's ready-mades. His theatre, Cricot 2, initiated interest in radical performance that rebelled against the institutionalized theatre. Kantor sought to redefine himself with every theatre work and artistic endeavor. He explored the function of objects which lead the way to a blurred distinction between reality and the stage.

Theatre Happening 1967 (1982)

(Theatre of Events.)

(Àpropos the performance of *The Water-Hen.*)

I do not treat theatre as a fenced-off or a professional field. Contemporary art undergoes multiple changes, which introduce radical reevaluations, eruption of new forms, destruction of the old; which are seemingly absurd; which trigger hatred, disapproval, mockery, or humiliation; which are prohibited; which are perceived simultaneously as shallow and profound; which are being forged by transient fashion, misapplication, and dilettantes;

Tadeusz Kantor, "Theatre Happening 1967" (1982), tr. and ed. Michal Kobialka, first published in 1982 as "Teatr Happening" and reprinted in *TDR* 30.3 (Fall 1986), 135–6. © 1982 by Tadeusz Kantor.

which are a mirror to the ideas that originated in the twentieth century and the facts that regenerate tirelessly the condition of human awareness. One should know of those changes and probe deeply into their complicated mechanism. Furthermore, one should take risks, create, and participate in the process of initiating those changes. If they are not introduced, nothing more than conventional and uncommitted forms will be created.

Today's theatre is impregnated with conformity. It tends to ignore all those changes (for reasons that are well known) and hide itself behind professional or academic studies, actions that, in the context of those changes, seem disturbingly limited, scholastic, provincial, and ridiculous. From time to time, this theatre puts a veil around us and tricks us into believing that it embarks on an adventurous trip into the forbidden zone. But when back, it turns the living forms, which it has stolen, into dead props.

In spite of the opinions of the opportunists – of all those half-dead personalities whose position is entrenched by their titles or of pseudo-intellectual aesthetes – THE AVANT-GARDE IS POSSIBLE AND WILL ALWAYS EXIST IN THEATRE. Today's Cricot 2 is not the theatre that transfers the experiments of visual art onto the stage floor. Its aim is to create and safeguard the existence of FREE AND DISINTERESTED ARTISTIC EXPRESSION. All conventional barriers separating the arts have been removed. An artist does not change this mundane, everyday reality with the help of his intuition or imagination; he simply takes and sets it ablaze. In this process, he keeps changing his condition and function; in turns and simultaneously, he becomes a winner and a victim! For the last few decades, the noble conditions in which art has been created have systematically and with consequence been impaired by MOVEMENT; AUTOMATIZATION, COINCIDENCE, DEFORMITY, AMBIGUITY OF DREAMS, DESTRUCTION, COLLAGES, etc.

As a result of this process, there occurred a CRISIS OF FORM, that is, the crisis of the concept that art should be the outcome of a maximum condensation of artistic activities such as forming, molding of forms, branding, gutting, anointing, constructing, and building.

To a certain degree, this ridiculed and butcher-like participation of an artist in the act of creation of his work has, however, introduced a new perception of an object.

Having gone through the deformed and sputtering matter of Informel and touched on the nothingness and the zero zone, one reaches the object "from behind," where the distinction between reality and art does not exist. Today's art has rediscovered an object and has held that object as if it were a ball of fire. Therefore, any questions of how to express or interpret the object seem too long, pedantic, and ridiculous in the context of this unprecedented situation.

The object simply exists. This statement has irrevocably depreciated the notions of expression, interpretation, metaphor, and similar devices.

In my treatment of [Witkiewicz's] The Water-Hen, I have tried to avoid an unnecessary construction of elements. I have introduced into it not only objects but also their characteristics and READY-MADE events that were already molded. Thus, my intervention was dispensable. An object ought to be won over and possessed rather than depicted or shown. What a marvelous difference! Important and unimportant, mundane, boring, conventional events and situations constitute the heart of reality. I derail them from the track of realness ("The Zero Theatre Manifesto," 1963);[1] give them autonomy, which in life is called aimlessness; and deprive them of any motivation and effects. I keep turning them around, recreating them indefinitely until they begin to have a life of their own; until they begin to fascinate us.

Then such questions as "Is this already art?" or "Is this still reality?" become inconsequential to me.

The dramatic text is also a "ready-made object" that has been formed outside the zone of performance and the audience's reality. It is an object that has been found; an object whose structure is dense and whose identity is delineated by its own fiction, illusion, and psychophysical dimension.

I treat it in much the same way as I treat other events and objects in the production. Caution: The terminology that has been used in the play is autonomous. It would be fallacious to apply it to draw conclusions concerning life. Chaos, destruction, disintegration, zero, anticonstruction, order, automatism, brutality, perversion, and obsession are the names of means and processes that are on equal footing in the arts and have neither negative nor positive coloring, as do their counterparts in life.

Note

1   See "The Zero Theatre" (1963), in Kandor, *A Journey Through Other Spaces: Essays and Manifestos, 1944–1990*, ed. and tr. M. Kobialka (Berkeley: University of California Press, 1993), 59–70.

Chapter 65

Jeffrey E. Huntsman

Jeffrey E. Huntsman, Professor in the English Department at Indiana University, illuminates Native American drama and theatre from a theoretical standpoint. Native American dramas, this essay contends, vary as much as the differing nations vary in their cultural, social, and ethnic milieus. Huntsman's essay reflects this diversity, encouraging a broad approach. The implication here is that it will require a book on Native American dramatic forms and theories to explore adequately the various permutations of Native theatre theory and performance. Jaye T. Darby notes that "Approaching Native theater involved an array of complexities because this work often fuses ancient ritual and performance elements from the oral tradition with more contemporary approaches. This complexity is compounded by the diversity among the many tribal nations with unique traditions, creation stories, aesthetics, forms of spirituality, histories, languages, and relationships to the land as well as centuries of cultural collusions, encounters, and convergences."[1] Huntsman takes these complexities into account.

Native American Theatre (1983)

Drama in Traditional Native American Societies

The impulse for the dramatic is universal in the societies of human beings, but its manifestations are as varied as the societies that bring it to life. Like other distinctive aspects of culture, dramatic events may serve to define a community, distinguishing its

Excerpts from Jeffrey E. Huntsman, "Native American Theatre," originally published in *Ethnic Theatre in the United States*, ed. Maxine Schwartz Seller (Westport: Greenwood Press, 1983), reprinted in *American Indian Theater in Performance: A Reader*, ed. Hanay Geiogamah and Jaye T. Darby (Los Angeles: UCLA American Indian Studies Center, 2000), 81–9. © Maxine Schwartz Seller. Reprinted by permission of Greenwood Publishing Group, Inc., Westport, CT.

members from others who do not share its aesthetic, metaphysical, and epistemological foundations. In societies informed by a common history and intellectual culture, the overt structure of dramatic events may remain largely constant, although ethnic, religious, racial, or class differences within heterogeneous cultures almost inevitably stratify the society at large. Such is the case in much of Europe and America, among the peoples whose dramatic events are the subject matter of most of this volume. Although the characteristics and values of the several Euro-American traditions differ, their dramatic *forms* are largely congruent, the result of the adoption of a "high" or "professional" dramatic structure the history of which is essentially pan-European, adapted from the varying elements of classical, medieval, and modern drama, whether religious or secular, folk, traditional, or professional.

For Native American[2] drama, the situation is quite different. Within the bounds of the continental United States alone, there were 15 to 30 million people in hundreds of separate nations when Europe's land-hungry reivers arrived. Even today there are approximately 1 million Indians, constituting perhaps 300 nations, despite both accidental and deliberate genocide by both individuals and governments, driven by misunderstanding, cultural chauvinism, and, too often, calculated treachery. Some of these native societies remain active and vital, maintaining many aspects of their traditional cultures while adapting few features from others, native or not. Others are failing, their languages receding as the old die and the young lose their interest or their bearings. Too many have gone completely, leaving tantalizingly few memories and fewer records. But even in the face of these losses, what endures is often rich, powerful, and rewarding.

The first difficulty, then, in approaching the drama of the Native Americans is that there are many dramas, conceivably as many as there are cultures. In addition to the affiliations that Indians themselves recognize, scholars have grouped the native peoples of North America in several different ways: by their languages, which fall into at least six unrelated families; by their material and economic cultures, which distinguish peoples who are chiefly hunters from farmers, fishers, and gatherers; by their religions, which range from relatively uncodified and unsophisticated beliefs in simple spirits to complex and subtle systems comparable with the world's better-known religions; by their sociological and geographical relationships, which vary from those of small bands of wandering gatherers centered on single, extended families to those of tightly-knit cities of thousands in which every member is connected to every other through numerous family, clan, and social relationships; or even by the history of their relations with Europeans, which have altered their precontact cultures in radically different ways.[3]

Clearly these many differences among Indian peoples will necessarily result in dramatic events of different forms and purposes, especially when the culture preserves in its dramatic ritual attributes of earlier times, as is typically the case when the dramatic events have major religious significance.[4] We should not expect a people like the city dwellers of the Southwest, whose cultural orientation is inward toward their communities, to have the same kind of drama as the highly individualistic horse people of the High Plains. The Pueblo peoples reflect in their literature those qualities that are most important to their way of life – cooperation, harmony, group identity – and their characteristic drama is fully choreographed, disciplined, and dramatically complex. The Lakota and Cheyenne, on the other hand, value the individual qualities of bravery, dauntlessness, versatility, and personal spiritual power, and their dramas, such as the Sun Dance, appropriately mirror those values. As a result of this diversity the term "drama," as it must be used with reference to Native American cultures, comprises a congeries of events ranging from the structured improvisations of shamans to hundred-hour-long, multi-dimensional celebrations like the great Navajo chantways, in which every costume, word, gesture, movement, and song are planned.

Considering the variety of Indian cultures and the fundamental differences between typical Euro-American societies and Native American ones, it is hardly surprising that Indian drama, as drama and not as an ethnographical curiosity, has been given scant attention by students of the theatre and students of Indians alike. Although many observers during the past century have commented on the "colorful" or "dramatic" nature of the Indian rituals they were privileged to witness, relatively few have used the terms in the precise ways of the Euro-American critical tradition. Even the best of the early studies are overly general, content to describe rather than to analyze, even when the writers gave the particular ceremonies and their Indian communities more than a passing visit. These observers were too interested in finding support for preconceived notions about "primitive" theatre or the "origin" of drama and often too unwilling to attribute the art they sometimes recognized to anything more than "primitive intuition." On the other hand, it is difficult and occasionally dangerous, given the diversity of Indian cultures, to make more than a few generalizations about Native American drama; that is perhaps why, although the literature on specific dramatic rituals is rich, there is little on Indian dramas taken together.

Standards of Traditional Drama

One of the defensible generalizations characterizes all small, coherent societies throughout the world, not just Indian ones. The shared culture of these societies frames a complex network of predictable reciprocal relationships. In the order of organisms, individuals are born, live some brief term, and die, leaving the enduring system of organization fundamentally unchanged. But the "progress"-loving societies of Europe and America generally value the innovative above the traditional, both personally and societally, and few generations fail to work major changes in the structure into which they are born. Naturally, that spirit of newness and adventure colors their drama. Their dramatic artists are inventors, creating purposefully unique artifacts, however much these artifacts inevitably reflect the experiences and the values of their communities.

But for Native American artists, as for their counterparts in other traditional societies, the artistic self is typically unobtrusive, and the dramatic work in effect proclaims the artist's involvement with the community, not his or her distance from it. The aesthetic principles governing the form, content, and meaning of the artist's work are established, in effect, by the community as a whole, although usually covertly if not unconsciously. The Indian artist comes to understand, often quite without knowing how, exactly what is expected of an artist in that community, and it has frequently been said that in Indian eyes every person becomes an artist of some kind. The artist's training in such traditional communities is typically an apprenticeship, whether formal or not, through which he or she learns in what ways the community's standards set limits to personal style and values. Learning in Indian communities characteristically takes the form of extended observation, imitative play not overtly urged by adults, and careful practice, which begins only when the child feels confident of a reasonably successful result.[5] This is true whether what is to be learned is specific tasks, like cooking, weaving, and fishing, or more general matters, like proper behavior, ethics, and religious beliefs. [...]

Thus traditional art is a fundamental aspect of the culture, its practices, and its values. Such art is firmly embedded in the community, temporally, spatially, and emotionally, and individual artists change but little the characteristics of the community or its aesthetic values.[6] These community standards are not often articulated because, like many other closely shared matters in small societies, they only rarely need to be. But to say that these standards are not often spoken about does not mean that they do not exist and are not followed. Few artists are competent philosophers of art – many are notoriously inarticulate about their work – nor is there any need for them to be. The dimensions of art exist independently of any attempts to explain them in words, in the Euro-American "high" culture as much as in other cultures. Further, even if we do not find among Native American peoples the kind of written commentary that the philosophers of Western European culture have created, there is abundant evidence that most Native American peoples have thought about their art in comparable ways. The cohesiveness of the art for each group and its high quality testify to the aesthetic principles that underlie its making. If some Indian artists in the past have been unwilling to talk about their creations, the reasons are more to be found in the lack of a common cross-cultural universe of discourse and experience between artist and critic and the often sacred matter of much dramatic art.

This emphasis on the continuity of aesthetic traditions does not mean that innovation or individuality is forbidden. The practices of any Indian people may change markedly as one group adopts a dramatic ritual from another. The Sun Dance ritual, for example, is or has been performed in varying ways and for differing purposes, by peoples ranging from the Mandan at the edge of the Eastern Woodland area to the Southern Ute of the Great Basin. An individual within a group may create a new drama; Black Elk's Horse Drama, which made manifest the power of his great vision, is perhaps the best-known example. Cultural changes may also influence the development of new elements within an existing ritual. In all these cases, however, the new dramatic event is naturally molded to the community norms; if Black Elk had been a Kwakiutl or a Cayuga instead of a Lakota, his vision and its dramatization would have had a different shape. Sometimes specific adaptations are precluded entirely by other aspects of a culture; the Navajo, virtually alone of the inland Western peoples, did not adopt the late-nineteenth-century Ghost Dance, with its promise of the return of all Indian people who had ever lived, because of their extreme fear of the dead. In short, alterations of either the forms or the values of traditional arts is evolutionary, not revolutionary, as the artist works within the frames established in the community for a given dramatic genre.[7]

The Sacred Source of Power and Significance

Another generalization is that there was little that any Native American living in a traditional community would do that was not charged, if only slightly, with religious significance. Naturally, the religious power that inhered in major rituals was greater than that connected with the beginning of a hunt or the making of a meal, if only because the major rituals drew more of the community into their center than personal observations did. The religious beliefs that motivate the Sun Dance drama are different in detail from those that underlie the Navajo chantway, but each ceremony draws on the most fundamental metaphysical tenets of its performers and each, in its own way, reaffirms the harmony, unity, and sacredness of all creation. Despite the myriad superficial variety in Native American drama, certain fundamental attitudes permeate virtually all of it, including (surprisingly) several obviously modern, realistic, and Western-styled plays, like Hanay Geiogamah's *Body Indian*.[8]

Fundamental to many, if not most, Native American ritual events are two beliefs that have few direct counterparts for Euro-Americans. The first is the concept of non-linear time – time that may be viewed cyclically from one perspective and eternally from another. The second is the concept of a dimensionless sacred place, the center of the universe and the locative counterpart of the ever-present time. These two concepts are congruent, in a sense identical, for each point in time or space is infinitely large, extending outward from the sacred event to include all creation, yet located around the event in a way that precisely fixes the position and assures the security of the participants. Joseph Epes Brown characterizes this notion well.

> The tipi, the hogan, or the long house...determined the perimeters of space in such a way that a sacred place, or enclosure, was established. Space so defined served as a model of the world, of the universe, or microcosmically, of a human being. Essential to such definition of space, so central to human need, were means by which the centers of sacred space of place were established. For without such ritual fixing of a center there can be no circumference. And with neither circumference nor center where does a person stand? A ritually defined center, whether the fire at the center of the plains tipi or the *sipapu* (earth navel) within the Pueblo *kiva*, obviously expresses not just a mathematically fixed point established arbitrarily in space. It is also taken to be the actual center of the world. It is understood as an axis serving as a bridge between heaven and earth, an axis that pierces through a multiplicity of worlds.... It symbolizes the way of liberation from the limits of the cosmos. Always, vertical ascent is impossible unless the starting point be the ritual center.[9]

Without such a centering in sacred time and place, Native American dramas would be mere displays, robbed of their meaning. Sometimes a special place is created for the drama, either permanent, like the kivas of the Southwest, or temporary, like the Sun Dance lodges of the High Plains. Sometimes the stage is the people's ordinary living space, like the Northwest Coast family houses, the Southwest village plazas, or the Plains lodges. But even in these latter cases, the mundane is typically made special by such devices as the creation of an altar in a dwelling, as for the Cheyenne or Lakota Pipe Ceremony, or by performance of a cleansing and sanctifying ceremony. Using the ordinary living space, in fact, adds an extra dimension to the sacred ceremony, for it reaffirms the continuity between the parts of the cosmos that human beings conventionally inhabit and those in which their presence is charged with an unusual significance.

Nowhere is this more apparent or more powerfully symbolized than in the great Navajo chantways, epic religious dramas of cosmic scope, the fundamental purpose of which is to restore and maintain the essential balance of the world, the lack of which produces sickness in mind and body. A sing, the actual curing event manifesting the chantway, restores health to the individual patient, to those gathered at the ceremony, to the nation, and ultimately to the cosmos.

Not only is the hogan the living space for the Navajo, it is also where rituals occur. It is created in the shape of rituals, its round floor and east-facing door are parts of the total alignment of human beings with the world of nature to which their rituals are addressed. Ritual space is not separated from daily life but integrated into it.... The great sandpaintings on the dirt floor of the hogan provide a two-dimensional diagram for the forces of nature. When the patient walks on the sand painting, the ritual creates a four-dimensional world where one is surrounded by and related to the holy power.[10]

Thus the moment of the dramatic event is one of extraordinary significance that envelopes everyone concerned, blurring the distinction, so crucial to Euro-American drama, between actor and audience. The apparently casual and selective attention of those not central to such ritual events does not indicate indifference, as many outside observers have concluded, but rather an unprepossessing recognition that their very presence, their watching participation, is their contribution to the drama at hand. In this way Native American drama is by its nature celebratory of the essential being of the community, emphasizing that ultimately all are affected by what the central participants do. The community, the audience, is an integral part of the creative process before, during, and after the fact of the performance, because the performance realizes an aesthetic and metaphysical immanence of the society.

From the outset, then, Native American drama differs in several profound ways from recent Euro-American drama. The fundamental embedding of dramatic events, whatever their particular character, in the metaphysical substratum of the society gives them an immediate power and importance that Western (in the sense of Euro-American) drama cannot command. Even religious rites in the Western mode for the most part lack the sacred central moment of eternal creation that characterizes Native American rites. Indian events assert a present and eternal reality; Western ones celebrate past realities or seek to invoke realities-to-be. The moment of transubstantiation in the Communion ritual is the only significant Western exception, and the extensive history of argument over its nature is eloquent testimony to the way it runs counter to prevailing habits of thought, even among theologians and other philosophers. [...]

Notes

1   J. T. Darby, "Introduction: A Talking Circle on Native Theater," in *American Indian Theater in Performance: A Reader*, ed. H. Geiogamah and Jaye T. Darby (Los Angeles: UCLA Press, 2000), iv.

2   The term "Native American" has recently come to be the preferred description in formal and legal contexts for Indian people taken together, although most individuals still think of themselves first as members of their separate nations (Bella Coola, Seminole, Melacite, and so forth). [...]

3   Obviously, within the limits of a single chapter, only some of these distinctions can be made for any groups discussed, and those often must be the minimum required to set their drama in an adequate form for presentation to the wide variety of readers of this book, some of whom may have extensive knowledge of Native American peoples, others considerably less. [...]

4   For example, the chantways of the Navajos, who for the past several centuries have been herders and planters, contain much that relates to their old way of living as hunters in northwestern Canada nearly a millennium ago. [...] There is an exact parallel in the Christian communion

ritual, where the eating and drinking of symbolic flesh and blood continues a hunters' rite of immense antiquity.

5   Such modes of learning are thus quite contrary to Western teaching methods, which typically encourage a child to "learn by doing," even at the risk of serious initial mistakes or failure. The inability of educators to contend with this difference has continually crippled attempts to instruct Indians in non-Indian schools.

6   The absence of a true understanding of a traditional culture would seem to lie behind the failure of the attempts during the 1960s to develop what some were calling "tribal" theatre. Although some manifestations of "radical" theatre, the best of it stemming from European theorists such as Antonin Artaud and Jerzy Grotowski, occasioned interesting theatrical moments, most were pointless except as reactions to outside events and conditions and hence were ephemeral. [...]

7   The term "frame" and "genre" are used here in technical senses [...] concerned with verbal acts as performances regulated in large part by cultural expectations.

8   H. Geiogamah, *New Native American Drama: Three Plays* (Norman: University of Oklahoma Press, 1980).

9   J. E. Brown, "The Roots of Renewal," in *Seeing with a Native Eye: Essays on Native American Religion*, ed. E. H. Capps (New York: Harper and Row, 1976), 31.

10   J. B. Toelken, *The Dynamics of Folklore* (Boston: Houghton Mifflin, 1979), 243–4.

Chapter 66

Bert O. States (b. 1929)

Bert O. States is a scholar and theoretician who chaired the University of California at Santa Barbara's drama department. His interests concerned dreams and phenomenology in their manifestation onstage. States examines the semiotics of theatre, its phenomenological sign system and its transmutation to the public. He builds on Saussurian linguistics and Brechtian estrangement, but seeks to expand the concept of the theatrical event. In this essay he builds on semiotic and structuralist theories in order to ascertain a critical position in theatre.

The World On Stage (1985)

If we approach theater semiotically we must surely agree with the Prague linguists that "all that is on the stage is a sign,"[1] and that anything deliberately put there for artistic purposes becomes a sign when it enters illusionary space and time. That is, it becomes an event in a self-contained illusion outside the world of social praxis but conceptually referring to that world in some way, if only in the fact that the illusion is *about* hypothetical human beings. As long as there is pretense, or playing, there is pretense of something, and this *of* constitutes a bridge between the stage and its fictional analogue of the world, or, if you wish, between the sign and its various significations.[2]

However, if we approach theater phenomenologically there is more to be said. For, among other considerations, there is a sense in which signs, or certain kinds of signs, or signs in a certain stage of their life cycle, achieve their vitality – and in turn the vitality of

Excerpts from Bert O. States, "The World On Stage," from *Great Reckonings in Little Rooms: On the Phenomenology of Theater* (Berkeley: University of California Press, 1985), 19–47. © 1985 by The Regents of the University of California Press. Reprinted by permission of The Copyright Clearance Center on behalf of University of California Press.

theater – not simply by signifying the world but by being *of* it. In other words, the power of the sign – or, as I will refer to it here, the image – is not necessarily exhausted either by its illusionary or its referential character. This may be obvious enough in itself, but some implications of the idea seem important enough to develop beyond the semiotic notion that such images are simply signs with a high degree of "iconic identity."[3] But putting semiotics aside, we tend generally to undervalue the elementary fact that theater – unlike fiction, painting, sculpture, and film – is really a language whose words consist to an unusual degree of things that *are* what they seem to be. In theater, image and object, pretense and pretender, sign-vehicle and content, draw unusually close. Or, as Peter Handke more interestingly puts it, in the theater light is brightness pretending to be other brightness, a chair is a chair pretending to be another chair, and so on.[4] Put bluntly, in theater there is always a possibility that an act of sexual congress between two so-called signs will produce a real pregnancy.

It comes down, of course, to a matter of perspective. Quite legitimately, to the extent that something is *not* a sign the semiotician would lose interest in it, since he is concerned only with the sign-ness of things, and what they do in their spare time is their own (or someone else's) business. And quite legitimately, the phenomenologist, in pursuit of "the essence" of things, will subsume their sign function – along with all other possible functions – under their phenomenal character as objects in the real world.[5] Of course, the literary critic may complacently ignore both of these concerns in his quest of the theme or the style or the historical import of any set of art images. All are, as it were, workers in the same field harvesting different kinds of crops.

By way of establishing my own perspective, it will be useful to begin with a well-known definition of art by Victor Shklovsky that will serve as a departing point for much of what I have to say in this chapter:

> Art exists that one may recover the sensation of life; it exists to make one feel things, to make the stone *stony.* The purpose of art is to impart the sensation of things as they are perceived and not as they are known. The technique of art is to make objects "unfamiliar," to make forms difficult, to increase the difficulty and length of perception because the process of perception is an aesthetic end in itself and must be prolonged. *Art is a way of experiencing the artfulness of an object; the object is not important.*[6]

Such a concept of art arises from, or at least leans into, the phenomenological attitude. Here art is perceived as an act of removing things from a world in which they have become inconspicuous and seeing them anew. Perhaps it would be better to say "seeing them as of old," for the presumption behind Shklovsky's theory is that we grow away, perceptually, from the contents of reality (habit being a great deadener) and that art is a way of bringing us home via an "unfamiliar" route. This much, at least, art has in common with phenomenological reduction: if art is a way of endowing the world with meaning it is also a way of allowing the world to express itself. If the objects of reality depicted in art carry some of their worldly meanings with them – and no one would deny that they do – they are now seen, by a trick of perspective, to have been partially concealed all along *by* the meanings. The meanings, instead of preceding the objects (as eye glasses precede vision), now trail them, like the tails of comets. The object comes forth, as in the trunks and limbs of Van Gogh's olive trees, and we experience "the unmotivated upsurge of the world."[7] As the phenomenologist would say, the object becomes "self-given," and "something can be *self-given* only if it is no longer given merely through any sort of symbol; in other words, only if it is not 'meant' as the mere 'fulfillment' of a sign which is previously defined in some way or other. In this sense, *phenomenological* philosophy is a continual *desymbolization of the world*."[8]

If we now come back to Shklovsky's idea that art imparts "the sensation of things as they are perceived and not as they are known," we see how the phenomenological attitude differs from the semiotic in its descriptive yield. Here is a possible basis for a distinction between *image* and *sign*. Let us agree that either term can be said to contain the other and that either can be defined in many ways, as we see in moving from relatively simple theories of the sign (Sartre, Rudolf Ainheim, the dictionary) to highly complex ones (Peirce, Husserl, Derrida). In any case, the term *sign* is, in itself, a sign of the semiotic attitude, which is heavily dialectical (or, in Peirce's case, triadic): the referential urgency of the word *sign* is reproduced in its sub- or correlative terms – signifier and signified – one of which always forms the background of intelligibility of the other. To speak of the signifier is already to begin gossiping about a signified, to be thrown back into an elsewhere of assignable meaning. In adopting the more aesthetic term *image* as any likeness, or representation, made out of the materials of the medium (gesture, language, decor, sound, light) I am under no illusion that I am freeing myself of the dialectical problem, nor am I denying that an image signifies (is an image of something) or hauls behind it, in Peirce's term, an "infinite semiosis"; I am merely trying to abridge the process of signification and throw the emphasis onto the empathic response. In the image, one might say, we swallow the semiotic process whole and imagination catches its disease. It is the disease that interests the phenomenologist, not the germ that causes it or the stages of its progress.

Or let us take Shklovsky's idea that art makes objects "unfamiliar" (a statement, incidentally, that allows us to ground revolutions like Brecht's in an aesthetic orthodoxy).[9] Art increases difficulty and length of perception. By difficulty, of course, Shklovsky is not referring to stylistic obscurity but to expressive density. The image detains, arrests. It carries, in Gaston Bachelard's splendid word, its own *exaggeration*, which imagination "seizes" and carries, sensationally, to its "ultimate extreme."[10] Unlike the sign, the image is unique and unreproducible (except as facsimile), whereas the sign is of no value unless it repeats itself; in fact, as Derrida says, "a sign which does not repeat itself, which is not already divided by repetition in its 'first time,' is not a sign."[11] In other words, the inclination of the sign is to become more efficient, to be read easily. In the strictly utilitarian sphere (which of course does not exhaust signification) the sign gets down to its referential business with as little flourish as possible: for example, the red stop signal or the trousered silhouette on the men's room door (really an icon). But if this inclination applied as strictly to plays and their images, we could cut a great deal of the text of *Macbeth*, or even reduce it, allegorically, to the sign of a dagger with a diagonal red line across it. But Macbeth is extremely "difficult" or inefficient, taken as a sign. The proof of this is not in its significative subtlety but in the fact that the play does far more than is necessary in order to mean whatever it may mean (the history of a Scottish king, a study in crime and punishment). It is, in addition, a sensory experience that cannot be accounted for by semiotic systems (for instance, Peirce's threefold classification of predominantly iconic, indexical and symbolic signs, or Barthes's hermeneutic, semantic, proairetic, cultural, and symbolic codes). As a single illustration, take the opening lines of Macbeth's soliloquy:

> If it were done when 'tis done, then 'twere well
> It were done quickly.
>
> (*I, vii, 1–2*)

These words certainly express the collision of Macbeth's hesitation and momentum: behind the words stands the moral man in conflict with his own ambition. But this is not why an actor wants to "speak the speech" or why, hearing it, we are thrilled by it, or why it is one of the most fondled moments of the play. It is, phenomenally, a unique claim staked on speech by sound, as if the sound *done* possessed a powerful instinct of self-preservation. Here, in fact, repetition conjures the endlessness of sound's very utility (three usages constitute a pattern, and a pattern is a potential infinity). In short, sound is not consumed in its sense: sound simply gives in to language, as marble gives in to the chisel; it consents to be the ground of a possible expressiveness. Finally, no semantic explanation – such as that sense is passing through sound, or that sound and sense are inextricable – can exhaust the marvel of what is left under: the fact that the body, in possessing the sound, is "gripped" by its vibrations; we can say of *done* what Merleau-Ponty says of the German word *rot* (red): it "pushes its way through my body. I have the feeling, difficult to describe, of a kind of numbed fullness which invades my body, and which at the same time imparts to my mouth cavity a spherical shape."[12] And so with the entire play: from the standpoint of its musical code – or should we say visceral code? – it is a field of sound (just as, in the scenic connection, it is a field of space and shape) in which meanings parasitically swarm.

Granted, this is a deeply subjective reduction. More than anything else, I am trying to "exaggerate" the medium of theater, its affective corporeality as the carrier of meanings. Primarily, the line *means* something: it comes out of the mouth of a character in a play about murder and its consequences; Macbeth is the image of a hypothetical man. And here we uncover another root difference between sign and image, stated most simply by Sartre: "The material of the sign is totally indifferent to the object it signifies.... But the relationship between the material of the physical image and its object is altogether different; the two *resemble* each other."[13] And a further implication immediately relevant to theater: "In every image, even in the one which does not posit that its subject exists, there is a positional determination. In the sign, as such, this determination is lacking.... The sign...does not deliver its object" (29–30). Here we arrive at the source of the peculiar "difficulty" of stage images: the sense, for example, of Macbeth being *here* before us yet absent, of his story being unreal but imprisoned "positionally" in real time and space. Moreover, the particular density of the theater image rests in the fact that the whole perceptual ensemble of theater introduces a resistance to the gathering of certain levels of meaning. If you were interested in *Macbeth* for the density of its significations, it would be better to stay home and read the text – not, as it is often said, because reading affords the leisure to go back and ponder (though this is obviously a factor), but because reading presents almost no phenomenal distraction. In one respect, a play read and enacted in the mind's eye is more "real" than one seen on stage. By "real" I mean nothing palpable or objectively real, obviously, but only that our mental enactment of *Macbeth*, however vague or fleeting, has something of the realism of a succession of dream images; it is an imagined actual experience that floats wherever the text leads. In a reading, everything is susceptible to envisionment; the mind may suddenly lose its image of Macbeth speaking and see only his "multitudinous seas incarnadine" or the "naked new born babe" striding the blast of his imagination. But however fantastic or surreal the image, it is all real in the sense of its springing to an imagined actuality. Whereas a theatrical presentation of the text is precisely marked by the limits of artifice: the frontal rigidity of our view, the positional determination of everything on stage, the condensation of Macbeth into a real form, the fact that the play has already passed through the screen of an interpretation by director and actors.

Naturally what literary critics study so assiduously is their own dreamed text of the play, and for this reason their interpretations have a way of treating Macbeth as a once (and still) real man whose life, thanks to Shakespeare, is an open book. It is because words on the page have no resemblance to the things they conjure that reading is such a transparent process. In reading, the eye is an anesthetized organ, little more than a window to the waiting consciousness on which a world of signification imprints itself with only the barest trace of the signifiers that carry it. In the theater, however, the eye awakens and confiscates the image. What the text loses in significative power in the theater it gains in corporeal presence, in which there is extraordinary perceptual satisfaction. Hence the need for rounding out a semiotics of the theater with a phenomenology of its imagery – or, if you will, a phenomenology of its semiology.

Let us begin at rock bottom with some instances of things that resist being either signs or images, at least in the sense that we have discussed them to this point. This may be difficult to document convincingly because we all have different capacities for settling into the theater illusion. Moreover, it is a simple fact that almost anything, under the right sociological conditions, can be "seen through" and pass into convention, the most outrageous being the convention of real blood in the Roman gladiatorial games. What we are trying to catch here, in Bachelard's words, is "the original amazement of a naive observer." And, as he adds immediately, "Amazement of this kind is rarely felt twice. Life quickly wears it down."[14] To this end, I have chosen a few things that have abnormal durability and might illustrate the idea that stage images (including actors) do not always or entirely surrender their objective nature to the sign/image function. They retain, in other words, a high degree of *en soi*.

I take the first from Walter Benjamin's essay, "The Work of Art in the Age of Mechanical Reproduction." "A clock that is working," Benjamin says, "will always be a disturbance on the stage.... Even in a naturalistic play, astronomical time would clash with theatrical time."[15] I doubt that such a clash would really occur in a naturalistic play in which theatrical time and real time were roughly identical. Why, then, do stage designers usually take the precaution of removing the minute hand or masking the clock face? Clearly, there is something about a working clock on stage that is minimally disturbing to an audience. But it has less to do with time per se than with our awareness that theatrical time is being measured by a real clock – an instrument that is visibly obeying its own laws of behavior. I doubt that this would be a very serious distraction, or would remain one for very long, or that a certain kind of theater project couldn't take advantage of a working clock heeding its own rhythms. I am simply saying that some things, by virtue of their nature, retain an exceptional degree of self-givenness on a stage. A better case might be made for fire or running water. A working fountain, for example, is mildly distracting, in the sense of being "interesting." It is not that circulating water (like fire) is a threat to the illusion, as would a glass of water accidentally spilled by an actor; in fact, it has been a standard enhancement of theatrical spectacle for a long time. But it is the sort of detail one would remember in describing the setting to others because real water – unlike real chairs, clothing, flower vases, or the painted façades of a village square – retains a certain primal strangeness: its aesthetic function does not exhaust its interest. It is a happening taking place within the aesthetic world: with running water something indisputably real leaks out of the illusion.

An even better example is the child actor. Who has ever seen a child on stage without thinking, "How well he acts, for a child!" or, of the doomed children in *Medea*, "Do they *understand* the play?" No doubt Elizabethan audiences at Paul's and Blackfriars got used to seeing children in adult roles and, to some extent, saw them only conventionally, as they saw male actors (often boys) playing female roles. But the children's troupes did not carry away "Hercules and his load" because they were magnificent actors. Their success – their *raison d'être* – depended heavily on the audience's "double vision," even to the point that the companies specialized in comedy and satire, the genres most closely linked to any audience's immediate world. Moreover, unlike the adult companies, they were permitted exceptional license in abusing the audience, including royalty in it. Various explanations have been offered for this privileged status, among them the "inherent innocence" of children, but Michael Shapiro is surely right in saying, in his book on the boy companies, that it comes down to "the disparity between the actors and their roles."[16] We can expand this idea, phenomenologically, by adding that it would have been a waste of a good thing to confine children to the acting of tragedies and serious plays that depended on a suspension of disbelief – something adult companies could have satisfied more easily [...]

Notes

1   J. Veltrusky, "Man and Object in the Theater," in *A Prague School Reader on Esthetics, Literary Structure, and Style*, ed. P. L. Garvin (Washington: Georgetown University Press, 1964), 84.

2   In strictly Saussurian terms, the signifier and the signified are indivisible aspects of the sign. Yet, some protostructuralists of Prague were more interested in the referential connections between language and the world than is generally supposed, and their work was, to some extent, phenomenologically inspired. [...] In this study I am less interested in the linguistic constitution of the sign than I am in the relationship of the sign (or image) and what [American pragmatist Charles Sanders] Peirce terms the *referent*, or the reality denoted by the sign.

3   K. Elam, *The Semiotics of Theatre and Drama* (London: Methuen, 1980), 22.

4   P. Handke, *Kaspar and Other Plays*, tr. M. Goloff (New York: Farrar, Straus, and Giroux, 1969), 10.

5   Throughout, I use the adjective *phenomenal* in the sense of pertaining to phenomena or to our sensory experience with empirical objects. The adjective *phenomenological*, of course, refers to the analytical or descriptive problem of dealing with such phenomena.

6   V. Shklovsky, "Art as Technique," in *Russian Formalist Criticism: Four Essays*, tr. L. T. Lemon and M. J. Reis (Lincoln: University of Nebraska Press, 1965, 12, italics Shklovsky's). [...]

7   M. Merleau-Ponty, *Phenomenology of Perception*, tr. C. Smith (New York: Humanities Press, 1970), xiv.

8   M. Scheler, *Selected Philosophical Essays*, tr. D. R. Lachterman (Evanston: Northwestern University Press, 1973), 143.

9   On this point, see T. Hawkes, *Structuralism and Semiotics* (Berkeley: University of California Press, 1977), 62–3.

10 G. Bachelard, *The Poetics of Space*, tr. Maria Jolas (Boston: Beacon Press, 1969), 219–20.

11 J. Derrida, "The Theater of Cruelty and the Closure of Representation," in *Writing and Difference*, tr. A. Bass (Chicago: University of Chicago Press, 1978), 246. [See Chapter 49, this volume.]

12 Merleau-Ponty, *Phenomenology of Perception*, 236.

13 J.-P. Sartre, *The Psychology of Imagination*, tr. B. Frechtman (New York: Washington Square Press, 1968), 27.

14 Bachelard, *The Poetics of Space*, 107.

15 Benjamin, *Illuminations* (New York: Schocken Books, 1977), 247.

16 M. Shapiro, *Children of the Revels: The Boy Companies of Shakespeare's Time and Their Play* (New York: Columbia University Press, 1977), 107.

Chapter 67

Victor Turner (1920–1983)

Victor Turner was an influential anthropologist who applied much of his work to performance. Using the medium of rituals, Turner examined the patterns of cultures through the signification of ritualistic styles and norms. Turner focused on the concept of liminality, the manner in which a society uses space to evolve through rites of passage. His insistence that theory must answer to social reality honored the societies he investigated. In his important work, *Dramas, Fields, and Metaphors* (1974), Turner emphasized field work and hands-on assessments reminiscent of Franz Boas and early twentieth-century anthropologists. Yet Turner wanted to shift the ground from structure to process, to perceiving cultures as fluid rather than fixed and containable.

Images and Reflections: Ritual, Drama, Carnival, Film, and Spectacle in Cultural Performance (1987)

In anthropology there has been a noticeable shift in theoretical emphasis in recent years from structure to process, from competence to performance, from the logics of cultural and social systems to the dialectics of sociocultural processes. This has not meant a jettisoning of structuralist discoveries but rather a reintegration of the insights gained from the study of symbol systems such as myth, ritual, and kinship terminology treated as abstract sets of interdependent binary oppositions and mediations into the mainline study of "man and woman alive," the ongoing developing and declining processes of interpersonal and intergroup behavior in communities and networks, and the cultural

Victor Turner, "Images and Reflections: Ritual, Drama, Carnival, Film, and Spectacle in Cultural Performance," in *The Anthropology of Performance* (New York: PAJ Press, 1987), 21–7. © 1987, 1988 PAJ Publications.

processes and products involved with these. We are to think of changing sociosymbolic fields rather than static structures.

Anthropology is currently sensitive to the "ethnography of speaking" – a field which lies between what grammars and ethnographies have taken separately – the former treating language essentially as a structure of abstract and self-contained codes, the latter (ethnographies) with the abstract and hence static patterns and structures of sociocultural life. Attention now is on the use of language – and other nonverbal types of communication, in the actual conduct of social life.

I want to move directly to the frame of this essay – which includes the ethnography of speaking but extends it to the modes of symbolic action – and that is the peculiar relationship between the mundane, everyday sociocultural processes (domestic, economic, political, legal and the like) found in societies of a given major type, tribal, feudal, capitalist, socialist, or whatever (and each of these has numerous variants) and what may be called, using Milton Singer's term, their dominant genres of "cultural performance." My thesis is that this relationship is not unidirectional and "positive" – in the sense that the performative genre merely "reflects" or "expresses" the social system or the cultural configuration, or at any rate their key relationships – but that it is reciprocal and reflexive – in the sense that the performance is often a critique, direct or veiled, of the social life it grows out of, an evaluation (with lively possibilities of rejection) of the way society handles history.

In other words, if the contrivers of cultural performances, whether these are recognized as "individual authors," or whether they as representatives of a collective tradition, geniuses or elders, "hold the mirror up to nature," they do this with "magic mirrors" which make ugly or beautiful events or relationships which cannot be recognized as such in the continuous flow of quotidian life in which we are embedded. The mirrors themselves are not mechanical, but consist of reflecting consciousnesses and the products of such consciousnesses formed into vocabularies and rules, into metalinguistic grammars, by means of which new unprecedented performances may be generated. My Africanist colleague Philip Gulliver writes about the "continuum of interaction amongst a given collection of people," as an object of study.[1] I would add here that the "discontinuum" of action among the same collection of people, culturally made possible by setting aside times and places for cultural performances, is equally part of the ongoing social process – the part where those people become conscious, through witnessing and often participating in such performances, of the nature, texture, style, and given meanings of their own lives as members of a sociocultural community.

Anthropologists, as you may have found, are always uneasy when too long separated from what Clifford Geertz calls the "whole vast business of the world," that is, "from what, in this time or that place, specific people say, what they do, what is done to them." It might be useful, then, to break into our major topic by taking a look at what Milton Singer has written on cultural performances, as he came to understand them in the South Indian context, before moving to redefinition of the term in cross-cultural and cross-temporal comparative frames.

Singer, trained in philosophy but enamored later by anthropology, with Robert Redfield as his *guru*, went to India to do fieldwork with a set of hypotheses in mind derived from Redfield's theories about the differences between Great and Little Traditions, and the gradations of the urban–rural continuum. He soon found that "the units of cogitation are not the units of observation."[2] All anthropologists discover this and it is the problem produced by this disparity which when met with undeterred zeal distinguished the vocational anthropologist from the mere manipulator of abstract anthropological findings. Singer found himself "confronted with a series of concrete experiences, the observation and recording of which seemed to discourage the mind from entertaining and applying the synthetic and interpretative concepts that I had brought with me. These experiences had an intrinsic fascination, which also tended to discourage the broad reflective view to which I had been accustomed" (70).

Among the most salient "concrete experiences" were what Singer found to be discriminable "units of observation" which he called "cultural performances." These were central and recurrent in the social lives of the Indians he studied in the Madras area. They included what "we in the West usually call by that name – for example, plays, concerts, and lectures. But they include also prayers, ritual readings and recitations, rites and ceremonies, festivals, and all those things which we usually classify under religion and ritual rather than with the cultural and artistic" (71). The performances became for Singer "the elementary constituents of the culture and the ultimate units of observation. Each one had a definitely limited time span, or at least a beginning and an end, an organized program of activity, a set of performers, an audience, and a place and occasion of performance. Whether it was a wedding, an upanayana (sacred thread) ceremony, a floating temple festival, a village Pongal festival, a ritual recitation of a sacred text, a bharatanatya dance, or a devotional movie, these were the kinds of things that an outsider could observe and comprehend within a single direct experience" (71). Singer found that "cultural performances" are composed of what he calls "cultural media" – modes of communication which include not only spoken language, but such nonlinguistic media as "song, dance, acting out, and graphic and plastic arts – combined in many ways to express and communicate the content of Indian culture" (76). He argues that "a study of the different forms of cultural media in their social and cultural contexts would reveal them to be important links in that cultural continuum which includes village and town, Brahman and non-Brahman, north and south, the modern mass media culture and the traditional folk and classic cultures, the Little and Great Traditions" (76–7).

This is an important point – rituals, dramas, and other performative genres are often orchestrations of media, not expressions in a single medium. Lévi-Strauss and others have used the term "sensory codes" for the enlistment of each of the senses to develop a vocabulary and grammar founded on it to produce "messages" – for instance, different types of incense burned at different times in a performance communicate different meanings, gestures and facial expressions are assigned meanings with reference to emotions and ideas to be communicated, soft and loud sounds have conventional meaning, etc. Thus certain sensory codes are associated with each medium. The master-of-ceremonies, priest, producer, or director creates art from the ensemble of media and codes, just as a conductor in the single genre of classical music blends and opposes the sounds of the different instruments to produce an often unrepeatable effect. It is worth pointing out, too, that it is not, as some structuralists have argued, a matter of emitting the same message in different media and codes, the better to underline it by redundancy. The "same" message in different media is really a set of subtly variant messages, each medium contributing its own generic message to the message conveyed through it. The result is something like a hall of mirrors – magic mirrors, each interpreting as well as reflecting the images beamed to it, and flashed from one to the others. The many-leveled or tiered structure of a major ritual or drama, each level having many sectors, makes of these genres flexible and nuanced instruments capable of carrying and communicating many messages at once, even of subverting on one level what it appears to be "saying" on another. Furthermore the genres are instruments whose full reality is in their "playing," in their performance, in their use in social settings – they should not be seen merely as scripts, scenarios, scores, stage directions, or other modes of blueprinting, diagramming, or guiding. Their full meaning emerges from the union of script with actors and audience at a given moment in a group's ongoing social process.

Milton Singer and many other cultural anthropologists see cultural performances and media as casting "much light on the ways in which cultural themes and values are communicated as well as on processes of social and cultural change" (77). I would agree with this, but only if it is realized that cultural performances are not simple reflectors or expressions of culture or even of changing culture but may themselves be active agencies of change, representing the eye by which culture sees itself and the drawing board on which creative actors sketch out what they believe to be more apt or interesting "designs for living." As Barbara Babcock has written: "many cultural forms are not so much reflective as reflexive." Here the analogy is not with a mirror but rather with a reflexive verb "whose subject and direct object refer to the same person and thing." Performative reflexivity is a condition in which a sociocultural group, or its most perceptive members acting representatively, turn, bend or reflect back upon themselves, upon the relations, actions, symbols, meanings, codes, roles, statuses, social structures, ethical and legal rules, and other sociocultural components which make up their public "selves." Performative reflexivity, too, is not mere *reflex*, a quick, automatic or habitual response to some stimulus. It is highly contrived, artificial, of culture not nature, a deliberate and voluntary work of art. A "reflex" would presuppose "realism," a picturing of people and things as it is thought in that culture they "really" are, without idealization or fantasization. But, of course, in art and literature even realism is a matter of artifice and what is real is ultimately a matter of cultural definition. Nevertheless, cultural realism, however "unreal," is some way from what I consider to be the *dominant* genres of cultural performance.

Since the relationship between quotidian or workaday social process (including economic, political, jural, domestic, etc., interactions) and cultural performance is dialectical and reflexive, the pervasive quality of the latter rests on the principle that mainstream society generates its opposite; that we are, in fact, concerned in cultural performances with a topsy-turvy, inverted, to some extent sacred (in the sense of "set apart," hedged around with taboo and mystery) domain of human action.

For such a domain to be truly reflexive, where the same person(s) are both subject and object, violence has to be done to commonsense ways of classifying the world and society. The "self" is split up the middle – it is something that one both is and that one sees and, furthermore, acts upon as though it were another. It is, again, not a matter of doting upon or pining over the projected self (as Narcissus did over the face in the pool) but of acting upon the self-made-other in such a way as to transform it. I am speaking in the singular; in practice, we are dealing with social and plural phenomena. Ritual and drama involve selves, not self; yet the aggregate of selves in a given community or society is often thought of, metaphorically, as a self. Nevertheless, in practice, the plural reflexivity involved allows freeplay to a greater variability of action: actors can be so subdivided as to allocate to some the roles of agents of transformation and to others those of persons undergoing transformation.

This opposition between social life and dominant genre is also related to what I have called in several publications "liminality." A *limen*, as the great French ethnologist and folklorist Arnold van Gennep has pointed out, is a "threshold," and he uses the term to denote the central of three phases in what he called "rites of passage." He looked at a wide variety of ritual forms, taken from most regions and many periods of history, and found in them a tripartite processual form. Rituals *separated* specified members of a group from everyday life, *placed them in a limbo* that was not any place they were in before and not yet any place they would be in, then *returned* them, changed in some way, to mundane life. The second phase, *marginality* or *liminality*, is what interests us here, though, in a very cogent sense, the whole *ritual process* constitutes a threshold between secular living and *sacred* living. The dominant genres of performance in societies at all levels of scale and complexity tend to be *liminal phenomena*. They are performed in privileged spaces and times, set off from the periods and areas reserved for work, food and sleep. You can call these "sacred" if you like, provided that you recognize that they are the scenes of play and experimentation, as much as of solemnity and rules. Western views of ritual have been greatly influenced by Puritanism. At any rate both the perform-ances and their settings may be likened to loops in a linear progression, when the social flow bends back on itself, in a way does violence to its own development, meanders, inverts, perhaps lies to itself, and puts everything so to speak into the subjunctive mood as well as the reflexive voice. Just as the subjunctive mood of a verb is used to express supposition, desire, hypothesis, or possibility, rather than stating actual facts, so do liminality and the phenomena of liminality dissolve all factual and commonsense systems into their components and "play" with them in ways never found in nature or in custom, at least at the level of direct perception.

One may perhaps distinguish between secret and public liminality, between performa-tive genres that are secluded from the gaze of the mass and those that involve their participation not only as audience but also as actors – taking place, moreover, in the squares of the city, the heart of the village, not away in the bush, hidden in cave, or secreted in a catacomb or cellar. I have discussed elsewhere various forms of secluded or isolated liminality – which again withdraw a selected group or category of persons from the wider society – men, women, adolescents, sometimes members of an elite of birth or wealth – in order to raise them to a higher rung of some structural ladder, inwardly transformed to match their outward elevation (most initiations are of this sort) and other rites which are concerned with reclassifying persons who are to pass through the life-crisis of birth, betrothal, puberty, marriage, elderhood, and death – as these are culturally defined. Here, though, the spotlight will be on forms of liminality in theory accessible to all or most members of a given group, where the subject matter of the performative genres involved will be their shared lives as seen from various angles – some of them quite new to audience and actors. The great genres, ritual, carnival, drama, spectacle, possess in common a temporal structure which interdigitates constant with variable features, and allows a place for spontaneous invention and improvisation in the course of any given performance. The prejudice that ritual is always "rigid," "stereo-typed," "obsessive" is a peculiarly Western European one, the product of specific conflicts between ritualists and antiritualists, iconophiles and iconoclasts, in the process of Christian infighting. Anyone who has known African ritual knows better – or Balinese or Singhalese or Amerindian.

Let us look at the relationship between social and ritual processes in nonliterate cultures of some complexity – such as the Swazi, Maya, or Pueblo Indians – with particular focus on calendrical or solstitial public ceremonies, such as first fruits, harvest, sowing, etc. I also intend to scan the dynamic relationship between popular festivity, such as the Careme-Carnaval cycle in France and the Mardi Gras masquerades in Brazil and Trinidad and what Geertz has called the "pattern of life" which informs them with meaning – in many cases the superimposition of new on traditional patterns, leading to the analysis of two world views in a single universe of symbolic action – expressed in the performance of popular festivity. We are now out of tribal and into medieval-feudal and early modern society.

In complex societies with some degree of urbanization stage drama emerges in its various subgenres as a performative mode *sui generis*. Drama is derived from the Greek *dran*, "to do," which itself derives from the Indo-European base *dra-*, "to work." Interestingly, as I have written in various publications, in many societies ritual, too, is described as "work," and the term "liturgy," prescribed forms for public ritual action, also derives from Greek terms meaning "people," *leos*, and "work," *ergon*. Work is indeed performed by these reflexive genres, the work of sustaining cherished social and cultural principles and forms, and also of turning them upside down and examining them by various metalanguages, not all of them verbal. One can work in the subjunctive mood as seriously as in the indicative-making worlds that never were on land or sea but that might be, could be, may be, and bringing in all the tropes, metaphor, metonymy, synecdoche, etc., to endow these alternative worlds with magical, festive, or sacred power, suspending disbelief and remodeling the terms of belief.

Dramas, at their simplest, are "literary compositions that tell a story, usually of human conflict, by means of dialogue and action, and are performed by actors" and presented to an audience, the nature and degree of whose involvement and participation varies from culture to culture. Unlike rituals and carnivals they tend to be assigned to individual authors though there are numerous examples of "folk" dramas and puppet theatre where the playwrights are anonymous. Yet, in performance a drama is a social performance involving many. A drama is never really complete, as its etymology suggests, until it is performed, that is, acted on some kind of a stage before an audience. A theatrical audience sees the material of real life presented in meaningful form. Of course, it is not just a matter of simplifying and ordering emotional and cognitive experiences which in "real life" are chaotic. It is more a matter of raising problems about the ordering principles deemed acceptable in "real life." Various theories exist about the origin of drama. Some see it coming out of religious ritual and myths which are ritual's charter. Others see it originating in choral hymns of praise sung at the tomb of a dead hero. At some point, a speaker was distinguished from the chorus singing the paean. The speaker acted out in dramatic mimetic gestures the key deeds in the hero's life. The acted part, it is held, became more elaborate and the chorus's role attenuated. Ultimately, the stories were performed as plays, their origins forgotten.

More secular theories exist. Some see drama coming out of story-telling round the old camp fire where hunting or raiding achievements were vividly and dramatically retold with miming of the events and roles. Whatever its origins, which probably vary from society to society, drama tends to become a way of scrutinizing the quotidian world – seeing it as tragedy, comedy, melodrama, etc., in the West, according to Aristotelian categories and their subsequent development in different cultures of that tradition (plot, character, thought, diction, music, and spectacle, and their subdivisions); and in other traditions, such as the Japanese Noh and Kabuki, as concerned with the aesthetics of salvation and honor as well. [...]

Notes

1   P. Gulliver, *Neighbors and Networks* (Berkeley: University of California Press, 1971), 354.
2   M. Singer, *When a Great Tradition Modernizes* (New York: Praeger, 1972), 70. [Further references are cited in the text.]

Chapter 68

Eugenio Barba (b. 1936)

Eugenio Barba is a theatre director and theorist who worked closely with Grotowski, was influenced by Brecht, and examined Indian theatre (Kathakali), Balinese dance, and other non-Western forms. In 1964 he began the Odin Teatret in Oslo and in 1979 he founded the International School of Theatre Anthropology. Barba's study of acting challenges the compartmentalization of the actor in Western culture. He compares the idea of the actor in other cultures to Western traditions, pinpointing the short-comings of limiting the actor to strict expectations. His work evolved from texts to improvisation, attempting to create what Artaud sought: a theatre of physical gestures and images devoid of words. The voice was used as an instrument, the body as an expression of emotions, and the language of the stage embraced as its own semantics. Barba's key writings are *The Dialed Body* (1985), *Beyond the Floating Islands* (1986), and *The Secret Art of the Performer: A Dictionary of Theatre Anthropology* (1991).

Eurasian Theatre (1988)

The influence of Western theatre on Asian theatre is a well-recognized fact. The important affect that Asian theatre has had and still has on Western theatre practice is equally irrefutable. But there remains an undeniable embarrassment: that these exchanges might be part of the supermarket of cultures.

Eugenio Barba, "Eurasian Theatre," tr. R. Fowler, *TDR* 32.3 (Fall 1988), 126–30. © 1988 by Eugenio Barba. Reprinted by permission of the author.

Dawn

Kathakali and noh, onnagata and barong, Rukmini Devi and Mei Lan-fang – they were all there, side by side with Stanislavski, Meyerhold, Eisenstein, Grotowski, and Decroux when I started to do theatre. It was not only the memory of their theatrical creations which fascinated me, but above all the detailed artificiality of their creation of the actor-in-life.

The long nights of kathakali gave me a glimpse of the limits which the actor can reach. But it was the dawn which revealed these actors' secrets to me at the Kalamandalam school in Cheruthuruty, Kerala. There, young boys, hardly adolescents, monotonously repeating exercises, steps, songs, prayers, and offerings, crystallized their ethos through artistic behavior and ethical attitude.

I compared our theatre with theirs. Today the very word "comparison" seems inadequate to me since it separates the two faces of the same reality. I can say that I "compare" Indian or Balinese, Chinese or Japanese traditions if I compare their epidermises, their diverse conventions, their many different performance styles. But if I consider that which lies beneath those luminous and seductive epidermises and discern the organs which keep them alive, then the poles of the comparison blend into a single profile: that of a Eurasian theatre.

Antitradition

It is possible to consider the theatre in terms of ethnic, national, group, or even individual traditions. But if in doing so one seeks to comprehend one's own identity, it is also essential to take the opposite and complementary point of view: to think of one's own theatre in a transcultural dimension in the flow of a "tradition of traditions."

All attempts to create "antitraditional" forms of theatre in the West, as well as in the East, have drawn from the tradition of traditions. Certain European scholars in the 15th and 16th centuries forsook the performance and festival customs of their cities and villages and rescued the theatre in Athens and ancient Rome from oblivion. Three centuries later the avant-garde of the young romantics broke with the classical traditions and drew inspiration from new, distant theatres: from the "barbarous" Elizabethans and the Spaniards in the Siglo de Oro, folk performances, the commedia dell'arte, "primitive" rituals, medieval mysteries, and Oriental theatre. These are the theatrical images that have inspired the revolutions led by all "antitraditional" Western theatres in the 20th century. Today, however, the Oriental theatres are no longer approached through tales but are experienced directly.

Why

Why in the Western tradition, as opposed to what happens in the Orient, has the actor become specialized: the actor-singer as distinct from the actor-dancer and, in turn, the actor-dancer as distinct from the actor-interpreter?

Why in the West does the actor tend to confine herself within the skin of only one character in each production? Why does she not explore the possibility of creating the context of an entire story, with many characters, with leaps from the general to the particular, from the first to the third person, from the past to the present, from the whole to the part, from person to things? Why, in the West, does this possibility remain relegated to masters of storytelling or to an exception like Dario Fo, while in the East it is characteristic of every theatre, every type of actor, both when she acts-sings-dances alone and when she is part of a performance in which the roles are shared?

Why do so many forms of Oriental theatre deal successfully with that which in the West seems acceptable only in opera, that is, the use of words whose meaning the majority of the spectators cannot understand?

Clearly, from the historical point of view, there are answers to these questions. But they only become professionally useful when they stimulate us to imagine how we can develop our own theatrical identity by extending the limits which define it against our nature. It is enough to observe from afar, from countries and uses which are distant, or simply different from our own; to discover the latent possibilities of a Eurasian theatre.

Every ethnocentricity has its eccentric pole, which reinforces it and compensates for it.

Even today, in the Asian countries – where often the value of autochthonous tradition is emphasized vis-à-vis the diffusion of foreign models or the erosion of cultural identity – Stanislavski, Brecht, agitprop, and "absurd" theatre continue to be means of repudiating scenic traditions which are inadequate to deal with the conditions imposed by recent history.

In Asia, this breach with tradition began at the end of the 19th century: Ibsen's *A Doll's House*, the works of Shaw and Hauptmann, the theatrical adaptations of Dickens's novels or of *Uncle Tom's Cabin* were presented not as simple imports of Western models, but as the discovery of a theatre capable of speaking to the present.

In the meeting between East and West, seduction, imitation, and exchange are reciprocal. We in the West have often envied the Orientals their theatrical knowledge, which transmits the actor's living work of art from one generation to another; they have envied our theatre's capacity for confronting new themes, the way in which it keeps up with the times, and its flexibility that allows for personal interpretations of traditional texts which often have the energy of a formal and ideological conquest. On one hand, then, stories that are unstable in every aspect but the written; on the other hand, a living art, profound, capable of being transmitted, and implicating all the physical and mental levels of actor and spectator, but anchored in stories and customs which are forever old. On the one hand, a theatre which is sustained by *logos*. On the other hand, a theatre which is, above all, *bios*.

Roots

The divergent directions in which Western and Eastern theatres have developed provokes a distortion of perception. In the West, because of an automatic ethnocentric reaction, ignorance of Oriental theatre is justified by the implications that it deals with experiences that are not directly relevant to us, that are too exotic to be usefully known. This same distortion of perception idealizes and then flattens the multiplicity of Oriental theatres or venerates them as sanctuaries.

Defining one's own professional identity implies overcoming ethnocentricity to the point of discovering one's own center in the tradition of traditions.

Here the term "roots" becomes paradoxical: it does not imply a bond which ties us to a place, but an ethos which permits us to change places. Or better: it represents the force which causes us to change our horizons precisely because it roots us to a center.

This force is manifest if at least two conditions are present: the need to define one's own traditions for oneself; and the capacity to place this individual or collective tradition in a context which connects it with other, different traditions.

Village

ISTA (the International School of Theatre Anthropology) has given me the opportunity to gather together masters of both Eastern and Western theatre, to compare the most disparate work methods, and to reach down into a common technical substratum whether we are working in theatre in the West or in the East, whether we consider ourselves as experimental or "traditional" theatre, mime or ballet or modern dance. This common substratum is the domain of pre-expressivity. It is the level at which the actor engages her own energies according to an extradaily behavior, modeling her "presence" in front of the spectator. At this pre-expressive level, the principles are the same, even though they nurture the enormous expressive differences which exist between one tradition and another, one actor and another. They are *analogous* principles because they are born of similar physical conditions in different contexts. They are not, however, *homologous*, since they do not share a common history. These similar principles often result in a way of thinking which, in spite of different formulations, permits theatre people from the most divergent traditions to communicate with each other.

The work of more than 20 years with Odin Teatret has led me to a series of practical solutions: not to take the differences between what is called "dance" and what is called "theatre" too much into consideration; not to accept the character as a unit of measure of the performance; not to make the sex of the actor coincide automatically with the sex of the character; to exploit the sonorous richness of languages, which have an emotive force capable of transmitting information above and beyond the semantic. These characteristics of Odin Teatret's dramaturgy and of its actors are equivalent to some of the characteristics of Oriental theatres, but Odin's were born of an autodidactic training, of our situation as foreigners, and of our limitations. And this impossibility of being like other theatre people has gradually rendered us loyal to our diversity.

For all these reasons I recognize myself in the culture of a Eurasian theatre today. That is, I belong to the small and recent tradition of group theatres which have autodidactic origins but grow in a professional "village" where kabuki actors are not regarded as being more remote than Shakespearean texts, nor the living presence of an Indian dancer-actress less contemporary than the American avant-garde.

Creating Contexts

It often occurs in this "village" that the actors (or a single actor) not only analyze a conflict, let themselves be guided by the objectivity of the logos, and tell a story, but dance *in* it and *with* it according to the growth of the bios. This is not a metaphor: concretely, it means that the actor does not remain yoked to the plot, does not interpret a text, but *creates a context*, moves around and within the events. At times the actor lets these events carry her, at times she carries them, other times she separates herself from them, comments on them, rises above them, attacks them, refuses them, follows new associations, and/or leaps to other stories. The linearity of the narrative is shattered by constantly changing the point of view, anatomizing the known reality, and by interweaving objectivity and subjectivity (i.e., exposition of facts and reactions to them). Thus the actor uses the same liberty and the same leaps of thought inaction, guided by a logic which the spectator cannot immediately recognize.

That which has often created misunderstandings about Oriental theatre, has confused it with "archaic" ritual, or made it appear as perfect but static form, is in fact that which renders it closest to our epoch's most complex concepts of time and space. It does not represent a phenomenology of reality, but a phenomenology of thought. It does not behave as if it belonged to Newton's universe. It corresponds to Niels Bohr's sub-atomic world.

This phenomenology of thought, this objective behavior of the bios, which proceeds by leaps, is what I have tried to render perceptible in *The Romance of Oedipus* with Toni Cots, *Marriage with God* with Iben Nagel Rasmussen and Cesar Brie, and *Judith* with Roberta Carreri.

Spectator

Eurasian theatre is necessary today as we move from the 20th into the 21st century. I am not thinking of Oriental stories interpreted with an Occidental's sensibility, nor am I thinking of techniques to be reproduced, nor of the invention of new codes. Fundamentally, even the complex codes which seem to make sense of many Oriental traditions remain unknown or little known to the majority of spectators in India as well as in China, Japan, and Bali.

I am thinking of those few spectators capable of following or accompanying the actor in the dance of thought-in-action.

It is only the Western public which is not accustomed to leaping from one character to another in the company of the same actor; which is not accustomed to entering into a relationship with someone whose language it cannot easily decipher; which is not used to a form of physical expression that is neither immediately mimetic nor falls into the conventions of dance.

Beyond the public there are, in the West as well as in the East, specific *spectators*. They are few, but for them theatre can become a necessity.

For them theatre is a relationship which neither establishes a union nor creates a communion, but ritualizes the reciprocal strangeness and the laceration of the social body hidden beneath the uniform skin of dead myths and values.

Chapter 69

Megumi Sata

Megumi Sata is a lecturer in Drama and English at Teikyo University. This important essay compares the critical ideas of Aristotle's *Poetics* and Zeami Motokiyo's *Teachings on Style and the Flower*. Zeami Motokiyo (ca. 1363–ca. 1443) was a Japanese actor, playwright, and drama theorist. He was the son of the itinerant actor Kan'ami Kiyotsugu (1333–84). Zeami began his career as patron and lover of the shogun Ashikaga Yoshimitsu. Despite political difficulties with authorities, he developed Japanese Nō (skill) theatre. For fifty years Zeami performed, wrote, and theorized under the protection of the shogun court. He is believed to have written over fifty plays incorporating myth, literary allusions, Zen, and restraint. He produced practical handbooks for actors and theoretical works dealing with the art of the Nō theatre. One of his pieces of advice to actors, reflecting Zen simplicity and compactness, was to "move seven if the heart feels ten."[1] The analysis by Sata examines the relationship of Zeami and Aristotle: each thinker explores the practice and theory of theatre, especially how theatre can maximize its emotional and intellectual impact.

Aristotle's *Poetics* and Zeami's *Teachings on Style and the Flower* (1989)

Two great classic theatres of East and West, Japanese *nō* and Greek tragedy, are said to share common characteristics and elements – use of masks, the presence of a chorus, universality of themes, and a profound understanding of the human psyche. On a deeper level one can point to both societies being polytheistic and both theatre forms having

Megumi Sata, "Aristotle's *Poetics* and Zeami's *Teachings on Style and the Flower*," *Asian Theatre Journal* 6.1 (Spring 1989), 47–56, University of Hawai'i Press. © 1989. Reprinted by permission of University of Hawai'i Press.

ritualistic origins. At the same time there are major differences between the two forms: spectacular productions, sweeping stone amphitheatres, and vast public audiences in Greece and small-cast performances, simple wooden stages, and invited court audiences in Japan. They are almost two millennia apart in time.

This is not the place to compare the multitude of similarities and differences between the two forms, however. Here I wish to analyze key concepts that appear in Aristotle's *Poetics* and Zeami Motokiyo's *Teachings on Style and the Flower* (*Fūshikaden*) – two superb theatrical treatises to which we owe much of our knowledge of tragedy and *nō*. Each deals comprehensively and conclusively with the theory of the art form, and each has exerted profound influence upon later generations. I want to compare the two authors' works in terms of imitation, play structure, effects, and definition of success, while taking into account the different perceptions held by people in the cultures whom Aristotle (384–322 BC) and Zeami (1363–1443) represented.

Imitation

Imitation is a key word in both treatises. Aristotle repeatedly says that "tragedy is the imitation of an action," while Zeami says that "this skill [role-playing] forms the fundamental basis of our art.... Role-playing involves an imitation."[2] Aristotle and Zeami also seem to agree that this imitation should be beautiful. In the *Poetics*, Aristotle says:

> Since Tragedy is an imitation of persons who are above the common level, the example of good portrait-painters should be followed. They, while reproducing the distinctive form of the original, make a likeness which is true to life and yet more beautiful. So too the poet, in representing men who are irascible or indolent, or have other defects of character, should preserve the type and yet ennoble it (45).

Zeami's ideas are similar:

> Role-playing involves an imitation, in every particular, with nothing left out. Still, depending on the circumstances, one must know how to vary the degree of imitation involved.... He must imitate down to the smallest detail the various things done by persons of high profession, especially those elements related to high artistic pursuits. On the other hand, when it comes to imitating laborers and rustics, their common-place actions should not be copied too realistically (10).

Both statements imply that there are proper *ways* to imitate. A closer look, however, reveals differences between the two theorists about what (or who) imitates what (or whom).

Aristotle approaches imitation through his famous elucidation of "six elements" which determine the quality of tragedy; in order of importance, these are plot, character, thought, diction, song, and spectacle. Plot, character, and thought are the objects of imitation; diction and song the media; and spectacle the manner. Further, although every play should have all six elements, Aristotle separates playwriting from the elements of theatre (considering spectacle least artistic and least connected with the art of poetry). In emphasizing the text, he even holds that when a dramatist writes a play, he need not think much about how it should be produced on the stage. Tragedy is the imitation of action, and life consists of actions by which characters are made happy or otherwise.

Aristotle claims that the essential tragic effect can be produced solely by plot and artistically constructed incidents.

For Zeami, imitation always refers to the actor's role-playing. In *nō* an actor imitates a character who has thought and emotion and who develops the plot by external portrayal – dance and chant. Zeami addresses the actor about the art of imitation. The actor must begin by imitating the external of the thing he is performing – taking a proper posture and dressing appropriately for the character. This is followed by imitation of the internal. *Nō* acting, then, requires both physical and psychological imitation. It is therefore essential for the actor to understand the character he is going to present. In *Teachings on Style and the Flower*, Zeami describes nine role types and talks about the actor's attitude toward both externalization and internalization. He also mentions that the highest stage of imitation an actor can reach is one in which a genuine internalization has been achieved, a state in which the imitation of externals is no longer a concern.

In *nō*, the imitator is clearly an actor and the object a character type. In Greek tragedy, the imitator is a poet and the object the action of a character type. In both theatres, characters are not individuals but types. Greek tragedy shows how a person of a certain type will, on occasion, act; *nō* shows an essential emotion of a certain character type. In Greek tragedy the poet writes action which is probable for the character, whereas in *nō* the actor imitates the character externally and internally.

This difference in the concept of imitation between the two theories can be attributed not only to the authors' different perspectives on theatre but also to their concepts of acting. In *nō*, actor and poet are one. The main actor writes a play, directs it, and performs the major role. Zeami is addressing the same person when he talks about acting and directing. On the other hand, in Aristotle it is the actor and the character created by the poet who are one. He speaks of "enactors," the doers of what is done, which enfolds both actor and character. This is only possible in Aristotelian acting:

> Aristotle's actor is an actor-mask, and his bond with the man in the story is forgotten through acting, through repetition, and not through impersonation; what was done by the man in the story is done again by the mask.... The actor-mask is not a portrait, not a likeness; it presents, it does not re-present....[3]

This is not true in *nō* theatre, though it too uses masks. In a *nō* play an actor imitates a character, and a mask represents the type of that character. In Greek tragedy the imitator creates a plot to be enacted in performance. In *nō* the imitator creates his imitation through his performance.

In both theories artistic imitation is an important element, yet it is conceptualized differently in each. In discussing imitation, Aristotle talks to a poet or tragedian; Zeami addresses an actor. Aristotelian imitation happens in playwriting, where a poet imitates, in words, the actions of a human being as a type; Zeami's takes place in performance, where an actor imitates a human being as a type.

Structure

When considering an individual play, both Aristotle and Zeami stress the importance of wholeness and a sense of unity. They think that every play should have a sense of completion, and they divide a play into three sections. Aristotle calls these sections a beginning, a middle, and an end; Zeami calls them *jo, ha,* and *kyū* (introduction, breaking, and rapid).

Zeami mentions the *jo-ha-kyū* concept in *Teachings on Style and the Flower* only in reference to the arrangement of *nō* plays in a performance program. In one of his later writings, *Finding Gems and Gaining the Flower* (*Shūgyoku tokka*), he develops this concept and applies it to play structure as well. It is the *jo-ha-kyū* concept presented in the latter essay which I will compare with Aristotle's "beginning, middle, and end."

Aristotle describes unity of structure by saying that "the structural union of the parts [should be] such that, if any one of them is displaced or removed, the whole will be disjointed and disturbed" (39). According to him, a superior poet constructs a plot in such a way that even without the aid of the eye, tragic pleasure can be felt by merely hearing what takes place (43).

To remind us of exactly what Aristotle said, let me quote him in full. He explains the three parts of a well-constructed plot:

> Tragedy is an imitation of an action that is complete, and whole, and of a certain magnitude; for there may be a whole that is wanting in magnitude. A whole is that which has a beginning, a middle, and an end. A beginning is that which does not itself follow anything by causal necessity, but after which something naturally is or comes to be. An end, on the contrary, is that which itself naturally follows some other thing, either by necessity, or as a rule, but has nothing following it. A middle is that which follows something as some other thing follows it. A well-constructed plot, therefore, must neither begin nor end at haphazard, but conform to these principles (37–38).

Zeami's words in *Finding Gems and Gaining the Flower* sound surprisingly similar to Aristotle's:

> Fulfillment is related to the process of *jo, ha,* and *kyū.* This is true because there is in the composition of the word Fulfillment itself a suggestion of the process that involves a sense of completion. If this natural process toward completion is not carried out, no feelings of Fulfillment can arise. It is that instant of Fulfillment in an artistic work that gives the audience a sensation of novelty. The proper sequence of *jo, ha,* and *kyū* provides the sense of Fulfillment.[4]

The only occurrence between the *jo-ha-kyū* principle and Aristotle's analysis is that *jo-ha-kyū* also suggests the inclusion of moving elements. *Jo-ha-kyū* is basically a concept of rhythmic order.

The *jo-ha-kyū* concept was not Zeami's invention, for it had already been elucidated as early as the eighth century in sophisticated court dances (*bugaku*). Zeami applies this principle to *nō*:

> Long or short, large or small, all are equal in their endowment of the principle of *jo, ha,* and *kyū.* If this principle is firmly understood, one's own consciousness of one's art will follow the proper process to genuine fulfillment (*Finding Gems,* 139).

The literal meanings of *jo, na,* and *kyū* – "introduction," "breaking," and "rapid" – may be interpreted rhythmically as "slow," "fast," and "faster." But these do not just follow in order; they must also relate and contrast with one another. It is not until *ha* and *kyū* have followed that *jo* is understood. In other words, the effect of *jo* is caused by the existence of *ha* and *kyū*, and *ha* and *kyū* must be inherent in *jo*.

When Aristotle talks about order and a sense of wholeness, he is thinking of the unity of a written plot within which an action starts and concludes. Zeami, however, is talking about the dynamics of live performance. Zeami believes it to be "a duty of acting to unify actions into one complete image by bringing out this rhythmic structure.... They can give the viewer the impression of an organic unity."[5] In sum, then, while Aristotle's sense of unity comes from the textual frame, Zeami's sense of unity comes from the internal coherence of performance. As theorists, Aristotle and Zeami both find a sense of unity essential to the structure of a play, but whereas Aristotle bases his ideas upon cause and effect within plot, Zeami grounds his concept in the Japanese rhythmic notion of *jo-na-kyū* within performance.

Effect

Both theorists make it clear that the effect of a play is achieved through imitation within a certain structure and, moreover, that the concept of effect involves a relationship with an audience. In the *Poetics* Aristotle calls the proper effect of tragedy catharsis, a concept attributed to him. Although the word "catharsis" appears only once in the *Poetics*, it has caused much argument. According to Gerald Else's interpretation, which is based on analysis of audience emotion, catharsis is a purgation of the tragic hero's actions through the audience's full understanding.[6] The audience acts as a judge in whose sight the hero's actions are purified. The catharsis brought about by the plot proves that the hero was blameless, and this knowledge allows the audience to have pity on him. Feelings of pity and fear are proper to tragedy, and the poet should try to produce these reactions by imitating events terrible and pitiful. To be specific: "Pity is aroused by unmerited misfortune, fear by the misfortune of a man like ourselves" (Aristotle, 42). The fatal or painful act is the basic stuff that constitutes the tragic plot. Therefore, the effect of catharsis is automatic and is produced by all tragedies. Else says that catharsis is "a process carried forward in the emotional material of the play by its structural element" (439).

In Zeami's theory the proper effects of *nō* are mysterious beauty (*yūgen*) and novelty (*hana/omosniro*). *Yūgen* indicates a quality of beauty which is suggestive, elusive, meaningful, and tinged with sadness. *Yūgen* is an ideal of beauty to be valued in itself. Novelty is the difference between the present performance and previously experienced performances. Novelty depends on the audience's knowledge and is appreciated only by the audience:

> The fulfillment of *jo*, *ha*, and *kyū* provides the spectators with a sense of novelty, and the creation of *jo*, *ha*, and *kyū* by the performers brings this phenomenon about. When the audience can express its astonishment as one with a gasp, the moment of Fulfillment has come (*Finding Gems*, 138).

Zeami claims that good performances should have both effects. Both *yūgen* and novelty are created by imitation, within a rhythmic structure, which in *nō* means acting, dancing, and chanting. Beautiful verse and excellent music help to create these effects, of course, and just as the degree of effect in Greek tragedy depends on the quality of the play, the effectiveness of *yūgen* and novelty in *nō* also depends on the individual play. But whereas catharsis can, by definition, be written into Greek tragedy, the same is not true for *yūgen* or novelty in *nō*.

For Aristotle, the effectiveness of a performance is not determined by the audience, since the relationship between poet and audience goes only one way. Because he expects the audience to react in a predictable manner, their taste does not need to be considered when assessing a tragedy's dramatic value. In *nō*, however, the sense of novelty is influenced by the taste of the audience. Novelty should be produced by the fulfillment of *jo*, *ha*, and *kyu* and the ingenuity of the actors' actions, but only the audience can decide whether it has felt a sense of surprise.

Success

When Aristotle declares a tragedy successful, he means that it is a properly written work with well composed plot. Aristotle's main concern is playwriting. He is addressing the poet and he spends most chapters describing how to write a good tragedy (although the time had long passed for that). Thus if the playwright constructs a unified plot concerning a hero of high reputation who experiences a change in fortune from prosperity to misery due to error rather than vice in which events occur rationally according to cause and effect, and so on and so on, the result is a successful work of tragic poetry. Aristotle is very precise in his instructions and very clear about what is good or bad, what is interesting or not. His aesthetic criteria are absolute: whatever is good is always good, everywhere. Not being involved in actual dramatic production himself, he easily concludes that, as a matter of course, the best-plotted play will be successful on stage: "The best proof is that on the stage in dramatic competition, such plays, if well worked out, are the most tragic in effect" (42). He holds that such a play will be praised by readers even if not performed. Aristotle, born unluckily late for his topic, naturally looks at the text of the play as a self-contained entity, and, as a philosopher for whom everything "must have a nature of its own,"[7] he defines tragedy by analyzing the nature of the text.

Zeami, too, is concerned with properly written plays: "Writing texts for the *nō* represents the very life of our art" (*Teachings on Style*, 43). But writing a good play means different things to the two men. Zeami's conception of an ideal play is less clearly defined. He says: "A successful play of the first rank is based on an authentic source, reveals something unusual in aesthetic qualities, has an appropriate climax, and shows Grace [*yūgen*]" (44). He gives some instructions on play construction, but he always relates them to actual performance. Zeami does not believe in an ideal form separate from practical circumstances. Being an actor and not a philosopher, he believes success to be very conditional. His words present a striking contrast to those of Aristotle: "Most spectators assume that if a good play is given a fine performance, the results will be successful, yet surprisingly enough such a performance may not succeed" (45). To Zeami, success in *nō* means a performance which is accepted and praised by the audience.

For Zeami, therefore, even when a text has the qualities of *yūgen* and novelty it can be judged successful only in consequence to its being performed on stage. Even then the particular performance and the audience's reaction to it must be taken into account. As a professional actor, Zeami knows that communicating with the audience is difficult and unpredictable, so he places great emphasis on acting – dancing and chanting – the skills with which the actor communicates. Zeami starts with *nō* as a performing art; consequently its aesthetic charm is found in acting, not the written text. In *Teachings on Style and the Flower*, Zeami deals with such essentials of the actor's work as training, attitude toward art, and levels of achievement, concerns that are naturally excluded from Aristotle's book on poetry.

While Zeami wrote as an actor striving to gain the audience's respect and approval, it is not unfair to say that Aristotle shows condescension toward both actors and audience: spectators are so uncultivated they require gesture in order to comprehend tragedy (54). Gesture (that is, acting) and spectacle, being undervalued, are merely accessories to the text. As Yamazaki points out, "we may deduce that classical Greek tragedies required highly stylized acting, but the fact that such acting was not of aesthetic interest to Aristotle was decisive for the history of dramatic theories of the West" (xxxi). The tradition of Western dramatic theory that Aristotle established has long viewed drama as a unidirectional process wherein the artistic achievements of the playwright are presented to an audience through the medium of language with the help of acting (gesture). Although the audience is the object of the tragic aim of catharsis, the catharsis does not depend on the nature of the audience. Aristotle's guiding concept that the poet-playwright's goal is achievement of an ideal work of art (his ideal tragedy) causes him to ignore the taste of the audience.

Zeami, on the other hand, does not speak of ideal dramatic form. His advice is to decide all matters in reference to the audience's taste, nature, and psychological condition. From his experience as an actor, Zeami knows that

> unfortunately... our art [*nō*] is based on the desires of our audience... [so that] successful performances depend on the changing tastes of each generation... [and] success can only be assured when various elements are properly matched – the level of the play, the skill of the performer, the discernment of the audience, the performing area, and the occasion itself (*Teachings on Style*, 47, 50).

Success with the audience is, for the actor, everything. But Zeami also aims at artistic perfection. He speaks of a highly sophisticated, skillful, and aesthetically excellent art form which *nō* players should pursue, but his ideal includes pleasing the audience as an integral component. By fixing as the ultimate achievement the ability to see and grasp the audience and adjust one's way of presentation accordingly, Zeami solves the conflict between the artist's ideal and the audience's desire, a conflict which the Aristotelian dramatist must struggle with even today. Zeami writes:

> In the case of those spectators who have real knowledge and understanding of the *nō*, there will be an implicit understanding between them and an actor who has himself reached his own level of Magnitude. Yet in the case of a dull-witted audience, or the vulgar audiences in the countryside or in the far-off provinces, spectators will have difficulty in reaching a proper level of accomplishment. How should an actor behave in such a case?... When the location or the occasion demands, and the level of the audience is low, the actor should strive to bring happiness to them by performing in a style which they truly can appreciate. When one thinks over the real purposes of our art, a player who truly can bring happiness to his audiences is one who can without censure bring his art to all.... However gifted a player, if he does not

win the love and the respect of his audiences, he can hardly be said to be an actor who brings prosperity to his troupe (*Teachings on Style*, 41).

In emphasizing the importance of pleasing the audience, Zeami's book is also a practical manual on theatre survival. As an artist, Zeami wants his art to survive, yet without compromising its quality. Zeami compares the charm which an artist must pursue to a flower (*hana*), and he concludes *Teachings on Style and the Flower* as follows:

> The Flower…must differ depending on the spirit of the audience. Which of those Flowers then represents the true one? The nature of the Flower truly depends on the occasion on which it will be employed…. This teaching [which should be passed down to one person in each generation] can provide the means to come to truly master that exquisite Flower that permits the understanding of a myriad virtues (62–63).

Each flower has its own season. People are amused and surprised by its beauty which comes in time. It was Zeami's strong wish that *nō*, too, would please the audience whatever the trend of the time.

Nō: A Pragmatic Survivor

To this day, the *nō* play has survived; it is still performed before appreciative audiences as a living theatre in Japan even after more than six hundred years, and in much the same style as during the days of Zeami. Greek tragedy was substantially modified and transformed as early as Roman times. In time the performing traditions of Greek tragedy died out, leaving behind only literary remains. Of course, these are magnificent remains. We can debate whether Aristotle's insistence upon valuing a script on its own merits influenced that historic process. His influence on later generations is incalculable and unquestioned. Even today, after more than two thousand years, his playwriting theory is one of the bases of Western dramatic thought. It has been both copied and opposed, but no discussion of Western dramatic theory can fail to consider it.

Zeami's dramatic theory based on acting performance, *Teachings on Style and the Flower*, is read even today not only by *nō* actors but by performers of all kinds. It is regarded as one of the basic texts on Japanese performing art. If *nō* lives today it is surely in part because *nō* has always been directed to a present-day audience. In Zeami's highest theoretical discussions, he considers the relationship between performer and spectator to be of the greatest value. In *nō* we have an example of a pragmatic survivor that nonetheless maintains high artistic goals. In this Japanese experience we can see an alternative to the art-versus-pandering schism which the impractical idealism of Aristotle introduced into Western theatre.

Notes

1   Quoted in *Cambridge Guide to Asian Theatre*, ed. J. R. Brandon (Cambridge: Cambridge University Press, 1993), 145.

2   Aristotle, *Poetics*, tr. S. H. Butcher, in *Dramatic Theory and Criticism*, ed. B. F. Dukore (New York: Holt, 1974), 36, 37; M. Zeami, *Teachings on Style and the Flower* (*Fūshikaden*), in *On the Art of Nō Drama*, tr. J. T. Rimer and M. Yamazaki (Princeton: Princeton University Press, 1984), 10.

3   J. Jones, *On Aristotle and Greek Tragedy* (London: Chatto & Windus, 1962), 59.

4   Zeami, *Finding Gems and Gaining the Flower*, in *On the Art of Nō Drama*, 137.

5   M. Yamazaki, "The Aesthetics of Ambiguity: The Artistic Theories of Zeami," in *On the Art of Nō Drama*, xliii.

6   G. Else, *Aristotle's Poetics: The Argument* (Cambridge, MA: Harvard University Press, 1963), n.p.

7   K. A. Telford, *Aristotle's Poetics, Translation and Analysis* (Bloomington: Indiana University Press, 1961), 59.

Chapter 70

Jill Dolan

Jill Dolan is one the leading feminist scholars in theatre. Her major work, *Feminist Spectator as Critic* (1991), revolutionized perceptions of the theatre and performance by reevaluating the way in which theatre is viewed and critiqued. Dolan, along with other important feminist critics Sue-Ellen Case, Helene Keyssar, Loren Kruger, Janelle Reinelt, Yvonne Yarbro-Bejarano, and Haiping Yan (among others), ushered in a new and important perspective on theatre theory. Feminist theatre theory, Gayle Austin remarks, "means paying attention when women appear as characters and noticing when they do not. It means making some 'invisible' mechanisms visible and pointing out, when necessary, that while the emperor has no clothes, the empress has no body. It means paying attention to women as writers and as readers or audience members." Lastly, it means "taking nothing for granted because the things we take for granted are usually those that were constructed from the most powerful point of view in the culture and that is not the point of view of women."[1] The three areas of feminist theatre referenced by Dolan consist of liberal feminism (emphasizing equality and parity), cultural feminism (accentuating difference), and material feminism (stressing the social construction of sexual identity). In this essay Dolan considers the specter of pornography, the male gaze, and the voyeuristic theatre that has become part of the theatrical landscape. Her investigation of theatre has also led her to consider the utopian possibilities of performance and the potential for the theatre to be a location for communication, healing, and renewal.

Excerpts from Jill Dolan, "Desire Cloaked in a Trenchcoat," *TDR* 33.1 (Spring 1989), 59–67, reprinted in Dolan, *Presence and Desire: Essays on Gender, Sexuality, Performance* (Ann Arbor: University of Michigan Press, 1993), 121–34. © 1989 by New York University and the Massachusetts Institute of Technology. Reprinted by permission of MIT Press Journals.

Desire Cloaked in a Trenchcoat (1989)

"Desire Cloaked in a Trenchcoat" is maybe a corny image to inform an investigation of pornography, performance, and spectators. But the man sitting alone in a darkened theater masturbating under his coat while staring at the screen is an image engraved on our collective imagination. Male arousal by pictures is an accepted part of dominant cultural discourse.

The provocative relationship between sexuality and representation is revealed perhaps most blatantly in pornography. Pornography is an important locus for feminist critical thought because it provides a site for the intersection of feminist sexual politics and the politics of representation.

Whether you are for or against pornography, or straddle the anticensorship fence with "First Amendment" painted on it, pornography has to be dealt with as representation. As Susanne Kappeler points out in *The Pornography of Representation*, "Representation is not so much the means of representing an object through imitation (that is, matching contents) as a means of self-representation through authorship: the expression of subjectivity."[2] Antiporn feminists condemning pornography as both image and educator of male violence against women look for a match of contents by equating pornography and reality.[3] But pornography is more than simple mimesis. As representation, it helps to construct subject positions that maintain the strict gender divisions on which the culture operates.

The subject/object relations delineated by pornography are also paradigmatic of those structured by representation in general. Feminist film and performance critics argue that representation is addressed to the gaze of the male spectator. He is invited to identify with the active male protagonist portrayed in the narrative through voyeuristic and fetishistic viewing conventions. The male spectator shares in the pleasure of the hero's quest to fulfill his desire for the story's passively situated female.[4]

If all representation is structured by male desire, then sexuality is as integral a part of constructing spectator subjectivity in a Shakespeare production at Stratford as it is in live sex shows in Times Square. Any representation can be seen as essentially pornographic, since the structure of gendered relationships through which it operates is based on granting men subjectivity while denying it to women.

Kantian aesthetics propose that the only way to contemplate a work of art is through a certain detachment from reality. Disengagement allows the artwork a separate, "objective" existence and hides the fact of its authorship within a particular historical moment governed by cultural and economic considerations. Kappeler argues after Kant that the principles of aesthetic distance and disinterestedness motivate pornography as well as art. She suggests that, in the peep shows where men masturbate while watching women perform behind glass windows, the goal is not actually to fuck women. Rather, the goal is what she calls the "feeling of life, the pleasure of the subject" derived from aesthetic distance (61–2). Kappeler says that the pornographic representation is even preferable, because it allows the total assertion of a man's subjectivity. Since there is no intersubjective action, the image of the woman behind the glass becomes a screen for the projection of a fantasy over which the male viewer has total control.

In "Bar Wars," written for *Esquire* in November 1986, Bob Greene provides a succinct example of the intersection of sexuality, pornography, and spectatorship on the representational economy. A bar called B.T.'s in Dearborn, Michigan, which usually presents topless female dancing entertainment, also offers what it calls "Rambo Wet Panty Nights." Black plastic Uzi submachine water guns are handed out to the customers. Then a woman – sometimes a regular B.T.'s dancer, sometimes an "amateur" volunteer – mounts the stage dressed in a skimpy T-shirt and underwear and stands covering her eyes and face while the men shoot their water guns at her vagina. Six or seven women perform each evening, and cash prizes are given to the women who do the "best" job of being shot at, according to the bar owner's subjective judgments. Greene doesn't describe the critical standards applied.[5]

This performative exchange is a cultural feminist's nightmare of the conflation of sexuality and violence. But, aside from this neat match of contents, it's an overt example of representation proceeding according to a pornographic model. The bar is packed with men drawn by a chance to become Rambo in the flesh. The elements of a prior representation, then, are mapped onto the performance at the bar. Sylvester Stallone and his Rambo movies are missing, but they're implied in the narrative.

In the Rambo films, as in most Vietnam films, the enemy – or the other – is an Asian race. In the paramilitary ambiance of B.T.'s bar, the woman onstage becomes the alien enemy, the other defined by her difference (62). The floor manager at B.T.'s encourages the men with guns to think of the woman onstage as Vietnam or Libya or even Nicaragua. It's a neat way of eroticizing imperialism and keeping sexuality imperialist.

The men with the Uzis are implicitly identifying with Rambo as they aim, and they experience visual pleasure by projecting their subjective fantasies onto the passive woman. One man tells Greene: "I got her. She's hot; I know she likes it. She likes it, and she knows that I know she likes it" (62). But, if the woman's eyes were covered, how could this man possibly think the performer was acknowledging and enjoying a spray from his gun, except by fantasizing because he wants it that way?

What do the performers at B.T.'s think about allowing their bodies to be used as substitutes for Third World nations and becoming screens for projections of male fantasy? One woman tells Greene, "It's a power game." Unlike most, she doesn't cover her eyes when she performs. "I try to look out into the audience and make eye contact with as many of the men with guns as I can. A lot of times, they'll turn away. If a woman looks them in the eye, they'll turn away." At issue here is the struggle for subjectivity. These men can't face the intersubjectivity of the woman's gaze. They must maintain the disengagement of desire inspired by the safe aesthetic distance of the representation.

Greene's article, of course, is governed by the exigencies of his own male gaze, and he doesn't mention whether there are female spectators in the bar. But, theoretically, where could a woman place herself in relation to this display? How could she position herself in front of a peep show window? The image of a woman sitting in a darkened theater wearing a trenchcoat is incongruous at best.

Whether or not female spectators can be placed in positions of power that might allow for the objectification of male performers or that might allow for the liberation of both gender classes from the oppressions of the representational gaze is an issue hotly debated in feminist film theory. As Kappeler and others have pointed out, simply trading gender positions isn't as easy as it sounds. While women in representation usually signify their gender class, the culturally sanctioned power of male subjectivity makes a similar signification very difficult. Women cannot simply express their subjectivity by objectifying men. A nude male in an objectified position remains an individual man, not necessarily a representation of the male gender class.

For example, Richard Schechner, while pondering these issues, described the activity at several sex clubs in Montreal in which males danced for females as examples of women adopting the male gaze. Schechner says that the male dancers

> stripped until fully naked. They played with their cocks and displayed the rest of their bodies in a way very parallel to what women do in strip clubs. . . . As a new male entered the stage, the dancer who was onstage went from table to table, and danced directly in front of women. The male dancer brought with him a little step stool so that his genitals were face level to the female spectator(s). The women tipped him. There was a lot of flirtation, kissing, and some genital playing.[6]

While this situation seems to reverse the traditional paradigm, male sexuality is still active, privileged, and displayed. The female spectators want the male performer to desire them. Similar conditions are implied by female dancers in clubs for male spectators. The female dancers aren't performing their own sexuality: their display implies penile satisfaction; their open legs and wet vaginas imply the possibility of penetration. In both situations the desire of female spectators or performers is subordinate to male desire.

According to the psychoanalytic model, since male desire drives representation, a female spectator is given two options. She can identify with the active male and symbolically participate in the female performer's objectification, or she can identify with the narrative's objectified female and position herself as an object.

I do not mean to propose a universalism when I use the term *female spectator*. For the materialist feminist women are differentiated along class, race, and sexual orientation lines that make it impossible for them to respond to any image as a unit. Part of the problem with the psychoanalytical model of spectatorship is just this tendency to pose universal "male" and "female" spectators who respond only according to gender. Part of my project here is to suggest that sexuality is as large a part of spectator response as gender and that, by altering the assumed sexuality of spectators, the representational exchange can also be changed.

Mary Ann Doane, in *The Desire to Desire*, writes, "There is a certain naiveté assigned to women in relation to systems of signification, a tendency to deny the process of representation, to collapse the opposition between the sign (the image) and the real."[7] Women remain part of Lacan's Imaginary realm, completely marginal to the signifying process. Since she cannot separate herself from the image, the female spectator cannot experience the mirror phase through which she might see herself reflected as a separate subject. Because Doane's psychoanalytic reading considers desire as a form of disengagement "crucial to the assumption of the position of the speaking subject," a woman cannot hope to articulate her desire in the representational space (11).

Since she can assume neither disengagement nor aesthetic distance from the image, she is denied the scopophilic pleasure of voyeurism. Fetishism, which also operates particularly in the cinematic apparatus to provide visual pleasure, is also unavailable to the female spectator, since her originary lack dictates that she already has nothing to lose.

Woman as a psychic subject, then, is unarticulated in representation. Doane goes on to propose that women as social subjects are constructed merely as passive consumers invited to buy the idealized, male-generated image of the female body as a commodity displayed in the representational frame.

If the female spectator chooses to accept this passively constructed consumer position, Doane writes, "The mirror/window takes on then the aspect of a trap whereby her subjectivity becomes synonymous with her objectification" (33). Buying the idealized image of herself, she turns herself into a commodity to then be sold, as the performer already has. The positions of the female performer and the female spectator are collapsed into one: they become prostitutes who buy and sell their own image in a male-generated visual economy. They are goods in the representational marketplace, commodities in an exchange by means of which they are both objectified.[8]

The women performing at B.T.'s, for example, are sheer spectacle in a representational exchange constructed for the male gaze. Some of the women admit that they do it for the money, prostituting their subjectivity to the demands of the representational space. The owner of B.T.'s, of course, doesn't see it in so mercenary a light. He romanticizes the women's involvement, speculating that they are willing to perform because they come from disturbed backgrounds and need attention – a variation of *A Chorus Line*'s "What I Did for Love."

The idea that specularized, objectified women do it for the love of the male gaze is a concept perpetuated by dominant cultural discourse. In "Confessions of a Feminist Porno Star," printed in a feminist anthology of personal narratives called *Sex Work*, Nina Hartley acquiesces to this view. She says she is an exhibitionist, a woman who is aroused by being looked at. But she also feels she has some control over the production of her image. "In choosing my roles and characterizations carefully," she writes, "I strive to show, always, women who thoroughly enjoy sex and are forceful, self-satisfying and guilt-free without also being neurotic, unhappy, or somehow unfulfilled."[9] Hartley proposes that she can subvert the representational apparatus by adjusting the content of its images and giving the positive, active roles to women.

This is a kind of liberal feminist, matching-contents argument that has been used to justify generating feminist erotica. Some feminists think that, if women controlled the means of producing pornography, its representations would be different. But the gendered component of heterosexuality, with its inevitable constant of male desire, problematizes positioning women as the producers or subjects of heterosexual pornography. Heterosexual feminist erotica, such as the magazine *Eidos*, and much feminist performance art indicate that disarming male desire in the representational space requires "feminizing" the represented males or avoiding sexuality as an integral issue. These attempts are for the most part either unsuccessful – since the erect male penis is still a power-filled image even if it's displayed in a feminine, "natural" context – or banal, as sexuality gives way to the obfuscating realm of spirituality (Dolan, "Dynamics of Desire," 157–61).

Debi Sundahl, in her *Sex Work* essay called "Stripper," acknowledges the subject/object problem inherent in heterosexual representation. Initially, she says:

> The hardest part of the job was dealing with my feminist principles concerning the objectification of women. Dancing nude is the epitome of woman as sex object. As the weeks passed, I found I liked being a sex object, because the context was appropriate.... I perform to turn you on, and if I fail, I feel I've done a poor job. Women who work in the sex industry are not responsible for, nor do they in any way perpetuate, the sexual oppression of women. In fact,

to any enlightened observer, our very existence provides a distinction and a choice as to when a woman should be treated like a sex object and when she should not be. At the theatre, yes; on the street, no.[10]

I find this a provocative statement. Sundahl suggests that subject positions onstage can be separated from those assumed in life. But she also suggests that bowing to the demands of objectification in theater is the only role a woman can play in the heterosexual representational space. Implicit in her argument is the idea that representation is driven by a kind of sexuality in which objectification is constantly assumed. But is all sexuality motivated by objectification? And, if not, what might happen to representation if the sexual desire motivating it were different?

There's a twist to Sundahl's story. She is a lesbian; she publishes *On Our Backs*, a lesbian porn magazine; and she started a women-only strip show at Baybrick's, a now defunct lesbian bar in San Francisco. Sundahl herself makes a distinction between her performance spaces, pointing out that the different cultural mandates of the heterosexual and lesbian contexts make the terms of the performative exchange very different, even if the images used or roles played are the same. Describing the show at Baybrick's, for example, Sundahl writes: "The dancers loved performing for the all-female audiences because they had more freedom of expression. They were not limited to ultrafeminine acts only; they could be butch and dress in masculine attire" (178). In other words, if they wanted to, the performers could assume the subject position rather than objectifying themselves. The butch–femme role play allowed the performers to seduce one another and the lesbian spectators through the constant of lesbian sexuality.

This context allows lesbian desire to circulate as the motivating representational term. The subject/object relations that trap women performers and spectators as commodities in a heterosexual context dissolve. The lesbian subject, according to Monique Wittig and others,[11] has free range across a gender continuum, and, to paraphrase Sue-Ellen Case, her role-playing through a "strategy of appearances"[12] disrupts the dominant cultural discourse representation mandates. Wittig says lesbians are "not women" and not men according to the way these gender roles are culturally constructed (110). Since they are already outside a strictly dichotomized gender context, they are free to pick and choose from both extremes. There are no prostitutes on the lesbian representational economy because the goods have gotten together.

In *Upwardly Mobile Home*, a production by the lesbian performance troupe Split Britches, Peggy Shaw has a monologue describing her character's trip to see the fat lady at the circus. She says the lights and the posters promised her entertainment, but she got much, much more. When she entered the fat lady's tent, Shaw says: "She knew I had come to see her being fat. She looked at me and I looked at her. I loved that fat lady." Rather than the fight for subjectivity that takes place in B.T.'s heterosexual bar, Shaw's exchange with the fat woman seems paradigmatic of the lesbian viewing experience. The recognition of mutual subjectivity allows the gaze to be shared in a direct way. Shaw tells *Upwardly Mobile Home* spectators, "You have paid to see me" – but the visual economy is now under lesbian control.

Lesbians are appropriating the subject position of the male gaze by beginning to articulate the exchange of desire between women. Lesbian subjectivity creates a new economy of desire. [...] Rather than gazing through the representational window at their commodification as women, lesbians are generating and buying their own desire on a different representational economy. Perhaps the lesbian subject can offer a model for female spectators that will appropriate the male gaze. The aim is not to look like men, but to look at all. [...]

Notes

1 G. Austin, *Feminist Theories for Dramatic Criticism* (Ann Arbor: University of Michigan Press, 1990), 1–2.

2 S. Kappeler, *The Pornography of Representation* (Minneapolis: University of Minnesota Press, 1986), 53.

3 Antiporn feminism is very much in line with the cultural feminist politic, which maintains that the biological differences between men and women are the basis of their psychological and social differences. This stance translates into often prescriptive dichotomies that describe men's behavior as violent, women's as pacifist. Andrea Dworkin is the most vocal and visible antiporn cultural feminist; her book *Pornography: Men Possessing Women* (New York: Pedigree Books, 1979) is the bible of the movement. See J. Dolan, "The Dynamics of Desire: Sexuality and Gender in Pornography and Performance," *Theatre Journal* 39.2 (May 1987), 156–74, for a further explication of antiporn feminism in terms of feminist performance and criticism.

4 See T. de Lauretis, "Desire in Narrative," in *Alice Doesn't* (Bloomington: Indiana University Press, 1984), 103–57; E. A. Kaplan, *Women and Film: Both Sides of the Camera* (New York: Methuen, 1983); and L. Mulvey, "Visual Pleasure and Narrative Cinema," *Screen* 16.3 (1975), 6–18.

5 B. Greene, "Bar Wars," *Esquire*, November 1986, 61–2.

6 R. Schechner, personal correspondence, September 7, 1987, 10.

7 M. A. Doane, *The Desire to Desire: The Woman's Film of the 1940s* (Bloomington: Indiana University Press, 1987), 1. [Further references are cited in the text.]

8 Gayle Rubin, "The Traffic In Women: Notes on the Political Economy of Sex," in *Toward an Anthropology of Women*, ed. R. Reiter (New York: Monthly Review Press, 1978), argues that women have been use-value in a male economy at least since the kinship systems studies by Lévi-Strauss. [...]

9 N. Hartley, "Confessions of a Feminist Porno Star," in *Sex Work: Writings by Women in the Sex Industry*, ed. F. Delacoste and P. Alexander (San Francisco: Cleis Press, 1987), 142.

10 D. Sundahl, "Stripper," in Delacoste and Alexander, *Sex Work*, 175–80. [Further references are cited in the text.]

11 See, for example, M. Wittig, "The Straight Mind," *Feminist Issues* (Summer 1980), 103–11, and "One Is Not Born a Woman," *Feminist Issues* (Winter 1981), 47–54.

12 S.-E. Case, "Toward a Butch–Femme Aesthetic," in *Making a Spectacle*, ed. Linda Hart (Ann Arbor: University of Michigan Press, 1989), 282–99.

Chapter 71

Judith Butler (b. 1956)

Judith Butler is a leading feminist scholar, philosopher, and theorist. She has pioneered the study of queer theory and the notion that gender, sexual identity, and other forms of individuation are socially constructed. We identify a person by dress, behavior, style, manner, and other forms of outward interaction in the public sphere. These behaviors are fluid, what Butler calls "performative." This term is borrowed from linguist J. L. Austin's theory of the distinction between performative, an utterance that performs an action (a command, an imperative, etc.) and "should be doing something as opposed to just saying something," and constative, which merely describes something already stated or completed.[1] Performance is marked by a collective agreement of what it means to belong to a gender or other forms of identity; this normalization process through regulating and iterative practices, according to Butler, has rendered identity invisible or difficult to discern: "The normative force of performativity – its power to establish what qualifies as 'being' – works not only through reiteration, but through exclusion as well."[2] Gender is performance because, Laurence Senelick observes, "Like a Berkeleian universe, gender exists only in so far as it is perceived; and the very components of perceived gender – gait, stance, gesture, deportment, vocal pitch and intonation, costume, accessories, coiffure – indicate the performative nature of the construct."[3] The body is merely adorned by accoutrements that mark its place in the social hierarchy. Such markings, Butler maintains, are nothing more than socially agreed-upon notions having little or nothing to do with one's birth or sense of self. Modes of performance, Alice Lagaay writes, are either "how one's behaviour establishes who the person is or perceived to be" or have to do with "what *is done to the subject*, how, for instance, a culture's language, and prevailing discourses within society, impose

Judith Butler, "From Parody to Politics," in *Gender Trouble: Feminism and the Subversion of Identity* (New York: Routledge, 1990), 142–9. © 1990 by Routledge, Chapman, & Hall, Inc. Reprinted by permission of Taylor and Francis Group LLC.

a certain identity on its people."[4] Butler's important books are *Gender Trouble: Feminism and the Subversion of Identity* (1990), *Bodies that Matter: On the Discursive Limits of "Sex"* (1993), *Excitable Speech: A Politics of the Performative* (1997), and *Giving an Account of Oneself* (2005). These works examine the transparency of sexual identity, suggesting a mutable relationship between desire and subjectivity.

From Parody to Politics (1990)

I began with the speculative question of whether feminist politics could do without a "subject" in the category of women. At stake is not whether it still makes sense, strategically or transitionally, to refer to women in order to make representational claims in their behalf. The feminist "we" is always and only a phantasmatic construction, one that has its purposes, but which denies the internal complexity and indeterminacy of the term and constitutes itself only through the exclusion of some part of the constituency that it simultaneously seeks to represent. The tenuous or phantasmatic status of the "we," however, is not cause for despair or, at least, it is not *only* cause for despair. The radical instability of the category sets into question the *foundational* restrictions on feminist political theorizing and opens up other configurations, not only of genders and bodies, but of politics itself.

The foundationalist reasoning of identity politics tends to assume that an identity must first be in place in order for political interests to be elaborated and, subsequently, political action to be taken. My argument is that there need not be a "doer behind the deed," but that the "doer" is variably constructed in and through the deed. This is not a return to an existential theory of the self as constituted through its acts, for the existential theory maintains a predical structure for both the self and its acts. It is precisely the discursively variable construction of each in and through the other that has interested me here.

The question of locating "agency" is usually associated with the viability of the "subject," where the "subject" is understood to have some stable existence prior to the cultural field that it negotiates. Or, if the subject is culturally constructed, it is nevertheless vested with an agency, usually figured as the capacity for reflexive mediation, that remains intact regardless of its cultural embeddedness. On such a model, "culture" and "discourse" *mire* the subject, but do not constitute that subject. This move to qualify and enmire the preexisting subject has appeared necessary to establish a point of agency that is not fully *determined* by that culture and discourse. And yet, this kind of reasoning falsely presumes (a) agency can only be established through recourse to a prediscursive "I," even if that "I" is found in the midst of a discursive convergence, and (b) that to be *constituted* by discourse is to be *determined* by discourse, where determination forecloses the possibility of agency.

Even within the theories that maintain a highly qualified or situated subject, the subject still encounters its discursively constituted environment in an oppositional epistemological frame. The culturally enmired subject negotiates its constructions, even when those constructions are the very predicates of its own identity. In Beauvoir, for example, there is an "I" that does its gender, that becomes its gender, but that "I," invariably associated with its gender, is nevertheless a point of agency never fully identifiable with its gender.

That *cogito* is never fully of the cultural world that it negotiates, no matter the narrowness of the ontological distance that separates that subject from its cultural predicates. The theories of feminist identity that elaborate predicates of color, sexuality, ethnicity, class, and ablebodiedness invariably close with an embarrassed "etc." at the end of the list. Through this horizontal trajectory of adjectives, these positions strive to encompass a situated subject, but invariably fail to be complete. This failure, however, is instructive: what political impetus is to be derived from the exasperated "etc." that so often occurs at the end of such lines? This is a sign of exhaustion as well as of the illimitable process of signification itself. It is the *supplément*, the excess that necessarily accompanies any effort to posit identity once and for all. This illimitable *et cetera*, however, offers itself as a new departure for feminist political theorizing.

If identity is asserted through a process of signification, if identity is always already signified, and yet continues to signify as it circulates within various interlocking discourses, then the question of agency is not to be answered through recourse to an "I" that preexists signification. In other words, the enabling conditions for an assertion of "I" are provided by the structure of signification, the rules that regulate the legitimate and illegitimate invocation of that pronoun, the practices that establish the terms of intelligibility by which that pronoun can circulate. Language is not an *exterior medium or instrument* into which I pour a self and from which I glean a reflection of that self. The Hegelian model of self-recognition that has been appropriated by Marx, Lukács, and a variety of contemporary liberatory discourses presupposes a potential adequation between the "I" that confronts its world, including its language, as an object, and the "I" that finds itself as an object in that world. But the subject/object dichotomy, which here belongs to the tradition of Western epistemology, conditions the very problematic of identity that it seeks to solve.

What discursive tradition establishes the "I" and its "Other" in an epistemological confrontation that subsequently decides where and how questions of knowability and agency are to be determined? What kinds of agency are foreclosed through the positing of an epistemological subject precisely because the rules and practices that govern the invocation of that subject and regulate its agency in advance are ruled out as sites of analysis and critical intervention? That the epistemological point of departure is in no sense inevitable is naively and pervasively confirmed by the mundane operations of ordinary language – widely documented within anthropology – that regard the subject/object dichotomy as a strange and contingent, if not violent, philosophical imposition. The language of appropriation, instrumentality, and distanciation germane to the epistemological mode also belong to a strategy of domination that pits the "I" against an "Other" and, once that separation is effected, creates an artificial set of questions about the knowability and recoverability of that Other.

As part of the epistemological inheritance of contemporary political discourses of identity, this binary opposition is a strategic move within a given set of *signifying* practices, one that establishes the "I" in and through this opposition and which reifies that opposition as a necessity, concealing the discursive apparatus by which the binary itself is constituted. The shift from an *epistemological* account of identity to one which locates the problematic within practices of *signification* permits an analysis that takes the epistemological mode itself as one possible and contingent signifying practice. Further, the question of *agency* is reformulated as a question of how signification and resignification work. In other words, what is signified as an identity is not signified at a given point in time after which it is simply there as an inert piece of entitative language. Clearly, identities *can* appear as so many inert substantives; indeed, epistemological models tend to take this appearance as their point of theoretical departure. However, the substantive "I" only appears as such through a signifying practice that seeks to conceal its own workings and to naturalize its effects. Further, to qualify as a substantive identity is an arduous task, for such appearances are rule-generated identities, ones which rely on the consistent and repeated invocation of rules that condition and restrict culturally intelligible practices of identity. Indeed, to understand identity as a *practice*, and as a signifying practice, is to understand culturally intelligible subjects as the resulting effects of a rule-bound discourse that inserts itself in the pervasive and mundane signifying acts of linguistic life. Abstractly considered, language refers to an open system of signs by which intelligibility is insistently created and contested. As historically specific organizations of language, discourses present themselves in the plural, coexisting within temporal frames, and instituting unpredictable and inadvertent convergences from which specific modalities of discursive possibilities are engendered.

As a process, signification harbors within itself what the epistemological discourse refers to as "agency." The rules that govern intelligible identity, i.e., that enable and restrict the intelligible assertion of an "I," rules that are partially structured along matrices of gender hierarchy and compulsory heterosexuality, operate through *repetition*. Indeed, when the subject is said to be constituted, that means simply that the subject is a consequence of certain rule-governed discourses that govern the intelligible invocation of identity. The subject is not *determined* by the rules through which it is generated because signification is *not a founding act, but rather a regulated process of repetition* that both conceals itself and enforces its rules precisely through the production of substantializing effects. In a sense, all signification takes place within the orbit of the compulsion to repeat; "agency," then, is to be located within the possibility of a variation on that repetition. If the rules governing signification not only restrict, but enable the assertion of alternative domains of cultural intelligibility, i.e., new possibilities for gender that contest the rigid codes of hierarchical binarisms, then it is only *within* the practices of repetitive signifying that a subversion of identity becomes possible. The injunction *to be* a given gender produces necessary failures, a variety of incoherent configurations that in their multiplicity exceed and defy the injunction by which they are generated. Further, the very injunction to be a given gender takes place through discursive routes: to be a good mother, to be a heterosexually desirable object, to be a fit worker, in sum, to signify a multiplicity of guarantees in response to a variety of different demands all at once. The coexistence or convergence of such discursive injunctions produces the possibility of a complex reconfiguration and redeployment; it is not a transcendental subject who enables action in the midst of such a convergence: There is no self that is prior to the convergence or who maintains "integrity" prior to its entrance into this conflicted cultural field. There is only a taking up of the tools where they lie, where the very "taking up" is enabled by the tool lying there.

What constitutes a subversive repetition within signifying practices of gender? I have argued ("I" deploy the grammar that governs the genre of the philosophical conclusion, but note that it is the grammar itself that deploys and enables this "I," even as the "I" that insists itself here repeats, redeploys, and – as the critics will determine – contests the philosophical grammar by which it is both enabled and restricted) that, for instance, within the sex/gender distinction, sex poses as "the real" and the "factic," the material or corporeal ground upon which gender operates as an act of cultural *inscription*. And yet gender is not written on the body as the torturing instrument of writing in Kafka's "In the Penal Colony" inscribes itself unintelligibly on the flesh of the accused. The question is not: what meaning does that inscription carry within it, but what cultural apparatus arranges this meeting between instrument and body, what interventions into this ritualistic repetition are possible? The "real" and the "sexually factic" are phantasmatic constructions – illusions of substance – that bodies are compelled to approximate, but never can. What, then, enables the exposure of the rift between the phantasmatic and the real whereby the real admits itself as phantasmatic? Does this offer the possibility for a repetition that is not fully constrained by the injunction to reconsolidate naturalized identities? Just as bodily surfaces are enacted as the natural, so these surfaces can become the site of a dissonant and denaturalized performance that reveals the performative status of the natural itself.

Practices of parody can serve to reengage and reconsolidate the very distinction between a privileged and naturalized gender configuration and one that appears as derived, phantasmatic, and mimetic – a failed copy, as it were. And surely parody has been used to further a politics of despair, one which affirms a seemingly inevitable exclusion of marginal genders from the territory of the natural and the real. And yet this failure to become "real" and to embody "the natural" is, I would argue, a constitutive failure of all gender enactments for the very reason that these ontological locales are fundamentally uninhabitable. Hence, there is a subversive laughter in the pastiche-effect of parodic practices in which the original, the authentic, and the real are themselves constituted as effects. The loss of gender norms would have the effect of proliferating gender configurations, destabilizing substantive identity, and depriving the naturalizing narratives of compulsory heterosexuality of their central protagonists: "man" and "woman." The parodic repetition of gender exposes as well the illusion of gender identity as an intractable depth and inner substance. As the effects of a subtle and politically enforced performativity, gender is an "act," as it were, that is open to splittings, self-parody, self-criticism, and those hyperbolic exhibitions of "the natural" that, in their very exaggeration, reveal its fundamentally phantasmatic status.

I have tried to suggest that the identity categories often presumed to be foundational to feminist politics, that is, deemed necessary in order to mobilize feminism as an identity politics, simultaneously work to limit and constrain in advance the very cultural possibilities that feminism is supposed to open up. The tacit constraints that produce culturally intelligible "sex" ought to be understood as generative political structures rather than naturalized foundations. Paradoxically, the reconceptualization of identity as an *effect*, that is, as *produced* or *generated*, opens up possibilities of "agency" that are insidiously foreclosed by positions that take identity categories as foundational and fixed. For an identity to be an effect means that it is neither fatally determined nor fully artificial and arbitrary. That the *constituted* status of identity is misconstrued along these two conflicting lines suggests the ways in which the feminist discourse on cultural construction remains trapped within the unnecessary binarism of free will and determinism. Construction is not opposed to agency; it is the necessary scene of agency, the very terms in which agency is articulated and becomes culturally intelligible. The critical task for feminism is not to establish a point of view outside of constructed identities; that conceit is the construction of an epistemological model that would disavow its own cultural location and, hence, promote itself as a global subject, a position that deploys precisely the imperialist strategies that feminism ought to criticize. The critical task is, rather, to locate strategies of subversive repetition enabled by those constructions, to affirm the local possibilities of intervention through participating in precisely those practices of repetition that constitute identity and, therefore, present the immanent possibility of contesting them.

This theoretical inquiry has attempted to locate the political in the very signifying practices that establish, regulate, and deregulate identity. This effort, however, can only be accomplished through the introduction of a set of questions that extend the very notion of the political. How to disrupt the foundations that cover over alternative cultural configurations of gender? How to destabilize and render in their phantasmatic dimension the "premises" of identity politics?

This task has required a critical genealogy of the naturalization of sex and of bodies in general. It has also demanded a reconsideration of the figure of the body as mute, prior to culture, awaiting signification, a figure that cross-checks with the figure of the feminine, awaiting the inscription-as-incision of the masculine signifier for entrance into language and culture. From a political analysis of compulsory heterosexuality, it has been necessary to question the construction of sex as binary, as a hierarchical binary. From the point of view of gender as enacted, questions have emerged over the fixity of gender identity as an interior depth that is said to be externalized in various forms of "expression." The implicit construction of the primary heterosexual construction of desire is shown to persist even as it appears in the mode of primary bisexuality. Strategies of exclusion and hierarchy are also shown to persist in the formulation of the sex/gender distinction and its recourse to "sex" as the prediscursive as well as the priority of sexuality to culture and, in particular, the cultural construction of sexuality as the prediscursive. Finally, the epistemological paradigm that presumes the priority of the doer to the deed establishes a global and globalizing subject who disavows its own locality as well as the conditions for local intervention.

If taken as the grounds of feminist theory or politics, these "effects" of gender hierarchy and compulsory heterosexuality are not only misdescribed as foundations, but the signifying practices that enable this metaleptic misdescription remain outside the purview of a feminist critique of gender relations. To enter into the repetitive practices of this terrain of signification is not a choice, for the "I" that might enter is always already inside: there is no possibility of agency or reality outside of the discursive practices that give those terms the intelligibility that they have. The task is not whether to repeat, but how to repeat or, indeed, to repeat and, through a radical proliferation of gender, *to displace* the very gender norms that enable the repetition itself. There is no ontology of gender on which we might construct a politics, for gender ontologies always operate within established political contexts as normative injunctions, determining what qualifies as intelligible sex, invoking and consolidating the reproductive constraints on sexuality, setting the prescriptive requirements whereby sexed or gendered bodies come into cultural intelligibility. Ontology is, thus, not a foundation, but a normative injunction that operates insidiously by installing itself into political discourse as its necessary ground.

The deconstruction of identity is not the deconstruction of politics; rather, it establishes as political the very terms through which identity is articulated. This kind of critique brings into question the foundationalist frame in which feminism as an identity politics has been articulated. The internal paradox of this foundationalism is that it presumes, fixes, and constrains the very "subjects" that it hopes to represent and liberate. The task here is not to celebrate each and every new possibility *qua* possibility, but to redescribe those possibilities that *already* exist, but which exist within cultural domains designated as culturally unintelligible and impossible. If identities were no longer fixed as the premises of a political syllogism, and politics no longer understood as a set of practices derived from the alleged interests that belong to a set of ready-made subjects, a new configuration of politics would surely emerge from the ruins of the old. Cultural configurations of sex and gender might then proliferate or, rather, their present proliferation might then become articulable within the discourses that establish intelligible cultural life, confounding the very binarism of sex, and exposing its fundamental unnaturalness. What other local strategies for engaging the "unnatural" might lead to the denaturalization of gender as such?

Notes

1   J. L. Austin, *How to Do Things With Words* (Cambridge, MA: Harvard University Press, 1962), 133.
2   J. Butler, *Bodies that Matter: On the Discursive Limits of "Sex"* (New York: Routledge, 1993), 188.
3   L. Senelick, "Introduction," in *Gender in Performance: The Presentation of Difference in the Performing Arts*, ed. Senelick (Hanover, NH: University Press of New England, 1992), lx.
4   A. Lagaay, *Metaphysics of Performance: Performance, Performativity, and the Relation Between Theatre and Philosophy* (Berlin: Logos Verlag, 2001), 25–6.

Chapter 72

Reza Abdoh (1963–1995)

Reza Abdoh was an Iranian-born performing artist, director, playwright, choreographer, filmmaker, and activist for gay and lesbian rights. By his early twenties he was diagnosed as HIV-positive. Rather than retreat into sentimental morbidity, Abdoh infused his work with urgency and passion. As well as works that include *The Hip Hop Waltz of Eurydice* (1990), *Father Was a Peculiar Man* (1990), *The Law of Remains* (1992), *Tight White Right* (1993), and *Quotations from a Ruined City* (1994), Abdoh directed *King Lear* and an adaptation of *The Brothers Karamazov*. Abdoh was, in Saul Bellows's phrase, a "first-class noticer." His astute observations of the Los Angeles landscape enabled him to transfer his insights onto the stage. His work examined images that inhibit the imagination, seeking to liberate preconceived notions of reality and power. Abdoh was influenced by the artistic director of the Wooster Group, Elizabeth LeCompte, and by other experimental artists such as Robert Wilson and Richard Foreman (see Chapters 60, 73). However, as Arnold Aronson observes, "there was a fundamental difference in that his work was clearly political – there was no ambiguity about intent, although specific meanings were not always clear. Abdoh was commenting on American society as seen from his perspective as an outsider living within the society."[1]

Los Angeles (1992)

Los Angeles has a unique concave and convex reality which happens at the same time, where many cultures are running on parallel tracks, maintaining their own identities, but at the same time meshing to assimilate with the dominant culture. In other places I've

Reza Abdoh, "Los Angeles," *Mime Journal* (1991/1992), annual published by the Pomona College Theatre Department. © 1991 by Mime Journal. Reprinted by permission of Mime, Pomona College Theatre Department.

worked that's not always true. Usually the diverse cultures have become part of the dominant one to a point that they are beyond recognition. Sometimes the dominant culture is too strong and has overwhelmed them, or the other cultures have intentionally not tried to maintain their individual identities.

New York is a unique case; there is an artistic tradition of dialogue between an audience and a creator which is lacking in California, and that dialogue between the creator and the viewer determines how a work is perceived and the direction that it takes. On the other hand, in New York there is a preformed set of rules, expectations, a norm or paradigm that you either try to uphold or try to break. When people go to see something they are always referring back to that model. There is a long tradition, especially in the performing arts, in New York. Here, in Los Angeles, that tradition simply does not exist.

I feel that the environment in L.A. enriches me; the unpredictability of it fuels my work. The aesthetic one forms here has the potential of becoming one's own aesthetic, as one is not necessarily conforming to a certain trend or an existing paradigm. In other places there is a push toward conforming to a certain model. There still remains a frontier spirit here. It's ironic because in the pop culture there is very much an emphasis on trend-making, on topicality, on fashion making, whereas in the sub-pop world, or in the subcultures, there is a frontier spirit.

Popular culture is the livelihood of this country, and a lot of it gets manufactured in Hollywood, because Hollywood is the apex of the industry of image making. Image making is equal to economic power and economic subjugation; popular culture is not just about what is being sold on television, but about how your thought is being processed for you, how your thought is being determined. A great deal of that is manufactured here. The marginality of the subcultures is something that you either believe or you don't. If you believe that you are marginal, then indeed you are. It is important to think about how subcultures affect the popular culture. The relationship is one of a vulture feeding on remains. A great deal of popular culture is a result of what happens in the subculture. Open a stylish magazine; the images that protrude are the result of what has happened in the last 70 years in the subculture. The trick is to break one's own rules so one does not become a consumer product, a prisoner of one's own conventions. Is it worthwhile to attempt to create a work that remains religious, a work that links one to the higher aspect of one's self. That effort is worthwhile, whether it is successful or not. James Joyce spent his life writing a book which is incomprehensible, and remains an enigma and a phenomenon of the twentieth century. Was it worthwhile? Yes.

The original impulse behind *The Hip Hop Waltz of Eurydice* was my gut reaction to systematic repression and erosion of freedom taking place around me. Instead of feeling helpless about it I decided to create a piece. I think on a multi-track; I never think mono. Art today needs to have a holistic nature; it's not the time for an atomistic, Newtonian approach to art. I don't believe in creating work that is too easily digestible. It's important to create work that resonates in every aspect of one's personal and universal self. That impulse grew into different aspects of the piece. *Hip Hop* summarizes what my struggle has been with my work in the last eight years or so. There are certain themes, certain preoccupations, certain obsessions, dreams, nightmares that I've had continuously which somehow were tied together in this piece, but not necessarily resolved.

A spiritual pigeonholing takes place in this culture; it is a feeling of my God as opposed to your God. Spiritual entrapment is shown in the spear shaking of morality in the name of decency. What is decent is to care about people, not to thumbtack them on the wall and say this is this and that is that. The mechanism of spiritual entrapment is important to the piece. The language of the piece conveys a verbal fascism that this culture continuously but very subtly lays on us, lays on itself really. The logorrhea that results is a defense mechanism that we like to use as a weapon. The tension between language and the body is shown in the way the body is made as an object of desire but an object that is memory, that is present but is also a memory in the same way that language is an object which is also present yet a memory; how is that controlled? In Hell, the relationship of the thought to the spoken word is shown in the way the body is moving continuously toward an imaginary and an actual fence and keeps bumping into it and keeps getting shoved back, the same way language continuously tries to break through this wall and it keeps getting shoved back. Ultimately what happens is that the unity of the body, thought and language breaks through the wall. It tries to refute the notion of dualism, the instance on either/or, the belief in Aristotilian [sic], Christian dualism. There is the possibility of cracking the binary system and replacing it with a holistic approach. In Hell, where the psyche of Orpheus, the psyche of Eurydice, and the psyches of the slaves interact, the language that you're hearing is at once the language that is being spoken functionally, language as a function, and language that is being spoken in order to subjugate, language of communication, language of support, language of memory but at the same time you are hearing a language that has nothing to do with any of these functions but is a language of the spirit. It ties into the history of the spirit rather than a history of material events. The history of the spirit ties into the language of the body as a function: it shits, it eats, it pisses, it fucks. The language of the body as the body/spirit is derived from the psychic physiognomy that needs all its parts in order to recreate itself. That ties into the history of the spirit as opposed to the history of the body. All these themes become united and embodied by the slaves, by the hounds, by Eurydice and by Orpheus, and are opposed by the character of the Captain, a fascist undertaker-overtaker of the underworld. When they come head to head, the wall breaks, opening the possibility of renewal, of a new birth, of love.

How does one embody abstract thought and physicalize ideas that are the essentials? This seems to be the most important question in theater. How does one manifest the invisible and the unknown without making it into a property? In order for this to happen the performers have to become primary creators. It is essential to think of the performer as a primary creator in this process because the act of becoming another person is not as urgent. What is of concern is to re-establish one's contact with an inner matrix which might not be at the forefront of one's consciousness. In order for this contact to be made the process needs to break down and regenerate continuously.

I've known these actors for a long time, and they're important to my work. Casting takes place without one's being conscious of it. Somehow it manifests itself in all its uniqueness and one does not have any choice, one sees it there. For the character of Captain, who embodies fascism, the dark nature, I wanted an actor who had savvy, coolness. I always wondered why people play Lady Macbeth so viciously, when it's more interesting to me if she appears benign; horrendous acts come out of her. Captain needed to be a poet, a Baudelaire, but grosser; he needed to be physically repellent. There's a moment when he talks about his complete loneliness, desperately clinging to a notion of immortality. There are those aspects of the character which could only be conveyed through an actor who had experienced these things but had repressed them at the same time, but who also had the technique and the savvy to convey it. In the cases of Orpheus and Eurydice, it was important to de-gender the play so it didn't become about the tensions of men–women, men–men, women–women, but was instead about the universal conflicts and specific conflicts that we deal with constantly on a human level, and about the kind of gender roles that are dictated to us. I needed to amplify and to emphasize those. The way to do that was to reverse the roles of the characters.

The quotidian movement that opens the play – Eurydice is chopping vegetables, Orpheus is typing – that reality, the surface reality, is a parallel text to the surreality, the higher reality, the super-consciousness that manifests itself through the movement of the *capoeira* dancers.[2] There is an id, an under-reality, a subconscious reality that manifests itself primarily through the activities of the underworld but it also manifests itself through the movement of the *capoeira* dancers. Certain everyday gestures are filled with psychic energy; body movement, gesture has a psychic history, a reservoir that comes with it. Certain quotidian gestures have that reservoir which one is not aware of. Motion is the one element in the human history which connects us to light, to space, and to history. In the piece motion operates by conveying those three layers of reality simultaneously.

The sub-level is the level in which the psyche speaks. In the piece Eurydice is tortured while hung upside down, Orpheus starts to pant and then he screams when he is shocked by the Captain. The panting and the scream link back to other primordial cries in the play. The *capoeira* dancers scream and make certain primordial sounds that confront their reality against something which is austere. The equivalent of this primordial level of speech is reflected in movement in act 4 in the Underworld when Orpheus suddenly starts moving not like a human being but like a four-legged animal. Orpheus's spine is suddenly misaligned.

The high volume of much of the sound in the piece is important, as sonic gesture carries a psychic residue which can't be carried in any other way. Sometimes it needs to be quite loud, and sometimes it needs to be subtle, as in the last act with the distant barking of dogs, the sound of sheep, the old man shivering.

I'm involved with the use of different media in theater rather than working purely theatrically. Media work has certain impulses which recognize the force that drives life into certain areas that become significantly mundane like the rotten fruits of St. Augustine. Light, space and motion interact through different media. The use of the rear-screen video in *Hip Hop* hooks you into the psyche of the world outside as well as the psyche of the world inside. When the Captain throws the coffin through the window, you see a world that shatters. The boy behind the window represents the forces behind the window which are facing us but which we choose not to see. At the start of the play, the figure behind the window, which was before reproduced, is now, at the end of the play, alive. That is translated through light into space, and in space translated to motion. On one level it is completely reproduced, it is not actual; on another level, it's actual, and that is only possible when you are using different media.

Footsteps in the Dark (*Pasos en la Obscuridad*) had a linear plot, rare for me, but I wanted to work with a certain formula to see how I could depart from it, how I can explore it, come to a certain understanding of the form. The form I was playing with was the trashy Mexican soap operas on Channel 34, and the Mexican game shows, both of which are the direct result of cultural colonialism. The game shows are, especially, with their simulated pleasure, pleasure created for you in order for you to feel rewarded. That notion in the Western world interests me, as there is a hunger, an addiction to being rewarded, to being pleased, to being made happy. A lot of that is simulated, is illusory, and that is especially apparent in the *tella novella* [soap opera] form, where the created reality seems, on the surface, to be about human relationships filled with troubles, but it is a step removed from that because the act of reproducing a misfortune lessens it. I was working with two of my favorite performers. One, a remarkable Mexican actor, embodies the spirit of Artaud; he acts with his entire being. His name is Carlos Nielba, who performed in drag in this piece, but the drag became totally irrelevant. His every gesture is a religious statement, as it links him to a higher aspect of himself. The way he moved his head, closed his eyes, every single gesture was formed because the impulse drove him to it. He was juxtaposed with a quintessential Los Angeles drag performer, Olga, who performs at a Hollywood drag bar. He has the same qualities as Carlos, but he is less aware of them, and he is clumsier. He is not the perfectionist that Carlos is, but he is an impassioned performer, a Maria Callas of the drag world, whose clumsiness makes him even more interesting. These two were the heroine and the anti-heroine, pitted against each other, enacting *tella novella* plots. At the end of the play there was so much darkness, there were so many pits that everyone kept falling into, that what took place was a redemptive act, an embrace. It's important to be generous, especially at this time, as we live in such chaotic and dark times. It's important, if you believe it, to offer a vision of redemption. And I do believe it; and by the end of the play there was that vision.

Before that I did a piece in New York entitled *Father Was a Peculiar Man*. The title was taken from vaudeville, which interests me a great deal. I took certain 19th century psychological realism and mixed it with vaudeville and American music hall. I'm influenced by reading about vaudeville, and also by television performers of the 1950s, who were vaudevillians: Jack Benny, Gracie Allen, Art Carney, Jackie Gleason. My hero is Buster Keaton, one of the great American artists. In fact, he is a character in *Father Was a Peculiar Man*. The point of departure for Father is *The Brothers Karamazov*; it deals with the family as a degenerating unit. We were dealing with things I'm obsessed with, like the killing of authority, in several different stages. The trajectory of the piece started with the killing of the father, patricide in the family, Karamazov; then the killing of the king, the president, the assassination of J. F. K.; then the killing of God, in the crucifixion. In the end there was a redemptive act, when after the crucifixion the audience and the actors sang "Dream a Little Dream" together. There were 60 performers, an entire marching band, and it took place in 4 street blocks of the meat packing district in New York. It is an area of cobblestone streets, abandoned storefronts and meat warehouses; it is very dark and it's all about what is happening behind closed doors in the psychic underbelly of the streets. The piece took place in some abandoned slaughter houses where you could still see the dry brown ash which remained from the blood that had been spilled there. That's where the vision of heaven and hell was created. The characters were J. F. Kennedy, Jackie O., Buster Keaton, Karamazov.

This piece played with 60s icons and the notion of icon making. It is now time for iconoclasm, time to destroy the myths we create to have something to cling to. We need to separate ourselves from them, break the icons, break the myths so that there is a possibility for renewal.

The unification of the spirit, the body, and the person is something that mystic poets write about and something I'm obsessed with. I hope to come to that one day. But there must be a purgation before certain psychic tumults can be cleansed. Until then, the chaos, the destruction is necessary. The Hindus believe in the *Kali* age, an age of destruction. This is important in order to make us aware of our responsibility to ourselves and our need to align ourselves with something which is less about our material selves and more about our spiritual ones. I say this unabashedly. It's the vogue now to believe that nature is a fake, that there is no nature, and I understand why there is a need to believe that, but even that is a paradox, because if you believe that nature is a fake, that there is no absolute truth, then simply by the act of believing you are refuting the belief that there is no belief. The sheer fact that you have the capacity to imagine a genesis, a beginning, makes it real. There is a there there.

Notes

1   A. Aronson, *American Avant-Garde Theatre: A History* (New York: Routledge, 2000), 196.
2   *Capoeira* is an African-Brazilian martial arts dance marked by acrobatics, feints, and kicks. – Editor's note.

Chapter 73

Richard Foreman (b. 1937)

Richard Foreman is an avant-garde theatre director and playwright. Founder of the Ontological-Hysteric Theater in New York, he explored the concepts of mind, pheno-menology, space, and time. Foreman has written over fifty plays, staged several plays by other authors (Brecht and Suzan-Lori Parks, for example), and has emerged as a leading figure of alternative theatre. His works countermand the Aristotelian notion of narrative and catharsis; Forman, instead, looks to Heidegger's concept of ''being-in-the-world,'' which rejects the Cartesian dualism of mind and body. Rather than catharsis as a subjective-mental reaction to plot, Forman creates theatre that underlies the immediacy of the visual and oral experience. He is influenced by Joseph Chaikin, Grotowski, and Brecht. While his plays are noted for their intellectual exercise, they are also enjoyable, employing frenzy, surprise, cabaret, and Grand Guignol. His well-known plays *Hotel China* (1971), *Egyptology* (1983), *Miss Universal Happiness* (1985), *My Head Was a Sledgehammer* (1994), and *I've Got the Shakes* (1995) express life's absurdities, folly, and chaos through the visual spectacle of bizarre and compelling images.

Foundations for a Theater (1992)

My theater has always tried to spotlight the most elusive aspects of the experience of being human. Human beings are to a great extent unknowable to themselves. Passing through each of us is a continual flow of motor and emotional impulses we are taught to give conventional names – "hunger," "lust," "aversion," "attraction." But these labels are neither

Excerpts from Richard Foreman, "Foundations for a Theater," in *Unbalancing Acts: Foundations for a Theater*, ed. Ken Jordan (New York: TCG, 1992), 3–31. © 1992 by Richard Foreman. Reprinted by permission of Pantheon Books, a division of Random House, Inc.

truthful nor accurate; condensing our wide field of impulses into a few nameable categories suppresses our awareness of the infinity of tones and feeling gradations that are part of the original impulse. As each impulse is shaped in accordance with the limited number of labels available in a society, the sense of contact with their original ambiguous flavor is lost. Perhaps your impulse has a certain flavor that relates it to "hunger" or "lust," but is neither fully one nor the other. Without a name of its own, its unique truth disappears, rechanneled into one of the already named desires.

Among the countless impulses passing through us at any moment, some surface in a manner that allows us to continue with our lives along the patterns we've inherited from our society. But any moment of true freedom suggests other structures, other textures, around which life could circle. My plays are an attempt to suggest through example that you can break open the interpretations of life that simplify and suppress the infinite range of inner human energies; that life can be lived according to a different rhythm, seen through changed eyes.

What I show on stage is a specific aspect of a chosen moment that suggests how the mind and emotions can juggle, like an acrobat, all we perceive. The strategies I use are meant to release the impulse from the straitjacket tailored for it by our society. Character, empathy, narrative – these are all straitjackets imposed on the impulse so it can be dressed up in a fashion that is familiar, comforting, and reassuring for the spectator. But I want a theater that frustrates our habitual way of seeing, and by so doing, frees the impulse from the objects in our culture to which it is invariably linked. I want to demagnetize impulse from the objects it becomes attached to. We rarely allow ourselves the psychic detachment from habit that would allow us to perceive the impulse as it rises inside us, unconnected to the objects we desire. But it's impulse that's primary, not the object we've been trained to fix it upon. It is the impulse that is your deep truth, not the object that seems to call it forth. The impulse is the vibrating, lively thing that you really are. And that is what I want to return to: the very thing you really are.

*

Society teaches us to represent our lives to ourselves within the framework of a coherent narrative, but beneath that conditioning, we *feel* our lives as a series of multidirectional impulses and collisions. We're trained to see our lives as a series of projects, one following the next along the road of experience, and our "success" depends upon how well we progress from project to project. But traveling this narrow road shuts out a multitude of suggestive impulses and impressions – the ephemeral things that feed our creative insight and spiritual energy. It's as if we were wearing blinders to restrict our emotional field, making us spiritually and psychically uneasy with the normal ambiguity of our everyday experience. So we compensate. We make self-righteous demands that noncontradiction be the basis of our value systems, but that inevitably means the suppression of all sensory richness. It reinforces our denial of the ambiguity inherent in life, which, when suppressed, makes the world seem rigid and frightening.

I like to think of my plays as an hour and a half in which you see the world through a special pair of eyeglasses. These glasses may not block out all narrative coherence, but they magnify so many other aspects of experience that you simply lose interest in trying to hold on to narrative coherence, and instead, allow yourself to become absorbed in the moment-by-moment representation of psychic freedom.

*

The aim of art, ultimately, is to speak to man's spiritual condition, his relationship with the universe. I have always felt that I'm a closet religious writer – in spite of the aggressive, erotic, playful, and schizoid elements that decorate the surface of my plays – and it is because of my essentially religious concerns that some critics have attacked my plays for not accurately representing what they refer to as "real people" with "real" interpersonal, psychological, humanistic concerns. But once you become truly interested in man's so-called religious dimension, you lose interest in making an art that only recreates the superficial dynamics of the contingent level of being that is daily life. You lose interest in the level of "personality," because you recognize it as a product of the conditioning of the social world. This conditioning interferes with our contact with the deeper ground of being by preoccupying us with the illusions of psychological, goal-oriented involvement. We live our lives focused on those forces of our culture that give rise to certain personality traits that are the warp and woof of daily life. But character and personality are accidents of circumstance. We don't choose the customs of the culture we are born into; we arrive in a culture by chance. Social life may focus our attention on character and its vicissitudes – and that's been the source from which most theatrical form has always come – but in my plays I want to evoke the deeper ground of being, the originating network of impulse, which precedes the circumstantial "I."

*

No work of art is absolutely truthful about life, but is a strategic maneuver performed on coagulated consciousness. As Picasso said, art is a lie that tells the truth. And it's a lie that tells the truth because it's a chosen, strategic maneuver, which is not the truth. No art could ever be "the truth," because it has to leave out ninety percent of life. But since even life's tiniest detail is an integral part of the interwoven whole, if you're not talking about all of life you're not really talking about the truth – you're talking about a selective distortion. Art is a perspective; all perspectives are lies about the total truth; so art is a lie that, if it is strategically chosen, wakes people up. Art is a lever to affect the mind. The truth of art is in the audience's, the individual's, awakened perceptions. It is not in the work of art.

*

In my plays I try to separate the impulse from the object that seems to evoke it, and in doing so, clarify the quality of the impulse itself. One strategy I use is to overdetermine each specific, manifest impulse, so that its origin is no longer traceable to a single object that would falsely paint it with its own qualities. For instance, in a scene where the character says, "I have difficulty getting out of the room," I try to offer several reasons why, not just one. I baffle the impulse to leave the room: first, by tying the character's foot to a table; then by putting a wall between him and the door; and finally by blinding him so he cannot see his way out of the room. This strategy overloads the context. It focuses attention on the impulse to leave the room, blocking the spectator's normal tendency to think: I know how he can leave the room – he can walk through the door. If the spectator is offered a clear solution to imagine (exit through the door), his focus will be on the mundane object ("Will he get through the door?") rather than on what is happening to the character's body and soul, or on how the character's life is changed when it is filled with the impulse, "I want to leave the room."

Paradoxically, bafflement can clarify. Bafflement can force you to refocus your vision. It is the same as making the sun so bright you're forced to look away, but as you avert your eyes you see the delicate flower you've never observed before.

*

There are several ways to isolate the impulse. One is through a strategy of interruption. Suppose an interaction between two characters is suddenly cut short by loud music, and they begin a silly dance. In this case the impulse of the scene is not allowed to fulfill itself; it's deflected. To take the example of the man who wants to leave the room, his impulse to leave might suddenly turn into a movement of the body that has nothing to do with leaving, but which suggests that impulse is still alive, though manifested in an alternate way, which allows you to observe it from a different angle.

Another way of isolating the impulse is to place it in the context of a so-called "double bind." Suppose a character sits at a table and laments to his friend, "I want to get out of the room." His friend opens a door and says, "This is the way to get out of the room." And the first replies angrily, "Why should I leave the room when I am already out of the room?" This diagrams in external dialogue a self-contradictory internal impulse, a paradoxical configuration. "Double bind" is a psychological term coined by Gregory Bateson and his associates in the fifties. In a classic double bind situation a mother asks her son, "Why don't you ever hug me? Don't you love me?" but she says it with her body tense, using a shrill tone of voice that makes it clear to the child that she has no real interest in being hugged. The child is given contradictory signals; that's the double bind. Bateson theorized that such crossed messages are at the root of schizophrenia. While I may not employ this strategy to drive people clinically crazy, I do find it useful to employ externalized double binds in my plays, because the frustration they create demagnetizes the spectator from normal avenues of conceptualization.

How can I frustrate the spectator's expectations, including his tendency to identify with the performance of a powerful actor? How can I frustrate the flow of the action within the play and prevent the inevitable drift into normal, narrative form? How can I frustrate the commonplace drive toward narrative understanding in the spectator that awakens in his consciousness a habitual identification with the goals, values, and mind-sets received from our social and cultural system? To frustrate habit is to uncover ways our impulses might be freed for use in more inventive behavior. So I try to build frustration into the very structure of my performances.

*

To make theater, all you need is a defined space and things that enter and leave that space. You could even make a play without an actor. A jar could be thrown out into an empty space, and a minute later a stick from offstage could push that jar one inch forward. That would function as theater.

Theater is presence and absence. Someone or something is either onstage, or offstage. The deeply metaphysical concerns of the playwright poet should include: who is offstage; who is onstage; who will be coming onstage; when they will come onstage; how can an entrance or an exit have real weight. "Offstage" is a term used only in a specifically theatrical context. There is no equivalent term relevant to the consideration of a painting or a poem. Referring to a painting, you might say something is outside the frame, but that does not have the weight of something that takes place "offstage" in the theater. In film, you assume that what you see on the screen is part of a contextual environment that is always present, "onstage," even though only one part of that environment is captured by the camera in an individual shot.

Most people claim that theater requires an audience. I disagree. I can imagine an entire audience walking out of a performance while the play continues to the end, and yet it remains a powerful piece of theater. I can imagine every member of an audience falling asleep and the play continuing to the end, turning into an objectification of the dream of that audience. Art, conceived as a revelatory process, can indeed spin its web in the void. Who knows who is really watching? When a huge audience seems to be watching, it may be only a mass collection of habitual responses planted in the seats of the theater. When nobody seems to be watching, perhaps an invisible god has his eyes on the performance. This may well be a different kind of theater than any that has ever existed. So be it. [...]

Chapter 74

Suzan-Lori Parks (b. 1964)

Suzan-Lori Parks is a playwright and screenwriter. Her plays, *Imperceptible Mutabilities in the Third Kingdom* (1986), *The America Play* (1990), *Venus* (1996), *In the Blood* (2000), and *Topdog/Underdog* (2004), examine the meaning of history and identity as they inform race and gender. Parks playfully casts famous people (Lincoln, for instance) as black in order to highlight the flexibility of received wisdom. She opposes the obvious, sentimental, and "message play," searching instead for modes of expression that explore new territory of language and gesture.

Elements of Style (1994)

I'm writing this essay for 2 reasons. First: to talk about my work – to give those readers, scholars, directors and performers of my plays a way in – so that instead of calling me up they can, with this "guide," dive into an examination with great confidence. Secondly, I want to examine what seems to me a real crisis in American dramatic literature. I'm hoping to form a sort of bulwark against an insidious, tame-looking, schmaltz-laden mode of expression that threatens to cover us all, like Vesuvius, in our sleep.

As a writer my job is to write good plays; it's also to defend dramatic literature against becoming "Theatre of Schmaltz." For while there are several playwrights whose work I love love love, it also seems that in no other form of writing these days is the writing so awful – so intended to produce some reaction of sorts, to discuss some issue: the play-as-wrapping-paper-version-of-hot-newspaperheadline, trying so hard to be so hip; so uninterested in the craft of writing: the simple work of putting one word next to another;

Suzan-Lori Parks, "Elements of Style" (1994), in Parks, *The American Play and Other Works* (New York: TCG, 1995), 6–18.
© 1995 by Suzan-Lori Parks. Reprinted by permission of Theatre Communications Group.

so uninterested in the marvel of live bodies on stage. Theatre seems mired in the interest of stating some point, or tugging some heartstring, or landing a laugh, or making a splash, or wagging a finger. In no other artform are the intentions so slim! As a playwright I try to do many things: explore the form, ask questions, make a good show, tell a good story, ask more questions, take nothing for granted.

This essay is intended primarily for the new generation of theatre makers. For those of us who haven't yet reached the point where we can say we've spent ½ our lives in theatre. I've been writing plays for 11 years now; all along I've felt that the survival of this splendid artform – an art that is not "poor film" or "cheap TV" but an art so specific and strange in its examination of the human condition – depends not only on the older guard but also on those of us who are relative newcomers.

There are many ways to challenge ourselves as theatre artists. Here are some ideas, feelings, thoughts, takes on the world, riffs, ways of approaching the word, the page, the event, the subject, the stage, that keep me *awake*.

theatre

Jesus. Right from the *jump*, ask yourself: "Why does this thing I'm writing *have* to be *a play*?" The words "why," "have" and "play" are key. If you don't have an answer then get out of town. No joke. The last thing American theatre needs is another lame play.

form and content

Form is never more than an extension of content. – Robert Creeley to Charles Olson

A playwright, as any other artist, should accept the bald fact that content determines form and form determines content; that form and content are interdependent. Form should not be looked at askance and held suspect – form is not something that "gets in the way of the story" but is an integral part of the story. This understanding is important to me and my writing. This is to say that as I write along the container dictates what sort of substance will fill it and, at the same time, the substance is dictating the size and shape of the container. Also, "form" is not a strictly "outside" thing while "content" stays "inside." It's like this: I am an African-American woman – this is the form I take, my content predicates this form, and this form is inseparable from my content. No way could I be me otherwise.

Playwrights are often encouraged to write 2-act plays with traditional linear narratives. Those sorts of plays are fine, but we should understand that the form is not merely a docile passive vessel, but an active participant in the sort of play which ultimately inhabits it. Why linear narrative at all? Why choose that shape? If a playwright chooses to tell a dramatic story, and realizes that there are essential elements of that story which lead the writing outside the realm of "linear narrative," then the play naturally assumes a new shape. I'm saying that the inhabitants of Mars do not look like us. Nor should they. I'm also saying that Mars is with us – right on our doorstep and should be explored. Most playwrights who consider themselves avant-garde spend a lot of time badmouthing the more traditional forms. The naturalism of, say, Lorraine Hansberry is beautiful and should not be dismissed simply because it's naturalism. We should understand that realism, like other movements in other artforms, is a specific response to a certain historical climate. I don't explode the form because I find traditional plays "boring" – I don't really. It's just that those structures never could accommodate the figures which take up residence inside me.

repetition and revision

"Repetition and Revision" is a concept integral to the Jazz esthetic in which the composer or performer will write or play a musical phrase once and again and again; etc. – with each revisit the phrase is slightly revised. "Rep & Rev" as I call it is a central element in my work; through its use I'm working to create a dramatic text that departs from the traditional linear narrative style to look and sound more like a musical score. In my first play, *The Sinners Place* (1983), history simply repeated itself. With *Imperceptible Mutabilities* (1986) and the others I got a little more adventurous. With each play I'm finding the only way that that particular dramatic story can be told. I'm also asking how the structure of Rep & Rev and the stories inherent in it – a structure which creates a drama of accumulation – can be accommodated under the rubric of Dramatic Literature where, traditionally, all elements lead the audience toward some single explosive moment.

Repetition: we accept it in poetry and call it "incremental refrain." For the most part, incremental refrain creates a weight and a rhythm. In dramatic writing it does the same – yes; but again, what about all those words over and over? We all want to get to the CLIMAX. Where does repetition fit? First, it's not just repetition but repetition with revision. And in drama change, revision, is the thing. Characters refigure their words and through a refiguring of language show us that they are experiencing their situation anew. Secondly, a text based on the concept of repetition and revision is one which breaks from the text which we are told to write – the text which cleanly ARCS. Thirdly, Rep & Rev texts create a real challenge for the actor and director as they create a physical life appropriate to that text. In such plays we are not moving from A → B but rather, for example, from A → A → A → B → A. Through such movement we refigure A. And if we continue to call this movement FORWARD PROGRESSION, which I think it is, then we refigure the idea of forward progression. And if we insist on calling writings structured with this in mind PLAYS, which I think they are, then we've got a different kind of dramatic literature.

What does it mean for characters to say the same thing twice? 3 times? Over and over and over and oh-vah. Yes. How does that affect their physical life? Is this natural? Non-natural? Real? In *Betting on the Dust Commander* (1987), the "climax" could be the accumulated weight of the repetition – a residue that, like city dust, stays with us.

After years of listening to Jazz, and classical music too, I'm realizing that my writing is very influenced by music; how much I employ its methods. Through reading lots I've realized how much the idea of Repetition and Revision is an integral part of the African and African-American literary and oral traditions.

I am most interested in words and how they impact on actors and directors and how those folks physicalize those verbal aberrations. How does this Rep & Rev – a literal incorporation of the past – impact on the creation of a theatrical experience?

time

I walk around with my head full of lay-person ideas about the universe. Here's one of them: "Time has a circular shape." Could Time be tricky like the world once was – looking flat from our place on it – and through looking at things beyond the world we found it round? Somehow I think Time could be like this too. Not that I'm planning to write a science book – the goofy idea just helps me NOT to take established shapes for granted.

[. . .]

etymology

I spend a lot of time reading the dictionary. The word "grammar" is etymologically related to the word "charm." Most words have fabulous etymologies. Thrilling histories. Words are very old things. Because words are so old they hold; they have a big connection with the what was. Words are spells in our mouths. My interest in the history of words – where they came from, where they're going – has a direct impact on my playwrighting [*sic*] because, for me, Language is a physical act. It's something which involves your entire body – not just your head. Words are spells which an actor consumes and digests – and through digesting creates a performance on stage. Each word is configured to give the actor a clue to their physical life. Look at the difference between "the" and "thuh." The "uh" requires the actor to employ a different physical, emotional, vocal attack.

ghost

A person from, say, time immemorial, from, say, PastLand, from somewhere back there, say, walks into my house. She or he is always alone and will almost always take up residence in a corner. Why they're alone I don't know. Perhaps they're coming missionary style – there are always more to follow. Why they choose a corner to stand in I don't know either – maybe because it's the intersection of 2 directions – maybe because it's safe.

They are not *characters*. To call them so could be an injustice. They are *figures, figments, ghosts, roles, lovers* maybe, *speakers* maybe, *shadows, slips, players* maybe, maybe *someone else's pulse.*

[. . .]

bad Math

x + y = meaning. The ability to make simple substitutions is equated with *clarity*. We are taught that plays are merely staged essays and we begin to believe that characters in plays are symbols for some obscured "meaning" rather than simply the thing itself. As Beckett sez: "No symbols where none intended." Don't ask playwrights what their plays mean; rather, tell them what you think and have an exchange of ideas.

the NEA hoopla

Overweight southern senators are easy targets. They too easily become focal points of all evil, allowing the arts community to WILLFULLY IGNORE our own bigotry, our own petty evils, our own intolerance which – evil senators or no – will be the death of the arts.

history

History is time that won't quit.

dance

If you're one who writes sitting down, once before you die try dancing around as you write. It's the old world way of getting to the deep shit.

humor

A playwright should pack all five, all six – all 7 senses. The 6th helps you feel another's pulse at great distances; the 7th sense is the sense of humor. Playwrights can come from the most difficult circumstances, but having a sense of humor is what happens when you "get out of the way." It's sorta Zen. Laughter is very powerful – it's not a way of escaping anything but a way of arriving on the scene. Think about laughter and what happens to your body – it's almost the same thing that happens to you when you throw up.

action in the line

The action goes in the line of dialogue instead of always in a pissy set of parentheses. How the line should be delivered is contained in the line itself. Stage directions disappear. Dialogue becomes rich and strange. It's an old idea. The Greeks did it and Shakespeare too, all over the place. Something to try at least once before you die.

sex

People have asked me why I don't put any sex in my plays. "The Great Hole of History" – like, duh.

a (rest)

Take a little time, a pause, a breather; make a transition.

a spell

An elongated and heightened (rest). Denoted by repetition of figures' names with no dialogue. Has sort of an architectural look.

LUCY		LINCOLN
BRAZIL		BOOTH
THE FOUNDLING FATHER	*and*	LINCOLN
LUCY		BOOTH
BRAZIL		LINCOLN
THE FOUNDLING FATHER		BOOTH
and		
THE FOUNDLING FATHER		

THE FOUNDLING FATHER
THE FOUNDLING FATHER

This is a place where the figures experience their pure true simple state. While no "action" or "stage business" is necessary, directors should fill this moment as they best see fit.

The feeling: look at a daguerreotype; or: the planets are aligning and as they move we hear the music of their spheres. A spell is a place of great (unspoken) emotion. It's also a place for an emotional transition. [...]

language is a physical act

> Language is a physical act – something that
> involves yr whole bod.
> Write with yr whole bod.
> Read with yr whole bod.
> Wake up.

opening night

Don't be shy about looking gorgeous.
I suggest black.

Chapter 75

Rebecca Schneider (b. 1959)

Rebecca Schneider is one of the important scholars of performance studies. She is concerned with feminism as a bodily performance. Her work covers early manifestations of feminist performance such as artists Carolee Schneemann, Shigeko, and Suzanne Lacy, as well as later 1980s work by stand-up comics and performers Annie Sprinkle, Cindy Sherman, Karen Finley, Ann Magnuson, Sandra Bernhard, Robbie McCauley, and the Native American theatre group Spider Women. For Schneider these performers "speak-back" to the audience, i.e., they turn the gaze back onto those seeking delectation. The value of their work challenges the explicit determination of who is viewing whom. Schneider considers the "break" with theatre's received concepts of perception and ontology in what she calls "the explicit body."

The Explicit Body in Performance (1997)

For decades now on sunny Sundays after brunch, fur-clad uptowners and in-the-know suburbanites have clogged downtown Manhattan's West Broadway sidewalks. Eyeballing each other at galleries and grazing in expensive shops, these *porno flâneurs* rub shoulders with black-leathered SoHo aesthetes, exchanging insignia of fashion. In 1985, a new breed of poster began to appear around and about downtown, especially near major SoHo art galleries. Strolling the avenue, a wandering eye might catch a boldfaced byline from one of these posters: ONLY FOUR COMMERCIAL GALLERIES IN NEW YORK SHOW BLACK WOMEN. ONLY ONE SHOWS MORE THAN ONE. In the late 1980s, art patrons might have stopped and thought before putting down money. As the posters gained in infamy [...] shoppers might have inquired within – were these posters, by the Guerrilla Girls, for sale?

On one poster, a list of twenty galleries is followed by the words "THESE GALLERIES SHOW NO MORE THAN 10 PER CENT WOMEN ARTISTS OR NONE AT ALL." Other posters pose pointed questions: "DO WOMEN HAVE TO BE NAKED TO GET INTO THE MET MUSEUM?" This particular poster features a naked woman in a gorilla mask beside statistics on the Metropolitan Museum of Arts modern artists (more than 95 per cent male) and nudes (85 per cent female).

The group responsible for the posters is a feminist "gang" of artists who call themselves The Guerrilla Girls. These "girls," all working artists, appear in public wearing gorilla masks. They keep their identities secret to protect an anonymity which frees them to speak openly, without fear of reprisal, but also insures that notoriety cannot accrue to an individual career. Large and hairy, their masks have the look of generic department-store Halloween stock. While the masks render anonymity, they also render literal a certain symbolic paradigm. Not only do "gorilla" masks pun on "guerrilla" acts to create a kind of side-stepping, material translation, but the masks wield performative punch – they make explicit a social contract which has historically marked women and people of color as less evolved, more "primitive," than the implicitly higher primate, white Man. Alluding to primitivity, the gorilla masks appear to quote the racist primitivism at the heart of colonialism as well as the mimesis of all things "primitive" at the base of modern art. The conflation of the "primitive" mask with the masked identities of the female artists suggests a complex interrelatedness between codings of race and gender, especially vis-à-vis the politics of representation and artistic authority.

Here, word play doubles as deeply serious body play, wrapped up with the ways words have played, with significant effect, upon bodies – bodies on the avenue, in the galleries, in the mirror, and framed as art. As the posters make abundantly clear, the appellations "female" or "black" are words which have historically overridden or amended the appellation "artist" when these words have been applied to the same person. Importantly, collapsing guerrilla and gorilla suggests a certain terror(ism) at the heart of hierarchical distinctions of difference, such as civilized/primitive or male/female. By collapsing the homophones across their own bodies in performative action, the artists render the symbolic literal. Their pun confuses the space between symbolic and literal reading, and in so doing it both plays with and questions dominant habits of comprehension. [...] Rendering a word in translation (here translated across homophones) as if words were *materially* interchangeable underscores a literal versus symbolic meaning and un-settles habitual modes of sense making. Though wrapped in a laugh, Guerrilla Girls arguably provoke a threat in the form of critical inquiry into implicit structures of comprehensibility which have delineated terrains of art and validity of artists according to bodily signatures of gender and race. With all the force of literal translation, the posters, and their anonymous simian signatories, work to make those masked structures apparent.

[...] I have coined the phrase "explicit body" as a means of addressing the ways such work aims to explicate bodies in social relation. Interestingly, the words "explicit" and "explicate" stem from the Latin *explicare*, which means to "unfold." Unfolding the body, as if pulling back velvet curtains to expose the stage, the performance artists [...] peel back layers of signification that surround their bodies like ghosts at a grave. Peeling at signification, bringing ghosts to visibility, they are interested to expose not an originary, true, redemptive body, but the sedimented layers of signification themselves.

A mass of orifices and appendages, details and tactile surfaces, the explicit body in representation is foremost a site of social markings, physical parts and gestural signatures of gender, race, class, age, sexuality – all of which bear ghosts of historical meaning, markings delineating social hierarchies of privilege and disprivilege. The body made explicit has become the *mise en scène* for a variety of feminist artists. [...]

Researching thirty years of feminist explicit body performance from its early manifestations in the 1960s, I found a number of recurrent themes. First, much explicit body performance replays, across the body of the artist as stage, the historical drama of gender or race (and sometimes, brilliantly, gender and race). Second, these artists critically engage ways of seeing, specifically perspectivalism, which has inscribed women as given to be seen but not as given to see. Third, these artists often tug at the plumb lines marking bodies for gender, race, and class in order to expose their link with representational structures of desire in commodity capitalism. And fourth, feminist explicit body work talks back to precedent terms of avant-garde art transgression, raising questions about modernist "shock value" and the particular fascination with a "primitive," sexual, and excremental body. At base, the explicit body in much feminist work interrogates socio-cultural understandings of the "appropriate" and/or the appropriately transgressive – particularly who gets to mark what (in)appropriate where, and, who has the right to appropriate what where – keeping in mind the double meaning of the word "appropriate." [...]

Ghost of the Avant-Garde

One of the complexities that riddles contemporary performance art is the status of transgression in art practice today. Inasmuch as postmodernity necessitates a distinction from modernity, cultural critics and postmodern theorists have made the claim that the avant-garde, and its "bad boy" hope in the political promise of transgression, died sometime in the 1960s. As the argument goes, late capitalism appropriates, incorporates, and consumes transgression into fashionable chic at such a rapid pace that the subversive impact of transgression has become impossible. [...]

Basically, there is cause for suspicion. Hasn't it historically been the case that boys are given to transgress while girls are meant to resist? That boys are expected to transgress re-marks the tradition of bad-boy art as always already normative, and rewrites the modernist avant-garde as less transgressive than structurally institutional. [...] But abandoning transgression might not be the issue so much as critically confronting the historical licensing of transgression in art practice. When women as active agents picked up the avant-garde tradition of transgressive shock, as they began to do with a certain *en masse* fervor in the 1960s, the terms of transgression necessarily shifted. Female transgression presented a structural impossibility – almost a double shock. After all, men transgress, women resist. [...]

At the very least, to suggest that nothing shocks anymore is certainly curious in an age of conservative right-wing anxiety over the "appropriate" cultural limits of aesthetic expression. Still, looked at from another angle, the abandonment of the avant-garde and the championing of "resistance" takes on an important political dimension. Conservatives are arguably nostalgic for modernist belief in the power of transgression, since transgression, or the inappropriate, certainly props the appropriate. If nothing can be considered transgressive, then nothing can be considered (in)appropriate. In their nostalgia for the (in)appropriate, the right wing make strange bedfellows with feminist, gay, and lesbian artists whom they see as providing contemporary transgression. [...] Looked at in this light, the politicized postmodern art world's claim that all transgression is defunct is in itself transgressive, disallowing the "transgression" upon which right-wing agendas depend. And yet the timing of this claim is suspiciously gender-, race-, and preference-marked, coming at a moment when the terms of transgression, the agents of transgressive art, had radically shifted. The terrain is tangled indeed. [...]

Desire and the Satiate Body

In much feminist explicit body performance art we can find, with the tools of feminist theory, an effort to make apparent the link between ways of seeing the body and ways of structuring desire according to the logic of commodity capitalism. [...] The image of the female body has, throughout the twentieth century, served as a symbol of desire in general. That desire might masquerade as "male," but it has recently been explored in its secret service, that is, its service to the general circulation of commodities in a dreamscape upon which late capitalism so intrinsically depends. Desire is bought into, just as any tangible object is bought. Like a commodity, desire is produced. And like the commodities it facilitates, desire bears a secret akin to Marx's secret of commodities. The secret of circulating, insatiable desire is the labor that goes into its construction. Desire must appear as unmarked, as "human nature." But, like commodities themselves, it is nature designed, packaged, and sold – marketed, outfitted, and set upon a runway of dreams where it is also marked for gender as if by some great accident of God: desire is masculinized; the desired, feminized.

The ways in which desire in late capitalism is instituted and circulated as insatiable, promoting infinite accumulation, has placed the emblematic female body in a particular relation to impossibility – always just beyond reach, symbolizing that which can never quite be acquired, even for those possessing a body marked female. I have worked in these pages to link the emblematic inaccessibility of the woman-as-commodity-mascot with the legacies of perspectival ways of seeing which have erected the female body as Prime Signifier of the Vanishing Point – Dominatrix *and* Madonna of Loss: This effort was inspired by what appears in so much explicit body art as a ribald refusal to vanish, an excess linked to disruptions of normative "appropriate" vision. Such disruptions have marked these artists' works as politically volatile – threatening, perhaps, to a comprehensibility structured, like our society, around the insatiability of commodity exchange.

In general, I am fascinated by the ubiquitous and nostalgic paradigms of loss which riddle a society devoted to accumulation. Western civilization is in thrall to a "Real" we are acculturated to accept as forever beyond our grasp – keeping us reaching, keeping us spending. Platonic shadowscapes of illusion on cave walls have hardly disappeared. We still grasp for a truer reality beyond or behind the scenes as Plato's cave shadows become the flicker of representation across ad-scapes and TV screens. In my own strivings for some "true-real" I attempt to be more materialist than idealist, but I am hinged to a contradiction. I am drawn to the paradox, explicated by feminist theory, that the female body in representation has emblematized *both* the obsessive terrain of representational fantasy *and*, as empress/impress of the vanishing point, that which escapes or is beyond the representational field. [...] Signifying desire, "she" is the obsessive emblem of representational fantasy – we see her body everywhere, selling a dream of a future real to a present posited always as "lack." Yet even as she is ubiquitously given to be seen, she simultaneously signifies a flirtatious impossibility of access, a paradoxical "reality" only of dream, of shadow, always beyond reach, always already lost.

Insatiable desire and paradigmatic lack are performative: the signs of desire and the drive of loss depend on bodies in exigency. Dramas of loss and insatiable desire are scripted across bodies, as images of men and women prop object relations driving commodity dreamscapes. Much explicit body performance art work aims to make explicit, to render literal, the symbolic foundations by which the thrall of loss and insatiability is exhibited in the space of the particular – across particular bodies engendered in social relation. The aim is not necessarily to erect a "True Woman," a "Real Woman," as much as to explicate the historical service of bodies to commodity dreamscapes and to wrestle with the effects of that service.

To render the symbolic literal is to disrupt and make apparent the fetishistic prerogatives of the symbol by which a thing, such as a body or a word, stands by convention for something else. To render literal is to collapse symbolic space. [...] It is to pose [...] a "direct threat" to the naturalized social drama of "comprehensibility." To render literal is also to interrogate the notion that relations between sign and signified are fundamentally arbitrary. Denying the arbitrary, a notion at the very base of modernist and capitalist sensibilities of abstraction and meaning, invites a kind of hysteria, or a psychosis of the overly real – a psychosis historically linked to women.

In exploring the explicit body in performance I look at ways in which perspectival vision and commodity fetishism are played back across *the body as stage*. I argue for a critical (and ironically distantiated) "take" on the very distance between sign and signified, like the distance between viewer and viewed, in normative habits of comprehension. The performers in this study use their bodies as the stages across which they re-enact social dramas and traumas which have arbitrated cultural differentiations between truth and illusion, reality and dream, fact and fantasy, natural and unnatural, essential and constructed. The performers make apparent the ways in which bodies are stages for social theatrics, propping hosts of cultural assumptions, and their works suggest that these social theatrics might be differently scripted, differently dramatized, differently realized. Social dramas of foundational loss and dances of insatiable desire smack against explicitly literal bodily renderings which suggest the satiate and finite. Indeed, rendered literal, symbolic constructs can become volatile, and full of critical potential. As if enacting Barbara Kruger's art slogan "Your Gaze Hits the Side of My Face," much explicit body performance work suggests a confrontational satiability (both of pleasure and pain), and a refusal of the logic of infinite loss. [...]

Chapter 76

Peggy Phelan (b. 1959)

Cultural theorist and performance studies scholar Peggy Phelan is the Ann O'Day Maples Chair of Drama at Stanford University. She has been in the vanguard of new concepts of performance theory. Along with Latin American performance scholar Diana Taylor, founder of the important Western Hemisphere Project which illuminates performance and politics in the Americas,[1] Phelan investigates the political efficacies of performance for social change. Influenced by Derrida, Phelan considers "embodied silence," the space where the presence of those "unmarked" (unreferenced) by their marginalization can be identified. In her important work, *Unmarked*, she says that the site of the unmarked "is not spatial; nor is it temporal; it is not metaphorical; nor is it literal. It is a configuration of subjectivity that exceeds, even while informing, both the gaze and language. In the riots of sound language produces, the unmarked can be heard as silence. In the plentitude of pleasure produced by photographic vision, the unmarked can be seen as negative."[2] *Unmarked* also defines the "ontology of performance," emphasizing the "liveness" of performance which only has life in the present: "Performance cannot be saved, recorded, documented, or otherwise participate in the circulation of representations of representation" (6). The following extract is from her other work, *Mourning Sex* (1997), which examines the complexities of loss and grieving in art and society.

Mourning Sex: Performing Public Memories (1997)

I once had a beautiful book with a shiny red vinyl cover. The book's title I cannot remember, something along the lines of "The Wonder of Science" or "Science for Children" or "Science and Other Mysteries." The book had gorgeously detailed illustrations of the interior of

Excerpts from Peggy Phelan, *Mourning Sex: Performing Public Memories* (London: Routledge, 1997), 1–5. © 1997 by Peggy Phelan. Reprinted by permission of Taylor and Francis Books UK.

thermometers and maps of how clouds formed. It was a fascinating book and I read it with a kind of unbounded thirst. I did not read according to the law of genre but I somehow knew that this particular book was different from my other favorite book, *Old Peter's Russian Fairy Tales*, a big gold-covered worn book with fabulous colored drawings of witches and cauldrons, and different still from the flat beige encyclopedia with small black and white diagrams of machines. What I loved about the red science book was its exhilaration, its sense of true wonder. This wonder was of a different sort from the "let's pretend" of most fairy tales and the secure facts of the encyclopedia.

The red book was also an alluring tactile object – its cover could handle my peanut butter and jelly-coated fingers, and on the last page there was a pop-up anatomy of a man that I quickly demolished. I don't remember why I tore it out, probably because I could. I liked to feel my strength in those days, and paper was a foe I could master. I remember looking at the hole I had made with great pride. I showed it to my sister, laughing about how this outline was a much better anatomy of a man than the one with red ink and blue veins provided by the book publishers. My sister did not understand my delight but she indulged me anyway and asked if I wanted to make another pop-up model. I did not, but I lacked the words then to tell her why.

Maybe it has taken me all these years to find the words to explain why I thought the loss of the pop-up model revealed the anatomy of the body more fully than the drawing. (Maybe such a claim will locate us more securely in the law of this genre: introduction to a critical book). The body's anatomy was the primary wonder of the wonder of science because it could not be represented without tearing the body open. When the body was opened, science rushed in. Anatomy established an interiority to the body that transformed representation itself (and was itself predicated on changes in representational technologies – most notably perspective). Even within the genre of science-for-5-year-olds, anatomy demanded and merited a form of representation denied to clouds and thermometers. The pop-up model was one way to signal this difference in representation.

Tearing out the pop-up art and refusing science's comprehensible mysteries, I created a gouged page that held the hole where the body once was. [...] I want to say that that gesture was my first piece of performance art. It was an act whose primary goal was to enact the disappearance of the manifest visual object. Performance and theatre are instances of enactments predicated on their own disappearance. Like a detective's chalk rendering of a murdered body, the demolished pop-up page illustrated the outline of a body in a state of arrested movement. The book now presented the shadow of a man lying down in a pale white casket, a man's outline asleep in the page's proscenium stage, a chiselled tracing of a body that I had forcefully and gleefully evicted from my red book. I wanted the outline of that body, its paper ghost, much more than I wanted the illustrated body.

If this was my first piece of performance art, an "if" that has a certain pedagogical virtue for me now, it was also my first sense of the deep relationship between bodies and holes, and between performance and the phantasmatical. I loved that red book in part because it illustrated something about what haunted me even then, the ghostly mysteries of what we cannot see. Theatre, of course, has had a long romance with ghosts and it would not be too much to say that the theatricality of spiritualism, parapsychology, and other ghostly (pseudo)sciences owes something to theatre's conviction that it can make manifest what cannot be seen. From the ghost of Hamlet's father to the ghost in the machine of contemporary theatre's special effects, Western theatre has had a sustained conversation with the incorporeal. The specific weight given to the physical sets and settings of theatrical performances create a kind of mausoleum, a space designed to summon the phantasmatical charge of the immaterial.

As our current cultural moment is buffeted on one side by the claims of virtual reality and electronic presence, and on the other by a politicized and commodified spirituality (from Christian fundamentalism to new age gurus), it behooves us to think more seriously about what theatre and performance have to teach us about the possibilities and perils of summoning the incorporeal. To what end are we seeking an escape from bodies? What are we mourning when we the catastrophe and exhilaration of embodiment? [. . .]

I am investigating, in *Mourning Sex*, the possibility that something substantial can be made from the outline left after the body has disappeared. My hunch is that the affective outline of what we've lost might bring us closer to the bodies we want still to touch than the restored illustration can. Or at least the hollow of the outline might allow us to understand more deeply why we long to hold bodies that are gone.

Performance and theatre make manifest something both more than and less than "the body." And yet the acts made visible in theatre and performance are acts that we attribute over and over again to bodies, often immaterial and phantasmatic ones. [. . .]

The enactment of invocation and disappearance undertaken by performance and theatre is precisely the drama of corporeality itself. At once a consolidated fleshly form and an eroding, decomposing formlessness, the body beckons us and resists our attempts to remake it. This resistant beckoning was the lure for this writing, a writing toward and against bodies who die.

I

The title *Mourning Sex* is meant to respond to the end of a certain possibility opened up by what social historians and fast-typing journalists have called the "sexual revolution." It never seemed to me that the "revolutionary" part of the sexual revolution stemmed entirely from the act, the performance of corporeal choreography that it denominated. Viewed from the sidelines where those too young to participate are always consigned to observe, the revolutionary aspect of the sexual revolution seemed to come from the self-consciously forged relationship between desire and act, between will and body, that made apparent a new social, psychic, and political relationship to making itself. The making in "making love" marks an allegiance to nothing more and nothing less than the force of the desire to make something in the present tense. The particular making enacted through sex, with sex, and in sex, quickly bleeds from the thing itself into social, psychic, and political making more broadly, more publicly, imagined. If people could copulate without coercion (an "if" that remains primarily phantasmatic for many women), if people could touch without the restraining influences of orthodox social codes (even while rapidly establishing new orthodoxies), how might making love and having sex become revolutionary acts? What language would be made in this making? What death? These latter questions, realized through the spectacle of the "liberation" of sexual acts, opened up a way of thinking that transformed social politics. Sex was in every way necessary to that opening but what was opened exceeded physical sexual acts.

The possibilities opened up by the sexual revolution, we have been told, have been foreclosed by the onslaught of AIDS. This claim is both shockingly inaccurate and deceptively true. The reasons for the foreclosure of those possibilities are many and AIDS is, among other things, a *tabula rasa* for the projections of multiple myths. But I am not interested here in providing another interpretation of the last thirty years of US cultural, sexual, political and social history. I am concerned rather with how we perform our mourning, how we recover from the trauma of loss. I find that the most compelling explanations for the intricate working through of mourning come from psychoanalytic theory. This theory accounts for the affective force of the sexual and psychic remaking that surviving loss entails. As we go about making new sexualities in the technologies and misprisions of "safe(r) sex" we all mourn the loss of the "liberation" (however phantasmatical) that stands behind this remaking.

One of the propositions informing this argument is one that I cannot prove but nonetheless find generative. What psychoanalysis makes clear is that the experience of loss is one of the central repetitions of subjectivity. It may well be that just as linguists have argued that syntax is "hard-wired" into the brain which allows infants to discern that specific sounds are language bits, perhaps the syntax of loss is hard-wired into the psyche which structures our encounters with the world. Severed from the placenta and cast from the womb, we enter the world as amputated body whose being will be determined by the very mortality of that body. Prior to recognizing the specific content of an affective grief, perhaps the human subject is born ready to mourn. Perhaps a psychic syntax of mourning is in place before the subject learns specific vocabularies of grief. Without such a syntax, the subject might be overwhelmed and find life-as-loss unbearable.

The psyche has no material form and yet in describing it we tend often to give it a body. From the mystic writing pad to the ghost in the microprocessor, we have attempted to speak of the psyche as a body, however phantasmatical. We talk about the psyche as something subject to wounds, to tears, to traumas. We believe it can be made healthy. We eat it, in short, as a body.

Throughout *Mourning Sex* I rely on "trauma" as a way to understand injuries to both body and psyche. Psychoanalysis gives us the idea that trauma is simultaneously untouchable and remarkably unattached to, untouching of, what surrounds it. Often trauma is not recognized until well after it has happened, in part because it is a complete, contained event. Trauma's potency comes in part from how well it is contained. When I say trauma is untouchable, I mean that it cannot be represented. The symbolic cannot carry it: trauma makes a tear in the symbolic network itself. [...]

Notes

1   The Western Hemisphere Project is a collection of student activists exploring a variety of social issues concerning people in the Western Hemisphere. They present several websites and radio shows.
2   P. Phelan, *Unmarked: The Politics of Performance* (London: Routledge, 1993), 27.

Chapter 77

Erika Fischer-Lichte

Critic, scholar, and theatre historian Erika Fischer-Lichte has contributed to the fields of theatre semiotics. Like Patrice Pavis (see Chapter 61), she is one of theatre's leading semioticians. Among her many important books are *The Semiotics of Theatre* (1992), *The Show and the Gaze of Theatre: A European Perspective* (1997), *History of European Drama and Theatre* (2004), and *Theatre, Sacrifice, Ritual: Exploring Forms of Political Theatre* (2005). Fischer-Lichte investigates the cultural signs of performance, the meaning of the actor in society, and the representation of gesture and action onstage. Among her major concerns is the division between dramatic and performance text. Her studies analyze how scripts translate to the stage and what processes are involved in such a translation.

Written Drama/Oral Performance (1997)

The Drama: Literature or Theatre?

Theatre in the West is essentially characterized by the tension between written drama and orality. Since Aristotle, there has been much dissent as to whether drama should be considered under literature as writing or under theatre as orality. While Aristotle sharply distinguished drama as literary text from its performance in the theatre [...] drama theorists today tend to classify drama as a "multimedial text."[1] This is a valid approach since literary theory has consistently neglected the dimension of performance. Some

Excerpts from Erika Fischer-Lichte, "Written Drama/Oral Performance," in *The Show and the Gaze of Theatre: A European Perspective* (Iowa City: University of Iowa Press, 1997), 319–37. © 1997 by The University of Iowa Press. Reprinted by permission of the publisher.

conclusions drawn on the basis of such an approach, however, may not always be entirely appropriate.

This is because there are fundamental differences between the performance of a drama and its literary text in terms of both the media and semiotics. Drama, with its fixed, written text, belongs to the class monomedial texts. The performance, on the other hand, which at the very least is communicated by two media – the stage and the actor – belongs to the class multimedial texts. While the literary text consists exclusively of homogeneous linguistic/written signs, and even complex signs (such as character and plot) arise through the combination of linguistic/written signs, the performance is made up of heterogeneous signs which may be verbal or nonverbal (mime, gesture, proxemics, mask, costume, props, set, sounds, music). The literary text of the drama belongs, therefore, to the category writing, the performance of the drama, on the other hand, to orality.

This important distinction between the drama and its performance in media and semiotics has far-reaching consequences in the study of the dramatic dialogue. For the dramatic dialogue primarily represents – even in the fixed, literary text – a face-to-face interaction which, by definition, must fall within the sphere of orality. Second, the language of the dialogue can be constructed so differently that its variants can range across a whole continuum extending between two extremes – a highly elaborate written language and a completely artless spoken language. The tension between writing and orality is thus both constitutive and productive for the dramatic dialogue as much in the literary text of the drama as in its performance.

Our point of departure stems from this unique feature of the dramatic dialogue. The dramatic dialogue is a specific meaning-generating system that is made up of the special alternating relations between writing and orality.

[. . .] In the context of our discussion, it is the dramatic dialogue in performance which provides the more interesting and varying functions. Since, however, it is most often based on a literary dramatic dialogue, an introductory systematic of the types of literary dramatic dialogue relevant to our theme is outlined below.

The Literary Dramatic Dialogue

Every literary dramatic dialogue is – as is the whole text of the drama – organized into "primary" and "secondary" text. The secondary text may be limited to giving the name of the person speaking – and thereby changes in who has the floor – or extended to the provision of detailed information on intonation, mime, gesture, posture, and movement of the speaker or listener. In some cases it may grow into an independent descriptive text of considerable size. Every literary dramatic dialogue thus consists of two different textual systems whose interference produces its particular meaning: one system which constitutes the character's speech and one system which typifies the character's behavior outside the actual dialogue. Thus, we must further distinguish the literary dramatic dialogue according to the extent to which each of the two textual systems is responsible for constituting meaning. Since such a criterion would imply an endless multiplicity of possibilities, we need to make a basic distinction between (1) dialogue whose secondary text is solely restricted to giving the name of the speaker, where meaning is provided through the speech text of the characters and through attribution to their names, and

(2) dialogue which, besides listing the names of the speakers, contains a reasonably extensive secondary text offering information not provided in the speech where the meaning is constituted – above and beyond the attribution of speech to name of speaker – solely through the various specific interferences between the speech text and the secondary text.

The dominance of the speech text characterizes, to varying degrees, genres that are as widely different as Shakespeare, classical French or German drama, and the lyrical drama of the *fin de siècle*.

Although there is face-to-face interaction in the lyrical drama of the *fin de siècle*, for example, no other characteristics here indicate orality. There is no explicit reference to the dialogue partner who speaks, the listener, or the situation. Rather, the dialogue is molded by various poetic systems where reflection, decontextualization, density of information, and elaborateness predominate. A situation of direct communication is enacted through the media of elaborate writing.

In German classical drama, the dominance of the speech text operates quite differently. Here the system of turn-taking is acknowledged by the speech text itself. Although, for example, in Goethe's *Iphigenia in Tauris* (1787) all dialogue partners speak in the same style (i.e., cannot be differentiated from one another according to individual styles of speech), the alternating changes between the speaker and the one who responds are so apparent, beyond any change of name in the speech text, that every indication of name for the purpose of ordering the speech and showing the system of turn-taking can be dispensed with. All this can be easily gained from the text itself.

On the one hand, speech is characterized by involvement, context dependency, expressivity, and affectivity. Nevertheless, the dialogue can still operate without a secondary text that would normally describe the various nonverbal signs which would be typical of this kind of situation in direct communication. Instead, all information is provided by a speech text characterized by a wealth of information, compactness, complexity, and elaborateness, based on a specific poetic modeling of the dialogue.

The second dialogue type, whose meaning is constituted by the specific *interference of speech text and secondary text*, always points to a more intense situation of direct communication than does the first type as it explicitly underlines the paralinguistic, mimic, and proxemic signs in the secondary text used by the dialogue partners in the course of the dialogue. Meaning can thus only be accorded to the dialogue when the linguistic signs of the secondary text that point to nonverbal signs are related to the linguistic signs of the speech text. This can be realized in far more different ways than can the absolute dominance of the speech text. If we are aiming toward a useful systematization, it would therefore make sense to limit our discussion to two possible extremes. Either the speech text contributes more to the constitution of meaning in the dialogue than the secondary text or the meaning of the secondary text dominates that of the speech text. Both positions are limited by the absolute dominance of the speech text in one case and by the absolute dominance of the secondary text in the other (as in Beckett's *Acts sans paroles* [Acts without Words] or Handke's *Das Mündel will Vormund sein* [*The Minor Wants to Be Guardian*]).

In the German domestic tragedies (*Bürgerliche Trauerspiele*) of the eighteenth century, the secondary text is systematically built up as an integral component of the dramatic dialogue through stage directions referring to the behavior of the characters. In Lessing's *Emilia Galotti* (1772), for example, the speech text and the secondary text complement each other, and this alternating cross-referral constitutes the meaning of the dialogue. The secondary text may list mimic and gestural behavior which strengthens the emotions already expressed in the choice of words or syntax or it may describe deliberate actions which complement the blanks in an incomplete speech text. Nonetheless, the speech text is of considerably greater importance than the secondary text. Through it, the most significant information is communicated, just as the emotions are principally expressed through its specifically linguistic form.

The tension between writing and orality is considerably reduced here in comparison to the first two examples, although not so much that one could speak of a simple – written – notation of a situation of direct communication. The dominant features are spontaneity, involvement, interference of situation, expressivity, affectivity, and an intense sense of process. These arise mainly through the interference of speech text and secondary text. They realize the aesthetic program of creating the illusion of reality, that is, a situation of direct communication.

On the other hand, the features complexity, elaborateness, and construction cannot be overlooked. They point to a conception of character that is determined by the rationality in principle of human beings, whose feelings, however, are natural phenomena given natural physical expression. Since the tension between writing and orality is greatly reduced in comparison to that in French (and German) classic drama, it thus draws attention to explicitly bourgeois values.

In naturalist drama, the tension is, in fact, so reduced that one can speak of simulation – and thereby notation – of a situation of direct communication. Here it often happens that the behavior of a character described in the secondary text does not conform to the speech acts performed by the character in the speech text. The linguistic signs of the speech text and the nonverbal signs carried out in the secondary text appear in undisguised contradiction to one another. While the character's words might portray indifference, for example, or at least disinterest, the character's nonverbal behavior betrays fierce emotional involvement, or vice versa. The meaning of the secondary text thus contradicts that of speech text.

While in the German *Bürgerliche Trauerspiele* of the eighteenth century the meaning of the secondary text solely intensifies, concretizes, or complements that of the primary text, here it modifies (in the sense of either expansion or dilution) and even stands in direct opposition to the meaning of the primary text. One might summarize the possible relations between the speech text and the secondary text as complementation, concretization, modification (intensification or dilution), and contradiction. In any case, the meaning of the dramatic dialogue can only be constituted by the outcome of the specific relations between the two textual systems.

The dominance of meanings carried in the secondary text over those of the speech text is clear. For they point to the actual feelings and inner thoughts of the character which are neither revealed nor spoken in the speech text. It is only through the secondary text that it is possible to deduce the character's dialogic strategy, which would be completely incomprehensible when drawn from the speech text alone.

Thus, it is the circumstances of communication as much as the strategies of speech in the naturalistic dialogue that point to the features of orality. In this way, on the other hand, an aesthetic program is realized that is comparable to the early bourgeois illusionist theatre inasmuch as it postulates an imitation of reality. Exclusive recourse to orality functions, however, as a sign of a fundamentally changed character conception. It focuses on a split in the character which the frequent contradictions between speech text and secondary text also highlight. It is only through the nonverbal behavior that the appropriate conclusions can be drawn concerning the inner world and thoughts of the character. While solely the physical expression is "true," the words lie, deceive, betray, or are simply inadequate. The character might not even consciously recognize the inner processes thus exposed. They seem to flow without the character's control and are thus removed from consciousness or awareness. Rational decisions are not possible. The character falls victim as much to circumstances as to lack of self-autonomy.

The shifts in the relations between writing and orality thus signalize, on the one hand, the comparability of general aesthetic conception and, on the other, fundamental differences in character conception.

The Theatrical Dramatic Dialogue

Unlike the literary dramatic dialogue, the theatrical dramatic dialogue not only points to a situation of direct communication, it also represents it. Its realization employs all those sign systems which are characteristic of a situation of direct communication: linguistic, paralinguistic, mimic, gestural, and proxemic signs. The meaning of the theatrical dramatic dialogue is thus created by the interference of different semiotic sign systems. As a result of this, the theatrical dramatic dialogue should be systematized according to each specific interference. To do this, it is necessary to begin by distinguishing between the two semiotic systems employed: verbal and nonverbal signs. Either group of signs may occur in various specific relation to the other.

> In the theatre, the linguistic sign system, which intervenes through the dramatic text, always combines and conflicts with the acting, which belongs to an entirely different sign system. All the other components, such as music, scenic sets, and so forth, can be eliminated by the text itself; by the same token, the intervention of the sign systems to which they belong can be reduced to "zero degree," unless they reenter the theatrical structure through the intermediary of the actor. Therefore, the general function of drama in the shaping of the semiotics of theatre can be brought out only by means of confronting two sign systems that are invariably present, that is, language and acting.[2]

From this in turn arise two fundamentally different possibilities. Either the verbal signs (language) dominate the nonverbal (performance) or vice versa. Thus, the theatrical dialogue can be systematized according to the dominance of verbal or nonverbal signs. Before examining those two extreme positions separately, I shall offer some preliminary thoughts on the relation between the literary and the theatrical dramatic dialogue and advance a general survey of the possible interrelations between verbal and nonverbal signs.

The Literary and the Theatrical Dramatic Dialogue

From a historical point of view, there is naturally a close correlation between (1) the literary dramatic dialogue, which realizes the dominance of speech text, and the theatrical dramatic dialogue, which is dominated by verbal signs, as there is between (2) the literary dramatic dialogue characterized by the interference between speech text and secondary text and the theatrical dramatic dialogue in which nonverbal signs predominate. [...]

Although the theatrical dramatic dialogue as a performed piece of face-to-face interaction clearly belongs to the sphere of orality, Goethe attempts to organize the nonverbal signs relating to orality (the paralinguistic, mimic, and gestural signs) so that the significant features of writing running through the speech text are maintained and also emphasized. The same underlying aesthetic concept forces the literary and the theatrical dialogue into direct relation with one another – the art of acting is subordinate to poetic art. [...]

Lessing, on the other hand, tried to create the illusion of reality onstage and present individual characters. He saw poetry and performance in quite a different relationship to each other. His aim was to create an art of acting that would be independent of poetry and that would ultimately be able to portray characters without it. Lessing, like Diderot, was convinced that the gestural signs in the art of acting are more capable of conveying emotions than linguistic signs and felt this to be the most important function in the art of acting. Not only do gestural signs realize the secondary text, they also authenticate the truth of the speech. When the actor deliberately reproduces the paralinguistic, mimic, and gestural signs of anger in the right way, for example,

> the nervous walk, the stomping feet, the raw, sometimes shrieking, sometimes bitter tone, the movement of the eyebrows, the quivering lips, the gnashing of teeth and so on – if he only ... imitates those things which can be imitated, if you like, and does it well, then without fail a dark feeling of anger will befall his soul which reacts throughout the whole body and produces there those changes which are not simply under our control; his face will burn, his eyes flash, his muscles swell; in short, he will seem to be truly angry.[3]

The true illusion of anger can only be produced by the art of acting. In this sense, according to Lessing, in realizing the aesthetic concept of the theatrical dramatic dialogue, the nonverbal signs are given a certain dominance over the verbal – at least in the case of the portrayal and expression of emotions.

Consequently, an analogy in the formation of the dominants in the dramatic dialogue between the literary text of the drama and its performance in theatre (the dominance of the speech text/the dominance of verbal signs, interference between speech and secondary text or the dominance of the secondary text/the dominance of nonverbal signs) can, as the examples given above show, be historically guaranteed. If these dramas were produced today, on the other hand, such an analogy is not necessarily valid. Goethe's *Iphigenia in Tauris* may, for example, be performed with a clear dominance of nonverbal signs, as Hans Neuenfels demonstrated in his production at the Schauspielhaus in Frankfurt (1989). In this respect, the historically guaranteed analogy must be balanced against a systematic definition of different types of dialogue.

Possible Relations Between Verbal and Nonverbal Signs

The theatrical dramatic dialogue belongs fundamentally to the sphere of orality. As the historical examples have shown, it can also occur in such a way that it emphasizes the characteristics of writing. It would thus seem necessary to begin by differentiating the basic possible relations between verbal and non-verbal signs. [...]

Nonverbal signs, coded or noncoded, can stand in place of verbal ones. If a nod of the head is employed as a sign of affirmation, or if a demonstrative gesture takes the place of a spoken instruction, then these signs can be interpreted on the basis of a code that is assumed to be generally known in our own culture. These gestures function as "emblems,"[4] as signs which have a quasi-lexical meaning. If, on the other hand, an entreating look should take the place of a spoken plea, it must be understood intuitively, instinctively (i.e., on the basis of the individual's personal experience).

Nonverbal signs can supplement verbal ones in different ways. A gesture or special intonation might, for example, illustrate the meaning of the linguistic signs by indicating the size, shape, or scale of the person or object being spoken of. Or nonverbal signs might act as repetition of the verbal ones: where the sentence "I feel sad" is spoken with the appropriate paralinguistic signs – for example, with sobbing or quivering voice – while the face adopts a typically sad expression and head and shoulders are lightly inclined, the nonverbal signs constitute the same meaning as the verbal signs: it is repeated and substantiated.

On the other hand, the meaning of the verbal signs might be weakened, strengthened, or slightly altered by nonverbal signs. A sentence which, according to its syntactic structure, may be interpreted as a statement can, for example, be transformed by certain emphasis into a question, an exclamation, a command, an expression of doubt, etc. In order to understand a sentence properly, it requires more than mere understanding of the performative verb and the preposition that follows it – the intonation of the sentence must also be considered. In this sense, for example, a gentle smile or a sympathetic gesture might weaken a command into a friendly request just as a cautionary word can be intensified through relevant emphasis, gesture, or facial expression into a threat.

One special kind of modification is neutralization: the meaning of the verbal sign is so diluted that it loses practically all validity. Where, for example, the sentence "I am so sorry, can I do anything for you?" expressing sympathy and pity is spoken in an indifferent tone and is accompanied by disinterested gestures and behavior, the meaning, though not completely lost, is nonetheless so changed that the sympathy expressed on the verbal level must be understood as purely conventional behavior and not as the expression of a deeply felt emotion.

Where the nonverbal signs not only neutralize the meaning of verbal ones but also constitute a wholly opposite meaning, they thoroughly contradict the verbal signs. If the above example is spoken in a tone that betrays the speaker's secret delight and is accompanied by a radiant – or perhaps stifled – smile, a glint in the eye, shoulders thrown back, etc., a contradiction between the meaning of the verbal and that of the nonverbal sign is produced. The meaning of this contradiction can now only be discovered by reference to the situation, to the relation between the dialogue partners, to the specific circumstances of the speaker, or to the usual predominant sign system of the theatre form in question. A contradiction such as this may function as a sign of the real existence of contradictory feelings in the speaker, as the sign of deliberate, unsuccessful deception, or as the sign of the prevalence of one of the two emotions shown according to the dominance of the sign system: if language is the dominant sign system, then pity outweighs the other emotion in the contradiction. If, on the other hand, the meaning of the nonverbal signs dominates, then the ruling emotion is one of delight.

Notes

1   M. Pfister, *The Theory and Analysis of Drama* (Cambridge: Cambridge University Press, 1988), 6–11.

2   J. Veltruský, "Dramatic Text as a Component of Theatre," in *Semiotics of Art*, ed. L. Matejka and J. R. Titunic (Cambridge, MA: MIT Press, 1976), 114ff.

3   Lessing, *Hamburgische Dramaturgie*, ed. O. Mann. 3 Vols. (Stuttgart: Kröner, 1948), 246.

4   P. Ekman and W. V. Friesen, "The Repertoire of Non-Verbal Behaviour: Categories, Origins, Usage and Coding," *Semiotica* I (1969), 49–98.

Chapter 78

Richard Schechner (b. 1934)

Theorist, playwright, and director Richard Schechner is one of the founders of performance studies in the United States. He is longstanding editor of the journal *TDR* (formerly the *Tulane Drama Review* and the *Drama Review*). His major works include *Public Domain* (1968), *Environmental Theater* (1973), *Essays on Performance Theory* (1976), *Between Theater and Anthropology* (1985), *The Future of Ritual* (1993), and *Performance Studies: An Introduction* (2002). Schechner advanced the science of performance studies by examining the idea of a performance in terms of its repeatability, doubling (copying from something else), and the connection between "acting" and "being." He is also an international stage director, his most well-known work being *Dionysus in 69* (1970), as well as founder of the Performance Group and East Coast Artist Exchange.

One of Schechner's principal contributions to performance studies is the concept of "restored behavior." It is the main characteristic of performance because it is behavior that can be "stored, transmitted, manipulated, transformed." The process of rehearsal is the essential element of restored behavior, but it is not the only one. Rituals, funerals, and other physically recreated actions in specified spaces are what he calls "symbolic and reflexive" behavior which in turn becomes "the hardening into theater of social, religious, aesthetic, medical, and educational process. Performance means: never for the first time. It means: for the second to the *n*th time." Performance is thus "twice-behaved behavior."[1] A similar manner of examining performance is what Joseph Roach, another important founder of performance studies, calls "surrogation." Surrogation is a "three-sided relationship of memory, performance, and substitution." Cultures

Richard Schechner, "What is Performance Studies Anyway?" in *The Ends of Performance*, ed. Peggy Phelan and Jill Lane (New York: NYU Press, 1998), 357–62. © 1998 by New York University. Reprinted by permission of New York University Press.

reproduce and reinvent themselves by a process occurring "in the network of relations that constitute the social fabric." Surrogation, he says, appears in the "cavities created by loss through death or other forms of departure," in which "survivors attempt to fit satisfactory alternatives."[2] Performance is also linked to memory and history, what Roach calls "performance genealogies" that yield "the idea of expressive movements as mnemonic reserves, including patterned movements made and remembered by bodies, residual movements retained implicitly in images or words (or in the silences between them), and imaginary movements dreamed in minds not prior to language but constitutive of it" (26). In her examination of Latin American performance and culture, Diana Taylor adds along similar lines that "Performance and aesthetics of everyday life vary from community to community, reflecting cultural and historical specificity as much in the enactment as in the viewing/reception."[3] In the following extract, Schechner traces the history of performance studies for which he, Roach, Taylor, and others have been leading advocates.

What is Performance Studies Anyway? (1998)

Is performance studies a "field," an "area," a "discipline?" The sidewinder snake moves across the desert floor by contracting and extending itself in a sideways motion. Wherever this beautiful rattlesnake points, it is not going there. Such (in)direction is characteristic of performance studies. This area/field/discipline often plays at what it is not, tricking those who want to fix it, alarming some, amusing others, astounding a few as it sidewinds its way across the deserts of academia. At present, in the United States, there are only two performance studies departments – full-fledged academic enterprises replete with chairpersons, the ability to tenure faculty, an independent budget, and so on. One of these, my own home base, is at New York University's Tisch School of the Arts; the other is at Northwestern University. It is worth sketching the development of these departments.

In 1965 Robert W. Corrigan founded the New York University School of the Arts. Corrigan had been at Tulane University, where he was my dissertation advisor/mentor. He was also the founding editor of the *Carleton Drama Review*, later the *Tulane Drama Review*, presently the *Drama Review* (*TDR*), which I edited from 1962 to 1969 and again since 1986. In 1965 I published "Approaches" in *TDR*, an essay in which I said that performance was an inclusive category that included play, games, sports, performance in everyday life, and ritual. In 1967 Corrigan invited me to head the Drama Department in the NYU School of the Arts. I came with *TDR* but declined the headache of administration, suggesting instead Monroe Lippman, who had resigned as chair at Tulane. In 1968, we brought to NYU Brooks McNamara, a Tulane PhD, theatre historian, and scenographer. His passion was for popular entertainments, mine for the avant-garde and Greek theatre (a combination that bore fruit in *Dionysus in 69*). In the early 1970s, adding Michael Kirby and Ted Hoffman to the faculty, we moved further and further away from a conventional drama department. I taught courses in ritual, using anthropological thinking and joining forces with Victor Turner.

In 1979, with the strong support of David Oppenheim, who became dean of the School of the Arts in 1968 (Corrigan having gone on to found the California Institute of the Arts), I began a series of courses entitled Performance Theory. These were the kernel of what was to become performance studies at NYU. As the flyer for the first such course proclaimed, "Leading American and world figures in the performing arts and the social sciences will discuss the relationship between social anthropology, psychology, semiotics, and the performing arts. The course examines theatre and dance in Western and non-Western cultures, ranging from the avant-garde to traditional, ritual, and popular forms." The visiting faculty for this initial offering included Jerzy Grotowski, Paul Bouissac, Donald Kaplan, Alexander Alland, Joann W. Kealinohomoku, Barbara Myerhoff, Jerome Rothenberg, Squat Theatre, and Victor Turner. Here, possibly for the first time together, were anthropologists, a Freudian psychoanalyst, a semiotician specializing in play and circus, a dance scholar, a poet and scholar of oral cultures and shamanism, and leading experimental theatre artists. The graduate assistant for the course was Sally Banes.

Over the next three years, Performance Theory counted among its visiting faculty Clifford Geertz, Masao Yamaguchi, Alfonso Ortiz, Erving Goffman, Eugenio Barba, Steve Paxton, Joanne Akalaitis, Yvonne Rainer, Meredith Monk, Augusto Boal, Colin Turnbull, Richard Foreman, Allan Kaprow, Linda Montano, Spalding Gray, Laurie Anderson, Peter Pitzele, Brian Sutton-Smith, Ray Birdwhistell, Edward T. Hall, Julie Taymor, and Peter Chelkowski. Victor and Edith Turner were frequent participants. Topics ranged from "Performing the Self" and "Play" to "Shamanism," "Cultural and Intercultural Performance," and "Experimental Performance."

By the end of the 1970s, we at NYU knew we weren't teaching "drama" or "theatre" in the ways it was taught elsewhere. Often we weren't teaching these subjects at all. So in 1980 we officially changed our name to Performance Studies. But we needed coherent leadership more than a name change. Enter Barbara Kirshenblatt-Gimblett, who came to NYU from the Department of Folklore and Folklife at the University of Pennsylvania with a PhD in folklore from Indiana University. Kirshenblatt-Gimblett's far-ranging interests spanned Jewish studies, museum displays (from colonial expositions to living history museums), tourist performances, and the aesthetics of everyday life. She became chair in the spring of 1981 and remained in the post for twelve years. It was Kirshenblatt-Gimblett who crafted a singular department out of what had been disparate and sometimes quirky interests and practices.

In such a short essay, I can't detail what happened from then to now. At NYU we follow a dictum of having people teach what is most important to them. We resist abstract plans. PS [Performance Studies] goes where faculty and student interests take it. We know that such a small department can't do it all, so we exist as a conscious partiality, a knowing slice of the pie. With the arrival of Marcia Siegel in 1983, dance was folded into the mix. When Peggy Phelan joined in 1985, a strong feminist tendency, informed by psychoanalysis, became a PS mainstay. Michael Taussig was at PS from 1988 to 1993, teaching his own conjunction of Marxism, postcolonial thought, and anthropology. Kenyan writer and activist Ngũgĩ wa Thiong'o holds a joint appointment from PS and Comparative Literature. Younger faculty May Joseph, José Muñoz, and Barbara Browning bring with them particular interests ranging from queer theory to samba. As of this writing, Diana Taylor is set to become chair. Because PS is in New York, we are able to draw a rich panoply of adjuncts, with interests ranging from Asian performance to jazz, orality to Artaud and Valerina, and much more.

What happened at Northwestern is parallel to but different from NYU. NYU's performance studies is rooted in theatre, NWU's [Northwestern University] in oral interpretation. These are not only genres, but academic traditions. The theoretical and historical foundation of NWU's program is rhetoric, broadly understood. In a 1993 Internet discussion of "What Is Performance Studies?" Nathan Stucky of Southern Illinois University wrote (in part),

> By the late 1960s and early 1970s many (then Oral Interpretation) programs were really practicing what was called "Performance of Literature." However, the view of literature quickly broadened to include cultural performances, personal narratives, everyday-life performances, non-fiction, ritual, etc.... By this point in time, ethnographic work, as well as folklore and anthropology, began to be of some interest.... So, along with the literary, theoretical, and critical models of performance that one might associate with "Interpretation" has been the emergence of interest in cultural and social elements, as well as interest in performance as a way of knowing. These threads connect logically and historically through relatively recent literary/critical foci to the oral tradition which has always been part of these approaches to performance.

In 1991 Dwight Conquergood, currently chair of NWU's Performance Studies Department and a major theorist of performance studies, raised what he called "new questions that can be clustered around five intersecting planes of analysis":

1   Performance and cultural process....
2   Performance and Ethnographic Praxis....
3   Performance and Hermeneutics....
4   Performance and Scholarly Representation....
5   The Politics of Performance....[4]

Conquergood's questions indicate how closely related the NWU approach now is to NYU's. A further demonstration of this convergence is the collaboration between the two departments on the recurring Annual Performance Studies Conference(s). The first was held at NYU in 1995, the second at NWU in 1996, the third at Georgia Tech in 1997. Of course, by now many PS graduates – from NYU and NWU – are teaching, have authored dozens of books with a PS approach, and are disseminating PS ideas. A number of performance artists and theatre directors have also been influenced by PS.

But what is performance studies, conceptually speaking? Can performance studies be described? Performance studies is "inter" – in between. It is intergeneric, interdisciplinary, intercultural – and therefore inherently unstable. Performance studies resists or rejects definition. As a discipline, PS cannot be mapped effectively because it transgresses boundaries, it goes where it is not expected to be. It is inherently "in between" and therefore cannot be pinned down or located exactly. This indecision (if that's what it is) or multidirectionality drives some people crazy. For others, it's the pungent and defining flavor of the meat.

PS assumes that we are living in a postcolonial world where cultures are colliding, interfering with each other, and energetically hybridizing. PS does not value "purity." In fact, academic disciplines are most active and important at their ever changing interfaces. In terms of PS, this means between theatre and anthropology, folklore and sociology, history and performance theory, gender studies and psychoanalysis, performativity and actual performance events, and more – new interfaces will be added as time goes on, and older ones dropped. Accepting "inter" means opposing the establishment of any single system of knowledge, values, or subject matter. Performance studies is unfinished, open, multivocal, and self-contradictory. Thus any call for or work toward a "unified field" is, in my view, a misunderstanding of the very fluidity and playfulness fundamental to performance studies. That sidewinder again, the endlessly creative double negative at the core of restoration of behavior.

Closer to the ground is the question of the relation of performativity to performance proper. Are there any limits to performativity? Is there anything outside the purview of performance studies? To answer, we must distinguish between "as" and "is." Performances mark identities, bend and remake time, adorn and reshape the body, tell stories, and allow people to play with behavior that is "twice-behaved," not-for-the-first-time, rehearsed, cooked, prepared. Having made such a sweeping generalization, I must add that every genre of performance, even every particular instance of a genre, is concrete, specific, and different from every other. It is necessary to generalize in order to make theory. At the same time, we must not lose sight of each specific performance's particularities of experience, structure, history, and process.

Any event, action, item, or behavior may be examined "as" performance. Approaching phenomena as performance has certain advantages. One can consider things as provisional, in-process, existing and changing over time, in rehearsal, as it were. On the other hand, there are events that tradition and convention declare "are" performances. In Western culture, until recently, performances were of theatre, music, and dance – the "aesthetic genres," the performing arts. Recently, since the 1960s at least, aesthetic performances have developed that cannot be located precisely as theatre or dance or music or visual arts. Usually called either "performance art," "mixed-media," "Happenings," or "intermedia," these events blur or breach boundaries separating art from life and genres from each other. As performance art grew in range and popularity, theorists began to examine "performative behavior" – how people play gender, heightening their constructed identity, performing slightly or radically different selves in different situations. This is the performative [J. L.] Austin introduced and [Judith] Butler and queer theorists discuss.

The performative engages performance in places and situations not traditionally marked as "performing arts," from dress-up to certain kinds of writing or speaking. The acceptance of the performative as a category of theory as well as a fact of behavior has made it increasingly difficult to sustain the distinction between appearances and facts, surfaces and depths, illusions and substances. Appearances are actualities. And so is what lies beneath appearances. Reality is constructed through and through, from its many surfaces or aspects down through its multiple depths. The subjects of performance studies are both what is performance and the performative – and the myriad contact points and overlaps, tensions and loose spots, separating and connecting these two categories.

Notes

1   R. Schechner, *Between Theater and Anthropology* (Philadelphia: University of Pennsylvania Press, 1985), 36.
2   J. Roach, *Cities of the Dead: Circum-Atlantic Performance* (New York: Columbia University Press, 1996), 3.

3   D. Taylor, *The Archive and the Repertoire: Performing Cultural Memory in the Americas* (Durham, NC: Duke University Press, 2003), 3.

4   D. Conquergood, "Rethinking Ethnography: Towards a Critical Cultural Politics," *Communications Monographs* 58 (June 1991), 190. [Dwight Conquergood was another significant figure in the implementation of Performance Studies in the academy.]

Chapter 79

Alina Troyano

Alina Troyano (a.k.a. Carmelita Tropicana) is a Latin American feminist performance artist. Her play (co-written with her sister Ela), *Carmelita Tropicana: Your Kunst is Your Waffen* (1994), is a radical three-person show satirizing sexual stereotypes. Troyano's work underscores lesbian and queer identity politics in the face of oppression. Like the lesbian theatre group Split Britches, Troyano dramatizes the conditions of queerness by employing non-traditional methods. Performing in drag and other cross-gender styles, Troyano displays Judith Butler's concepts of gender performativity and the fluidity of identity. Here Troyano mixes German with English and Spanish to stress the playfulness of language and the destabilizing of subjectivity, mixing theory and irreverence in a way that is characteristic of postmodern performance art.

I, Carmelita Tropicana (2000)

The pen is the tongue of the mind. Did I say that? No, it was that other linguist Miguel de Cervantes. I, Carmelita, say:

> *Hello people you know me I know you*
> *I don't need no American Express card*
> *Ich bin schoenheitzkonigin*
> *Reina de belleza de Loisaida*
> *Carmelita Tropicana*
> *Ms. Lower East Side Beauty Queen*

Alina Troyano, "I, Carmelita Tropicana," excerpted from Alina Troyano, with Ela Troyano and Uzi Parnes, *I, Carmelita Tropicana: PeRforMinG Between CultuRes*, ed. C. A. Norigea (Boston: Beacon Press, 2000), xiii–xxv. © 2000 by Alina Troyano. Reprinted by permission of the author.

Famous nightclub entertainer
Superintendent and performance artiste

I love to be a performance artist because you get to travel a lot. And I have a talent that is very good for traveling. I pick languages up pretty fast. First there was Spanish in Cuba where I was born and then English in America where I got reared. And of course on my first international tour of Germany I pick up the language the Deutsche and a lot more – I pick up Kunst, Art.

In Search of Kunst

NYC, downtown, the eighties. That is when I first began my search for Kunst.

A happy fun time for artists, playful, innocent; there was enough money for an artist to make art, survive, hang out. Clubs and art galleries flourished. It was the best of times: Art was more about process than product, more about esthetic edification than career, more about transgression than mainstream assimilation. It was the worst of times: AIDS hit, clubs and galleries closed, the NEA started defunding, the culture wars began.

But to go back to the happy times when my life changed. It happened one night at the Women's One World (WOW) International Festival, held in multiple venues on the Lower East Side. My eyes were ablaze at the spectacle of so many women in all colors, sizes, shapes doing every art imaginable – music, poetry, theatre, cooking. I thought I'd found paradise. I was especially moved by the play *Split Britches*, performed by a theatre troupe with the same name, made up of Deb Margolin, Peggy Shaw, and Lois Weaver. As the future Carmelita would exclaim: It made me cry in one eye and laugh in the other. At last, feministas with a sense of humor! I was hooked. So when the girls that put the Festival together opened up the WOW cafe, I followed.

There's a Place for Us

I became a member of WOW, a loose collective of wayward girls, mostly lesbians, a place that offered an artistic salon on East 11th Street. There were art exhibits, poetry readings, variety nights, thematic parties like the Military Drag Ball and the WC-Rated Xmas, workshops in butch, femme, and stand-up comedy. All accompanied by melted brie sandwiches. A place where the credo for everywoman was "Express yourself." A place that said if existing theatre does not represent women like us, let us create that theatre. A place seething with untapped talent.

One such talented member was Holly Hughes, who had written *The Well of Horniness* and cast me as Al Dente, Chief of Police, and Georgette, a butch girl. The role of Al Dente became easier to tackle once Jack Smith, infamous filmmaker and performance artist (who I met through Ela Troyano and Uzi Parnes) admired by many, from Federico Fellini to Nan Goldin, watched the rehearsal and gave me three magic words: Bark the part. Bark the part, of course. I had imagined Al Dente as a cross between Marlon Brando's Godfather and a bulldog. Georgette was harder. Playing butch hit closer to home. All those voices from my adolescence came back to haunt me: "Don't laugh that loud." "Don't walk that way, pareces una carretonera." "You look like a truck driver." I had been sent to charm and etiquette school to cure my gruff demeanor. Now I was being asked to play a butch girl and revel in it. When I stepped on stage, took off my shirt exposing bare arms in a tank T-shirt, and flexed my muscles, the girls went "Oooh." I had a revelation: This wasn't so bad.

It was at the WBAI radio station in the studio, waiting to perform *The Well of Horniness*, that I came up with the name of my alter ego. As the clock showed two minutes before the on-the-air sign was about to go on, my pulse raced and with a rush more euphoric than that from cocaine, I came up with my new name Carmelita and last name Tro – Tropicana. I hit the jackpot.

Now I had a name and the name was especially helpful for the comedy class I was taking at WOW. I had felt too naked and self-conscious to do stand-up; with the name came a character, and the character had red lipstick, a beauty mole, an accent. But what to wear? That was solved when my future collaborators Ela Troyano and Uzi Parnes presented me with their Christmas gift. I opened the box and touched the thick, rich, red velvet cloth with big purple and pink roses, I thought for upholstering my couch, but as I took it out of the box I saw it wasn't for my couch, it was an evening gown. Now I was ready. The moment to strut my stand-up stuff had come. I waited backstage. My teacher signaled me to go on and Carmelita opened her mouth: Hello people.

Etiquette and Esthetics

If WOW had an esthetics it was that of the Ridiculous Theatre and Split Britches. It was camp. It was queer. It was comedy. In fact it was at WOW that I got to see live stand-up for the first time. It was a double bill of Marga Gómez and Reno. So it made sense then for WOW to offer a workshop in stand-up comedy.

The teacher giving the stand-up workshop, although she had a wry sense of humor, was not a counter-culture, downtown type and did not share this sensibility. She was a professional who had been playing comedy clubs and was hardened by the experience of hearing nightly routines full of dumb dick jokes. She thought WOW was too soft a spot, it was not the real world. Her advice focused on how to make it to mainstream and get on [David] *Letterman*. She warned me about using foreign words and expressions that middle America, the target audience, was not familiar with. Chutzpah and oy vey had to go. But the sensuous pleasure I got from rolling meshuggener around my lips and tongue I couldn't give up, or the idea of teaching a vocabulary word, or playing in the backyard of a different culture. My political resistance came in the way of a Jewish poem titled "Oy Vey Number 1."

The teacher was right – WOW was a soft spot embracing gender discourse and that was not the rest of the world. I found that out when I got a gig at the Limelight for a modeling show. They wanted all kinds of street people. I thought I'd go butch. I wore a man's suit, men's shoes, hair slicked back, hung a big gold medallion from my neck and did not wear any lipstick. I looked like a heavy hitter butch Latina who would have been at home at the old La Escuelita on 9th Avenue, full of queens and working-class folks. The reaction I got from the other models in the show was icy. They avoided looking at me. The photographer posed everyone for a group picture and left me out. These people had no etiquette. My teacher was right. She didn't promise me a butch garden. This was the real world.

There's a Place for Us – The Other – And it's Uptown

If WOW was a theatre space grounded in gender and sexual politics, Intar was the Latin hood where we could check out our roots. Intar, an arts complex with two spaces – one on 42nd Street and the other on 53rd Street – nurtured Latino talent through its theatre, art gallery, and two significant workshops, the playwriting workshop led by Maria Irene Fornes and the musical theatre workshop led by George Ferrencz and Graciela Daniele. I was chosen to join the musical theatre workshop with a stipend attached. Money for art, that was a novel concept for me. How lucky can a girl get? All I had to do was write the book for a musical. So I agreed and went to ask Lois Weaver of Split Britches what that meant.

It was not easy. I had never written more than a few monologues in the voice of Carmelita. A play seemed a Herculean task. ([The TX show] Xena had not yet arrived). And a musical to boot. I'd only seen one live musical, *Fiddler on the Roof.* I couldn't do it. I tried summoning Chekhov but he would not come. Desperate, I begged [playwright] María Irene [Fornes] to let me audit a few classes at her lab.

Irene is a formidable teacher as well as La Grande Dame del Teatro. Any Latino writing today has been through Irene and Irene has been through them. The lab began with yoga. After yoga you would get coffee and sit at desks perfectly laid out in a circular shape making sure all desk corners touched. This was very important. She would begin the writing exercises "Close your eyes and..." I squinted and saw some people with heads raised like the blind trying to see; others had contorted bodies, but all were concentrating. What I wrote was self-conscious and did not ring true. She advised me that writing was quiet observation. If I imagined that outside it was snowing and there was a man with a snow shovel, the man could be shoveling or not. I had to observe. The man could speak or not. I should not put words into people's mouths but let them speak for themselves. This seemed the opposite of the active comedy writing I was doing. One day I wrote in that quiet way, observing, and reached that deep state of concentration where your surroundings disappear and you go into your writing. After that class in that dreamlike state, outside on the street, a car honk stopped me from getting run over. This was dangerous writing and the kind that would come in handy at a later date; for now I felt inspired.

I went back to the musical theatre workshop and my lab director told me to forget Chekhov and write for Carmelita. So I did and gushed at the thrill of hearing my lyrics set to the ingenious melodies of composer Fernando Rivas.

Like WOW, Intar was significant for the network it provided. It was there I met Maria Irene, Graciela Daniele, and Max Ferra, as well as other writers and musicians that were starting out, like Manuel Pereiras, Ana María Simo, Lorraine Llamas, Alfredo Bejar, Micky Cruz, Bobby Sanabria, Luis Santeiro. It was here that I was paired up with Fernando Rivas and our styles meshed so well that we became collaborators in and out of Intar. But he was not my first collaborator.

Reflections through a Cuban Eye

My first collaborators were Uzi Parnes and my biological sister Ela Troyano, who are both filmmakers, directors, and writers. To this day I collaborate with each one in some capacity, whether as director, dramaturg, or cowriter. Their artistic generosity allows me to adapt work we have created together and present it as recycled solo performance. They are still the two people I trust most for feedback.

As a triumvirate of two cubists and one Jewish (an Uzi-ism), we created work that made Carmelita the protagonist, a super Latina heroine who, when pitted against evil forces, always triumphed in the end.

Ela and Uzi added a flamboyancy to Carmelita – Uzi by creating fruited boas and hat chandeliers that light up my life and the stage, Ela by saving a charred sequined bustier from a fire I had in my apartment, adding glittered fruit to the burnt left breast so I could appear at a TV interview looking intact with just a hint of smoke. Together they created exquisite visuals in multimedia that made spectacles of our pieces and helped shape the work by providing plot development and narrative structure. As artists both are analytical and versatile enough to mix intellectual semiotics and structural theory with pop culture. But they do have their differences. Uzi is like a painter with a flair for using big extravagant brush strokes; Ela uses finer brush strokes with lots of details. As I see them, Uzi is more attuned to the musical comedy, Ela to the screwball comedy. As directors they begin their approach at opposite ends. They are like belly buttons: Ela is an innie, Uzi an outie. I remember when I asked them to help me with a character I was playing that I felt I had not gotten. Uzi gave me suggestions of physical tasks to do on stage; Ela asked me questions that led me to delve deeper into the character. I found both approaches effective and eventually leading to the same end.

Memories from the Corners of my Medulla Oblongata

First times usually occupy a dulce, sweet spot in one's heart. So it is with *Memorias de la Revolución/Memories of the Revolution*, my first play written with Uzi Parnes. *Memorias* was fun to do, was critically well received, and set the tone for my future collaborations with Uzi. As with other works, we took on multiple jobs. Uzi wrote, directed, and designed and I acted, wrote, and helped produce.

We found that an effective shortcut to writing a play was knowing the talent and writing parts for them. At WOW auditions were unthinkable, but there was plenty of talent. We had three of the future Lesbian Brothers: Maureen Angelos, Peggy Healey and Lisa Kron. We knew Peggy and Lisa were not only funny, but could also sing, so we could give them musical numbers. Maureen Angelos was wonderful at male drag and cut a dashing figure that made both straight women and lesbians swoon. She was cast as Carmelita's brother Machito, a recurring character in other plays. Diane Jeep Ries had done a Marlene Dietrich and was good with a German accent; she became our German spy. Holly Hughes and Allison Rooney, fabulous writers and performers, both exuding Americana, played the American tourists. Kate Stafford's performances had a comic edge suited to the Chief of Police, and Quinn added to the cabaret ambience as the cigarette girl and the go-go dancer Dance Machine. Uzi was thrilled at the gender-bending possibilities that an all-female cast, with some playing male roles, would bring.

Besides the obvious reason of the name I had chosen, there were other reasons for setting Act I of *Memorias* at the Tropicana nightclub in Havana 1957. Act III takes place in a replica of the club Tropicana A-Go-Go in New York City in 1967. This suited the narrative as well as eliminated a big set change. For Uzi, who loved musicals, the setting was a chance to stage musical numbers. To create the cabaret environment he set up tables and chairs for the audience. For me the Tropicana conjured up bedtime stories of the greatest nightclub and memories of my relatives, exiles who romantically yearned for a pre-revolutionary Cuba.

Like many of the downtown shows of the period, *Memorias* owed much of its color scheme to Material for the Arts, an organization that takes fabric, paints, and all kinds of supplies and furniture from businesses and recycles them for artists. Material for the Arts had bolts of green and orange fabric. Uzi was imaginative with the flaming red-orange lame and a neon lime-green polyester, using both for the curtains and the costumes. He added a more subdued faux Henri Rousseau as a set backdrop. My stand-up comedy teacher thought it odd and asked why Lisa, who played the chanteuse, was dressed like the curtain. Lisa in turn milked her entrance proudly, pointing to her dress and the curtain.

With *Memorias* we realized the importance of titles and names. *Memorias de la Revolución/Memories of the Revolution* fit symmetrically both English and Spanish. It was grand and ludicrous enough for Carmelita and reminiscent of the great film by Tomás Gutiérrez Alea's *Memorias del Subdesarrollo/Memories of Underdevelopment.* If a title hooked an audience, a name fed the imagination. When I heard the name Pingalito in a conversation, I stole it immediately. Pingalito, little Dick, a typical macho Cubano, sauntered off the page with guayabera and cigar.

Although *Memorias* was a comedy, my favorite moment in the play came from a not-so-funny image I had of someone being tortured to a seductive jazz tiff. I told Uzi my image and he turned it into a musical number where Carmelita's protégé and singer Rosita dances with the sadistic Chief of Police, who demands she sing a love song, abusively twisting her arm, pushing her around, and finally dropping her on the floor.

Uzi thought that what *Memorias* was missing was religious iconography. He conceived Act II somewhere near the Bermuda Triangle. Carmelita, who has escaped the revolution, is in a boat with two cohorts, lost at sea. The Virgin could appear to Carmelita, but if she's Jewish and speaks Yiddish, who could we get to play a Yiddish mama? After a storm at sea, Carmelita prays and two little angels open up a triptych in the background, revealing on film the apparition that is Uzi as the Virgin.

Cooking Performance Art

I'm like a short-order cook when I make performance art pieces, quickly whipping up a piece for a specific event and audience. When the Dance Critics Association asked me to be on a panel on performance art, I concocted the *Performance Art Manifesto* according to Carmelita. I can then toss the *Manifesto* liberally into other performances, e.g., a performance for the Bad Girls Exhibit at The New Museum of Contemporary Art.

> Recipe for Carmelita's Bad Girls Show
> at The New Museum of Contemporary Art
> INGREDIENTS
> *1/3 Pingalito (Carmelita in male drag) recites*
> *"Ode to the Cuban Man" from* Milk of Amnesia
> *1/3 Carmelita delivers* Performance Art Manifesto
> *1/3 The Art Quiz Show*
> HOW TO MAKE THE ART QUIZ SHOW

Sprinkle clues for the audience to guess the artwork
  or artist recreated in live tableaux
Add a pinch of art commentary to taste and blend
  with 1 generous dollop of modern dancer
Jennifer Monson whisked rapidly for
  Duchamp's Nude Descending a Staircase.
Set aside.
In a separate pan mix
1/2 cup of Jennifer as Cupid with piercing arrow and
1/2 cup of Carmelita moaning, hanging on museum
  fire escape
Simmer to Wagner's Tristan und Isolde *and stir*
  until both harden into Bernini's sculpture
  The Agony of St. Theresa.
Set aside.

In separate bowl create the creme fraiche of one of the baddest girl artists beaten into soft peaks until stiff but not dry, a half-and-half bisexual, add to it the fuzzy peach of one who disdains depilatories and plucking and lace it with 80 percent proof mezcal, garnish with sugar skulls and candied flowers for an artist who can withstand excruciating pain and paint and paint because art is her life and Kunst is supreme Frida Kahlo. One hundred percent artist.
  Buen Provecho and Bon Appétit

Ch Ch Ch Ch Ch Changes

The gloom of the latter part of the eighties spilled onto the new decade. The effects of the AIDS epidemic were devastating the arts community, the economy took a nose dive, homelessness was on the rise, the culture wars took their toll on artists and arts organizations, and everyone scrambled to survive.

For me the nineties was a period of transition. The Parnes–Troyano–Tropicana trio dissolved and we all produced work independently. I took on more work as an actress and solo artist and, prompted by "The Decade Show," I began experimenting with a different style of writing.

"The Decade Show: Frameworks of Identity in the 1980s," a collaboration of three museums (The New Museum of Contemporary Art, the Museum of Contemporary Hispanic Art, and the Studio Museum of Harlem), brought together curators, artists, and critics to examine representative "nonmainstream or oppositional art" and provide an understanding of the period. As an artist asked to perform, I began to take stock of the work I'd been creating, and this inevitably led to the question, "What's next?"

My performance at "The Decade Show" was a collage of old and new work. I adapted excerpts from *Memorias de la Revolución, The Boiler Time Machine,* and *Candela* and seized the opportunity to write more personal autobiographical monologues. But without the Carmelita fruits I felt naked, which is why I did the monologues in the dark, for after all, as a born and bred ex-Catholic our confessions take place in the dark.

Remember Walking in the Sand?

I once read that the act of remembering is like xerox copying. You remember a memory, and then the next time you remember it's the memory of the memory you are remembering, and after that it's the memory of the memory of the memory, and so on. My trip to Cuba as an adult in 1993 brought back many memories and gave me the topic for my solo *Milk of Amnesia*. *Milk* was conceived as if inside the brain; when you tapped a certain area, a memory would unfold.

Ela, who acted as director and dramaturg, was invaluable in the creation and development of the piece. She urged me to combine the more personal autobiographical style with the campy satire of earlier work. With *Milk* my schizophrenia blossomed, and I was able to combine the voice of Carmelita with mine, that of the writer, and sprinkle it with assorted animals whose voices gave us a glimpse of Cuban history.

Unlike earlier, more colorful and flamboyant work, Ela wanted *Milk* to be subdued, intimate, and she suggested we hire Kukuli Velarde, a Peruvian sculptor, to design the show.

One of the most exhilarating times in the collaborative process is when you get together with your collaborators, kicking ideas around, and you watch as these ideas evolve and get incorporated into the show. The images of milk and childhood memories in the text were embodied in the visuals. Kukuli translated milk and amnesia into white; she wanted everything painted white, including the theatre. This had to be scaled down at Performance Space 122 [in New York], where we premiered the show, to a white cube and white costume. The three of us started to free associate childhood images and came up with balloons. I told them I'd visited a friend in the hospital who had a brain injury and had wires attached to her head resembling a hat. Kukuli created a hat with white balloons which Carmelita wears in the hospital sequence when she is suffering from amnesia. Kukuli and I proposed helium ballons in the hat so it could ascend upwards. Ela pops our balloon and comes up with the next image: pinata. She tells us one of the most memorable performances she has seen was Jack Smith's adaptation of Ibsen's *Ghosts*, where a little stuffed animal went across the stage and spilled glitter from its body. Kukuli sculpts a six-foot papier-mâché pig with the face of one who is about to be slaughtered. Just like the pinata bursts open and candy spills on the ground, so too, our pig had a tampon. When it was pulled, glitter gushed from its neck, forming a puddle of glittered blood on the white linoleum floor. The red glitter blood is a stolen homage to Jack Smith.

Milk is the show I have toured the most, but as with all touring, since presenting organizations vary in terms of space and resources, one must improvise. Alas, the pig, though magnificent at six feet, is too difficult as a traveling companion. In Barcelona the pig substitute was a whole ham serrano, in London it was can of Spam, and in Los Angeles a two-foot-tall Mexican piggy bank.

In the Year 2017 Will *Chicas* Be Alive?

Chicas 2000 had a lot in common with *Memorias*. I had a cast, a director, and a booking, and had to write a press release before there was a play. Ellie Covan of Dixon Place got us commissioning funds from the Joyce Mertz Gilmore Foundation and booked it for June as part of the Toyota Comedy Festival. Since *Chicas* was part of the festival it had to be funny, and since we were in mid-March I had to write pronto.

At the time I wanted to set aside solo work and longed for a bigger show like *Memorias*; I longed to gather live girls on stage with me. It was also around that time that Dolly was cloned and the scientific possibilities gripped me.

My cast was made up of Rebecca Sumner Burgos and Ana Margaret Sánchez, young, tall, voluptuous latinas. I thought, What if Carmelita was cloned and Ana and Rebecca were her clones? That worked for me.

I had to be very fertile with so close a deadline and this is when everything becomes grist for the mill. I heard a greeting on my answering machine: "Oye, chusma." It was the affectionate greeting of José Muñoz, NYU professor of Performance Studies. Chusma. The word is used in Latin America and it means loud, tacky, excessive behavior and tastes associated with "lower classes." The American equivalent of chusma is bottom feeder, white trailer trash, except that this is people-of-color trash. I married cloning to chusma and came up with the premise of the show. Carmelita, who has the chusma gene, a gene deemed harmful to society, is cloned by the stalking wanna-be chusma, Dr. Igor. To cure her disease a futuristic society has created jails known as Behavior Modification Units, where Carmelita and her clones are interned.

I thought meeting informally with the cast would get my creative juices going. I asked them if they had a fantasy of doing something on stage, what would that be. Uzi said he wanted to direct but also wanted to play a small role. Ana Margaret said she wanted to use her body in odd ways, to express herself physically, not necessarily through dance. Rebecca talked about cannibalism, its meaning and necessity, both metaphorically and not, and said she also wanted to sing a song. I tried honoring their wish list. Uzi got to play the mad scientist, Dr. Igor. Ana got to use her legs as the hands of a giant clock opening and closing in a musical number. Rebecca got a monologue about her urges to eat human fingers ("They don't even need hot sauce").

We were very lucky to have Charles Scott Richards as the designer for *Chicas* at both Dixon Place and Performance Space 122.

Persona Grata and Not

It is hard to believe, but I've encountered times when Carmelita has been persona non grata. It must have been las frutas, which Enrique Fernandez, a critic, referred to as "dangerous fruits." Those dangerous fruits had been my collaborator's signature piece and pièce de résistance.

It was after my performance at "The Decade Show" that my girl-friend of two months, a politically liberal woman, confessed to me that the fruits I wore made her ill. Latina stereotype, she thought. But now she understood and liked what she saw on stage. The same happened to a photographer I met at the taping of the TV show *Cristina* on nightclubs in New York City. Carmelita's topics ranged from real estate on the Lower East Side of New York City to performance art and finally nightclubs, as I recalled the night at a nightclub called MK's where I met Donny the human horse, who wore a saddle and gave me a ride. The photographer said when he saw the fruits he thought I was a crazy stupid woman, but after listening to me talk he liked what I had to say.

And there was that other incident that caused me to ponder how the persona is received. It happened riding a limo with an upper-class Cuban couple after a gala I had entertained at. Even though I said I was Cuban in my routine, the Cuban couple still could not believe it and asked: "You are Puerto Rican, aren't you?" They did not see the fruits, the accent, the loud behavior reflected in their own Cuban mirror.

At present Carmelita has put away her classic fruit and opted for donning camouflage, Desert Storm, and animal prints, faux snake, faux leopard, faux cow, no faux Foucault.

As a writer, I do confess to being jealous of Carmelita and, ingrate that I am, have wanted to kill that persona who has served me so well, who ironically gave me my voice, that persona who lets me see beyond the printed word. Oh, how I cried when a Boston reviewer described me as one who had horn-rimmed glasses, orange hair with black roots and buck teeth. But it was Carmelita who said buck up, girl: black roots, that's right, be proud of your African black roots; buck teeth, I say delicious overbite à la Brigitte Bardot and Patricia Arquette, and watch out cause I bite. Grrrr.

I Exit You Enter

And now, dear reader, I hope that as you turn these pages, you'll find that the work entertains you; that the work moves you, tugging at your heartstrings; but that the work is also thought provoking and ponders universal questions like the African saying that asks: Con qué culo se sienta la cucaracha? With what ass does the cockroach sit?

Chapter 80

Herbert Blau

One of the leading scholars of Samuel Beckett and performance theory, playwright and artistic director Herbert Blau, like Bert O. States (see Chapter 66), considers the phenomenology of theatre and the roots of performance. Director of the Repertory of Lincoln Center, Blau has written important books including *To All Appearances: Ideology and Performance* (1992), *Nothing in Itself: Complexions of Fashion* (1999), and *Sails of the Herring Fleet: Essays on Beckett* (2000). Here Blau considers the "limits of performance," the capacities and boundaries of the theatre.

Limits of Performance: The Insane Root (2001)

[. . .] "When you think about it, it is a strange thing that we do," said the New York Giants linebacker Jessie Armstead a couple of years ago, when the NFL was, as it still is, going through a reassessment of degrees of violence in the game, crack-back blocks, leg whips, face masks twisted, kicks in the groin, thumbs in the nostrils, fingers bent and bitten, or other vulnerable parts, gouged eyes, head butts, or after a smashing tackle, gratuitous elbows in the massive piling on. Not every player, coached to perform "like a bunch of crazed dogs," as Lawrence Taylor once put it, can do so with the marauding grace of his lethal instincts, but there is among the league's statistics a ferocious inventory of serious damage, surreptitious or flagrant, intended and unintended, from repeated quarterback concussions to shredded tendons, snapped clavicles, ripped ligaments in the

Excerpts from Herbert Blau, "Limits of Performance: The Insane Root," in *The Dubious Spectacle: Extremities of Theater, 1976–2000* (Minneapolis: University of Minnesota Press, 2002), 307–20. Originally published in *Psychoanalysis and Performance*, ed. Patrick Campbell and Adrian Kear (London: Routledge: 2001), 21–33. © 2001 by Routledge. Reprinted by permission of Taylor and Francis Books UK. The essay is a revised and expanded version of a talk given in May 1999 at the Stanford Presidential Symposium on "Limits of Performance: Sports, Medicine, and the Humanities."

line. "During a game we want to kill each other," Armstead remarked. "Then we're told to shake hands and drive home safely. Then a week later we try to kill each other again." This is not to mention the subtler brutalities of psychological dominance that may erupt, too, in physical violence, or the physical violence that goes the other way, as when, before Bill Parcells brought them together as teammates, the Bears linebacker Bryan Cox, stunned and upended by the Jets 300-pound tackle Jumbo Elliott, went down punching him in the ribs. As they grappled then on the ground, the simple question was this, posed by Elliott with his hands on Cox's throat: "Do you know who's in control of this situation?"[1]

It would seem that acting in the theater is a somewhat tamer game, but at the extremities of performance – where, when you think about it, a strange thing is being done, and in certain modes of performance, outside the precincts of theater (e.g., body art, from Viennese actionism to Chris Burden's crucifixion to Orlan's cosmetic surgeries), even stranger yet – the same question may be asked: "Do you know who's in control of this situation?" And indeed, if the performance does not rise to the level of that question – as it must, too, in the knot, the negative transference – it is not likely to be very much of a performance. Which is to say that, if we are really talking of limits, it must include the kind of performance that occurs in dubious peril just this side of a loss of control – not only strange but wondrous when the peril is only a seeming. If this is not quite the case with a wide receiver who, going up for the ball, risks being sliced in midair, it may be so with the actor who in a kind of hallucination, like the blinded Gloucester in *King Lear*, jumps from the cliffs of Dover – the "crows and choughs [winging] the midway air" (4.6.13) – or in conceiving a role like Macbeth, rehearses the impossible as if, as Banquo puts it after the witches vanish, having "eaten on the insane root" (*Macbeth* 1.3.84).

I may have been eating on that root many years ago, back in the early sixties, when I wrote – with a determined psychic violence and potential loss of control, feeling "like the lunatic Lear on the heath, wanting to 'kill, kill, kill, kill, kill!' " – the first paragraphs of *The Impossible Theater*, in which I said that "if politics is the art of the possible, theater is the art of the impossible. 'Seeming, seeming' is what it's made of," as if there were no future but the future of illusion, as Nietzsche believed and Freud had to concede, given the ineliminability of civilization's discontents. What I had in mind, more immediately, was the instrumentality of illusion and the demands on intelligence at the perceptual limits of the form. But given at the time, amidst the insanities of the Cold War, the woeful condition of our theater – institutionally, aesthetically, in every conceivable way, from the consensual humiliations of actors to the vacuity of most productions to the absence of continuity making for teamwork in performance – I added "that among the meanings of the word *impossible* I have in mind is the one you get when you say it raging with your teeth clenched."[2] I will not rehearse what has happened to the theater since, except to say that, as always, the impossible takes a little time, while the insanities persist, some of them undreamed of during the Cold War.

But let us stay at the limit of performance where doing the impossible, or nearly so, remains a constant dream, though what I have in mind at the moment is, if insanely rooted, also up in the air, and, as it turns out, if not without illusion, somewhere beyond seeming – as if performance were occurring somehow in phantasmic figures on the other side of the dream. For it is even higher up in the air than the body artist Stelarc, who thinks the body obsolete, and on that forbidding premise did a series of events – beautiful at a distance, at sites around the world: over the waves in Japan, above a street on the Lower East Side of Manhattan, and way above the Royal Theater in Stockholm – in which his body was suspended by fishhooks through the flesh. [...]

[...] [I]t suggests those figures crossing an abyss, "like Ideas in Plato's cave," in the van den Leyden painting admired by Artaud in his essay on "Metaphysics and the Mise en Scène," because it suggests "what the theater should be, if it knew how to speak the language that belongs to it."[3] It is a language, of course, which must be for Artaud material, tactile, "affecting the brain directly, like a physical agent" (35), yet as a "poetry of the senses" (37) nothing less than transcendent, though what he is describing, it seems, is the pictographic language in the dramaturgy of the unconscious. So with his notion of the actor, like a victim "burnt at the stake, signaling through the flames" (13), at that limit of performance never quite realized, nor maybe realizable, not by Artaud himself, nor by those of us, stirred by his enraptured vision, who were not quite up to that suicidal idea, but who tried to remember in all the psychophysical exercises of a generation ago – pushing the narcissistic body beyond limits to some sensation of a *déchirement*, the originary splitting contained by thought that actors in the West had forgotten how to scream. He did not mean the indulgent noise that characterized some performance in the sixties but rather, in the "essential theater," what released the body that matters from logocentric repression into its "complete, sonorous, streaming naked realization," which is also, as in the dreamscape of the Eleusinian mysteries, a "transfusion of matter by mind" (52). Unachievable as it may be, Artaud's conception of a theater of Cruelty – mystical, alchemical, where all the "perverse possibilities of the mind" (30) are localized and exalted, opening up the "gigantic abscess" (31) of repression and deceit – nevertheless ups the ante on the crucial question of control, which in the more familiar regions of theater is part of the psychopathology of the rehearsal process that must shake off, in time, "the asphyxiating inertia of matter which invades even the clearest testimony of the senses" (32). It is as if in the deepest sense, as in the protocols of the death wish beyond the pleasure principle, the organism does not want to act, or with the illusion of commitment – as to a predictable plot or image – acts by a kind of default.

As for the Nietzschean "true illusion," which requires from the actor, according to Artaud, an inescapable commitment to "the truthful precipitates of dreams, in which his taste for crime, his erotic obsessions, his savagery, his chimeras, his utopian sense of life and matter, even his cannibalism, pour out, on a level not counterfeit and illusory, but interior" (92). As there are conventional forms of theater that hardly dream this way, and theories of theater that, from Brechtian alienation to the queerer deconstruction, distrust the energy of an "interior," or think of it as a fiction, there are evasive practices of rehearsal that try to defer it or ward it off, as there must be with working it up in practice on a football field, or for that matter, in the associational process of the analytical session. But when push comes to shove, that is where the action is, and the best of actors know it, to the point of obsessive compulsion that can make a rehearsal endless, and thrilling to the degree that it is always on the edge. Or to return to the image after Macbeth's encounter with the witches, close to the insane root, where it is sometimes impossible to ascertain who exactly is in control or, as we trammel up the consequence, "smother'd in surmise, and nothing is / But what is not" (1.3.141–42), not who, but *what*.

Of course, to begin with, like the coach with firing power, head tricks, and playbook or, more subtly, the analyst introjecting the patient's idiom – presumably a "shadow ego"[4] but, in the counter transference, something more than that – the director may be in control; or in the commodified theater of Broadway, the producer who puts up the money; or moving from stage to screen, with Miramax, Disney, or Dreamworks, the source of megabucks. That may even produce, as it did recently, in *Saving Private Ryan* or *The Thin Red Line*, powerful images of fear and courage at the excruciating limits of performance, where teamwork exists at the edge of the imbecilic. If the harrowing realism of it depends on a prior teamwork of actors, crew, editors, stunt men, and wizards of special effects, what is achieved by camera and cutting is unavailable to the theater, whose teamwork always returns to the susceptible thing itself, the unaccommodated body that at any performative moment may really lose control, as in something so elemental as a case of stage fright. It should be apparent, though it is not, that while it may be superbly sublimated, stage fright is the latency of any performance, as it is there in the batter's box or down in the sprinter's crouch, or even in the supposed privacy of the analytic encounter, where the patient forgets the dream or stutters through made-up experience or, in a seizure of dislocation, is made speechless by the uncanny. Harrowing as it may be, the symptoms of stage fright, like the blanking out on lines, still occur in a situation that you cannot shoot over again. Laurence Olivier was quite aware of that when, at the height of his career, having made his film of *Hamlet* and played triumphantly as Othello, he was directing the National Theater and about to perform in *The Master Builder*. It was then, after some vague "feelings of misgiving" at an afternoon dress rehearsal, that he experienced "a much-dreaded terror," which he thought of as the punishment his pride always deserved, but "which was, in fact," as he wrote of it in his autobiography, "nothing other than a merciless attack of stage fright with all its usual shattering symptoms."[5] For which, and other reasons, he had entered into analysis.

Meanwhile, the vicissitudes of control are endemic to the art of acting, and in the exacerbation of rehearsal – with its associational process – a director may work on that, escalating a certain danger that, in the reciprocity of actors, may really get out of hand, not only in scenes of violence but, as lyrical or tender as it may be, in a love scene as well: more of that, yes, it's splendid (so the director thinks, sometimes saying it, sometimes not), but if the sensuosity increases, whatever the text says, text or no text, the bodies becoming the book, when do you stop? and why? since the actors are into it now, and then again, if one of them is not, how do you get them to take it a little further? one controlling the situation, one ever so slightly resisting, and if the truth were known, you not sure that it isn't too much already. "Do it again," you say, but the demoralizing thing in rehearsal – what the French call *répétition* – is not really knowing what *it* is, "it all, it all," as Beckett says, the intangible referent that always escapes you, not that, *this*, not this, *that*, nor do you really want to repeat it, not that merely, because it wouldn't be the same if it were only the same, it would be nothing but a repetition, not as right as it was, spontaneous, as when it happened for the first time, because the actors were, as they say, "living the moment," not what was, but what *is*, while the desire to get at it, whatever it (again) is, drives the rehearsal even more, sometimes driving it crazy. Which suggests that, at some limit, you are dealing with the impossible, arousing an interior violence, which is the mythic source of theater, if we can believe the canonical drama (which moved into psychoanalysis), back through Oedipus to Dionysus, the root not only insane but insatiable as well. Arid when there is, indeed, physical violence on a stage (which can neither be achieved, escalated, cut away from as on film), a sword fight, a murder, a rape. Othello smothering Desdemona, you always want more, more, but how far do you go, you wonder, before somebody does get hurt, emotionally or physically, you are not always sure which is worse.

That may become an incessant question when there is a sustained history among the actors, with mixed feelings of attraction and aversion, or along with devotion, inflexions of animosity, intensified by dependence, with the director as shadow ego (or as with the analyst drawn into the "emotional constellation," a kind of "somatic double" [Bollas, 12]), caught up in the displacements and condensations that eventually shadow them all, as intrinsic to what they do as the atmosphere they breathe. What they come to know about each other could naturally be an asset, drawn upon in performance, but it could also be a burden, cutting off surprise. That was certainly our experience at The Actor's Workshop of San Francisco, as it developed from a studio with 8 actors to a company of about 150, at a time in the American theater, through the early fifties into the sixties, when (as I have said) there were no examples of continuity, and almost nothing like a company concept. As a performative proposition, the mixed feelings were addressed, even more intimately, in my work with the KRAKEN group (young people whom I trained, some of them famous now), where no matter what we did, whatever the theme or surface appearance, it was always at some level about relations among the performers and – whether on the brain-struck ramparts of *Elsinore*, a work derived from *Hamlet*, or forced to cannibalism in the Sierras in *The Donner Party, Its Crossing* – the psychic condition of the group, with none of the easy escape routes of therapeutic consciousness-raising.

So it was only to be expected when, at the exhausting limit of one improvisation, which was part of an exhaustive interrogation (some of these went on for hours) of materials resembling *Othello* that, when one of the men in the group started to smother one of the women, there was nothing like the accustomed Desdemona about her, certainly nothing submissive, as she threw him off in a rage, and shouted ceaseless obscenities, every scurrilous word of it meant, what they felt about each other being not merely a subtext, but rather the compulsively abrasive substance of the event. "You bastard, you shit, don't you ever do that again!" she cried, as he backed away, "you always do that, always!" – *what* wasn't entirely clear – "don't you ever put your filthy hands on me again!" Whereupon he looked at her and said simply, "But I can't help it, it's written," and started moving toward her, big and powerful, overwhelmingly so, in a muted rage of his own, and I let him go until he touched her, because I really *wanted to see it*, you always want to *see* it, and then had all I could do to stop it – she there flailing, scratching, cursing when he grabbed her – because they were no longer simply acting and he was almost ready to kill her, and if I hadn't interfered it would have been something more than a fiction or mimicry of abuse. And it was something more than that, too, when it was reflected upon, debated, worked through in other sessions, then displaced to another context (over the months of analysis) and, in another imagistic form, dispersed among the actors, entered into the structure of a developing work, charged as it might not have been if the outbreak had never happened or, since I saw it all coming, if I wasn't entirely sure – in letting it go the limit, and wanting it to go beyond – that I hadn't, almost, lost control of the situation. [...]

Notes

1 Quotation from M. Freeman, "A Cycle of Violence, On the Field and Off," *New York Times*, Sept. 6, 1998, 27, 34.

2 Blau, *The Impossible Theater: A Manifesto* (New York: Macmillan, 1964), 1, 5.

3 Artaud, *The Theater and Its Double*, tr. M. C. Richards (New York: Grove, 1958), 36–7.

4 C. Bollas, *Cracking Up: The Work of Unconscious Experience* (New York: Hill & Wang, 1995), 39.

5 L. Olivier, *Confessions of an Actor: An Autobiography* (New York: Simon & Schuster, 1982), 261.

Chapter 81

Mitsuya Mori

Mitsuya Mori is a Professor of Theatre in the Department of Art Studies at Seijo University, Japan, and an acclaimed theatre director. He has written studies of Japanese theatre as well as of Ibsen and Strindberg. His books (in Japanese) include *Scandinavian Theatre* (1980), *Ibsen's Realism* (1984), *Comparative Theatre* (1994), and *Ibsen's fin de siècle* (1995). In the following extract he explicates the semiotics of Japanese theatre, fleshing out its distinctions and identity. His triangular concept of theatre has much in common with Meyerhold's notions in this anthology (see Chapter 8), and both authors bear fruitful comparison.

The Structure of Theater: A Japanese View of Theatricality (2002)

The Western concept of "theater" did not exist in pre-modern Japan. *Engeki* was the word chosen to translate "theater" when it was introduced to Japan in the second half of the 19th century.[1] It still sounds a little foreign to Japanese people. Traditionally Japan had a word, *shibai*, which was almost equivalent to "theater," but was, and still is, applied only to Kabuki and Bunraku (puppet theater) and not to Noh. The modern westernized theater is not usually called *shibai*, either, for this sounds too colloquial or too non-literal. The adjective forms of *shibai*, *shibai-jimita* or *shibai-gakatta*, imply "pretentious" or "insincere" behavior, a definitely pejorative nuance, equivalent to the negative meaning of the English term "theatrical."

Excerpts from Mitsuya Mori, "The Structure of Theater: A Japanese View of Theatricality," in *Substance 98/99: Special Issue, Theatricality* Vol. 31.2 and 3 (2002), 73–93. © 2002. Reprinted by permission of The University of Wisconsin Press.

"Theatricality," on the other hand, is rendered in Japanese as *engeki-sei*. The suffix *-sei* makes an abstraction of the preceding noun. The foreignness of *engeki* is reinforced by this suffix, for the abstraction of theatricality is also a Western way of thinking, imported into Japan only in modern times. Grammatically, it would be possible to add *-sei* to *shibai* as well, but *shibai-sei* sounds odd and is not in common usage. This means that there is no Japanese word that is exactly equivalent to the slightly pejorative "theatricality." Instead, *engeki-sei* (theatricality) is used to mean the spectacular quality of theater, or the qualities unique to theater – i.e. particular qualities that construct the kind of performance we could call theater. It is in this sense that the word was often uttered to describe the new trend of Japanese theater since the late 1960s. But some representatives of this "underground" theater would like to call their activities *shibai* rather than *engeki*, as a revolt against "modern theater." They have even declared themselves to be closer to the old conception of performance art in Japan, *geinoh*.

Geinoh ("gay-noh") is another Japanese word, fairly equivalent to "theater" but covering the broader or narrower realm of performance arts, depending on the context. [...] Though the word itself first appeared in literature in the 10th century,[2] much earlier than *shibai*, today the word is also commonly used, and obviously intersects with *engeki-sei*. The distinction between *engeki*, *shibai* and *geinoh* is not a clear-cut one, and it becomes almost meaningless to attempt to define the words at all. (Such confusion is an inevitable result of modernization, and is seen in many fields of culture in Japan.) But if our goal is not simply defining terms, but understanding what theater is, then we need to move beyond the definition of concepts. Our understanding of the topics will be deepened in the course of discussing them. Our topics are theater and theater-like performances, which still exist in abundance in Japan.

There are many ways to analyze theater. I will limit my arguments here to the structural analysis of theater events – i.e. basic characteristics of theater to be distinguished from other performative activities, in order to clarify "theatricality" to some degree.

From Creator to Audience

Theater is play and so is music. As an art form, theater and music have some structural similarities. In the aesthetic classification of art forms, theater and music are put into the same category – performing arts.

A composer writes a piece of music, which is perceived by someone else. This "someone else" is usually a musician who plays the score to be perceived by the audience. This sequence can be schematized as follows:

Composer → Musical Composition → Score reader
|
Musician → Musical performance → Audience

The upper and the lower levels have a similar structure in the way they are produced. For this reason, music is called an art form of "double productions."

Different musicians may play the same score differently, but it would not be unreasonable to say that what the composer composes and what the musician plays are almost the same. In a competition of musical composition, the nominated works are performed in front of the judges. What the audience finally perceives is supposed to be the same as what the composer originally had in mind. The audience and the composer share the same artistic experience. We can modify the diagram to the cyclic structure as follows:

Composer → Musical Composition → Score reader
|
Audience ← Musical performance ← Musician

The second production repeats the first one but in reverse.

Theater is also an art form of double productions. Therefore, on the surface, the analysis of its structure is similar to that of music.

Dramatist ⟶ Drama ⟶ Drama reader
|
Actor ⟶ theater performance ⟶ Spectator

However, unlike music, the second production does not repeat the first one in reverse. A theater performance onstage is quite different from a drama on paper, and what the spectator conceives is not at all the same as what the dramatist had in mind. It used to be said that the dramatist imagines the stage production as he writes, so that one can read in the drama – provided it is a good one – every detail of the stage production. Obviously this is wrong. Even the realist Ibsen would not possibly have imagined the way *A Doll's House* or *Ghosts* might be performed today. This is because a theater production is a combination of two different aspects: drama and play. [...]

If what the musician plays is fairly much the same as what the composer composes, the above written diagram of the music structure could be as simple as this:

Composer ⟶ Musical Piece (Score-Musician-Playing) ⟶ Audience

But the diagram of theater structure cannot be shortened. It remains:

Dramatist ⟶ Drama ⟶ Actor ⟶ Playing ⟶ Audience

Structurally speaking, the musician is a mediator between the composer and the audience or an interpreter of the score (a musical performance is sometimes called an interpretation), while the actor is a creator of a kind of art form that is different from a written drama. This is another way of saying that music depends only on our sense of hearing, but theater on both hearing and sight. True, we enjoy the pianist's passion-filled bodily movements, but the sight is not supposed to affect our evaluation of his or her musical performance.

Actor Plays Character for Audience

The unique feature of theater lies in its process of performance. Hence any discussion of theater tends to focus on the performance level. Peter Brook says in the opening passage of his *The Empty Space*, "A man walks across [...the] empty space whilst someone else is watching him, and this is all that is needed for an act of theater to be engaged."[3] This statement is rather misleading. The man who crosses the empty space may be an actor and the man who watches him a spectator, but Brook mentions no character that the actor plays. Nevertheless, the man's action of crossing the empty space implies his playing something or somebody else. Therefore, we can find even in Brook's statement three basic elements of theater: Actor plays Character for Audience.

Admittedly, this formula has been challenged in the second half of the 20th century, and various theaters, which seemingly lack one of those elements, have been advocated and practiced. But it seems that no one has proposed more than these three as the primary agents composing a theatrical event. So, this formula can still be a good point of departure.

First, the relationship between these three elements is to be seen not as linear but as triangular. The diagram can be drawn thus:

$$A(ctor) \quad\text{————————}\quad C(haracter)$$
$$\searment$$

A(ctor) ———————— C(haracter)

Au(dience)

This kind of triangular relationship is meaningless in art forms other than theater. The impossibility of technological reproduction of a theater performance also derives from this structural relationship.

This triangular diagram may be viewed in two ways: either from each corner point, or from each line between the two corners. The latter view is preferred here, for in this way we have a chance to grasp a theater production as a whole without cutting it up into pieces to be examined one by one. If we look into the triangle from the line between A and C, for example, we see Au beyond the line so that Au is not at any moment excluded from our view of the A–C relationship. In this way the whole theatrical event could be viewed, if not in its completeness, at least adequately enough.

Each line of the triangle – i.e. the relationship between each two of the three agents – is closely related with each of the three basic aspects of theater: playing, drama, theatrical space. The relationship between Actor and Audience transforms a physical place, where they simultaneously exist, into a theatrical space. The aspect of playing stands in the relationship between Actor and Character, and Drama is not something Actor presents to Audience, but something formed between Audience and Character. The triangular diagram, therefore, can be enriched as follows:

Playing

Space ——→ A ——— C ←—— Drama

Au

Creating a Theatrical Space

When and how is a physical place transformed into a theatrical space? Peter Brook refers to empty space as if it exists before a man crosses over it. But "empty space" does not exist in this world. In both an open-air theater and a proscenium-arch theater, many things have been in existence before the man crosses over the space. In fact, it is the man's crossing it that makes the place into the "empty space" for the one who watches. The actor's action makes every pre-existing thing (except those set up for his action) invisible to the audience.

This is apparent particularly in the indoor theater, which became common in the 18th century, both in Europe and in Japan. Before that, most theatrical performances took place in open- or semi-open-air theaters, surrounded by nature. [...] One of the oldest Noh stages in Japan stands in seawater, and the audience, sitting in another building, can notice the sea-level change as the performance proceeds. Even the Shakespearean theater, already encircled by walls, must have made best use of the effect of the movement of the sun during the performance. I would like to call this characteristic of the theatrical place "field" in contrast to empty "space." It is an interesting coincidence that both European and Japanese theater history had a transition from "field" to "space" in the 16th and 17th centuries. In Europe in this period, the tradition of medieval drama lost its vigor and modern secular drama came to be formed, while in Japan, the long-established Noh drama made room for the newly-emerging Kabuki theater form. Apparently, on both sides, this change was reinforced by a new type of dramatic character on the stage – a type that was more realistic than in previous dramas.

The "space" characteristic of the stage is closely related to realism in theater. Realism demands that the audience ignore the pre-existing decorations and forms of the stage and see characters as if they were really living there. The more realistic the drama becomes, the more the stage is required to be "space," and vice versa. The "space" also cosmopolitanizes drama, because a drama's "space" can be transferred to any other theater without essential alterations. This was not possible for Shakespearean drama, for example, which still retained the "field" aspect to a considerable degree.

Nevertheless, a physical place cannot transform itself into a theatrical place without acquiring aspects characteristic of "space." An absolute "field" will remain a natural place of daily life. Thus the question, "When and how is the physical place transformed to theatrical space?" can be modified to, "When and how is field transformed into space?"

Field and Performance

The "field" aspect of the performing place is nowhere more apparent than in folkloric rituals, which still today are regularly seen in Japan and other Asian countries. The place can be a rice field, the area around a shrine, a village market place, etc. Every ritual must be performed in its particular "field" and cannot be moved to any other place.

However, the "field" of the ritual is not a mere natural, everyday field. An actual rice field, which is chosen for the rice ritual on a specific day of the year, is decorated in a special way for the performance by girls selected in the village for this occasion. This is no longer an ordinary rice field, but the one devoted to a divine being in a wish to have a good harvest, not only for this particular field, but for all the fields in the village. The "space" aspect already creeps in here. The selected girl performers and the surrounding village people have a special relationship with each other in their wishes, which transforms this rice field into a ritual space or, we may say, a theatrical space.

Let us take another example. A ritual performance at the Nigatsu-do Hall of the Todaiji Temple in Nara is called *Todaiji-shunie* and takes place in the middle of March. The climax comes after dark. Monks carry eight or nine burning torches (ca. 10 meters long and half a meter in diameter), each held by several monks, up to the wooden veranda of the Hall, about 20 meters above ground level. They are laid side by side on the edge of the floor, the burning heads being thrust in the air. Hundreds of thousands of people come to watch this performance, standing on the ground below, so that sparks of fire fall upon them. This is truly a spectacular sight. While the torches are burning on the veranda, a group of monks conducts a special rite in a small room inside the Hall. They continue the rite all night long, sometimes sitting on the floor, sometimes walking or jumping around an altar, but all the time chanting prayers. At around three o'clock in the morning, a monk brings another burning torch into this small room and hits the wooden floor with full force. Sparks of fire spread out and monks jump over them. This is an incredible performance, even more spectacular than the performance outside. Only those who have obtained special permission from the Temple are allowed to witness this rite from a side room. No women are allowed. They must remain outside, but may watch through a grill. The monks completely ignore the spectators, the rite being conducted first and foremost for themselves. I cannot deny the great excitement I felt when I saw the enactment of this rite. And yet I had no personal feeling toward the monks, but rather an impression of a great panoramic picture, like an erupting volcano or an awesome ocean wave. It was an event completely of another world, so to speak, which we were peeping into, similar to a cinematic experience rather than a theatrical one. No definite theatrical relationship between the performers and the spectators was formed.

It was different in the case of the ritual that I once experienced in the region of Kofu, in central Japan. The performance took place inside curtain walls set up around the village shrine, so that the performance was totally hidden from the spectators. Nevertheless, we, standing outside, clearly felt related to those performers inside. I say "we" because I could sense the festive atmosphere prevailing among us while waiting for the end of the performance. This feeling, I assume, came from the fact that we had talked with the village performers and had walked behind them to the shrine before the performance. The whole process was a ritual, only a part of which was the performance inside the curtain walls. So we were participating in the ritual not only by having followed them to the shrine, but also by waiting outside the curtain walls. It was odd indeed that we had a feeling of being related to the performers whom we could not see – a kind of feeling one did not have for the other performers whose spectacular action had made an awesome impression. Although I did not share the belief of the village people in their divine being, I at least could understand their belief. Herein lies the crucial point of our relationship. Both I and the village people perceived something existing outside our relationship, or better said, something that assured our close relationship. Even if it is doubtful that this "something" could be called Character in our diagram of the theater structure, it was, without doubt, because of this "something" that the area of the village shrine became a theatrical space, which the small room for the rite in the Nigatsudo Hall was not. I had been struck by the sight of the monks' performances, but almost completely alienated from their belief.

Without at least a glimpse of C, the relationship will be reduced to that of Player–Spectator. I mean by "Player" the performer who performs for him/herself, and by "Spectator," the one who watches the performance as a mere bystander. The Player–Spectator relationship is, in fact, no relationship. This is the case with sports, games or music. Some sports, and certainly music, are played *for* spectators (or listeners), and some may claim that musical performers are influenced by the audience's responses. This is true especially in popular music concerts, but these come close to being theater performances. Spectators are not essential for players of music, nor are players necessary for "spectators." We enjoy recorded music as a substitute for live performances, even if it is not a completely satisfactory one. This is not the case with theater, as anyone knows.

Actor and Character

The relationship between Actor and Character is the most problematic one in the triangular structure of theater. We say that an actor plays a character, but this activity is called acting. The difference between playing and acting corresponds to the distinction between Player and Actor, respectively. Acting implies "playing a character," but the "play" element, being situated between Actor and Character, stands independent of both. In actuality, A, p and C are combined together in a person acting in front of the audience, but in theory these three can be separately examined. I have done so in some detail on another occasion, basing my arguments on the following schema:[4]

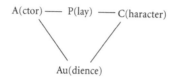

As is easily understood, realistic theater tends to hide p, or tries to make p unseen to Au. In non-realistic, or stylized, theater, p is emphasized rather than hidden, and when a certain pattern or form of p is repeated by one actor or one generation of actors after another, what is called *kata* in Japanese is born. This is the case with the stylized movements in Kabuki and Noh.[5] And the traditional puppet theater in Japan, today called Bunraku, is an interesting example by which we can illustrate each element of this scheme – A, p and C – not in theory, but in actuality.

Any puppet theater consists of three basic elements: the puppeteer, the puppet, and the narrator. The puppeteer manipulates the puppet according to the dialogue or narrative spoken by the narrator. In most puppet theaters the puppeteer and the narrator are the same person who hides himself from the audience so that they see only the puppet. But in Bunraku, all three elements are in sight. The narrator chants the story with the *shami-sen* (three-stringed instrument) musical accompaniment, played by a *shami-sen* player. Both narrator and musician sit side by side on the small platform, stage-left. A puppet is two-thirds the size of an actual human being, and is operated by hand by three puppeteers; the main puppeteer handles the head and the right hand, the second the left hand, and the third, the legs. Usually puppeteers cover their heads and bodies in black so as not to distract the audience's attention from the puppets, but curiously enough, the main puppeteer shows his face in important, dramatic scenes of the play.

These three elements of Bunraku – puppeteer, puppet and narrator (with music player) – correspond to the above-schematized three structural elements of acting, A, p and C, respectively. This rare case of Bunraku reveals that C cannot be a theatrical element without being bodily expressed by p, and that p could not be theatrical p, no matter how stylized it may be, without being framed by C. But the most interesting thing to see is that A and p are indeed two separate entities in acting. The Audience can see p without paying attention to A, or even both A and p at the same time but separately. The audience can see all the structural elements of theater performance independently. In this respect Bunraku manifests the most basic structural characteristic of theater performance.

Of course this manifestation is not possible in an ordinary theater. But what is really revealing in Bunraku for the present argument is the fact that A does not play C in the sense that A's movements represent C to Au. Au watches p, or A and p together, but C is given independently from a different side. In Bunraku, what the narrator chants is not only the dialogue of the characters but the whole narrative story. It can be appreciated as a free-standing form of literature. Herein lies a key to the everlasting question concerning acting: is it the actor or the character that the audience is watching on the stage?

Actor/Character

Our perceptive organs can perceive only one object at a time, never two or more. It is not possible for us to watch both the actor and the character at the same time. Some think that we watch them alternately. But this is absurd, for then the character is split into pieces, and each member of the audience may have entirely different portions of the character. Some also think that the actor is a real person and the character an imaginary one, so that both are compatible. But real or imaginary, we cannot perceive two objects at the same time. What is wrong about the above-asked question is the presupposition that character is a "person," real or imaginary. For in fact, a character is not a person but a conception, which is formed in the audience's mind.

When a person appears on the stage, we notice him, of course, but do not know if he is an actor playing a character or not. He may be the man we call Hamlet, but he may turn out to be the man who is going to apologize for the delay of the performance. Even a man who we suppose is playing Hamlet can take off his pretense at any moment and come back to himself as an actor. This means that we cannot be sure of having a complete character until the final curtain falls. We have a character only when the play ends. But when the play ends, the character is gone. He remains only in our minds, as a conception. Therefore, we may say that, watching the movements of the actor and hearing his lines, we build up the conception of the character little by little. Sometimes he may surprise us by an action, which his previous behavior had not led us to expect from him, but we adjust our hitherto built-up character to that new behavior and amend the conception accordingly. No matter how much his behavior confuses us at a certain moment in the play, we get a total conception of the character at the end. If we do not, we feel that the character is incomprehensible.

Although everything in theater is pretense, a pretense that the audience is well aware of all the time, the audience can believe in the character all the same. This belief is supported by the fact that a man on the stage is a real human being, which is not the case in cinema or the novel. So, coming back to the question of actor–character confusion, the audience's illusion of character is based on the reality of the actor's being. And if

Character is a conception that we complete only at the end of the play, it is to be understood in the genuine sense of the word "character" – *ethos* in Greek.

Aristotle put the primary importance on *mythos* rather than *ethos*, in his analysis of Greek tragedy in the *Poetics*. *Mythos*, usually rendered into English as *plot*, is a series of actions. Hence his definition: "Tragedy is a representation of an action." But we humans have the amazing ability to discern the plot of a play that consists only of dialogues. In a theater, we hear only actors' lines, with no explanations by the author or any one else, but we can still discern the story of the play as if it were narrated. This ability is obviously related to our ability to understand language. In the same way that we conceive the meaning of a sentence in a linear sequence of words, we weave the texture of the story little by little as we see actions going on. The story grows bigger and bigger from the series of small stories within each scene, until we get the whole story – the plot of the play – at the final curtain.

If the series of actions does not form a plot, everything we see is on the level of bare reality, and there is no formation of character, either. If one were to diagram the formation of both character and plot, they would be the same, since character and plot are actually one and the same thing. A character cannot stand alone, but can exist only in relation to other characters.[6] That a character is complete at the end of the play means that all the relationships between characters are completed, which is nothing but the plot of the play. We make up a character, little by little, in our minds, as we gradually make up the plot. Here arises the question of Drama. But before pursuing this question, I would like to take a couple of examples to illustrate how reality and fictionality intersect on the stage. [...]

Notes

1　Sino-Japanese characters for *engeki* did exist early in the 19th century, but labeled not as *engeki* but as *kyogen* (see Mori, "Thinking and Feeling," in *Japanese Theater and the International Stage*, ed. Stanca Scholz-Cionca and Samuel Leiter [Leiden, Boston and Cologne: Brill, 2001], n.p.).

2　The meaning of *geinoh*, which originally came from Chinese usage, first meant "skill," but went through a considerable degree of change from the 10th to 14th centuries (see Tsuyoshi Moriya, "Introduction," in *Nihon Geinoh-shi* [*The History of Japanese Geinoh*], Vol. I [Tokyo: Hosei University Press], 1981, n.p.).

3　Brook, *The Empty Space* (New York: Atheneum, 1968), 9. [See Chapter 52, this volume.]

4　See Mori, "Noh, Kabuki, and Western Theater: An Attempt at Schematizing Acting Styles," *Theatre Research International*, Spring Supplement, Oxford University Press, 1997, n.p.

5　*Kata* is described in the *New Kabuki Encyclopedia* as follows: "*Kata* essentially are fixed forms or patterns of performance and, while the term most commonly refers to acting, may be found in all production elements, such as the arrangement of a program, of scenes, and the traditions of scenery, props, wigs, makeup, music, and costumes. [...] A *kata* may be said to have been born when an actor created an appropriate *interpretation* of the spirit of a play and his role in it (in terms of movement, speech, appearance, and so on) and this interpretation was transmitted as a convention to the next generation of actors..." (S. L. Leiter, *New Kabuki Encyclopedia*, a *Revised Adaptation of Kabuki Jiten* [Westport, CT: Greenwood Press, 1997], 289). However, in my opinion, *kata* in Kabuki is more a pattern, while *kata* in Noh is more form, or Form in the sense close to the Platonic idea. *Kata* as pattern can be changed, as we see in the history of Kabuki, but *kata* of Form cannot, since Noh will no longer be Noh if its *kata is* changed (see Mori, 1997, II).

6   B. O. States holds a similar view of character: "All characters in a play are nested together in 'dynamical communion,' or in what we might call a reciprocating balance of nature: every character 'contains in itself' the cause of actions or determinations, in other characters and the effects of their causality...Hamlet is made of Gertrude and Claudius, Osric and Horatio, Rosencrantz and Guildenstern, et cetera and vice versa. Seen from the characterological view-point, Hamlet is a collection of relationships" (*Great Reckonings in Little Rooms* [Berkeley: University of California Press, 1985], 146–8). [See Chapter 66, this volume.]

Chapter 82

Heisnam Kanhailal (b. 1941)

Heisnam Kanhailal established the theatre group Kalakshetra Manipur in 1969. Rather than a production company, it is engaged in research theatre. For 35 years, the group has been working to create a theatre idiom based on physical rather than psychological language, driven by instinct and intuition, and exploring the specific powers of theatre in the context of Manipuri indigenous culture. Kanhailal's theatre focuses on the experiential: understanding is approached not through the intellect but through an evocation of empathy in the performance. In Kanhailal's theatre, for example, the actor's body is not so much disciplined to behave in certain acceptable ways as expressive of nuanced physicality, rhythm, and gesture. The effect is one of simplicity, high lyricism, and moving humanity. At its most fundamental level, Kanhailal's theatre upholds the poetry of the human spirit while at the same time commenting on social inequalities and injustices, informed by the repressive violence and corresponding insurgency affecting Manipur. With his wife and leading actress Sabitri, Kanhailal creates theories of theatre and life. Both performers are highly acclaimed in India. Their creative partnership performed *Tamnalai* (*Haunting Spirits*, 1972), *Kabui Keioiba* (*Half Man Half Tiger*, 1975), *Imphal '73* (1974), *Pebet* (1975), *Huranbagi Eshei* (1977), *Laigi Machasinga* (1978), *Mrityu Shwor* (1984), *Memoirs of Africa* (1985), *Rashomon* (1987), *Migi Sarang* (1991), *Karna* (1997), *Draupadi* (2000), *Nupi* (2002), and *Dakghar* (2006). Kanhailal's additional projects include the "Nature-Lore": a move away from the conditioning of the city towards a "home-return," exploring the openness of the rural. This is a continuation of his work to engage and overcome the racial biases and attitudes that exist in Manipuri.

Heisnam Kanhailal, "Ritual Theatre (Theatre of Transition)," in *Theatre India: National School of Drama's Theatre India* 10 (Nov. 2004), 3–16. Reprinted by permission of Heisnam Kanhailal.

Ritual Theatre (Theatre of Transition) (2004)

We are disillusioned with the spirit of the time. We reject the clichéd and often-made claim that nothing can be changed. Ours is an entirely different kind of awareness, reflecting on the past and the present. The importance of our continuous work consists in that we have breathed new values into the empty shell of theatre. Therefore, we believe in distilling new meanings from that social rapport, which is theatre. We believe in such productions that can shatter the ways of seeing and doing theatre.

What we have learnt from our past heretics like Stanislavski, Meyerhold, Craig, Copeau, Artaud, Brecht, Grotowski and Badal Sircar and Habib Tanvir in India is, to be in transition which invents personal value *of our own* theatre. Transition is itself a culture. In the universal perspective, every culture must have three aspects: material production by means of particular techniques, biological reproduction making possible the transmission of experience from generation to generation, and the production of meanings. Meanings are essential for a culture. In the absence of it there is no culture.

We are now in a culture of transition which creates for us an environment of continual exercises in learning the unknown in search of new possibilities. The work we have produced so far does not value the finished product which is not saleable, not mobile, and cannot be possessed by the future generations. So we do not value it for what it is; on the contrary, we do it for the promise of skill, technique or something that will come out in the future. What they will learn is again to be in transition.

In our practice of making theatre, we entered the culture of transition to pursue a rebellious way of life and expression. A journey towards an *unknown* world of creativity – wandering bewildered into the ethnic jungle of impulses – made our work vulnerable, because we denied the theatre which appeared itself as "orphan." Believing in the autonomy of theatre we swallowed the text and absorbed it into our body instead of speaking out the lines through lip movement, facial and finger gestures. We shattered the whole network of illusion on the stage. We were no longer burdened with the heavy light, set, costume and make-up. We cleaned the stage as an empty space where we began to unfold the autonomy of theatre – the drama of biological evolution accomplished by the bare body of the performer.

Here, it would be highly necessary to trace the sources of this theatre of transition in the context of culture-specificity as we are the progeny of our continual ethno-social tradition. We are aware of the historical process that our traditional forms of expression tend to change whenever we face paradoxical situations in the body behaviour because of tensions of the time. The reaction is the survival instinct manifested in movement and sound naturally produced by the body. So, the form is created by the body. We are not blind and romantic when we are exposed to the exotic and spectacular forms of our tradition. It makes us conscious of the continuity of tradition which lies in its spirit, not in its form. Our intention is thus to elicit the essence – the spirit of our *ancestral* tradition. "Not forms, but the marrow of forms," as Garcia Lorca says. "And that which seems to be a flower is in fact honey."

Let our body-mind be rocked by the sensuous memory of Mother's arm – the cradle of our *ancestral* tradition. Let us feel the blood and skin of Mother's arm which holds us near her breast as one with her body in a joyful play of impulses. Whenever Mother took us at such play we felt a great sensation that made us laugh and cry following each other in a natural course of actions – impulses and counter-impulses. In the dark nights Mother took us on her lap, and her image-filled tales carried us away to the strange world of the spirits. We always felt haunted. During the moonlit nights, we were on her back. Her lullaby transported us to the land of the moon which appeared to us as the presence of a human form radiating the calmness – the solitude. Thus her rhythmic movement of the trunk in tune with the soft, whispering but penetrating sound of *hum* removed our inner tensions and made our senses asleep. Whenever we were on her back in the daytime Mother made us feel the nature of all kinds of household labour, and sensitive to the process of the work-rhythm, tempo, organicity and flow. By "natural fooling" Mother taught us the art of mimicry and entertaining. Exposing us to the family and community rituals, Mother led us into the mythical world which infused into our body the unknown world of cosmic energy, and inspired us to enter the world of the collective unconscious.

When we do reflect on the blood and skin of Mother's arm, we grasp her as the performer and ourselves as spectators. As a performer she could make us, the spectator, "alert" sensorial "informed" body. Thus she could transport us to the dream as necessarily done by the performer to the spectator. Objectively, it is because of the truth of the intimacy between the two, an organic dialogue or encounter on the sensory level could occur. We can understand that the inter-human activity comes "alive" amidst the sensorial awareness in the event of action and reaction. Another analogy too we can trace out in the culture of prayer and ritual in a real community experience. On this occasion, though our body is immobile, we become involved with our whole being of the body, and at the same time identified with the group, singing men and women, lights, incense, colours. Awakening the energy within and outside of oneself, the intention-action is seen at work. The "ritual" spirit – the origin of our theatre – is deeply rooted in this sensorial environment of the culture of faith which gives way to the discovery of the lost "eternal human" – the psychic power and archetype. Therefore, we oppose the culture of corrosion now parading itself before us where immobility imprisons you, makes your feet sink into the earth and does not allow you any other reaction. The parade is the display of a stage set of geometrically lined up body which exhibits the mechanical "appearance" of attention without the slightest understanding of the inner action which makes any outer verity alive and credible.

Our theatre is an extremely localized theatre committed to identity, nationalism, difference, of finding an original outlet to channel the silent feelings and instincts of the oppressed. Our work, in many ways anti-establishment, has peculiar ideological concerns politically and culturally about how it defines its notion of itself. Our theatre is therefore "new, edgy, shrill" and "does not appeal" to both traditionalist-revivalists, and sophisticated modern and westernized minds. Their interest lies in aesthetics only. And also in academic and intellectual theatre. They do not want to see that the senses and ideas they have chosen and fallen for in their life style are deeply disturbed. To them, the traditional theatre or theatre of aesthetics is the great art. This theatre is highly privileged because it succeeds in catering to their taste and making itself international – "the most plugged into the global grid." Westerners simply love to see this traditional theatre, and they rate it as the work of genius.

However, we are antagonistic to the sophistication and vices of the great art because of the oppressive implications and cult atmosphere inherent in it. Here, vice does mean that our body-mind is clamped to the ceiling unable to feel the earthly social experience because of their "other-worldly" perception in making the form de-humanized. This is the basis of the perception of aesthetics created by "Devas" for the sanctity of their godly identity while marginalizing the "Asuras" to the identity of demons, wild and hostile, who live the life of "lokayata" – "this-worldly," indicative of the social sanction of material production. On the other hand, our culture of transition does not allow us to imitate any given form or style blindly. Technically, one is trained to cope with a given style. As a result of this, one is bound to produce the style itself. In our theatre, we need a force which can liberate our body-mind to respond to the tensions of the time – a body that can create the forms of social experience. *Form is social experience solidified.* For the content in respect of its fullness of humanity we have the legitimacy "not always to have to start at the beginning but to carry on from a point already attained, to transform an existing style into something new as a moment in the historical development of art." This is true not only of the arts but of all social phenomena. This is how our culture of transition is meant really for the "expression" which continues as "work-in-progress" in contrast to the "exhibition" of "Public Theatre," the professionally finished product of the culture of *Theatre as Industry* which basically works to meet the art consumer's demand in the global market. It encourages commodifying the traditional artifice in the wrong notion of glorifying the past and popularizing it internationally.

How does our theatre crystallize the most critical realities of oppression and resistance in a predominantly non-verbal dramaturgy of rhythm, gestures and movements in organicity? How does the body of the performer, through songs, cries, lullabies, evocation of dreams, incarnate resistance in alerting its spectators to the resilience of the human spirit in countering the dominant tensions of our times?

Before giving a concrete and technical answer to the above, we feel the need for cleansing the premises of our empirical research in the continuity of our ancestral tradition of body culture. Our theatre of transition is deeply rooted in the intra-cultural exercise, but in universal perspective, in terms of creating a practical objective impact. The memory of human nature transmitted orally from generation to generation in the case of our ethnicity which was founded on nature-lore and folk-lore reveals the hidden history of the biological evolution of an organism-in-life. When we locate this organism-in-life into the identity of an Asian performer in the larger Asian context, the body is traditionally trained to cope with the ecosystem and natural environment through various body techniques, movement, vocabulary, martial art, dance, yoga, mantra and understanding of myth and legend. The difference between the cultures of Asia lies in gradation only, not in contraposition as we find between the East and the West. Multigradations of cultural expression are the characteristics of Asian identity.

This is the story of a contemporary Asian performer who reflects on the past and present socio-culturally for a culture of transition. The body, as the human resource of the performer who is supreme in the performance, is the only answer. When we objectify the body's behaviour in its naturalness with analytical approach, we have discovered a body which could identify with the biological evolution of organism-in-life in its pristine purity (though the word purity has some vague implications), this is the body of the primeval character of natural human behavior, which transforms the natural into the artificial. This is the experience of the historical need of the body transmitted to us orally from generation to generation in the continuity of our ancestral tradition.

To accomplish the natural human body is to be conscious of "Body-in-life...the polyphony of tensions tied together by invisible, internal consistency," in the words of Eugenio Barba [see Chapter 68]. The body is thus charged with the complexity of energy, biological, social and creative, in our performance context. This complexity of energy merged into a single vital force makes the dynamics of inner action-energy flow from one quality (course) to another (subtle). It is the cognitive development of the human brain that internalizes input supplied by the senses and uses this stored information to externalize or express itself. We strive to develop these two aspects of cognitive function – sensitization of the brain so that it can distinguish subtler stimuli and internalize it, and expertise and skill in form of expression to encompass what one knows and feels. Where expression occurs, what is inside is reorganized through a series of complicated processes and is externalized. In the sensorial environment of the body, what the performer does is to internalize the most intricate of details of the external world and absorb that information which, in turn, inspires the most intriguing forms of expression. Let the energy flow in the organic transformation of vitality to subtlety.

We borrow certain terms from Barba for a better communication between the director and performer. We find that he is the best analyst and inventor of the jargon of words for the professional practice in theatre. Whatever we have experienced in the process of biological evolution are the assertions of new body techniques. These techniques, according to Barba, are the extra-daily body techniques for the conscious process of creativity where the maximum energy is used for a minimal effect. In contrast to this, the daily body technique belongs to the unconscious behavior making the minimum input of energy for the maximum benefit.

The extra-daily body technique enthuses the performer to create the physical and scenic presence, and radiates the vibrations pertaining to the celebration of feelings of joy and terror of life in its authenticity and originality. Of course, in the sensorial context of expression, vibration turns out to be the language which is shaped by psychology, logic and physics transforming the physical into the spiritual. This language makes the spectators "alert" and "deeply disturbed" at the sensory level. It further creates a perception in them in order to justify the efficacy of art – the perception of the "meaning" produced, ground between experience and reflection.

Justifying the artistic process of a given performance through tests of validity makes us also conscious of similarity of principles, that whatever we do on the stage is *real*, but not *realistic*. In making art we bear the naturalness of the thing intact, instead of the nature, and we do abstract and throw light as artificial but believable. This similarity of principles works everywhere, despite the diverse cultural milieux, styles, and genres of different geographical locations. [...]

In summing up the way we happened to be a part of this culture of transition, that is, a culture of faith, we keep reminding ourselves of the following passages of Ernst Ficher:

This curious description, reminiscent of the reports of certain mystics, expresses Goethe's pantheism. Makarie is a symbol of the world unity of creative man, and the astronomer at her side is a personification of science. True, the "superabundance of her condition" lacks a social element, that of the creative human being's unity not only with the natural world but also with the rest of mankind. Such "superabundance" in society as we have known it until now, has been the lot and the heavy burden of only very few men and women; but in a truly human society, springs of creative power will gush forth in many, many more; the artist's experience will no longer be a privilege but the normal gift of free and active man; we shall achieve, as it were, *social genius*. Man, who became man through work, who stepped out of the animal kingdom as transformer of the natural into the artificial, who became therefore the magician, man the creator of social reality, will always stay the great magician, will always be Prometheus bringing fire from heaven to earth, will always be Orpheus enthralling nature with his music. Not until humanity itself dies will the arts die.

[...]

The concept of the "Ritual of Suffering" thus reveals the essence: We suffer because our natural body behavior becomes imprisoned by the forces of increasing urban sophistication and the "speed" of the time. Our behavior appears terribly mechanical, unable to activate and use the spine. As a result, the neck-upward-culture is produced. We fail to produce effective response when we face the paradoxical situation in our body because of the times. On the other hand too, we suffer because our people are bitterly marginalized and oppressed though we are becoming aware of our "pain" and "anguish," and the need of "sacrifice" and "martyrdom" in the expression of the instinct of the people: freedom. Our body is located in this human condition. Therefore, with the sensorial awareness of a natural human being, we felt the need of discovering the psychic power and archetype in the process of a ritual theatre so that our body incarnates *Resistance*. Why we need the discovery of psychic power and archetype is related to the idea that this is the root, the "eternal human," transforming itself into a powerful expression of silent but inarticulate feelings of the oppressed people.

The way we continue our "doing" in order to breathe a new life into the work as generated by love and cooperation in the core of family environment is the new perspective of theatre sociology. The democratic principles of right and equality are thus newly valued in our human relationship in the group. We, as teachers and leaders of the work, are responsible to see that colleagues as well as apprentices feel themselves extremely liberating in ensuring their own individuality without affecting the core of the group. Simultaneously, we strive to sustain the spirit of the group in its emotionality and objectivity too. As teachers, we look forward to passing the real knowledge of the older one to the younger, of *"do it"* to *"yes,"* rejecting all oppressive intrigues and a mainly cult atmosphere. For us, theatre is thus worked out in its ritual value of *art as breath* – the liberating force of a new life.

Our theatre does not assert ideology obviously in the function of making "propaganda" and "teaching" of a political theatre. Our theatre does not appear in such a form which subordinates art to ideology. Our theatre is predominantly an art which conceals ideology, embodies the nuances of the instinct of the people and expresses itself in the form of a logical, sensuous and lyrical performance text: a theatre of the senses that dances and sings. [...]

Theatre in Theory: Working Units

The following is a list of clustered units for teaching theatre in theory. It is recommended that each course follow its own pattern and ideal.

Avant-Garde and Happenings

Wilde	Craig	Yeats	Marinetti	Witkiewicz
Stein	Artaud	Bentley	Ionesco	Kantor

Comedy

Bergson	Pirandello	Hurston	Dürrenmatt

Ethnicity

Walker	Locke	Du Bois	Hurston	Valdez	Boal	Soyinka
Shange	Huntsman	Barba	Sata	Mori	Kanhailal	

Epic Theatre

Brecht	Benjamin	Barthes	Abel	Szondi

Feminism and Queer Theory

Dolan	Butler	Schneider	Phelan	Troyano

Naturalism and Realism

Strindberg	Bryusov	Shaw	Lukács	Goldman
Miller	T. Williams	O'Casey	Weiss	

Performance Studies

Turner	Schneider	Phelan	Schechner

Political, Folk, and Ritual

Rolland	Locke	Du Bois	Brecht	Hurston	Lorca
R. Williams	Valdez	Boal	Soyinka	Turner	Barba

Poststructuralism and Postmodernism

Derrida	Müller	States	Parks	Blau

Semiotics and Structuralism

Brušák	Honzl	Barthes	Burke	Kirby
Pavis	Fischer-Lichte	Mori	Kanhailal	

Symbolism and Expressionism

Maeterlinck	Meyerhold	Kaiser	Eliot

Theatre of the Absurd

Stein	Artaud	Ionesco	Sartre	Esslin	Ludlam

Theatricality (Set Design, Directing, Mask)

Meyerhold	Appia	O'Neill	Wilder	Dürrenmatt	
Fergusson	Grotowski	Brook	Wilson	Sata	Foreman

Tragedy

Yeats	Anderson	Miller	Gassner	Steiner

Selected Bibliography

I have profited from other theory and criticism texts. Several have been mentioned in the Introduction: Marvin Carlson's *Theories of the Theatre* (Cornell, 1984, expanded edition, 1993); J. L. Styan's *Modern Drama in Theory and Practice* (Cambridge, 1981), three volumes; Shannon Jackson's *Professing Performance: Theatre in the Academy from Philology to Performativity* (Cambridge, 2004); Martin Puchner's *Stage Fright: Modernism, Anti-Theatricality and Drama* (Baltimore, 2002); Graham Ley's *From Mimesis to Interculturalism: Readings of Theatrical Theory before and after Modernism* (Exeter, 1999); Jenelle Reinelt and Joseph Roach's *Critical Theory and Performance* (Michigan, 1992, expanded edition, 2007); David Krasner and David Z. Saltz's *Staging Philosophy: Intersections of Theater, Performance, and Philosophy* (Michigan, 2006); and *Sources of Dramatic Theory*, edited by Michael J. Sidnell (Cambridge, 1991, 1994). Some, such as Bernard Dukore's *Dramatic Theory and Criticism* (Harcourt, 1974), E. T. Kirby's *Total Theatre: A Critical Anthology* (Dutton, 1969), Daniel Seltzer's *The Modern Theatre: Readings and Documents* (Little, Brown, and Co., 1967), Robert W. Corrigan's *Theatre in the Twentieth Century* (Grove, 1963), and Barrett H. Clark's *European Theories of the Drama* (Crown, 1947), are either out of print or lack sufficient representation of the second half of the twentieth century. Eric Bentley's *The Theory of the Modern Stage* (Penguin, 1989) and Daniel Gerould's *Theatre/Theory/Theory* (Applause, 2000) offer few essays but those represented are significant. The selections from Richard Drain's *Twentieth-Century Theatre: A Sourcebook* (Routledge, 1995) and Bert Cardullo and Robert Knopf's *Theater of the Avant-Garde, 1890–1950* (Yale, 2001) emphasize the avant-garde. Michael Huxley and Noel Witt's *Twentieth-Century Performance Reader* (Routledge, 1996), George Brandt's *Modern Theories of Drama* (Oxford, 1998), and Henry Bial's *The Performance Studies Reader* (Routledge, 2004) are worthy collections covering important material outside of theatre and drama (dance and performance art, for example). An excellent source in German is *Texte zur Theorie des Theaters*, edited by Klaus Lazarowicz and Christopher Balme (Stuttgart, 1991). Oscar Lee Brownstein and Darlene M. Daubert's *Analytical Sourcebook of Concepts in Dramatic Theory* (Greenwood, 1981) is a thematically arranged compilation of quotations by theorists. Mark Fortier's *Theory/Theatre* (Routledge, 1997) is a recommended introduction to theatre in theory.

Index

ᵀᴬ information can be obtained at www.ICGtesting.com
in the USA
¹027220814

¹⁄00002B/4/P